W9-CNR-654

# LOCAL GOVERNMENT FINANCE
## Concepts and Practices

*Edited by John E. Petersen and Dennis R. Strachota*

GOVERNMENT FINANCE OFFICERS ASSOCIATION

180 N. Michigan Avenue
Suite 800
Chicago, Illinois 60601



Library of Congress catalog card number 90-85877

ISBN 0-89125-152-9

Printed in the United States of America

First printing, May 1991

# *Contents*

# *Foreword*

Fifteen years have passed since the Government Finance Officers Association published *Concepts and Practices in Local Government Finance.* Co-authored by Lennox Moak and Albert M. Hillhouse, the book has been widely read by practitioner and student alike. GFOA owes a great debt of gratitude to those two gentlemen who conceived of such a volume and pioneered in bringing together the range of disciplines that make local government finance. As in other fields, however, developments and trends in the financial environment of local governments dictate re-examination from time to time. The publication of *Local Government Finance: Concepts and Practices* represents such a timely re-examination.

This book offers a comprehensive overview and cohesive reference of policies and practices in the assorted disciplines that make up local government finance. It examines the new forces influencing this environment, including reduced levels of federal assistance, an expanded state role in domestic policy, and financial practices increasingly shaped by professional standards, technology and financial markets. As with the original publication, this book brings together into a single volume the many and diverse elements of local finance. John Petersen and Dennis Strachota who co-edited this book, the authors who contributed individual chapters, and the many others who assisted in its preparation are to be commended for this latest installment on GFOA's obligation to the advancement of local governmental financial practice. I am especially grateful to Dennis Strachota whose special efforts brought this project to a successful completion.

Jeffrey L. Esser
Executive Director
Government Finance Officers Association

April 1991

# *Preface*

The purpose of this book is to provide a comprehensive overview of the many disciplines that go under the general heading of local government finance. As the table of contents will attest, this subject embraces a wide array of functions and activities. Even at that, the editors had to be discriminating, if not arbitrary, in choosing topics to keep the metes, bounds, and mass of the book within reason. While the book does presuppose some knowledge of local government, its primary orientation is toward the practitioner, student or informed citizen who wants to know more about local government finance. With that goal in mind, we have sought to develop a balanced presentation that introduces concepts, explains their rationale, discusses contemporary issues and illustrates applications at the local government level.

The reader should bear in mind that there is a tremendous range and texture to the local finance function. This diversity in large part reflects the political framework in which finance is practiced among thousands of local governments in the United States. While many of the financial disciplines covered in this volume share much in common with those found in the private sector, in practice they serve the unique purposes of the public sector where emphasis is on control and accountability. These distinctions of purpose become even more pronounced when the organization of local government is taken into account. Local governments reflect the peculiar concerns and heritages of states from which their powers are derived. Such diversity provides for bold contrasts and numerous comparisons and frequently limits the ability to generalize when it comes to specifics of practice.

The original concept of this volume stretches several years when it became clear that the original treatise authored by Lennox Moak and Albert M. Hillhouse was becoming dated. Unlike the original book, which was primarily the handiwork of the two authors, specialists were enlisted to write about their individual areas of expertise. As the phrase "concepts and practices" implies, these contributors undertook the burden of authoring chapters that blended the theoretical with the applied, in the conviction that understanding why things are done in such a way was equally important as explaining how they are done.

In addition to the contributing authors, who patiently updated early drafts and responded to editorial musings, we wish to thank several individuals who assisted in the preparation of the book. First, thanks go to Girard Miller who originally served as a co-editor and assisted with the original design of the book when he served as Director of GFOA's Technical Services Center. Our thanks also go to Lisa Cole, Paul Shinn and Ann Stephani who assisted with the editing of selected manuscripts and Robert Addelson, Arthur Blumenfeld, Timothy Kays, Joni Liethe, Linda Patterson, Sharon Quigley, Timothy Riordan, Kent Rock, Philip Rosenberg and Michelle Saddler who reviewed and commented on individual chapters. Our appreciation also goes to Geoff Garvey, Director of Link Book Development, who served as copy-editor, Sharon Fucone who proofread the manuscript, Carol Kutner who typed several chapters, Benjamin Mays, who created original graphics and Shirley McLaughlin, who typed several versions of each chapter.

John E. Petersen
Dennis Strachota

# 1
# Introduction

DENNIS STRACHOTA AND JOHN E. PETERSEN

FUNDAMENTALLY, finance is the raising and spending of money. In government finance, however, the money is the publics and spending is for the public good. Because the ways, means, and purposes are different, government finance in many respects differs from that found in the private sector. Yet, at the same time, many of the techniques and disciplines used are the same. The chapters in this volume present a comprehensive view of the concepts and practices of finance as employed by local governments in the United States.

Structurally, the book is organized into the following broad areas. The first chapters deal with overall financing patterns and economic role of local governments and the allocative decisions found in budgeting for both current operating and capital spending. The following chapters deal with the revenue-raising function and the major sources available to local governments. Next, the functions of accounting, reporting, and auditing, especially essential in government, are considered. The management of assets and creation of liabilities and the practice of borrowing are examined as are other techniques for raising capital funds and acquiring goods and services. Local government finances frequently are organized in ways to carry out specific and specialized purposes and the concluding chapters focus on the subjects of enterprises, employee retirement systems, and the pervasive effect of state involvement in local government finances.

Highlights from each of these chapters are grouped by topic area and presented below.

### *FRAMEWORK*

The first and last chapters offer a good start and finish to an examination of local finance. In chapter 2, "Financing Local Government," Robert Rafuse lays the groundwork with his review of the basic principles underlying local finance.

Rafuse examines the allocation, distribution, and stabilization functions of government and the role that local governments play in each.

Following a discussion of the basic objectives of local finance, the author briefly describes the sources of local revenue and trends in local government spending.

Because states ultimately can determine the makeup of local finance, chapter 22, "State Involvement in Local Finance," offers a fitting conclusion. Dennis Strachota reviews the nature and extent of state involvement in many of the finance activities covered in the other chapters. He describes various state regulatory and assistance roles and their implications for local finance objectives. Strachota concludes with an examination of several factors that most influence state involvement.

## *REVENUE RAISING*

Local governments rely on a variety of sources for raising revenues. They fall into one of two categories: "own-source" and "intergovernmental" revenue. Major own-source revenues include taxes, user charges and fees, and debt proceeds. Intergovernmental revenues originate from the federal and state governments in the form of grants and payments.

Separate chapters are devoted to the four largest sources of own-source revenue—property taxes, nonproperty taxes, user charges, and debt. Federal and state financial assistance are covered in a chapter on intergovernmental revenues. In addition, a chapter is devoted to an examination of local revenue capacity.

### *Property Taxes*

Far and away the largest source of local revenue and one of the most controversial forms of taxation is property taxes. Although local reliance on property taxation has fallen over the last three decades, property taxes still constitute 75 percent of total local tax revenues and nearly half of all local own-source revenue. In chapter 6, Michael Bell and John Bowman trace trends in local property-tax reliance and tax burdens as well as the current pattern of property-tax use by local governments.

Bell and Bowman examine the inner workings of property taxation in their review of variations in property-tax bases, principal methods of valuation, and measurements of assessment quality. The authors present evidence that property taxes can be consistent with both the ability-to-pay and benefits principles of taxation while they offer differing views on who ultimately "pays" for these taxes. Lastly, Bell and Bowman describe a variety of measures that have evolved to provide taxpayer relief.

### *Nonproperty Taxes*

In chapter 7, "Nonproperty Taxes," Holley Ulbrich outlines the costs and benefits of revenue diversification, a driving force behind the increased use of nonproperty taxes by local governments. Ulbrich describes the basic characteristics and rationales of the second- and third-largest sources of local tax revenue—sales taxes and personal income taxes.

Ulbrich concludes that local sales and income taxes, as well as a variety of lesser taxes that she profiles, offer ways to capture revenue from nonresidents and to generate revenue from taxpayers whose wealth is not derived from real property.

### *User Charges and Fees*

Playing an even larger role as an alternative to property taxes are user charges and fees. As defined by Kurt Zorn in chapter 8, user charges and fees are payments for voluntarily purchased, publicly provided services that benefit specific individuals.

Zorn reviews the advantages and disadvantages of financing publicly provided goods and services with user charges and fees. The author explains the difficulty in determining the appropriate level of charge for services that are good candidates for user-charge financing. Zorn describes three approaches to pricing services in addition to suggesting implementation guidelines for governments contemplating the use of user charges.

### *Borrowing*

While local governments use all the aforementioned sources of revenue to finance their operating needs, they rely principally on borrowing to finance large-scale capital projects as well to meet cash-flow needs. John Petersen describes how the tax-exempt market works in chapter 15, "Debt Markets and Instruments." Petersen explains how the forces of supply and demand and changes in the legal environment, especially tax laws, have created changes in the design of debt instruments and securities transactions.

Against this backdrop, the author describes how tax-exempt rates are determined and the risk and reward tradeoffs that occur in the creation of innovative techniques. Among the innovative debt instruments profiled in the chapter are tax-exempt commercial paper, variable-rates, puttable securities, call options, refunding, zeros, direct issuance, hedges, forward delivery, swaps, and taxable municipals.

### *Intergovernmental Revenues*

A diminishing, yet significant, source of revenue for most local governments is intergovernmental revenues. In chapter 9, Jed Kee and John Forrer cover both federal and state financial assistance, including federal aid that passes through states to local governments. The authors offer a historical look at the structure and funding levels for intergovermental assistance and speculate as to its future course.

Kee and Forrer review the major types of financial aid and their economic effects. They examine recent trends in federal and state assistance, including the downsizing and restructuring of federal aid and the state response to those changes. In contrast to federal aid, the authors present evidence that state assistance is fashioned largely by the structure of state-local relations.

### *Fiscal Capacity*

A government's ability to generate own-source revenues is defined as its fiscal capacity. Although considerable research has been done on the relative fiscal capacity of multiple jurisdictions, in chapter 10, Freda Johnson and Diana Roswick focus instead on the individual locality and its ability to raise resources to support its own operating and capital needs. Because a community's fiscal capacity is closely linked to its economic base, the authors describe measures of economic activity, population trends, and socioeconomic and housing characteristics.

Johnson and Roswick devote most of their chapter to describing methods to assess the contribution that various own-source revenues can make to local fiscal capacity. They conclude with a review of the legal, political, and administrative constraints that can limit a local government's ability to tap its revenue base.

## *SPENDING*

The ability to raise revenue usually is a precondition for spending. Most spending decisions by local governments are made as part of a budgeting process. For many local jurisdictions, this process is split for operating and capital-spending purposes.

Local governments typically adopt annual operating budgets that constitute their spending plans for current operations. Although the operating budget may include appropriations for major capital projects, many governments prepare a separate capital budget as part of a multiyear capital improvement plan. The discussion of budgeting in this book parallels this separation between operating and capital spending.

### *Operating Budgets*

Diverse is the adjective that best describes budgeting practices at the local level. In chapter 4, Lon Sprecher stresses that the budgeting process must be tailored to meet the unique needs of each jurisdiction. He explains how the budget and the budget process are shaped by the environment, issues, and participants in each locality. Sprecher describes budgeting as a unified series of steps undertaken to link four functions: policy development, financial planning, service/operations planning, and communication.

The author depicts budgeting as a conflict-resolution process as he describes the chronological steps in the process: planning/preparation, integration, selling/passage, and execution/feedback. Sprecher explains how these steps, taken as a whole, translate the values and priorities of budget participants into programs and policies.

### *Capital Planning and Budgeting*

Many local governments prepare multiyear capital improvement plans to forecast major capital project needs. As described by Susan Robinson in chapter 5, these plans offer a comprehensive approach to identifying needed capital projects and coordinating project financing and timing. Robinson explains that the capital budget, which represents the current year of that plan, authorizes specific projects for the ensuing fiscal year.

The author explains the rationale for long-range capital planning and describes the advantages that it offers for local governments. In addition, Robinson provides a detailed description of the annual cycle for capital planning and budgeting from resource and demand inventories to project implementation.

## *ORGANIZATION AND ADMINISTRATION*

Decisions to raise revenue and spend money are not made in isolation. Financial systems and procedures are put in place to plan and carry out these financial decisions in an effective, efficient, and accountable manner. A major portion of this book is devoted to the systems and procedures that comprise financial administration, including their organization.

### *Organization*

Local financial administration crosses organizational and program lines. As Ed Lehan states at the outset of chapter 3, "Organization of the Finance Function," integration has been the key organizational issue in local government finance since the turn of the twentieth century. Lehan traces the evolution of an integrated finance function from efforts to deal with fragmented finance activities.

From this historical perspective, the author reviews the contemporary finance organization, observing that integration may be rooted more in theory than in practice. Whatever the organizational scheme, Lehan concludes that the local finance administration must stress planning and analytical objectives as well as their historical concerns of coordination and control.

### *Computers*

Electronic data processing has probably had the single greatest impact on the finance organization. With the price of computing having fallen from 5,000 to 1 over the last three decades, computers have become a key tool in local financial administration. In chapter 21, Jerry Mechling traces the evolution of computing in government and, in particular, government finance.

Mechling takes a look at the major computer applications for government finance: transaction processing, decision support, and office automation. He concludes with a discussion of management issues and future developments in local government computerization.

### *Public Retirement Systems*

In chapter 19, "Public Employee Retirement Systems and Benefits," Paul Zorn describes the organizational, legal, actuarial, accounting, and investment features of public pension plans that distinguish from other areas of local finance.

Zorn provides an overview of the nearly 9,000 public employee retirement systems (PERS) administered by state and local governments, including benefit types and plan administration. The author presents a comprehensive review of funding methods, asset valuation and investment, and reporting requirements for these plans. Zorn concludes with some predictions for the future of PERS given current demographic and economic trends.

### *Enterprises*

Although user charges and fees are covered elsewhere in the book, in chapter 20 Lawrence Pierce and Kenneth Rust examine the organization of self-supporting local government activities that rely primarily on user charges to finance their operation.

Pierce and Rust profile nine service areas (e.g., water supply, public parking) and describe how the nature of each service, its customer base, and its policy objectives affect the pricing of public charges for those services. The authors describe the various organizational forms under which these enterprises are operated in addition to the methods that can be used to measure their financial performance. Pierce and Rust conclude with a review of special charges that are used to finance capital improvements for local enterprises.

### *Accounting and Reporting*

Two activities that cut across all other areas of financial administration are accounting and financial reporting. As described by Stephen Gauthier in chapter 11, they form the "informational infrastructure" of public finance. Gauthier describes the elements of accounting that are essential to effective control and decision making. In addition, he explains how the financial data generated from the accounting system is used for external and internal reporting.

The author focuses on the key features of generally accepted accounting principles (GAAP) that govern the preparation of local government financial reports. Gauthier concludes with a review of pending changes under consideration by the standard-setting body for government accounting standards.

### *Cash Management*

One area of finance accounted for and reported in the accounting system is the management of cash. In chapter 13, Girard Miller describes cash management in its simplest terms as a combination of cash mobilization, controlled disbursement, and an investment program.

Within this context, Miller reviews seven basic cash-management functions: receipts, deposits, custodial functions, disbursement of funds, relations with financial institutions, investments, and short–term borrowing. The author highlights, in particular, the expanded use of sophisticated investment practices and techniques at the local level and the advantages and pitfalls that they present.

### Purchasing

A major form of spending at the local level is the procurement of goods and services from private-sector. In chapter 17, "Purchasing," Stephen Gordon stresses that legal requirements pervade every facet of this support function. Gordon reviews the three major phases in the procurement cycle: planning and scheduling, vendor selection, and contract administration. In addition, the author raises several policy and management issues that affect the design and performance of this element of financial management.

### Leasing

One way to acquire the use of equipment and real property is through leases. As pointed out by Percy Aguila and John Petersen in chapter 16, "Leasing and Service Contracts," leasing has evolved into an increasingly important alternative in the financing of major capital assets. Aguila and Petersen attribute this growth in leasing to several economic and legal factors, including legal limits on borrowing.

The authors describe the major types of leases, including operating leases, lease-purchases, and master leases, in addition to the structure of typical lease transactions, their tax treatment, and other distinguishing characteristics. They also offer a brief look at service contracts, which finance the combined costs of operation and capital services in a single package.

### Debt Administration

Local governments have a variety of ways in which to finance capital outlays but the traditional manner has been through the use of long-term debt. In chapter 14, John Petersen and Tom McLoughlin first view the administration of debt as part of the overall capital financing process. They then describe the variety of instruments and marketing methods that may be used to access the capital markets.

Particular stress is placed on the decision-making process in the selection of particular forms of borrowing, the steps by which securities are offered in the market, and the documents that need to be produced to inform potential investors. Petersen and McLoughlin conclude by reviewing the important role played by various professionals in the design and marketing process and how these services may be procured and managed.

### Risk Management

Another activity that can have a significant bearing on government finances is risk management. In chapter 18, Brad Johnson and Bernard Ross point out that public risk management has taken on greater importance and visibility as a result of the insurance crisis of the mid-1980s. In their description of the risk-management process, Johnson and Ross explain how and why risk management involves much more than the purchase of insurance coverage.

### *Auditing*

How well do local governments perform the finance activities described above? The answer will be provided, in part, through audits. In chapter 12, Stephen Gauthier describes how financial and performance audits can assist local government managers as well as taxpayers, oversight bodies, investors, and creditors.

Gauthier offers a comprehensive look at financial auditing, including a description of the major types, how and who performs them, and the reporting and resolution of audit findings. The author contrasts these financial audits with performance audits, which can be conducted by internal staff, and which address the more fundamental question of whether management is meeting its responsibilities efficiently and effectively. Gauthier also examines the role of audit committees in advising local governing bodies on both external and internal audits.

## *CONCLUSION*

As the authors of the chapters in this volume demonstrate, the subject matter involved in government finance are many, diverse, and dynamic. No aspect of the finance official's job is insulated from the ever-changing financial and political environment. As a result, policies, techniques, and tools will always be in transition. We believe that the following chapters will not only provide an update on the state of the art in the various financial disciplines, but will serve as points of departure for the additional study and analysis that is needed to stay abreast of developments.

# 2

# *Financing Local Government*

Robert W. Rafuse, Jr.

In the history of public finance in the United States during the third of a century since the Korean War, one constant stands out. It is the remarkable stability in the relative importance of local governments in the delivery of domestic public services. In 1954 local entities accounted for 44 cents of every dollar of direct general expenditures by all governments in the nation for these services.[1] In 1988 local governments accounted for 45 cents. In all the intervening years, the figure was never higher than 47 cents nor lower than 42 cents.

The stability of the local role in spending masks dramatic shifts in the ways that role has been financed. This chapter is mostly about the revenue side of local government though limited attention is given to the expenditure side. It begins with a brief discussion of the essential functions of government and the key issues involved in paying for those functions. Then the primary objectives of local finance are considered along with the most important constraints on financing decisions. Finally, the major sources of local revenues are examined. Recent trends in those sources and in the overall size and fiscal condition of the public sector are briefly reviewed.

## *BASIC CONCEPTS*

It seems appropriate to begin this brief inquiry into the financing of local government by considering some basic principles. These relate to the reasons governments exist at all in nations like the United States—where consumer sovereignty and the market are the warp and woof of the economy—and to the basic functions governments are called upon to perform.

President Eisenhower was fond of quoting as an expression of his own philosophy a statement by Abraham Lincoln on the appropriate role for government:

> The legitimate object of government is to do for a community of people whatever they need to have done, but cannot do *at all,* or can not *so well do,* for themselves—in their separate and individual capacities. In all that the people can individually do as well for themselves, government ought not to interfere. [Emphasis in original.][2]

As a general statement of political philosophy, this is a useful beginning. Unfortunately, it does not suggest how we should identify the things the people "cannot do at all or can not so well do for themselves."

## *THE ESSENTIAL FUNCTIONS OF GOVERNMENT*

In the United States, people do most things for themselves in the marketplace. This suggests that an appropriate rephrasing of the Lincoln statement would characterize the role of government as stepping in when the market fails altogether or in some significant degree, but as not otherwise interfering with the operation of the market.

The question of market failure and its implications for the role of government has been addressed in the economic literature in considerable detail over the past two centuries. One of the best discussions appears in Richard A. Musgrave's monumental treatise on public finance.[3] It outlines a widely accepted triad of functions that government must perform in the interest of the objectives of an efficient allocation of resources, equity, and a stable economy. Professor Musgrave refers to the functions as allocation, distribution, and stabilization.

### *Allocation*

The allocation function comprehends the actions of governments that change the deployment of resources from the allocation the market would otherwise produce. Government involvement in the resource-allocation process is necessary because the market can produce the socially optimal amounts of goods and services—that is, the quantities demanded by consumers at prevailing prices—only when it is possible to exclude from the benefits of consuming those who are unwilling to pay.

For example, the "right" amount of bread is produced by private bakeries without government intervention because all the benefits from consumption of the product are realized by the purchaser. When exclusion is completely out of the question, however, as in the case of a mosquito-spraying operation, the service is a pure public good, which must be provided by government if it is to be available at all.[4]

This does not mean that the pure public good must be produced by the government. It may well be purchased by the government from a private firm, a form of what recently has come to be known as "privatization." The central point is that the demand for the good must be articulated by a government on behalf of its residents, who could not otherwise express their willingness to pay for the service.[5]

The more common case is the good or service characterized by "externalities," that is, benefits or costs that are not enjoyed or incurred solely by those who make the purchase in the market. Elementary education is a classic example of a service with external benefits. Most of the benefits are enjoyed by the children, who could be denied them if they (or their parents) were unwilling to pay tuition. But society as a whole also has an interest in the education transaction. Everyone benefits from a literate citizenry familiar with the history and cultural heritage of the nation, the state, and the community.

At the same time, the consumption of other goods and services purchased by individuals in the market may generate costs (or even benefits) for others. Real estate is a clear example. How a parcel is developed is very likely to affect the value of neighboring properties. Local governments have, of course, long recognized this potential and have sought to control the externalities by enacting zoning ordinances.

### *Distribution*

The distribution function relates to the influence of government on the distribution of income and wealth among individuals. Though free-market zealots occasionally lose sight of the fact, the social legitimacy of the allocation of resources produced by the market rests on the acceptability of the distribution of income and wealth among the consumers who generate that allocation when they exercise their sovereignty in the marketplace.

Local governments have played a role in ensuring that the poor have a place to sleep and food to eat since the early days of the Industrial Revolution. Since the Great Depression, a clear consensus has existed on a major role for the national government (and the states) in the distribution of income and wealth in the United States, and an income-maintenance system of extraordinary complexity has developed.

### *Stabilization*

The stabilization function involves the influence of government on the overall level of economic activity. The actions of all levels of government affect economic activity to some degree. As a practical matter, however, it is generally agreed that only the national government is in a position to design its monetary and fiscal policies with explicit attention to the general health of the economy. An exception to this generalization is the efforts of state and local governments to influence the level of activity and the pace of economic growth within their jurisdictions by so-called development programs.

### *Some Other Considerations*

A basic reality of local government in the U.S. federal system is that all of the complex array of entities comprehended by the term are creations of the states, which are the direct parties—with the federal government—to the great compact known as the Constitution. The legal forms, structures, responsibilities, and sources of revenues of local governments are prescribed by the states.

What follows from this arrangement is what could be expected. A second overarching reality of local government in the United States is its extraordinary diversity. The Bureau of the Census reports that there are about 80,000 units of local government. Roughly half of these are classified by the Bureau as "general-purpose" governments, that is, they perform a range of governmental functions and have at least a minimal degree of independent taxing power.

The entities other than general-purpose governments include school districts, water districts, park and recreation districts, and just about every other type of special district imaginable. Some states, such as California, have made special districts a major element of their structure of grass-roots government. Other states assign virtually all responsibilities to general-purpose governments.

### *Basic Issues in Financing Government*

A fundamental concept of economics is that the cost to society of a government program or activity is the value of the output that would have been produced in the private sector if the resources had not been diverted to public use. This concept is sometimes referred to as opportunity cost.

Abstracting for the moment from the nature of the program or activity being performed, the fundamental issue of government finance is how the opportunity costs are to be distributed among individuals and over time. How the costs are distributed depends on how the government obtains the resources, and there are only three basic options: (1) "drafting" the resources, (2) purchasing them in the marketplace, and (3) such mixed methods as the exercise of eminent domain.[6]

Resources are "drafted" when government takes them from their owners in an involuntary transaction and pays compensation less than market prices. In a pure draft, the resources are simply confiscated, and no compensation is paid. The cost of the government activity using the resources clearly rests on the owners of the confiscated property. The draft we are all familiar with—the military draft—was not a pure draft because some compensation was always paid to the individuals involved. The compensation was much less than market price, however, so a major share of the cost of the nation's defense rested directly on the draftees.

A draft can be distinguished from the exercise of eminent domain by the fact that, in the latter instance, a court proceeding is involved. The purpose of the proceeding is to establish a fair market value for the property taken by the government from the unwilling owner.

Purchase in the marketplace is generally the only option available to a local government. When resources are purchased, the distribution of the costs depends on how the government obtains the money. The cost does not rest on the owner of the resources sold to the government because the owner receives the market price. This is at least equal to the value of the resources to the owner, or the sale would not have occurred. The major options are

- "Printing" the money (an option only for the federal government [7])
- Borrowing from the public (an option for most localities only to finance capital outlays and for purposes of short-term cash management)

- Taxation
- Sale of services
- Sale of assets
- Transfers from other governments

Each of these methods offers the prospect of a somewhat different distribution of the government costs.

The distribution effected by printing money depends on economic conditions at the time. If the economy is strong, and unemployed resources are not abundant, printing money is inflationary. In this event, the costs are borne by those who lose from inflation—notably creditors in general and retirees on fixed incomes. If the economy is weak, on the other hand, printing money may enable the government to buy resources that would otherwise have been unemployed. That is, the government activity may have zero opportunity cost because the idle resources would otherwise have produced nothing. At the same time, the expenditure of the printed money would not be inflationary, so the action would impose no burden on the economy, at least in the short run.

Borrowing from the public shifts the costs of the financed government program to the future, when interest payments must be made and the principal eventually repaid. (The federal government can roll over debt, potentially in perpetuity, without necessarily jeopardizing its premier credit rating. A state or local government could not do so without eventual adverse consequences.) Those who purchase the securities clearly do not bear the costs of the government spending because they are at least as well off owning the securities as they would have been had the government outlays not been made.[8] Therefore, the incidence of the costs depends on the method used to finance the interest and principal payments.

The distribution of costs that results from taxation depends on the incidence of the taxes—that is, on who ultimately bears the burden. For example, a general sales tax in almost all circumstances is paid by the retailer, who shifts the burden to the purchaser by, in effect, raising prices. Such shifting is promoted by the common statutory requirement that the tax be quoted separately as an addition to the posted retail price.

When government services are financed by the proceeds from their sale in voluntary transactions equivalent to those in the marketplace, the costs are paid by the purchasers. As voluntary transactions are involved, however, the purchasers are at least as well off as they would have been without the government activity, so it cannot be said that they are burdened in any way.

If a government produces a commodity or service that can be sold in the market at a price that covers the cost of producing it, one may legitimately wonder why the government is involved at all: odds are that private production would be more efficient—read lower in cost. If the government is producing and competing successfully by virtue of some advantage conferred by statute—an example is a state liquor-sales monopoly, as in Virginia—the chances are that the consumer is paying a price that exceeds the one that would prevail in a free market. In this case, the consumer effectively is paying a sales tax.

The sale of government assets generates revenues that do not impose the costs of programs on the purchasers, assuming that the sales are entirely voluntary. Rather, the costs rest on future residents of the jurisdiction, if the assets were worth more in the long run to the government than their sales price. If they were not, everyone is better off as a result of the transaction, assuming only that the proceeds from the sale are applied intelligently to programs or activities (including even a tax cut) that pass reasonable cost-benefit muster.

Transfers from other governments shift the costs of the aided programs (or other components of the recipient government's budget) to the taxpayers of the other governments.

A given local government typically does not have the legal authority to raise money by all the possible methods inherent in the array of options discussed in this section. For example, states commonly prescribe the types of taxes local entities may use, and they often impose limits on the rates and ways the taxes may be administered.

## *OBJECTIVES OF LOCAL FINANCE*

The general objectives of local finance are accountability, equity, and efficiency. Each is discussed in turn in this section.

### *Accountability*

In general, accountability is achieved when the level and mix of government spending and the distribution of its cost are decided in a climate of full disclosure by the elected representatives of the residents of a jurisdiction. Key elements of full disclosure are the maintenance of a rigorous system of internal accounting controls, financial reporting on the basis of generally accepted accounting principles, and the engagement of an annual audit of financial statements conducted in accordance with generally accepted government auditing standards prescribed by the Comptroller General of the United States.

Under most circumstances, accountability is promoted when the elected officials who decide how public funds are to be spent are also responsible for raising those funds.

### *Equity*

The objective of equity, or fairness, is usually presented as having two basic dimensions: horizontal and vertical. Horizontal equity can be defined fairly rigorously, and it is rarely a matter of major controversy. It is achieved when individuals (or families, depending on how the taxpaying unit is defined) in equal relevant circumstances are treated equally. Such controversy as arises with respect to horizontal equity tends to involve the definition of relevant circumstances. Examples are the not-uncommon disputes about whether all types of income, property, or retail transactions should have equal value in the base of a tax.

Vertical equity is another matter. It is achieved when the appropriate—that is, equitable—treatment is accorded to individuals in different relevant circumstances. Clearly, value judgments play a major role here. In concept, the major options are regressivity, proportionality, and progressivity. That is, the taxpayer with the larger tax base should pay a lower, the same, or a higher rate than the taxpayer with the smaller base.

An approach to this issue that has enjoyed increasing popularity in the past decade is referred to as the benefit principle. This principle lies behind the major shift, discussed in detail later, toward user charges and fees in local finance. The benefit principle holds that, in general, the fundamental objective in financing local government should be to distribute the costs to the maximum extent possible to those who benefit from the services. The benefit principle flows readily from the view of the role of government as stepping in when the market fails.

In essence, the benefit principle defines "relevant circumstances" as the value of the benefits received from a public service. Vertical equity, in this case, requires proportionality of treatment. That is, as in the case of market transactions (and the benefit principle derives its logic and appeal from market-based reasoning), everyone should pay the same price per unit of benefit, just as everyone (with exceptions, as in the case of volume discounts and price discrimination) pays the same price per unit in the marketplace. The common objection to user charges—that they are unfair to the poor—loses weight when the role of government in the allocation function is understood, and where the distribution function is appropriately performed.

Note that the deductibility of certain local taxes in calculating taxable income for state and federal purposes drives a wedge between apparent and actual tax burdens. This reality has significant implications for equity, efficiency, and accountability in local finance.

### *Efficiency*

In the financing of local government, efficiency can have several meanings. In its narrowest sense, it refers simply to economy, that is, whether a given activity is being carried out with as few resources as possible, or whether the best results are being achieved within a given budget.

In a more general sense, efficiency concerns the issue of the "right" level and mix of public services from the perspective of the overall economy. The textbooks say that, for government outlays in general, the amount of a service provided should be increased until the marginal social benefits equal the marginal social costs.

For a local government, the rule is that the amount of a service supplied should be raised until the marginal *local* benefit equals the marginal *local* cost. These benefits and costs may be the same as the social benefits and costs. They may not be, however, if (1) there are benefit or cost spillovers (externalities), or (2) the state or the federal government provides a grant to help pay for a service—if the grant has the effect of reducing the net local cost of the last unit of the service provided.

The way revenues are raised can help in the decision about the level of services. A major advantage of user charges, for example, is that the stream of revenues itself provides direct feedback from the consumers of the service on whether the right quantity is being delivered. Experimentation with charges is also possible to test consumer sentiment, and they can be varied over time to discourage congestion and to encourage use of facilities at times when they might otherwise go unused.

## *CONSTRAINTS ON LOCAL FINANCING DECISIONS*

The major constraints on local financing decisions are state law, federal "mandates," and intergovernmental competition. As it defines the basic responsibilities and revenue sources of local governments, state law clearly constitutes the primary body of constraints on local finance.

Federal law and regulations constrain local financing decisions in a number of ways.[9] In most cases, the constraints merely apply to states and localities—as employers—as they do to all other employers in the United States. For example, federal wage and hour laws apply to state and local governments (with certain exceptions for the unique circumstances of police and fire employment) just as they do to private employers.

Other federal constraints on local options are conditions of grant programs. Many of these conditions are ill-conceived, unnecessary, and even counterproductive. Nonetheless, it is the indisputable prerogative of a grantor to define the terms on which the funds are to be available. Progress has been made in recent years in the simplification of the regulations applicable to federal grant programs, but considerably more could be done. Many aspects of grant policy are poorly designed from the perspective of the effectiveness of their contribution to the achievement of the objectives of the programs.

Intergovernmental competition is a third type of constraint on local financing decisions. No locality's tax rates can get too far out of line with those of neighboring jurisdictions without risk of emigration of residents and firms. The same applies to the quality of the public services delivered by a local government. On balance, this competition is probably healthy because it tends to promote more efficient service provision.

## *SOURCES OF LOCAL REVENUES*

Local governments raise revenues from their own sources and receive payments from other governments.

### *Own Sources*

The major sources of revenue a local government can raise from its own sources are taxes, sales of services, other nontax revenue, and the sale of debt.

Taxes are compulsory payments by individuals or private organizations to a government, customarily associated with no specific, explicit *quid pro quo*. Some types of levies are often referred to as "benefit" taxes because they are linked somehow to identifiable benefits from particular public services. Sometimes the linkage is plausible and direct, as in the case of a frontage tax. The liability for this tax is defined by the footage of a property on a public street. The proceeds are used for such purposes as the construction of curbs and gutters. Despite the linkage, these charges are taxes because the property owner has no choice about paying them. The variety of taxes available to many local governments has increased in recent decades, but an individual government typically may rely only upon the specific types authorized by its state government.

Some types of taxes are especially well suited to administration by a particular level of government, taking into account the costs of administration (including taxpayer compliance), ease of avoidance, and the potential for evasion. For example, the real property tax is generally regarded as most appropriate for local government. The obvious consideration is that land and improvements cannot easily be moved to escape the tax. Net income and general sales taxes, on the other hand, are ill-suited for local governments because there are substantial economies of scale in administration. In addition, evasion and avoidance are much more difficult when such taxes are administered at the state or national levels.

It is important to note that the judgment that a sales or income tax can be administered most efficiently by a state government need not mean that local jurisdictions must be denied access to the sales and income tax bases. Access is easily provided by the device of the optional supplement to a state income or sales tax. Roughly half of the states authorize local governments to enact supplements to state sales taxes, though the range of authority varies tremendously.[10] Although local governments in 13 states tax income to one degree or another, in only 3 is the option of a supplement to the state's income tax available.[11]

The sale of services provided by a local government is a second major source of revenues—one that has been growing rapidly in recent years. Such revenues are distinguished from taxes by the voluntary character of the transactions, which are essentially identical to those between private parties in the market. When the sale of a service is practicable, that is, when an individual can be prevented from benefiting from it if he or she is unwilling to pay the price, equity and efficiency are served when the service is sold rather than given away. In such cases, however, the underlying question deserves careful attention. If those unwilling to pay can be excluded, why is the service being provided by government at all?

Other nontax revenues run the gamut from interest earned on invested cash balances to the proceeds from the sale of property owned by the local government.

The fourth major source of receipts from own sources is the issuance of debt. Typically, local government debt is limited by state law to short-term issuances for cash-management purposes and long-term issuances to finance the construction of capital facilities that will last for many years. State law usually requires that paper issued for cash management, commonly referred to as tax-anticipation notes (TANs) or revenue-anticipation notes (RANs) be retired before the end of the fiscal year in which it is sold.

The objective of selling debt to finance a capital facility is to spread the cost among residents of the jurisdiction over the life of the facility. By contrast, paying for the construction from current revenues imposes the costs entirely on those who happen to be residents of the community at the time the facility is built.

A distinguishing feature of most debt issued by local governments is that the interest paid on it is exempt from federal (and, in some cases, state) income taxation. This makes it possible for localities to market debt at lower interest rates than they would have to pay if the interest were taxable.

Exemption of interest income from taxes reduces federal income-tax collections. Hence, for debt of all maturities, the Federal Internal Revenue Code constrains local options—whatever state law may provide—if the interest on the securities is to be exempt from federal income taxes. The basic purpose of these provisions is to restrain the volume of tax-exempt debt in order to limit the federal revenue loss.[12]

### *Payments from Other Governments*

There are three primary rationales for intergovernmental transfers. The first is that the government making a grant seeks to induce the recipient to provide more of the aided service than it would in the absence of the grant. The second is reduction in disparities in the fiscal capacities of recipient governments. The third is more mundane: the intergovernmental transfer of funds is simply for the purpose of compensating a government for the costs of services provided to the one making the transfer.

Three major types of intergovernmental payments generally correspond to the three objectives. These are discussed in this section, as is a fourth type, the block grant, which is something of an anomaly.

*The Categorical Grant.* The first type of intergovernmental payment is the categorical grant, which is characterized by extensive restrictions on the uses to which the funds may be put by the recipient government. The restrictions are intended to ensure that the money is spent for a specific purpose, and that the recipient government increases its outlays on the aided service.

The quintessential condition of the categorical grant is that the recipient must "spend" the money for the indicated purpose. With this condition alone, however, the grant would have the intended effect of increasing outlays for the purpose only if the recipient's spending on the service in the absence of the grant would have been less than the amount of the grant. Then outlays for the aided service would have to rise in order for the recipient to prove that the full amount of the grant was spent for that purpose.

This is the reason categorical grants commonly have matching requirements. These condition the availability of the funds on the willingness of the recipient government to spend on the aided service a total equal to at least the amount of the grant plus the required local "match."

For example, suppose that a federal or state grant of $10,000 were available with a 50-percent-local-matching requirement. A local government would have to demonstrate spending of at least $20,000 on the aided function to receive the full amount of the grant. Again, whether the grant induces an increase in outlays for the aided function depends on the amount the locality would have spent for the purpose in the absence of the grant.

*General Fiscal Assistance.* The second type of grant is general fiscal assistance, often referred to as "revenue sharing." Such intergovernmental transfers are not intended to affect spending on any particular function (or even on all functions taken together). Rather, their purpose is to improve the overall ability of the recipient to finance its public-service responsibilities. As a consequence, such assistance is accompanied only by very limited restrictions. It is—as in the case of the Federal Revenue Sharing Program, which expired in 1986—"no-strings" aid.

One type of intergovernmental transfer is somewhat ambiguous. This is "shared taxes," which some prefer to classify as local tax collections. Shared taxes are tax revenues of a state government that are distributed, with few if any restrictions, to local governments on the basis of the "origin" of the revenue. They are not local tax collections because the local government has no role in the decision to collect the taxes in the first place. This being the case, shared taxes should be regarded as general-assistance grants, and they should be evaluated with a view to their effects on disparities in fiscal capacities. From this perspective, shared taxes are a fiscal device of dubious value. No locality receives a nickel that does not originate in that jurisdiction and, as a consequence, a shared tax is inherently incapable of reducing fiscal disparities.

*Reimbursement of Costs.* The third type of intergovernmental transfer is nothing more than reimbursement paid by one government for the costs of services rendered to it or its residents by another government. A special case of reimbursement has gained increasing attention in the past few years. This involves the cost to a locality of complying with mandates imposed on it by its state or the federal government. Some state governments have enacted legislation requiring them to compensate local governments for these costs, and a campaign has been mounted to persuade the Congress to approve similar legislation. Very serious questions have been raised by the experience in the states about the practicability of an effort to require across-the-board reimbursement for the costs of all types of "mandates."

*The Block Grant.* A fourth type of intergovernmental transfer has grown rapidly in importance in the past few decades at the federal level. This is the block grant, which is characterized by fewer restrictions than categorical grants. In particular, the funds typically may be used for any purposes in a fairly broad functional area, such as elementary and secondary education or social services.

The idea of the block grant originated several decades ago as a response to the charge that the categorical grant system had become excessively complex, expensive to administer, and even counterproductive. The concept was that a set of categorical grants in a particular functional area would be combined into a single block grant with many fewer restrictions and nominal compliance requirements. The funds would have to be spent for the general functional purposes addressed by the superseded categoricals, but there would be no matching or elaborate reporting requirements.

The block grant is best viewed as what economists refer to as a "second-best" policy option. That is, it might be proposed and defended as a politically appealing improvement over a "congested" set of categorical grants. But this would make sense only if it were determined that the categoricals could not be reformed to meet reasonable standards of efficiency and equity (the "first-best" option).

Standing on its own, the block grant is an anomaly. Having no matching or maintenance-of-effort requirements, it cannot do what a well-designed categorical grant potentially can—that is, induce a recipient government to increase the amount it provides of the aided service. Hence a block grant is clearly unsuited to the first rationale for grants: raising service levels.

*Summary.* All four types of intergovernmental payments are used by the federal government and by most states in varying degrees. The sunset of the Revenue Sharing Program in 1986 reduced by more than half federal outlays for programs classified by the Office of Management and Budget as general fiscal assistance. Such assistance continues to be made available under a complex array of federal payments in lieu of taxes to states and localities. The funding for federal block grants rose steeply in the early 1970's and again in the early 1980's. In the latter instance, the rise in funding was largely at the expense of categoricals as a substantial number of such programs were consolidated into an array of new block grants.

State payments to local governments may be financed by revenues from state taxes and fees or by federal grants. In the latter instance, the federal funds are often characterized as being "passed through" to localities by the state governments that are the direct recipients of the aid.

## RECENT TRENDS IN THE SOURCES OF LOCAL REVENUES

Table 2-1 shows the percentage distribution of the major sources of local revenues in fiscal year 1988 and a decade earlier. A number of significant trends are readily apparent.

First, over the ten-year interval, local governments became more reliant on revenues from their own sources (those collected by them applying their own taxes, charges, and other miscellaneous revenue items). Between 1978 and 1988, own-source revenues as a share of total revenues increased from 61 percent to 67 percent, with all three components—general revenues, utility revenues, and other revenues—showing increased importance.

Looking specifically at the composition of general revenues, which is shown detailed in the lower half of table 2-1, the decline in reliance on property taxes is the most striking development. The yield of these taxes as a proportion of total general revenue from local sources plunged from 64 percent to 47 percent during the decade. All other types of taxes contributed larger shares of local general revenues in fiscal year 1988 than in fiscal year 1978. General sales taxes are the second most important type of local tax, and their share of revenues rose the

TABLE 2-1

*Recent Trends in the Sources of Local Government Revenue, Fiscal Years 1978 and 1988*

| Source | PERCENTAGE DISTRIBUTIONS | |
|---|---|---|
| | FY 1978 | FY 1988 |
| Total Revenue | 100.0%‡ | 100.0% |
| Revenue from Own Sources | | |
| General Revenue | 51.6 | 54.8 |
| Utility Revenue | 7.6 | 9.3 |
| Other Revenue* | 1.6 | 3.0 |
| Intergovernmental Revenue | | |
| State | 30.1 | 29.4 |
| Federal | 9.0 | 3.5 |
| General Revenue from Own Sources | 100.0% | 100.0%‡ |
| Taxes | | |
| Property | 57.9 | 46.9 |
| General Sales | 5.6 | 6.7 |
| Selective Sales | 2.8 | 2.9 |
| Income | 3.7 | 3.8 |
| Other Taxes | 2.6 | 3.0 |
| Current Charges | 19.1 | 22.2 |
| Miscellaneous Revenue† | 8.3 | 14.6 |

* Consists of insurance-trust and liquor-store revenue
† Sales of assets, interest earnings
‡ Detail does not add to total because of rounding
SOURCE: U.S. Bureau of the Census, *Governmental Finances in 1977–78.* (Washington, D.C.: GPO, February 1980) tables 4 and 12; *Governmental Finances in 1987–88*, GF85 5 (Washington, D.C.: GPO, January 1990), Table 6.

most—by one-fifth, but they still account for less than 15 percent of the amount contributed by taxes on property.

The major replacement for property taxes in the revenue system of the typical local government was nontax revenues. Charges produced substantially larger shares of local revenues in 1988 than they had a decade earlier.[13] Miscellaneous revenues, including interest earnings and proceeds from land sales, accounted for nearly twice the proportion of local revenues at the end of the period that they had at the beginning.

The relative contribution of intergovernmental revenue from state governments declined slightly, while that of the federal government dropped precipitously during the decade. Thus, almost all the increase in the importance of own-source revenues is attributable to the decline in the share of federal aid.

## SIZE AND PERFORMANCE OF THE STATE AND LOCAL SECTOR

Table 2-2 provides a concise overview of the size of state and local sectors in relationship to the economy as measured by percentages of the gross national

TABLE 2-2

*Total Direct Expenditures, Own-Source Revenues, and Outstanding Debt of State and Local Governments as a Percentage of Gross National Product Selected Fiscal Years 1932–1988*

| | 1932 | 1940 | 1950 | 1960 | 1970 | 1980 | 1988 |
|---|---|---|---|---|---|---|---|
| **Panel A. Total Direct Expenditures** | | | | | | | |
| State share | 3.3% | 3.5% | 3.8% | 4.4% | 5.7% | 6.6% | 7.1% |
| Local share | 11.0 | 7.7 | 5.9 | 7.7 | 9.3 | 9.8 | 10.4 |
| Total | 14.3 | 11.2 | 9.8 | 12.0 | 14.9 | 16.4 | 17.5 |
| **Panel B. Total Own Revenues** | | | | | | | |
| State | 3.9 | 5.0 | 4.0 | 5.2 | 6.9 | 8.1 | 9.2 |
| Local | 9.3 | 5.8 | 4.1 | 5.4 | 6.0 | 5.9 | 7.1 |
| Total | 13.2 | 10.8 | 8.1 | 10.6 | 12.9 | 14.0 | 16.3 |
| **Panel C. Total Debt Outstanding** | | | | | | | |
| State | 4.9 | 3.6 | 1.8 | 3.7 | 4.2 | 4.6 | 5.9 |
| Local | 28.2 | 16.7 | 6.6 | 10.1 | 10.2 | 8.1 | 10.2 |
| Total | 33.1 | 20.3 | 8.4 | 13.9 | 14.4 | 12.7 | 16.1 |

SOURCES: Office of State and Local Finance, U.S. Department of the Treasury, *Federal-State-Local Fiscal Relations* (Washington: G.P.O., tables III.1, III.4 and III.7, and U.S. Bureau of the Census, *Government Finances in 1987–88*, GF-88-5 (January 1990), tables 6, 10 and 13; *Economic Report of the President, 1990* (January 1990), p. 294.

product (GNP) for selected years of the period 1932 through 1988. Panel A displays state and local direct expenditures as a percentage of GNP, while panel B gives total own-source revenues in similar terms. Rising ratios of expenditures and revenues to GNP indicate that the sector (or states and localities within the sector) are growing more rapidly than the economy as a whole. The percentages also reflect the shifts between the state and local levels in relative importance in terms of revenue-raising and spending. Panel C provides information on the relative size of the outstanding debt of state and local governments in relationship to GNP.

Several trends are apparent. As panel A of table 2-2 indicates, total state-local spending during the Depression year of 1932 was 14.5 percent of GNP; outlays by localities alone equalled 11 percent of GNP. As the nation recovered from the Depression and moved through World War II, the relative importance of the state and local sector shrank. Postwar prosperity, the baby boom, and recovery from the austerity of the Depression and War, and a surge in new programs, however, propelled rapid growth in the sector through the 1970's. Growth tapered off in the 1980's; but even so, state and local spending reached 17.5 percent of GNP by 1988. In addition, the composition of spending changed markedly over the period. The states, which had accounted for 24 percent of the sector's direct spending in 1932, by 1988 accounted for 41 percent.

Panel B of table 2-2 tells a similar but even more dramatic story. State and local own-source revenues also retreated from the high levels of the Depression and then grew in the postwar period (expenditures consistently exceed own-source revenues because of intergovernmental aid from the federal government and because of capital outlays financed by borrowing). Accompanying the growth in revenues was a shift in revenue-raising responsibility from the local to the state level. Between 1932 and 1988, the share of revenues raised by the states increased from 30 percent to 56 percent. Thus, in both revenues and expenditures, there has been a growing concentration of activity at the state level. Two major factors in this development have been the shifting of the welfare function from the localities to the states and the great increase in the scope of such programs and the growing role of the states in financing education at both the public school and higher education levels.

Panel C of table 2-2 provides insight into the trends in total debt outstanding of states and local governments, including both the general-obligation and limited-obligation ("revenue bond") forms of indebtedness. In the midst of the Depression, state and local debt amounted to a very high 33 percent of GNP. The nation's GNP had fallen drastically as a result of the economic contraction (in 1927, before the crash, total debt had represented only 14 percent of GNP). Reflecting the shrinkage of the sector during World War II, debt declined through 1950 and then began to grow slowly and, especially since 1970, fitfully. At the local government level, the relative debt declined between 1970 and 1980, resurging somewhat by 1988. Heavy volumes of borrowing, especially for private-activity purposes, have somewhat inflated the state and local debt figure. Since 1985, the volume of borrowing has abated and it is likely that debt outstanding will grow more slowly than GNP in the near future.[14]

A question frequently asked is how well state and local governments are performing in the aggregate in balancing their revenues and expenditures and the degree to which the sector overall is experiencing fiscal stress. That question is difficult to answer given the nature of the aggregate data that are available, and analysis of conditions really must be directed at indicators other than simply total expenditures and receipts. As a practical matter, it is most unlikely that the operating budgets of states and localities will ever get very far out of balance for any period of time. This is because all the states (save Vermont) must balance their operating budgets under either constitutional or statutory requirements and the great majority of localities must conform to a similar fiscal discipline.[15]

Thus, except for the opportunity to borrow for funding capital spending, state and local governments faced with deficits must draw down reserves (which seldom exceed a few weeks of spending needs), raise revenues, or reduce expenditures. These transitions may be accommodated by short-term borrowing to help smooth out the adjustment process.

Keeping in mind certain shortcomings, it is nonetheless possible to use the National Income Accounts to gain a sense of the fiscal pressures the state and local sector is experiencing. In doing so it is important to focus on the "operating account" of the sector, netting out the activities of the insurance trust funds (primarily pensions). A major difficulty in looking at the operating account is

FIGURE 2-1
*State and Local Surpluses and Deficits (Operating Account) as a Percentage of Receipts, 1955–89*

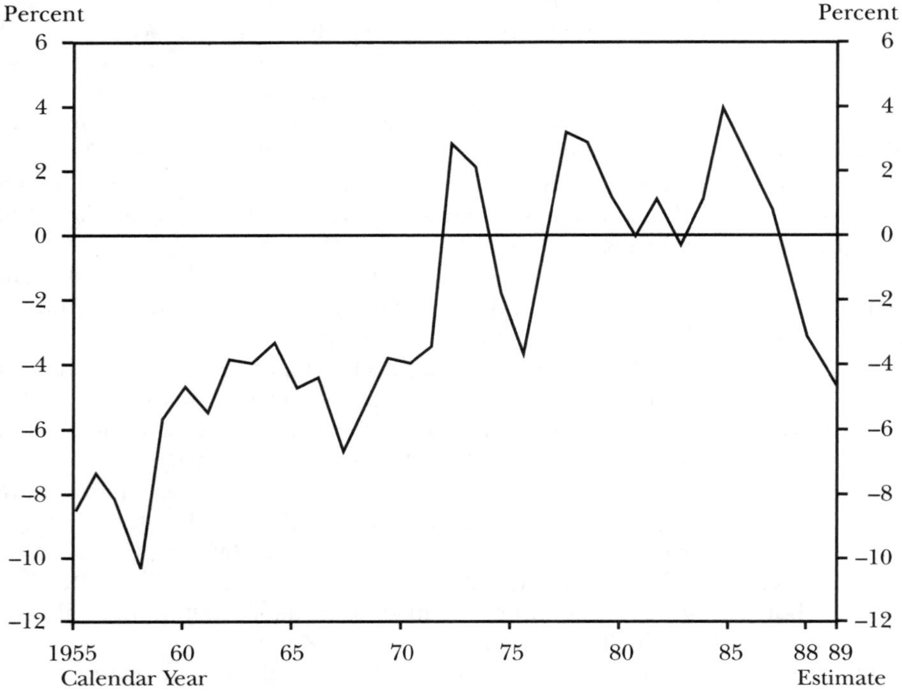

Note: Excludes Social Insurance Funds
SOURCES: Executive Office of the President, *President's Fiscal Year 1990 and 1991 Budget: Special Analyses* (Washington, D.C.: GPO) and *Survey of Current Business* (March 1990), Table 3.3.

that by the conventions used in the national income accounts, all capital outlays are treated as "operating" expenditures, but the proceeds of the borrowings that finance much of those capital outlays are not treated as receipts.[16]

Figure 2-1 presents the operating account of the state and local sector for the period 1955 through 1988, with the surplus or deficit measured as a percentage of total receipts, using the National Income Account definitions. The current account was in deficit every year through 1971. The persistent deficit largely reflected the fact that substantial capital outlays were being debt-financed, while year-to-year variations in the size of the deficit reflected changing economic conditions. That is, the deficit tended to increase in times of recession and to decline in times of prosperity. Short-term borrowing was heavily relied upon during recessions to finance temporary deficits and to carry governments until prosperity returned.

In 1972, the state and local operating account jumped into surplus as a direct result of the initiation of payments under the Revenue Sharing Program.

The account remained in surplus most years through the mid-1980s, mostly because of the decreased importance of capital spending financed by borrowing. The severe recession of 1982 and 1983 produced a small deficit in 1982, but the strong recovery of the mid-1980s, coupled with tax increases and spending restraint, saw a rapid recovery in the fiscal balance of states and localities. Since 1984, despite the generally strong economy, the trend in the operating account has been into deficit, as a result of reductions in federal assistance and increasing reliance on the debt financing of capital spending.

By the end of the 1980s, state and local governments found themselves in a deficit position comparable to that of the 1960s.[17] In view of the enormous changes that have occurred in the economy and the U.S. fiscal system since the 1960s, the plunge of the state-local sector into deficit since 1984 deserves careful analysis that is, regrettably, beyond the scope of this chapter.

## *NOTES*

1. Domestic public services include all general expenditures except those for national defense, international relations, and interest on the national debt. Those familiar with the accounts of the U.S. Bureau of the Census, from which these data are drawn, will recall that the concept of general expenditures does not include insurance trust expenditures. The most notable of these are the federal government's outlays for Social Security, which rose at a rate nearly 60 percent faster than all domestic general expenditures during the period.

2. Dwight D. Eisenhower, *The White House Years: Mandate for Change, 1953–56* (New York: Doubleday, 1963), p. 327.

3. Richard A. Musgrave, *The Theory of Public Finance* (New York: McGraw-Hill, 1959), pp. 3–27.

4. Another way of characterizing this distinction is that most goods are inherently "rival" in nature—what I consume you cannot, as in the case of bread. The consumption decision is how much is to be purchased in the market at various prices. Some goods (or services) are nonrival by their very nature. That is, whatever quantity is produced is consumed equally by all. As a consequence, the production decision must be made by some collectivity on behalf of all of the residents of the area affected by that decision. When few people are involved, the decision may be handled by a voluntary organization, such as a club or a neighborhood association. As a practical matter, however, the decision-making entity must be a government in most situations. The issues are, of course, how much is to be produced and what share of the cost is to be paid by each resident of the jurisdiction.

5. As Musgrave observes in a different context, the difference between private and public goods "Is not a matter of ideology but an objective or 'technological' distinction." (*Fiscal Systems: Studies in Comparative Economics* [New Haven, Conn.: Yale Univ. Press, 1969], p. 10.)

6. In feudal times, the public sector was largely supported by the produce of the land belonging to the Crown, an option available to few governments in the twentieth century.

7. The money is not literally printed, in the sense that the Bureau of Engraving

and Printing works overtime and trucks the output to the nearest bank for deposit to the account of the U.S. Treasury. Rather, printing is a shorthand way of referring to the effect of the sale of Treasury securities to the Federal Reserve System. The Fed pays for the purchase by crediting the government's account. By doing so, it creates the money in the account. The sale may occur indirectly, to the same economic effect, if the securities are sold to "public" (in federal finance, this means any party other than the Fed) and the Fed purchases in the open market an equivalent amount of previously issued Treasuries. The Fed, of course, is an agency of the U.S. government. This status, coupled with its power to purchase Treasury securities, gives the federal government the ability to "print" money. No comparable institutional arrangements exist at the state level today, although they did in the early nineteenth century.

8. The bondholders do assume two risks: that the issuer may not service the debt on schedule, and that they may be unable to liquidate their holdings before the securities mature without experiencing capital losses if interest rates rise. Default on the debt, as in the case of the $2.5 billion of bonds issued by the Washington Public Power Supply System that were declared in default in 1982, rests the costs of the government activity funded by the debt on the bondholders. This is, of course, the equivalent of a draft—or confiscation—of the resources, in this case the money paid for the bonds.

9. See Advisory Commission on Intergovernmental Relations, *Regulatory Federalism: Policy, Progress, Impact and Reform,* Report A-95 (February 1984); and Department of the Treasury, Office of State and Local Finance, *Federal-State-Local Fiscal Relations: Report to the President and the Congress* (September 1985), pp. 80–92.

10. See the discussion of the arrangements in 26 states by John F. Due and John L. Mikesell, *Sales Taxation: State and Local Structure and Administration* (Baltimore: John Hopkins Univ. Press, 1983), pp. 298–314.

11. Eligible local jurisdictions are counties in Indiana and Maryland (including the City of Baltimore) and school districts in Iowa. Supplements are authorized in Iowa when the state comptroller determines that a district's costs exceed the revenue yield at the property tax limit and the available state aid.

In Maryland, a supplement of 20 percent of a taxpayer's state liability is mandatory, but a rate as high as 50 percent may be enacted. In this case, only the rate in excess of 20 percent is a true supplement. The mandated minimum rate of 20 percent clearly is a state tax whose proceeds are returned to the locality of origin (see the discussion of shared taxes later in this chapter).

The New York State Department of Taxation and Finance has administered New York City's income tax since 1976. As the base of the tax is state taxable income and the tax was enacted by the city, this clearly is a supplement rather than a shared tax. Since its fiscal crisis in 1984, the City of Yonkers has been required to levy a supplement, administered by the state. The current rate of the supplement is 19.25 percent of individuals' net state tax liability after a property tax credit. Because the city has no alternative, this is really a special state tax whose proceeds are returned to the locality of origin. See Advisory Commission on Intergovernmental Relations, Significant Features of Fiscal Federalism: 1990, Vol. 1, *Budget Processes and Tax Systems,* Report M-169 (January 1990), table 21; and Clara Penniman, *State Income Taxation* (Baltimore: Johns Hopkins Univ. Press, 1980), p. 262.

12. The Code does this by attempting to ensure that tax-exempt debt is not used to finance (1) capital outlays that do not really support essential functions of local government, and (2) income-earning investments by local governments. The sale of tax-exempt debt to finance investments in higher-yielding paper rather than capital outlays is commonly

referred to as arbitrage, and the earnings captured from the spread in rates are called arbitrage profits. Current federal law, with limited exceptions, imposes what amounts to a 100 percent tax on arbitrage profits—that is, all arbitrage profits must be paid to the U.S. Treasury. This includes the profits associated with schemes that can be very subtle and complex, and that may not at first appear to involve arbitrage. An example is the locality that sells TANs to finance a seasonal cash-flow dip even though one or more of the government's own funds has a balance that could be borrowed to finance the deficit. For a discussion of the extensive restrictions placed on the use of tax exemption in the 1986 Tax Reform Act see John E. Petersen, *Tax-Exempts and Tax Reform* (Chicago: Government Finance Officers Association, 1987). State and local governments have actively protested many of the restrictions placed in the code by the 1986 Act. See *Preserving the Federal-State-Local Partnership: The Role of Tax Exempt Financing,* Report of the Anthony Commission (Chicago: Government Finance Officers Association, 1989).

13. U.S. Bureau of the Census, *Government Finances in 1987–1988* (Washington, D.C.: Government Printing Office, January 1990), figures 3 and 4.

14. See Petersen, [note 12], pp. 2-1–2-10.

15. U.S. Treasury, [note 9], p. 393.

16. There are numerous other inconsistencies between the way governments keep their books and the way the National Income Accounts are computed. For example, purchases of land, and existing structures are not treated as expenditures, utilities are treated on a net basis after expenditures are subtracted from receipts, and the various revenue receipts are accrued that many governments recognize on a cash basis. See U.S. Office of Management and Budget, *Special Analyses, Budget of the United States Government, Fiscal Year 1990* (Washington: GPO), p. H.31.

17. See "Budgetary Pressures Drive Short-Term Market," *Credit Review,* Standard & Poor's Corporation (December 11, 1989), p. 1.

# 3

# *Organization of the Finance Function*

EDWARD ANTHONY LEHAN

SINCE the turn of the twentieth century, the key organizational issue of local government finance has been integration.

Before the onset of computers, which complicated the integration issue, expert opinion defined the problem simply as an undesirable fragmentation of authority. In the early decades of the twentieth century, organizational arrangements for finance work typically embraced elected finance officials, multimember boards exercising finance functions, and frequently numerous appointed finance officers reporting function by function to various boards, legislative bodies, and senior officials. The prescription for this fragmentation called for the concentration of finance supervision in a finance director reporting to a chief executive. Although this prescription has been adopted by numerous local governments, integrated finance directorates have by no means supplanted the fragmented approach to finance organization, particularly in the larger jurisdictions. The incomplete realization of the integration ideal represents an important item of unfinished business for those interested in the efficient and effective management of local government and its finance.[1]

Looking back, the concept of finance directorates was rooted in turn-of-the-century campaigns to free local governments from the grasp of the spoilsman—and cannot be truly understood apart from that struggle. The theory of "good" government, defined as public accountability, is better served by a concentration of authority, rather than its dispersion. The idea of concentrating the supervision of finance work in a finance directorate appeared as a necessary and logical extension of this theory. Facing entrenched spoilsmen, the turn-of-the-century reformers sought to concentrate administrative authority in chief executives as the best means of ensuring local government accountability. They also saw, as a practical matter, that the financial aspects of administration should be concentrated in the hands of an officer reporting to a strong chief executive to make that office effective.

Seizing on the strategic fact that finance cuts across all programs, the architects of the early finance directorates expected incumbent directors to exploit the advantage of their position to

- enforce local government policies by means of finance-related controls
- represent and enforce the values of economy and efficiency through the government, and
- provide broad policy advice on issues facing the government

Looking inward, finance power is intrusive. Its arithmetic reaches into every nook and cranny of local government. The organizational and procedural arrangements for the exercise of finance power provide a basic system of order and a prime vehicle for regulating the execution of governmental policies. Looking outward, the exercise of a government's fiscal power regulates its relationship to the financial and economic marketplace, affecting the arithmetic of the community. In various degrees, this relationship is most precisely formulated at budget time, when, in addition to defining its service agenda, appropriation decisions invoke collateral decisions on taxes, service charges, and loans.

In historical perspective, the influential advocates of finance directorates advanced "coordination" and "control" values as the principal rationale for a hierarchically integrated finance organization.[2] By providing a single authoritative source, this hierarchical integration was also seen as a way to reduce conflicts and contradictions in advice and information supplied by finance officers to policy-making officials. As their experience did not embrace computers, the early advocates of hierarchical integration did not envision the collateral issue of "data integration," with its organizational and procedural implications.

On this latter point, at the end of their chapter "Organization" in the 1975 edition of *Concepts and Practices in Local Government Finance*, Moak and Hillhouse acknowledged that computer technology was "forcing major changes in the organization for financial management," and then offered the following qualified speculations:

> Perhaps the centralized department of finance will evolve into a centralized department of administration, which means that the latter will absorb the former as a subordinate unit. Initially, responsibility for the data processing activity has been placed where the best use can be made of expensive equipment and where technical know-how exists. This has often been the case with activities which have been added to the department of finance.
>
> As for the future, it is not possible to predict, of course, the outcome of more automation in city hall, but we would expect some lasting, and perhaps drastic, changes.[3]

Since this comment by Moak and Hillhouse, the power and speed of computers increased exponentially, the relative price of computer power decreased significantly, integrated financial software became readily available and widely used, a very useful "spreadsheet" software was invented and spread rapidly, compact "personal" computers invaded office after office and could be tied together in local area networks, and, with the advent of the laser printer, anybody could compose and produce first-class illustrated documents.

In the fifteen years since Moak and Hillhouse wondered about the "outcome of more automation in city hall," the organizational and procedural consequences of computers have become clearer. Finance employees work less at traditional tasks, such as posting, transcribing, calculating, stamping, logging, listing, etc., as computers do more processing and manipulation. Collaterally, finance employees increasingly work at "controlling" the status and flow of computerized data. Because they extend the reach of the human nervous system and expand the human memory, computers are revolutionizing work. And mark this: Even more than organizations, computers empower persons. In a thoroughly computerized environment, the concept of supervision, which traditionally defined a hierarchical relationship, seems more appropriately applied to data, rather than persons. Endowed with access to computer resources, including software that facilitates data manipulation, finance workers become creative personnel—if you will, supervisors of databases—and as such are beyond the reach of traditional techniques of supervision.

## *THE CONTEMPORARY SITUATION*

Although systematic survey data is not available to document the form of finance organization decade by decade, a certain amount of evidence can be adduced that indicates comparatively less interest in the comprehensive finance directorate during the post–World War II era than during the first four decades of the century, including the Great Depression. Consider the following generalizations:

- Prosperity encouraged and permitted the leaders of local government to emphasize programmatic values. As a result, service programs proliferated and expanded, willy-nilly, straining the power of chief executives to direct and coordinate operations by traditional means. Many governments responded to the growing programmatic confusion by establishing "super departments," including departments of management or administration under the control of an executive appointee. In many cases, the local government's chief financial officer was required to report to this appointee instead of the chief executive, a sharp and serious departure from the classical concept of the finance directorate.
- Improvements in budgetary technique, deemphasizing the accounting nature of the format and process in favor of its policymaking and managerial aspects, often resulted in a shift of important budget duties from finance directors to a member of the chief executive's immediate staff or to the aforementioned departments of management or administration.

- Data processing, in most cases originally introduced into local government by alert and progressive finance directors, grew to the point where the systemwide applications and implications led some governments to reduce or eliminate the supervisory role of finance directors for this fabulous technology, an ironic twist.

As a case in point, the experience of the City of Hartford, Connecticut, reported below, reflects the impact of these general trends and forces conditioning the organization of the finance function in the post–World War Two years.[4]

In 1947, the city adopted a new charter, establishing the council-manager form of government, including provisions for a finance department headed by a finance director appointed by the city manager. But, as is so often the case in government reorganizations, the power and prestige of incumbent officials received respectful consideration. As a result, the treasury and property assessment units were not included within the ambit of the finance department. Under the 1947 charter, the city treasurer is elected. The city assessor is appointed by the city manager, but enjoys civil service protection against removal. In effect, the city has three finance leaders, one of whom is completely beyond the formal coordinating power of the city's chief executive; another, partially so.

Taking 1959–60 as a benchmark year, the 69-position finance department included the data-processing function, then called machine records, and a 3-position budget and research division. Machine records, with 12 positions, functioned as an activity of the accounting division. As provided by the charter, the 5-position treasury and the 19-position assessment functions were assigned departmental status.

Over the next sixteen years, with the exception of machine records, which was renamed data processing and assigned divisional status in the finance department, Hartford's finance establishment grew in size but remained organizationally stable.

In 1976–77, the data processing division was transferred from the finance department to the city manager's office. This move portended a broader role for the division in the city's information and decision-making process, and the city manager's expressed interest in "an independent means of evaluating the rest of the city organization."

The following year, the budget and research division, renamed management and budget, was shifted from the finance department to a new management services department headed by an assistant city manager. In his budget message of April 18, 1977, the city manager indicated his dissatisfaction with the existing organizational arrangement, stating that this new assignment to his office would result in the "implementation of a major budget modification, incorporating the benefits of MBO and a project evaluation and monitoring system." At the same time, the data processing division was also shifted from the city manager's office to this new department. As the transfer of the budget and research division left it without staff resources, a 4-position financial management division was established within the finance department.

Continuing to evolve organizationally, data processing was assigned departmental status in 1985–86; in the following year it was renamed the department of information services.

In 1987–88, without interpretive comment in the annual budget document, the management and budget unit, with 10 positions, was returned to the jurisdiction of the finance director.

As noted above, the city has three finance leaders, rather than the single leader prescribed by the integrated model. How common is the integrated finance organization today?

In a study of 254 local government finance establishments across the United States conducted in the mid-1960s, Marshall W. Meyer reported that "less than half of these 254 departments have centralized all major financial responsibilities under the control of one department head."[5]

Reporting the results of a survey of 551 local governments in 1985, the Government Finance Officers Association (GFOA) found a single finance leader accountable for all of the 22 listed finance functions, if practiced, in 29 percent of those governments.[6] The listed finance functions included assessments, pre-audit, post-audit, *budgeting, central accounting, cash management,* data processing, *debt administration, debt issuance, disbursements,* grants management, internal audit, *investment management,* inventory, pension administration, *policy analysis and research,* purchasing, *payroll, revenue collection,* risk management, tax billing, and utility billing.

When the list was narrowed to ten "core" functions, italicized above, the proportion of the 551 jurisdictions with a single accountable finance leader jumped to 44 percent.

Additionally, the report noted that the tendency to adopt an integrated finance organization is inversely related to size, with the proportion using an integrated approach declining as the size of the jurisdictions increased. In jurisdictions with populations of 100,000 or less, 48 percent reported using the same supervisor for the ten "core" functions. In jurisdictions with populations of 500,000 or more, the proportion dropped to 20 percent.

In both surveys, the sample was provided by members of the Government Finance Officers Association. Based on these samples, taken twenty years apart, one may cautiously observe that, although integrated finance establishments have been widely adopted, they are probably not, at the time of this writing, the predominant form of finance organization in local governments in the United States.

Both surveys provide insight into the internal organization of finance establishments. Meyer reported that establishment size has significant effects on important organizational variables, including the number of supervisory levels, the number of divisions and division sections, and the number of employees reporting to first-line supervisors, all of which increase as the size of the establishment increases.[7] Table 3-1 summarizes his findings.

The GFOA survey reported a tendency for certain of the 22 listed finance functions to be assigned to the same supervisor. Pre-audit, payroll, disbursements,

TABLE 3-1
*Organizational Features by Size of Work Force*

| ORGANIZATIONAL CONCEPT | AVERAGE TOTAL NUMBER OF EMPLOYEES | | | |
|---|---|---|---|---|
| | 20–34 | 35–59 | 60–99 | 100+ |
| Supervisory Levels | 3.5 | 3.6 | 4.0 | 4.7 |
| Divisions | 4.4 | 5.3 | 5.7 | 7.9 |
| Sections | 6.7 | 9.5 | 10.5 | 21.8 |
| Reporting to Line Supervisors | 4.5 | 5.5 | 7.1 | 11.6 |

SOURCE: Marshall W. Meyer, *Bureaucratic Structure and Authority* (New York: Harper & Row, 1972).

debt administration, and central accounting formed one such organizational grouping that appeared with very high frequency among the 551 jurisdictions. Cash management and investment management appeared as another strong combination put under common leadership. On the other hand, tax billing was frequently found to stand alone with its supervisor. The 14 other functions showed a variety of inconstant combinations.[8]

Meyer also took note of this organizational diversity, advancing the following comment:

> So varied are the departments of finance that it is difficult to describe a typical one. Some are only accounting offices; responsibility for the budget, collection of funds, and maintenance of the treasury lies elsewhere. At the other extreme, a few departments in addition to their administrative activities direct services such as management of government-owned real estate and operation of parking garages.[9]

Meyer even discovered a finance department supervising a county morgue. Certainly, to formulate an adequate organizational philosophy for the conduct of local government finance, one must cut through this operational variety to locate the basics of the job.

## ORGANIZATIONAL RATIONALE: THE GOALS OF FINANCE WORK

Organizations are justified by goals sought and attained. Despite respect for this axiom, it must be acknowledged that goals tend to be elusive, no less in finance work than in other fields of human endeavor. Indeed, the same environmental pressures that are compelling contemporary governments to "do more" paradoxically work to make goal attainment increasingly problematical.

In differentiated modern society, the values of responsibility and accountability are at war with one another. In this context, *accountability* refers to authoritative action exercising the discretionary powers of an office in accordance with law or a code of official conduct. *Responsibility* refers to authoritative action subject to correction by those subject to it. If one is totally responsible, one has no authority. (On the contemporary scene, the distinction between accountability and responsibility can be clearly seen in the controversy over the review of police action by citizen boards.) As the complexity of modern society advances, administrative organizations differentiate in an effort to respond, that is, satisfy the conflicting demands of a steadily growing array of subgroups, subcultures, and differentiated environments. Under the impact of differentiated interests, official responses to the stimuli tend to replace the reasoned exercise of authority.

Further, goals are particularly hard to define and communicate in governments, as they do not enjoy the seeming clarity that the "bottom line" confers on profit-seeking organizations. Yet, despite the ambiguities that beset governmental enterprise, the goals of local government finance work must be defined. This is the indispensable, irreducible ingredient of organizational thought applied to finance work.

Another caution is in order. Organization provides a framework for management. It is not management. Nor can organizational forms guarantee management performance. Management behavior is not a natural human attribute. It must be learned, and once learned, steadfastly practiced, lest it atrophy or, worse, pass into an instrument of personal caprice or opportunism.

Although each local government strives to attain goals unique to it and its situation, its finance targets should be related to the following financial concerns:

- The *availability* of money
- The *cost* of money
- The *productivity* of money

*Availability* refers to cash and the ability to meet obligations when due. To think about availability is to focus on a jurisdiction's credit repute, reserves, tax strategies, billing cycles, payment procedures, past-due receivables, and the investment of loan proceeds and cash balances. Liquidity is the *sine qua non* of finance management. Achieving goals related to liquidity and cash management require coordinated actions involving every sector of a local government.

The *cost* of money refers to (1) interest charges on borrowed funds and (2) the financial burden of administering the finance function. As pure "overhead," the finance function normally embraces the "core" functions previously cited, plus others. Every local government should strive to reduce net interest costs and the cost of finance management, not only in the finance establishment proper, but also in all service program centers. Needless to say, economical finance management cannot be achieved without strong centralized leadership and unremitting attention to the details of daily work.

The *productivity* of money refers to the net benefit earned by the allocation of funds to the various purposes of the local government. Most actively applied at budget time, local government policymakers use some form of investment criteria to weigh the merits of various spending proposals, seeking the "best" distribution of funds, measured in terms of relative "return." Although this process will always reflect the subjective judgments of elected leaders, every local government should strive to enlarge the role of formal allocation criteria in their decisions by including benefit estimation data in budget documents and finance reports. Progress in this difficult task depends on government-wide collaboration and a close working relationship between chief executive, finance director, and budget staff.

## ORGANIZATIONAL IMPLICATIONS

*Liquidity.* Acquiring capital, and having it ready to pay wages and other due bills is the prime duty of every finance establishment. In precise terms, annual revenues must equal or exceed authorized expenditures.

The credit rating agencies show great interest in the history of local government liquidity, rightly seeing it as the telltale indicator of fiscal probity and, perforce, creditor security. Because they are fundamentally concerned with a jurisdiction's ability to pay its creditors in the future, the rating agencies place the liquidity issue in a context of socioeconomic trends, assessing the long-term ability of the local government to draw capital from its environment to finance essential services and debt payments. In this connection, governments that maintain multiyear plans, particularly for their capital investments, and actively support community development and tax-enhancing projects generally enjoy better credit ratings.

In governments of general jurisdiction, cash flows toward the treasury from a complex of sources, including an ever-changing mix of taxes, regulatory fees, service charges, loans, and grants. All these receivables require unremitting management attention to ensure timely receipt, deposit, and subsequent investment. To ensure maximum investment earnings, every local government needs formal goals for the receivables process, particularly tax delinquencies, disbursements, and the idle funds investment program, reviewing performance periodically.

Fundamentally, investment earnings depend on the interplay of investment amount, investment duration, and, interest rates. Of these three variables, interest rates are the most problematical, being set by market forces. Because interest rates fluctuate, reflecting the mutability of market conditions, and increasingly the volatility of world capital markets, finance officials cannot be held strictly accountable for making good on their forecasts of total investment earnings. They can, however, be held accountable for their predictions of investment size and duration. In contrast to the capriciousness of interest rates, the size and duration of investments are much more controllable and can be favorably influenced by coordinated management action, provided the finance establishment can transcend its own boundaries to supply government-wide leadership for a formal cash management program. Formal cash management programs foster the needed collaboration by fixing attention on the managerial factors affecting investment earnings.

In thinking about liquidity and any subsidiary cash management procedures, local government leaders confront an organizational problem of considerable complexity. Cash management is by no means a costless activity, nor is it to be considered as a treasury sideline, based on ad hoc decisions, guesswork, and "rules of thumb." To maximize investment potential, cash must be a prime subject of government-wide managerial thinking, planning, and collaboration. Many variables are involved, such as intelligent management of receivables, prompt cash depositing, and accurate disbursement forecasting by all service program managers. Recognizing that important variables lie in hands outside the treasury, indeed, outside the finance establishment, local governments are advised to provide a high order of financial leadership for cash management, vesting this function in a finance director. A local government may gain as much, or more, from this leadership as it might from the exercise of pure investment savvy. Furthermore, as the requirements for a separate treasury office disappear under the impact of computerization and integrated data management, local governments with finance directorates are well advised to assign the treasurer's duties to the finance director.

***Reducing Costs.*** It costs money to manage money! Inspired by this self-evident truth, local governments should keep a sharp eye on the relative costs to get, store, reckon, and spend its money. From this viewpoint, the finance establishment appears as a set of procedural problems that can be successfully attacked by applying the traditional forms of management analysis, such as work measurement, work simplification, the rationalization of forms and procedures, and the matching of costs to workloads and work output standards. For example, assuming an accurate assignment of costs, the annual investment in, let us say, accounts payable, can be related to an appropriate measurement of output, the number of settlements, and the resulting unit cost reduced in the future by deliberate management effort.

Of course, this assumes that finance personnel have sufficient motivation to strive for higher productivity. Given the low-key atmosphere of many local governments, finance personnel may tend to dwell on the dark side of the motivational issue, stressing productivity inhibitions and barriers, pointing to missing ingredients, making excuses for low productivity—thus shunning responsibility for improvements. Such tendencies can be successfully counterbalanced only by aggressive finance leaders who insist on pursuing procedural studies across functional lines. Due to this cross-functional aspect, it is highly unlikely that governments with fragmented finance leadership can muster the power and persistence to pursue and implement such studies.

Paradoxically, isolated attempts to bring each finance procedure to a peak of efficiency may not produce an efficient overall pattern of procedures if finance units are permitted to process and reprocess the same information. In those governments that do not maintain an integrated approach to finance management, an observer will undoubtedly find the same information (purchase order numbers, vendor addresses, invoice numbers, assessments, payroll data, etc.) recorded and rerecorded, filed and refiled, reported and rereported as it moves through one unit to another. Further, when finance personnel are observed at work, they are often occupied in transcribing existing data, creating new records. While some data redundancy is useful for proving and checking, most transcription work is sheer waste, particularly in computerized work environments. To counter this inevitable tendency, all procedural studies should be dominated by the theory of integrated data management, a perspective that demands the elimination of redundant data and superfluous routines in favor of continuous assembly of outputs.

Clearly, this requires a "systemic" approach, since finance-related data is to be created or captured but once, then stored and transmitted in a common medium such as paper, film, magnetic tape or disk, etc., which make the data repeatedly useful with minimal or no further input. As the only sure road to efficient, economic finance work, the systemic approach both implies and produces an integrated finance organization. This conception of integrated finance is not limited to centralized finance functions; it also applies to "line" agency "business affairs."

Characteristically, the service functions of local government are assigned to "line" departments, offices, or agencies. If a jurisdiction has centralized its finance functions, these fiscally dependent line units must assign staff to manage their business affairs, which commonly embrace the forms and procedures related to payrolls, requisitions, purchase orders, receiving reports, vendor payments, and expenditure controls. In governments of general jurisdiction, these scattered assignments are a significant cost and a source of much redundant data handling and storage. The relationship between line agency business affairs personnel and central finance units is rarely harmonious or efficient. Even in those jurisdictions where the finance director exercises a good deal of functional supervision over line agency business affairs personnel, the relationship tends to be the locus of tension, confusion, and error. The spread of computers and their linkage provides an opportunity to rethink this relationship in terms of the integrated data management ideal.

Despite the claims of computer manufacturers, there are few technological shortcuts to lower operating costs. Simple grafting of computer technology onto existing forms and procedures is quite common. Indeed, the advent of inexpensive desktop computers sharply *increases* the potential for idiomatic, repetitive recording of data—the practice already identified as the source of inefficient finance work, computerized or not. While reliance on a single centralized computer facility promotes various degrees of data integration, the concept of decentralized computer resources provides no such incentive. Obviously, in a government that provides its finance staff—and the line agency business affairs personnel—with decentralized computer resources, the integrated data management ideal will be more difficult to attain. In the years ahead, the availability of small, powerful computers will produce an irresistible demand for such decentralization. It is already happening. Only strong, continuous planning for integrated data management, via coordinated files and coding protocols, can offset the inherent waste and duplication that will accompany a planless distribution of these fabulous resources.

The tendency to think about finance procedures in planless, segmented ways is nowhere better illustrated than in the haphazard introduction of micrographic technology. One frequently hears of microphotography applied to inactive records. Far less frequently does one hear of a local government applying micrographic technology in daily operations. Rarer still is the jurisdiction that has developed a comprehensive plan to carefully balance and integrate the use of "hard copy" micrographic and computer records.[10]

In addition to measures that might help reduce the administrative costs of finance management, attention must be directed to the ways and means of reducing the cost of borrowed capital. Obviously, it is best to do no borrowing at all, thereby eliminating interest payments. Indeed, using this pay-as-you-build approach, the funds appropriated to pay for the project can be temporarily invested, earning interest. With a little lead time to build up reserves, even large projects can be financed without incurring debt. Next best is to borrow for short periods, as the short-term market offers the lowest interest rates. Local governments are usually permitted to finance projects with short-term notes for a limited time. If a government feels compelled to issue bonds, the most costly financing alternative, the term should be as short as possible to limit interest costs. Generally, the credit rating agencies look with favor on a government that limits the life of its bond issues to 10 years or less.

***Increasing Returns.*** The comparative merit of programatic investments is undoubtedly the transcendent concern of local government leaders. Obviously, success in this endeavor hinges on the ability to match accurate program costs with credible estimates of program benefits. Every government, large or small, can assign relatively accurate costs to its array of service programs, provided it maintains a budgeting and accounting system that distributes all charges, direct and indirect, including capital charges, to an appropriate scheme of cost centers. The estimation of program benefits, however, is another story. Placing a value on program outputs is a challenging task, requiring the development and maintenance of a suitable database and a planning and analytical capability.

The relative worth of publicly financed programs can best be established by comparing rates of return, expressed as net benefits (gross benefits minus costs) or as percentages of investment. Benefits can be ascribed and monetized for a certain number of public programs. In those cases where benefits cannot be ascribed and monetized, making the preferred benefit/cost approach impossible, outputs still can be numerically or physically specified or one can apply performance ratios or the cost/effectiveness approach. If these approaches are deemed impractical, comparative values can be established by using weighting and scoring schemes.

This brief reconnaissance cannot do justice to the many technical refinements that enter into the application of formal allocation criteria to local government program investments. It seemed sufficient, however, to establish the concept that quality finance management is insolubly linked to the efficient use of capital by the local government as a whole. As this work is usually assigned to budget units, this brief discussion also seemed sufficient to introduce the most important issue of finance organization, the placement and role of the budget function.

*Budgeting.* To budget is to ration scarce resources among competing purposes. As such, budgeting is certainly not finance or accounting; yet budgeting is absolutely dependent on finance and accounting activity for information, structure, and process. For some, this dependency, and the consequent staff interplay, provides sufficient rationale for locating the budget function within the ambit of the finance directorate. For others, the symbiotic advantages of placement within a finance directorate are less advantageous than an identification of the budget function with the chief executive's office. Is there a solid institutional answer to the placement question? Or should the placement of the budget function depend on personal perception and needs, as it was in the City of Hartford case, previously cited?

A recent survey of budget offices in 358 local government jurisdictions distributed across the United States reported four patterns of organizational placement: 52 percent of these offices were located within finance establishments, 18 percent had departmental status, 16 percent were assigned to a chief executive's office, and 13 percent served in multifunction administrative organizations.[11]

Every well-ordered government expects sound advice from its budget staff, such advice embracing economic and financial considerations, resource availability, operational feasibility, and reliable estimates. Ideally, this advice should reflect the application of formal allocation criteria, including reasoned judgments on program efficiency and effectiveness. Budget work is reflective work. It is best done by disinterested persons endowed with an analytical cast of mind.

In terms of the specifications outlined above, what are the hazards of a nonfinance placement of a budget office? The following comments trace the likely ramifications of direct supervision of a budget division or department by a chief executive.

First, chief executives, and their aides, are typically immersed in the concerns of the day, fending off attacks, checking things out, "fighting fires," etc. Considering the unremitting pressure, it is not surprising that they reach for additional staff resources. Lacking a buffer to regulate its involvement, the budget staff is easily drawn into the hothouse atmosphere of a chief executive's office, with predictable and deleterious effects on the objectivity of its advisory output. To do its best work, a budget unit needs relative detachment and a relatively remote time horizon.

Secondly, a chief executive's relationship with line department heads, while fundamentally hierarchical, is frequently grounded on consultation and reciprocal loyalty. The reflective work of budget units is often seen as threatening by those affected. Those who observe close relationships tend to impute subjectivity. People who are thought to have the "king's ear," so to speak, find it difficult to maintain a reputation for objectivity. Recommendations produced by budget units closely identified with a chief executive's office may be preceived to represent the chief executive's true position, even if the chief executive disavows them as damaging important relationships with political forces or the department head(s) concerned.

To an extent not usually appreciated, even by practitioners, budgeting is a search for truth. Effective budget work depends on a deserved reputation for the employment of evidence, logic, and objectivity. Budget units should not be placed in administrative environments that cannot, by their very nature, protect the credibility of analytical work.

Finally, it is highly unlikely that budget units reporting to chief executives or their executive aides, can get the required depth and breadth of supervisory review of an agenda of reflective work, or the proper supervisory encouragement of that work as it progresses.

The assignment of budget units to a department of administration or to some such organization embracing general housekeeping services and either some or all of the finance functions at least provides a buffer between the budget staff and the chief executive's office.

On balance, however, if a jurisdiction has a comprehensive finance directorate, the budget unit should be placed under the supervision of its director, with the understanding that the chief executive determines the analytical agenda in consultation with the finance director and the director of the unit. This placement maintains the required "administrative space" between the executive office and the work of the budget unit and provides easy access to the information and advice of the finance director and the leaders of all finance functions. In this regard, it is important to note that finance directors are usually the most competent officials in local government to review proposed policy and procedural proposals, including budget recommendations, for administrative and financial feasibility. It is the only office within government where program and financial values consistently intersect.

Of course, the institutional validity of this arrangement depends on the orientation of finance directors, who must habitually express an enthusiastic interest in analytical and planning values in addition to the values of coordination and control traditionally manifest in finance work. By not having a budget unit within their purview, finance directors find it very difficult to muster the analytical resources and talent needed to assess the productivity of the capital applied to local government operations, much less to discover and support those uses for capital producing the highest rates of return for the community as a whole. In this connection, again referring to the Hartford experience, it is instructive to note that, in partial compensation for the shift of the budget unit to the city manager's office, the finance director established a new unit to provide the directorate, and the city, with indispensable financial and economic analysis.

Institutions thrive and spread when they offer the best way to serve important values and attain goals. Today and for the foreseeable future, local governments need finance establishments that not only efficiently assess and collect revenue, keep books, pay bills, and husband resources, but can assist them to prefigure their economic and fiscal future. Intrinsically, the tasks required for fiscal and economic analysis and planning demand more talented and imaginative leadership than do the tasks associated with coordination and control.

Governments that persist in maintaining fragmented finance organizations are bound to experience serious difficulty in recruiting and retaining the requisite talent. Governments with a comprehensive directorate, on the other hand, offer a position with enough power, prestige, and continuity to attract and retain the requisite talent and provide that talent with ready access to the staff resources and information needed for analytical and planning work. In this connection, in many local governments burdened with multiheaded finance establishments, one notes that frustrated chief executives frequently try to provide a base for finance leadership by appointing a special assistant for fiscal affairs. Predictably this assistant, weary of begging needed information and cooperation from relatively "independent" controllers, treasurers, collectors, assessors, etc (who may not be on very good terms with one another or with the chief executive), leaves for a more lucrative job, probably with some finance-related firm. In addition to suffering a damaging discontinuity in policy development, the local government loses the knowledge acquired by the special assistant. On the evidence, such ad hoc arrangements are no substitute for a solid institutional approach to the requirements of finance leadership.

It is axiomatic that job design has powerful effects on recruitment. That is, a known demand for certain skills calls forth a supply. The amazing spread of the council-manager form of local government is a telling example. The availability of a sufficiently honored city manager career stimulated and sustained a supporting recruitment system. Indeed, the osmotic effect of the council-manager plan produced an informally organized nonpartisan urban career service. If finance directorates are to emphasize analytical and planning values in addition to the traditional values of coordination and control, there is every reason to believe that the very design of the job will have the desired osmotic effect of attracting persons with the requisite temperament and skill.

## *A CONCLUDING NOTE*

A government's credit rating provides an important clue to the overall quality of its finance management. These ratings, provided to the investment community by private rating services, reflect appraisals of the relative riskiness of debt instruments. Because these ratings tend to influence interest rates, and thus the cost of debt capital, local governments are advised to pursue fiscal policies and practices that enhance their reputation with the rating agencies. Since the agencies base their appraisals on information displayed in local government documents, such as annual financial reports, budgets, and the "official statements" for bond issues, local governments should strive to improve the quality of these documents and the supporting planning and analytical capability.

Information is the raw material of finance management. If not properly focused, information and advice distract and confuse, wasting the time and energy of busy policymakers and administrators. As information and advice illuminate issues, spotlight options, and stimulate thought, the organization and presentation of information and advice must not be left to chance or to caprice. Even before computers increased the availability and utility of information, reporting was never a trivial point of organizational theory because reporting requirements, such as budget formats and the layout of finance reports, were known to have profound affects on managerial attention and procedure.

What of the future? It is abundantly clear that the pursuit of coordination and control no longer provides an adequate philosophy for the organization of finance work in the local governments of North America, and, perhaps, the world. Local governments also need planning and analytical finance organizations that can assess the fiscal consequences of the interplay of social and economic tendencies and help citizens and officials understand the impact of worldwide and regional trends on local interests. As the manifold challenges of a worldwide economic system increasingly impinge on local economies, local government finance organizations must be governed and energized by analytical and planning values, without slighting their indispensable coordination and control contributions. Nothing short of a comprehensive, well-led finance directorate can attract and retain the talent necessary to balance and forcefully express the coordinate values of coordination, control, analysis, and planning.

### *NOTES*

1. In the preparation of this chapter, the author drew freely on his previous work, including "The Future of the Finance Directorate," Chicago: Municipal Finance Officers Association, MFOA Study #3, 1/2/78; "Then Management of Finances," unpublished monograph, 1978; "Technology in the Countinghouse," *Governmental Finance* Nov. 1979, pp. 25–28; and "Finance Management," in *A Handbook and Policy Reader for Connecticut's Local Elected Officials* (Storrs, CT: Institute of Public Service, University of Connecticut, 1985).

2. Leonard D. White, *Public Administration* (New York: Macmillan, 1926), chapters 5 and 6.

3. L. L. Moak, and A.M. Hillhouse, *Concepts and Practices in Local Government Finance* (Chicago: Municipal Finance Officers Association, 1975), 46.

4. Revised Charter of the City of Hartford, CT, 1968, and Annual Budgets 1959–60 through 1989–90.

5. Marshall W. Meyer, "Centralization and Decentralization of Authority in Departments of Finance," pp. 40–41 in *Municipal Finance* (Chicago: Municipal Finance Officers Association, August 1967).

6. John E. Petersen, Pat Watt, and Paul Zorn, *Organization and Compensation in Local Government Finance* (Chicago: Government Finance Officers Association, 1986), 45–55.

7. Marshall W. Meyer, *Bureaucratic Structure and Authority*. (New York: Harper Row, 1972), 33.

8. Petersen, Watt, and Zorn, *op.cit.*

9. Meyer, *Bureaucratic Structure,* 19.

10. Myron E. Weiner, *Photomation* (Storrs, CT: Institute of Public Service, University of Connecticut, 1972).

11. Daniel E. O'Toole and James Marshall "Budgeting Practices in Local Government: The State of the Art," pp. 11–16 in *Government Finance Review* (Chicago: Government Finance Officers Association, 1987).

# 4
# *Operating Budgets*

LON SPRECHER

OPERATING budgets are multifaceted items. A budget can be a process, a document, an accounting ledger, a plan, something that's always out of balance (media perspective), or a system. A historical perspective really doesn't help clarify what is meant by the word *budget.* Jesse Burkhead notes that "In Britain, the term was used to describe the leather bag in which the Chancellor of the Exchequer carried to Parliament the statement of the Government's needs and resources."[1] Over time, the budget came to refer to the statement rather than the bag itself.

Whether the budget be the bag or what's in the bag that politicians let out, suffice it to say that each local government defines *budget* to best serve its unique circumstances. No one would ever argue that the governments of New York City; El Paso, Texas; and Eau Claire, Wisconsin, deal with the same issues. No one should argue that each of these cities should have the same view or definition of a budget or budget process.

## *DIFFERING VIEWS; DIFFERING NEEDS*

Each local government's budgeting process is unique—it is the product of geographical, historical, economic, political, and social factors peculiar to that jurisdiction. Rather than throw up our hands and say it is impossible to discuss local budgeting because each unit is different, the task is to define a conceptual framework. This framework should allow the practitioner (elected or civil service) as well as the casual observer to understand a given locality's response to budgeting in relation to other governmental units.

Not only will each unit of government define the budget differently, each player within that government will also have different views based on the role and position played in the government. Budgetary decisions consist of the actions of executive officials (mayor, finance director, line agencies), legislative officials, interest/neighborhood groups, citizen committees, and the media.

This chapter is organized around the premise that budgeting is a unified series of steps undertaken to link and implement four functions:

- Policy development
- Financial planning
- Service/operations planning
- Communications

This chapter begins with a brief set of definitions for each of these four functions—what a service/operations plan includes and what relationship that has to the financial or policy plan.

This budget is viewed as the process that provides the backdrop for the integration of these functions. The environment and the actors unique to a given municipality will dictate the extent to which the linkage occurs and the form of the linkage. The forces that throw together various actors and environmental concerns with the express charge to allocate scarce resources to competing demands breed conflict and fragmentation. The budget is the conflict resolution process.

The chapter uses a chronological approach to illustrate the development and the linkage of the four functions or goals of budgeting. The local budget cycle is segmented into four phases: planning/preparation, integration, selling/passage, and execution/feedback.

## THE FRAMEWORK

### Policy Development

Whether local governments realize it or not, their budget processes are more than just a "bean counting" exercise or a handy way of balancing revenues and expenditures. Budgets are

- A way to rationalize the allocation of scarce resources
- A change vehicle—a way to accomplish social change in the legislative arena
- An accepted way to propose new fiscal and nonfiscal issues as defined by the decision maker
- A political strategy—a way to integrate a chief executive's political and policy agenda and values to provide vision and direction for the bureaucracy and citizens

The budget as a policy instrument requires a clear articulation by the chief executive and legislative body of the goals, objectives, and strategies that underline the budget. The budget provides an opportunity to explain the substantive impact of policy changes on operations, service levels, and the financial well-being of the community. The flip side of proposing policy changes is accountability. If the new policy is implemented, it is generally useful to explain at the outset exactly how the new or revised policy will be implemented and how performance will be monitored.

### *Financial Planning*

A local budget, by law, generally has to balance revenues and expenditures. Therefore, a key budgetary function is to provide a financial plan that will govern the fiscal operation of the municipality for the next year. At a minimum, the financial planning process will include

- A projection of the government's financial condition at the end of the current year and at the end of the proposed fiscal year
- Current and past-year financial activity by department or program so that decision makers know where current appropriations are being spent as a comparison to proposed expenditures
- A formal revenue estimate that includes a listing of all the current and proposed sources of revenue, how much has historically been produced by each source, how much is expected in the proposed budget, and the underlying sensitivities of the revenue projections (economic, seasonal, demographic, or activity changes) resulting in either more or less revenue than projected; this will provide the decision makers with an idea of the potential fiscal volatility with which they are dealing
- A look to the future to anticipate events or conditions that would require changes in operations in order to ensure financial stability or solvency
- An explicit relationship of the capital budget to the operating budget; the capital budget is largely debt-financed, which requires that a local government budget from annual appropriations a sum sufficient to service the debt—i.e., meet the interest and principal payments required under the debt instrument (A capital budget project financed through a debt instrument today will bind the city to debt service appropriations usually funded over the next 10 operating budgets.)
- To ensure that debt service remains under control and that sitting decision makers do not unwisely mortgage the future, many jurisdictions have instituted a guideline that seeks to contain debt service as a specified ratio of debt to general fund expenditures; while debt service receives first draw on municipal expenditures, a good financial plan will try to set a rational debt service level for a multiyear period

### *Service/Operations Planning*

The budget not only sets the financial, policy, and political plan for a government, but it is also the blueprint that governs the amount of service provided and how that service is provided. It is the basic direction-setting tool that the chief executive and legislative body have to direct the bureaucracy in delivering services to the community. The budget provides approved expectation levels in the form of objectives and performance measures, targets, and timetables for projects.

Budgetary directions to managers are usually not day-to-day operating procedures, but they could include

- Departmental goals and objectives
- Approved reorganizations
- Funding and staffing limits
- Newly mandated services that need to be provided regardless of funding levels
- Changed service levels, such as collecting brush every four weeks rather than every seven

### *Communications*

As well as being a policy instrument, the budget is a concise way for a local government's decision makers to communicate changes in priorities, rationale for decisions made, and a changed vision for the future. The budget process can be an effective tool in helping citizens understand the need for change and the reasons behind the policy and political decisions.

Many jurisdictions use public forums or "town meetings" to communicate the budget to the people. Other localities provide the chief executive with a forum to present either a "state of the municipality" or a budget message or both. Neighborhood meetings conducted by department officials regarding the budget's impact on the neighborhood are also an effective communication outgrowth of the budget process.

## *THE ENVIRONMENT AND THE ACTORS EQUAL CONFLICT*

One of the basic premises for budgeting is that it is a way to allocate scarce resources by translating values or priorities into programs and policies. Any time two or more actors come together to make a decision, there is a potential for conflict. Environmental factors, such as economic or demographic changes, can also heighten the potential for conflict.

### *Environment*

Many municipalities subscribe to the "fair share" budgeting philosophy—when more resources are made available, they should be divided "fairly" among various competing agencies.[2] Many line departments assume that there is a "rotation" theory for resource allocation. If one department makes out well one year, it will have to wait its turn until all other departments have had their needs met in succeeding budget periods.

Overall budget levels usually change (either up or down) in a very incremental manner.[3] Fairly cataclysmic events must take place, such as a major plant closing, a Proposition 13, or a significant shift in the mix of a population, for overall budget levels to change dramatically or quickly.

Departmental or specific program budgets, however, can and do change rather dramatically from one year to the next. Perceived needs as expressed by neighborhood associations or legislators or key businesses in the community can initiate substantial changes within departmental budgets. While the municipal budget as a whole may not change by more than a couple of percentage points, the police budget may increase dramatically if there is a major increase in neighborhood vandalism and burglary, for example.

***Actors***

The actors and their values (priorities) will respond to the environment in different ways, in most instances adding to the level of conflict. The key actors in the budget process are the chief executive, executive agencies, the legislative body, the media, and citizen committees. Larger jurisdictions also have a central budget office (CBO), a finance director, a controller, or an administration director as an executive-branch actor.

All these actors' roles vary according to the issue, the stage of the budget process, and their own views of their roles. In addition, the legal structure of the jurisdiction also affects the interaction of the actors. While there are an almost infinite number of structures, there are two extremes that bound the rest. Most larger municipalities have moved to an executive form of budgeting. Here the chief executive prepares or directs the preparation of the budget document. The budget reflects the values of the chief executive and is a statement of his or her priorities. The department heads submit their proposals and resource needs to the chief executive or the finance director for analysis and possible inclusion in the executive budget.

The contrast has been characterized as a less complex although no less rigorous approach to budgeting, with the legislative and executive branches jointly making the budget decisions—in essence, a legislative budget. The department heads bring their resource needs to a joint executive-legislative body, usually chaired by the chief executive and called the board of estimates or a similar name. This body, with analysis usually provided by a city or county administrator or clerk/treasurer, makes the decisions in a collegial fashion.

The *chief executive*, even in weak-executive forms of government, is responsible for promoting and achieving coordination among the competing demands for resources and policies. The chief executive is generally the main change agent in local decision making. He or she has an agenda for policy change and needs to assimilate enough of the other actors' agendas into his or her own to gain passage and movement.

Chief executives battle not only with council members and interest groups over their vision of change and policy innovation; many of their more important battles are with unresponsive executive-branch bureaucracies.

*Department officials* focus their attention on serving their constituencies (their definition), and on the initial budget request and the final appropriation. The truly effective department head will not only be competent in the substance of his agency, but will be an aggressive player in the competition for resources. At times, this competition will pit the agency head against other agencies, the chief executive, the legislative body, the central budget staff, and perhaps the media.

The *legislative body* is the ultimate holder of the purse strings. The chief executive has to convince a majority of this body to approve the executive's vision, policy changes, and financial and operations plan. Once decisions reach the legislative body, whatever coordination the chief executive has achieved to date has the best chance of coming unraveled here.

The legislative body offers one last chance to the executive agencies that were unsuccessful in getting their requests included in the chief executive's budget. The legislative body represents different views on almost all issues—there is no one voice. Couple this divergence with the splitting of the budget issues among several committees before it comes back to the full body, and *fragmentation* becomes the watchword. It is this fragmentation that creates the most visible conflict in the process.

The *media* role is a bifurcated one. It can create issues by running in-depth "cover stories" or analysis pieces. It can heighten conflict by selectively covering citizen committee meetings, visible debates but not the behind-the-scenes conflict-resolution meetings, or agency heads' disagreements with the chief executive. For the media, conflict equals news. If everybody agrees, the story is boring.

The skillful chief executive will hold special one-on-one discussions with influential reporters, go to editorial boards regularly, and hold regular press conferences. To be sure, not every chief executive has found the need to curry the media in order to be reelected. Effective media relations is, however, a key ingredient in utilizing the budget as a communications device.

*Citizen committees or neighborhood associations* also play a key role in the budget process at the local level. While there is a growing trend toward paid representation rather than ordinary citizens appearing on their own behalf, the citizen committee is still a factor in determining what is ultimately included in the budget. Citizen committees are usually one-issue committees (e.g., better schools, more police, more open government) and play an important role in helping focus the decision makers on an issue that may not have been on the policy agenda previously.

*Central budget offices* are the chief executive's main tool in coordinating and controlling the conflict inherent in the resource allocation-process. The effectiveness of the CBO depends upon its location in the hierarchy.

If the CBO is located in a general administration department, which can include such housekeeping units as data processing and central purchasing, it tends to be considered more administrative and less policy-oriented. Under this organizational structure, the chances of its playing a major policy or analytical role are slim. Its conflict-resolution role is also submerged in this location.

The CBO can be a part of the chief executive's office, which will give it visibility and clout but may give it a "political hack" reputation rather than a professional, analytical personna.

If the CBO is located in the finance department with an appointed finance director and analysts who hold civil-service status, it might attain the best of both worlds: the clout of the chief executive and the perception of some objectivity. In any case, the CBO determines, in very significant ways, the packaging of information for the decision makers and the media.

## *THE BUDGET AS CONFLICT RESOLUTION PROCESS*

The sources of conflict are many when it comes to deciding how much money to take from the taxpayer, what services should share in the largesse, and whose vision of change should be implemented. The budget process will determine how well the conflict is resolved.

While each jurisdiction will approach the budget process differently, there are generally four chronological steps in any budget process: planning/preparation, integration, selling/passage, and execution/feedback. Figure 4-1 depicts a typical budget cycle.

The four steps can be undertaken annually (most common in local government) or biennially. The planning stage can take two or more years under a sophisticated budget process. Even for an annual budget cycle, the elapsed time for all four steps to occur could be as long as twenty-four months.

### *Preparation/Planning*

*Service Plans.* Many local and state governments undertake formal service planning and evaluation techniques. The budget process is more than an accounting exercise—it is an opportunity to explicitly tie dollar costs to alternative service levels and alternative policies that will affect those service levels.

Before a municipality can use the budget process to identify alternative policy choices or alternative visions for the community, the nuts-and-bolts budget framework should be in a format that will foster such analysis.

Specifically, the budget could be organized around programs or, at a minimum, discrete services. The next step is for the managers and elected officials to agree on specific objectives for these services or programs. Objectives are

- Results-oriented
- Measurable within a given time
- Related to the overall department goal

The final step in securing a framework within which the needs of policy setting, financial planning, service planning, and communication can work is the development of quantitative performance measures.

Harry Hatry and others have defined a variety of performance measures and techniques.[4] Generally, there are four types of measures: demand measures, workload measures, efficiency measures, and effectiveness measures.

*Demand measures* indicate the scope of the program or the need for the

FIGURE 4-1
*Local Government Budget Cycle*

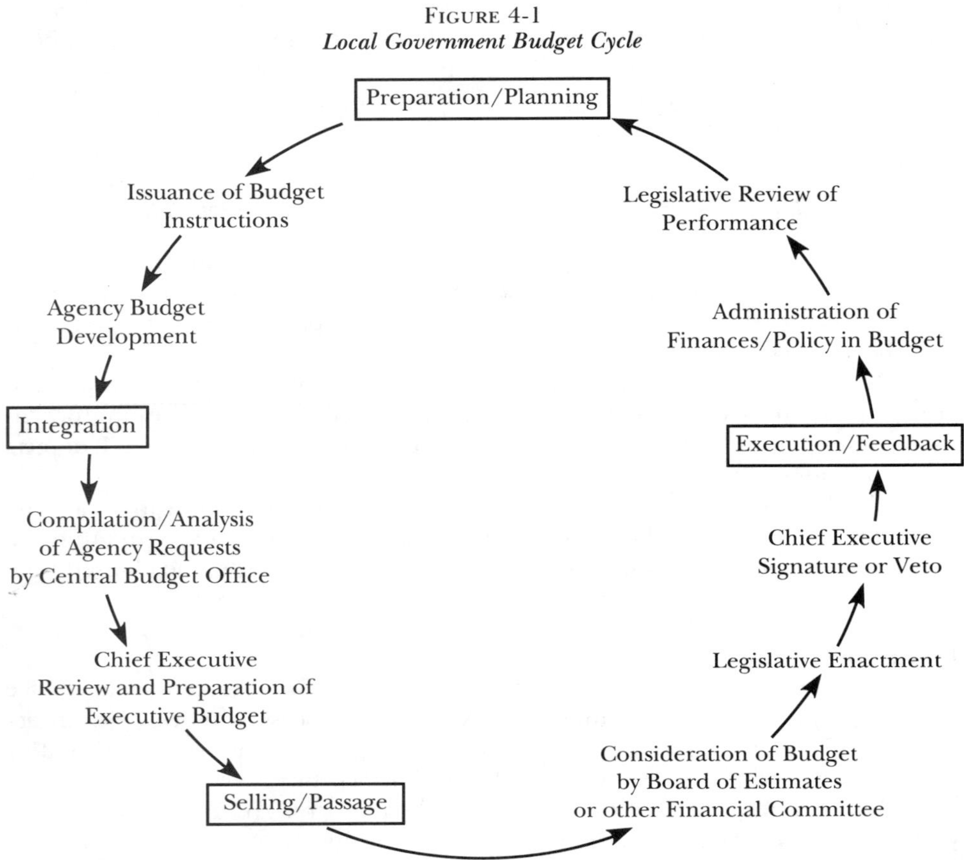


The local government budget process is a continuous cycle, moving from submission of agency budget requests to legislative authorization of appropriations to agency expenditure of appropriations and then beginning again with subsequent agency budget requests.

service. Examples include the number of residences in a fire district and the amount of garbage picked up in previous years in a given area. Demand measures do not directly assist in the choice among competing policy or funding priorities, but they do provide a backdrop to help budgeters to put in perspective the gross budget numbers being requested.

*Workload measures* go one step further than demand measures—they indicate the amount of work actually performed on a particular activity. Examples of these measures include the number of fires responded to, property loss as a result of fire, and number of garbage pickups.

*Efficiency measures* relate the workload measures to resources required and results obtained. Examples include the number of fires per district, the number of garbage pickups per crew, and the number of patrol hours per officer.

*Effectiveness measures* build on efficiency measures and tell how well an activity meets an objective. These measures are results-oriented and are the most useful to decision makers in determining priorities for resources. They can help isolate programs that may be efficient but are not meeting intended results. For example, the traffic engineering department may have installed all the required stoplights efficiently, but the ultimate program objective—reduced accidents—may not have been accomplished. The next issue raised would be "are traffic lights the best accident deterrent or are there other, more effective ways to meet the operational objective?"

Budgets based on objectives and service plans generally allow the decision makers the opportunity to play "what-if" games. "What if we reduce funding for parks patrols? Will vandalism go up?" It also allows the identification of alternative ways of performing the service. The planning process also allows the monitoring of expected and actual service performance, which becomes an important factor in subsequent budget rounds. If there is a quantitative measure that shows that a department consistently meets the workload, efficiency, and effectiveness measures established for it, a level of confidence is established for future programming and budgetary decisions.

***Budget Instructions.*** At the beginning of the budget cycle, the chief executive, budget officer or (in smaller cities) a legislative committee develops the key fiscal/operational and policy guidelines that will govern the preparation of the ensuing budget. The budget instructions usually combine the political and policy tone setting of the chief executive with the necessity of getting the right budget numbers from the agencies in some standard format. Figure 4-2 shows four types of documents (budget instructions, agency request, executive budget summary, and monitoring documents). Each set of documents includes specific forms of information.

The preparation/planning stage of the budget process generally utilizes the budget instructions and agency request documents. The selling/passage stage includes the final budget summary document. The executive feedback stage contains the monitoring document.

The budget instructions are the result of numerous meetings between the chief executive, key advisers, the head of the CBO, and, potentially, select legislative members. These discussions take place well before the agencies have begun their planning and deliberations in earnest. In a larger jurisdiction, the CBO has taken on a policy-analysis role as well as a purely fiscal advisory role. Before the budget instructions are released, the decision makers have reviewed analyses performed by either the CBO or finance staff that include many of the following:

- Current expenditures versus budget and the prospects for a carry-forward surplus
- Major cost items that will fall due in the budget year
- Trends in inflation and local economic conditions
- Revenue assumptions for the next 1 or 2 years (including state and federal aid)

FIGURE 4-2
*Budget Documents*

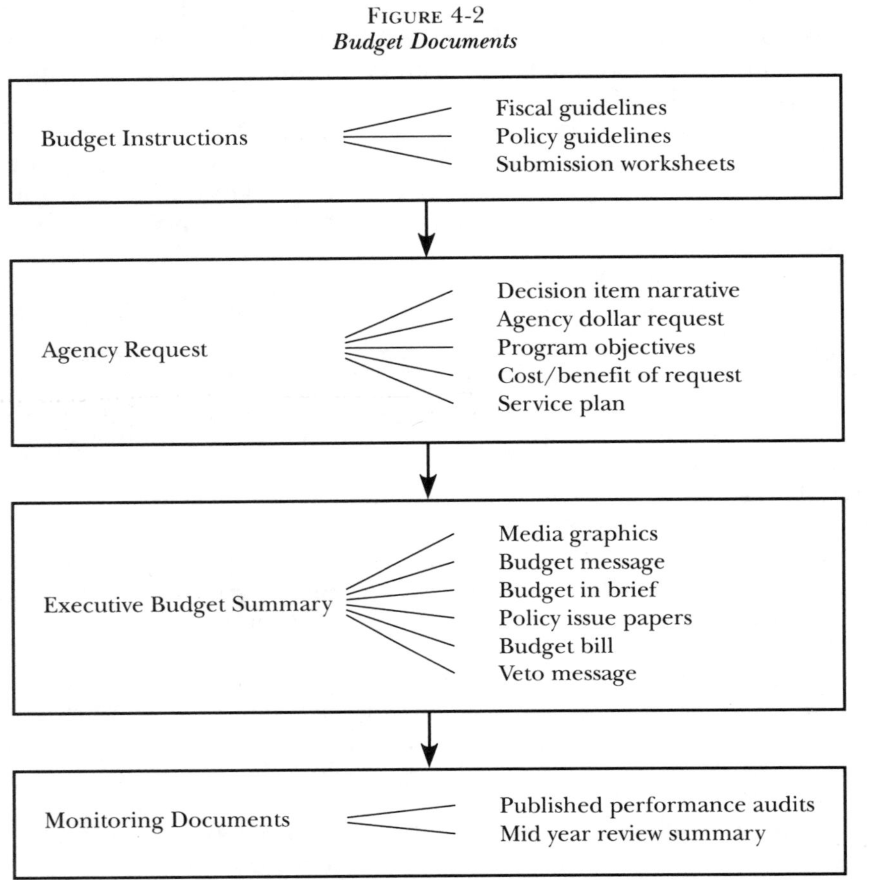


Not all documents will be used by a given jurisdiction. Some entities may devise other documents unique to their situation.

- Acceptable levy increases—keeping the levy to an acceptable percentage of local gross or disposable income
- A listing of possible policy and program issues that could confront the chief executive
- Analysis of general alternatives to accomplish the chief executive's policy or political agenda

*Fiscal and Operational Guidelines.* Before the budget can be used as a policy instrument or a political vision, the financial and operational foundation needs to be laid. These guidelines set the general parameters within which department heads can structure their requests. The guidelines can include such items as

- Guidelines for budget increases due to inflation
- Salary-increase guidelines for employees
- A statement of tax and fee policies to be followed
- An indication of what service/operational areas should be strengthened or deemphasized to meet evolving priorities
- Inclusion of all forms that will need to be completed so that all requests are on a comparable basis and easily summarized for executive and legislative review and publication. The forms can include detailed worksheets for personal services, supplies, and equipment requests
- worksheets that describe in detail new position requests
- a source-of-funds worksheet that details whether the service will be funded from general funds (usually property-tax money), federal or state funds, or enterprise revenues

*Policy Guidelines.* Once the financial/operational guidelines are in place, the chief executive can develop policy instructions within the framework of what is affordable.

Sometimes the executive will precede the budget instructions with a broader and less fiscal overview of priorities. This address usually gives an overview of the progress made in the past year and the goals and challenges for the succeeding year. This message usually tempers expectations and tries to lay out realistically what government can and can't expect to accomplish in the succeeding year. This message sets the stage for the more specific fiscal-related communication contained in the budget instructions or budget message.

The agencies are not the only audience for the budget instructions. The instructions are written "to" the agency head, but the real audience is the public and the media. The budget instruction is a way to communicate the chief executive's agenda and signals the kickoff for the next round in allocating resources to achieve the policy change that the chief executive desires.

The budget instructions detail what the executive expects to be accomplished in the next budget period. Invariably, the message stresses frugality and the analysis of alternatives. The message also highlights the executive's priority programs. The inference is: if it is not on the list, it is not in line for major new resources and may even be on the hit list.

The instructions can include agency-specific budget and policy targets that have been predetermined by the CBO, either separately or in conjunction with the agencies. Agencies generally like to have some idea of what is acceptable behavior and what is clearly out of line. Fiscal, service, and policy targets give the agency that feedback and also show the public and the media that the chief executive is in control and has a game plan governing the budget.

*The Agency Request.* Meanwhile, the agencies have not been sitting around waiting for the instructions. Most department heads know the rules of the game—

budgets are generally incremental and successful requests have a demonstrated need or constituency.

The successful department will have been using the time since the last budget was approved not only to administer that budget, but also to set in motion the data gathering, constituency, and program enhancements for the next budget.[5] The budget instructions tell department heads whether they will have an easy time or a more difficult time in getting their priorities to mesh with the executive's.

How does an agency know what to ask for? Agencies must approach the budget from two perspectives: the more mechanical one of applying a sharp pencil to the numbers requested; and the more visionary one of clearly articulating and selling their programs' priority.

From a purely mechanical perspective, agencies need to develop budgets for each program, breaking expenses into at least three categories: personal services, operating expenses (supplies and services), and equipment.

The CBO has usually established worksheets and formats for the agencies to complete. By identifying the number of new positions required plus the number of continuing positions, the agency has accounted for about 70 percent of the total budget in most departments.

In addition, the operating expenses are largely driven by the number of positions and can usually be calculated on a per-position basis using historical levels adjusted for inflation as a guideline. Contractual services are also a key variable operating cost. Some municipalities contract for garbage removal, while others use contracts only to analyze specific problems such as where most effectively to locate a new fire station. Regardless of the extent of contractual services, the budget should contain a clear and concise rationale for the need of the service and the outputs expected. Many times, the CBO requires the completion of a special worksheet to justify contracts.

The last major component of the budget request is the equipment budget—those things with a designated useful life (e.g., more than 2 years) and a cost exceeding a specified amount (e.g., of more than $500). Again, there will be specific worksheets to complete to justify such items as computers, typewriters, and communications equipment.

Agency requests should be justified on the basis of the service plans developed earlier in the planning stage of the budget. Simply requesting an incremental change from the previous year's budget does not utilize the full potential of the budget as a planning or policy tool. Department heads should identify priority programs as well as important fiscal and nonfiscal issues in their budget requests. They should also show that they have examined current programs and have explored whether there are more efficient or effective alternatives to accomplish desired objectives. From a policy and political perspective, over the years many agencies have used some or all of the following strategies to gain support for the budget request:

- First and foremost, the agency needs a clientele, preferably large and vocal. The agency's role in budgeting is to serve the clientele, expand it, and focus it to tell the chief executive and legislative body that it needs the service changes the agency is proposing. If no one is saying they need the service, it is a likely cut-back target.

- Agencies need to be assertive. The agency may decide to "satisfice" overall but to be entrepreneurial in a select few areas where there is a documented need for a new or significantly expanded service.
- Agencies should always remember that they are usually the only original source of data. No one else keeps track of workload data or the number of students not passing minimal reading thresholds. The CBO and others can manipulate and analyze the data, but they are confined, in most cases, to analyzing the agency's data.
- Agencies may use outside experts and task forces to help document the need for a service.
- Agencies should try to fit their requests under one of the major priority headings identified by the executive or legislative body in speeches or the budget instructions.

Submitting a budget that follows these steps does not guarantee success, but it will help the agency justify its request in the competition for resources.[6]

### *Integration*

The integration stage is where the CBO comes into its element. Until the budgets are submitted to the CBO, they are fragmented. Very little discussion among agencies takes place. Each has viewed the budget process as a zero sum game, and accordingly each has tried to grab as much as it could reasonably justify.

The chief executive's main tool in realizing any vision for policy change and coordination is the CBO. The first time the budget is considered as a whole is when the CBO has analyzed it and made tentative recommendations to the executive.

Many governments use program budgets and decision-item narratives to help the CBO, the executive, and the legislative body understand the interrelationships between various agency requests. Decision-item narratives include a brief description of the program, why a change is necessary, the priority of the change compared to all other agency requests, and how the change will help accomplish one or more of the department's goals. These narratives can be in any form or in specialized formats across all departments. These standardized formats also help the CBO priority requests and match them to executive priorities.[7]

The CBO focuses and distills the executive's policy intent into dollars and programs. The CBO head has enormous power if the executive lets him or her exercise it. The CBO generally sets the briefing schedules. It also distills the essence of complex program issues into relatively short briefings structured around dollars, people, and policy as the end product. Agency heads as well as legislative representatives may be present for these briefings, if the structure and size of the municipality and the desire of the chief executive warrant.

The CBO briefings generally start by giving the chief executive an overview of how agency requests, in general, compare to the executive's priorities, how the requested expenditures compare to the revenue estimates (how much needs to be cut), and how the CBO plans on proceeding to make the policy and dollars fit the executive's stated objective.

Once the "big picture" overview is completed, the agency-by-agency briefings start. A tally of dollar and position decisions as well as major policy decisions is kept.

The CBO staff generally includes much of the following in the analysis of agency budget requests, using a critical review of agency service/operations and financial plans as the backdrop:

- Past program performance evaluations
- An independent forecast of service needs (Is the program needed?)
- Relative cost effectiveness—this program compared to an alternative way of solving the same problem or an alternative use of the resources to solve another problem
- Efficiency analysis (Is this the least cost way to solve the problem?)
- Workload data
- Council or citizen-group demand for the program

By following this process, the CBO rationally leads the executive through the vast number of agency requests. In this way, the CBO helps the executive pick and choose from the requests to develop a policy budget consistent with the executive's values, priorities, and desired policy changes.

The literature portrays the CBO as merely a reactive budget cutter.[8] A progressive executive will want the CBO to be a proactive policy initiator and synthesizer. The effective CBO will initiate recommendations for the executive's consideration when no request has been made by an agency. The CBO, early in the game, develops its own policy agenda, which may or may not be shared with the agencies.

For example, the executive may know that the health department has not been very receptive or creative in dealing with an AIDS awareness program. The executive may ask the CBO to develop a proposal. The CBO will get necessary data from the department, but the actual design of the program and resource identification will be the product of the CBO staff. This assures the executive that there will be a program and could force the health department to step forward with its own program or be forced to administer the CBO-designed program. The health department program could be integrated with the CBO program, thus giving the executive the best that both agencies have to offer.

By making decisions based upon agency requests and CBO-initiated items, the chief executive has completed the budget recommendations. The chief executive now has only a few more days before submitting the budget to the legislative body. Those final days are generally spent performing yet one more revenue reestimate and dealing with agency appeals. It also marks the beginning of legislative and media briefings regarding the general content of the budget.

### *Selling/Passage*

The chief executive now takes center stage in packaging and selling the budget. The budget substrategies of the agencies have been covered, the integrative role of the CBO has been described, but now the real question—how does the chief executive convert all of this competing advice into *the budget?* The executive, while making the choices, needs to have a clear picture of how he or she wants the budget characterized—how will the headlines and editorials portray it? The chief executive's analysis will probably take into consideration many of the following questions:

- What audiences' concerns are not addressed in the solution?
- What is the environment for action—do legislators or citizen groups want a real solution or only one that appears to be a solution? (Sometimes it is politically more beneficial for "eye wash and window dressing" to be the proposal.)
- Which audiences are essential to make the recommendation happen, and is their primary interest elsewhere during this budget cycle?

In characterizing the budget, the chief executive makes implicit and explicit decisions about constituencies and where he or she stands or wants to stand with each group. Executives are elected to be reelected. The chief executive categorizes the electoral constituency into four groups:

- Those who will have no place else to go no matter what
- Mobile constituents who need to be kept happy
- Potential new constituents who are marginally in the other group's camp
- Those who are not and never will be constituents

As a constituency, the trick is to avoid being lumped into either the first or last category—to be taken for granted has the same consequence as being ignored.

The chief executive has made his or her policy choices. Now he or she needs to frame them with the various constituencies in order to get the best play from the policy and the affected constituency.

Once the politics of the budget have been sorted out, the executive begins to weave the elements of the budget message—the characterization of the key policy and program elements and the major fiscal and operational assumptions underlying the budget. The message is also likely to include a listing of major issues the legislative body must address and significant changes in the proposed budget compared to the current budget. The budget message is generally delivered in person to the legislative body, but again with the media and, ultimately, the public being the real audience.

Budgets are generally viewed as time-release capsules—it is virtually impossible for the public or the media to digest all the good things in the budget at one sitting. The executive will generally leak some of the smaller decisions as they are made, driving the CBO and finance director up the wall in the process. The executive will keep two or three of the most inviting pieces under wraps to assure that the budget gets the headline that he or she wants at the time of the budget message.

The budget message is just one of the documents that can be produced to ensure that the budget is indeed a communications device. In larger jurisdictions, the message is accompanied by several other documents prepared by the CBO:

- A budget in brief, which summarizes expenditures and revenues by agency and in total, outlines key program changes by function or agency, and includes graphics for television or newspapers to use
- Policy issue papers, which provide a detailed rationale for key programs highlighted by the executive in the budget message
- The budget bill itself, which includes the detailed appropriations, revenues, and statutory or ordinance language

The completed budget documents will also include a detailed justification of the budget recommendations.

A well-constructed set of budget documents will augment each other and will provide an analysis of policy changes, quantity of services provided, and changes in service priorities.

Once the budget is delivered to the legislative body, the selling of the budget continues. After one brief moment of being considered as a whole, the budget is again fragmented. The first step the legislative body usually takes is to refer the budget to several standing committees as well as a finance or board-of-estimates committee.

Usually either the CBO or chief executive or both present the budget to the legislative body and answer questions about the numbers as well as the policy content. The presentation will generally include

- Revenue estimates broken down by revenue source
- A summary of proposed expenditures by major category
- A department-by-department breakdown of requested positions and requested expenditures by source of funds and major category of cost compared to the CBO and chief executive's recommended levels
- Narrative statements justifying the recommended levels

At this point, the interest groups and interested citizens have the opportunity to discuss their perceptions of the positive and negative aspects of the budget. The legislative members may meet in small working groups to make recommendations on pieces of the budget either to a committee of the whole or to the board of estimates, which in turn will make a recommendation to the full body.

At this stage, the CBO head is busy explaining the numbers as well as the policy choices contained in the budget. Generally, the CBO does not perform the purely political job of negotiating tradeoffs with individual legislative members. However, that role can be undertaken if the executive desires.

The budget, at this stage, involves the executive bargaining and compromising to pass, largely intact, the most important parts of his budget. The executive budget probably contained some "lightning rod" or throw-away programs that can be used as trade bait to ensure the passage of the real policy changes sought by the executive. The skillful weaving of lightning rods with the true policy desires provides insight into successful executive budgeting.

During legislative deliberation, the CBO should keep an account of all changes the legislative body has made in the budget and determine the impact each change has on the projected surplus at the end of the budget year. If the surplus is made too large or small by the legislative actions, the legislative body as well as the executive need a timely reminder of the numbers so corrective action can be attempted before passage.

The budget is passed as an appropriation ordinance, which sets the spending ceiling and authorizes all departmental budgets. The final budget is published and either in its entirety or in a summarized version made available to all officials as well as the public.

Once the budget is passed, many localities provide for another step before execution. The chief executive may either veto in full or in part any aspect of the budget that is inconsistent with his or her fiscal or policy desires. Needless to say, the prospect of vetoing the entire budget over several policy differences is not an appealing thought for a chief executive.

If the chief executive has line-item authority, the CBO keeps track of all objectionable issues and consults with agencies, interest groups, and council members to recommend which issues can be cured through a veto and which vetoes will likely be sustained. The executive then exercises the veto pen to excise objectionable fiscal or policy items. The legislative body then has the option of sustaining or overriding the vetoed portions, usually with a two-thirds vote required to override.

### *Execution and Feedback*

As the name implies, the execution stage is an executive function. The CBO therefore plays a significant role at this stage in coordinating the bureaucracy to carry out legislative and executive intent.

There is a push and pull between flexibility and control.[9] It is easy to overemphasize the control features of this stage of the budget cycle. As local governments move more toward program budgeting, the questions become more difficult—it is no longer enough for an administrator to say the year ended with money left over. The question is, what did that administrator accomplish with the dollars that were spent?

Traditional control serves two purposes: to prevent budget deficits (an embarrassing situation to say the least), and to ensure that administrative actions produce desired policy and program accomplishments.

The first type of control uses the following financial management techniques:

- Establishing monthly or quarterly spending plans (allotments) and monitoring progress against them
- Reporting actual expenditures against detailed budgets
- Reviewing and recommending departmental requests to transfer funds between appropriation lines
- Position and payroll expenditure control
- Monitoring revenues on a periodic basis
- Instituting procedures necessary to adjust budgets to reflect changes in revenue availability or changed service requirements

One of the main reasons for these fiscal controls is surplus management. In some municipalities, surplus is a four-letter word. The implication is that a surplus, particularly a growing one, indicates that money is being burgled from the unsuspecting citizenry and should be given back immediately. The Wall Street version is that if a municipality wants to maintain an AAA rating, it better maintain at least a 5 percent budget surplus. Most finance directors, out of political necessity, are happy if the unappropriated surplus account is somewhere in between these two extremes.

The obvious values of having an unappropriated surplus are (1) to avoid having to short-term borrow or go back to the taxpayer in midyear if the revenue estimates prove too low, and (2) to use some of it to help balance next year's budget. If the surplus is truly used to smooth the peaks and valleys of revenue collections and not just the peaks and valleys of the chief executive's popularity, good fiscal management can be served through the accumulation of unappropriated surpluses.

The second type of control requires a more sophisticated follow-up system. The budget has been built on workload measures and program accomplishment statements. The obvious need is for the agency to prove that each of these requirements has been met. The consequences of not complying is a reduced budget or a less-than-cordial hearing during the next budget cycle.

The efficiency measures (volume and cost) are easily monitored. The budget execution feedback system should ideally produce information that can be used to review program effectiveness. Questions about whether the objectives are worth pursuing and whether the programs are meeting those objectives are difficult to address under this system. Program audits, conducted by internal auditors or external consultants are a step toward achieving this second control or feedback goal.

The CBO and executive stay in close personal contact with department heads to discuss project problems and progress. The monitoring system requires the establishment of standards and procedures to measure progress toward identified performance targets. Monitoring provides the input to determine if the department or program is meeting the goals established in the approved budget. Monitoring also provides the baseline data to use in the following year's planning and preparation stage.

Some localities go so far as to provide for a formal midyear review. This review can give a midyear analysis of the data gathered from the monitoring process as well as an update on revenues and unappropriated surplus balance. The midyear review allows the jurisdiction to reallocate resources and also provides sufficient lead time to correct fiscal problems before they become major crises.

## *CONCLUSION*

Each local government has its own needs and unique problems. The budget and the budget process will depend on the environment, issues, and actors in the locality. Yet there are common threads that provide a conceptual framework, which allows some generalization about local budgeting. To be effective, a budget process must link four functions: policy development, financial planning, service/operations planning, and communications. The effective linkage of these functions allows the budget process to resolve conflict, help chief executives coordinate various issues and agency's efforts, allocate scarce resources, and result in change.

Budgeting entails choice. Choice implies that there are priorities. Elected officials base resource-allocation decisions upon these priorities.

Planning is the key that encourages integration of the policy, financial, and operational aspects of municipal budgeting. "Planning is the process of preparing a set of decisions for action in the future, directed at achieving goals by preferable means."[10]

The planning emphasis in budgeting provides a systematic way to determine objectives and alternatives through policy-analysis techniques. By providing information that links costs and results, analysis enables decision makers to quantify alternative ways to achieve their priorities. Planning and analysis can also help determine tradeoffs between competing priorities.

This chapter has segmented the budget process into four phases: planning/preparation, integration, selling/passage, and execution/feedback. Budgeting is a series of steps undertaken to implement a government's policy objectives. It provides a documented work program (service plan), the careful linkage of that program with a formal comprehensive financial plan, and the basics of an operational plan to assure the administrative accomplishment of the entire scheme. It also provides for communication of the choices made and encourages midcourse or next-cycle correction of errant policies or programs. A good budget process helps the decision makers and the administrators of those decisions to plan, check, and correct.

## NOTES

1. Jesse Burkhead, *Government Budgeting* (New York: Wiley, 1956), p. 2.
2. Aaron Wildavsky, *The Politics of the Budgetary Process* (Boston: Little, Brown, 1964), p. 62.
3. *Ibid.*, pp. 74–89.
4. Harry Hatry, Louis Blair, Donald Fisk, and Wayne Kimmel, *Program Analysis for State and Local Governments* (Washington, D.C.: The Urban Institute, 1976), pp. 33–85.
5. Thomas J. Anton, "Roles and Symbols in the Determination of State Expenditures," *Midwest Journal of Political Science* 11, 1 (February 1967): 30–32.
6. Fremont J. Lyden and Marc Lindenberg, *Public Budgeting in Theory and Practice* (New York: Longman, 1983), pp. 127–129.
7. Fremont J. Lyden and Ernest G. Miller, *Public Budgeting,* 4th ed. (Englewood Cliffs, N.J.: Prentice Hall, 1982), pp. 107–44.
8. See James W. Martin, ed., *Approaches to the State Central Budget Process* (Lexington, Ky.: National Association of State Budget Officers, 1970), for a full discussion of the literature on CBO staff roles.
9. S. Kenneth Howard, "Budget Execution: Control vs. Flexibility," *Midwest Review of Public Administration* 2, 1 (February 1968): pp. 20–27.
10. Yehezekl Dror, *Ventures in Policy Sciences* (New York: American Elsevier, 1971), p. 106.

# 5

# *Capital Planning and Budgeting*

Susan G. Robinson

Congestion on the nation's roadways, growth limits resulting from inadequate wastewater-treatment capacity, and collapsing bridges are all symptoms of what many refer to as the infrastructure crisis. A number of recent studies have concluded that the nation's stock of capital goods has not kept pace with economic and social needs.[1] During the 1980s, the nation's infrastructure was wearing out faster than it was being replaced. Decreases in federal financial assistance and expanding government responsibilities in other program areas contributed to public-sector neglect of capital facilities. Increasingly stringent health and environmental standards that govern the design and operation of public works exacerbated the problem. Federal regulations imposed on wastewater-treatment plants, for example, have increased the costs of constructing and operating that essential element of community infrastructure.

Even assuming popular support to increase funding for capital infrastructure, communities often find it difficult to decide among competing demands for capital investment. Many face pressures to extend infrastructure to rapidly developing areas; at the same time, they are urged to rehabilitate infrastructure in older, established neighborhoods. In addition, funding is often inadequate for the maintenance of facilities that are aging but not yet severely deteriorated. Insufficient funding allows for little more than emergency repair, not a rigorous program of routine inspection and regularly scheduled maintenance and replacement.

The need for investment in public facilities—the physical system of roads, bridges, water supply, wastewater treatment, and drainage facilities that support activity in our communities—has been well documented on a national level. For local jurisdictions, the aggregate numbers that make up the "infrastructure crisis" translate into capital investment requirements. In both mature and rapidly growing communities, this includes spending for sewer and water-treatment facilities, administrative buildings, parks and recreational facilities, schools, fire trucks, ambulances, and police cars, to name just a few. They are the investments that make our communities healthy, safe, and economically viable and physically attractive places to live.

## *PLANNING AND BUDGETING*

Whether or not a jurisdiction has a formal capital budgeting system, each year it probably goes through the sometimes painful process of deciding which of several capital projects it will fund. Capital expenditures are a major component of local government spending. The buildings, streets, parks, facilities, and equipment required by the public sector attract widespread attention because they represent large, "lumpy" expenditures and provide tangible evidence of public spending. Without a plan, however, this process can go awry. Most jurisdictions face a continual gap between identified needs and the resources available to meet those needs. Strategies to close the gap include the assignment of priorities to capital-investment needs and examining strategies to increase revenues available to fund capital projects.

The orderly process of capital-facilities planning is called capital budgeting. This general term differentiates the endeavor of financing long-lived physical improvements from the operating budget, which applies to those annual or routine activities financed from current resources. The capital budget usually follows an annual cycle and often is integrated directly into the operating budget process. Done properly, however, the capital budget in any given year is the current slice of a multiyear plan. To differentiate between the capital spending element of the annual budget and the longer-term capital financial planning process, a distinction is often drawn between the *capital budget* and the *capital improvement program.*

### *Capital Improvement Program*

A *capital improvement program* (CIP) is a multiyear plan (usually covering five or six years) that forecasts spending for all anticipated capital projects. The plan addresses both repair and replacement of existing infrastructure as well as the development of new facilities to accommodate future growth. It enables one to identify needed capital projects and to coordinate facility financing and timing. An effective CIP consists of both an administrative *process* to identify the location, scale, and timing of needed capital projects and a fiscal *plan* to provide for the funding of those projects.

The CIP links a jurisdiction's planning and budgeting functions. It can help implement past policy decisions by establishing priorities among existing and competing capital needs but can also be used to measure and evaluate the merits of new proposals. The capital improvement program should be a logical extension of a jurisdiction's comprehensive land-use plan. Typically, the CIP describes each capital project proposed for development over the planning period by listing the year it is to be started, the cost to be incurred by year, and the proposed method of financing. Based on these details about each project, annual cost schedules for capital expenditures, as well as summaries of financial requirements and resources (i.e., current revenues, general obligation bonds, intergovernmental assistance), are developed.

### *Capital Budget*

The *capital budget* represents the first year of the capital improvement plan. The primary difference between the capital budget and the CIP is that the capital budget is a legal document that authorizes specific projects during the ensuing fiscal period. The capital plan, on the other hand, includes the first-year projects as well as future projects for which financing has not been secured or legally authorized. The "out years" of the CIP are not binding and are therefore subject to change.

The CIP process is a dynamic one. It helps a jurisdiction plan for major expenditures in the future and adjust capital projects as needs and circumstances change. The CIP's multiyear perspective allows projects to be planned ahead of actual need. The yearly repetition of the CIP process also ensures that each project undergoes several stages of review before it is finally approved and funded. Ideally, it ensures that new facilities will be evaluated within the context of a comprehensive land-use plan and weighed against demands for the repair and replacement of existing infrastructure. The best capital planning process

- Considers all proposed projects simultaneously
- Produces a planning document that considers both available financing sources and feasible timing
- Measures the impact of capital spending and financing sources on the jurisdiction's overall financial position
- Relates a community's perception of itself and its goals to a coherent program of investments

### *The State of the Art*

The capital budget is the linchpin of financial management for local governments. Not only are capital expenditures significant in terms of their dollar volume, but they play an essential role in public service delivery and in the economic welfare of the community. Many of the most compelling local government policy issues are articulated in the capital budget. On an organizational basis, the capital-planning function is one that has potential for bringing together various departmental personnel and technical disciplines. It also provides opportunities to involve the public—and particularly special-interest groups such as developers, neighborhood associations, business groups, and taxpayer associations—in defining and creating the community's future.

If a community has developed a strategic plan, it will likely be implemented through the capital improvement plan. There is a symbiotic relationship between the comprehensive land-use plan and the capital budgeting process as well. Many jurisdictions, especially those that are growing rapidly, use fiscal impact models to estimate future revenues and expenditures over time and under changing conditions. An important component in determining the impact of new growth is the establishment of public costs through the capital planning process. Some governments have developed highly refined consensus-building and collaborative problem-solving techniques around the capital budgeting process. And finally, in a few instances, local governments are looking at their capital budgets in rigorous mathematical terms, using capital-budget-planning computer models.

## *THE RATIONALE FOR CAPITAL PROGRAMMING*

The capital budget and capital plan are closely associated with the long-term operating program and budget, since the reason for each capital project is to facilitate the accomplishment of an operating objective. The following section discusses why it is necessary to develop a separate capital-budget process. These reasons include the special characteristics of capital investments as well as the political and administrative incentives for capital planning and budgeting.

### *Characteristics of Capital Expenditures*

Despite their close interrelationship with the operating budget, infrastructure or capital facilities have special characteristics that "justify" their inclusion and analysis in a special capital budget:

- Essential public purpose
- Long useful life
- Infrequent and expensive
- Related to other government functions
- Local government's general responsibility to provide them

*Essential Public Purpose.* Since the provision of infrastructure is a primary function of local government, it affects the community as a whole and the public decision-making process in particular. Without a sound physical infrastructure, government could not provide the services necessary to maintain a community's public health and welfare. Capital investments such as parks, senior centers, and transit enhance the quality of life in the community; in some jurisdictions they are viewed as absolutely essential. In all cases they must compete with other infrastructure needs for financing sources.

The relationship between a community's provision of adequate, well-managed public works and its ability to retain and attract commercial and residential development is clear. In addition to such determinants as the availability of skilled labor and the cost of energy, the condition of public facilities affects a community's ability to retain existing businesses and attract new ones. For instance, an efficient infrastructure system can reduce the costs of waste disposal, water supply, and other essential municipal services and, as a result, lower business costs and encourage private firms to invest in new facilities. The increase in economic efficiency also enables businesses to expand their markets and make better use of their resources. In addition, local government's timely provision and maintenance of infrastructure sends a clear message to both residents and businesses that government is committed to a stable community. These factors are often considered by businesses in their location, relocation, and expansion decisions and can help a jurisdiction attract new industry without tax abatements and other costly incentives.[2]

As with businesses, individuals consider the availability and condition of public facilities when making investment decisions. The quality of public services (supported by a well-functioning physical infrastructure) enhances the value of residential housing along with such factors as location and other community amenities. The cost of providing adequate infrastructure can also, however, affect housing affordability at time of purchase as well as the carrying costs associated with maintaining a residence.

*Long Useful Life*. Capital facilities have a relatively long useful life. Unlike operating expenditures that may undergo annual or more frequent adjustments to accommodate changing circumstances, capital expenditures once made cannot easily be modified.

*Infrequency and Expense*. By their technical and physical nature, most capital projects involve large, infrequent expenditures that must be made before the benefits are realized. For example, it is either inefficient or technically impossible to build half a wastewater treatment plant or a bridge that stops in the middle of a river. As a result, communities make major capital expenditures only infrequently and for specific purposes, but the outlays are particularly large. Of course, the larger the jurisdiction, the more frequent and regular is the need for certain large outlays such as street repaving.

*Relatedness to Other Government Functions.* Each community requires certain physical structures and systems to provide residents and businesses with the urban services necessary to live and conduct business. The capital investments made by a government to support infrastructure are interrelated and are part of a system or network that provides the public with a set of goods and services. In general, all system components must be in place before the system can function properly. The relationship of capital facilities to other programs and services requires careful timing to ensure that necessary facilities are in place when development occurs.

*Responsibility.* Local governments shoulder the largest share of financial responsibility for providing, operating, and maintaining most public works. This is due, at least in part, to the fact that local communities and their residents are the primary users of public works. During the 1980s the national trend of shifting functions and fiscal responsibility from the federal government to the state and local levels continued. With the notable exception of highway financing, federal programs for capital projects at the state and local levels are approaching extinction. Most states lack the financial resources, administrative structure, and/or political initiative to offset the decline in federal assistance. Unfortunately, the increase in local responsibility has not been accompanied by a parallel increase in the resources needed to do the job. Communities that cannot or will not make up the growing gap in infrastructure financing risk the loss of both population and businesses to communities that are willing to find ways to help themselves.[3]

### *Advantages of Capital Planning and Budgeting*

Local governments that employ capital budgeting and programming systems are likely to derive several advantages.

*The Capital Program as a Reporting Document.* The capital planning process can involve citizens in shaping their community's future and help minimize complaints and after-the-fact objections to major capital projects. Input from community residents and businesses can be critical to success, and increased citizen participation in planning capital improvements can lead to enhanced understanding of the factors involved in building and maintaining facilities.

The complex interrelationships among overlapping and underlying jurisdictions such as towns, cities, school districts, special districts, counties, and regional governments often make capital planning especially difficult. Ideally, these jurisdictions should integrate or, at a minimum, coordinate their capital programs. Because such cooperative capital planning rarely occurs, the capital improvement document often serves as the only mechanism for coordination in the timing and location of related projects.

The CIP can be used as a means of reporting to the governing board, civic organizations, citizens, and neighboring jurisdictions. Capital projects often generate community interest because they directly affect the quality of life and daily activities of its citizens. The CIP has the potential to be an important method of communicating the financial position of the government, as well as its goals, policies, management performance, and community vision. It can illustrate the issues and concerns facing the jurisdiction, examine possible alternatives, and indicate what impact the planning and financial decisions will have on both the community and individual futures.

*The CIP as a Financial Management Tool.* The CIP is a useful financial management tool. It helps policymakers determine the amount of infrastructure and equipment spending required to accommodate anticipated growth and development and provide for the orderly replacement of existing capital facilities and equipment. A well-developed capital program provides a useful frame of reference for all participants in the acquisition, construction, and financing processes.

The CIP can be employed to forecast future capital demands on current revenues, borrowing power, and levels of outside assistance. As resources or demands change, policy makers can move capital projects forward or back in time to other years, to reevaluate project priorities, or to change the revenue mix. The ability to shift capital projects and outlays is particularly important when a significant portion of the capital budget is financed from current revenues, since it allows the jurisdiction to allocate "lumpy" capital projects over the forecast period in such a way as to stabilize or smooth out the property-tax rate.

Because of its multiyear time horizon, the CIP can provide local government agencies and departments the opportunity to carry out required plans, engineering surveys, land acquisition, architectural sketches, and site-plan reviews. The financial analysis integral to a capital improvement plan highlights the impact that capital expenditures will have on the operating budget.[4] If the capital budget explicitly acknowledges the personnel and maintenance costs associated with capital projects, it can provide a basis for realistic operating budget assumptions and expectations.

Since the CIP schedules the timing of capital projects, it helps avoid duplication and overlap. It also encourages the principles of value engineering—the notion that a leaky roof should be repaired or replaced before a new ceiling is installed. In this sense it facilitates optimal use of public funds, reducing the possibility of overlapping or conflicting projects. Finally, because the CIP encompasses the entire jurisdiction, it can ensure that no one functional area (e.g., streets) receives more attention than others or that any one geographic area receives more public facilities than others.

*The CIP's Contribution to Long-Range Policy Development.* The CIP focuses attention on community goals and needs and can ensure that major capital expenditures are in line with community expectations, anticipated growth, and projected financial capability. A number of policy areas can be enhanced by the preparation of a comprehensive capital improvement program. Among the most important areas are: the formalization of capital funding objectives, that is, adopting standards that permit efficient allocation of limited financial resources; and the development of carefully structured debt policies.

The CIP process includes a system to prioritize spending for capital facilities. Establishing formal policies to guide the ranking of capital-project requests can provide justification for spending decisions. For example, the policies typically give greatest weight to projects or equipment required to address public-health and safety concerns. If consensus on spending priorities is reached between elected officials and staff in advance, the annual evaluation of project requests can be streamlined and made more efficient.

In recent years an increasing number of state and local governments have found that the adoption of debt policies gives them greater control over the mix of issue types, redemption schedules, and credit implications of their borrowing programs. These are easily developed in concert with the implementation of the capital improvement program. The CIP can be designed to evaluate automatically the impact of proposed borrowings on the existing debt structure. This represents an added degree of management control.

*The CIP as a Positive Credit Rating Consideration.* Because a capital improvement plan has intrinsic value as a financial planning tool, it gives credit-rating agency and credit market analysts some assurance that the government has carefully planned for its future capital requirements and has assessed the financial resources likely to be available to meet those requirements. It should be kept in mind that credit ratings are a judgment of the kind and degree of risk that will be acceptable to investors. Individual securities or bonds are not avoided or acquired because of the ratings, but rather because of the characteristics that are reflected in the rating.

As part of the credit-rating process, rating agencies base their analysis on four key variables: financial condition, economic factors, indebtedness, and administrative factors. The fact that a local jurisdiction has developed and implemented a comprehensive capital plan has a positive effect on each of these areas.

## *THE CAPITAL PROGRAMMING PROCESS*

The benefits described above emphasize the value to a jurisdiction of an orderly and routine method of planning and financing required capital improvements. Like the operating budget, an effective CIP process involves several steps or activities, each of which is repeated every year. In most local governments, the CIP and the operating budget are developed separately, although some jurisdictions have successfully incorporated the overall process into the annual budget cycle.

### *Process Initiation*

The legal basis for capital budgeting usually lies in a local charter or ordinance. In some states, the process is mandated by law. Whatever the legal foundation, each local government should establish specific policies and procedures for submitting and evaluating projects and assessing funding sources. This usually includes (1) appointing a person or group to serve in a central review and coordination function and (2) developing a system to collect, analyze, and monitor capital requests, future needs, and potential resources. A timetable for the submission of projects, procedures for initiating projects generated internally by staff and externally by the public, and a method of evaluating and ranking projects are also necessary.

The importance of two policy or procedural issues should be emphasized here. The first is the determination of exactly what kinds of items and projects will be included in the CIP. Deciding which items should be included in the capital budget or plan and which in the operating budget is essential. As a general rule, items in a local government budget are classified as capital or operating by cost and frequency. Both criteria should be applied simultaneously to determine whether a project belongs in the capital budget.[5]

Capital costs represent a significant outlay for the government—something out of the ordinary. Accordingly, smaller governments frequently require lower minimum dollar amounts for capital expenditures than do larger jurisdictions. For instance, in a small community, vehicles may qualify as capital expenditures because of their cost in relation to other government supplies, while in another jurisdiction they are routine operating expenditures. An important criterion is that any facility or item financed by long-term debt should always be considered a capital expenditure. It is not fiscally prudent to debt-finance any item that has a useful life that is less than the repayment term of the loan (or bond).

In terms of frequency, only expenditures that *do not* occur annually should be included in the CIP. For example, some governments classify items or projects as "nonrecurring" if they have a useful life of three years or more. These distinctions are useful, however, only as guidelines to help avoid confusion and increase consistency. There will always be "gray areas" that must be resolved locally. Each government must make its own decisions regarding the appropriateness of including items (usually maintenance and replacement) that recur regularly but infrequently, i.e., every five, ten, or twenty years.[6]

A second concern is the identification of prospective participants in the process. The government's infrastructure role vis-à-vis other jurisdictions and political subdivisions necessarily dictates some of the participants in the CIP process. Within the jurisdiction's own organizational structure, the main players include the operating departments (e.g., public works, parks, schools), which submit project proposals; and a central review agency such as the planning department or the budget/finance department or a CIP committee that assesses and selects projects. The chief administrative officer is generally responsible for submitting the CIP to the governing board.

The role of the legislative body varies from jurisdiction to jurisdiction. In some cases, the CIP must be approved by both the planning commission and the governing board. These bodies may take a relatively passive role, merely approving the CIP as submitted, or they may actively participate in the selection of projects and financing mechanisms used.

Likewise, the participation of residents and business interests will vary. In some communities, citizens (or citizen CIP committees) identify projects and are involved in modifying the priority-setting process by determining what selection criteria and weighting factors will be used. In others, the process is more ad-hoc, with citizens being given the opportunity to submit project requests and allowed to comment at public hearings.

There are advantages and disadvantages to both methods of involvement. Active citizen participation can require considerable staff time and to be successful requires in-place systems of volunteerism and activism in the community. But extensive citizen participation can also make it easier to implement controversial infrastructure improvements. It frequently provides decision makers with information about the public's perception of community needs and its willingness to incur new costs.

### *Resource and Demand Inventory*

Local governments usually compile and periodically update an inventory of their physical plant. Because many capital project proposals will request expansion or replacement of existing facilities, it is important to be aware of the age, general condition, and original acquisition cost of all fixed (capital) assets owned or leased by the government. This information will help to track the condition of equipment and forecast replacement needs. Some indices that might be used to inventory and assess the condition of infrastructure are presented in table 5-1. It is also a good idea to determine the status of previously approved capital projects, both to monitor the CIP and to aid in the preparation of the new capital budget.[7]

The local government may also "inventory" future demands that, at a minimum, includes an annual review and forecast of changes in population, land-

TABLE 5-1
*Inventory and Condition Assessment Indices*

| Inventory | Condition/Performance |
|---|---|
| Unit (e.g., street, bridge, pipe) | Current Condition Rating and Date |
| Type of Material | Percentage of Capacity in Use |
| Location | Repair History |
| Physical Dimensions | Type of repair |
| Initial Value/Cost | Cost |
| Responsible Department | Date |
| Funding Source/Eligibility | Trends in Performance of Key Variables |

SOURCE: Stephen R. Godwin and George E. Petersen, *Guide to Assessing Capital Stock Condition* (Washington: The Urban Institute Press, 1984), Table 1.

use patterns, and other demographic information. The "future demands" inventory identifies locations for new development, as well as any changes in the type or number of businesses or industries locating within the jurisdiction. Once this information is in hand, the data can be compared to the land-use plan and the impact on the capital plant can be estimated.

### *Project Identification and Priorities*

As with the operating budget, the capital programming process begins with the collection of proposals from departments, agencies, and sometimes private individuals or community groups. Typically, forms are issued by the central review agency. For projects that previously were included in the past year's capital program, the resubmission requires only revisions of cost estimates or other new developments. For first-time submissions, or for proposals that previously went unfunded, however, considerable information may be requested. Information typically required in the project-request form includes a narrative description of the project, its costs broken down by year of expenditure, the rationale for the project, its impact on the operating budget, and proposed funding sources. Supplemental information, such as project scheduling, construction cost estimates, and maps also may be required. Many jurisdictions require separate forms for equipment items because they do not fit readily with their capital-facilities-request forms. Thus, a CIP request packet typically involves several forms and may even require a summary form for the submitting department to complete.

Many local governments require that the submitting department assign priorities to the projects requested. This introduces one of the most common problems associated with capital budgeting—the weighting of priorities in order to allocate scarce resources. The allocation problem becomes even more significant later, but it is important to realize that the assignment of priorities can be difficult even at the level of the originating department.

Generally, the chief administrative officer will send a letter to each department head and to citizen groups calling for project submissions, outlining procedures to be used, the CIP implementation schedule, and anticipated funding levels and requirements. Often this intergovernmental transmittal letter also includes guidelines for ranking projects within each department or division. In some systems each project is rated according to specific categories, such as:

*Urgent Projects:*
- to meet emergency situations
- to perform work required by state or federal law

*Necessary Projects:*
- to eliminate safety hazards/correct code violations
- to meet contractual obligations
- to perform required renovation or repair

*Desired Projects:*
- to replace equipment
- to extend/enhance service
- to match state or federal funds

*Ongoing Projects:*
- to continue work in progress

*Deferrable Projects:*
- to perform nonessential renovations/improvements
- to perform projects with questionable timing or need

The departmental ranking system may also include some more subjective evaluation. For instance, those submitting requests may be asked to answer the following questions:

- What improvement do we need most?
- Which capital projects can be postponed without jeopardizing health, safety, or other program objectives?
- How will these project decisions affect the level of service currently provided?
- Do any of the projects contain "frills" that could be cut without essentially changing the request?
- Have all alternatives and solutions been fully examined?

Once each of the projects has been given a priority rating by departmental staff, they can also be ranked (first, second, third) to indicate their overall importance when compared to items with similar priorities. These rankings typically are then sent to the central agency for review and comparison with systemwide needs.

### *Project Evaluation*

The capital project "wish list" will probably not be fully fundable with the resources available. To compare and choose among dissimilar projects, the local government will institute procedures to evaluate each project and rank each in order of priority on a systemwide or jurisdictionwide basis.

Once departmental requests have been collected, they must be evaluated. Many jurisdictions begin by referring capital development proposals to the public works or engineering department to ascertain technical feasibility. In some cases, this is accomplished before the submission is documented on the forms. Likewise, equipment items are often reviewed by the general services director or other responsible officials. Once these technical reviews are completed, the more difficult process of comparing competing projects must be undertaken.

Some states require a formal review by the local government planning commission usually to ensure conformity with the master plan. Useful suggestions regarding other proposed activities which may have been overlooked by the original submitting agency or individual may surface at this point. This review is not likely to produce priority changes, but rather provides an opportunity for improved scheduling of interrelated physical developments. Further, the jurisdiction's planners are alerted early to proposed future projects that could affect private development.

Upon completion of the planning review, many mid-size and large jurisdictions appoint a review committee to assign priorities and to screen or rank the various proposals. Although ultimate responsibility for recommending a capital program may be assigned to the chief administrative officer, this internal process helps to establish objective criteria and provides a comprehensive effort that cannot be accomplished single-handedly. Although certain recommendations inevitably will be overruled, and other projects may be inserted into the ultimate capital program, the product of committee review typically proves to have enduring value.

Even if the system used to evaluate and compare projects is a numerical or quantitative one, the final decision will be based on value preferences and policy choices. In order to have an effective project-selection process, the government should have clearly defined and agreed-upon criteria and a system to rank each project request. Although there are some rules of thumb for ranking projects, those making the selection decisions must ultimately rely on their own knowledge of the locality and their confidence in staff.

Most public officials find that the development of evaluation criteria and setting priorities are the most difficult part of capital programming. No matter how much care is taken, there will always be those who disagree with the ranking system. Many find that a two- or three-tier ranking system is most helpful. Frequently used general criteria for evaluating projects are

- Fiscal and budgetary impact on the jurisdiction
- Health and safety effects
- Community economic effects
- Extent of facility use
- Environmental, esthetic, and social effects
- Disruption and inconvenience caused
- Distributional effects
- Prior commitments and feasibility
- Implications of deferring the project
- Amount of uncertainty and risk
- Effects on interjurisdictional relationships
- Advantages accruing from relation to other capital projects[8]

To assist in the rating process, jurisdictions may assign numerical scores to each project based on criteria that have been developed over time. Although such quantitative approaches are attractive at first, many suffer from high degrees of subjectivity, with a bias toward one type of spending. For example, replacement equipment could receive lower scores than new development under a skewed scoring system that emphasizes growth.

If the flaws can be worked out of these systems, objective scoring programs do serve a useful purpose. They also provide guidance to project requestors, who quickly learn that certain suggestions are unlikely to be funded on the basis of objective ranking. Some governments use a two-stage evaluation procedure in which a "core" list of projects is identified first. Then a second stage of evaluation is added to allow first-time rejections to resurface and be reconsidered before a final recommendation is made. This avoids the embarrassment of submitting a mechanically pure list to the governing body for consideration, knowing very well that certain worthy projects have been excluded because they lack an adequate "point count." Ultimately, of course, subjectivity enters into the process—as it must in a public decision-making system.

*Cost-Benefit Analysis.* For many years, economists have advocated that the public-sector capital-budgeting process could be improved through rigorous application of economic analysis techniques. In formal quantitative models, a stream of future social benefits are calculated, and the discounted present value of the benefits compared to the project cost. In a capital planning model, the formula would look something like this:

$$NPV_B = -I + \frac{B_1}{(1 + r)} + \cdots + \frac{B_n}{(1 + r)^n}$$

Where: $NPV_B$ = net present value of benefits
$I$ = investment (capital cost)
$B$ = benefits in each future year
$r$ = rate of interest (social cost of capital)
$n$ = number of years

Unfortunately, applying this elegant model can prove elusive in practice. Although it may retain value in a few specialized instances, the problems of quantification can be immense. Primarily, this is because it is quite difficult to quantify monetarily the benefits of public spending. In the case of toll bridges and water-supply facilities, where pricing is possible, the value to consumers can be measured and captured through tolls and charges. Most public facilities, however, are built by the public sector *because* they provide some social benefits that presumably escape the pricing system. For example, public parks provide considerable value to their users, although people rarely pay each time that they enjoy the open space. Only when limited numbers of facilities are available—that is, exclusion becomes a factor—does pricing work. Generally then, the quantification of social benefit becomes a true quagmire for the analyst.

A second problem relating to net present value analysis is the issue of the social cost of capital and the rate of discount to employ. Most local governments can borrow capital funds at a low, tax-free interest rate—usually below the rate on U.S. Treasury bonds. On the other hand, the local government's investment portfolio may receive higher returns on taxable government securities. Which interest rate should apply? Or should the analysis use the cost of money to private taxpayers who must finance costs through taxes and fees and thus detract from their future accumulation of personal wealth? In general, the lowest, usually tax-exempt, interest rate has been used for net present value calculations, although this introduces a bias toward completing as many public projects as possible because the denominators of the calculation are reduced—which mathematically increases the net present value that will be derived. As a consequence, most practitioners believe that the net present value methodology, while useful in the comparison of like projects, should not be the rationale in assigning priorities.

***Financial Analysis.*** Once projects have been identified, the planning and engineering feasibility of each evaluated, and a preliminary rank-ordering process begun, it is necessary to conduct a financial analysis. Analysis is needed at the aggregate level, as well as on a project-by-project basis. On the project level, the economics of project financing must be examined closely. The central review agency must assess the feasibility of the project, the impact of the cost of the project on the jurisdiction, and the effect of future maintenance and operational expenses on the operating budget.

At the macro level, the financial capability of the local government is estimated—How much capital spending and debt financing can be supported by the local tax base and the local economy? To determine the government's capacity to absorb additional debt and to finance capital spending from current revenues, several tax and debt-burden studies can be undertaken. First, the total overlapping tax burden on local taxpayers is determined. To calculate the total overlapping tax burden, the tax levies for county, city, township, school district, and special districts are added together. Relative tax information is collected and compared. A jurisdiction's total tax rates can then be compared with averages for their region, state, and the nation. Because of differential tax structures, national comparisons may not be relevant, but at the regional level comparative analysis can be fruitful. Jurisdictions with high total tax rates relative to their neighbors may be vulnerable to future taxpayer backlash. The exception to this rule is that affluent suburbs with high tax rates are often both able and willing to sustain above-average levels of public expenditure.

In addition to competitive position and taxpayer attitudes, local officials also should determine whether there will be any risk of overburdening local properties during periods of business downturns (recessions). Communities with highly cyclical economies must be particularly careful to gauge their capacity to bear high debt burdens when local industries operate at less-than-average capacity.

The next area of analysis is an examination of overlapping debt burdens. Local governments may encounter resistance to new bond issues from taxpayers in localities that already have absorbed above-average levels of debt. Certainly, the bond rating and underwriting communities will be likely to discourage aggressive capital spending programs in such jurisdictions. This suggests that the costs of borrowing will be higher in riskier, high-debt localities. Debt statistics can be presented in per-capita terms or as a percentage of aggregate property valuations or personal income.

Financial analysts also will be inclined to study the trend of a government's borrowing and its overall leverage. Unless driven by economic growth, jurisdictions with rising per-capita debt and rising debt as a percentage of property value will be looked upon unfavorably as having overly ambitious capital programs.

Another helpful analytic technique is an examination of the existing debt-service schedule. By plotting existing debt-service payments over time, policy-makers can determine their future "spending opportunities." A well-planned capital program can take advantage of this "envelope" by slotting spending programs into the future so that tax rates could remain stable even though new capital spending increases. Some jurisdictions also have established policies that require that debt be redeemed at a predetermined rate, which limits the ability of local officials to burden future taxpayers with principal payments that balloon in the distant future.

Looking beyond historical information, projections of future revenue capacity also should be made. This creates several estimation risks and analytical complications. Revenue growth depends on several key variables, including demographic trends, tax policy, and the general business cycle. Communities that experience population growth may find it difficult to make accurate determinations of their future financial condition.

To forecast revenues, it is necessary first to understand the nature of the local tax and user-charge structure. Some governments have elastic tax bases, relying heavily on income taxes, sales taxes, and fees related to growth. Others may find themselves dependent on stable, but relatively inelastic, property taxes. In states with constitutional tax limitations, the probability of revenue increases must be discounted. Future tax increases to finance specific improvements may be a direct function of the capital improvement program and the ensuing political campaign needed to "sell" it. In some cases, a status quo estimate of future revenues on the basis of existing tax rates, assuming no new voted millage or tax-revenue sources is made.

***Funding Source Identification.*** Only a limited pool of resources is available to fund all the requested capital projects. The challenge is to identify the full range of resources available (both current and borrowed) and to determine how these funds can be used to meet the needs with the highest priorities. Among the major sources of funding that should be considered are

- *Pay-as-you-go financing*—costs are paid directly from current income, such as taxes, fees and user charges, and interest earnings
- *Grants* from other governments
- *Debt financing*—tapping external funds through the issuance of debt in the capital market
- *Public/private ventures,* including privatization

Most governments find that current revenues are inadequate to fund all the projects in their capital plan. For this reason, a well-structured capital improvement program should include a review of all financial resources that might be available to meet current and future capital needs. The mix of financing methods that will be used to fund a CIP is likely to be one of the most important decisions made in developing and executing a capital planning effort. In the case of debt financing, for example, amortization rates and repayment schedules are determined by the parameters established by the mix of financing tools used. Each method of financing has advantages and disadvantages, and each should be viewed in the context of its applicability and its effect on the jurisdiction's spending levels and overall fiscal health.

No one method of financing is appropriate for every project or capital facility. Prudent financial management calls for a combination of sources and methods to be used to fund the capital requirements of a local government. Too much reliance on one source or method jeopardizes the entity's fiscal health and its ability to respond to changing economic and demographic conditions.

In most large jurisdictions, each department typically submits funding-source recommendations with their project requests. The central reviewing agency must then determine the appropriateness of each source recommendation.

There are no hard-and-fast rules for determining a "good mix" of financing methods. Every jurisdiction must develop its own set of criteria that recognizes the legal and practical limits of each approach. These decisions are based on the characteristics (cost, location, timing) of the capital expenditure in question, as well as on the financial analysis (fiscal capacity, requirements for operating purposes and debt service, limitations on the revenue system), and finally on historical, economic, and political constraints operating within the jurisdiction.

### Project Scheduling

After projects have been evaluated and rated, and potential sources of available resources identified, the next task is to determine the timing of all the projects. The projects must be placed into time slots that fit both the jurisdiction's needs and the availability of resources. The end result will be a sequential listing of projects that can be reasonably financed, designed, constructed, and implemented.

This is, however, generally a trial-and-error process. Some projects will be interrelated; the sequence of developments sometimes take precedent over finances. Bond referenda may be required. Engineering capability and staffing also may impose constraints on the volume of work that can be undertaken in any given year. Known political priorities of the governing body may also enter into the decision making, particularly for capital programming activities. Like the operating budget, the capital budget or CIP is sure to go through many iterations after review by various participants in the process. A preliminary CIP is usually submitted to the governing body, with the final adopted plan published after action by that body.

Urgency and feasibility will likely dictate the initial field of candidates for the capital budget. If funding capacity remains—which rarely occurs—projects with lower priorities can be considered. The more frequent occurrence, however, is that projects initially scheduled or desired for the early years must be deferred pending funding ability. For the remaining projects, the timing of development will likely reflect tactical factors, such as a replacement schedule, the prospects for funding from outside sources, or political factors.

Once a government has formalized its capital planning process through the adoption and implementation of a CIP, subsequent years' efforts are usually simplified. As the prior year's capital budget is implemented, completed projects can be crossed off, and the second year of last year's CIP becomes the beginning list for the subsequent capital budget. Also, new suggestions can be entertained, and projects that were considered but not included in the prior CIP can be added if funding priorities change. Sometimes, a multiyear education effort is required to develop political and community support for projects that would properly belong in the capital program if revenue constraints were removed by action of the governing body or voters. Some governments therefore add a final column to their presentation, showing projects that are desirable, but for which funding is not available.

An important but often overlooked aspect of the capital program is the orderly process of planning for the replacement of existing facilities and equipment. Although some governments do not maintain sufficiently precise records to assist them in the capital-facilities-replacement process, a growing number have developed impressive processes. In some localities, a facilities inventory is used to establish clear documentation of the condition of available capital facilities and the probable timing of needed improvements. This can include a formal decision to allocate a fixed percentage of annual revenues for capital facilities and equipment replacement, making it possible to engage in pay-as-you-go financing on a regular basis, eliminating the tendency to defer replacements, which results in greater maintenance costs. Replacements and renovations thus take priority over new developments or program expansion.

For equipment financing, many local governments have created motor-pool funds or other internal-service funds and include depreciation in the rental charges that are levied against user departments. The advantage of this approach is that the depreciation process ensures that cash will be available when the time comes to replace equipment. For small communities, this eliminates the need for borrowing to finance major equipment such as fire trucks and public works vehicles. Many local governments initiated such replacement programs during the early phases of the now-defunct Federal Revenue Sharing program using newly found "windfall" revenue to initiate the funding program. Unfortunately, jurisdictions that now attempt to implement such programs in periods of economic constraint find it difficult to locate the "seed money" to fund accumulated depreciation. A further drawback of this funding mechanism is the problem of intergenerational equity. By charging depreciation to existing taxpayers through service charges that ultimately are funded through taxation and user fees, the replacement of future capital equipment is ensured. It will be future generations, however, not the present generation of taxpayers, that will benefit from the eventual replacement of today's equipment and facilities. So why should today's taxpayers incur the cost of future benefits? Further, some analysts argue that tax-exempt financing for general governmental equipment produces lower costs than the depreciation and pay-as-you-go approach implicit in the internal-service fund approach. From a long-term standpoint, however, equipment financing is a very minor element in the overall CIP. The costs absorbed by today's taxpayers in funding a depreciation system often work out to less than 10 cents per household. This would appear to be a minor price to pay for the assurance that the future has been provided for.

### *CIP Adoption*

Generally, a preliminary capital improvement program and capital budget are prepared and presented to the governing body. This effort provides an opportunity for informative discussions of key financing and policy issues, as well as a detailed presentation of proposed projects. The CIP usually includes a transmittal letter from the chief administrative officer, capital budget policies, long-term financial forecasts, financial summaries, summaries of revenues and expenditures by category or function, project descriptions and project summaries, special analyses, maps and charts or graphs, and a glossary or other reader aids.

During the review of the preliminary CIP, the policy dimension of the capital programming comes into focus. In jurisdictions with elected executives, the CIP often provides an opportunity for strong executive leadership. Public hearings customarily are held before final deliberation by the governing body. These opportunities for public input may represent the final opportunity for citizen involvement. In many jurisdictions, a subsequent public hearing may be required at the time of debt authorization or appropriation of public funds. Nonetheless, the public hearings attendant to the capital program offer an important vehicle for individuals and interest groups to represent themselves in the context of a capital priorities system. Once the capital program is approved, the first year of the CIP, the capital budget, is authorized.

### *Implementation*

The capital budget appropriates funds for the projects in the first year of the CIP and recommends the authorization of necessary bond issues. This legislative authority does not extend to the remaining years of the CIP, thereby requiring an annual update of the program. The progress of all authorized capital projects and expenditures should be monitored throughout the year. Each project may be assigned a project manager, who is responsible for ensuring timely completion. Regular reports from project managers will ensure that the projects are on schedule and can also serve as the basis for the following year's CIP submissions. Monthly or quarterly reports are typically provided to the chief administrative officer so that deviations, delays, change orders, and overruns are detected immediately. Similar information (in a more condensed format) can also be provided to the governing body, permitting elected officials the opportunity to review systematically the overall program instead of individual pieces.

As the year progresses, new projects and ideas will surface, and one or two projects may fall behind the original timetable. The resulting changes help the preparation of the next year's CIP planning effort, which will begin before the current year's projects are completed. Eventually, a cyclical rhythm will develop, and officials will become accustomed to the discipline and rationale inherent in the capital programming process.

## *CONCLUSION*

Capital planning and budgeting is an essential element of financial management. Local governments increasingly are using the capital plan as a policy tool and as a vehicle for public communication. The CIP represents a framework for decision making. It provides a forum to discuss and resolve the political choices that a jurisdiction makes about what to build, where and when to build or buy it, and how much to spend for it.[9] For many of the local governments that use it, the CIP provides the only forum in which decisions regarding the physical development and maintenance of the community interact with those concerning its financial and fiscal future.

## *NOTES*

1. For a review of needs studies done between the early 1970s and mid-1980s see "Infrastructure Needs Studies: A Critique," a paper prepared for the National Council on Public Works by George Petersen, Ted Miller, Nancy Humphrey, and Christopher Walker, July 1, 1986.

2. Apogee Research, *Financing Infrastructure: Innovations at the Local Level* (Washington: National League of Cities, 1987), pp. 6–7.

3. Significant portions of the preceding section are from *Building Together: Investing in Community Infrastructure* (Washington: Government Finance Officers Association, National Association of Home Builders and National Association of Counties, 1990).

4. *A Practical Guide for Local Governments,* Office of Local Development Programs (Virginia Department of Housing and Community Development, 1986), p. 3.

5. Rosenberg, Philip, and Rood, Sally, "Planning for Capital Improvements," *MIS Report* 16, 8 (Washington: International City Management Association, 1984.)

6. *Ibid.*, p. 11.
7. *Ibid.*, pp. 11–12.
8. Annie Millar, "Selecting Capital Investment Projects for Local Governments," *Public Budgeting and Finance* (Autumn 1988): 66–68.
9. Rosenberg, p. 4.

# 6
# *Property Taxes*

MICHAEL E. BELL AND JOHN H. BOWMAN

## *INTRODUCTION*

Property taxation has been a major source of government revenue at the state or local level in the United States since colonial times. Even now, it is far and away the largest source of local government tax revenue. But it has not survived unchanged over 200 years. Rather, it is a dynamic tax source that is continually adapted to changing circumstances. Changes both in the extent and the definition of the tax base and in the structure of the rates have altered the tax substantially, as we shall see, making the tax less general than it was several decades ago. And the degree to which governments rely upon property taxation for their revenues has diminished.

Critics of the property tax have been many and vocal. Jens Jensen, for example, has said, "If any tax could have been eliminated by adverse criticism, the property tax should have been eliminated long ago."[1] George W. Mitchell, addressing the 1956 annual conference of the National Tax Association, went so far as to predict the demise of the tax: "Over the next two decades, I would expect to see the property tax all but wither away. Further relative decline is a foregone conclusion, but I would go beyond this and predict that in absolute terms, the property tax is headed for oblivion."[2] Some thought this prediction, although clearly wrong in its details, acquired some credence in 1978, by the fact that California voters approved Proposition 13 to force nearly a 60 percent property-tax cut in the largest state. Many thought the ensuing "tax revolt" would cripple the property tax.

But the property tax is a vital tax, a survivor. In 1957, about the time of Mitchell's forecast, local property taxation raised $12.4 billion (86.7 percent of local taxes), and by 1977 the figure had risen to $60.3 billion (80.5 percent of local taxes).[3] Property-tax collections in fiscal 1988 were $127.2 billion (about 74.1 percent of local taxes).[4] Thus, despite continued long-term *relative* decline, *absolute* property-tax amounts have grown substantially, averaging 7.9 percent growth per year between 1957 and 1988, and 6.8 percent between 1977 and 1988.

What features of property taxation have made it a target for criticism and the subject of voter referenda to restrain it? And, despite these, why has the tax endured so well? A number of considerations come into play, including:

- Public attitude toward the tax, which, due in part to unique aspects of property taxation, historically has been adverse
- Property-tax relief measures that narrow the base, limit the rates, limit the levy amounts, and/or substitute other revenue sources
- Trends in intergovernmental aids to local governments
- Trend toward revenue centralization
- Proliferation of special-purpose local governments, often lacking property-tax authority

Many of these factors are interrelated, and some exert opposing influences on the role of the property tax. Relief, for example, may seem to reduce revenues, but it also may improve acceptance and revenue productivity of the tax. Glenn Fisher has argued a strong revenue source of its own is essential to strong local government, that property taxation is better suited to local use than other major tax forms, and that many changes in property taxation over the decades reasonably can be viewed as adaptations to stress on local governments that have helped to ensure preservation of both the property tax and local autonomy.[5]

Before turning to a detailed consideration of property taxation, we first explore some of the above factors, with emphasis upon public opinion and fiscal federalism developments.

While many would argue that no tax is a *good* tax (or that good taxation is no taxation), taxes do play an important role in civilized societies, and some taxes are better than others. There are standard criteria by which to evaluate taxes[6] that provide a better yardstick than public opinion, but opinion polls clearly command the attention of politicians.

Historically, the property tax has been held in low esteem, as suggested by the Jensen quote, above. More recently, when the Advisory Commission on Intergovernmental Relations (ACIR) began sponsoring a regular public-opinion poll on government and taxes in 1972, the property tax was the runaway choice as the worst among major taxes. When asked, "Which do you think is the worst tax—that is, the least fair?" 45 percent chose the local property tax, compared to only 19 percent for the runner-up, the federal income tax. For the next few years, the percentage finding the property tax most objectionable fell sharply while the percentage bestowing that honor on the federal income tax rose sharply, thereby placing the two taxes in a virtual dead heat. Since 1979, however, the federal income tax has beaten the local property tax in garnering worst-tax votes, often by a wide margin. In many recent years, the property tax has been viewed the worst tax by fewer than 30 percent of respondents, a big improvement over the first survey.

To the extent that improvement in the property-tax image is due to changes in the tax resulting from the reform and relief movements, the opinion survey numbers might seem reasonable and the findings important. But headlines about particular tax problems, or about the general need for income-tax reform, probably have played an important role in shaping the results. Moreover, year-to-year shifts of several percentage points have not been uncommon, making the polls a rather unstable guide for policymakers. It may be significant, however (especially for revenue centralization and diversification at the state or local level), that, throughout the 1972–1986 period, the state income and sales taxes have been held in higher regard (or lower disregard) than property taxation.

Several reasons have been given to explain why the property tax might be unpopular relative to other state and local taxes. One might be its magnitude. As noted, historically property taxation has been the largest tax source at the state or local level, and it still is, although by a reduced margin. Because most state income taxes follow federal income-tax law rather closely, the very wide gap between the percentages of the public holding one or the other to be the worst tax seems explicable only by the fact that state tax rates are so much lower than the federal rates. Other considerations go to the nature of the property tax compared to income and sales taxes:

- The property tax, in part, taxes unrealized capital gains.
- For most properties in a given year, there is no market transaction that determines the size of the tax base (i.e., the value of the property), so the property-tax base, unlike those of the income and consumption taxes, must be estimated by the taxing governments.
- The property-tax bill can rise even when the taxpayer's cash position does not improve because it is a tax on accumulated capital value, rather than on current economic flows, and thus may become quite high in relation to current income.
- Property-tax rates tend to fluctuate (generally rise) more often than income-tax and sales-tax rates, because historically the property-tax rate has been set at the level needed to balance local budgets.
- Property-tax bills generally are paid in a small number of large payments (usually one or two, but perhaps as many as twelve in the case of those paid with mortgage payments).

Several of the property-tax developments discussed in later sections of this chapter have eased some of these perceived problems.

## *THE ROLE OF PROPERTY TAXATION IN LOCAL GOVERNMENT FINANCE*

Into the early years of the twentieth century, property taxation was the major tax source for state governments. At the turn of the century, over 50 percent of state governments' tax revenues came from property taxation. State tax diversification more than halved the property-tax share of state taxes between 1902 and 1927.[7] But it was the Great Depression of the 1930s that brought actual state property-tax reduction (including its abandonment in some states in favor of local use of the tax) and serious state tax diversification into taxes thought to be more in accord with taxpaying ability, such as general sales taxes (a new form of tax) and income taxes. By 1940, less than 8 percent of state tax revenue came from property taxes.[8] The figure now is below 2 percent.[9]

Thus, the property tax is also almost wholly—over 96 percent—a local tax (Table 6-1). To be sure, local governments also have diversified their tax structures.[10] Chief among nonproperty taxes are those on consumption (both general and selective sales taxes) and on income. The local share of revenues from both these tax types increased sharply from the mid-1950s to the mid-1980s, but it remains small for each: about 12 percent for consumption taxes and less than 2 percent for income taxes (Table 6-1). Moreover, even after large percentage increases, consumption and income taxes in the late 1980s account for relatively small shares of total local tax dollars: roughly 15 percent and 6 percent, respectively.[11] The growth in such taxes has been sufficient to reduce the property-tax share, but it has not been sufficient both to offset the slowed growth of property taxes and to match the growth of state own-source revenues. Thus, the local share of all taxes has varied between 15 percent and 19 percent over the last 30 years, showing no clear trend (Table 6-1).

TABLE 6-1

*Local Government Share of Tax Revenues by Type of Tax, Selected Years, 1957–1988*

| | TYPE OF TAX | | | | |
|---|---|---|---|---|---|
| Year | Total | Property | Consumption | Income | Other |
| 1957 | 14.5% | 96.3% | 5.0% | 0.3% | 12.0% |
| 1967 | 16.5 | 96.7 | 5.4 | 0.9 | 10.0 |
| 1972 | 18.9 | 97.1 | 7.4 | 1.5 | 9.9 |
| 1977 | 17.8 | 96.4 | 9.9 | 1.5 | 10.9 |
| 1975 | 15.4 | 96.2 | 10.5 | 1.3 | 12.6 |
| 1981 | 14.6 | 96.1 | 9.8 | 1.4 | 12.0 |
| 1982 | 15.4 | 96.2 | 10.6 | 1.5 | 10.5 |
| 1983 | 17.0 | 96.3 | 11.0 | 1.6 | 12.0 |
| 1984 | 16.8 | 96.0 | 11.2 | 1.7 | 13.1 |
| 1985 | 16.7 | 96.2 | 11.9 | 1.7 | 13.4 |
| 1986 | 17.1 | 96.3 | 12.6 | 1.7 | 8.8 |
| 1987 | 16.8 | 96.2 | 12.7 | 1.7 | 15.7 |
| 1988 | 17.2 | 96.2 | 12.5 | 1.7 | 16.1 |

SOURCE: Census Bureau data, as reported by the: Advisory Commission on Intergovernmental Relations. *Significant Features of Fiscal Federalism 1987 Edition*, Report M-151 (Washington, D.C.: Government Printing Office, 1987), Table 32.2; and U.S. Bureau of the Census, *Government Finances in 1986–87* and *1987–88*. (Washington, D.C.: Government Printing Office, 1988 and 1990), Table 2.

### *Trends in Local Property-Tax Finance, 1957–1988*

Given the history of criticism of property taxation, predictions of the tax's demise, the recent tax revolt (Proposition 13 in California, Proposition 2½ in Massachusetts, etc.), and the general centralization of fiscal authority in the United States in this century, perhaps one of the most striking facts of the property tax is its strong revenue growth. From 1957 through 1988, local property-tax revenue increased from $12.4 billion to $127.2 billion (Table 6-2), a 7.8 percent compound average annual growth rate. The slowest average annual growth rate in any of the five-year periods shown in Table 6-2 (5.5 percent) was for 1977–1982, the period encompassing the major tax revolt activities, including those in California and Massachusetts. But in the subsequent 6-year period (1982–1988), the growth rebounded to 8.3 percent per year, a bit above the 31-year average and higher than in three of the other six periods.

*Local Reliance on Property Taxation.* Despite the fairly strong property-tax growth over the past three decades, the tax's relative position in the local revenue structure deteriorated—and rather sharply, by some measures (Table 6-2). By the narrowest of these measures—property tax as a percentage of all taxes—local reliance fell from over 85 percent to under 75 percent, reflecting local tax diversification. The property-tax role among all local own-source general revenues slipped even more, from 69 percent to 47 percent, or about one-third. The greater deterioration in the property-tax role in own-source revenues reflects a trend toward greater local reliance on nontax revenues. A major source of such revenues is user fees, which have found greater favor in recent years. Also, higher interest rates in the 1970s and early 1980s increased the role of interest earnings.

TABLE 6-2

*Local Property Tax Revenue, Absolute Amounts in Current Dollars and Relative to Various Revenue Measures*
*(Selected Years, 1957–1986)*

| Year | Property Tax Revenue (Millions) | Average Annual 5-Year Growth | PROPERTY TAX PERCENTAGE OF Local Taxes | General Revenues Own-Source | General Revenues Total |
|---|---|---|---|---|---|
| 1957 | $ 12,385 | 8.4% | 86.7% | 69.3% | 48.5% |
| 1963 | 18,414 | 8.3 | 87.7 | 69.0 | 48.0 |
| 1967 | 25,186 | 6.5 | 86.6 | 66.2 | 43.2 |
| 1973 | 41,620 | 10.6 | 83.7 | 63.5 | 39.5 |
| 1977 | 60,267 | 7.7 | 80.5 | 59.1 | 33.7 |
| 1982 | 78,952 | 5.5 | 76.1 | 48.0 | 28.1 |
| 1988 | 127,191 | 8.3* | 74.1 | 46.9 | 29.3 |

* Six-year period, 1982–1988.

SOURCE: U.S. Bureau of the Census, *1982 Census of Governments, Volume 6, Number 4, Historical Statistics on Governmental Finances and Employment* (Washington, D.C.: Government Printing Office, 1985), Table 14; and U.S. Bureau of the Census, *Government Finances in 1987–88,* (Washington, D.C.: Government Printing Office, 1990), Table 2.

The role of the property tax in total local general revenue generation declined the most from the mid-1950s to the mid-1980s: from nearly half to less than 30 percent, a drop of more than 40 percent. Why?

While continued relative decline of the property tax is the trend over the three decades considered here, it is noteworthy that the rate of decline has dropped significantly in the 1980s. Whether the comparison is to total local taxes, total own-source general revenues, or total local general revenues, the average annual drop in the property-tax role was slower between 1982 and 1988 than in any of the five-year periods starting with 1972. And the property tax as a percentage of total local general revenue actually rose slightly between 1982 and 1988, the result of the stronger growth of the property tax itself in that period coupled with the much slower growth of federal aid. Property-tax levels above the trend line were chosen both over much larger increases in other local revenue sources and over lower levels of local spending.

*Trends in the Local Property-Tax Burdens.* Everything else equal, a tax is more burdensome if it takes a larger percentage of available economic resources, and less burdensome if it takes a smaller percentage. Common measures of resources available to taxpayers, or the size of the economy, are personal income and gross national product (GNP). Because personal income is a relatively steady share of GNP, expressing the property tax as a percentage of either of these two economic indicators yields very similar results, but with larger values for the narrower (personal income) measure.

In 1988, the property tax accounted for about the same percentage of personal income as it had in 1957—3.51 percent in 1988 versus 3.56 percent in 1957. This resulted from the reversal of a long-term decline.

Between 1982 and 1988—the period of accelerated property-tax growth and slowed federal-aid growth—the property tax rose in relation to personal income. The increase from 3.07 percent to 3.51 percent represents an average annual increase of about 2.3 percent (not percentage-point) in the property-tax share of personal income. Whether this renewed relative increase in the property tax continues will depend upon a number of factors, including the health of the economy, the level of intergovernmental-aid funding, and local preferences for property taxes in relation to other local revenue sources and to local services.

While income is the most general measure of taxpaying ability, many believe that, because the property tax is a tax on the value of accumulated property (wealth) rather than on income, the level of the tax should be expressed as a percentage of the value of the taxed property. Unfortunately, data limitations preclude expressing the property tax as a percentage of the market value of all taxable property. About the best that can be done on a basis that is comparable across states is to use FHA statistics on effective property-tax rates (i.e., the property tax as a percentage of market value) for single-family residences with FHA-insured mortgages.[12]

Expressing the property tax for these homes as a percentage of their market values gives a pattern similar to that relating property taxes to personal income: the 1986 national average effective rate (1.16 percent) is lower than the 1958 effective rate (1.34 percent), and both are lower than the early-1970s peak (1.98 percent in 1971). Thus, since the early 1970s, property taxes have fallen relative to income, GNP, and property value, but the decline has not been uninterrupted in any of these cases.

Another way of evaluating the level of property taxes is their magnitude in inflation-adjusted, or "real," dollars. As inflation rises, a larger nominal property-tax bill may be less burdensome (given that taxpayer incomes tend to rise in line with inflation over time) and capable of buying a smaller quantity of real services. While the aggregate property tax increased about tenfold between 1957 and 1988, after adjusting for both inflation and population change, the per capita real property-tax level increased by about 60 percent. The high inflation between 1972 and 1982 caused per capita real property-tax amounts to fall, even though nominal amounts rose.

### *Current Pattern of Local Property-Tax Use by Type of Government*

While the property tax is the major local tax, the degree to which local governments use and rely upon it varies substantially among the types of local government, by population size of the taxing unit, and by state and region. We will consider only the variations by type of government.

The Census Bureau reports data for five types of local governments, which, in the aggregate, numbered 83,186 in 1987, including three categories of general-purpose government and two of single- or dual-purpose governments:[13]

- 3,042 counties, including what are known as boroughs or parishes in some states
- 19,200 municipalities—cities, towns, and villages
- 16,691 townships, multifunction units that generally lie outside incorporated municipalities
- 14,721 school districts that provide only educational services and are independent of county or municipal units
- 29,532 special districts that usually perform one function (but not education), such as fire protection, sewer service, mosquito control, toll roads, or parks

Local governments in 1987–88 raised 74.1 percent of total taxes and 46.9 percent of total own-source general revenues via property-tax levies (Table 6-3). Thus, while local revenue systems now are rather diversified, the property tax still accounts for three-fourths of all local taxes, and nearly half of all locally raised general revenues. This dominant position of the property tax in local revenue systems is attributable, in part, to the age and tradition of property taxation in the United States. Unique among local taxes, property-tax authority and use are virtually universal among local governments, with the major exceptions being some special districts.[14] The degree of property-tax reliance, though, varies substantially by type of government.

TABLE 6-3
*Property Tax Use by Type of Local Government, 1988*

| Type of Government | Tax Amount (Millions) | Percent Distribution | PERCENTAGE OF Total Taxes | PERCENTAGE OF Own-Source General Revenue |
|---|---|---|---|---|
| All | $127,191 | 100.0% | 74.1% | 46.9% |
| County | 29,680 | 23.3 | 73.1 | 44.0 |
| Municipal | 29,948 | 23.5 | 50.1 | 30.7 |
| Township | 8,336 | 6.6 | 91.9 | 74.1 |
| School District | 54,611 | 42.9 | 97.4 | 80.4 |
| Special District | 4,617 | 3.6 | 75.8 | 17.0 |

SOURCE: U.S. Bureau of the Census, *Government Finances in 1987–88*, (Washington, D.C.: Government Printing Office, 1990), Table 2.

Counties and municipalities, the two major types of general-purpose (multifunction) local governments, account for almost exactly the same percentage of total local property taxes, a bit less than one-fourth (Table 6-3). Counties, however, rely more heavily upon property taxation; county revenue systems, on average, are less diversified than those of municipalities. Property taxes were 73.1 percent of all taxes and 44.0 percent of own-source general revenue for counties, but only 50.1 percent of taxes and 30.7 percent of general revenues for municipalities.

Townships, the third set of multifunction governments, are nearly as numerous as municipalities, yet impose property-tax levies only about one-fourth as high—6.6 percent of 1987–88 local property taxes (Table 6-3). Yet townships are even more reliant than counties on property taxes to raise their taxes (91.9 percent of total township taxes) and their aggregate own-source general revenues (74.1 percent of such revenues). Clearly, township revenue structures are less diversified than those of other sorts of multifunction local governments, and their property taxes are less. At least two considerations help to explain this. First, most townships lie outside incorporated municipalities, and public service levels tend to be lower in such areas. Also, the range of services provided by townships generally is less than for counties or municipalities.

The most intensive users of property taxation are the (independent) school districts. In 1987–88, they raised 42.9 percent of all local property-tax dollars, almost as much as counties and municipalities combined (Table 6-3). Moreover, property taxation accounts for almost all local school-tax revenue (97.4 percent in 1987–88) and the vast majority of all own-source general revenue of school districts (80.4 percent in 1987–88). Small wonder that property taxation sometimes is referred to as "the school tax."

Even for school districts, though, the property-tax role has dropped considerably when viewed in the broader context of total general revenues. Before the round of school finance equal-protection cases that began in the early 1970s, the property tax accounted for about 47 percent of total school district general revenue, compared with about 45 percent for intergovernmental aid.[15] But equal-protection litigation focused on financing disparities associated with local tax-base disparities; increased state and federal aid for education were seen as part of the solution.[16] By 1988, the intergovernmental-aid share of total school district general revenue had risen to 54 percent, and the property-tax share had dropped to 37 percent.[17]

Finally, there are the so-called special districts, which typically are single-purpose units and over half of which lack property-tax authority.[18] Thus, although these are the fastest-growing type of government and also by far the most numerous, they account for a very small portion of local property-tax levies—3.6 percent in 1988 (Table 6-3). This small amount of property-tax revenue, however, was enough to represent 75.8 percent of special districts' total taxes, but only 17.0 percent of their own-source general revenue. These figures reflect the high reliance of such units on nontax revenues, especially charges and fees.

## DETERMINING THE PROPERTY TAX BASE

The property tax can be either general or selective in its application. A general tax applies to all types of property and treats the various types uniformly. Non-uniformity can be introduced by total exclusion of some property types from the base, by differential tax treatment for various property types, or by a combination of these two.

A truly general property tax would be imposed on all classes of property—not only such tangible items as land, improvements, machinery, household goods, automobiles, and business inventories, but also financial (intangible) instruments—in a uniform manner irrespective of the nature of the asset, its use, or ownership. The property-tax levy within a taxing jurisdiction would be determined by applying a single tax rate to the estimated market value of all assets. 

Alternatively, a selective property tax would be imposed on a well-defined subset of all classes of property. Depending on the type of asset, its use, or its ownership, its value may be totally or partially excluded from the property-tax base, and/or differential rates might be applied.

The property tax in the United States initially was a specific property tax imposed on selective classes of wealth easily identifiable in an agrarian economy—e.g., land, improvements, cattle. Rates generally were *in rem,* or specific —i.e., levied at so many cents per unit, rather than as a percentage of value. During the early nineteenth century the forms of tangible wealth multiplied and intangible property made its appearance. In an effort to broaden the property-tax base to include these new forms of wealth, the property tax evolved during the early- to mid-nineteenth century into a general *ad valorem* (percentage of value) property tax uniformly applied to most varieties of property.

Personal property—tangible and intangible—for a time was an expanding component of the base. Tangible personal property —business inventories, machinery, jewelry, livestock, pets, household furnishings—was generally divided into business and household categories. Intangible personal property included corporate stocks and bonds, bank deposits, and mortgages. However, the main component of the property-tax base continued to be real property consisting of two separate elements—land (residential, commercial, agricultural, and vacant) and improvements (buildings, structures, and other capital improvements).

Not long after adopting very general property taxation in the mid-1800s, states began to provide for exceptions. For the last several decades, property taxation in the United States has become increasingly a tax on real property. Personal property as a share of the property-tax base has dwindled substantially. This is true especially for intangible property, but also (and increasingly) for tangible property, and is the result of changes in state constitutions and statutes. The changes have been motivated by both practical and philosophical considerations.

Intangibles are very difficult for the assessor to locate and, assuming success in discovering such properties, often difficult to value. Moreover, noting that intangibles—particularly stocks, bonds, mortgages, and the like—are merely claims on real and tangible personal properties that also are generally part of the tax base, many have argued that the taxation of intangible property constitutes an undesirable form of double taxation.

Others argue that repeal of intangibles taxes seriously impairs the equity and the neutrality of property taxation, and that administration is technically feasible. The proponents, however, appear to have lost the battle. The Census Bureau's periodic surveys in the census of governments reveal that most states either wholly or largely exempt intangibles, at least for local tax purposes. In 1986, there were 13 states that allowed local property taxation of intangible assets, but only 3 (Idaho, Kansas, and Tennessee) had available the aggregate assessed value of such personal property.

Taxation of tangible personal property also has declined, again for both administrative and philosophical reasons. Given the movable character of many forms of tangible personal property—e.g., inventories, railroad cars—tax avoidance often is relatively simple. Philosophically, some have argued that the tax, particularly as applied to inventories, is perverse in its effect: it tends to rise during an economic downturn (as inventories rise) and to fall during expansions. Popular and political unwillingness to take the administrative steps necessary to discover and list household personal property in general, together with the difficulties inherent in valuing such items, resulted in many states exempting such property, although several tax such property in business use (e.g., chairs in a doctor's waiting room). Where household property in nonbusiness use remains legally taxable, enforcement and compliance often are quite lax. Almost all states exempt at least some types of agricultural personal property, and most exempt motor vehicles, often for political reasons rather than administrative considerations.

By 1986, complete exemption from the local property tax was accorded these major categories of tangible personal property by the number of states shown for each: motor vehicles, 31; household personal property, 33; agricultural personal property, 18; business inventories, 30; and other commercial and industrial property, 9. These numbers include 8 states that exempted all tangible personal property—up from 5 states in 1979.[19] As a result of these trends, the personal property share of locally assessed taxable property declined nationwide from 15.7 percent in 1961 to just 9.8 percent in 1986.[20]

In reality, the property-tax base (net assessed value) is often only a fraction of the estimated full market value of these different taxable assets. However, the ratio between market value and the portion of that value subject to the tax (i.e., the assessment ratio) varies across jurisdictions, property types, and, in some instances, among individual properties of the same type within the same jurisdiction. In some cases, e.g., Minnesota, where differences in assessment ratios are legally mandated, they are *de jure;* in other cases, differences in assessment ratios are *de facto*—they exist without legal basis. *De facto* assessment differences often are superimposed upon *de jure* differences. Both sources of difference cause the effective property-tax rate (the nominal millage rate times the assessment ratio) to vary across jurisdictions, types of property, or individual properties.[21] The further from uniformity a jurisdiction moves, the greater the potential for horizontal inequity and inefficiency because different effective rates result from the assessment errors.

### *Valuation Approaches*

The property tax is the only tax with an unobservable base. Both consumption and income taxes are based on current flows or transactions, the values of which are relatively clear. But the valuation of property is inherently subjective. Assessing property requires the talents of highly trained and experienced personnel. However, because no two individuals have exactly the same experiences, individual assessors differ in the weights they assign factors, such as view and neighborhood quality, which influence the value of a property. Since there is no objectively discernible true market value for an individual property, especially ones not recently sold, the goal of the assessor is to provide what amounts to a "best guess" of what the property would sell for on the open market at a given time. Written procedures, establishing the parameters or rules governing subjective judgments that an individual assessor must make, can help reduce the variation in estimated market value between different assessors. These can result in less variation in property values, thereby minimizing some of the confusion on the part of both practitioners and the general public.

Whatever the exact provisions of a state's assessment law, assessors employ the three common approaches to the valuation of property that are endorsed by the American Institute of Real Estate Appraisers:

1. *Cost Approach*—the current cost of reproducing a property minus depreciation from deterioration or functional and economic obsolescence

2. *Income Approach*—the value that the property's potential net earning power will support, based on a capitalization of net income
3. *Market Data Approach*—the value indicated by recent sales of comparable properties in the marketplace

Typically, each of these traditional approaches to valuing property is applied to a specific subset of property uses. For example, market data are more commonly used in valuing homes than in valuing factories, because factories are relatively heterogeneous and sell relatively infrequently. However, each approach to value, if accurately carried out, should give approximately the same answer. Thus, these alternative approaches should *not* be considered mutually exclusive; rather, alternative valuation techniques may be used to verify the results of the "traditional" approach of valuing each property type (commercial, residential, farm, etc.).

***The Cost Approach.*** The cost approach is used frequently in the appraisal of new construction and special-purpose properties. The assessor first determines the value of the land by examining sales of comparable land. Next, the assessor estimates the cost of replacing a building at the time of the reassessment based on available cost data. Thus, as construction prices increase or decrease, so will the estimated cost of replacing a building. When applied to existing buildings, the replacement cost is depreciated according to the building's age and functional or economic obsolescence.

***The Income Approach.*** Generally, the income approach is used to value investment properties, i.e., commercial and industrial properties and apartments. A fundamental relationship involved in the income method is value × interest rate = income. Thus, if one year's information is representative, and if the average (market) rate of return on investment is 10 percent, a property costing $1,000,000 would have to produce at least $100,000 annual income to be an attractive investment at that price ($1,000,000 × .1 = $100,000).

This same relationship is used to determine value when the market interest rate and the (potential) income from a given property are known. Rearranging the above equation: value = income/interest rate. If a property yields an annual income of $1.5 million, and if the prevailing interest rate is 12 percent, the value of that property is $12.5 million [$1.5/.12 = $12.5]. Thus, for a given level of income, an increase in the interest rate (the opportunity cost of money) implies a reduction in value of a given property.

The application of the income approach requires information on income and operating expenses for the property being valued. In some instances, this information is readily available from schedules filed by the property owner. In other cases, general income and expense information may be obtained from standardized tables available to assessors.

The next step in the valuation process is to capitalize net income at a rate of return prevalent in the market at the time of valuation. The choice of a capitalization rate often is difficult because the appropriate rate—that which is sufficient to attract investment capital—changes over time.

> Such a rate is influenced by many considerations, including the degree of apparent risk, market attitudes with respect to future inflation, the prospective rates of return for alternative investment opportunities, historical rates of return earned by comparable properties, supply of and demand for mortgage funds, and the availability of tax shelters. Because the rates of return used in the capitalization approach represent *prospective* rates, as distinguished from historical rates, special consideration is given to market perceptions of risk and changes in purchasing power.[22]

Two subjective factors pose problems for the income capitalization approach. The intent is to estimate the value of the property (land and permanent improvements), as distinct from the value of entrepreneurial and other factor services used along with the property to generate the observed level of net income. But actual income reflects both managerial skill and "goodwill," both of which can vary considerably and also are hard to quantify.

***Market Data (Comparable Sales) Approach.*** The comparable sales or market approach to valuation involves a comparison of the property being appraised with similar properties that have sold recently in *arm's-length sales*—i.e., exchanges between a willing buyer and a willing seller who are unrelated. Differences, minor and major, are enumerated and evaluated according to the judgment of the appraiser. The value of the property being appraised is thereby related to the prices of comparable properties that have sold. Depreciation in this approach is not measured by the appraiser. The result of the appraisal is market value in which all depreciation has already been determined by the market itself. This method is used generally for valuing residential and small apartment or commercial properties. It is based on the principle that the value of a property tends to be set by the cost of acquisition of an equally desirable substitute property.

### *Measuring Assessment Quality*

The property tax is an ad valorem tax based on the value of property as estimated above.

> An estimate of market value, or value in exchange, is the purpose of most valuation assignments. Such an estimate reflects the appraiser's interpretation of the buyers and sellers in the marketplace and the conditions that prevail when property is offered for sale.[23]

Market value, then, is the target for the assessor and represents the usual selling price that could be obtained from an arm's-length sale. Since the actual market price is observed only when a sale takes place, the natural question arises: How well does the assessor estimate the market value of property in the jurisdiction? That is, to what extent does the assessor's estimated market value—which is the product of the assessment process described above—reflect the "true" market value as indicated by actual sales data?

One of the primary objectives in property-tax administration is the assessment of property in a uniform manner. It is important that uniformity be attained not only among local property owners but also between taxing districts, since property valuations serve as a basis for

1. tax levies by overlapping governmental units, e.g., counties, school districts, and special districts
2. determination of net bonded indebtedness, which often is restricted by statute to a percentage of either the local assessed value or market value
3. determination of authorized levies restricted by statutory tax-rate limits
4. apportionment of state assistance to local governmental units, e.g., school aid formula, local government aid formula

The consequence of nonuniform assessment is an unwarranted shift in the tax burden elsewhere to the benefit of some, but the detriment of other property owners. An equitable distribution of the tax burden is achieved only if built upon uniform assessment.

*Assessment/Sales Ratios.* In order to evaluate the degree of uniformity across properties and jurisdictions, reasonably accurate and acceptable statistical measures are needed. The technique most commonly used to measure the degree of assessment inequality is that of determining *assessment/sales ratios,* or the relationship of the assessor's estimated market value to the sales price of a particular property that sold. The assessment/sales ratio for an individual parcel of property sold is simply the relationship, expressed as a percentage, between the assessor's estimated market value and the actual sales price. For each parcel of real estate sold, the assessment/sales ratio is found by dividing the assessor's estimated market value by the full consideration paid as illustrated in Table 6-4. If perfect assessment uniformity existed in an area, the assessor's estimated market value for a property that sold would be 100 percent of the actual sales price, and no ratio would deviate from that level. In practice, however, individual assessment/sales ratios may vary substantially.

One important way of describing a group of individual assessment/sales ratios for an area or class of property is by the use of averages. Usually three

TABLE 6-4

*Assessment/Sales Ratios: Examples*

| Parcel | Assessor's Market Value | Sales Price | Ratio |
|---|---|---|---|
| 1 | $ 20,900 | $ 19,000 | 110.0% |
| 2 | 28,500 | 30,000 | 95.0 |
| 3 | 22,950 | 25,500 | 90.0 |
| 4 | 33,200 | 41,500 | 80.0 |
| 5 | 31,200 | 52,000 | 60.0 |
| TOTAL | 136,750 | 168,000 | 435.0 |

measures of average are considered: the mean, median, and the aggregate average ratio. The mean, or arithmetic average, is one measure of central tendency and provides a simple numerical description of a group of individual assessment/sales ratios. The mean is derived by first computing the assessment/sales ratio for each parcel sold, adding those ratios, and dividing the total by the number of items. In the above example, the mean is 435.0/5 = 87.0. The mean is the most commonly used, easily understood measure of central tendency, but extreme individual assessment/sales ratios affect the mean even without undue distortion in assessment practices.

The median, as the mean, is a measure of central tendency used to describe a group of individual assessment/sales ratios. Unlike the mean, however, it is not affected by extreme ratios. The median is found by arranging the individual assessment/sales ratios in order of magnitude from highest to lowest, then selecting the middle ratio in the series. In the above example, the median is 90.0. The *aggregate,* or *weighted, average* is an alternative measure of central tendency. This measure is computed by dividing the *total* assessor's market value for the properties sold by the *total* sales prices of those properties. In the above example, the weighted average ratio is 136,750/168,000 = 81.4. In the aggregate average ratio, unlike the mean, each property sold is given a weight according to its sales price. Higher-priced properties sold, of course, play a more important role than lower-priced properties in such an average. This effect is justified if the sale of higher-priced properties bears the same relationship to all properties in the sample as those properties bear to all properties in the taxing district. Because of its statistical properties, the aggregate ratio generally is accepted as the most appropriate measure to be used in the equalization of aids.

*Assessment–Sales Dispersion.* The second dimension of the quality of assessment that needs monitoring is the degree to which actual assessment ratios are dispersed around the measure of central tendency. For example, for any particular taxing jurisdiction, the median assessment ratio may equal 1.0, indicating that the estimated value of the median property exactly equaled its actual selling price. However, this provides no information about the variation in the individual ratios in the jurisdiction—i.e., how closely clustered around the median are the individual ratios?

The concern here is with the variability of assessment ratios. While any of several measures is conceptually appropriate to measure the uniformity of assessments, the coefficient of dispersion is perhaps the most commonly used measure. It measures the deviation of parcel ratios from the average ratio as a percentage of the average ratio. The higher the coefficient, the less uniform are the assessments.

An example may help to clarify the nature of the coefficient of dispersion. Presented in Table 6-5 are data (also used in illustrating the sales ratios) for five hypothetical homes that have recently sold—assessed values, sales prices, assessment/sales ratios, and absolute deviations of the individual parcel ratios from the median ratio.

Individual assessment/sales ratios are subtracted from the median ratio,

TABLE 6-5
*Deviation in Assessment/Sales Ratios in Table 6-4*

| Property | Assessed Value | Sales Price | A/S Ratio | Absolute Deviation |
|---|---|---|---|---|
| 1 | $20,900 | $19,000 | 110.0% | 20 |
| 2 | 28,500 | 30,000 | 95.0 | 5 |
| 3 | 22,950 | 25,500 | 90.0 | 0 |
| 4 | 33,200 | 41,500 | 80.0 | 10 |
| 5 | 31,200 | 52,000 | 60.0 | 30 |

and the difference is recorded without regard to its sign (absolute deviation from the median). Next, these absolute deviations are summed and divided by the number of homes in the sample (65/5 = 13). Finally, this average absolute deviation is expressed as a percentage of the median ratio: (13/90) × 100 = 14.4 percent. Thus, in this example, the value of the coefficient of dispersion is 14.4 percent.

Generally, only residential properties are represented in assessment/sales ratio studies because they account for most real property transactions and, therefore, the ratios are most reliable for this type of property. Because of the greater amount of sales for residential properties, it is often argued that assessors can be expected to perform better in valuing such properties; focusing on residential assessment performance, therefore, should place assessors in a relatively favorable light.

## *REVENUE STABILITY*

The absolute dollar amount produced by the property tax in any single year is calculated as the product of the property-tax rate and the property-tax base. The nominal property-tax rate is determined by the legislative process. The property-tax base—the assessed value—changes as a result of a change in the level of assessment. This, in turn, is largely a function of the frequency of assessment and the degree to which assessed values capture changes in market values resulting from real and nominal economic growth. Thus, given a constant assessment ratio, the base would increase in direct proportion to the growth in market values.

In such a circumstance, assuming a constant property-tax rate, the property tax will generate a known and stable revenue stream.[24] The responsiveness of property-tax revenue to economic growth, when such growth is measured by income growth (the income elasticity of property-tax revenues), depends upon (1) the responsiveness of market value to economic growth and (2) the ability of the local assessing jurisdiction to capture changing market values through the assessment process.

A stable tax typically will generate revenues that change *relatively* more slowly than income—i.e., the revenue is income inelastic.[25]

In general, depending on assessment procedures and the extent to which increased market values are reflected in the property-tax base, the property tax is characterized as being a unitary elastic revenue source.[26] Thus, if a jurisdiction relied totally on the property tax as a source of revenue, it would continually face a fiscal gap as the economy grew, since the demand for services is income elastic, but property-tax revenues are not. The resulting fiscal gap would create constant pressure on local officials to increase the property-tax rate.

Alternatively, to the extent a jurisdiction diversifies its revenue structure by de-emphasizing the property tax in favor of more income-responsive revenue sources—e.g., the income tax—this problem becomes less critical.

## *RATIONALE FOR PROPERTY TAXATION*

The property tax is consistent with both the ability-to-pay and the benefits principles of taxation. From the standpoint of ability to pay, the case for a property tax rests largely upon imperfections in the taxation of income.[27] The preferred measure of income is a comprehensive one. Comprehensiveness is desirable to promote neutrality (economic efficiency); if there is no escape from the tax, the tax is not a factor in economic choices. This requires that *all* additions to wealth—whether in the form of money income, imputed income (i.e., nonmonetary benefits, such as the value of housing services from owner-occupied housing), or increases in asset values—be taxed alike. But this is not standard income-tax practice, in part for practical reasons.

Whenever the flow of benefits from property totally or partially escapes income taxation, equity and efficiency concerns require that the asset that creates the benefits be taxed. The value of the asset is taxed because it represents the capitalized value of the stream of benefits; the tax rate applied to the asset value appropriately would be lower than the rate applied to an annual income flow.[28]

An example may help to illustrate this notion. Suppose that Morris and White each have wages of $50,000 and assets of $150,000; the only difference is the form in which they hold their assets. White owns the $150,000 home in which she lives, while Morris has a $150,000 bank account. Both assets generate benefits, and an ideal income tax of the sort discussed above would tax both benefit streams equally. In practice, however, Morris's bank account yields interest payments that are subject to income taxation, while White's house provides her with a nonmonetary stream of housing services that are not subject to income taxation. This difference in income-tax treatments produces a horizontal inequity that can be redressed by property taxation. It also creates incentives that tend to influence economic choices.

In general, the foregoing reasoning suggests that the case for property taxation (or for relatively high property taxes) is strongest in the case of owner-occupied residences, the benefits from which completely escape income taxation.

Perhaps next strongest is the case of farmland, given the apparent underreporting of farm income. The inequity from the failure to tax the imputed rental value of owner-occupied homes is exacerbated by the allowance of deductions from *other* income the costs of generating these tax-exempt benefits—i.e., property taxes and mortgage interest.

The property tax also is consistent with the benefits principle of taxation. It is argued that property taxes, to a considerable degree, are used to finance local government expenditures—police, fire, streets, etc.—that are site-oriented services, benefitting local property owners and thereby increasing the value of their properties.

In a recent evaluation of this argument, Hamilton concluded that the supply of local public services is pretty well matched to the demand through voting, both by ballot and by feet (i.e., by geographic mobility).[29] In other words, the property tax does serve, to a significant extent, as a benefit tax sending signals to both property owners and local governments. Support for this view is provided by evidence of nearly full capitalization of service benefits and prices paid into housing values.[30] Thus, an increase in public expenditures financed by an equal  increase in property taxes would have no net effect on housing prices, indicating that the supply and demand for services are in balance.

This argument, however, implicitly assumes that benefits are distributed across properties in proportion to their property-tax liabilities (and under the usual standard of tax uniformity, this implies benefits in proportion to market value). This in turn implies that expenditure benefits are, in fact, capitalized in the value of the properties. Thus, the property tax on two homes of equal value and in receipt of equal service benefits must, for equity under the benefits principle, be taxed the same. Any tax nonuniformities tend to depart from the theory underlying the benefits-received case for the property tax, as they cause tax shares to diverge from benefit shares. Nonuniformities can arise from either extralegal differences in tax treatment (assessment error) or intentional differences (exemptions for homeowners with no comparable break for rental properties).

The assumptions underlying the benefits principle may not be true for all goods and services provided by local government. For example, the *direct* benefits of education are not likely to be distributed across all properties in proportion to property values, but rather according to the number of public-school children in the household. This does not suggest, however, that property owners without children in public school should be exempt from the school portion of their property tax. First, public education not only provides *direct* private benefits to those attending school, but also provides *indirect* benefits to those living in the community (e.g., a more informed population, local sports activities, the physical plant is available for public use, etc.). At least to the extent of such communitywide benefits, then, everyone in the community should contribute to funding local public education.

Second, and perhaps more important, there is a redistributive intent. The property tax is not strictly based on the benefits principle of taxation, but rests as much on an ability-to-pay rationale; it is a tax on wealth, not a user charge based on *direct* benefits received. Property-tax liabilities, therefore, are defined in relation to the value of real estate, not direct benefits received.

## *WHO PAYS THE PROPERTY TAX? SHIFTING AND INCIDENCE*

The *gross* property-tax liability for any property owner is determined by multiplying the property-tax rate by the assessed value. Often, property owners may qualify for property-tax credit programs that reduce the amount of taxes the property owner actually must pay. For example, homestead credits are deducted from the gross tax liability to calculate the actual *net* amount that the taxpayer must pay to the local government.

Each year property owners pay local governments an amount equal to their net property-tax liability. This transfer of funds—from property owner to the local government—represents the *initial* burden of the property tax. The property owner may be able to shift all or part of the net property tax to others through changes in the prices of things sold and/or purchased. This tax shifting may be either "forward" to users or "backward" to suppliers. The ability of the property owner to shift the property tax will depend upon both the type of asset taxed and market conditions. The type of asset is important because the mechanism by which shifting occurs is supply reduction, and the feasibility of this differs across asset classes. In any event, the *ultimate burden* (incidence) of the property tax is likely to differ frequently from the initial burden.

The entire tax, whether imposed initially on business or not, ultimately becomes a burden on, and reduces the real incomes of, people. The question is whether the burden falls on people in their role as consumers of business products, in their role as suppliers of labor and other resources bought by business, or in their role as the owners of the taxed properties. The answer no doubt is that it falls on all these activities, with differences in market conditions determining which activity bears the heaviest burden.

### *Land*

The property-tax base includes a variety of property types— land, improvements, and personal property. The assumptions about the potential for shifting that portion of the property tax falling on each component differ. Economists generally agree that a tax on land results in a decrease in the land's value and a capital loss to the landowner *at the time the tax is imposed or increased*.

The supply of land is considered to be fixed. As a result of the fixed supply of land, potential users need bid no more for the land than they did before the imposition of the property tax. Indeed, since the owners of the land must pay the tax, the increased tax will lead prospective land buyers to offer less after the increase than before because the higher annual tax payment reduces the net return to land ownership to the extent it does not increase services provided to the property. It turns out that the reduction in the land's value would be exactly equal to the increased property-tax liability capitalized at the appropriate rate. In this case, therefore, the initial and final burden coincide and fall on the owners of land at the time of the tax increase. Given such capitalization, the level of property taxes on land at the time of purchase does not burden the buyers, who are the future landowners and taxpayers.

### *Improvements*

The tax on improvements and tangible personal property owned by business is more complicated. Because the supply of improvements, unlike that of land, is not fixed over time, shifting of the tax is possible. But the nature of any shifting—forward to consumers or backward to resource suppliers—and the degree to which it occurs will depend upon the nature of the product and resource markets. Therefore, the outcome is less clear.

According to the "traditional view," the property tax on improvements is shifted forward in the form of higher rents. The property tax is viewed as an excise tax on capital improvements, thereby reducing the rate of return and slowing the rate of investment in (reducing the supply of) the taxed good—e.g., new structures, rehabilitation, and maintenance. A tax increase tends, initially, to make the existing stock of structures become less valuable, which tends to make future investment less attractive. The resulting supply curtailment causes users to pay higher rents for a restricted capital stock. This restriction on supply will continue until the after-tax rate of return is equal to the rate of return existing before the imposition (increase) of the tax—assuming the local supply restriction is not offset by an increase elsewhere. Therefore, rents will increase by the amount of tax and the property tax on the improvements will be shifted forward to the renter.

The renters or users of the improvements, in turn, may be able to shift the tax either forward or backward. The ability of the business to shift that portion of the property tax falling on improvements and personal property depends on (1) the market structure of the industry, (2) the availability of substitutes for the product, and (3) the degree of influence the firm has in determining factor input prices.

As opposed to this "traditional view" of property-tax incidence, the "new view" starts from the premise that there is some level of property taxation that is common to all types of property and all jurisdictions. The analysis treats this portion of the tax as a uniform general property tax.[31] For this level of tax, the initial and ultimate burdens again coincide and fall on the owners of capital, since all forms of capital are subject to a uniform rate and there is no untaxed sector to which capital can be shifted.

The second dimension of the "new view" of property-tax incidence is an analysis of the effects of that portion of the tax that is not universal.

In summary, the "new view" leads to a number of implications that extend those associated with the "traditional view." First, that portion of the property tax common to all property across jurisdictions falls on the owners of capital in the form of lower rates of return than would be expected in the nontax situation. Second, in addition to their share of the average nationwide property-tax burden, property owners bear a major portion of the above-average tax-rate differentials, particularly in urban areas. Conversely, in those areas with below-average tax levels, property owners tend to benefit from the low taxes and, therefore, are able to absorb some increase in taxes without depressing their returns to investment below national norms. Third, that portion of the property tax that is shifted to consumers is much less important than believed in the "traditional view."

It should be emphasized that the "new" and "traditional" views are complementary and not competing views. If the concern is a change in the national average property tax, the "new view" is most appropriate and leads to the conclusion that the tax change is primarily borne by the owners of capital. If, however, the concern is the relative change in a local property tax or differentials between sectors or regions, the "traditional view" provides the appropriate framework for analysis focusing on the "excise" effects of local differentials.[32]

## APPROACHES TO PROPERTY-TAX RELIEF

Property-tax relief can be defined quite broadly to include anything that reduces the reliance on property taxation for public revenue.[33] Such a definition includes not only homestead exemptions, circuit breakers, deferrals, and classification, but also various local nonproperty taxes, local nontax revenue sources, and intergovernmental aid programs. Those in the first group are referred to as *direct* property-tax relief; they directly reduce the tax bills for individual property parcels, even though they may not affect total property-tax levies of governments. Approaches in the second group provide *indirect* property-tax relief by providing local governments with alternative revenue sources and, thereby, permitting property-tax levies to be lower than they otherwise would be.

### Direct Relief Mechanisms

Many programs offer direct property-tax relief, working within the property-tax framework to reduce either the tax or the tax-base amount. Most modify the calculation of individual property-tax bills. Circuit breakers are exceptions, since they typically provide refunds after property-tax bills have been calculated and paid. While uniform relief to all property types is possible, direct property-tax relief programs generally discriminate among property-use types (residential, commercial, etc.). Thus, they tend to redistribute the property-tax load among classes of property.

*Partial Exemption.* The property tax is the product of the tax base (assessed value) and the rate. A partial exemption reduces the base by subtracting some amount from assessed or market value. While the exempt amount could be expressed as a percentage of gross value, standard practice is to exempt some absolute number of dollars. This practice means that a larger percentage of the value of lower-valued properties is exempt.

*Credit.* A credit is subtracted from the tax bill after the liability has been calculated. Despite the apparent difference between a credit and an exemption, a credit can be designed to have exactly the same effect as an exemption. In practice, however, the property-tax credit often is different from the exemption approach because property-tax credits are calculated as a specified percentage of the gross tax. The fact that with a credit program a gross tax amount is calculated before the tax relief is subtracted may make decisionmakers more aware of the costs of their decisions and, therefore, more likely to bear them.

*Refund or Rebate.* The refund or rebate mechanism (hereafter, simply refund) works much the same as a credit, except that with a refund, receipt of property-tax relief is not simultaneous with payment of the gross property tax. With a credit, the taxpayer pays only the net property tax after relief; with a refund, however, the full tax is paid and a separate refund is provided.

Because most property-tax refund programs are circuit breakers, this relief form is targeted to lower-income groups more than property-tax credits. The refund can be made through a separate administrative arrangement, or this function can be piggybacked on the state income tax (or some other nonproperty tax).

*Freeze.* Another approach to direct relief is to freeze property taxes. A freeze can apply at any point in the calculation of the property tax—the base (assessed value), the rate, or the tax amount itself. Freezing the tax amount obviously is the most effective way to keep the tax from rising; if only the base or the rate were frozen, changes in the other still could serve to increase the tax. Distinctions must be made, however, between the aggregate levy and the bills of individual taxpayers. If a tax freeze means only that the aggregate levy is frozen, the property-tax bills for individual parcels may change. In this case, any increases in individual tax bills would be matched by decreases for others.

*Use-Value Assessment.* Since the advent of general ad valorem property taxation in the mid-nineteenth century, valuation according to highest and best use, rather than actual use, has been the standard. In many cases, current use and highest and best use will be the same. As property values escalate in transitional areas, properties used in pursuits whose value in the market is relatively low tend to experience rising property taxes compared to the income generated by those uses. One result can be pressure to provide relief by ignoring highest and best use (market) value and to look only at actual-use value. The divergence between use value and market value apparently is greatest for agricultural land in rural-urban fringe areas.

*Classification.* The hallmark of classification is different effective tax rates for different property classes. Because effective rate differences result from anything that affects the actual tax amount, the line between what generally is called classification and other relief programs is difficult to draw. The broadest definition would consider all the foregoing direct-relief mechanisms to be classification (if nonuniform effective rates result). Here, however, we apply the classification label only to those programs that entail a legally provided split property roll.

The most common approach to establishing effective tax-rate differentials is the application of uniform nominal rates to differential assessment levels—about two-thirds of the classification states use this approach. On the other hand, West Virginia and the District of Columbia classify by applying differential nominal rates to supposedly uniform assessed values. New York authorizes local adoption of such an approach. Either approach can be effective, but some argue that the practice of establishing assessment level differences is inferior because it (1) makes it harder for taxpayers to evaluate the appropriateness of their assessed values, (2) increases the potential for abuse of the assessment system and appears to make the assessor part of the tax-setting process, and (3) affects debt limits and other policies tied into assessed value figures.[34]

*Circuit Breaker.* Circuit breaker relief programs, like other property-tax relief mechanisms discussed so far, also provide favorable effective rates for claimants' property taxes, but circuit breakers are more narrowly targeted. Because circuit breakers take many forms, generalization about them is difficult. What they have in common is that relief is inversely related to income. When property taxes rise to levels that are thought to constitute an "overload" relative to income, the relief program "breaks" the load. This analogy to electrical circuit breakers and power overloads gives the relief form its name. Circuit breakers accept both property ownership and income as indicators of economic well-being (ability to pay taxes), but the decision to provide relief is based on income when income is relatively low. Thus, benefits can be targeted to those considered to be most in need of tax relief. Targeting provides a given level of relief to those for whom the property-tax amount is truly onerous in relation to income—presumably the group of most concern to tax-relief advocates—with a lower total outlay.[35]

*Deferral.* A deferral program simply delays the time by which the property tax, or a portion of it, has to be paid. Property taxes may impose hardships on those with property wealth that is large relative to current income, even though their property holdings raise them on the economic ladder beyond the point at which it might seem desirable to stop any subsidy. But the hardship posed by cash-flow fluctuations may be aggravated by an inability to borrow (at least on reasonable terms) against the asset value. A state (or local) tax deferral may be viewed as a means of overcoming adverse cash-flow problems or imperfections in capital markets. The deferred portion of the tax would be a loan that creates a lien against the property. The loan would come due when the property changes hands, or when other possible conditions (e.g., income level) change. If the full amount of deferred tax, plus interest at a market rate, ultimately must be paid, deferral—unlike the other relief forms discussed—does not provide a subsidy.

*Broad versus Targeted Relief.* It is useful to divide direct relief into two general categories: broad and targeted. *Broad* relief may be given in a manner that preserves the legal requirement of uniform effective tax rates for all properties within the same taxing jurisdiction, or it may introduce intentional effective tax-rate nonuniformities. The nonuniform approach is more common. It defines property types (classes) across which effective rates are to be nonuniform, although uniformity still is required within each class in a given taxing jurisdiction. The classes used for broad direct relief are defined by reference to some aspect or aspects of the property—its use, its location, or its value. In short, while global uniformity may be abandoned, the impersonal nature of the tax is preserved. *Targeted* relief, by contrast, modifies the traditional nature of property taxation through personalization, taking into account one or more attributes of the owners (or occupants), such as age, income, disability, and military service. These attributes serve as the targeting variables.

To illustrate, a homestead exemption that is available to all owner-occupants of residential property is, by this terminology, a broad relief mechanism; owner occupancy defines the property-use category rather than any personal attribute of the owner-occupants. A homestead exemption restricted to owner-occupants aged 65 years and over, however, is available to only a portion of the whole class of owner-occupants; such relief is targeted. In general, all the direct-relief approaches discussed in the preceding section can be either broad or targeted; the exception is the circuit breaker. By its nature, a circuit breaker always is targeted, because it determines relief in part by reference to the income of the owners or occupants, thereby personalizing the tax.

Two or more personal attributes may be used simultaneously in defining a targeted relief mechanism. A homestead exemption restricted to elderly owner-occupants, for example, may be further targeted to such persons having less than $15,000 income.

In practice, much direct relief is targeted, even though broad, classwide relief is generally feasible. A 1981 count by Steven Gold of the National Conference of State Legislatures (NCSL) found 30 circuit breakers, all of which, by definition, were targeted by income, and 21 of which were further restricted to the elderly.[36] The same study also found 43 homestead exemption programs, of which 23 were only for the elderly and 14 were limited to those below certain income levels. Other sorts of personalization of the property tax were found in Indiana, where an exemption is available only to homeowners with mortgages or contracts on their homes, and Kansas, where a circuit breaker for all ages is extended to the nonelderly only if a dependent child under the age of 18 is in the household. Although such detail was not recorded by the NCSL survey, in practice many relief programs are targeted to certain disabled persons and to military veterans, and—reversing the Kansas circuit-breaker treatment noted above—a New York exemption is available to the elderly only if they do not have school-age children in the household.

Two programs that have become quite popular in the last two decades, classification and circuit breakers, exert opposing influences with regard to targeting. Classification, by its nature, is broadly provided; while different property-use classes are treated differently, all within a class are to be treated uniformly. Circuit breakers, on the other hand, are inherently targeted by income, and two-thirds of these programs are further targeted to the elderly.

### *Indirect Relief*

In addition to direct property-tax relief, there are many indirect-relief programs. Direct relief, as discussed, (1) is keyed to the property tax, (2) reduces individual property-tax bills in ways that generally redistribute the property-tax load across classes, or even within classes, but (3) may or may not affect the total property-tax levy. Indirect property-tax relief, on the other hand, (1) works outside the property-tax system, but (2) also may or may not affect the total property-tax levy.

Indirect relief includes greater reliance on local nonproperty taxes (income and sales, whether general or selective), local nontax revenues (user charges, interest income, etc.), and intergovernmental assistance. These revenue instruments may simply displace property-tax revenue, thereby providing property-tax relief, or they may to some degree augment property-tax revenue, permitting an increase in the overall level of services. Leaving aside the question of the effect of nonproperty-tax sources on the overall level of local public services, these sources can be viewed as property-tax relief mechanisms in the sense that, for a given level of services financed with some contribution from these sources, the amount of revenue to be raised from the property tax is less than it otherwise would be.

The diminished reliance on property taxation made possible by these indirect-relief mechanisms, taken alone, will result in proportionate property-tax relief for all property-tax payers. Thus, indirect relief is inherently broad, rather than targeted.

## *CONCLUSION*

For a time in the 1970s, the public rated property taxation the worst, or least fair, of the major taxes, and in the late 1970s the much-heralded tax revolt set in. Still, the tax has hardly faded away. Its staying power no doubt lies, in part, in the fact that taxpayers truly do not like any tax, but also do not want dramatic cuts in public services—perhaps especially education and some other local services that rely heavily on property-tax support. Thus, while repeal of the property tax without replacing it is not politically feasible, neither is raising other revenues by enough to replace the property tax. So we have had a number of adjustments that seek to balance these considerations, including slower growth of the property tax, increased importance of local nonproperty taxes, an increased state role in raising state-local revenues, and probably growth in public spending at a rate below what would have occurred absent the pressures to restrain property-tax growth (or even cut the tax) and to hold the line on other taxes.

## *NOTES*

1. Jens P. Jensen, *Property Taxation in the United States* (Chicago, Illinois: University of Chicago Press, 1931), 478; as quoted in Dick Netzer, *Economics of the Property Tax* (Washington, DC: Brookings Institution, 1966), 3.

2. George W. Mitchell, "Is This Where We Came In?" *Proceedings of the Forty-Ninth Annual Conference on Taxation* (Sacramento, CA: National Tax Association, 1957): 492.

3. U.S. Bureau of the Census, *1982 Census of Governments, Vol. 6, No. 4, Historical Statistics on Governmental Finances and Employment* (Washington, DC: Government Printing Office, 1985), table 14.

4. U.S. Bureau of the Census, *Government Finances in 1987–88*, GF88-5 (Washington, DC: Government Printing Office, 1990), table 2.

5. Glenn W. Fisher, "The Changing Role of Property Taxation," in *Financing State and Local Governments in the 1980s: Issues and Trends*, ed. N. Waizer and D. L. Chicoine (Cambridge, MA: Oelgeschlager, Gunn Hain, 1981), 37–60.

6. These often are listed as equity, efficiency (both economic neutrality and avoidance of undue costs of compliance and administration), revenue adequacy, and stability.

7. U.S. Bureau of the Census, *1982 Census of Governments, Historical Statistics*, table 13.

8. ibid.

9. U.S. Bureau of the Census, *Government Finances in 1987–88*, table 2.

10. For a recent survey of local taxation, see: John H. Bowman and John L. Mikesell, *Local Government Tax Authority and Use*, State-Local Backgrounder Series (Washington, DC: National League of Cities, 1987).

11. U.S. Bureau of the Census, *Government Finances in 1987–88*, table 2.

12. Advisory Commission on Intergovernmental Relations, *Significant Features of Fiscal Federalism*, 1988 Edition, vol. 1, table 30.

13. U.S. Bureau of the Census, *1987 Census of Governments, Government Organization*, GC87-1(1) (Washington, DC: Government Printing Office, 1988), table 3.

14. The Census Bureau reports that "all county, municipal, township, and school district governments are legally authorized to levy property taxes, [but] over half of the special district governments are not." (*Ibid.*, p. xvi.) A 1987 survey, however, received reports from state municipal leagues in seven states indicating that not all municipal units in those states impose property taxes (John H. Bowman and John L. Mikesell, *Local Government Tax Authority and Use*, State-Local Backgrounder Series [National League of Cities, 1987], table II-2).

15. U.S. Bureau of the Census, *1982 Census of Governments, Historical Statistics*, table 15.

16. For a discussion, see, for example: Robert D. Reischauer and Robert W. Hartman, *Reforming School Finance* (Washington, DC: Brookings Institution, 1973).

17. U.S. Bureau of the Census, *Government Finances in 1987–88*, table 2.

18. For more information, see U.S. Bureau of the Census, *1987 Census of Governments, Government Organization*, especially tables 3 and 23.

19. Delaware, Hawaii, Illinois, New Hampshire, New York, North Dakota, Pennsylvania, and South Dakota.

20. *Table Property Values, 1987 Census of Governments*, Vol. 2, U.S. Department of Commerce, Bureau of the Census, (Washington DC: U.S. Government Printing Office, March 1989), table B.

21. The legislated property tax rate, or nominal rate (often expressed in dollars per hundred dollars assessed value), when multiplied by the assessment ratio for each property, equals the effective tax rate. For example, if the legislated property tax rate (the nominal rate) was $2.00 per $100 assessed value, and the assessment standard was legislated to be 100 percent, the nominal rate will equal the effective rate, $2.00 per $100 market value. But if the assessed value attained was only 50 percent of the market value, the assessment ratio of 50 percent times the $2.00 nominal tax rate yields an effective rate of only $1.00 per $100 market value.

22. *The Appraisal of Real Estate*, 8th ed. (Chicago: American Institute of Real Estate Appraisers, 1983), p. 340.

23. *Ibid.*, p. 39.

24. Actual property tax collections usually do not grow as rapidly as implied by the growth in market values; in part because assessments do not keep pace with the growth in market value, and new exemptions and exclusions have the direct result of reducing the base. On the other hand, property taxes can be responsive to inflationary pressures, especially when assessments are made on a timely basis using modern techniques. See David Greytak and Bernard Jump, "The Effect of Inflation on State and Local Government Finances, 1967–74," Occasional Paper no. 25, (Syracuse, N.Y.: Syracuse University, 1975).

25. This is the standard definition used in the economic literature for revenue stability. Fox and Campbell have recast this definition by distinguishing between the short-run and long-run stability of tax revenue. They argue that the income elasticity of a tax is an endogenous variable that varies over the business cycle, i.e. no consistent relationship need hold between short-run and long-run elasticities over the business cycle. Given this view, a tax is regarded as being relatively stable if the short-run elasticity rises during recessions and falls during expansions so the tax revenues fluctuate *less* than income. See William F. Fox and Charles Campbell, "Stability of the State Sales Tax Income Elasticity," *National Tax Journal* (June 1984): 201–12.

26. An income elasticity of 1.0 indicates a proportional revenue source where the base (and revenues) increase at the same rate as income, a value greater than 1 indicates an elastic revenue source, and a value of less than 1 indicates an inelastic revenue source.

27. For a discussion, see Richard A. Musgrave and Peggy B. Musgrave, *Public Finance in Theory and Practice*, 4th ed. (New York: McGraw-Hill, 1984), pp. 232–40.

28. The tax is currently applied to gross wealth and might be more appropriately applied to net wealth, e.g., the equity one has in a home, not the total market value of the home.

29. Bruce W. Hamilton, "A Review: Is the Property Tax a Benefit Tax?" pp. 85–107 in George R. Zodrow, ed., *Local Provision of Public Services: The Tiebout Model after Twenty-Five Years* (San Diego, California: Academic Press, 1983.)

30. Howard S. Bloom, Helen F. Ladd, and John Yinger, "Are Property Taxes Capitalized into House Values?" pp. 145–63 in George R. Zodrow, ed., *Local Provision of Public Services: The Tiebout Model after Twenty-Five Years* (San Diego, California: Academic Press, 1983.)

31. For a discussion, see Henry J. Aaron, *Who Pays the Property Tax?: A New View*, (Washington, D.C.: Brookings Institution, 1975); and a useful clarification offered by Charles E. McLure, "The 'New View' of the Property Tax: A Caveat," *National Tax Journal* (March 1977): 69–75.

32. McLure, *op. cit.*

33. Steven D. Gold, *Property Tax Relief*, (Lexington, Massachusetts: D.C. Heath, Lexington Books, 1979).

34. Advisory Commission on Intergovernmental Relations, *The Property Tax: Reform or Relief? A Legislator's Guide*, Report AP-2 (Washington D.C.: ACIR, 1973). For a recent, more complete discussion of real property classification, see John H. Bowman, "Real Property Classification: The States March to Different Drummers," pp. 288–96 in *Proceedings of the Seventy-Ninth Annual Conference on Taxation* (Columbus, Ohio: National Tax Association–Tax Institute of America, 1987).

35. For a discussion of policy issues concerning circuit breakers, see John H. Bowman, "Property Tax Circuit Breakers Reconsidered," *American Journal of Economics and Sociology* 39 (October 1980): 355–72.

36. Steven D. Gold, "An Overview of Property Tax Relief for Homeowners," (Denver: National Conference of State Legislatures, 1982), table 1.

# 7

# *Nonproperty Taxes*

HOLLEY H. ULBRICH

FROM colonial times until the Great Depression, the property tax was the mainstay of local government finance. When property values and property-tax revenues fell while demands on local governments rose in the Depression era of the early 1930s, a search intensified for alternatives to the property tax—other revenue sources that could complement the property tax, offset some of its less desirable features, and provide a cushion of stability and growth for local governmental revenues. Although there were scattered uses of other local taxes prior to the 1930s, that decade marked a sharp increase in the use of the two principal alternatives to the property tax, the local general sales tax and the local personal income tax.

A second wave of growth in adoption of local nonproperty taxes took place in the 1960s and 1970s, first in response to the fiscal crises of large cities and later as a way to address the property-tax revolt. Today, local general sales taxes are authorized in 31 states, and local income or payroll taxes are used in one form or another in 16 states. Other local taxes—primarily selective sales and business-income taxes—are also in place in a number of states. There is still some potential for expanded use of local nonproperty taxes through new authorizations for local taxes in the remaining states, but much of the potential for further growth in nonproperty-tax revenues lies in expanded use of nonproperty taxes in those states where they have already been authorized.

Table 7-1 presents a summary of the revenues of local governments from various types of local taxes and their relative importance. As this table suggests, nonproperty-tax revenues play a particularly important role as a revenue source for municipalities, followed at a distance by special districts and counties. Special districts are not primarily dependent on taxes as a revenue source; only about 20 percent of their own-source revenues derive from taxes. Typically special districts provide services such as fire protection or water and sewer, which are

TABLE 7-1

*Revenue from Local Nonproperty Taxes, 1985–86*

In Dollars ($000,000)

| Source | All Local | County | Municipality | Township | School District | Special District |
|---|---|---|---|---|---|---|
| All Own-Source Revenues | $233,406 | $58,046 | $84,931 | $9,163 | $57,997 | $23,269 |
| All Tax Revenues | 144,997 | 34,049 | 50,873 | 7,270 | 48,040 | 4,766 |
| Property Tax | 107,356 | 25,366 | 25,061 | 6,741 | 46,777 | 3,412 |
| General Sales and Gross Receipts | 15,889 | 5,157 | 9,034 | — | 423 | 1,274 |
| Selective Sales: | 6,739 | 1,047 | 5,623 | 10 | 57 | 1 |
| Motor fuels | 313 | 209 | 104 | — | — | — |
| Alcoholic bev. | 261 | 97 | 164 | — | — | — |
| Tobacco | 200 | 60 | 140 | — | — | — |
| Public utilities | 4,024 | 306 | 3,654 | 7 | 57 | — |
| Other | 1,941 | 376 | 1,561 | 4 | — | 1 |
| Income | 8,536 | 908 | 7,074 | 167 | 387 | — |
| Individual | 6,948 | 908 | 5,486 | 167 | 387 | — |
| Corporate | 1,588 | — | 1,588 | — | — | — |
| Licenses | 587 | 309 | 274 | 3 | — | — |
| Motor vehicle | 568 | 309 | 255 | 3 | — | — |
| Other | 19 | — | 19 | — | — | — |
| Other Local Taxes | 5,890 | 1,261 | 3,806 | 348 | 296 | 79 |
| | | | As Percent of Local Tax Revenue | | | |
| Property Tax | 74.0 | 74.5 | 49.3 | 92.7 | 97.4 | 71.6 |
| General Sales and Gross Receipts | 11.0 | 15.1 | 17.8 | — | 0.9 | 26.7 |
| Selective Sales | 4.6 | 3.1 | 11.1 | 0.1 | 0.1 | — |
| Income | 5.9 | 2.7 | 13.9 | 2.3 | 0.8 | — |
| Licenses | 0.4 | 0.9 | 0.5 | — | — | — |
| Other Local Taxes | 4.1 | 3.7 | 7.5 | 4.8 | 0.8 | 1.7 |

SOURCE: U.S. Bureau of the Census, *Government Finances in 1985–86*, (Washington, D.C.: U.S. Government Printing Office, 1987), p. 46.

financed primarily with fees and charges. Where special districts derive revenue from nonproperty taxes, the general sales tax is the most important revenue source—particularly for transit districts. Counties are far behind municipalities in relying on nonproperty taxes; these taxes account for only 25 percent of county own-source revenues versus 50 percent for municipalities.

The most widely used local tax, although not the most productive in terms of revenue, is the motor-vehicle-license tax. Income from this tax is reported for counties in 27 states, municipalities in 25 states, and townships in 2 states. The most important single local nonproperty tax in terms of revenue is the general sales tax, followed by income taxes and selective sales taxes of various kinds. General sales taxes are reported as a local revenue source for counties in 25 states, municipalities in 23 states, townships and special districts in 1 state each, and school districts in 3 states. Income taxes provide revenues for counties in 10 states, municipalities in 17 states, townships in 3 states, school districts in 2 states, and special districts in 1 state. "Other local taxes" provide revenues for municipalities in all 50 states; for counties, in 45; for townships, in 19; for school districts, in 11; and for special districts, in 5.[1]

## *COSTS AND BENEFITS OF A DIVERSIFIED LOCAL TAX BASE*

An important rationale for local nonproperty taxes is that a diversified revenue structure can be more equitable and more efficient than a revenue system that depends primarily on a single source. A diversified tax base promotes equity because it can capture revenues from individuals who can avoid some taxes but not others. The property tax is a wealth tax. But not all wealth generates income with which to pay the tax, and not all forms of wealth are subject to the property tax. Other local taxes, particularly general sales and income taxes, can extract revenue from citizens with more income but fewer taxable property assets. Such shifting of the burden can offer some tax relief to households with tangible property wealth but low income and low spending. In cities, property-tax relief can reduce the deterioration of inner-city properties and encourage rehabilitation. In rural areas, farmers—traditionally land-rich and cash-poor—may benefit most from local revenue diversification.

A diversified revenue base can also promote efficiency, because it reduces the distortion of economic decisions resulting from overreliance on any particular tax. High property-tax rates discourage improvements to buildings, encourage flight to the suburbs, and offer incentives to shift wealth into nontaxable forms. High income or payroll taxes encourage firms to substitute capital for labor, encourage locating in untaxed areas, and may even discourage work effort. High sales taxes discourage consumption and can encourage the flight of commercial facilities to outside taxing jurisdictions.

Diversification keeps all tax rates lower than they would otherwise be. To the extent that local taxes influence consumption and production decisions and locational choices, lower rates cause fewer distortions of economic decisions.

Finally, a diversified tax base offers local governments the same advantages that a diversified portfolio of financial assets offers investors. Any given tax has strengths and weaknesses in terms of stability, growth, sensitivity to inflation, and other qualities. A diversified revenue base can offer a better mix of such attributes than dependence on a single tax.[2]

There are two drawbacks to diversification. First, nonproperty taxes often cause greater distortions of economic decisions than the property tax at the local level. It is easier to work or shop outside the local taxing jurisdiction to avoid an income or sales tax than to remove one's property from it to avoid the property tax. It is for this reason that the property tax held such long, unchallenged sway as the mainstay of local tax revenues.

Second, additional local taxes create additional costs of administration and compliance. In general, local income and sales taxes are less costly to administer (per dollar of revenue) than the property tax. Nevertheless, an increase in property-tax rates (either the mil rate or the assessment rate) will raise more revenue without much (if any) increase in compliance and administrative cost. Diversifying, even to a tax that is relatively inexpensive to collect, will call for a whole new set of tax collection procedures, records, and employees. Thus, a diversified revenue base will cost more to administer than a single-tax system, and the greater the variety of taxes used, the more complicated the tax system and the more likely that additional collection and compliance costs will be incurred.

## *THE LOCAL SALES TAX*

### *Basic Characteristics*

The local sales tax is the largest single local nonproperty tax in both revenue generated and number of jurisdictions in which it is employed. Like other nonproperty taxes, some basic guidelines for its use are usually set by the state. Typically the state in its authorizing legislation sets a rate, a maximum rate, or a range of rates, and specifies which types of local governments are allowed to use the tax. Usually the state's sales-tax base is the local base as well. A few states, however, allow their home-rule cities considerably more freedom in setting rates and designing the base.

The range of rates among state and local goverments is large, but local rates are generally much lower than state sales-tax rates. The most commonly used local rate is 1 percent, while the average state rate is in the 4.5 to 5 percent range. At present, the New York City rate of 4.25 percent is the highest local rate in the nation; it exceeds the 4 percent sales-tax rate of its parent state of New York.

Municipalities are the largest users of the local sales tax; 5,488 municipalities in 24 states use this tax. It is a very significant revenue source for municipalities, particularly large cities. In 1985, for example, cities of a population of one million or more derived $324 per capita in sales-tax revenue, much of it from nonresidents. In smaller cities the per capita revenue ranged from $52 to $140, with an all-city average of $58.41. Counties, by contrast, averaged $21.46 in per capita revenue from the local sales tax.[3] The tax is used by 1,065 counties in 18 states.

It is also used by boroughs in Alaska, by school districts in Louisiana, and by 95 transit districts in 10 states.

### *Rationale*

Any nonproperty tax will be justified on the basis of property-tax relief and revenue diversification. In addition, however, each type of tax offers certain advantages that may make it compare favorably with alternative tax instruments. An important evaluation criterion for both economists and public officials is incidence, or who actually bears the burden of the tax. Does the burden of the sales tax fall primarily on the buyer or the seller? the worker or the owner? local residents or transient shoppers? rich or poor? To the extent that the price paid by the buyer rises because of the tax, the burden rests on the buyer. To the extent that the tax is absorbed in a lower net price received by the seller, it will fall on workers and owners of the retail firm or on its suppliers.

For a state (or national) sales tax, it is expected that most of the burden falls on the consumer in the form of higher prices, although some small part of the tax (including compliance cost) may fall on the vendor. A larger share of the burden will fall on sellers when they have competitors in adjacent jurisdictions with lower sales taxes or no sales tax—a border problem for states. At the local level, if the sales tax is used in some communities but not all, more of the burden is likely to fall on the seller, because there are alternative sellers available to the buyer in nearby jurisdictions offering lower tax rates and therefore lower prices. Thus, the local sales tax falls partly on the seller and partly on the buyer, especially for big-ticket items, for which the trip to another area is worth the time and effort.

Incidence merely tells us who *does* pay; it does not tell us who *should* pay. Economists suggest two principles for determining who should pay: the benefit principle and ability to pay. A benefit-principle tax is one for which a citizen's share of the tax burden is proportional to the benefits he or she receives from the services financed by that tax. Property taxes are often at least partially justified on the benefit principle, because many local services—fire, police, sanitation, street maintenance—can be regarded as services to property, whose value to the taxpayer is roughly proportional to the value of property owned.

The benefit principle case for a local sales tax is not strong, but a case can be made. The share of the sales tax falling on the seller can be claimed as a benefit tax, since the vendor enjoys all the municipal services that support its operation and bring in its customers. It can also be argued that application of the benefit principle justifies levying sales on purchases by both residents and nonresidents who shop in the local jurisdiction.

Those who shop in the city, including commuters who both work and shop there, use the services of local government. They park in the parking lots, walk on the sidewalks, drive on the streets, fill the trash cans, consume the city's cultural services, and benefit from fire and police protection. However, they generate little tax revenue to local governments that depend primarily on the property tax. Thus, the sales tax offers a way to charge for the services that these nonresidents enjoy. A sales tax levied by a transit district that ferries shoppers and commuters into and out of the central city is a particularly good instance of a benefit-principle local sales tax, a fact that may help to account for the popularity of such taxes in urban areas.

Not all economists agree that suburban commuters and shoppers are "exploiting" the central city. David Bradford and Wallace Oates, for example, argue that local taxes go overwhelmingly to support services to residents and particularly to schools, which benefit residents rather than commuters.[4] Nevertheless, the opportunity to "export" some part of the local tax burden to the surrounding suburbs is an important element of the appeal of a local sales tax.

A second criterion for selecting a tax is whether the burden of the tax adequately reflects ability to pay. Ability to pay is widely interpreted to imply a proportional or progressive tax, i.e., one for which the tax burden rises in proportion to or faster than income as income rises.

The state or local sales tax is generally believed to be regressive, especially in states that tax food and exempt services. That is, the percentage of income that is paid in tax is higher for lower-income families. A recent study in Kentucky, for example, found that the burden of the sales and use tax (plus the motor vehicle tax) ranged from 27.1 percent of income for incomes less than $3,000 to 1.1 percent of incomes above $35,000.[5]

In addition to being regressive, the sales tax is horizontally inequitable. Horizontal inequity simply means that households with the same incomes can pay vastly different percentages of their income in sales tax, depending on how much of their income they spend rather than save and how their spending is allocated between taxed and untaxed purchases.

In general, local sales taxes parallel the state tax in the base, so tax treatment of such items as services and food is the same at both levels. A regressive state sales tax means a regressive local sales tax, and a horizontally inequitable state tax will still be inequitable at the local level when the same tax basis is used.

On the other hand, an adequate measure of ability to pay needs to be broader than simply earned income. This is so for two reasons. First, it is possible to conceal income from the tax collector by a host of means, some legitimate and some not. Second, current money income is not a good measure of longer-term income and thus of ability to pay taxes. Two additional measures of ability to pay are wealth and consumer expenditures. The property tax attempts to capture the wealth component of ability to pay, while the sales tax captures some part of the expenditure measure. Thus, the sales tax has at least some role to play even in a tax structure based on ability to pay when that ability is broadly defined.

### *Locational Effects*

A major issue in deciding whether to use a local sales tax and what rate to set is how consumer purchases will respond to the tax. Will sales be lost to outlying areas or other communities that do not have the tax? How large a tax differential will consumers tolerate before they start shopping elsewhere? Will the tax induce retailers to locate outside the city, aggravating the existing trend toward suburban shopping malls?

Several studies suggest that local sales taxes do indeed affect the location of retail activity and decisions by consumers about where to shop. They are less likely to affect the location of nonretail business or residential choice.

One study by Mikesell found that the effect of the sales tax on retail sales was significant; it estimated that a 1-percentage-point increase in the rate would lower per capita retail sales by amounts ranging from 1.69 percent to 10.97 percent.[6] Of the various local taxes—income, property, and general sales—he found that the border effects were largest for the sales tax. In a more recent study, Fox found that a tax rate differential reduced retail sales and employment in three Tennessee border communities—Clarksville, Chattanooga, and the Tri-Cities area. All three were competing with retailers in adjacent states with lower sales tax rates.[7]

Due and Mikesell summarized a number of studies of the border-city problem and drew the following conclusions:

> 1. The extent of the border city problem has been reduced by the spread of the sales tax to almost all states. . . . Any state, however, that raises its sales tax rate can still expect some influence on sales. . . . The magnitude of the problem depends on the border situation of the state.
> 2. For states, the problem is aggravated when a substantial population is near the border, and the principal shopping center for the area is across the state line in the lower tax area.
> 3. For cities, strong empirical evidence shows that a rate differential causes significantly lower per capita sales. . . . This evidence speaks strongly for the use of county-wide taxes when sales loss is feared.
> 4. The problem for states reaches its extreme form where a city straddles the border and part of its business district is in each state. Not only can sales loss be substantial, but tax administrators, retailers, and consumers face difficult problems in the collection and enforcement of sales taxes on either side of the border.[8]

The border problem is usually most severe near state lines, where a combination of state and local tax differentials can make it worth the consumer's time to travel a little farther to shop. Shopping centers spring up to take advantage of the border trade. In response to this problem, the state of Washington levies a lower state sales tax in counties bordering Oregon, which has no general sales tax. The limited use of local sales taxes in the Northeast may also reflect the relatively short driving distances to state lines to shop elsewhere.

The border problem is not always an overwhelming reason for avoiding local sales taxes, or for keeping rates very low. It may be offset by other special advantages the taxing location may offer. Tourist areas, concentrations of shopping facilities, or special locational advantages may permit a municipality to charge a relatively high local sales tax and still not suffer serious loss of retail sales or retail firms.

### *Yield and Stability*

The yield of a local sales tax varies considerably from one city to another. Per capita sales-tax revenues are highest in large cities, generally reflecting their role as a commercial center for the surrounding area rather than high rates of tax. The local sales tax produces from 6 percent to 36 percent of local own-source revenues (revenues exclusive of state and federal aid) in large cities. Small cities (less than 100,000 population) rank highest in share of local own-source revenues derived from the sales tax, followed by the second-tier group of large cities (those with populations of 500,000 to one million). The importance of this tax relative to other local taxes or other local revenue sources (including fees and charges) varies tremendously among and within states and among size classes. In general, the sales tax seems to be most heavily used by the cities and counties just below the largest size range.

What accounts for the variety of yields? Part of the difference reflects the percentage of jurisdictions using the tax and the rates levied. Due and Mikesell identify some other factors. They estimated the per capita sales-tax revenue per 1 percent of tax rate at the state level for 1981. This method permits comparison among states with different tax rates. According to their estimates, the per capita yield per 1 percent of sales-tax rate ranged from a low of $29.30 in Pennsylvania to a high of $141.12 in Wyoming.

These figures reflect two important factors; one is reduction of the base through exemptions, of which the most important is food, and the other is exporting taxes, particularly through tourism. Exemption of food consumed at home reduces the yield by 15 to 20 percent.[9] Pennsylvania, with the lowest per capita revenue per 1 percent of tax rate, has the greatest variety of exemptions. Tourist states such as Florida and Hawaii have much higher yields per 1 percent of tax rate.[10] (Both states also have a fairly broad base.)

Due and Mikesell also measured sales-tax revenue as a percentage of personal income per 1 percent of tax rate in 1981. Yields ranged from 31 cents in Massachusetts (closely followed by Pennsylvania at 32 cents) to $1.45 in Hawaii. The relative yield among states can again be best explained in terms of exemptions and tax exporting through tourism.[11]

The sales tax, like the income tax, is relatively responsive to growth and fluctuations in income. That is, it has a relatively high income elasticity. This aspect of the sales tax makes it an attractive complement to a property tax; the property tax will offer a stable revenue base in recessions, while the sales tax will yield increases in revenue when business expands.

At the state level, a 1 percent increase in total income results in an increase in sales-tax revenue between 0.8 percent and 1.27 percent, with the most frequent response being right at 1 percent. In the formal language of economics, income elasticity ranges from 0.8 to 1.27, and averages about 1.0. The elasticity of the income tax is greater, while the property tax is less sensitive to changes in income.[12]

Thus, the sales tax is more stable but less sensitive to growth and inflation than the income tax, while it occupies the opposite position with respect to the property tax.

Fox and Campbell examined changes in the sales-tax base (that is, expenditures on items subject to sales tax) relative to changes in income over the course of recessions and expansions in the economy. Consumer durables are quite sensitive to variations in income, while nondurables such as food and clothing were highly stable. Fox and Campbell found that the overall base tends to fluctuate, but by somewhat less than the fluctuations in total income. When the level of state or community income changes, the various components of the sales-tax base change in the same direction by amounts ranging from 16 percent to 92 percent of the percentage change in income.[13] Since the local base is usually the same as the state base, local sales-tax revenue would be subject to the same modified fluctuations—less than fluctuations in income, but more than fluctuations in property-tax yield.

### *Administrative and Compliance Costs*

While no figures could be found for local sales-tax administrative costs, for the state general sales tax costs range from 0.30 percent of revenue in Arizona to 1.68 percent in Nevada, with a median of 0.73 percent for 23 states for which data was available.[14] Collection costs as a percentage of revenue generated are higher where there are more exemptions from the base, where rates are lower, or where administration is done locally.

Little hard data exists about how much it costs sellers to comply with the sales tax at either the state or local level. One study found that compliance cost averaged 3.93 percent of tax due. Costs tend to be highest for smaller stores or those with a high percentage of exempt items. Another estimate indicated that compliance costs for a department store with a 4 percent tax rate were about 2.51 percent of tax liability. (The higher the tax rate, the lower the compliance costs will be as a percentage of the tax liability.)[15]

Some local sales taxes are state-administered while others are locally administered. Both Rodgers[16] and Due and Mikesell[17] describe the procedures for administering a local sales tax. Rodgers identifies several features that increase both the government's cost of collection and the seller's cost of compliance. These features are dissimilar state and local tax bases, differences in tax rates among local jurisdictions, and using place of delivery rather than vendor location as the site of the tax.[18]

Due and Mikesell argue strongly for state administration because it facilitates collection of local use taxes (where applicable) on interstate transactions, simplifies coordination of taxes in overlapping jurisdictions, and reduces the need to provide compensation to vendors for compliance costs.[19]

Some large cities have chosen to collect their own tax where they are allowed to do so. In some cases, tax administrators in these cities argue that they feel they can do a better job of local audit. Others complain about state collection fees or slowness in returning the revenue. Local administration will permit use of a tax base that is different from that of the state, and can also facilitate collection of local use taxes on purchases made by city residents elsewhere in the state.

Critics of local collection argue that it will cost more than state collection. Not only will the local government incur collection costs, but the compliance costs for the retailer will also rise because of the need to provide duplicate state and local sales tax forms and maintain duplicate records. Even when they are centrally administered, local sales taxes can discourage retailers from locating within the taxing jurisdictions. The extra compliance costs associated with local administration may offer a further inducement to locate on the fringes of taxing cities or counties.

### *Tax Situs and Local Use Taxes*

An important design issue, even more critical for local sales taxes than state sales taxes, is tax situs. Is the relevant location for a tax on a retail sale the site of the vendor or the site of delivery? In most sales the two sites are one and the same, but if a buyer from one jurisdiction makes a purchase in another jurisdiction for home delivery, there is a question of which jurisdiction is entitled to the tax. Mail and phone orders and delivery of large items (computers, appliances, home furnishings, etc.) by truck or other method add up to a significant component of the potential sales-tax base. Who is entitled to the tax revenue? If the answer is the jurisdiction of the vendor, then there is substantial potential for tax "exporting," i.e., for one state or city to derive substantial sales-tax revenue from nonresidents. If the answer is the jurisdiction of delivery, then some mechanism must be found to extract the tax either from the "foreign" seller (since the sellers usually serve as collection agents) or from the buyer. That mechanism is the use tax.

Both state and local use taxes are intended to collect tax revenue on purchases that would otherwise escape taxation. Without a use tax, many purchases would not be taxed either in the state of purchase or in the state of destination. The use tax is designed to close that loophole, although it is difficult to enforce (except for automobiles, because they must be registered). For other big-ticket items such as boats, appliances, and computers, states have developed cooperative information exchanges to facilitate collection. In most cases, if a sales tax were collected by the state of origin, it would be credited against use-tax liability in the destination state. If the state administers the local sales tax, then local use taxes will be collected on out-of-state purchases, but not on purchases in other local jurisdictions within the state.

The potential for exporting taxes from one jurisdiction to another within a state can be quite great, particularly in large urban retail centers or resort areas. The choice of vendor location rather than delivery as the tax situs enhances the ability of local governments to export local sales taxes both to residents of surrounding jurisdictions and to out-of-state buyers.

All but 10 of the states with local sales taxes use vendor location rather than delivery site as the basis for collecting the tax. In those states, the local use tax is not an issue. Delivery is the determining site for tax liability, however, in 10 states: Alabama, Colorado, Georgia, Louisiana, Minnesota, Nebraska, New York, North Carolina, South Dakota, and Wyoming. This list includes a few states that are major users of the local sales tax, and in these states the local use tax is an important issue. Since the local use tax is even more difficult and costly than the state use tax to collect and enforce, this choice is expensive in terms of both lost revenue and administrative costs. Many states forbid local use taxes or allow them only on out-of-state purchases. A few states allow taxation of all purchases by residents outside the local taxing jurisdiction.

The choice of vendor location makes the tax much more attractive to large retail centers, who depend on tourists, commuters, and business visitors to pay a large part of the tax. To the extent that these nonresidents are paying for benefits received from the retail center, vendor location is an appropriate tax situs. To the extent that the sales tax is used to finance services that primarily benefit residents, the point of delivery (destination or residence) is a more appropriate choice.

### *Statewide Uniformity or Local Option*

The question of state or local administration is closely linked to other aspects of local choice in the sales tax, particularly the choice of rates and the choice of using the state base or modifying it. In some states the state does not merely decide that the tax is available but actually mandates its use by a particular kind of local government.

Local option within a range of rates specified by the state is the most common form of local sales tax. In 26 states with local sales taxes, less than 100 percent of any type of local jurisdiction use that type of tax, although it is very widely used in several states.

When the tax is universal at a mandated rate, as in Virginia and Nevada, it is more like a state tax that is shared with local governments on an origin basis. This type of tax reduces distortions in locational choice within the state, and should result in lower administrative costs for the government and lower compliance costs for the retailer. There are some advantages, however, in tailoring the tax to local needs and preferences that are lost in the process. Many states have leaned toward allowing greater local choice in rates and whether to use the tax. At the same time, states typically place some limits on the freedom of local governments to modify the sales-tax base, to charge rates outside certain limits, or to charge local use taxes. The rationale for these restrictions is to minimize compliance costs, to reduce locational effects from tax differences, and to facilitate state rather than local administration.

### *Tax Overlapping*

In some states more than one type of local government is allowed to use a local sales tax, resulting in a potential problem of tax overlapping. Taxpayers could be paying sales tax simultaneously to a city, a county, a school district, and a transit district, all encompassing that person's residence and shopping area. Such overlap would result in a high combined local-sales tax rate and might significantly distort business location and consumer shopping decisions. Most often this problem arises for counties and the cities they contain. Where transit districts use the sales tax, the rates are usually quite low.

## *THE LOCAL PERSONAL INCOME TAX*

The local income tax is primarily a supplementary revenue source for large cities. Local income taxes, like local general sales tax, are often used to reduce dependence on the property tax and to collect revenue from those who work in the central city but live in the suburbs. In 1987, a total of 3,545 local government units—primarily cities but also boroughs, towns, townships, counties, school districts, and transit districts—levied some form of income, wage, or payroll tax.

Personal income taxes rank third in local tax-revenue sources, behind property and sales taxes. They are most often authorized for use by general-purpose local governments, although Iowa, Ohio, and Pennnsylvania allow use by school districts. Generally, states do not permit the same local government unit to use both a general sales tax and a local income tax. Only 5 states (Alabama, California, Missouri, New York, and Ohio) permit the use of both local income or wage taxes and local sales taxes, and there are only 7 cities—Birmingham, Alabama; Los Angeles and San Francisco, California; Kansas City and St. Louis, Missouri; and New York City and Yonkers, New York—that levy both. Ohio limits use of the income tax to cities and the sales tax to counties. Local income taxes are only found in those states that have a broad-based state income tax.[20]

### *Basic Characteristics*

While local general sales taxes are fairly similar from state to state, there are three very different types of local income taxes employed: the wage or payroll tax, the piggyback tax, and the locally designed broad-based income tax.

*Payroll Tax.* The most widely used of the three types is the payroll tax, also known as the wage tax or the earned-income tax. This tax typically consists of a single flat rate and is collected by payroll withholding. Income from sources other than wages and salaries is not taxed. The payroll tax has no exemptions, deductions, or filing of tax returns. While administration is simple, the payroll tax is more regressive than other kinds of income taxes.

Of the 14 states now employing local income taxes, 9 use some form of a payroll tax: Alabama, California, Delaware, Kentucky, Missouri, New Jersey, Ohio, Oregon, and Pennsylvania.[21] Local income taxes in Michigan are also of this type, except for the city of Detroit. In California, Oregon, and New Jersey, the payroll tax is legally imposed on employers rather than employees, so these taxes are often not counted among local income taxes in official tabulations. Most economists would argue, however, that a substantial part of the burden of such a tax falls on the employee, and thus it is effectively the same as the payroll tax is on employees in other states.

*Piggyback Tax.* The second variety, in which the local income-tax liability is linked directly to federal or state income taxes, is used in Iowa, Indiana, and

Maryland, and in the cities of Detroit, Michigan, and Yonkers, New York. In Iowa and Maryland the local income tax is a percentage of the state income-tax liability. Detroit and Indiana county income taxes are computed on the basis of federal adjusted gross income rather than state income-tax liability. An advantage is that such taxes are relatively inexpensive to administer and to comply with because they are linked to a return that the taxpayer is already obligated to file. Because of the broader income base, such a tax is also less regressive than a payroll or wage tax. While the payroll tax usually collects taxes from all workers in a jurisdiction, the piggyback type of tax is designed to collect from residents, an issue considered below.

*Broad-Based Tax.* New York City's local income tax is unique. It is a broad-based, graduated income tax with locally set exemptions and deductions. Until 1976, New York City residents filed separate city returns. Now, they can use state income-tax forms to file their city returns, but there are still differences that raise taxpayer compliance costs.[22]

Local income and payroll taxes are now used by 3,545 local governments in 14 states, of which 2,782 are in the state of Pennsylvania. In that state the income tax is available to cities, boroughs, towns, townships, and school districts. Ohio is the next-largest user, with 482 cities and 6 school districts. Local governments in Maryland have also relied heavily on the local income tax.[23]

In most states, the local income or payroll tax requires state authorization. Included in the enabling legislation are such restrictions as the form of the tax, the permissable range of rates, and the treatment of nonresidents. Only Maryland has required its use; elsewhere it is optional. Other stipulations may address overlap between different jurisdictions (e.g., cities and counties) and whether state administration is required.

### Yield and Stability

Local income taxes rank third as a local tax-revenue source behind property taxes and sales taxes. Nationally, the local income tax accounts for only 5.8 percent of all local tax revenues. It is more significant in certain states, however; in the states of Ohio, Pennsylvania, and Maryland, local income taxes provide (respectively) 14 percent, 15 percent, and 29 percent of local tax revenues.[24] For individual cities, its importance is even greater. Philadelphia, for example, derives almost half its general-fund revenue from this tax; it accounts for 21 percent of local revenues for Kansas City, 25.8 percent for St. Louis, and 23 percent for New York City.[25] In San Francisco, increases in the payroll tax (from 1.1 percent to 1.5 percent) in 1980 helped to offset the effects of Proposition 13 on the city's revenues.[26]

An income tax is usually more responsive to both inflation and to real economic growth in a community than the property tax, especially if the local income tax is a broad-based income tax rather than a payroll tax. Responsiveness, however, is a two-edged sword; revenues from a local income tax are more likely to drop off more sharply than sales-tax or property-tax revenues in a recession, forcing curtailment of public services. Some estimates suggest that revenues from a broad-based income tax would increase (or decrease) by an average of 1.7 percent for every 1 percent increase (or decrease) in the community's total income base. This figure would vary considerably with the design features of the local income tax. In general, however, a local income tax that copies the progressive features (deductions and exemptions reflected in the base and progressive rates) of the federal or parent-state income tax is more likely to show wide revenue swings in response to the ups and downs of the local economy. From this perspective, the payroll type of local income tax may be more appealing. One study of the revenue fluctuations in four major cities (three of which used payroll-type local income taxes) found that the revenues from this source were highly stable despite ups and downs in the local economy.[27]

### *Rationale*

Like the local sales tax, the local income tax is difficult to justify on the basis of the benefit principle; it has a stronger case on the ability-to-pay principle and, like any nonproperty tax, can be implemented as a form of revenue diversification or property-tax relief. The benefit principle calls for a close link between the tax base and the services the tax is used to finance—gasoline tax and highways, alcoholic beverage tax and alcohol abuse programs, etc. No such one-to-one correspondence exists for the income tax; but at the local level, the income tax often succeeds in capturing revenues from those who benefit from the city's services by earning an income there. That is, it collects some tax revenue from nonresidents who commute to work in the taxing city. This argument is made for both the local sales tax and the local income tax. An income or payroll tax on nonresidents that finances such services as streets, trash collection, public safety, and cultural amenities heavily consumed by commuters into the city might loosely be regarded as a benefit-principle tax. Since commuters do pay property taxes where they reside, and since local services (particularly education) benefit residents more than nonresidents, many cities and counties tax nonresidents at a lower rate.

The income tax is usually considered an ability-to-pay tax. The relationship between local income taxes and ability to pay depends on which type is used. Generally the piggyback form of the tax (percent of state or federal tax liability, or tied to federal or state taxable income) conforms more closely to widely accepted measures of ability to pay. Such a tax is usually mildly progressive and comes fairly close to treating households equally if their income (adjusted for more dependents or high expenses of certain kinds) is the same. The payroll tax is more nearly proportional, if not slightly regressive, and does not score as high on a measure of ability to pay as the other types.

### *Who Pays? Residence or Workplace*

The benefit argument gives rise to the question of where the worker's tax liability lies—in the jurisdiction of residence or the place of employment. The question of whether to tax residents or workers is resolved differently in different states.

In addition to capturing revenues for central cities to pay for services of benefit to commuters, this issue is entangled with the problem of duplicate taxation. While duplication is mainly a problem of overlapping jurisdictions for the sales tax (e.g., both city and county levying the same tax), the far more serious problem for the income tax is the competing claim of the residence and the workplace. In most states overlap is not a problem for the local income tax, because typically only one type of local government (county, city, or school district) may use the tax.

Usually double taxation of workers who live in one jurisdiction but reside in another is avoided within a state by assigning priority to one jurisdiction. In Alabama and Kentucky, where the tax is technically an occupational license tax, there is no possibility of double taxation; it is clearly a workplace tax. Local governments in Maryland, Michigan, and Pennsylvania (except for Philadelphia) tax residents only. Philadelphia, as the largest city, is given prior claim on taxes from nonresidents, who may then credit their Philadelphia income tax against any local income tax in their cities of residence. Ohio residents are allowed a credit in their city of residence for taxes paid to the city of employment, giving the employment city prior claim.[28] In several states, nonresidents pay a lower tax rate than residents.

If place of residence has a prior tax claim, more revenues will accrue to suburban communities. A prior claim for the workplace tends to favor central cities, although less so than formerly, as many workplaces have moved to the suburbs. Tax credits may be used to balance the claims of the two competing jurisdictions.

### *Locational Effects*

In a small community with a high tax rate, a local income tax is likely to influence taxpayers to locate their work, residence, or business establishment outside the city to avoid the tax. Larger cities with other attractions that tax incomes at lower rates are less likely to see serious locational effects. Even in central cities, however, where a major reason for using the tax has been to capture revenues from commuters, there has been observable loss of residents and jobs in some cases due to the tax.

San Francisco's payroll tax has some particular features that have resulted in changes in the kinds of firms located in the city. Firms are excused from the tax if they would owe less than $2,500 (which would mean a payroll of less than $166,667). Banks, insurance companies, and regulated utilities are exempt by state law. The exemption has encouraged these three types of firms to locate in downtown San Francisco, but there is some evidence to suggest that labor-intensive firms have fled to the suburbs.[29] Inman and Hines's study of the Philadelphia income tax also found that Philadelphia's very high local income tax had some measurable effects on jobs and relocation.[30]

If most local jurisdictions in a region have an income tax, and the rates are low, locational effects will probably be minimal. There will be few places to move to escape the tax. In addition, if the income tax reduces the burden on the property tax, or significantly improves the quality of local public services, firms and residents will be less likely to relocate.

### *Administrative and Compliance Costs*

In general, income taxes are less costly to administer than property taxes, and about the same as sales taxes (depending on the relative complexity of each). A payroll-type local income tax that relies on withholding means that taxpayers do not have to file returns. The compliance-cost burden falls on the employer, and with a small number of relatively uncomplicated returns from employers, administrative costs would be fairly low. The second type of tax, tied to state or federal tax liability or state or federal taxable income, is somewhat more complex to monitor. The compliance cost for the taxpayer is relatively low, since most of the necessary information has already been generated for state or federal income-tax purposes and the additional form is usually quite simple. If such a tax is locally administered, however, then the local tax authorities must police avoidance and evasion by comparing local residence (or employee) records to state or federal income-tax rolls. The type of local income tax unique to New York City is the most costly of all, since it requires a separate administration that does not make use of state and federal income-tax information as effectively as the second type.

### *Local or State Administration*

To some extent, the answer to the question of whether the local income tax should be administered by the state or by the local government depends on which type of tax it is. The payroll-type tax can be administered efficiently at the local level, since the roster of local employers is available from either the property tax rolls or the business-license tax in most cases. In Ohio, for example, local governments pool their resources; agencies in three large cities provide income-tax collection services to surrounding local governments.[31]

If the local income tax is linked to the state income tax, or if both the local and state income taxes are keyed to the federal definition of taxable income, there is an opportunity for cost savings for both local officials and taxpayers if the tax is administered by the state using the same form. Most local income taxes are of the payroll type, however, and except for Pennsylvania and Maryland where state law requires central collection, local income taxes tend to be locally administered.[32]

### *Statewide Uniformity or Local Option*

Bowman and Mikesell argue that administrative costs can be minimized (while, at the same time, the tax will be fairer and cause fewer distortions in locational decisions) if the local tax uses the state base, the tax is state-administered, and the tax is widely used or even universal within the state.[33] In practice, only Maryland requires that the tax be levied in all local governments of a particular type (counties). Where local income and payroll taxes are used, the state usually imposes some rate uniformity.

A universal local income tax at a uniform rate within a state reduces the temptation to relocate for tax reasons. However, uniformity means that the tax cannot be modified to meet local needs and preferences. Faced with the benefits of uniformity and the pressure for local autonomy, most states have steered a middle course between total local independence in designing local income taxes and complete uniformity in use, administration, rates, and other features.

## *OTHER LOCAL NONPROPERTY TAXES*

General sales taxes and local personal income or payroll taxes dominate the tax instruments alternative to the property tax at the local level. An assortment of other taxes are used in most states, of which the most important are selective sales taxes. Other widely used local nonproperty-tax revenue sources are motor-vehicle licenses, real-property-transfer taxes (under various names), and corporate-income/business-license taxes, some of which are subsumed under either income taxes or sales taxes.[34]

### *Selective Sales Taxes*

Selective sales taxes are imposed on a specific or limited number of goods or services. According to the 1982 Census of Governments, municipalities derived 19.7 percent of their local tax revenue from selective sales taxes while all local governments (including municipalities) derived 4.4 percent from this source. Selective sales taxes of one kind or another are used by local governments in 45 states. Municipalities accounted for 84 percent of total local selective sales taxes. Thus, this group of taxes is primarily municipal. In 1985–86, per capita revenue from local selective sales taxes was $37.51, compared to $167.20 for the property tax, $60.27 for local general sales tax, and $47.19 for local income tax.[35]

Within the category of selective sales taxes, the largest revenue producer by far is the public-utilities tax, accounting for 92.6 percent of municipal selective sales-tax revenues and 61 percent of all local selective sales-tax revenues.[36] Of the 45 states with some local selective sales taxes, 39 have localities that tax sales by public utilities. This tax is commonly known as a franchise tax and is levied as a percentage of utility charges.

Other local selective sales taxes are levied on motor-vehicle fuels, tobacco, alcoholic beverages, accommodations, and meals. Again, the largest users of these taxes in terms of revenue are municipalities.[37] The tax is used in only a handful of states. It is a significant revenue source in a few large cities. Among cities with populations over $300,000, this tax was used by 7—New York, Memphis, Nashville, New Orleans, Atlanta, Baton Rouge, and Washington, D.C. For those seven cities, alcoholic beverages provided $67 million in revenues in 1985–86.[38] Tobacco closely follows alcohol as a revenue producer, even though it is used by local governments in only 6 states.

Motor fuels, taxed locally in 12 states, were a minor revenue source for municipalities (1.5 percent) but somewhat more significant for all local governments (3.2 percent), suggesting that this tax is largely collected outside the cities.

A variety of other selective sales taxes in 37 states provide the remainder of the selective sales-tax revenue.

Selective sales taxes are criticized on grounds of both equity (who pays?) and efficiency (decisions about where to shop or to locate a business facility). Like general sales taxes, or for that matter most local taxes, selective sales taxes tend to be regressive on the whole. A tax on tobacco is the most regressive, while taxes on meals, alcoholic beverages, and motor fuels are the least burdensome on lower-income groups. Selective sales taxes are likely to create some shifting of shopping patterns in border cities and may encourage flight to the suburbs for some types of facilities.[39] In general, the attractions of a downtown location are likely to offset the disadvantage of meal and accommodation taxes in major cities, where they are most likely to be used. Where they are targeted to visitors and commuters, however, the taxes can be exported, with the burden falling on those from outside the region.

### *Corporate-Income and Gross-Receipts Taxes*

This catchall category of local taxation of business income is difficult to separate from the local income and sales taxes. Local taxes on business firms are variously known as business-license, employers'-expense, mercantile-privilege, occupational-privilege, and gross-receipts taxes. Typically they are levied on the basis of gross receipts, payroll, number of employees, or gross income, and thus overlap both sales and income taxes. Often the revenues are grouped with one of those two taxes for reporting purposes, making it difficult to ascertain the revenue yield and extent of use of local taxes on business.

There are 6 states—Georgia, Missouri, Michigan, New York (only New York City), Ohio, and Pennsylvania (only Philadelphia)—that permit taxation of local business income. In addition, 2 states have local business-license taxes that are roughly equivalent (Kentucky and Oregon). The tax is authorized but not used in Georgia; widespread use is found only in Ohio and Kentucky. In other states the tax is confined to a few large cities. Rates normally range from 0.5 percent to 2 percent, but the New York City rate is 9 percent, where it yields 13 percent of local tax revenue. The usual base is federal taxable income.[40]

Such a local business-income tax has two problems, one in implementation and the other in its effects. The implementation problem is one familiar to state administrators of business-income taxes; the apportionment of the firm's income among its multiple locations. What share of the firm's income can fairly be attributed to the local taxing jurisdiction? The other problem is the impact of such a tax on business location. It is probably fair to say that fear of driving away existing or potential employers and property-tax payers is a major reason for the present limited use of local business-income taxes.[41]

### *Motor-Vehicle-License Taxes*

Local governments in 27 states reported revenue from motor-vehicle licenses. This tax accounts for only 1 percent of municipal tax revenues and less than 0.5 percent of all local tax revenues in 1982. Although it is widely used, the revenue per household or per vehicle is very low because of low rates. Thus, at present it is a very minor revenue source, but one with potential for expansion.

### *Miscellaneous Local Taxes*

A variety of other taxes complete the miscellaneous local tax-revenue picture. Many of them are other forms of selective sales taxes. Local severance taxes are used in a few areas with substantial mineral resources. One other tax source that is closely linked to the property tax is the real-estate-transfer tax, known by a variety of other names (deed transfer, real property transfer, etc.) This tax is used in 36 states and the District of Columbia, but only in 12 states is it used at the local level. Rates range from 0.5 percent in Illinois counties and Virginia cities and counties to 2.5 percent in the city of Philadelphia. It is widely used in Pennsylvania; in 1980, this tax yielded revenues of $43 million to 1,801 municipalities and $39 million to 455 school districts.[42] It has also been a productive revenue source for the city of New York.[43]

Steven Gold suggests some other taxes that could be used or some existing taxes that have potential for wider use. The hotel-motel accommodations tax has considerable potential for areas with a high volume of tourists or business travelers. This tax is easy to administer and captures some of the costs created by tourists and other travelers. Amusement taxes (including admissions, coin-operated machines, etc.) and cable-television taxes are other possibilities in the selective sales-tax area. Gold also suggests that there is potential to expand the use of some existing taxes, particularly motor-vehicle-license fees and excise taxes on alcoholic beverages, tobacco, and motor fuels, although some of these run the risk of increased bootlegging.[44]

## *SUMMARY AND CONCLUSIONS*

While the property tax remains the mainstay of local government tax revenues, alternatives to the property tax have assumed an increasingly important role over the last fifty years. Local sales and income taxes, as well as a variety of lesser local taxes, have provided property-tax relief, diversification, revenue growth, a way to capture revenue from nonresidents, and a way to generate revenue from those whose consumption and income suggest ability to pay that is not reflected in ownership of real tangible property.

Each alternative to the property tax offers some unique attributes, both positive and negative. Sales taxes are more sensitive to changes in income and population and capture revenue from nonresidents who come to shop in cities, but they may encourage retailers to locate outside the taxing jurisdiction and shoppers to go elsewhere. Income taxes offer similar advantages and drawbacks, but are generally less burdensome on the poor than property and sales taxes. Selective sales taxes of various kinds can take advantage of a community's particular assets to generate revenue from tourists, commuters, or consumers of specialized goods or services. Business taxes of various kinds can recoup the cost of some local public services that particularly benefit businesses, but again at the risk of encouraging firms to locate outside the city, county, or school district in a more "tax-friendly" neighborhood.

The city, county, school district, or other local government has a menu of revenue choices. The diversity of the menu depends on what its state government has made available. Local governments can continue to depend on the mainstay, the property tax, but will likely increasingly sample from an array of alternatives as they continue to search for ways to finance the provision of local public services.

## *NOTES*

1. U.S. Bureau of the Census, *Government Finances in 1985–86* (Washington, DC: U.S. Government Printing Office, 1987).

2. For an evaluation of state and local taxes in a portfolio model, see Fred C. White, "Trade-Off in Growth and Stability in State Taxes," *National Tax Journal* 36 (March 1983): 103–14; and Walter S. Misiolek and D. Grady Perdue, "The Portfolio Approach to State and Local Tax Structures," *National Tax Journal* 40 (March 1987): 111–14.

3. *City Government Finances* (Washington, DC: U.S. Government Printing Office, 1985); and *County Government Finances* (Washington, DC: U.S. Government Printing Office, 1985).

4. David F. Bradford and Wallace E. Oates, "Suburban Exploitation of Central Cities and Government Structure," in Harold Hockman and George Peterson, eds., *Redistribution through Public Choice* (New York: Columbia Univ. Press, 1974), pp. 43–48.

5. William J. Stober, "A Study of State Tax Incidences—The Kentucky Case," *Revenue Administration* (1983), pp. 191–97.

6. John L. Mikesell, "Central Cities and Sales Tax Differentials: The Border City Problem," *National Tax Journal* 23 (June 1970): 206–14.

7. William F. Fox, "Tax Structure and the Location of Economic Activity along State Borders," *National Tax Journal* 23 (June 1970): 206–14.

8. John F. Due and John L. Mikesell, *Sales Taxation: State and Local Structure and Administration* (Baltimore: Johns Hopkins Univ. Press, 1983), pp. 316–17.

9. *ibid.*, pp. 66–69.

10. *ibid.*, pp. 10–11.

11. *ibid.*

12. James D. Rodgers, "Sales Taxes, Income Taxes, and Other Nonproperty Revenues," p. 233 in J. Richard Aronson and Eli Schwartz, eds., *Management Policies in Local Government Finance*, 3rd ed. (Washington, DC: International City Management Association, 1987).

13. William F. Fox and Charles Campbell, "Stability of the State Sales Tax Income Elasticity," *National Tax Journal* 37, 2 (June 1984): 201–12.

14. Due and Mikesell, *Sales Taxation.*

15. *ibid.*, pp. 323–27.

16. Rodgers, "Nonproperty Revenues," pp. 235–38.

17. Due and Mikesell, *Sales Taxation*, p. 280.

18. Rodgers, "Nonproperty Revenues," p. 238.

19. Due and Mikesell, *Sales Taxation*, p. 280.

20. For a description of key features of local income taxes, see U.S. Advisory Commission on Intergovernmental Relations, *Significant Features of Fiscal Federalism*, M-155

(Washington, DC: U.S. Government Printing Office, 1988). Current information on local income taxes is available in *State Tax Reporter* (Chicago: Commerce Clearing House), annual.

21. Kansas has a very limited tax on interest income which is not included in this discussion because the base is so narrow.

22. Washington, D.C., uses a similar tax, but it is not included because it is more similar to a state than to a city for local tax purposes.

23. *State Tax Reporter,* various issues; ACIR, *Fiscal Federalism,* 1988 edition, vol. 1.

24. Computed from data in *Fiscal Federalism,* 1986 edition. The term *local revenues* refers to all sources, including state and local aid. Local own-source revenues is exclusive of federal and state aid but includes user charges, fees, interest, etc. *Local tax revenues* refers only to revenues raised through local taxes, not any other means.

25. Carolyn Sherwood-Call, "The Labor Tax as an Alternative Revenue Source," *Proceedings of the 79th Annual Conference* (National Tax Association, 1986), pp. 86–93.

26. Wiseman, Michael, "Whatever Happened to the Proposition 13 Blues?" *Proceedings of the 79th Annual Conference* (National Tax Association, 1986) pp. 77–85.

27. Rodgers, "Nonproperty Revenues," p. 250.

28. *ibid.,* pp. 245–46.

29. Wiseman, "Proposition 13 Blues," pp. 77–85.

30. Robert Inman and Sally Hines, "Philadelphia's Fiscal Management of Economic Transition," in T. S. Luce and A. A. Summers, eds., *Local Fiscal Issues in the Philadelphia Metropolitan Area* (Philadelphia: Univ. of Pennsylvania Press, 1987), p. 98–115.

31. Rodgers, "Nonproperty Revenues," p. 246.

32. *ibid.*

33. John H. Bowman and John L. Mikesell, "Fiscal Disparities and Major Local Nonproperty Taxes: Evidence from Revenue Diversification in Indiana, Maryland, Ohio, and Virginia," *Proceedings of the 70th Annual Conference* (National Tax Association, 1977), p. 413.

34. For a good summary of these other revenue sources, see Steven Gold, *How State Government Can Assist Local Governments to Raise More Revenue,* Legislative Finance Paper No. 25 (Washington, DC: National Conference of State Legislatures, 1982).

35. *Government Finances 1985–86.*

36. U.S. Bureau of the Census, *1982 Census of Governments* (Washington, DC: U.S. Government Printing Office, 1983).

37. John H. Bowman and Michael D. Pratt, "Selective Excise Taxation as a Means of Local Revenue Diversification: Patterns, Trends, and Policy Issues," *Proceedings of the 76th Annual Conference* (National Tax Association, 1983), pp. 179–89.

38. U.S. Bureau of the Census, *City Government Finances in 1985–86* (Washington, DC: U.S. Government Printing Office, 1987).

39. Bowman and Mikesell, "Selective Excise Taxation," p. 180.

40. Catharine Kweit and Marilyn Rubin, "Local Business Income and Licenses and Taxes," *Proceedings of the 76th Annual Conference* (National Tax Association, 1983), pp. 190–99.

41. *ibid.*

42. Roger H. Downing, "Real Property Transfer Taxation in Pennsylvania and Ramifications of the Linkage with the Local Property Tax System," *Proceedings of the 79th Annual Conference* (National Tax Association, 1986), pp. 94–96.

43. James M. Suarez, "New York City's Real Property Transfer Tax on the Transfer of Economic Interest: A Progress Report," *Proceedings of the 79th Annual Conference* (National Tax Association, 1986), pp. 96–98.

44. Gold, "How State Government Can Assist," pp. 15–17.

# 8

# *User Charges and Fees*

C. KURT ZORN

LOCAL governments traditionally have relied heavily on the property tax as a source of revenue. During the past two decades local governments have substantially diversified their revenue structures, thereby reducing the importance of the property tax in the local revenue structure.

A number of factors have contributed to the diminution in the role of the property tax in local government fiscal structures. First, the late 1970s and early 1980s were an era of tax limitations, as taxpayers expressed their unhappiness with rising taxes. The effects of the tax revolt were widespread and—with the property tax being the most prominent of local taxes—focused on limiting property tax increases. Second, federal aid to local governments grew during the 1970s, becoming a larger contributor to total general revenue for local governments.[1] Third, local governments were suffering varying degrees of fiscal crisis due to recessions, losses of tax bases to suburban and regional competitors, and changing state and federal policies. As a result, local governments were looking for ways to diversify their revenue structures in order to stabilize revenues and enhance revenue streams without raising taxes.

Faced with these pressures to reduce reliance on the property tax and to increase their own source revenues, local governments expanded the use of other sources of revenue. One source that gained importance in local governments' revenue stream was broad-based taxes. In 1987, local government nonproperty tax revenues accounted for 8.8 percent of total revenue, 10.1 percent of own source total revenue, and 26.3 percent of total tax revenue as compared to 6.1 percent of total revenue, 9.7 percent of own source revenue, and 14.9 percent of total tax revenue in 1970.[2]

Nontax-revenue sources also began to play a more prominent role. Charges, miscellaneous revenue, utility revenue, and liquor-store revenue accounted for 41.8 percent of total local government revenue and 62.6 percent of own-source revenue in 1987, up markedly from 22.0 percent of total revenue and 29.5 percent of own-source revenue in 1970. Acknowledging the growing role of nontax revenues in local government finance, this chapter provides a detailed look at one component of these revenues, specifically user charges and fees, and analyzes their role in local government finance. Because of the ambiguity in what constitutes user charges and fees, the first section is devoted to a discussion of the range of definitions used for user charges and fees and delineates the definition employed in this chapter. Recent trends in local governments' dependence on user charges are discussed in the next section. In the third section, the basic rationale behind definitions of and distinctions between user charges and fees is presented, including basic theory, advantages and disadvantages associated with their use, and pricing considerations. Guidelines for implementing user charges and fees are presented in the next section, along with an example of implementation by a local government. The final section provides a brief summary.

## *DEFINING USER CHARGES AND FEES*

One clear thing about user charges and fees is that there is a lack of agreement about what should be included under the rubric "user charges and fees." At one end of the spectrum, user charges have been associated with marketlike transactions in the public sector; transactions possessing a link between a special payment paid and a special benefit received. Utilizing this broad definition, user charges can include

> fees and charges, rents and royalties, earmarked excise taxes, permits and licenses . . . revenues from the sale of government property, interest on government loans, premiums collected for disaster or other special insurance, receipts of public enterprises, the revenues raised from government-created property rights, and premiums or annuity payments for government retirement or health programs.[3]

Another definition for user charges portrays them less broadly as a subset of beneficiary charges. Beneficiary charges are defined as payments made by consumers in "direct exchange for government services received"[4] and include user charges and fees, license and permit fees, and special assessments. User charges are defined as payments that can be avoided by not using the service without regard to whether the service possesses public good characteristics. License and permit fees represent payments by consumers for government-produced services (such as inspection and regulation). Special assessments are directly linked to benefits received by property and its owners.

A narrower definition of user charges states they are "prices charged for voluntarily purchased, publicly provided services that, while benefiting specific individuals, are closely associated with pure public goods."[5] This definition excludes revenues raised by local government utilities—including water, sewage, electric, and gas utilities—because utility charges are public prices for publicly provided products that are truly private in nature. Also excluded are license and permit fees—because they are associated with privileges granted by government, not publicly provided goods—and special assessments because they are not voluntary.

This third definition is employed as the definition for user charges and fees in this chapter; it focuses on distinctly public-sector activities that do not compel individuals to contribute. User charges and fees are payments for voluntarily purchased, publicly provided services that benefit specific individuals, but exhibit public-good characteristics or are closely associated with public goods.

Goods that exhibit public-good characteristics or are closely associated with public goods often are referred to as *merit goods*.

> [A] merit good [is] a private good that has some public good characteristics. . . . Part of the benefit is 'seen' by the individual consumer and part by . . . the public in general. Although it is possible to levy user charges, total production could be subsidized to the extent that collective benefits are perceived.[6]

In other words, it is possible to exclude individuals from the consumption of a merit good if they are not willing to pay for the good and the benefits associated with consumption of the good clearly can be linked to an individual or group of individuals. However, there are external benefits associated with the consumption of the good and thus there may be a rationale to subsidize its provision.

The term *beneficiary charges* is used in this chapter to describe a group of nontax-revenue sources that broader definitions often include under the heading "user charges and fees": utility revenue, special assessments, and license and permit fees, and user charges and fees as defined above.[7]

Table 8-1 helps to clarify the definitions being employed for user charges and fees and beneficiary charges. The role that utility charges, user charges and fees, special assessments, and license and permit fees play in the local-government revenue structure is clearly delineated and differences among these local revenue sources are highlighted. *Utility charges* are, in essence, public prices levied on publicly provided private goods that the public sector has chosen to provide. *User charges and fees* are public prices that are levied on publicly provided goods that possess public-good characteristics; they create direct or indirect external benefits that may argue for subsidization of the good to ensure efficient levels of provision. *Special assessments,* despite being linked to identifiable beneficiaries and being associated with public goods, are compulsory, not voluntary. *License and permit fees* do not purchase a government-provided good or service; they are exchanged for a privilege.

Table 8-2 lists an assortment of sources of local government beneficiary charges. The sources are categorized as utility charges, user charges and fees, special assessments, and license and permit fees in order to further clarify the distinction among these four nontax-revenue sources. Admittedly, determining what should be placed in each category is somewhat subjective. For example, the distinction between sources of utility charges and sources of user charges hinges on whether the good exhibits public-good characteristics or is closely related to

TABLE 8-1
*Definitions*

| Revenue Source | Characteristics | Examples |
|---|---|---|
| Utility charges | Analogous to private market prices; benefits accrue to identifiable individuals; payment varies with consumption | Charges for sewer, water, and publicly provided electricity |
| User charges and fees | Similar to private market prices but may involve a subsidy to specific users; voluntary; payments normally based on an individual's consumption of merit goods and services | Fees for public swimming pools, trash collection, health services, public museums |
| Special assessments | Compulsory payments imposed on real property for specific benefits generated by public investments or services; in theory, costs are allocated in line with benefits received; includes exactments from developers and development fees | Local assessments for sidewalks, street paving and lighting, and fire-protection fees |
| License and permit fees | Payments required to cover the costs of government regulation of private activities; should be considered an excise tax if charges exceed reasonable costs of regulation | Automobile inspection fees, building permit and inspection charges, professional licenses |
| Narrow-based benefit taxes | Taxes on specific activities or purchases that are generally, but often indirectly, related to the use of public facilities, such as highways; revenues are usually earmarked for particular expenditure categories | Motor vehicle and fuel taxes |
| General taxes | Compulsory payments that are used to finance general government programs; tax payments are not linked, directly or indirectly, with an individual's consumption of specific goods and services | Sales, income, and property taxes |

SOURCE: Based on Figure 1 in Advisory Commission on Intergovernmental Relations, *Local Revenue Diversification: User Charges* (Washington, DC: ACIR, 1987), p. 4.

a public good. However, making this determination may involve a degree of normative judgment.

Some goods and services clearly are private goods without public-good characteristics and therefore are sources of utility charges—electric, gas, telephone, and cable television utilities. Water, sewerage, and transportation services are characterized in Table 8-2 as sources of utility charges, but some would contend that they are more appropriately classified as sources of user charges. The rationale is that these services are almost exclusively provided by the public sector and therefore must be merit goods. An equally strong argument, however, is that these services are not merit goods. Historically water, sewerage, and transportation services were franchised to the private sector and the public sector took over their provision only after rampant abuse of the franchise privilege occurred. If it were not for this historical precedent, it would be possible today to have efficient private sector provision of these services with public regulation.

TABLE 8-2
*Assorted Sources of Beneficiary Charges*

*Police Protection* (C)
Special patrol services
Police services at private events
Fingerprinting
Accident reports

*Fire Protection* (C)
Outside-city fire calls
False alarms

*Other Public Safety* (C)
Building, electrical, and plumbing inspection
Zoning and engineering services
Residential, commercial, and industrial refuse collection
Street lighting installation
Tree planting and removal

*Transportation* (U)
Subway and bus fares
Bridge tolls
On-demand transit
Landing and departure fees
Hangar rentals
Concession rentals
Parking-meter receipts

*Health and Hospitals* (C)
Laboratory services
Inoculation charges
X-ray services
Outpatient clinics
Hospital charges
Emergency ambulance services
Nursing homes
Concession rentals

*Education* (C)
Book charges
Library charges
Tuition charges

*Recreation* (C)
Golf courses
Swimming pools
Tennis courts
Skating rinks
Picnic grounds
Ball fields
Museums, zoos, galleries
Concerts and plays
Convention centers
Admission fees

*Water and Sewerage* (U)
Water-meter permits
Water-service charges
Sewerage-system charges

*Other Utilities* (U)
Electricity
Telephone
Gas
Cable television

*Special Assessments* (S)
Builder exactments
Developer fees

*Licenses and Permit Fees* (L)
Advertising
Amusements
Circuses and carnivals
Dog tags
Lodging
Occupation
Solicitation
Vendors

*Key*
U = Utility Charge
C = User Charges and Fees
S = Special Assessments
L = License and Permit Fees

SOURCE: Based on Selma J. Mushkin and Charles L. Vehorn, "User Fees and Charges," *Governmental Finance*, (Chicago, IL: Municipal Finance Officers Association, November 1977), p. 48; and United States Conference of Mayors and Arthur Young and Company, *User Fees: Towards Better Usage* (Washington, D.C.: U.S. Conference of Mayors, April 1987), p. 3.

## *TRENDS IN USER CHARGES AND FEES*

The U.S. Bureau of the Census defines current charges, a category used in its statistical compilations, as

> amounts received from the public for the performance of specific services benefiting the person charged, and from sales of commodities and services except by govern-

> ment utilities and liquor stores. Includes fees, assessments, and other reimbursements for current services, rents and sales derived from commodities or services furnished incident to the performance of particular functions, gross income of commercial activities, and the like. . . . Current charges are distinguished from license taxes, which relate to privileges granted by the government or regulatory measures for the protection of the public.[8]

Due to the limitations inherent in the Census Bureau definition of current charges—it excludes utility charges and license and permit fees, but includes assessments—it is not possible to focus specifically on trends in the utilization of user charges and fees as defined in this chapter. Instead, trends in "generic user charge" financing are discussed, in deference to data and definitional limitations. This operational definition, which is consistent with available census data, is employed in a recent study of user charges conducted by the Advisory Commission on Intergovernmental Relations (ACIR).[9] The ACIR defines user-charge financing to include current charges, special assessments, and utility charges.

Table 8-3 shows that local governments have been increasing their reliance on user charges since at least 1957. In 1957, for every $1 raised in tax revenue, $0.40 was raised by user charges. By 1977 this percentage had risen slightly to more than $0.45 for every $1 in taxes. The ratio of user charges to taxes rose significantly between 1977 and 1983, the period when most of the state and local tax limitations and two significant recessions were experienced. By 1983, user charges amounted to $0.64 for every $1 in taxes, a ratio maintained through 1987.

Without exception, all categories of user charges represented in Table-3 grew more quickly than local taxes during the 1977–83 period. Sanitation, parks and recreation, special assessments, water revenues, and other utility and transit charges experienced the largest increases relative to pre-1977 growth rates. Between 1983 and 1987 most categories, except education, either equalled or exceeded the annual compound growth rate in local taxes, but none experienced growth rates greater than their 1977–83 rates.

A survey published in 1987 by the United States Conference of Mayors (USCM) provides further information on the implementation of user-charge financing by U.S. cities. The USCM definition of user-charge financing differs from ACIR's; it excludes special assessments but includes license and permit fees. (Table 8-2 lists the major service categories covered by the survey.) Of the 402 cities that responded to the survey, 39 percent had 50,000 or fewer inhabitants, 32 percent had populations between 50,000 and 100,000, 17 percent had between 100,000 and 250,000 inhabitants, and 12 percent had populations in excess of 250,000.[10]

Fifty-one percent of the respondents indicated they had adopted user-charge financing primarily to generate revenue rather than to regulate demand for services. Respondents indicated that sewerage, sanitation, and recreational services were best suited as income generators and had the greatest profit-making potential among services financed by user charges. Regulation of demand and

TABLE 8-3

*Local Government User Charges, Fiscal Years 1957 to 1987*

| | MILLIONS OF DOLLARS | | | | AVERAGE ANNUAL RATE OF GROWTH (PERCENT) | | |
|---|---|---|---|---|---|---|---|
| Revenue Source | 1987 | 1983 | 1977 | 1957 | 1983–87 | 1977–83 | 1957–77 |
| User Charges Total | 101,046 | 72,655 | 34,030 | 5,764 | 8.6 | 13.5 | 9.3 |
| Current Charges | 54,299 | 39,433 | 18,977 | 2,536 | 8.3 | 13.0 | 10.6 |
| Education | 6,860 | 5,703 | 3,429 | 665 | 4.7 | 8.9 | 5.7 |
| Hospitals | 17,323 | 13,935 | 5,722 | 459 | 5.6 | 16.0 | 13.4 |
| Sewerage | 9,139 | 5,809 | 2,488 | 219 | 11.9 | 15.2 | 12.9 |
| Sanitation | 2,859 | 1,644 | 662 | 76 | 14.8 | 16.4 | 11.4 |
| Parks and recreation* | 2,294 | 1,572 | 756 | 131 | 9.9 | 13.0 | 9.2 |
| Housing and urban renewal | 2,124 | 1,496 | 916 | 280 | 7.8 | 8.5 | 6.1 |
| Other | 13,760 | 9,282 | 4,941 | 706 | 10.3 | 11.1 | 10.2 |
| Special Assessments | 2,257 | 1,569 | 862 | 284 | 9.2 | 10.5 | 5.7 |
| Water Revenues | 14,374 | 9,498 | 4,994 | 1,235 | 10.9 | 11.3 | 7.2 |
| Other Utility and Transit | 30,116 | 22,145 | 9,197 | 1,709 | 8.0 | 15.8 | 8.8 |
| Local Taxes | 158,216 | 113,145 | 74,852 | 14,286 | 8.7 | 7.1 | 8.6 |
| User Charges as a Percentage of Local Taxes | 63.8% | 64.2% | 45.5% | 40.3% | | | |

* Includes natural resources.

SOURCE: Advisory Commission on Intergovernmental Relations, *Local Revenue Diversification: User Charges* (Washington, D.C.: ACIR, 1987); and U.S. Bureau of the Census, *Governmental Finances in 1986–87* (Washington, D.C.: Government Printing Office, 1988).

reduction in waste and abuse was linked most closely with charges levied on public safety services, including building licenses and inspections, false alarms, and zoning.

The survey indicated that interest in user-charge financing continues. Approximately 70 percent of respondents had adopted fees within the last ten years and 15 percent had instituted charges during the past five years. In this latter group, 32 percent of the adoptions occurred in the public-service category, 23 percent in the recreation/cultural category, and 25 percent in the category "other." This last category includes cable television; license and permit fees; library fees for video and film rentals, database searches, and microfiche printers; electricity; telephone; cemeteries; subway and bus fares; on-demand transit; bridge tolls; and airport landing and departure fees. The services that experienced the greatest activity in new-charge adoptions share two characteristics. First, fees can be collected easily and relatively cheaply. Second, there is general popular support for the institution of charges.

## *UNDERSTANDING USER CHARGES AND FEES*

As was pointed out earlier, user charges and fees suffer some ambiguity but are unique among beneficiary charges because they represent true public prices for public products. The three remaining revenue sources composing beneficiary charges do not. This section is devoted to further sharpening the distinction among the four components of beneficiary charges and focuses on an explanation of user charges and fees.

### *Distinctions and Definitions*

*Utility Charges.* Utility charges are public prices for private products that the government has chosen to provide. Municipal utilities provide goods and services that are essentially private in nature, possess little or no public characteristics, and have no direct link with a public good. The public sector provides the service, but there is no reason the service could not be provided efficiently by the private sector with public-sector regulation. As a result, prices for municipal utilities should be structured in a manner that is similar to the way regulated private-utility prices are structured; they should be based on the quantity consumed and cover full cost.[11]

*Special Assessments.* Special assessments are compulsory payments levied against property in a specified and limited geographic area to cover the cost of improvements that provide special benefits to the property. The improvements usually involve infrastructure, such as street paving, sidewalks, and storm sewers. Although the benefits are closely tied to property, there is some public (or external) benefit associated with the provision of the service being financed by the special assessments. Therefore spillover benefits may be realized by property (and its owners) not in the special-assessment geographical area.

Special assessments are not voluntary; they are compulsory. Consequently special assessments are a form of local taxation and are not user charges. They differ, however, from general forms of taxation, such as property taxes and motor-fuel taxes, because the group benefiting from the service is more easily defined. Thus, the level of special assessment taxation should be set close to cost-recovery levels, but there is good reason to subsidize part of the cost due to the spillover effects associated with the good or service financed by the assessments.

*License and Permit Fees.* License and permit fees are related to the granting of a privilege by government rather than the direct sale of a good or service. They are a necessary condition for carrying out an activity; license and permit fees basically are taxes—they are compulsory if one engages in an activity. They may be levied at a flat rate, may be graduated by type of activity, may be related to business receipts, etc. Basically fees are intended to cover part or all of the cost realized by government as a result of granting the privilege.[12]

*Private versus Public Goods.* Before user charges and fees can be conceptualized fully, the distinction between public and private goods must be understood. Pure private goods are distinct from pure public goods; the former display characteristics of rivalry and exclusion while the latter exhibit nonrivalry and nonexclusion. Rivalry means the individual consuming the good enjoys all of its benefits; the benefits are completely internalized. Exclusion requires payment for the good before an individual can consume it and enjoy its benefits. Nonrivalry and nonexclusion are at the opposite end of the spectrum; no one can be excluded from consuming the good and an individual's consumption of the good does not diminish the benefits others receive from the good.

Three necessary conditions must be satisfied before user charges can be employed to finance a good or service—benefit separability, chargeability, and voluntarism.[13] First, there must be an identifiable set of individuals or firms, not the whole community, that directly benefits from provision of the good. Second, it must be possible to exclude individuals from consuming the good if they do not pay. Third, individuals must have the right to choose whether to consume the good. All three of these conditions are absent in pure public goods but are present in pure private goods. Therefore, the feasibility and practicality of applying user charges and fees is enhanced when the publicly provided good is closer, in characteristics, to a pure private good than a pure public good.

An examination of the aforementioned necessary conditions and how they relate to utility charges, special assessments, and license and permit fees sharpens the distinction between user charges and other beneficiary charges. The services financed by *utility* charges satisfy all three necessary conditions perfectly. However, these goods and services possess insignificant merit-good characteristics; they are essentially pure private goods. *Special assessments* display a significant amount of benefit separability but fail the chargeability and voluntarism test. The reason assessments are compulsory is that it is not feasible to exclude noncontributors from realizing the benefits of the financed activities. Also, due to the compulsory nature of the assessment, an individual is not able to choose whether to participate in the consumption of benefits emanating from the financed activities. While *license and permit fees* satisfy all three necessary conditions, they differ from user charges and fees. License and permit fees are exchanged for privileges granted by government, not for a publicly provided good or service.

### *Advantages of User Charges*

There are numerous advantages associated with financing publicly provided goods and services with user charges and fees rather than by taxation.

*Demand Signals.* User charges can provide clear demand signals, something that is lacking when government relies on tax finance. Prices serve a pivotal role in the market economy by answering three basic economic questions: what to produce, how to produce it, and for whom to produce it. Charges, which are public prices for public products, potentially can provide the same information about consumer preferences to decision makers in the public sector that prices provide private-sector producers.

Determining what services to offer, their quality, and their quantity is difficult for a local government in the absence of demand signals. Suppose a city is trying to decide whether to erect lights on its tennis courts. One approach is to place lights on a handful of courts to test demand. When the city sets user charges at a level that covers the cost of the lights, their maintenance, and operation, the level of demand for the courts clearly indicates the value of lighted courts to the citizenry. Based on the existence and size of excess demand for the test group of lighted courts, reasoned decisions about adding lights to other courts are straightforward. In the absence of charges, the city will have to base its decision on less conclusive criteria, such as interest expressed in public hearings or citizen petitions.

*Reduction of Waste.* User charges can reduce the possibility of oversupply or waste of publicly provided goods and services. Charges enable the consumer to see a direct connection between the price paid and service provided, something lacking with taxes. Financing by taxation often obscures the true cost of the service being provided and can conceal subsidies associated with delivery of the service. User charges can assist in uncovering hidden costs related to the activity, allowing for a complete and thorough evaluation. As a result, there is a more efficient allocation of productive resources.

If a city chose to pay for the installation, operation, and maintenance of tennis-court lights with general-fund revenues instead of user charges, there would most likely be excess demand for and oversupply of lighted tennis courts. The increase in property-tax rates needed to cover costs related to lighted courts would be insignificant relative to the overall tax rate; most citizens would fail to notice the rate increase or fail to make the connection between the tax increase and additional lighted tennis courts. Consequently, there would be little or no public pressure to reduce or eliminate this specialized service. At the same time, tennis players would not experience any differential between day and night court-rental fees, therefore valuing both equally. The result is a higher demand for night tennis than would be the case if the greater expense associated with the provision of the service were charged to the benefactors.

If, however, the installation, operation, and maintenance of tennis-court lights were financed with user charges, the hidden subsidy for night tennis would be removed. There would be a differential between day and night court time and tennis players would be forced to determine whether the benefits associated with night play were worth the additional expense. The end result would be less demand for night tennis in the presence of fees relative to what there would have been if taxes had financed the service.

*Revenue.* An additional advantage is that user charges and fees represent an additional source of revenue for local governments. In the wake of taxpayer revolts and during an era of reduced federal aid, local governments have looked for ways to diversify their revenue base. User charges and fees provide a robust source of revenue that also is popular with voters and politicians. Programs and activities that are largely self-supported by user charges and fees are less likely to suffer the inevitable budget cuts and reductions in service that occur during periods of fiscal austerity. Reducing or eliminating an activity that enjoys little or no general tax-revenue support will do little to balance the budget because there will be little or no effect on reducing the discrepancy between revenues and expenditures.

*Privatization.* Yet another benefit is that user charges and fees provide a strong response to those who advocate the privatization of public-sector activities. Not all activities lend themselves to privatization because of associated public-good characteristics that private pricing and provision fail to take into consideration. By charging public prices for these programs and activities, the public sector can realize the efficiency gains associated with prices without sacrificing its promotion of the merits associated with the activity.

*Equity.* User charges and fees is the dramatic improvement of equity in the public provision of goods and services. If goods and services are financed by general tax revenue, all citizens in the jurisdiction must contribute whether or not they use the services. By allowing those activities that possess characteristics of benefit separability, chargeability, and voluntarism to be financed by user charges and fees, only those that use the services must pay, eliminating the subsidy provided by nonusers to users inherent in general tax financing.

*Reduction of De Facto Subsidies.* An associated benefit of user charges and fees is the reduction in subsidies provided to nonresidents and properties not on the tax rolls. Financing government services and activities through general tax revenues does not allow the exclusion of those that do not pay taxes to the local jurisdiction. Refuse collection financed by property taxes is available to charitable, religious, and educational institutions despite the fact their properties are exempt from the property tax. User charges for refuse collection eliminate this subsidy from property-tax payers to these institutions. Nonresidents using lighted tennis courts enjoy a subsidy from the city's taxpayers unless user charges are used to finance the lights.

### *Limitations of User Charges*

Despite increased interest in user charges and fees as a substitute for taxation and a supplement to local government revenues, there are difficulties associated with their use that limit their practicality.

*External Benefits.* Many services provided by the public sector do not fit the requirements necessary for user-charge financing. If the activity has substantial external benefits, those that are not realized by its principal recipients, then it fails to meet the benefit separability test. Accident reports prepared by the police after an automobile accident are good candidates for user-charge financing because most, if not all, of the benefits are realized by those involved in the accident as they file insurance claims. On the other hand, basic police protection is not appropriate for user-charge financing because of the substantial external benefits associated with it. If one individual pays for police protection, the presence of the police will automatically provide increased protection for others who did not contribute to provision of the service.

Lack of chargeability also eliminates many government services from user charge financing. Despite the presence of a clearly identifiable beneficiary group, it may not be practical to charge a price. It is relatively easy to charge a price for the use of lighted tennis courts; tennis courts are fenced, so access can be denied if payment is not received. However, it is impractical to charge a fee for the use of a city park because it is impractical to construct barricades to deny access to nonpayers.

***Equity.*** Equity may be adversely affected if government services are intentionally subsidizing low-income or disadvantaged recipients. Charges would eliminate the subsidy and could exclude individuals who are unable to pay the price.

It is possible, however, to structure user charges so they improve equity and do so more efficiently. Provision of government services free of charge (financed by general tax revenues) is not a well-targeted subsidy; all users of the service benefit regardless of economic status or need. The subsidy can be better targeted by charging a price for the activity and then adjusting that price in consideration of special circumstances. Adjustments that are feasible include:[14]

1. Lifeline rates, which establish a low price or no price for minimal levels of service. Rates rise for service above this minimal level. For example, minimal levels of refuse collection could be financed by general tax revenues. One container per residence would be provided for no charge, while additional containers could be rented for an added fee.
2. Discounts that are offered to target groups. For example, refuse collection could be offered on a fee-per-container basis. The target group (e.g., poor, elderly) would be offered a discount on the container rental fee.
3. Neighborhood rebates. Charges are structured to vary by neighborhoods. For example, reduced rental fees on refuse containers could be offered to various neighborhoods based on median family income in the neighborhood.

***Legal and Political.*** Employment of user charges may be limited by state law.[15]

User charges are not deductible from federal income taxes. Property taxes and local income taxes are deductible. Thus, a dollar raised in property or income taxes is less expensive to the consumer of government services than a dollar raised by user charges.

*Cost of Administration.* User charges and fees may be costly to administer. Although it is feasible to establish charges for the use of the city park, it would be costly to erect a barricade and to pay personnel to enforce compliance with the charge. Also, there is the cost of collecting information necessary to set efficient prices for services amenable to user-charge financing. These informational needs may require establishing a more extensive cost-accounting system.

### *Pricing Considerations*

Just because a particular service is amenable to user-charge financing does not imply that determining the appropriate level of charge is easy. Stocker observed that

> pricing policies used by municipal governments are often fairly unsophisticated, perhaps understandably so in light of the difficulty of determining price elasticities, marginal costs, distribution of benefits and other things that enter into economic models of optimal pricing.[16]

Two approaches generally are proposed for determining the appropriate level of user charges—full-cost pricing and marginal-cost pricing. Full-cost pricing sets the user charge at a level that covers all costs associated with the provision of the service. These costs include operations, maintenance, capital, overhead, and debt service.

Unfortunately, not all costs lend themselves to easy linkage with a specific good or service:

> Exactly how overhead expenses or other joint costs are to be realistically attributed to a particular service of a multiservice agency will always remain a process of accounting rule, not economic reality.[17]

The allocation of these costs, however, is a problem not only for publicly provided services; private firms ultimately must cover all costs in order to remain a viable enterprise.

If there are some external benefits associated with the provision of the service, user charges should not be set at a level that covers full costs; there should be some subsidy provided from general tax revenues. This case, however, does not argue against using the full-cost principle as a pricing guide. Even when a subsidy is warranted, it is important to compute all costs associated with the activity in order to provide local policymakers with the information needed to make the most enlightened decision possible regarding an efficient allocation of resources.

> All expenses . . . including operating, maintenance, overhead, capital and debt service should be documented and accounted for. . . . Overlooking indirect or other costs leads policymakers to an inaccurate cost assessment that may result in under-

> pricing and, so, subsidizing the service. While a service may be priced at less than full cost, such a decision should be a policy decision by the local elected officials and not the result of data nonavailability during the policymaking process.[18]

Marginal-cost pricing is a more economically efficient method of user-charge pricing. It sets the charge at a level that covers the costs associated with the provision of the last unit of the good. While it is a more efficient method of pricing, it often is criticized because it does not provide for the recovery of full costs and may provide insignificant amounts of revenue.

A third approach, incremental pricing, has been suggested to avoid the difficult problem of allocating joint costs when full cost pricing is employed. It also overcomes the revenue-flow problem affiliated with marginal-cost pricing.[19] Incremental pricing focuses on costs directly associated with provision of the good or service, not indirect costs. Incremental costs are the costs that are avoided if a program or activity ceases operation:

> The logic of this approach maintains that many costs are costs associated with existence of a public agency, regardless of its annual program or particular facility use. . . . The cost that charges for a program should seek to recover are those resulting only from the program's existence.[20]

The full-cost approach to pricing is worth considering when agencies are responsible for one activity and that activity is suitable for support by charges. All resources acquired by the agency are obtained because of the charge-financed activity. Consequently, users of that activity deserve to bear all costs of the agency, including overhead and capital costs. The clearest examples of such publicly provided goods and services are water, sewerage, and other utilities that governments often provide on a monopoly basis. Thus, the use of full-cost pricing for utility charges is a sensible approach.

Incremental pricing is appropriate when an agency delivers a mix of services, particularly when some services lack the benefit separability and chargeability features requisite for user-charge financing. The agency typically exists to provide the public good; other services, the ones amenable to user charges, frequently are an afterthought. The costs on which the charge ought to be based are those emerging from the addition of that service—the incremental cost of the service to the agency. Any general overhead captured in a price ought to be considered as a contribution to general operation, not recovery of cost. Thus, a police department's charge for servicing of private alarm systems would not recognize an allocation of the chief's salary because that cost would continue despite the presence or absence of the alarms.

## *IMPLEMENTING BENEFICIARY CHARGES*

Clearly there is, and will continue to be, lasting interest in user charges, and beneficiary charges in general, as local governments look for ways to diversify their revenue bases. With this in mind, it is logical to consider some guidelines that can be used by local governments as they contemplate adopting or expanding their use of user charges and beneficiary charges.

### *Implementation Guidelines*[21]

Issues surrounding the adoption by a local government of user charges and fees are complex and demand a systematic analysis of user-charge feasibility before efficient and effective charges can be implemented. First, programs that are appropriate for user-charge financing must be identified. This initially involves determining which services can efficiently and equitably be financed through the pricing mechanism and which are better suited for tax financing. It has been suggested that use of the pricing mechanism is an appropriate alternative to financing by taxation if

1. Benefits are primarily direct, so that charges will not cause significant loss of external benefits
2. Demand has some elasticity, so that the use of prices aids resource allocation and eliminates excess utilization
3. Charges do not result in inequities to lower-income groups, on the basis of accepted standards
4. Costs of collection of charges are relatively low, or alternative taxes measured by use can be employed

On the other hand, use of the pricing mechanism is less acceptable when

1. External benefits are significant and will be lost in part if charges are levied
2. Equity standards require that the lower-income groups be assured of obtaining the services
3. Collection costs are relatively high, and alternative tax measures related to usage cannot be devised.[22]

License and permit fees and special assessments, while categorized as beneficiary charges, are not public prices. The services they finance fail to meet all of the criteria for use of the pricing mechanism. In the case of special assessments, the cost of collection associated with prices would be prohibitive due to the difficulty of excluding consumers who choose not to pay. The activity being financed by license and permit fees is the exchange of a privilege rather than the exchange of a good or service. As a result, the measurement of benefits is imprecise. Both are better suited for tax financing. Because these beneficiary charges are compulsory, there is a lack of sensitivity to market forces.

Once services are identified that are appropriate for special assessment or license and permit fee financing, the goal should be to set the charges at a level high enough to cover the costs of providing the services.

For those publicly provided services that meet the criteria for pricing, the task is to decide which truly are services that possess public-good characteristics and which are publicly provided private goods. If the latter is true, as is the case with municipal utilities, prices should be structured using the same guidelines private utilities use.

The second step for those services deemed appropriate for user charges and fees involves developing a basic rationale that supports the employment of user charges and fees. Third, operational data, specifically cost data, must be collected in as much detail as possible. Fourth, a determination must be made of the best pricing rule to use. Fifth, attention must be paid to market forces—what prices competitors charge, what increase in charges will be acceptable before there is a marked effect on demand for the service, etc. Sixth, consideration must be given to the possible equity effects of the pricing decision. Seventh, the formulation and implementation of user charges and fees must be sensitive to the political environment.

## *SUMMARY*

As local governments continue the quest for diversification of their revenue systems, attention will remain focused on beneficiary charges and, specifically, user charges as an alternative to tax financing of publicly provided goods and services. User charges and fees are attractive to local governments because they imitate private prices. Charges provide for efficient allocation of resources in the public sector and, if properly structured, can actually improve equity.

Clearly, not all publicly provided goods and services are suitable for user-charge financing. Taxes and other beneficiary charges, such as license and permit fees, special assessments, and utility charges, are more appropriate finance mechanisms if the service fails to satisfy three necessary conditions—benefit separability, chargeability, and voluntarism. Once those goods that are suitable for user-charge financing are identified, care must be taken to ensure that the charges are implemented efficiently, equitably, and effectively.

## *NOTES*

1. The 1980s, however, saw a reduction in federal aid to local governments as the federal government phased out its general revenue-sharing program and made cuts in domestic programs in response to Gramm-Rudman-Hollings constraints.

2. U.S. Bureau of the Census, *Governmental Finances in 1969–70; 1985–86* (Washington, DC: U.S. Government Printing Office, 1971 and 1987).

3. Fred L. Smith, "Prospective and Historic Role of User Charges as an Alternative to Taxation," *Proceedings of the National Tax Association—Tax Institute of America* 1981: 55.

4. Anthony Pascal, *A Guide to Installing Equitable Beneficiary-Based Finance in Local Government* (Santa Monica, CA: The Rand Corporation, 1984), p. 1.

5. John L. Mikesell, *Fiscal Administration* (Chicago: The Dorsey Press, 1986), p. 370.

6. Jerome W. Milliman, "Beneficiary Charges—Toward a Unified Theory," in Selma J. Mushkin, ed., *Public Prices for Public Products*, (Washington, DC: The Urban Institute, 1972), p. 40.

7. Pascal, *Equitable Beneficiary-Based Finance*, p. 1. It should be noted that the term *beneficiary charges* also is ambiguous. See Selma J. Mushkin and Richard M. Bird, "Public Prices: An Overview," in Selma J. Mushkin, ed., *Public Prices for Public Products* (Washington, DC: The Urban Institute, 1972), p. 4.

8. U.S. Bureau of the Census, *Governmental Finances in 1985–86* (Washington, DC: U.S. Government Printing Office, 1987), Appendix A.

9. Advisory Commission on Intergovernmental Relations, *Local Revenue Diversification: User Charges* (Washington, DC: ACIR, 1987).

10. U.S. Conference of Mayors and Arthur Young and Company, *User Fees: Towards Better Usage* (Washington, DC: U.S. Conference of Mayors, April 1987). The survey was sent to 800 cities with populations above 30,000 and 402 cities responded.

11. It is not claimed that all existing private-utility pricing schemes are efficient. Instead, the same efficient pricing principles that apply to private utilities are applicable to public utilities. See Mushkin, *Public Prices for Public Products*, for discussions of efficient pricing principles for public utilities.

12. Mikesell, *Fiscal Administration*, pp. 371–373.

13. Benefit separability and chargeability are terms for rivalry and exclusion used in an excellent discussion of user charges and fees by Mikesell, *Fiscal Administration*, pp. 371–382.

14. See Pascal, *A Guide to Installing Equitable Beneficiary-Based Finance in Local Government*, pp. 13–17, for a more complete discussion.

15. See Advisory Commission on Intergovernmental Relations, *Local Revenue Diversification: User Charges*, pp. 39–40.

16. Frederick D. Stocker, "Diversification of the Local Revenue System: Income and Sales Taxes, User Charges, Federal Grants," *National Tax Journal* 29 (September 1976): 320.

17. John L. Mikesell and C. Kurt Zorn, "The Implications of Alternative Cost Approaches for the Pricing of Municipal Services," *Proceedings of the National Tax Association—Tax Institute of America* 1982: 158.

18. Patrick C. Glisson and Stephen H. Holley, "Developing Local Government User Charges: Technical and Policy Considerations," *Governmental Finance* 11, 1 (March 1982): 5.

19. Mikesell and Zorn, "Alternative Cost Approaches," pp. 156–160.

20. Mikesell and Zorn, "Alternative Cost Approaches," p. 158.

21. For a good service-specific discussion of implementation and pricing considerations, see ACIR, *Local Revenue Diversification*, pp. 43–56.

22. John F. Due and Ann F. Friedlaender, *Government Finance: Economics of the Public Sector* (Homewood, Illinois: Richard D. Irwin, 1981), pp. 89–90.

# 9

# *Intergovernmental Revenues*

JAMES EDWIN KEE AND JOHN J. FORRER

THE DECADE of the Eighties witnessed a quiet but profound revolution in intergovernmental revenue trends—the change in flows of fiscal aid from the federal and state governments. Some observers argue that these changes are the product of a fundamental reordering of intergovernmental relations and fiscal federalism. They see a new era of federalism, roughly corresponding to the "Reagan era," not only signifying a departure from past practices and trends, but a significant alteration in the balance of power within our federal system of government.[1]

Others, while acknowledging the scale in the changing flows of intergovernmental revenues, interpret these events as less portentous. Changes occurring in fiscal federalism are understood as part of a political ebb and flow, a pendulum constantly swinging to one approach or another as governments contend with the next policy or fiscal "crisis" with an active or passive response. Recent changes, as large as they are, may simply reflect short-term political judgments and policy preferences rather than a fundamental restructuring of intergovernmental power.[2]

Whichever the case, great changes in intergovernmental revenue flows have taken place. Federal grants-in-aid, once dominating the fiscal landscape, remain significant but are receding in importance. State governments, in response, are reappraising program spending priorities. Local governments are becoming more reliant on own-source revenues.

Recent changes in the flows of intergovernmental revenues are a mirror that reflects larger trends in the changing pattern of intergovernmental relations. Grants from the federal government to state and local governments and grants from state governments to local governments—their size, distribution, and composition—reflect public policy priorities, balances of power among the federal government, the states and their localities, and fiscal capacity and effort.

FIGURE 9-1
*Intergovernmental Revenue Flows and Recipient Own-Source Revenues, 1987–88*
*(in billions)*

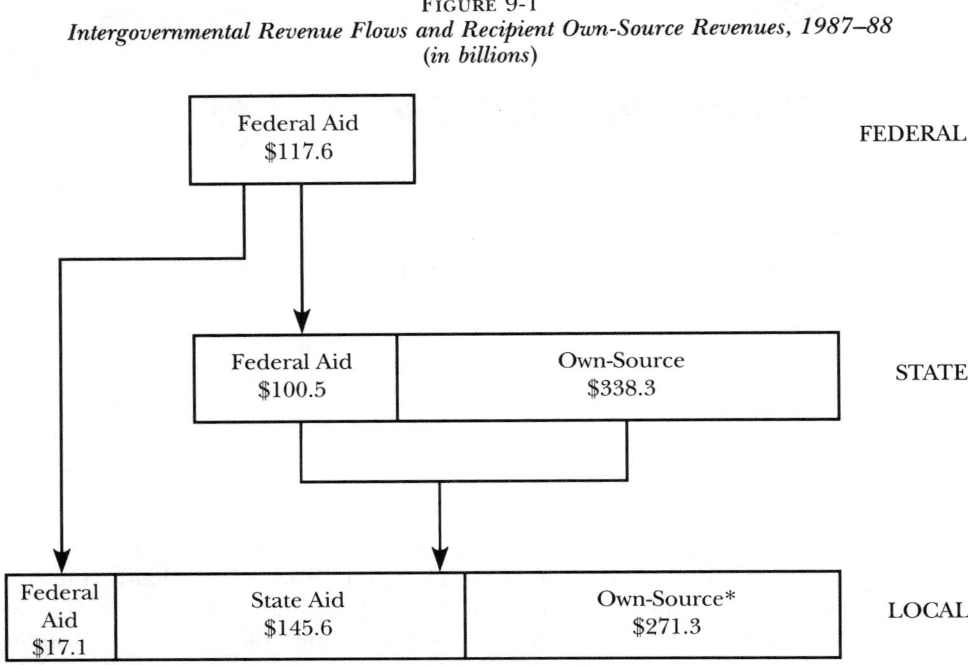


* Includes $6.8 billion of local aid paid to states and $3.0 billion to other localities.

SOURCE: U.S. Department of Commerce, *Government Finances in 1987–88* (Washington: GPO, 1988), table 6.

Figure 9-1 provides an overview of intergovernmental revenue flows during fiscal year 1988 and relates those flows to the revenues state and local governments raise from their own sources through taxes, charges, and other forms of income. Of the $117.6 billion in federal aid to state and local governments, $100.5 billion went to state governments and $17.1 billion directly to local governments. The $100.5 billion of federal aid represented about 22.9 percent of total state revenue of $438.8 billion, the other $338.3 billion representing state own-source revenue, a combination of taxes, fees, and charges. States provided $145.6 billion of aid to localities, an amount equal to 33 percent of their total revenues. A portion of state aid to localities represented federal funds that "passed through" the states on the way to localities. In addition, there were small flows of aid up from localities to states and among localities.

This chapter first discusses the rationale behind intergovernmental fiscal assistance and then reviews changes that have occurred in intergovernmental revenues, focusing on the last ten years. Suggestions are made on why these changes occurred and their implications for other aspects of intergovernmental relations and public policy.

## RATIONALE FOR INTERGOVERNMENTAL GRANTS-IN-AID

There are numerous political and economic rationales for fiscal assistance from one level of government to another. The economic justifications for grants-in-aid may be summarized as (1) corrections of "spillover" effects, or externalities, (2) stimulating local production of "merit goods," (3) using superior revenue-raising ability to achieve redistribution goals, and (4) equalizing fiscal inequities.[3]

### Externalities

Externalities are defined by economists as spillover effects on third parties that are not transmitted through the price system and that arise as an incidental by-product of another person's or firm's activity.[4] Spillovers may be positive, such as one government's expenditures on health care and education benefiting those beyond its borders, or negative, such as one government's pollution policies affecting the environment of surrounding jurisdictions.

For governments, the presence of externalities means potential inefficiencies in the allocation of services. A state or local government might spend less on a particular government service than is otherwise warranted by the total net benefits, including spillovers, to the region or nation. For example, the federal government provides significant matching funds to states for the construction of interstate highways because in the absence of that assistance each of the states is likely to spend only the dollars necessary to benefit its own residents. Federal aid is designed to induce the design of a system and total spending on interstate highways that correspond with the national benefit. Similarly, a state might provide assistance to local school districts in recognition that benefits of educating students in particular districts spill over to the benefit of the state as a whole.

### Stimulation of Merit Goods

Grants may be provided to encourage the production of goods or services that are available in the private sector for a price, but at a level of production or a price that limits access for many people. Governments may subsidize production of the desired good in several fashions, through grants, procurement, or tax incentives. Grants from the National Endowment for the Arts and Humanities are often designed to encourage state and local expenditures on activities that the president and the Congress deem especially worthy or meritorious. Federal- or state-funded daycare, recreation, and many health programs might also fall in this category.

### Redistribution

It is difficult for states and nearly impossible for localities to engage in significant redistribution of income. Because of the mobility of people, assets, and transactions, redistribution activities encourage an exodus of high-income taxpayers from a local jurisdiction and an influx of the needy into it. To the extent that such a redistribution is desirable, the jurisdiction having the superior revenue-raising ability (the one with the widest and most diverse base) is best able to design and finance programs of general assistance to the poor. The major "safety net" programs aimed at income redistribution include Aid to Families with Dependent Children (the nation's general welfare program), Medicaid (medical assistance), and food stamps. Usually managed at a state level, these programs are heavily financed by the federal government, with significant state financing as well.

### *Equalization*

States and localities do not have equal fiscal capacities, the ability to raise equivalent revenue from similar tax structures. Some have higher-income families, some have greater natural resource bases or locational attributes such as ports, some are affected by the location of a particularly large public or private facility. In other federal systems, significant national aid is directed at equalizing fiscal disparities.[5] In the United States, only general revenue sharing had this as one of its goals. Many federal grants, however, include formula funding provisions that recognize in their matching requirements the differences in states' fiscal capacities.

At the state level, the most significant equalization efforts have occurred in education, an area in which some states have made strides in reducing the disparity in per-pupil educational expenditures. States have also addressed the problem of fiscal disparity among localities by assuming the financing for some functions—such as welfare, Medicaid, and court costs—which are often difficult for localities to predict or control.

### *Political Factors*

Grants-in-aid are often made to achieve certain political purposes that may have little to do with underlying economic arguments. Funds are provided (the carrot) and requirements are imposed (the stick) to foster desired outcomes. While the aid may or may not cover the full costs of implementing the provision, it softens the sting of the new mandate. When one level of government is not responding to political pressures for policy changes as desired, higher levels of government are approached by advocates of change to design and implement solutions. Special-interest groups often resort to soliciting assistance from a different levels of government on different issues because they are not strong enough locally or in the individual states to secure the program, nor unified enough to achieve a wholly federal program.[6]

## *TYPES AND ECONOMIC EFFECTS OF INTERGOVERNMENTAL AID*

Intergovernmental aid may be classified in a number of ways. George Break has suggested a breakdown according to three broad criteria: (1) how funds are used by recipients, (2) how funds are allocated to recipients, and (3) the degree of participation by the grantor of the aid.[7] In addition, grants might be classified by their economic effect on the recipient's provision of services. Do they stimulate additional effort? Do they add to the current effort of the recipient? Do they substitute for dollars the recipient would have spent anyway?

The grant instrument used to allocate the aid has a direct impact on the economic effects of the level of services provided by the recipient. Four types of grants and their implications are discussed below: unrestricted assistance, categorical, project, and block.

### *Unrestricted or General Assistance*

From the recipient's standpoint, the best form of aid is general assistance, with few or no strings attached. This aid is often in the form of shared taxes, where a portion of a federal or state tax revenue is shared with the state or locality, either based on "point of origin" (where the tax was collected) or distributed by formula, frequently based on population. Other types of general assistance are provided as appropriations from the grantor's general funds through the budget process. At the federal level, general revenue sharing was a grant program with few restrictions that was distributed by a complex formula based on population, fiscal capacity, and tax effort. Its termination in 1986 eliminated the last unrestricted federal assistance program. At the state level, general aid constitutes a small portion of total state assistance. All together, about 15 percent of state aid to local governments, or $17 billion out of $136 billion in 1987, was unrestricted.

The effect of unrestricted aid is to increase the money available to recipient governments, but without changing the relative price of public versus private goods for their citizens. However, depending upon local demand for public goods and services, such aid may substitute for local taxes, in effect providing the recipient government with tax relief. The primary justification for unrestricted grants-in-aid is the superior revenue-raising capacity of the higher-level jurisdiction, which allows the recipient to provide the services it chooses without increasing local taxes.[8]

### *Categorical Aid*

By far the most common form of aid, at both the federal and state level, is categorical aid, which is assistance provided to defined program areas. These grants-in-aid may be matching or nonmatching. If nonmatching, they add to local resources. If the jurisdiction is not already performing the program, it will do so if it accepts the grant, and the aid may stimulate additional spending by the recipient. If the jurisdiction already has a program in the area of the grant, the aid may more closely resemble an unrestricted grant in its fungibility, unless there is some "maintenance-of-effort" requirement. The recipient has a choice of whether to spend more money in the program area, divert some of its own money it is now spending to another program area, or substitute the grantor's money for its own and provide for tax relief. The latter rarely happens because of the so-called "flypaper effect," i.e., funds from grants tend to stick to those purposes where they are allocated. The tendency of the recipient jurisdiction, at least in the short run, is to increase spending in the program of the grant. In the long run, however, the grantor's funds may substitute for money that the recipient would have spent on the program. In the process, the grant recipient becomes dependent on the grant to support other operations.[9]

Matching grants have a stimulative effect on total spending by recipient governments. They have the effect of lowering the price at which recipients may purchase particular goods and services, thereby making those goods less expensive and more desirable than other public or private goods. In the example of a "1 for 2" grant, $1 in recipient funds is matched by $2 of grant funds. The recipient gains $3 of spending benefits for $1 of revenue-raising effort. This will alter local choice on priorities (which is what the grantor wants) and typically will stimulate greater spending in the program area. The federal Medicaid program has encouraged states to develop highly diversified medical programs for low-income families because of the federal match, and states have tried to design more of their programs to be eligible for Medicaid matching funds.

State matching programs to localities are rare. Where they do exist, they often involve cost sharing for infrastructure development.

### *Project Grants*

Project grants, a specific type of categorical aid, require that potential recipients compete with one another for the grants by submitting detailed plans for their use. Some jurisdictions may choose not to compete because they lack the technical expertise or because they lack interest in the program area. Project selection is based on criteria contained in the legislation or developed through regulation by the granting agency. For the grantor, this provides an opportunity to select high-priority proposals. For the recipient, this enables it to fund a program that either would not be funded (because of lower local priority) or that would have been funded with local funds, thereby saving local revenue for other projects or permitting tax reduction. The economic effects, therefore, are on both price and income and it is problematic to say whether the grant has stimulated or substituted for local effort unless there is some maintenance-of-effort requirement.

### *Block Grants*

A recent trend in federal assistance has been the consolidation of like-kinds of categorical aid into block grants. Such grants involve less central control and are easier to administer for the recipient government. They allow the grantor jurisdiction the ability to establish broad public policy objectives while providing considerable discretion in how the programs are implemented by the recipient jurisdiction. The broader the block grant, the more it looks like general assistance to the recipient. Economic effects are much like those of nonmatching categorical grants. They do little to stimulate local effort and over the long run may substitute for local revenue. The expanded use of block grants has not been copied by state governments. This reflects their greater control over localities on the use of assistance.

## *A BRIEF HISTORY OF FEDERAL AID*

The dramatic reversal in the late 1970s of what had been the consistently increasing effort by the federal government to provide financial assistance to state and local governments dominates all discussions of intergovernmental revenue trends. After a fifty-year buildup of federal grants-in-aid, and increasing dependence on that aid by state and local government, the last ten years have seen a decreasing federal commitment to assist state and local governments. This reflects a decreased interest by the federal government to support programs where they otherwise would not operate and to offset fiscal inequities throughout the nation.

### *Federal Aid to State and Local Governments*

As shown in Table 9-1, federal grant-in-aid outlays, when measured in nominal dollars, have continued to increase, but the rate of growth has slowed since the late 1970s. When, moreover, the trend is examined after adjusting for inflation, as a percentage of total federal outlays, or as a percentage of state and local outlays, federal fiscal assistance to state and local governments reached a peak in 1978 at 26.5 percent of state/local spending. From the mid-1980s through the end of the decade, assistance has just kept even with the growth in prices, and has ebbed as a percentage of both the federal and state and local budgets.

Direct grants from the federal government to local governments, bypassing the states, expanded rapidly from 1952 to 1978 as the federal government initiated programs in response to a variety of urban problems. Corresponding with the overall pattern, this trend in intergovernmental revenue to local governments was also reversed in the late 1970s. Since that time, direct grants to local governments have held constant at around $20 billion through the late 1980s. Federal

TABLE 9-1

*Federal Outlays to State and Local Government*
*(in billions of dollars)*

| Year | Amount | FY 1982 Dollars | Percentage of Federal Outlays | Percentage of State and Local Outlays |
|---|---|---|---|---|
| 1940 | .8 | 7.4 | 9.2 | 8.7 |
| 1950 | 2.3 | 10.4 | 5.3 | 10.4 |
| 1955 | 3.2 | 12.7 | 4.7 | 10.1 |
| 1960 | 7.0 | 24.7 | 7.6 | 14.6 |
| 1965 | 10.9 | 35.4 | 9.2 | 15.2 |
| 1970 | 24.1 | 61.2 | 12.3 | 19.2 |
| 1975 | 49.8 | 87.1 | 15.0 | 22.6 |
| 1978 | 77.9 | 109.7 | 17.0 | 26.5 |
| 1980 | 91.5 | 105.9 | 15.5 | 25.8 |
| 1985 | 105.9 | 94.0 | 11.2 | 20.9 |
| 1988 | 117.6 | 94.3 | 11.0 | 18.6 |
| 1989 | 121.8 | 93.4 | 10.7 | 17.7 |

SOURCE: Executive Office of the President, President's *Fiscal Year 1990 and 1991 Budget: Special Analyses* and *Fiscal Year 1990: Historical Tables* (Washington, D.C.: GPO).

assistance as a percent of local government own–source revenue, however, declined substantially from 15 percent in 1978 to 5 percent in 1988.

Changing relationships between federal, state, and local governments have been given a host of labels to demarcate time periods or transformations: dual federalism, "layer cake" federalism, cooperative federalism, "marble cake" federalism, the "New Federalism" of Presidents Nixon and Reagan, and more recently, "competitive federalism." In discussing historical changes in fiscal federalism and intergovernmental revenue over the last sixty years, three distinct periods can be discerned.[10]

### *Great Depression to World War II*

The period 1929 to World War II was a radical departure from the preceding era. While federal and state governments have never operated within neatly defined constitutional parameters, prior to 1929 there was a general acceptance of the distinct roles played by the two levels of government and a justification for the small amount of intergovernmental revenues that flowed from the federal government to states. The federal government provided for the national defense, postal services, customs, regulation of interstate commerce, and foreign affairs. States, and especially their local governments, provided for the maintenance of public safety, transportation, public education, and social services. Government's role was modest. In 1929, total government spending equaled only 10 percent of the nation's GNP, with federal spending amounting to only 2.6 percent of GNP. What little aid flowed from the federal government to the states, primarily for roads, was clearly related to the federal promotion of commercial activity and the development of the West.

The stock market crash of 1929 symbolizes the beginning of a decade of activism by the federal government that rearranged the neatly ordered division of labor among levels of government. The Supreme Court, at first, denied the federal government's constitutional right to initiate a host of spending programs and economic regulation. But by 1937 there was a reversal of these judicial interpretations and approval was granted for the expanding New Deal programs. Reflecting this change, federal government spending quadrupled as a percentage of GNP by the outset of World War II. State and local spending held fairly constant throughout this period.

The growth in federal expenditures was accompanied by a concomitant expansion in federal aid to state and local governments. Funds for highway and bridge construction, work relief, and emergency fiscal relief ballooned at the nadir of the Depression. Direct federal grants to local governments also became a mechanism for revenue transfers. A federal-local public housing program was established, creating a new intergovernmental revenue connection. While many of these programs were terminated as the United States entered World War II, several seminal patterns of fiscal federalism and intergovernmental relations were established that proved to endure until the late 1970s. Among these patterns were

1. Allocation of funds on the basis of fiscal capacity and financial need
2. Use of federal aid as countercyclical spending to stimulate growth
3. Lobbying by cities for assistance in solving urban problems

One of the most significant programs established in this period was the Social Security Act of 1935. Federal aid under this act included old-age assistance, unemployment compensation, child welfare, aid for the blind, and aid for dependent children. Whereas the emphasis prior to 1929 was on federal construction grants for roads and universities, the new social welfare grant programs were aimed at providing assistance for individuals, and those grants exceeded construction grants by the beginning of World War II.

### *Post–World War II to the Late 1970s*

After a few years of postwar adjustment, new urban-oriented programs, including airport construction, urban renewal, and urban planning, were established. The Highway Act of 1956 established a dedicated-tax trust fund and funded the interstate highway system through grants to states. By 1959, federal grants for construction once again exceeded those aimed at assisting individuals.

The 1960s saw the creation of Medicaid as an addition to the Social Security Act and the establishment of the Elementary and Secondary Education Act. These major programs were directed at aiding the poor. In addition, a torrent of categorical grants were established to fund initiatives of the "Great Society" during the Johnson administration.

In addition to expanding the dollar volume of aid, federal grants were used as an instrument to promote changing federal policy interests. These interests were sometimes at odds with the policy priorities of state and local governments. This federal activism was based on the belief that many states and local governments—if left to their own devices and resources—could not, or would not, provide services to the poor and cities.

A second notable feature of this period was the fiscal environment of "easy money" for the federal government. The federal income tax proved to be bounteously elastic, providing strong tax-revenue growth from the robust U.S. economy. As U.S. defense needs stabilized, Congress was able to tap the revenue-raising power of the tax system to shift dollars from defense to domestic priorities. One of the important rationales for federal assistance to state and local governments was to rechannel tax dollars collected by the fiscally stronger federal government.

The 1970s also brought about some restructuring of federal grant-funding mechanisms. In place of myriad categorical grants, the Community Development Block Grant (CDBG), the Comprehensive Employment and Training Act (CETA), and the Law Enforcement Assistance Act (LEAA) "block grants" were created. General Revenue Sharing was also created at this time. The second structural change was an increased emphasis in federal grants paid directly to local governments, bypassing the states. Grants for public-sector employment, public works, economic development, and fiscal assistance were provided by the federal government directly to local governments.

### *The 1980s and the Reagan Era*

By the late 1970s, a strong federal presence in state and local governments' fiscal affairs, manifested by substantial federal grants-in-aid as sources of state and local revenue, had come to be accepted as part of the fiscal federalism landscape. This federal presence and its influence on state and local government fiscal decisions had two notable effects. One was the expansion of public services and investments provided by state and local institutions that was mandated or made possible by federal assistance. The role of federal grants in expanding services to individuals, supporting investments in communities, and improving government's fiscal position was particularly beneficial to jurisdictions with weak fiscal capacity or that faced dependent populations that placed high demands on social services. At the same time, federal grants had the effect of distorting allocation decisions by state and local government officials. The benefits of "free" federal money became a strong enticement for jurisdictions to make many fiscal decisions primarily based on the availability of a federal grant. Frequently, the answer, "The federal government's paying for it" was the rejoinder to the inquiry "Do we really need it?" Many state and local governments established offices solely for the purpose of finding and applying to federal grant programs. By the late 1970s, the political winds began to change.

Putting the brakes on federal assistance to state and local government was initiated by the Carter administration, reacting to federal deficits and the taxpayer revolts of Proposition 13 in California and Massachusetts Proposition 2½ and foreshadowing the "Reagan Revolution." President Carter's last two budgets made cuts in fiscal assistance, local public works, wastewater treatment, and public service employment. General Revenue Sharing to the states was also terminated.

The Reagan administration, coming to power in 1981, accelerated the trend toward deemphasis of federal assistance with severely reduced grant-funding levels, greater restrictions in grant eligibility, and reduced block-grant-funding levels for health, education, employment and training, and community services. The only grant program area that experienced increased funding was transportation.

## *RECENT TRENDS IN FEDERAL AID*

### *Downsizing and Redesigning Assistance*

In 1982, President Reagan, as part of his New Federalism, proposed a fundamental sorting out of domestic program responsibilities between the federal and state governments. The initial proposal called for the federal government to pick up all the Medicaid costs while the states would assume responsibility for food stamps, AFDC, and 61 other grant programs. After much wrangling and politicking with the states, and considerable skepticism in Congress, the proposal was dropped. Yet eight years later, something of a de facto sorting out has occurred.

In fiscal years 1981 through 1989 of the Reagan administration, payments for individuals, administrated through state and local governments, including AFDC and Medicaid, nearly doubled in nominal terms from $36.9 to $66.5 billion. Even after accounting for inflation, these grants increased 30.5 percent, reflecting increased participation, program scope, and medical costs that outstripped inflation.

In contrast, federal funding to state and local governments for capital investments declined 11.5 percent in real terms during this same period. The decline was selective: the five-cent gas tax increase of 1982 went to pay for increased transportation-funding assistance. Offsetting this was the fact that other capital programs suffered declines, including wastewater construction and rural water grants, economic development and public works, and housing and urban development.

"All other" grants to state and local governments declined by $3.3 billion between 1981 and 1989, nearly 10 percent in nominal dollars and almost 40 percent in constant dollars. The major reduction in this category was General Revenue Sharing to local governments. Other program reductions included labor and training, work incentives, community service, energy, and law enforcement.

During the Reagan era, federal support for grants to individuals has grown, keeping ahead of inflation. But grants to state and local governments for capital investments and the "all other" category have suffered declines in real terms. Figure 9-2 shows the changing composition of federal assistance to state and local governments. Notable is the expansion of federal aid for health grants (Medicaid) and its role in keeping federal grants to individuals dominant and the de-emphasis on grants to capital and other projects that have governments as the final recipients. These changes in the composition of federal grants, along with the need for state and local governments to increase reliance on own-source revenue to fund activities the federal government no longer supports, looks very much like the Reagan New Federalism plan that was rejected earlier in the decade.

### *Changes in the Structure of Federal Assistance Grants*

Two aspects of intergovernmental revenues that have changed over the last decade are the federal government's choice of grant-funding mechanisms and their requirements, both of which directly influence the flexibility state and local governments have in spending federal assistance within their jurisdiction.

Block grants became a more common vehicle for transmitting program revenues to state and local governments in the Reagan administration. President Reagan suggested transforming many more grant programs into block grants than Congress adopted. The most significant structural change happened early: the combining of 57 grant programs into 9 block grants in the 1981 Omnibus Budget Reconciliation Act (OBRA). In the Reagan era, block grants were created as a means for reducing federal domestic spending. Consolidation of individual grants into block grants was accompanied by a reduction in total funding for grants-in-aid; that is, the total size of the block grant was less than the sum of

FIGURE 9-2
*Composition of Federal Grants-in-Aid to State and Local Governments*

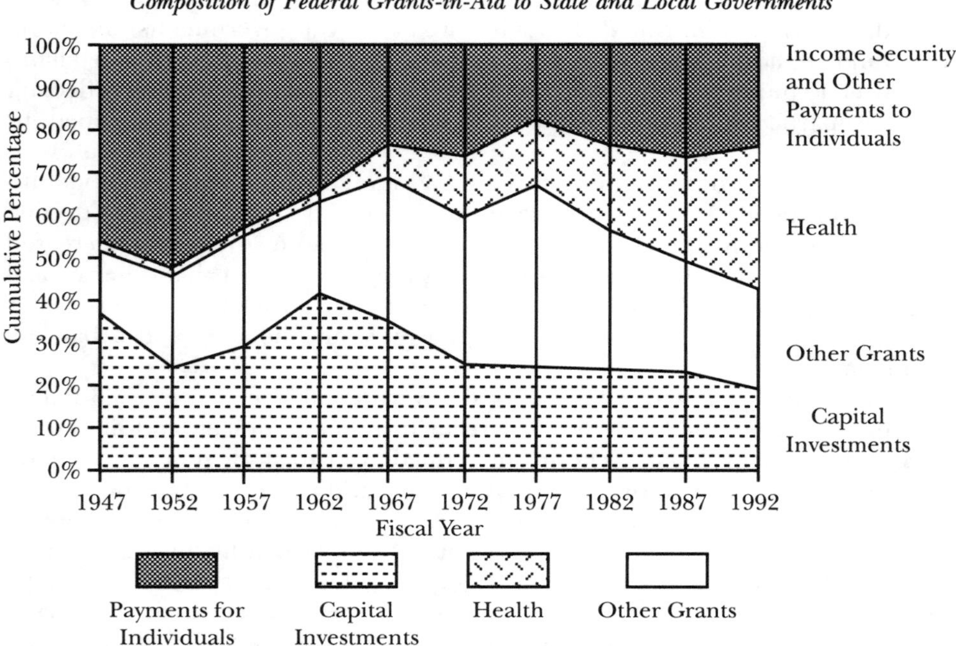


SOURCE: "Special Analysis: A History of Federal Grants-in-Aid to State and Local Governments." Victor Miller, *Federal Funds Information for the States*, Washington: 1988.

the individual grants. While the federal government reduced its support for state and local grants in many areas, the use of block grants was seen as an offset by allowing greater control at the local level over how the money was to be spent.

Federal requirements associated with federal grants also changed in the Reagan era. Some of these changes corresponded to the overall effort to reduce federal assistance. Others appeared to be a reaction to lessening federal funding for grants-in-aid. Four of these factors and their implications are particularly important: funding formulas, matching, earmarking, and mandates. Taken together, these changes may actually result in increased federal control over the use and distribution of federal assistance. If so, the results contradict the impression of the devolution of greater control and discretion to state and local governments that one would be predict from the use of block grants.

***Funding Formulas.*** Funding formulas prescribe the basis by which grant funds are to be allocated to jurisdictions. Formulas are a legislative attempt to allocate funds on the basis of factors that are proxies for need. Frequently used, factors are fiscal capacity, cost, and effort. The active use of alternative funding formulas as a means of influencing the distribution of federal assistance is a notably recent initiative. In the ten-year period prior to FY 1987, few changes were made to funding formulas for allocating state and local assistance.

In FY 1987 and FY 1988, however, an array of grant programs underwent funding-formula revisions. Differences between the old and new formulas are difficult to generalize due to the unique aspects of each program. One attribute that can be said to be common to all is more formula specificity, an attempt to increase the targeting of grants. Examples of this targeting include specific population cohorts and poverty criteria in lieu of population; greater targeting of education assistance to low-income families; and built-in incentives to the states for providing services to those most at risk.

One notable change in funding formulas that may be a harbinger of alterations in other programs was made in the Alcohol, Drug Abuse Treatment and Rehabilitation (ADATR) block grant. The previous formula used per-capita income as one allocation formula factor. Per-capita income is a traditional surrogate measure of the fiscal capacity for state and local governments. Under the revised formula for ADATR grants, per capita income is replaced with the three-year average of total taxable resources. This formula change introduces a change in the measure of fiscal capacity, signifying possible new fiscal-capacity indicators in future funding formulas.[11] The desire to change formulas results from federal budgeting pressures. With Congress unable to increase federal grants-in-aid, changing funding formulas has become one way to target aid to reflect congressional priorities more accurately.

*Matching Requirements.* Federal grants typically require state or local governments to match federal assistance with funding of their own as a requirement for eligibility. An examination of matching requirements shows that the federal government has made efforts to increase state and local government contributions to programs through tougher matching requirements.

Changes in matching requirements by the federal government do not provide a clear picture of how these changes influence state and local control over how funds are spent. An examination of changes in matching requirements in individual grant programs shows, however, a continued effort by the federal government to increase state and local share of welfare program costs. While the state and local matching requirements grew by nearly 50 percent between FY 1979 and FY 1984, this matching burden has started to recede again. Two countervailing factors have influenced changing grant-matching ratios. The elimination of matching requirements for state and local governments that accompanied the consolidation of categorical grants into block grants raised the matching ratio in favor of state and local governments. The expansion of Medicaid expenditures, on the other hand, with its lower-than-average federal-to-state matching requirements, has lowered the ratio.

Three of the largest grant programs providing payments for individuals (Medicaid, AFDC, Child Nutrition) have undergone significant changes in their matching requirements. Beginning in FY 1985, the minimum nonfederal share for Medicaid was lowered to 17 percent from 22 percent for the poorest states, while the maximum match remained 50 percent. This expansion in federal share for Medicaid reflects the federal government's commitment to grants for individuals, particularly for health. The state and local matching requirements for

AFDC and the National School Lunch program, however, have been raised, reflecting the federal government's efforts to get state and local governments to shoulder a greater share of costs for welfare programs.

*Earmarking.* Earmarking is Congress's specific designation of projects to receive funding. While funding formulas and matching requirements have changed mostly in grants to individuals administered by state and local governments, the practice of earmarking has increased particularly in capital-investment programs. Discretionary capital grants are generally awarded competitively on the basis of applications from eligible jurisdictions.

Earmarked demonstration projects now comprise more than 50 percent of interstate highway discretionary funding. Earmarking has also been growing noticeably in grants to science and technology centers and laboratories on university and college campuses. For example, in response to scandals at the Department of Housing and Urban Development, Congress increased the secretary's discretionary funds; but a substantial portion of those funds were earmarked to projects of special congressional interest.[12]

The increase in earmarking may be seen as a reaction to the overall decrease in federal support for capital investments and an effort of Congress to "micromanage" an otherwise discretionary program. Lower funding for capital-investment grants has no doubt increased the lobbying by state and local governments and other potential recipients for support of specific projects. Increased earmarking is a sign of congressional efforts to compensate for reduced spending by expanding its control over where funds shall be directed.

*Mandates.* The federal government may seek to alter behavior by mandating that states and localities meet certain requirements. Insufficient funding to carry out mandated regulations will always be an issue of contention between the federal government and state and local governments.[13] There are many examples of federal mandates without the funding support for their implementation and management, as well as mandates that accompany federal assistance to states and localities, allowing the federal government to leverage their funds to get certain acts performed.

A few examples are used to illustrate how grants are used to leverage mandates:

- **Handicapped Education:** The Education for All Act requires public schools to serve all handicapped students. Although Congress planned to provide 40 percent of the excess costs caused by the mandates, the FY 1989 appropriation covered only 7 percent of those costs, down from the original appropriation of 12 percent.
- **Environment:** The Clean Water Act of 1987 requires that federal mandates be met in FY 1991, despite the fact that federal support for wastewater treatment construction grants will be terminated in that year and supplanted by a revolving loan fund. Federal mandates to remove asbestos from schools is estimated by EPA to cost \$3 to \$5 billion, with only \$20 million provided in annual federal assistance to meet those objectives.

- **Transportation:** Federal highway aid to states was put at risk if states failed to raise the minimum legal drinking age to 21. States would lose 10 percent of their federal funding if they did not comply.

The fiscal burden that federal mandates place on states and local governments is difficult to discern because it is impossible to predict what localities would have done in the absence of the mandate. Impacts vary widely among state and local governments. For example, the costs of water-pollution control vary greatly among states on a per-capita basis and vary even more so among localities. Since state and local programs are increasingly funded from own-source revenues, federal mandates may lead to a potential recipient's rejection of federal grants because of the conditions imposed by the grants. On the other hand, Congress may increasingly use its "police power" to order states and localities to comply with federal policies, whether or not there is any funding provided.[14]

The trends in federal aid to state and local government demonstrate a clear pattern of reduced federal effort. Block grants have been expanded in the name of increasing local control. Changes in grant requirements, however, have at the same time been reducing the discretion of state and local governments. Rather than gaining greater autonomy, it may be that state and local governments will not only have fewer federal funds but also less control and authority over the use of federal grants.

The pattern of increased federal influence in grant spending through tighter requirements has as its source the Congress rather than the executive branch. While both recent administrations have stressed the elimination of red tape, deregulation, and increased use of waivers of federal requirements as part of the devolution of responsibility to the states, the Congress has reacted in the opposite direction. The rise of earmarking is a direct refutation of administrative flexibility on project spending priorities through the interjection of congressional preferences.

Thus, the intergovernmental fiscal legacy of the Reagan administration will be twofold: (1) a reversal of a fifty-year trend of increasing federal assistance to state and local governments and a devolution of program responsibility; and (2) a centralization of congressional power over the use of federal assistance, overriding the increased discretion of state and local governments associated with block grants.

## *STATE INTERGOVERNMENTAL AID TO LOCAL GOVERNMENTS*

State governments have undergone significant changes since World War II. State programs have expanded greatly in diversity and ambition. As the missions of states have grown, their fiscal capacity has become stronger and more stable. Also, over the last decade, federal policy has stressed the role of the states in the federal system. These changes suggest that states are playing a more prominent role today in fiscal federalism than they were just ten or fifteen years ago. But evidence of this change must be judged cautiously. When considered in aggregate,

TABLE 9-2
*State Grants to Local Governments*
*(in billions of dollars)*

| Year | Amount | As a Percent of Local Own-Source Revenue |
|---|---|---|
| 1952 | 5.0 | 35.5 |
| 1962 | 10.9 | 34.6 |
| 1972 | 35.1 | 46.8 |
| 1978 | 64.7 | 50.0 |
| 1982 | 95.4 | 48.0 |
| 1987 | 136.8 | 43.7 |
| 1988 | 145.6 | 43.8 |

SOURCE: Calculated by the authors from ACIR, *Significant Features of Fiscal Federalism, 1989* (Washington: GPO, 1989), table 12; and Bureau of the Census, *Government Finances in 1987–88* (Washington: GPO, 1990), table 6.

states comprise a heterogeneous group. Those who study state aid need to account for the diversity of states' service roles and fiscal circumstances, which makes generalizations about their behavior tenuous. The diversity in the size of states can also distort aggregate data, with a few of the largest dominating the results.

Table 9-2 presents the trend in state assistance to local governments for selected years since 1952, comparing the aid to the level of revenues raised by localities from their own sources. The results show a pattern of increasing aid, with state assistance representing a peak of $1 for every $3 raised locally in 1978, and then retreating from that level in the 1980s.

The heavy involvement of states in local government finance is not surprising given the fact that localities are progeny of the state. Moreover, it is important to realize that states have a choice of either performing a function themselves or helping local governments to perform it and supplying assistance. How states make that choice varies greatly from state to state and will change over time.

Measuring trends in total state aid to local governments is difficult. State assistance includes a portion of federal aid to the states that is passed through to local governments and reported as a state grant. Thus, it overstates the amount of actual state grants to local governments. On the other hand, no accounting is made in the calculations for differences in the division of responsibilities between states and localities and for state assumption of local functions, which results in an understatement of the amount of assistance states are providing to local governments. As an illustration of the difficulty in measuring state aid, if, to make up for declining federal pass-through grants, a state increased its aid to local governments from its own revenue sources or increased its direct spending on a functional area, the total amount of the state aid would appear not to change or perhaps even to decrease while, in fact, the state effort had increased. Recent analysis of developments in this area is discussed later in this chapter.

### *Intergovernmental Aid and State-Local Fiscal Relations*

States provide aid to local cities and counties and especially to their school districts. According to the definitions used by the U.S. Bureau of the Census, state aid to local government consists of categorical grants, general assistance, shared taxes, and payments in lieu of taxes. Table 9-3 gives an overview of the percentage distribution of state aid for the period 1954 through 1987. The most notable trend has been the decline in the proportion of aid going for highways and public welfare and the increasing importance of education. In the case of welfare, the decline is attributable to states' increasing their direct outlays for welfare (often in the context of passing through federal monies to individuals). State aid to local government for welfare is highly concentrated in two states, New York and California. Most other states have assumed total financing of the state/local portion of the welfare program.

State aid has always been dominated by aid to local education: over 63 cents out of every dollar in 1987. Not surprisingly, local schools look to state aid to provide over half their funds in the aggregate.

The rationale for state aid to localities is much the same as for federal aid to state and local governments with one important distinction. States are ultimately responsible for determining local government areas of service responsibility, fiscal processes, and revenue-raising authority. Localities, absent specific constitutional or statutory home-rule provisions, have no independent taxing authority. This is because of circumscriptions of local powers according to "Dillon's Rule," which generally holds that localities are creatures of the states. State legislatures determine the size, number, characteristics, function, and fiscal powers of local governments.[15] Legislatures typically delegate taxing authority, but they also may impose revenue and expenditure limits and mandate spending purposes and

TABLE 9-3

*Percentage Distribution by Categories of State Intergovernmental Expenditure to Local Governments: Selected Years 1954–87*

| | General Support | Education | Highways | Public Welfare | Other | Total |
|---|---|---|---|---|---|---|
| 1954 | 10.6 | 51.6 | 15.3 | 17.7 | 4.8 | 100.0 |
| 1964 | 8.1 | 59.1 | 11.8 | 16.3 | 4.8 | 100.0 |
| 1974 | 10.5 | 59.4 | 7.0 | 16.2 | 6.8 | 100.0 |
| 1984 | 10.1 | 63.3 | 5.3 | 11.2 | 10.1 | 100.0 |
| 1987 | 10.3 | 63.5 | 4.9 | 12.5 | 8.9 | 100.0 |

SOURCE: ACIR, *Significant Features of Fiscal Federalism, 1989* (Washington: GPO, 1989).

levels. In other words, intergovernmental aid is but one of a wide range of ways states structure and influence local government fiscal behavior.

The degree of local fiscal discretion allowed by the states varies widely.[16] Furthermore, depending on the division of responsibility between the levels of government, the degree of fiscal centralization or decentralization within each state also varies. One way to consider state-local fiscal relations is to examine which level raises the revenue and which provides the services.

Nationwide, about two-thirds of state and local taxes are raised at the state level. States with similar total per-capita state and local taxes can, however, have strikingly different collection patterns. In 1987, for example, both Delaware and Maryland had combined state and local per-capita taxes of about $1,700. The State of Delaware levied 92.5 percent of its total state/local taxes, and the State of Maryland levied 65.9 percent. Since local governments rely on user fees more heavily than do states to fund a portion of their government services, their share of combined state and local own-source revenue rises from 34 percent to 43 percent when total government revenue raised is considered (i.e., both taxes and nontax revenue).

Although there is wide variation across states, there has been a trend toward fiscal centralization at the state level. States, in the aggregate, have increased their share of own-source revenue as a percentage of combined state/local own-source revenue from 50 percent in 1952 to 57 percent in 1987. The centralizing tendencies in revenue collection are also reflected on the spending side, although the majority of programs in most states are still delivered at the local level. Sixty percent of all state and local expenditures occur at the local level. Nevertheless, there continues to be a trend toward centralization of expenditures at the state level. Between 1982 and 1988 a National Association of State Budget Officers' (NASBO) survey found cases in 22 states in which local services had been assumed by states. In 16 of those states, services dealing with the legal system were involved. A striking feature of survey findings is the extent to which states had assumed responsibility for the larger social-welfare functions, health care and welfare, during the 1960s and 1970s.

One way to summarize the states' pattern of fiscal relations with their localities is to place states in a matrix according to revenue raising and expenditure roles. In the matrix, states are considered centralized in either their expenditures or revenue-raising system if the state government total exceeds 50 percent of the state/local total; otherwise, they are considered decentralized.

Figure 9-3 presents the results of the centralization test for 1987. The results show 14 states where state expenditures and revenues exceeded 50 percent, up from 10 states in 1977 and 9 states in 1983. Even more impressive is the sharp reduction in the number of states that had both decentralized revenue-raising and expenditure systems. These dropped from 23 in 1977 to 11 in 1983 to 8 in 1987. The twin centralizing tugs of states assuming proportionately more of the expenditure areas and revenue raising are readily apparent; even where states leave expenditures at the local level, they tend to collect the revenue themselves and transfer funds to their localities.

FIGURE 9-3
*Expenditure and Revenue-Raising Centralization, 1987*

| Revenue-Raising Responsibility | Expenditure Responsibility: Centralized | Expenditure Responsibility: Decentralized |
|---|---|---|
| Centralized | Alaska<br>Connecticut<br>Delaware<br>Hawaii<br>Kentucky<br>Maine<br>Massachusetts<br>North Dakota<br>Rhode Island<br>South Carolina<br>South Dakota<br>Utah<br>Vermont<br>West Virginia | Alabama<br>Arizona<br>Arkansas<br>California<br>Idaho<br>Illinois<br>Indiana<br>Iowa<br>Louisiana<br>Maryland<br>Michigan<br>Minnesota<br>Mississippi<br>Missouri<br>Montana<br>Nevada<br>New Jersey<br>New Mexico<br>North Carolina<br>Ohio<br>Oklahoma<br>Oregon<br>Pennsylvania<br>Tennessee<br>Virginia<br>Washington<br>Wisconsin<br>Wyoming |
| Decentralized | | Colorado<br>Florida<br>Georgia<br>Kansas<br>Nebraska<br>New Hampshire<br>New York<br>Texas |

SOURCE: Calculated by authors from U.S. Department of Commerce, *Government Finances in 1986–87* (Washington: GPO, 1988).

In summary, the structure of state-local fiscal relations will often determine the level of state assistance to local governments. States that are revenue-centralized and expenditure-decentralized will rely heavily on grants-in-aid to get the revenue in the coffers of the local governments that supply the services. On the other hand, those states that are more centralized on the expenditure side (effectively those that pick up responsibilities that elsewhere are performed at the local level) need to provide less aid to their local governments.

### *State Response to Federal Cuts*

A major question related to state aid to local governments is the impact of reduced federal assistance to states. Have states cut back on state aid to localities, passing the burden of the reductions in federal aid on to local governments, or have they relied on their own-source revenues to replace federal funds?

A traditional view of states' role in fiscal federalism is that they will reduce aid to local governments when they themselves face revenue shortfalls. Evidence for this position is found upon examining census data on state aid to local governments during recessionary periods in the early 1980s.[17] A constraint on this conclusion is the inability of census data to distinguish federal pass-through revenue from state own-source revenue.

More recent evidence indicates that state assistance to local governments from general state funds has been increasing, to some extent offsetting lost federal assistance. Total state spending for aid to local governments grew 62 percent between 1982 and 1988. During this same period, state general-fund spending, for all activities, increased only 47 percent. While increased education funding is a major reason for the growth in state aid, the growth also appears to be a response to the decreasing federal support in social services and urban programs. Rather than simply reducing services in response to the federal retrenchment, states have used their own revenues to maintain levels of program services. States appear to be increasing their effort to aid local government and that aid is assuming a larger share of state budgets.[18] One recent analysis on this question supports the argument that states have been using their own-source revenue to replace lost federal funds. State aid was found to replace federal reductions almost dollar for dollar.[19] It seems plausible that state governments, in their new role in the federal system, are reacting differently to changes in fiscal fortunes and are less likely to cut local aid in times of fiscal austerity.

### *State Mandates on Local Government*

State mandates on local government are much more numerous and undoubtedly just as intrusive as those of the federal government on states. Local officials accuse state governors and legislatures of insensitivity to the costs of those mandates, especially when the local officials must use their tax base to fund services someone else takes credit for. In addition, mandating reorders local priorities just as surely as do federal mandates.[20] Fourteen states have enacted legislation to provide reimbursement for their mandates on local government; a U.S. General Accounting Office study, however, found those laws to be widely ignored or circumvented and that they had only a limited impact on reducing the burden of mandates on localities.[21]

Two key factors that seem to make reimbursement requirements effective at the state level are public initiation of the requirement through a referendum or a constitutional amendment and the existence of a healthy fiscal climate in the state. Some of the difficulties with mandate reimbursement legislation are determining the real cost of mandates, determining what the locality would have done absent the mandate, and determining whether to reimburse jurisdictions that were complying before the mandate was in force. Alternatives to mandate reimbursement legislation include block grants or general aid, legislative fiscal notes on bills that impose mandates, and annual reports estimating total costs of mandates on lower levels of government. The latter two proposals are attempts to increase legislative sensitivity to the costs of mandates.

## THE FUTURE OF INTERGOVERNMENTAL REVENUES

Federal aid to state and local governments has been crowded out in a period in which competition for scarce federal revenues has intensified. The 1981 Tax Act (Kemp–Roth dramatically reduced personal income taxes and indexed tax brackets and the value of the standard deduction and personal exemptions for inflation. The 1986 Tax Reform Act reduced the number of brackets to three (15, 28, 33), while broadening the tax base. The net effect of these changes was to make the federal personal income tax less elastic, reducing the rate of real growth in income tax revenue. The popular public policy of "no tax increases" (although ignored on occasion) has curbed government revenue growth.

The passage of the Gramm–Rudman–Hollings Act mandated federal budget deficit reductions on a forced-march schedule. With Congress tying itself to spending targets, the opportunity costs associated with each program became crystal clear. A spending increase for one program meant a corresponding decrease elsewhere. State and local governments lost out to other interests as Congress began to cannibalize federal programs to meet budget deficit targets.

The 1980s will be remembered as the decade in which the United States recognized that its domestically produced products were failing to compete in a global economy and had to deal with a large trade deficit. This lack of competitiveness meant that U.S. industries were using up greater resources than their competitors to produce goods. Lower productivity has meant a reduction in buying power of workers' wages and a struggle for business to reduce their production costs. This financial squeeze felt by families and firms has created a pressure on governments at all levels to reduce the tax burdens on both and reduce social welfare activity.

Where much of federal assistance has been spurred by considerations of distributing federal wealth to less-fortunate individuals and less-developed regions of the country, this period of flagging productivity has spawned a retrenchment of what had become an accepted federal role. Programs like UDAG, CDBG, and EDA have been eliminated or greatly reduced. States are now playing the leading role in efforts to stimulate economic activity through specific programs.

The primary constraints on state spending, however, including aid to local governments, continue to be those that have always existed: limited fiscal diversity, volatility in state economies, and regional competition. In the 1980s, many states enjoyed economic growth. New programs have been initiated, particularly those intended to help their citizens and industries become more competitive in a global economy. But very few states have been able to sustain this growth without interruption. Commodity-based state economies are still subject to depressed market prices. States with energy-based economies showed their economic and fiscal vulnerability to larger economic forces when their economies collapsed with the collapse of OPEC pricing targets. The Midwest states are still highly dependent on the ability of manufacturing firms to compete in global markets, and the Northeast states are now suffering budget deficits after a decade of being the envy of other states. It appears that no state is immune from changes in economic fortunes that quickly turn prosperity and revenue surpluses into austerity and budget deficits.

If domestic program leadership indeed has shifted to the states, we may see a continuation of new state initiatives in education, infrastructure development, and health care. Progress will be uneven and will depend on political leadership at the state level and on state economic conditions. State experiments may, however, prove an example for federal initiatives in the future, when and if the federal government gets its fiscal house in order.

Federal control, through mandates and earmarking and formula changes, will continue and perhaps become stiffer as congressional committees fight over the allocation of diminishing federal resources. The ability of the states and local governments to fight back against arbitrary federal actions will depend upon how well they are politically organized.

Finally, equalization may become increasingly important at the state level. The 1989 Texas Supreme Court decision in *Rodriguez*, declaring the Texas system of educational finance unconstitutional, may signal a renewed attention to intrastate equalization.[22] Whether this eventually leads to a greater concern for interstate equalization in Congress is debatable. It is more likely that the federal government will continue to address the equalization issue through categorical grants to the states for individuals rather than more general aid to jurisdictions.

## *NOTES*

1. John Shannon and James Edwin Kee, "The Rise of Competitive Federalism," *Public Budgeting and Finance* 9 (Winter 1989): 3.

2. Richard P. Nathan, "America's Changing Federalism," in Anthony Kin, ed., *The American Political System* rev. (Washington: The American Enterprise Institute, forthcoming).

3. Richard and Peggy Musgrave, *Public Finance in Theory and Practice* (New York: McGraw-Hill, 1976), 626–27; see also George F. Break, *Financing Government in a Federal System* (Washington: The Brookings Institution, 1980), 76–87.

4. Steven F. Rhoads, *The Economist's View of the World* (New York: Cambridge Univ. Press, 1985), p. 67.

5. Roy Bahl, "The Design of Intergovernmental Transfers in Industrialized Countries," *Public Budgeting Finance* 6 (Winter 1986): 3–22.

6. This concept was first noted by Phillip Monypenny, "Federal Grants-in-Aid to State Governments: A Political Analysis," *National Tax Journal* 13 (March 1960): 1–16.

7. George F. Break, *Financing Government in a Federal System* (Washington: The Brookings Institution, 1980), table 3–1, p. 74.

8. A concise discussion of the economic impacts of grants by types is found in *Federal–State–Local Fiscal Relations* (Washington: U.S. Department of the Treasury, 1985), chapter 7.

9. Economic analysis suggests that every dollar of unmatched, unconstrained aid should result in 10 cents of additional community spending on governmental services as

would any other increase in community income. Federal grants, however, with certain design and matching requirements generate between 20 and 40 cents of additional state and local spending, with block grants least stimulative and categorical grants with high matching requirements the most stimulative. The degree of stimulation is found to decline, however, over time. See *Federal–State–Local Fiscal Relations,* pp. 162–66.

10. This section draws heavily on Shannon and Kee, "The Rise of Federalism," and Victor Miller, "A History of Federal Grants-in-Aid to State and Local Governments" (Washington: Federal Funds Information System, 1988).

11. For a discussion of fiscal-capacity indicators and the index created by the Advisory Commission on Intergovernmental Relations, see John Kincaid, "Fiscal Capacity and the Tax Effort of States," *Public Budgeting and Finance* 9 (Autumn 1989): 1.

12. "House Hypocrisy," *Wall Street Journal,* October 27, 1989, A16.

13. U.S. Advisory Commission on Intergovernmental Relations, *Regulatory Federalism: Policy, Process, Impact and Reform* (Washington: ACIR, 1984).

14. The implications of the Supreme Court's decision in *Garcia v. San Antonio Mass Transit District,* 469 U.S. 528 (1985) is that Congress is free to interpret the commerce clause of the Constitution as empowering it to impose mandates on states and localities without court interference and without ties to federal funding.

15. See Office of State and Local Finance, Department of the Treasury, *Federal–State–Local Fiscal Relations* (Washington: GPO, 1985), pp. 103–18.

16. U.S. Advisory Commission on Intergovernmental Relations, *Recent Trends in Federal and State Aid to Local Governments,* (Washington: ACIR, 1980).

17. Steven Gold and Brenda Erikson, "State Aid to Local Governments in the 1980s," Legislative Finance Paper 63 (Denver: National Conference of State Legislatures, 1988).

18. National Association of State Budget Officers, "State Aid to Local Governments" (Washington: NASBO, 1989).

19. Helen F. Ladd, "State Aid to Local Governments in the 1980s," paper prepared for 1989 APPAM Conference.

20. A study of state mandates for local governments identified 2,632 individual mandates on New York counties alone. See "Mandate Reimbursement for New York" *State–Local Issue Briefs* (Albany, N.Y.: Commission on Intergovernmental Relations, 1988).

21. U.S. General Accounting Office, *Legislative Mandates, State Experiences Offer Insights for Federal Action,* HRD-88-75 (Washington: GAO, 1988).

22. David Maraniss, "Texas Schools' Financing Ruled Unconstitutional," *Washington Post,* October 3, 1989.

# 10
# Local Fiscal Capacity

Freda S. Johnson and Diana L. Roswick

Fiscal capacity can generally be defined as the ability of a jurisdiction to generate taxes and other revenues from its own sources. Fiscal capacity is critical to all local jurisdictions, large and small, for local governments need financial resources to carry out their functions. To make any financial policy decision—whether the decision entails potential new bond issues, new operating programs, or extensions of existing programs—a key step in the decision-making process is an assessment of the fiscal capacity available to support that decision.

In analyzing local fiscal capacity, several points must be kept in mind. First, local governments are creatures of a state and the parameters of a community's fiscal capacity are defined by the state constitution, statutes, and regulations. One key difference between the fiscal capacity of states and that of localities is scope; the state has at its disposal—at least in the first instance—all the tax and revenue bases within its boundaries. A locality has only those that have been granted to it by the state constitution or legislature.

Second, differences in fiscal capacity among types of governmental entities may reflect their different roles. General-purpose governments, such as counties and cities, usually have more fiscal capacity than limited-function jurisdictions, such as school districts, sanitation districts, library districts, or park districts. This disparity reflects the broader service responsibilities of the typical general-purpose government and is based on its historical functions and state mandates. Certain types of special-function districts, most notably school districts, frequently receive substantial amounts of state aid and need to rely less on local resources to provide funds.

Third, even among similar types of jurisdictions the need for fiscal capacity is relative; different amounts will be required by different communities. Consequently, fiscal capacity should be evaluated in the context of a jurisdiction's economic role, the extent of its operating and capital needs, and the cost of service delivery. A local government providing a broad range of services will typically need more fiscal capacity than one that has a more limited role. All else being equal, a community that is growing rapidly and that must make substantial capital improvements is likely to need more fiscal capacity than a mature community with a well-maintained infrastructure already in place.

Many variables should be considered when measuring local fiscal capacity, most of which are interrelated. Fiscal capacity stems directly from a community's tax and revenue base, and most measures of fiscal capacity attempt to quantify this base. The base consists of forms of economic activity—income flows, transactions, and asset holdings—that constitute the real or potential objects of taxation or charges. There are, however, certain aspects of the tax and revenue base that cannot be measured directly but must be imputed from other types of measures. Moreover, it is impossible to understand the tax and revenue base without understanding the economic and sociological framework within which that base exists.

Consequently, some measures of fiscal capacity will be economic and socioeconomic in nature. Various legal and practical limitations on obtaining access to the tax and revenue bases must also be addressed; these present very real constraints that significantly reduce the ability of a community to use its resources.

In measuring fiscal capacity, the need for current data cannot be emphasized enough. Because fiscal capacity should be analyzed over time, data that are available at regular intervals over many years are the most useful. Equally important is the need for information to be presented in a consistent manner from one reporting period to the next, or at least for inconsistencies to be clearly spelled out and taken into account. One of the key reasons for evaluating measurements of fiscal capacity over time is to use past trends to make informed judgments about the future. Such judgments are likely be more accurate if data are consistent.

We have offered above a general definition of fiscal capacity and a context for the discussion of local fiscal capacity. Fiscal capacity can, however, have a range of more specific definitions in other contexts. In each case, the definition of fiscal capacity will be tailored to the needs of the users, the perspective of the analysts, and the nature of the data available.

Much of the research on governmental fiscal capacity has focused on the relative fiscal capacity of various entities. One key purpose of such studies is to develop a standard measure that can be used to determine the need of each entity for fiscal assistance, so that aid can be distributed equitably. Studies of fiscal capacity have also been used to satisfy other informational needs of governmental policymaking bodies, as well as for academic purposes.[1]

The purpose of this chapter is to serve as both an introduction to fiscal capacity and a guide to a local jurisdiction that desires to assess and understand its fiscal resources. The focus is on the individual community and its ability to provide resources to support its particular set of operating and capital programs. Thus, the definition of a "good" level of fiscal capacity will vary with the nature of the jurisdiction and its changing circumstances over the years.

This chapter does not address issues of equity, nor does it attempt to find a means to rank all communities in terms of their relative fiscal capacity. Therefore, we try neither to develop nor to advocate the use of one standard formula that can be consistently applied to all jurisdictions. Because a community's fiscal capacity is the sum of a complex set of factors that include constantly changing, nonquantifiable components such as voter tolerance of tax-rate increases, such formulas by necessity leave out certain key variables and are only valid for a very limited time. The goal here is to identify factors that are typically used in assessing fiscal capacity and to discuss how they are used in such analysis.

## *THE LOCAL ECONOMY*

To understand the tax and revenue base from which a community's fiscal capacity derives, the economic context in which this base exists must be understood. First, housing values and other property values reflect local economic conditions. Second, other components of the tax and revenue base, particularly income and sales taxes, are sensitive to economic cycles. Finally, the ability of residents to pay any tax or user charge depends on their assets and income. A poor community has less ability to raise revenues than a wealthy one; a community where virtually all residents are employed has a higher ability to pay than one suffering from double-digit unemployment.

The relationship between a community's economic base and its fiscal capacity is complex. To fully evaluate the economic framework in which a community must function, the economy of the entire area where the community is located should be examined. Since many residents of a community will work outside the community, some of a jurisdiction's income streams and wealth levels will be integrally tied to the economic bases of other communities.

A key concept to keep in mind when examining the economic base is the distinction between assets and income. With the exception of property taxation, local governments do not tax assets, and ultimately even property taxes are paid from the income streams of the property owners. In evaluating fiscal capacity, one must understand the derivation of the community's income. Some communities have economies that export income earned within its boundaries, while other communities have economies that import income. Typically, a central city will export a substantial amount of income earned from employment within its boundaries while a suburb will import income earned elsewhere. This is why, for most communities, the nature of the industrial and sector mix of their county or metropolitan area is more critical than the actual employment opportunities within the community's own boundaries.

Many measures can be used to evaluate the local economy. The discussion below will focus on five areas particularly pertinent to measuring fiscal capacity. These are (1) the employment base, (2) unemployment rates, (3) other measures of economic activity, (4) population trends, and (5) resident socioeconomic and housing characteristics.[2]

### *The Employment Base*

One way to understand the economic base to which a community's fiscal capacity is tied is to examine how the community's residents are employed, since it is from employment that most residents will earn their income. A key source of information on employment comes from the U.S. Bureau of the Census, which provides sector analyses of local employment bases in conjunction with the census taken every ten years.

More current sector analysis and certain additional detail on sector employment can be obtained from the Bureau of Economic Analysis (BEA). Due to differences in data collection and categorization, however, these figures are not directly comparable to census data and are not available for local jurisdictions below the county level.

The U.S. Bureau of the Census groups resident employment into fourteen general categories. These categories include construction, manufacturing, transportation, communications, retail trade, finance, insurance, real estate, and educational services, among others. The manufacturing category is further divided into durable goods and nondurable goods industries.

There are a number of other statistics that can be derived from U.S. Census data. The retentiveness ratio, developed by Moody's Investors Service, is one that is particularly useful. Retentiveness is the percentage of the labor force that both resides and works within an area. Retentiveness can help assess to what extent the fiscal capacity of a jurisdiction's residents is tied to economic bases outside the community's geographic boundaries. As might be expected, the retentiveness for states was very high, or 96 percent according to 1980 figures. It was relatively high for central cities—about 68 percent—but low for suburban cities—about 27 percent.

Generally, the more diverse a community's resident employment base, the less vulnerable that community's economy is to national recessions or cyclical problems within one particular industry. Those communities that in 1980 had above-average concentrations in durable goods manufacturing, in general, suffered more during the recession of the early 1980s than those with economies less reliant on manufacturing. How well a local economy fares in times of economic stress is also determined by its concentration in particular industry subsectors. For example, not all communities with heavy concentrations in durable goods manufacturing suffered severely; those dependent on automotive and steel concerns were hurt more than communities whose manufacturing was based in high technology. Thus, a broad sectoral analysis of the employment base must be supplemented by knowledge about the major area employers and the outlook for their industries.

Also important is an understanding of the changing context in which a locality's employment base exists. What is at one time a growth industry and a source of strength for an area may at another time be a vulnerability. Not that many years ago, the presence of automotive and steel industries was, on balance, an economic strength. Now a predominance of those industries tends to be viewed as a potential weakness. Similarly, with oil prices soaring in the mid and late 1970s, mineral-based economies were often viewed as strong. Since then, with oil price declines, conservation measures, and increased oil production, communities reliant on energy-based industries have suffered.

Many communities are trying to attract high-technology firms to revitalize their economic bases. It is unclear, however, whether "high tech" is the answer for everyone. Indeed, in some places, there are signs that an overconcentration of high-technology firms has created problems, in part because many of the computer-assembly and other technological jobs offer lower salaries than the old-line manufacturing jobs they may have replaced.

In the past, a local economy with a sizable service sector has generally been less vulnerable than others during recessionary periods. Experience will tell, however, whether this continues to be the case as the dominance of services increases in many communities. Moreover, the identity of the recipients of the services is critical; if the industries served are declining, then fewer services will be needed. While the presence of hospitals, governments, and universities is often a stabilizing factor, these also can be unfavorably affected by factors outside the community's control. For example, changes in Medicare and Medicaid reimbursement policies have resulted in the implementation of cost-control measures that often lead to a reduction in hospital staff. One benefit that large cities often have is a degree of diversity made possible by their size and their roles as regional trade and service centers. Conversely, a risk for some smaller cities is an over-reliance on one large employer or one type of industry. Smaller jurisdictions dependent on farming run into special problems, as farm product prices and land value have fluctuated. Smaller communities dependent on mineral-based economies often suffer more than the more diversified major city nearby.

### *Unemployment Rates*

Unemployment rates provide data that are useful for many purposes, including measuring the overall level of economic activity. Changes in unemployment rates may indicate the direction and extent of future changes in both resident income levels and, over the longer term, wealth levels. Depending on its size and rate of increase, a rise in resident unemployment rates could be a cause for concern, as it is likely to foreshadow other unfavorable changes.

Unemployment statistics are available from the U.S. Bureau of Labor Statistics (BLS) on an annual as well as a monthly basis. Since 1980, the bureau has limited collection of unemployment data to cities with populations of 50,000 or greater, although recently it has begun to collect this data for communities with populations of at least 25,000. For other jurisdictions, unemployment data for the county in which they are located will need to be used, unless information is available from another source, such as the state.

Unemployment rates should always be analyzed in the context of labor-force trends. For example, if unemployment rates are stable but the size of the labor force is declining, then the unemployment rates in and of themselves are likely to be misleading. When using BLS unemployment data, it is important to note that there are frequent changes in "benchmarking"; that is, in how data are collected and manipulated. Such changes can create inconsistencies from one reporting period to the next.

### *Other Measures of Economic Activity*

The nature of the community will often determine which other economic indicators are appropriate to monitor. Levels of economic activity can be measured by the level of retail sales; the number of utility connections; the level of water consumption; the amount of trucking, freight, or waterborne cargo; the value added by manufacturing; the number of bank accounts and amount of bank deposits; the enrollment at institutions of higher learning; the number of tourists; and the commercial vacancy rates, among others. One indicator of economic activity that is very useful and available for most communities is annual data on the value, number, and type of building permits. Such figures provide a sense of the level of construction activity and the potential increase in the property-tax base that will result from this construction.

Any measure of economic activity that is used should be carefully analyzed. For example, increases in utility connections may reflect a new influx of population or may be due to connecting water and sewer lines to a previously unserved area. Increases in water consumption may be attributable to increased industrial activity or just to a long hot summer, requiring more air conditioning and lawn watering. Enrollment increases at the local college or university may mean that the institution has become more competitive or that more people are attending school because of decreased employment opportunities.

### *Population Trends*

Population trends are often a key to a variety of other trends. A community with a growing population is more likely to see growth in the tax and revenue base than one in which population is declining. Presumably, a trend of increasing population is reflecting new job opportunities and attractive housing stock, etc. Population can also grow, however, because of other factors, most notably annexation. Annexation activity added almost a quarter of a million persons and more than 750 square miles to municipalities in 1985 alone.[3]

### *Resident Socioeconomic and Housing Characteristics*

The U.S. Bureau of the Census publishes socioeconomic and housing data that provide information about the characteristics of a community's residents and the nature of its housing stock. The most commonly used of these statistics are probably data on income. Income levels of residents—which can be calculated on a per capita, per family, or per household basis—provide an indication of the overall ability of a community's residents to pay taxes and charges. Measures of the distribution of income provide an indication of whether the economic status of residents is homogeneous or disparate, while the portion of the population below poverty level indicates the size of the dependent population.

The median value of owner-occupied housing can serve as a proxy for measuring income and overall wealth levels. Other housing data provide additional information about the nature of a particular community. For example, data on the proportion of housing built prior to World War II and the proportion built since the last census can indicate how recently the community was developed and the relative age of the housing stock.

In addition to income levels and housing characteristics, other characteristics of a community's residents are important. The age of the population, their education, and their skill levels indicate how many are of working age and the types of jobs they are able to fill. This is useful in assessing the income that the population might potentially earn and their ability to adapt to changing job markets. It can also be key to firms' location decisions in that it provides an evaluation of the potential labor pool.

Because of differences in the cost of living and other factors, resident socioeconomic and housing characteristics should be evaluated in the context of regional norms. For example, based on 1980 U.S. Census data, the median family income was $21,933 in the Far West, $17,136 in the Southeast, and $19,011 in the Mideast. A family with an income of $22,000 would have been average if they lived in California, but above average if they lived in South Carolina or Pennsylvania.[4] The location within a state also makes a difference, because urban areas tend to have higher incomes than rural areas.

Data measuring income and wealth levels must also be considered in the context of the community. For example, a university town typically will have below-average per-capita income and an above-average percentage of the population below the poverty line because of the large number of students. This has different implications for fiscal capacity than would be the case for a community with the same income levels but made up primarily of families in an area with high unemployment rates.

One of the difficulties in evaluating resident socioeconomic and housing data is that most figures are available only at ten-year intervals, when the U.S. Census is undertaken. For example, the lack of availability of more current, nationally consistent housing data can create difficulties in evaluating a community's housing stock. Census data on the true worth of residential properties can be particularly problematic for areas such as New York City where housing values rose dramatically throughout much of the 1980s—in many cases more than doubling since the 1980 Census. Current statistics from local real-estate concerns are often more realistic. Since the method of data collection is not consistent across the country, however, caution should be exercised when comparing communities in different regions or states.

The BEA provides more current and more frequent data on personal income for regions, states, metropolitan statistical areas, and counties. Although such data are not comparable to census data because of differences in sampling methodologies and definitional categories, these statistics can provide additional information that is useful in analyzing the economic context in which a smaller jurisdiction exists.

## *THE TAX AND REVENUE BASE*

A community's economic base encompasses all its resources. The tax and revenue base—the direct source of a jurisdiction's fiscal capacity—defines which of these resources are potentially available for the community to use to finance its needs. The components of a community's tax and revenue base can be classified into four broad categories. These are the property-tax base, the sales-tax and excise-tax base, the income-tax base, and the user-charge-and-fee base. Although many jurisdictions benefit from sizable amounts of federal and state aid, such aid is not included here because it is not generated from the jurisdiction's own resources.

In some ways, the various tax and revenue bases are overlapping and duplicative. That is, taxpayers in a particular community have a finite ability to pay for government services and capital programs on the one hand and for their private consumption on the other. The ability to pay a property tax, an income tax, a sales tax, and/or a user charge stem from the same asset base and income streams.[5] This is why, for some studies of fiscal capacity, one figure, such as per capita income, is used to represent a rough estimate of the whole of an entity's fiscal capacity. The purpose of this chapter, however, is to analyze separately each potential form of taxation in order to assist local governments in weighing which aspect of fiscal capacity would be most appropriate for a particular purpose.[6]

### *The Property-Tax Base*

Most local governments have an ability to levy taxes on property. Because of its near-universal availability, property-tax-base data are frequently relied upon for many purposes, including determining the distribution of state aid among school districts and other local jurisdictions. In analyzing the property-tax base for purposes of evaluating fiscal capacity, one must examine the property-tax base over a period of time, preferably at least five years.

To evaluate property-tax-base trends, the base must first be quantified and then viewed from two perspectives. The first is the base's economic foundation and the forces that will be affecting property values. Key to analysis from this perspective, of course, are the structure and dynamics of the underlying economy. The second perspective is one of defining which types of property are assessed for taxation purposes and how these assessments are made. Ideally, in analyzing tax-base trends, the sources of all changes leading to the net change in aggregate tax-base figures should be identified. Growth in property valuation can be attributable to the addition of new property, to the rehabilitation of existing property, to increases in the economic worth of property from such factors as the community's proximity to employment centers, and to inflation. Conversely, declines in property valuation may reflect elimination of properties from the tax roll, depreciation of existing property such as industrial plants, or a general decline in the economic worth of property due to the condition of the local economy. Both growth and decline can also be due to changes in the types of property that are included in the tax base and how these are valued for taxation purposes.

### *Quantifying the Property-Tax Base*

The worth of property can be quantified using assessed valuation, equalized valuation or full valuation figures. Assessed valuation, which is available on an annual basis for virtually all communities, is a legal measure of the property-tax base. The assessed valuation of a particular property is the value legally assigned to a property by the local (or in some cases the state) assessor for tax purposes.

Equalized assessed valuations are local assessment figures that have been adjusted, typically by the state, to establish consistency within and among various localities.

In some states, assessed valuation or equalized valuation may be equal to full-market valuation, which is the most comprehensive property-value measure. Estimations of full value (that is, at what price the property would sell were it to be sold in the free market) are typically done through statistical studies entailing various sampling methodologies, in an effort to estimate the market value of property in a particular jurisdiction. Full-value figures should, at least theoretically, be comparable among states. In part because of differences in sampling methodologies, however, this is not the case. Moreover, estimates of full valuation—as well as of assessed valuation and equalized valuation—reflect the value only of property that is selected for inclusion in these figures. This is why the definitional aspect of property-value figures, discussed later in this section, is so important.

When examining the property-tax base for the purpose of evaluating fiscal capacity, the figures that should be relied upon in most cases are those from assessed valuation or equalized valuation—whichever is used for taxation purposes. Although full valuation seldom measures the actual valuation that can be taxed, it is also an important measure even with its imperfections. It provides a better sense of total property wealth, for example, and a community's true ability to pay property taxes for operating or debt—if one must use only one measure—than do assessed or equalized assessed valuation figures.

### *The Economic Foundation of the Property-Tax Base*

An understanding of the nature of a community's property-tax base and its relationship to the local economy can be obtained by determining what portion of the property-tax base is represented by different types of property and by examining the major taxpayers. Real property comprises the overwhelming share of valuation for most communities, representing approximately 90 percent of all locally assessed property valuation nationwide. This percentage has been increasing, reflecting the enormous escalation of real-estate values as well as a trend toward reducing reliance on personal property for taxation purposes.[7]

Real property can be classified by use. Most real property will be used for either residential, commercial, or industrial purposes, although the property-tax bases of rural communities often have a sizable agricultural component, while those in mineral-based areas have substantial oil, gas, and other mineral properties.

In general, diversity in the kinds of property adds strength to a property-tax base. There are many affluent suburbs across the nation, however, that are predominantly residential and have extremely strong tax bases. The property wealth of these communities derives from the high income of its residents, most of whom derive their incomes from sources outside the community.

Key to evaluating the residential component of the property-tax base will be the quality and nature of the housing stock. Some of the variables mentioned earlier—such as the median value of owner-occupied housing and the distribution of the housing stock between new and old housing—will provide a foundation for this analysis. Also of significance are the types of housing being built as well as the amount of land remaining for further residential development. The quality of life, as viewed by residents and outsiders, is also important. Is this a community with a good school system and other amenities that will continue to attract residents and increase property values? Or is it a community that is perceived as having problems and is unattractive to potential newcomers?

Finally, one will want to know the identity of large employment centers and the community's proximity to them—and this is one of the many areas where the link between the tax and the employment bases is critical—because the value of residential property will very often depend on the health of the areawide economy. If a new large employer locates in a nearby city, demand for local housing may increase. Conversely, if a large employer closes down, this may reduce the demand for and the value of housing in the area, particularly if the community's employment base stems primarily from that one employer.

For communities with sizable industrial or commercial sectors, the opening or closing of a major facility even more directly affects the community's property-tax base. When a large taxpayer is also a large employer, the community is doubly vulnerable—it relies on the company both for the company's share of property taxes and for the income the company provides to its residents.

If the company represents a large share of a community's tax base but is not a major employer, as is usually the case with a power plant, the impact of the loss of that taxpayer will depend on the community's overall tax and revenue structure. The loss of a large taxpayer will often require the community to increase the property-tax rate in order to maintain the same level of services unless alternative revenue sources are available. Having one large employer or several large employers all in the same industry increases the vulnerability of the property-tax base to any declines in that type of business. Therefore, the more diverse the commercial and industrial sector, the more property-tax-base stability one is likely to see.

### *Defining the Property-Tax Base*

While the nature of the properties composing the tax base is critical, equally important is the relationship between the true worth of all property in a community and the valuation given to various properties for assessment purposes. In analyzing property-tax-base trends, one must keep in mind the arbitrary nature of many assessment standards and the periodic changes that are made in how various classes of property are valued for assessment purposes. Changes that can cause discontinuity in the comparability of assessed valuation figures from year to year should be taken into account. For example, just as with population trends, any evaluation of property-tax-base trends should be adjusted for the impact of annexations.

### *Properties Subject to Assessment*

Quite simply, a property that can be assessed is one that is not exempt from taxation, and therefore from assessment. Exemptions can take many forms.

First, certain classes of property will be exempt by state statute. Intangible personal property is rarely assessed due to the difficulties of obtaining information. In addition, communities in almost every state exempt certain types of tangible personal property from taxation. The most common types of personal-property exemptions are for household property and motor vehicles. In eight states—Illinois, Hawaii, Delaware, New Hampshire, New York, Pennsylvania, North Dakota, and South Dakota—virtually all tangible personal property is exempt from taxation.[8]

Second, in every community, some property will be tax-exempt because of the nature of the entity owning the property and the use to which the property is put. The most significant type of property in this category is property owned by governmental bodies and nonprofit organizations. A community that includes a large military base or university is likely to have a taxable property base that is smaller than its economic base. The City of Boston is an example of such a community because of its large number of educational institutions and its sizable health-care sector.

Third, assessed valuation figures for real property can be affected by exemptions that stem from social policies, such as providing tax relief to certain categories of residents. One of the most common types is the homestead exemption, whereby the assessed valuation of every homeowner's residential property is reduced by an amount that is typically determined by the state. More broad-based adjustments to assessed valuation can also be made to carry out social policy. In the Minneapolis–St. Paul metropolitan area, for example, 40 percent of the growth occurring since 1971 in a community's commercial and industrial property is shared with the other communities in the seven-county area. The community in which the commercial or industrial development has occurred thus directly benefits from only 60 percent of the additional valuation. This sharing of assessed valuation is seen as a way to compensate for the disparity in fiscal capacity among various jurisdictions.

Fourth, assessed valuation can be constrained by the use of exemptions to promote various economic development policies. To provide incentives to developers, many communities will either exempt property from taxation or abate taxes for some period of time. When evaluating fiscal capacity, a community must take into account the fact that these new projects will not add to assessed valuation in the immediate future.

Finally, although not a tax exemption, a related development tool that will have an impact on the availability of a community's assessed valuation for general taxing purposes is the use of tax-increment districts. This technique, which is an option to localities in 35 states, involves selecting a particular area in which development is desired and establishing a tax-increment district. The incremental valuation, while still a part of the community's total tax base, is restricted to the use of the tax-increment district. Thus, while providing fiscal capacity to fund a tax-increment program or set of projects, the incremental valuation does not provide fiscal capacity available for funding a community's general operations or non-tax-increment debt.

Before ending the discussion of exempt property, it should be noted that even though a governmental or nonprofit property is excluded from assessed valuation figures, a community may nevertheless be able to include the entity in its revenue base. Frequently some arrangement, typically so-called "in lieu of tax" payments, can be made to compensate the locality at least partially for the fact that it cannot assess and therefore cannot tax. Hence, even if an entity is not included in assessed valuation figures, its property base can still contribute to a community's fiscal capacity. Furthermore, governments can often tap such entities through the use of user charges and fees from which they are not exempt.

### *Assessment Practices*

Assessment practices vary widely both among states and, from a practical (if not a legal) viewpoint, even within a state. When examining assessed valuation trends in the context of evaluating fiscal capacity, one should keep in mind the following points.

First, appraisal procedures and the timing of reappraisals can affect assessed valuation enormously. Property assessments often lag behind true market value. In some states, individual properties are reappraised annually, while in others, only periodically. One of the most extreme cases is New York, where some property has not been reassessed for decades. The timing of reassessments has a significant impact on equity among properties within the same jurisdiction. If two homes have the same market value, but only one of them has been reassessed recently, the owner of the reassessed home will be required to pay higher property taxes despite the fact that the true value of the property is identical to that of his or her neighbor's. Continual lack of reassessment over the years makes it increasingly difficult to reestablish equity by reassessment, for such reassessment will result in a substantial shift in how the property-tax burden is distributed. Clearly, regular reassessment is preferable.

Second, although assessed value is intended to have some prescribed relationship to the full value of the property in question, in some instances full market value is not the method for setting assessment levels. For example, in most states, with the notable exception of Texas, assessments of mineral property are based on how much is extracted from the ground, not on the market value of the reserves. Farmland value is often based on some measure of soil productivity rather than the estimated resale value of the land.

Third, different categories of property are often assessed at different rates. It is not uncommon to find that residential property is assessed at a rate that is lower—relative to its full value—than commercial and industrial property, in effect shifting a greater portion of the tax burden to the business sector. While such discrepancies can benefit the majority of the taxpayers (typically homeowners), it can also discourage new businesses from locating in the area, particularly if assessment practices in neighboring communities are more favorable.

Fourth, growth in assessed value can be limited by state law. For example, in California during 1978, assessed valuation was "rolled back" to 1975 levels. At the same time, the future growth in assessed valuation of existing properties was limited to no more than 2 percent per year. In Iowa, local assessments statewide are allowed to increase in aggregate only by 4 percent; any further increases are rolled back. Under constraints such as those found in California and Iowa, the fiscal capacity provided by a jurisdiction's property-tax base may not grow as fast as the economic value of that base. On the other hand, at least in Iowa's case, if assessments grow less than 4 percent, previously rolled back valuations can be returned to the base, thereby adding to fiscal capacity in years when the property-tax base growth is minimal.

Finally, even after all of the above considerations, assessed valuation figures cannot necessarily be taken at face value. Frequently included in these figures is valuation that is being contested by various taxpayers. Consequently, a portion of the existing as well as future valuation is subject to uncertainty.

### *Other Components of the Local Tax and Revenue Base*

Property taxes are typically the domain of local governments, and it is from this base that most local governments derive the major share of their fiscal capacity. There are other potential sources of fiscal capacity available to local communities, but in practice many of these other tax and revenue bases are used by the state, thereby preempting use by the locality. For example, the large mineral base of a county could provide a source of fiscal capacity; but states typically collect severance taxes on oil and mineral extraction, whereas localities do not. Most states also impose statewide sales and/or income taxes, and in these cases will be using some of the fiscal capacity provided by the sales and income bases of all communities. Nevertheless, local governments are relying increasingly on sources other than the property-tax base. In 1957, local governments derived about 87 percent of local tax revenues from property taxes; by 1985 this percentage had dropped to 74 percent.[9]

Most components of the tax and revenue base other than the property-tax base involve taxation of economic activity. Any evidence of economic activity implies a potential source of fiscal capacity. Of course, whether a community can turn this potential source into one that it can actually use depends on a variety of factors, some of which are discussed below and others of which are discussed in the section on fiscal constraints. The nature of the services the respective jurisdictions provide will help determine which components of local fiscal capacity are most appropriate. Water and sanitary districts, for example, may have the power to tax property but will often derive fiscal capacity primarily from their user-charge bases.

### *The Sales-Tax and Excise-Tax Base*

After the property-tax base, the second-largest local revenue base for many jurisdictions is the sales-tax and excise-tax base. An excise tax can be levied on the manufacture, sale, or consumption of a particular commodity or service. A broader definition of excise taxes would also include the various taxes on privileges, such as business licenses and fees. Like the property-tax base, how the sales-tax and excise-tax base is defined is key to how much fiscal capacity it actually provides.

The fiscal capacity stemming from a community's sales-tax and excise-tax base will depend on the nature of the community. For example, the retail sales base of a community with several large shopping malls will stem largely from the purchase of clothes, jewelry, and other tangible items; the sales-tax and excise-tax base of a resort community will stem primarily from hotel, motel, and restaurant use and related types of use or consumption; the sales-tax and excise-tax base of a community with a large commercial and industrial sector may stem in large part from a range of franchise activities.

Of the various types of excise taxes, the retail sales tax is, nationwide, the one that provides the largest source of fiscal capacity for local jurisdictions. In 1986, about 6,700 local jurisdictions in 28 states imposed a general retail sales tax.[10] Overall, general sales taxes accounted for a little over 10 percent of local government tax collection nationwide.

The underlying base for a retail sales tax may be extremely broad. In the most comprehensive sense, the retail sales base includes all goods sold at retail in a particular community. In reality, however, certain classes of goods are typically exempt from taxation. These generally include items that are viewed as basic necessities, such as food and drugs, but may also include other items, such as clothes. Usually the items included in the local retail sales base is determined at the state level.

Communities can also charge sales taxes selectively on specific items, either instead of a general broad-based tax or in addition to it. For example, taxes can be charged on purchases of tobacco products, alcoholic beverages, or gasoline and other types of motor fuel. Sales taxes on hotel and motel use, restaurant and food consumption, and amusements are particularly popular with resort communities and tourist areas, since some of the tax burden can be transferred to nonresidents.

Some localities tax insurance-policy premiums. Real-estate transfer taxes are used by others, often big cities. One of the most common types of sales taxes is on the consumption of utility services such as telecommunications, gas, and electricity provided by private utilities. This is a valuable tax base, because although utility usage varies with weather conditions and economic cycles, most residents and businesses need some basic level of utility services. In addition to various classes of exemptions, the size of the retail sales-tax base may also be restricted to transactions below a specific dollar amount. For example, the City of Peoria, Illinois, had a purchase tax on transactions of $500 or less until just recently. A limit such as this can provide fiscal resources to a locality while discouraging residents from buying large-outlay items such as automobiles or major appliances outside the city's geographic limits.

Increasingly there has been consideration of including services in the sales-tax base. As postindustrial economies become more service-oriented, this potential source of fiscal capacity grows. As with a tax on consumer goods, which services are included is critical to determining the amount of fiscal capacity available. Services ranging from haircuts and dry cleaning to legal counseling and financial advice can be taxed.

Sales and other excise taxes are very sensitive to economic trends, and the fiscal capacity provided by such tax bases will fluctuate. Whenever possible, sales-tax-base and excise-tax-base activity should be analyzed in relation to state, regional, and national trends. For example, if the growth in retail sales in a particular jurisdiction has declined but at a slower rate than that of the state or the nation, the decline in local retail sales activity is more likely reflecting the impact of a cyclical condition than a fundamental change in the locality's retail sales base.

The impact of economic cycles on a community's sales-tax and excise-tax base will in part reflect the composition of that base. A sales-tax base heavily reliant on so-called "big ticket" items such as furniture and cars will be more vulnerable to economic downturns than one that is more diverse. Hotel, motel, and amusement taxes are more likely to be sensitive to economic cycles than utility taxes. Utility taxes are subject to other forces, however, such as the breakup of the American Telegraph and Telephone Company and changes in the cost of gas and heating oil. In implementing any new tax or fee—but particularly a sales or excise tax—a jurisdiction needs to assess the ability of residents and others to avoid the tax. For example, consumers may attempt to avoid retail sales tax by keeping transactions on a cash basis, making enforcement of the tax more difficult. Consumers can also purchase many items elsewhere with relative ease; consequently, implementation of a new sales tax may result in loss of some of the sales-tax base to other jurisdictions. This risk is sometimes moderated by agreements with neighboring jurisdictions to charge, when feasible, sales tax based on the place of residence, rather than on the place of the transaction. Jurisdictions might also charge a use tax based on where the item is used rather than on where it is purchased.

The U.S. Bureau of the Census publishes data every five years on the number of retail establishments, the number of retail employees, and the value of retail sales. The sales data should be adjusted for inflation to assess whether growth has been real or nominal. Obviously, more current figures are preferable. If a state charges a sales tax, this data may be readily available from state sources.

Although the above discussion has focused primarily on retail sales and related tax bases, other types of excise taxes are very important to some localities. For example, many jurisdictions in the State of Washington rely heavily on business franchise taxes. Rapidly growing communities across the nation frequently derive a substantial amount of fiscal capacity from various building permits and fees.

### *The Income-Tax Base*

Both personal and business income are potential tax bases for most communities, although less than one-third of the states allow localities to tap these bases. The economic activity that has generated these income streams can come from the community's own economic base or, as is often the case with resident income, from neighboring economic bases. When a jurisdiction is permitted to charge income taxes, the tax base is likely to be limited to personal income. Although business-income taxes are an option for some jurisdictions, local business taxes more commonly take the form of license and privilege taxes.[11]

The personal-income-tax base is typically shared with the state and that base is often linked to the state definition of income for state taxation purposes. In states that allow local taxation of personal income, the tax base may be further limited to salaries, wages, and other earned income. A selected number of localities charge local employers a payroll tax, which, if passed on to employees, in effect becomes a personal income tax. Nationwide, income taxes account for approximately 6 percent of all local government tax resources.[12]

The localities that have personal income taxes frequently tax those who both live and work within the community's boundaries at a higher level than those who are employed in the community but live elsewhere. New York City, for example, has income-tax rates that are significantly lower for commuters than for residents. Attempts to raise nonresident income taxes have met with strong resistance. On the one hand, the lower nonresident tax rate can be justified by the more limited use of services by nonresidents and also by the role such tax rates might play in expanding the labor pool for local employers. On the other hand, it can be argued that the disparity is too large and that commuters are benefitting from more government services than they are paying for. Public officials are in essence put in the position of having to balance the needs of businesses and commuters with the needs of the local voters.

Like sales and other excise taxes, income taxes fluctuate with economic conditions. Increases in inflation and upturns in the economy will be captured more quickly by the income-tax base than by the property-tax base. On the other hand, high unemployment rates may be accompanied by declines in income-tax revenues. Understanding the sensitivity of a community's income-tax base to economic cycles will allow for a better assessment of the long-term fiscal capacity stemming from this base.

As with sales taxes, implementing a new income tax will raise concerns about competition with neighboring localities; imposition of an income tax may encourage residents to move to a jurisdiction without income taxes. Moreover, fewer localities have income or sales taxes than have property taxes, and implementation of a sales or income tax is generally viewed as a much more significant action than is an increase in the property tax.

### *User Charge and Fee Bases*

Reliance on user charges by local governments—that is, payments for the performance of specific goods and services benefitting those charged—has increased substantially in recent years. In part, this reflects the impact of increased vote concern about rising property taxes and related attempts to increase the efficiency of government operations. In addition, an equity argument can be made that the consumers that benefit from particular public services should pay for them.

Charges can be imposed on a range of goods and services. A city or other general-purpose government that provides many services will have the largest potential user-charge base. A special district such as a sanitation district or a park district will have a user-charge base limited to its own particular services. Certain other types of jurisdictions, most notably school districts, will have no significant user-charge base because the service they provide is considered a basic right, not dependent on ability to pay. Even jurisdictions with potentially large user-charge bases will not be able to charge for all services. It is generally not feasible, for example, to charge for police protection services, although other "basic" services such as wastewater treatment, water supply, and solid-waste collection are increasingly subject to a charge.

Typically, the revenues generated from a user-charge base only can be used to fund the service for which the charge has been imposed. These charges will pay for service delivery and system capital improvements. On the other hand, some jurisdictions rely on their user-charge bases to help finance general-fund expenditures. This is particularly attractive when an enterprise system provides services to tax-exempt entities or neighboring communities. In the latter case the user-charge base extends beyond a jurisdiction's geographic boundaries and the jurisdiction can use the monies paid by nonresidents to help finance basic resident services. But there are limits: perceived abuse by such a service supplier can lead to the creation of a new local supplier willing to charge reduced rates.

## *CONSTRAINTS*

A community may have a vibrant economy and a large revenue base, but if it is under legal or other constraints it will be unable to obtain full access to that base. Almost all local governments are subject to at least some state-imposed tax limitations and borrowing restrictions. Even if legal constraints are relatively few, such as with home-rule communities, a local jurisdiction is often subject to various political, competitive, and administrative constraints on its ability to realize its fiscal capacity.

### *Legal Constraints*

States impose a wide range of legal limitations on the taxing and borrowing activities of local governments. First, the state determines which components of a community's tax and revenue base are available to the different jurisdictions that serve the community and how the respective tax bases are to be defined. Second, the state has the authority to impose limits on tax rates, levies, fees and charges, spending, and even required year-end fund balances. Third, the state defines which resources can be pledged to debt retirement and sets debt limitations for both long-term and short-term borrowing. Finally, the state imposes certain procedural constraints, such as requiring public hearings before passage of a budget, prior approval of a new user charge by a state commission, or a voter referendum prior to imposition of a tax-rate increase. While these various limitations are intended to protect the taxpayers' interests, they almost always have an unfavorable impact on a jurisdiction's fiscal capacity.

Local jurisdictions across the country have operated under state-imposed limitations for years. There was increased focus on these limitations, however, with the taxpayer revolts of the late 1970s and early 1980s. As a result of taxpayer initiatives, additional limitations on local governments were implemented in a number of states. For example, Proposition 2½ in Massachusetts, the Headlee

Amendment in Michigan, and the Hancock Amendment in Missouri all limited the extent of annual increases in local property-tax levies. Proposition 2½ also capped the absolute dollar amount of tax levy to 2½ percent of full valuation, while the Hancock Amendment froze property-tax rates at the level in effect for 1982.

Most of the limitations implemented in recent years have been aimed at the property tax, which was and remains the major source of revenue for most local governments. In some instances, however, there were also implications for other revenue bases as well as for the ability of local governments to issue debt. For example, the Hancock Amendment also affected the ability to increase fees and charges related to enterprise systems. The Headlee Amendment made it virtually impossible to issue unlimited general-obligation tax debt without voter approval.

One of the most dramatic and possibly the most publicized voter-initiated tax-reform measures occurred with the enactment of Proposition 13 in California. Examining how California localities fared after the passage of Proposition 13 serves as a useful case study of how fiscal capacity can be constrained and how governments react.

### *Proposition 13*

Proposition 13, passed in 1978, imposed a range of limitations on revenue-raising and debt-issuing abilities of local governments in California. It rolled back assessed valuation to 1975 levels and limited annual increases in the valuation of existing property to 2 percent. It rolled back tax rates and established a maximum rate of $10 per $1,000 of assessed valuation. Proposition 13 also required noncharter cities to obtain voter approval for increases in utility and other special taxes. Finally, Proposition 13 prohibited the use of unlimited taxes for general-obligation bonds, unless the bonds were already authorized or outstanding.

Communities responded to Proposition 13 in various ways. Some of the most immediate responses included use of accumulated surpluses to balance current-year budgets, deferral of maintenance of capital facilities, and reductions in services and staffing levels. Over the longer term, however, these types of actions could not fully address problems of lost fiscal capacity. Those jurisdictions that had the authority to rely less heavily on property taxes started to do so. After the enactment of Proposition 13, localities across the state instituted a plethora of fees and charges. While California municipalities do not have the authority to impose an income tax, there has been an increasing reliance on the sales tax. Although charter cities have the greatest flexibility to diversify their revenue base, other types of jurisdictions have also diversified their revenues. For example, since the enactment of Proposition 13, more school districts have levied fees on developers. In some instances, the state provided new forms of financial assistance. For example, in 1986, the state established a lottery, which is being used to provide additional funds to school districts.

Although many California communities have reduced their reliance on property-tax revenues, the property-tax base has not been hurt as badly as many had initially feared. This is because economic factors have mitigated the impact of the limits placed on assessed valuation growth by Proposition 13. First, the state's economy has generally been favorable, resulting in much new development. Because new properties can be assessed on current market value, the valuation for these properties was not constrained by rollbacks and other limits imposed by Proposition 13. Second, the mobility of residents during the 1980s—and the consequent large number of resales of existing homes—helped many localities, since property can be reappraised at resale without regard to Proposition 13 limitations. Finally, inflation boosted the value of real estate, thereby substantially increasing the valuation added by new property and resales of existing property.

Because Proposition 13 made it impossible to issue general-obligation debt, local governments had to use alternative financing mechanisms. Many jurisdictions borrowed for capital purposes by entering into lease-purchase agreements with "shell" entities and selling certificates of participation evidencing an interest in these lease payments. The fiscal capacity supporting these forms of debt is significantly less than the unlimited full-faith-and-credit tax pledge securing general-obligation bonds. In 1986, a voter initiative allowed localities to again issue general-obligation debt. Since approval of two-thirds of the voters is required to issue such debt, however, local governments have persisted in using lease-rental and special-district financing for capital improvements.

The manner in which California localities responded to Proposition 13 illustrates several points. First, local jurisdictions' need for fiscal capacity cannot easily be reduced and if one source—in this case, the property-tax base—is reduced, localities will seek other sources, such as user charges or sales taxes. Second, local financial stress caused by a reduction in fiscal capacity places more pressure on the state either to give local jurisdictions new revenue-raising authority or provide direct aid from state sources (such as the lottery). Third, local jurisdictions can defer capital needs over the short term, but eventually infrastructure needs must be addressed. Borrowing will take new forms if old ones have been cut off.

Finally, the local economy plays a significant role in determining the extent of damage done by revenue and borrowing limits. In California's case, economic trends, on balance, have been favorable. A slowing of economic growth coupled with low inflation, however, may allow the full effects of Proposition 13 to be experienced. Moreover, the practice of assessing existing properties only at resale has created inequities that may be remedied by implementing additional rollbacks and placing further restrictions on assessed valuation. In a sense, the true power of Proposition 13 has not yet been fully tested. In addition, Proposition 13 was followed by the Gann Amendment, which imposes certain expenditure limits and requires revenues exceeding these limits to be rebated to taxpayers. Until recently modified, the Gann Amendment had begun to limit local fiscal capacity for a number of localities.

### *Political Constraints*

Requiring voter approval for new debt and tax rate increases is one of the most restrictive political as well as legal constraints that many localities face. This constraint is particularly strong if the required voter approval is greater than a simple majority. When such limits exist, local jurisdictions often attempt to avoid them if there is a legal method for doing so. For example, in Illinois, a number of local jurisdictions use public building commissions to issue debt on their behalf; this both avoids the need to obtain voter approval for the debt and also allows the jurisdiction to levy an unlimited tax to pay operating as well as debt-service costs of the facilities financed with the commission's bonds.

Even if a local government does not need voter approval for a tax increase or a new bond issue, voter sentiment is likely to play a key role in whether the tax increase is implemented or the bond issue is sold. While there may not be a formal constraint on taxing or borrowing, the political climate may create practical constraints.

Moreover, because the same taxpayers are usually paying property taxes to several different jurisdictions, an awareness of the taxing needs of other jurisdictions is critical. For example, the ability of a city to use the property-tax base may be effectively constrained if the local school district has just raised its taxes to fund a new program or build a new school. This is the reason that any evaluation of fiscal-capacity base must take into account the total tax burden in an area. In many instances, other bases in addition to the property-tax bases must be considered. For example, if a county has just imposed a sales tax, it may find it hard to increase property taxes the following year.

The existence of special districts only adds to the number of jurisdictions tapping the same tax base. For example, in Illinois, a community may be served not only by the city and the county, but also by several school districts, a park district, a library district, and a sanitation district. In New York, special districts provide a host of services to specific areas within a community. And a number of metropolitan areas—for example, Atlanta, Chicago, and San Francisco—have transit districts that cover wide geographic areas and encompass many communities. As the number of districts increases, the amount of revenue available to any one jurisdiction may decrease.

### *Competitive Constraints*

In addition to political constraints within one's own community, local governments also must be aware of the tax burdens and policies in neighboring communities, in the sense that communities compete for residents and for economic activity. As mentioned earlier, instituting a local sales tax when none of the neighboring communities have one may encourage some residents to purchase items elsewhere. High property taxes can deter residents and businesses from moving to a community. In fact, any sort of additional tax, fee, or user charge can have an economic impact and will often be evaluated in the context of what other communities do.

Because of the ability of residents and businesses to "vote with their feet" by moving elsewhere, jurisdictions with many different kind of taxes are particularly vulnerable to losing part of their tax and revenue base to neighboring jurisdictions. While tax policy is not the sole and not even the most important criterion in determining business location, it does play a role. Tax rates and tax composition will also be one of the factors taken into consideration when a family decides where its next home will be and whether it can afford a particular community. Any significant exodus of people and businesses from a jurisdiction that charges many taxes and fees can provide the impetus for an overhaul of local tax policy.

### *Administrative Constraints*

Finally, even if a local jurisdiction has the legal authority to impose a particular kind of tax or fee, has voter support for doing so, and has no concerns about competition from other communities, such a tax or fee may be difficult to impose because of administrative constraints. These constraints may involve practical limitations that make implementation difficult or financial limitations that make the cost of implementation prohibitive.

Smaller communities often face administrative constraints because of their size. For example, a small village may provide water to its residents but be unable to charge a fee based on usage because it has neither the resources to conduct a rate study to determine what appropriate charges should be nor the means to monitor usage. It may be simpler for the village to cover any costs of operating the water system through other revenue sources such as the property tax.

Although large jurisdictions may have fewer administrative constraints because of their size, even major cities can face administrative constraints in some areas. For example, a city could charge fees for docking a boat in the municipal marina; it would be very difficult, however, to charge for many other types of harbor-area use, such as admission to parks running along the shoreline.

And sometimes imposition of a tax or fee may not be cost-effective because of the small number of people affected. For example, a university town with many students might find it worthwhile to impose a bicycle registration fee, since many students own bicycles. Another locality, however, with proportionally fewer bike riders, could find the cost of administering such a fee greater than the revenues derived from the fee.

### *In Summary*

Fiscal capacity is an integral component of local government financial planning. It has an effect on both operating and capital policy decisions. The evaluation of a community's fiscal capacity entails a series of analytic judgments based on qualitative as well as quantitative factors.

In determining fiscal capacity, the community's local economy, its tax and revenue base, and various limitations facing the jurisdiction are considered. Measurements such as resident employment and income, unemployment rates, and population trends provide an economic framework within which fiscal capacity can be analyzed. Tax and revenue bases can be quantified, but the sensitivity of each revenue source to different independent variables is important to recognize. In addition, legal, political, competitive and administrative constraints often exist that will affect a community's fiscal capacity, and they should be identified.

The evaluation process is complex, but a local government's awareness of its fiscal capacity provides a solid base for preparing both short-term and long-term financial policies. Such policies may then be planned based on a thoughtful and thorough determination of the government's ability to support its service and capital-related goals.

## *NOTES*

1. For a compilation and discussion of the research on state fiscal capacity, see U.S. Department of the Treasury, Office of State and Local Finance, *Federal-State-Local Fiscal Relations: Report to the President and the Congress* (September 1985), pp. 207–43, and *Technical Papers,* vol. 1 and 2 (September 1986), pp. 1–261 and pp. 829–54, and Advisory Commission on Intergovernmental Relations, *Measuring State Fiscal Capacity: Alternative Methods and Their Uses* (Washington, D.C.: ACIR, September 1986).

For examples and discussion of studies on local government fiscal capacity, see *Federal-State-Local Fiscal Relations: Report to the President and Congress,* pp. 103–21 and pp. 244–48, and *Technical Papers,* vol. 1, pp. 263–95.

2. For a useful review of economic base and fiscal capacity, see Robert Berne and Richard Schramm, *The Financial Analysis of Governments* (Englewood Cliffs, N.J.: Prentice-Hall, 1986), pp. 98–115.

3. Joel C. Miller, "Municipal Annexation and Boundary Change," *The Municipal Yearbook, 1987* (Washington, D.C.: International City Management Association, 1987), p. 65.

4. Moody's Investors Service, Public Finance Department.

5. Berne and Schramm, *op. cit.,* ch. 4.

6. For a more theoretical discussion of revenue sources and their characteristics, see Richard Musgrave and Peggy Musgrave, *Public Finance in Theory and Practice* (New York: McGraw-Hill, 1984).

7. U.S. Department of Commerce, Bureau of the Census, *Taxable Property Values and Assessment-Sales Price Ratios,* vol. 2, *1982 Census of Governments,* p. *x.*

8. *Ibid.,* pp. *xvi–xvii.*

9. Figures exclude charges and utility and liquor taxes. See Advisory Commission on Intergovernmental Relations, *Significant Features of Fiscal Federalism,* 1987 ed. (Washington, D.C.: ACIR, 1987), p. 44.

10. *Ibid.,* p. 92.

11. *Ibid.,* p. 83; and *Federal-State-Local Fiscal Relations,* pp. 110–11.

12. ACIR, *Fiscal Federalism,* pp. 84–85.

# 11

# Accounting and Financial Reporting

STEPHEN J. GAUTHIER

ACCOUNTING and financial reporting play a vital role in all aspects of government finance at the local level. In fact, it would be no exaggeration to state that these two activities form the informational infrastructure for public finance. As such, they are of interest not only to accountants and auditors but to anyone responsible for financial decision making in the public sector.

Of course, there are many similarities between accounting and financial reporting in the public and in the private sectors. Indeed, governmental standards of financial reporting have incorporated many features of private-sector practice. Nevertheless, governmental accounting and financial reporting remain unique in many important respects. Accordingly, newcomers to local government, including accountants and auditors new to the public sector, cannot rely solely on private-sector experience, but must make a special effort to familiarize themselves with the specialized practices and standards governing accounting and financial reporting in the public sector.

This chapter is designed to give public finance officials a broad overview of accounting and financial reporting for local governments. Throughout, particular emphasis has been placed on practices unique to government.[1]

## ACCOUNTING

The term *accounting* is commonly used to describe the collection and processing of financial data. Such data are needed by management and others for effective control and decision making. In order to collect and process financial data, governments make use of a complex mix of personnel, equipment, procedures, and documentation that is commonly referred to as the government's "accounting system." This accounting system, in turn, is one of three elements forming a government's internal control structure, the other two elements being the *control environment* and *control procedures*.[2] The goals of an effective internal control structure include

- Providing information needed by management for decision making
- Gathering information needed for external financial reporting
- Safeguarding assets from theft or misuse
- Providing the information needed to demonstrate compliance with legal requirements

### *Control Environment*

The first of the three elements of a government's internal control structure is the control environment. Some factors that may enhance or detract from a government's control environment are readily apparent (e.g., the presence or absence of an audit committee or effective internal audit function). Other factors are more subjective. Management's attitude toward the internal control structure, for instance, may set the tone for nonmanagement employees. If management attaches importance to maintaining a sound internal control structure, nonmanagement employees are likely to be careful to observe established control procedures; if not, these procedures may simply be dismissed as "red tape." While a good control environment alone cannot be expected to make up for weaknesses in other internal control structure elements, its absence may render even the best-designed systems and procedures ineffective.

### *Accounting System*

The second element of a government's internal control structure is the combination of personnel, equipment, procedures, and documentation known as the accounting system. Specifically, a sound accounting system should ensure that for each period all financially relevant transactions and events are properly identified, measured, classified, recorded, and reported. Typically, accounting systems are structured around a number of "transaction cycles," such as treasury/financing, revenue/receipts, purchases/disbursements, and external financial reporting. These transaction cycles, in turn, comprise a variety of accounting applications such as

Billings
Receivables
Cash receipts
Purchasing and receiving
Accounts payable
Cash disbursements
Payroll
Inventory control

Property and equipment
General ledger[3]

In most respects, the transaction cycles and accounting applications used by local governments are quite similar to those used by commercial enterprises, but important differences do exist.

As mentioned earlier, one of the goals of an internal control structure in the public sector is to ensure and demonstrate compliance with legal requirements. The most important such legal requirement for local governments is the annual (or biennial) appropriated budget. Therefore, to ensure compliance with the appropriated budget, local governments, unlike most commercial enterprises, integrate specialized budgetary accounts into their accounting system. For example, governments typically record APPROPRIATIONS,[4] ESTIMATED REVENUES, and ENCUMBRANCES[5] as *budgetary* accounts and compare balances in these accounts against amounts in related accounts to monitor budgetary compliance and performance.

To facilitate such comparisons, budgetary accounts are normally recorded as a reflection of the accounts against which they will be compared (e.g., budgetary accounts with debits are used to match accounts with credits). For example, if a government appropriated $500,000 for a given activity, it would record a $500,000 "credit" to APPROPRIATIONS.[6] The government's accounts would then be structured so that APPROPRIATIONS was continually compared to expenditures and ENCUMBRANCES (both "debit" accounts) to determine the remaining uncommitted balance of the appropriation:

| APPROPRIATIONS | Expenditures | ENCUMBRANCES | Remaining Balance |
|---|---|---|---|
| ($500,000)[7] | $350,000 | $75,000 | ($75,000) |

Similarly, ESTIMATED REVENUES would be compared to revenues. Other budgeted amounts (e.g., ESTIMATED OTHER FINANCING SOURCES) would be handled in the same way. Having served their purpose, the budgetary accounts would be removed from the books at the end of the budgetary period; they would *not* be reported in the financial statements.

Some form of budgetary integration is essential for at least some of a local government's activities.[8] The extent to which formal budgetary integration is employed, however, will depend on the complexity and specific circumstances of individual local governments.

Governmental accounting systems also differ from similar systems found in the commercial sector in that they often must be designed specifically to monitor compliance with certain grant requirements. Accordingly, local government accounting systems commonly collect grant-related data involving recipient eligibility, matching or level-of-effort requirements, specialized grantor reporting, cost allocation, and the monitoring of subrecipients.

### *Control Procedures*

The third and final element of a government's internal control structure is composed of the control procedures established by the government to ensure

- Proper authorization of transactions
- Segregation of incompatible duties
- Maintenance of proper records and supporting documentation
- Controlled access to assets and records
- Periodic independent checks on performance

For conceptual purposes, it is possible to separate the accounting system, as described earlier, from these control procedures. In practice, however, control procedures normally are an integral part of a single system that identifies, measures, classifies, records, and reports financial data (i.e., the accounting system). Therefore, the term "accounting system" is often used in a nontechnical sense to refer to both the accounting system and the control procedures as just described.

In reviewing the various types of control procedures, special emphasis should be placed on the segregation of incompatible duties. Employee duties should be divided in such a way that an employee acting alone cannot commit and conceal an irregularity. Accordingly, employees who record transactions (i.e., the accounting department) should not also be responsible for authorizing transactions or maintaining custody of assets. Therefore, activities such as authorizing salary changes and receiving shipments are best handled by nonaccounting staff.

When a government's internal control structure, including all three elements just described, is functioning properly, management should be able to obtain the financial information it needs to meet its responsibilities, including financial reporting to third parties.

### *External and Internal Financial Reporting*

Provided that a government's internal control structure is adequately designed and functioning properly, management should be able to obtain the information it needs in whatever format it deems appropriate. Accordingly, *internal* financial reporting reflects the information needs and preferences of management, and often provides information on the government's budgetary basis of accounting, which may or may not differ from the budgetary basis of accounting used by similar governments. Others with a vital interest in a government's finances, however, typically do not enjoy such direct access to financial information. Groups such as citizens, legislative and oversight bodies, and investors and creditors must rely on a government's *external* financial reporting to meet their financial information needs.

Although all these users of external financial reports share a common interest in the finances of local governments, the focus of their interest may vary. It is probably not practical to design a single financial report that would completely satisfy all potential users. Nonetheless, it has been possible, in both the public and the private sectors, to establish criteria for the preparation of a single report designed to meet the *basic* informational needs of a wide variety of potential users. These criteria have come to be known as "generally accepted accounting principles" (GAAP).

### THE NATURE AND SOURCES OF GAAP

In spite of the terminology "generally accepted *accounting* principles," GAAP, properly speaking, apply more directly to financial reporting than to accounting. That is to say, the information needed for external financial reporting can be seen as a subset of the total financial data collected and processed by the accounting system. Accordingly, it is both common and acceptable for governments to keep their underlying records or "books" on some other basis of accounting (e.g., budgetary basis), provided their accounting system also collects and maintains the information needed to prepare periodic external financial reports in accordance with GAAP.[9]

For state and local governments, the primary source of GAAP is the Governmental Accounting Standards Board (GASB). This five-member body is the ultimate arbiter of GAAP for all state and local governmental entities, including government hospitals, utilities, and colleges and universities.[10] The GASB's guidance on various topics can be found, arranged by subject matter, in the *Codification of Governmental Accounting and Financial Reporting Standards* (*Codification*).

Although the GASB exercises ultimate jurisdiction over financial reporting by state and local governments, other sources of GAAP may need to be consulted for transactions and events not specifically treated by the GASB. One such source of GAAP can be found in the audit and accounting guides and statements of position issued by the American Institute of Certified Public Accountants (AICPA). Widespread practice also can constitute a source of "unwritten" GAAP in the absence of specific GASB or AICPA guidance to the contrary. Similarly, private-sector accounting standards issued by the Financial Accounting Standards Board (FASB) may be relevant in the absence of GASB guidance.[11] Finally, a wealth of nonauthoritative books and articles (e.g., the Government Finance Officers Association's 1988 *Governmental Accounting, Auditing and Financial Reporting*) may also serve as a source of GAAP in the absence of guidance in any of the other sources just cited.

Of course, GAAP may sometimes come into conflict with legal or contractual provisions. For example, some grantors may not wish for grantees to recognize certain types of expenditures/expenses until a disbursement takes place, whereas GAAP may require that they be recognized when incurred. In such situations, the question arises whether GAAP or legal compliance should take precedence. The correct response to this question is that neither GAAP nor legal compliance should be seen as taking precedence; rather, external financial reporting should provide the information needed for both purposes. In most situations, potential conflict can be resolved by preparing the basic financial statements in accordance with GAAP, while providing whatever supplemental schedules may be needed to demonstrate compliance with relevant finance-related legal or contractual provisions. In certain extreme situations, when such a solution is not practical, a government may need to consider issuing a separate report to demonstrate legal compliance.

## KEY FEATURES OF GOVERNMENTAL GAAP

Although the concept of GAAP is common to both the public and the private sectors, there are important differences between GAAP applicable to governments and GAAP used by commercial enterprises. Before attempting to understand government financial statements, finance officers should familiarize themselves with the following important features of local government financial reports.

### Fund Accounting

For financial reporting purposes, the various activities of a government are not typically considered to form a homogeneous whole. Instead, a local government is considered to comprise a number of separate fiscal entities known as "funds." Such funds are established to segregate specific activities or objectives of a government in accordance with special regulations, restrictions, or limitations.

All funds established by a government must be classified in one of seven "fund types" for financial reporting purposes. These fund types may be described briefly as follows.

*The General Fund* is used to account for all activities not reported in some other fund type. Typically, the general fund is the chief reporting vehicle for a government's current operations. Each government may report only one general fund.

*Special Revenue Funds* are used to account for specific revenue sources that legally may be expended only for specified purposes (e.g., noncapital grants). Special revenue funds are not used for amounts held in trust or for resources that will be used for major capital projects.

*Capital Projects Funds* are used to account for major capital acquisition or construction. These funds are *not* used, however, for construction financed by proprietary or trust funds.

*Debt Service Funds* are used to account for the accumulation of resources to pay principal and interest on general long-term debt.

*Enterprise Funds* are used for one or both of the following reasons: (1) to account for activities that are financed and operated in a manner similar to business enterprises (i.e., all costs, including depreciation, are recovered primarily through user charges), or (2) to provide the government with information on revenues, expenses, and net income where such information is useful for capital maintenance, public policy, accountability, management control, or some other purpose.

A good example of the first use of an enterprise fund would be a public utility that attempts to charge users all or most of the cost of providing service.

An example of the second use of an enterprise fund would be a public transportation authority that relies heavily on public subsidies to support its operations, but where the government believes it is important to determine the extent to which public transportation is being subsidized by taxpayers.

*Internal Service Funds* are used as cost-allocation devices for services provided to other departments within the government or to other governments or not-for-profit organizations. Governments often use internal service funds to account for motor pools and risk-management activities.

*Trust and Agency Funds* are used to account for assets held by a government in a trustee or agent capacity.

The trust and agency fund type is further divided into four "subfund types." These subfund types reflect variations in how assets are held and how they may be used.

*Expendable Trust Funds* are used to account for resources held in trust that may be expended in their entirety for the purpose or purposes specified in the trust agreement.

*Nonexpendable Trust Funds* are used to account for resources held in trust when only earnings may be expended and the principal must remain intact.

*Pension Trust Funds* are used to account for resources accumulated to finance pension benefits.

*Agency Funds* are used to account for assets held on behalf of others in a custodial capacity. A common example of the use of an agency fund would be for taxes collected by one government on behalf of another government or other governments.

### Fund Categories

Just as individual funds are classified into one of the fund types just described, so too fund types themselves are further classified into one of three categories. The general fund—as well as special revenue, capital projects, and debt service funds—are all classified as *governmental funds.* Enterprise and internal service funds are classified as *proprietary funds.* Trust and agency funds are classified as *fiduciary funds.*

Although GAAP require that all funds used by a government be classified into one or more of the fund types just described, with one exception, GAAP do *not* specify the number of individual funds of a given fund type that may be used.[12] As a result, the number of individual funds used in practice may vary significantly from one government to another. As a general rule, however, GAAP call for governments to use the minimum number of funds consistent with legal requirements and the needs of sound financial management.[13]

Sometimes governments use more individual funds than necessary because of a failure to distinguish between the needs of accounting and those of financial reporting. For example, some governments report numerous debt service funds in an effort to meet bond indenture requirements. In fact, however, bond indenture requirements for separate "funds" typically are intended only to ensure that a government's accounting system will collect and maintain the data specified by the indenture for use by the bondholders as needed. Accordingly, in such situations there normally is no need to complicate GAAP financial reporting by establishing numerous debt-service funds, provided that the accounting system collects and maintains the information mandated by the indenture.[14]

### *Pyramid Reporting*

As just noted, governments make use of a variety of fund types and individual funds in their financial reporting. To minimize the potential complexity that could result from the use of multiple funds and fund types, governments employ a "pyramid" approach to the presentation of funds and fund types as illustrated in figure 11-1. Under this approach, information is presented on a "combined

FIGURE 11-1
*The Financial Reporting "Pyramid"*

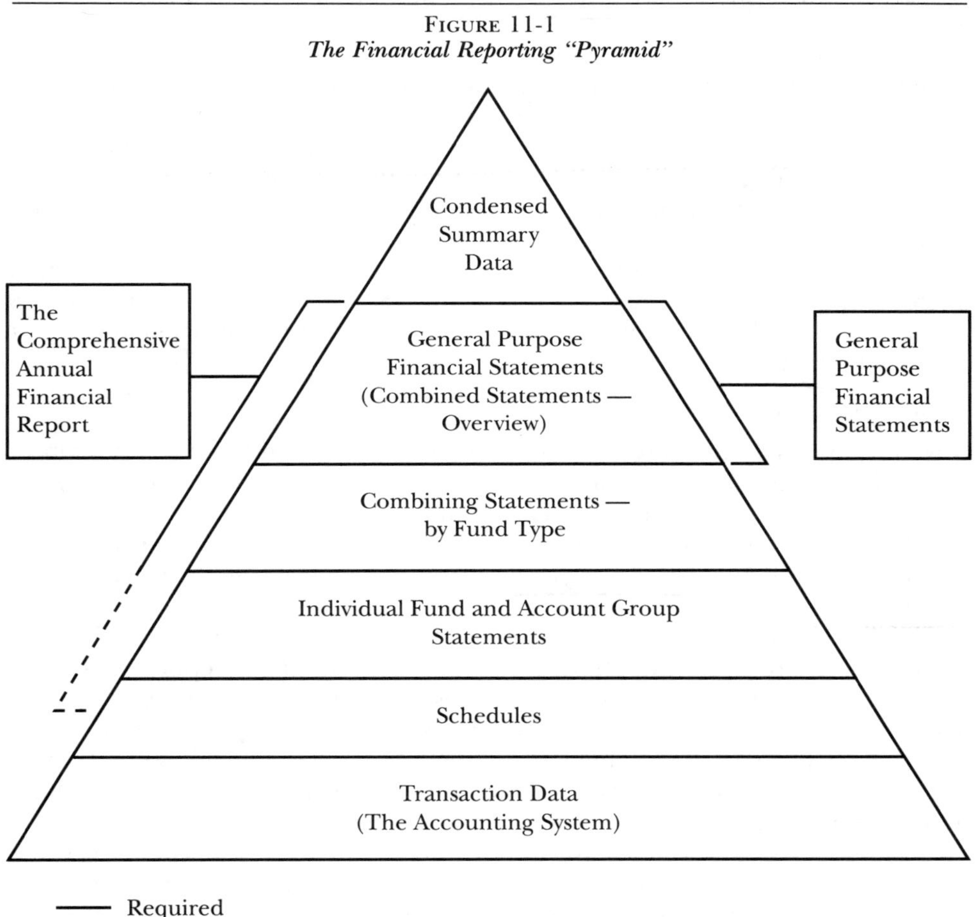


SOURCE: Statement No. 1, *Governmental Accounting and Financial Reporting Principles* (Chicago, Ill.: National Council on Governmental Accounting, March 1979), p. 20.

basis" first, and then supported by combining and individual fund information, as needed. Assume, for example, that a government has a general fund, four individual special revenue funds, a debt service fund, and a capital projects fund. The combined financial statements would report a single, separate column for each fund type used by the government. Accordingly, the single balance-sheet column reported for special revenue funds would reflect the combined assets, liabilities, and fund balance of all four individual special revenue funds:

| | Special Revenue Funds |
|---|---|
| Assets | $1,270,000 |
| Liabilities | 950,000 |
| Fund Balance | 320,000 |

Combining financial statements would then provide readers with detail on each of the four individual special revenue funds, with a total column that matched the single column for special revenue funds reported in the combined financial statements. Continuing with the preceding example, the combining balance sheet for special revenue funds of the government would appear as follows:

| | Fund 1 | Fund 2 | Fund 3 | Fund 4 | Total |
|---|---|---|---|---|---|
| Assets | $900,000 | $160,000 | $110,000 | $100,000 | $1,270,000 |
| Liabilities | 750,000 | 90,000 | 70,000 | 40,000 | 950,000 |
| Fund Balance | 150,000 | 70,000 | 40,000 | 60,000 | 320,000 |

Although combining financial statements provide information on each of the funds used, sometimes additional information on individual funds is also needed. For example, a government may wish to present comparative financial data from the preceding year or budget-to-actual comparisons. In most cases, such information could not be included in the format of a combining financial statement without undue complexity. Therefore, individual fund financial statements are normally used in such cases to supplement the combining financial statements. Similarly, governments may wish to report individual fund financial data at a level of detail not compatible with combining financial statements.[15] In this case also, the use of individual fund financial statements to support the combining financial statements would be appropriate.

At a minimum, GAAP require that governments present combined financial statements. As will be discussed later, GAAP also recommend that all governments prepare and issue a comprehensive annual financial report (CAFR) or a component unit financial report (CUFR).[16] If a CAFR/CUFR is prepared, combining statements must be reported for all fund types composed of more than one fund. Individual fund financial statements, however, are required in a CAFR/CUFR only when individual fund financial data cannot be efficiently presented in combining financial statements.

### *Measurement Focus*

Accountants use the term "measurement focus" to refer to the types of resources that are measured and presented in financial statements. Unlike private-sector enterprises, a single government typically uses two different measurement focuses in its financial reporting. Governmental funds and expendable trust funds use a "flow of current financial resources" measurement focus. Proprietary funds, nonexpendable trust funds, and pension trust funds, on the other hand, use the same "flow of economic resources" measurement focus used by private-sector enterprises. Table 11-1 lists the measurement focus and basis of accounting for each fund type.

The goal of the flow of current financial resources measurement focus is to report whether a given fund is better or worse off *financially* in the short term as a result of transactions and events of the period. Accordingly, financial statements prepared using the flow of current financial resources measurement focus report sources, uses, and balances of *current financial resources* (i.e., resources that are appropriable or "spendable").

The goal of the flow of economic resources measurement focus, on the other hand, is to report whether a given fund is better or worse off *economically* as a result of transactions and events of the period. Therefore, financial statements prepared using the flow of economic resources measurement focus report sources, uses, and balances of *economic resources* (i.e., all resources, regardless of whether they are appropriable or "spendable").

One highly visible difference between the two different measurement focuses involves the treatment accorded capital outlays. When a governmental fund purchases a fixed asset, that transaction is reported as a reduction of the fund's

TABLE 11-1
*Fund Accounting Summary*

| Fund Type | Fund Category | Measurement Focus | Basis of Accounting |
|---|---|---|---|
| General | Governmental | Flow of current financial resources | Modified accrual |
| Special Revenue | Governmental | Flow of current financial resources | Modified accrual |
| Debt Service | Governmental | Flow of current financial resources | Modified accrual |
| Capital Projects | Governmental | Flow of current financial resources | Modified accrual |
| Enterprise | Proprietary | Flow of economic resources | Accrual |
| Internal Service | Proprietary | Flow of economic resources | Accrual |
| Trust and Agency: | Fiduciary | | |
| Expendable Trust | | Flow of current financial resources | Modified accrual |
| Nonexpendable Trust | | Flow of economic resources | Accrual |
| Pension Trust | | Flow of economic resources | Accrual |
| Agency | | Not applicable | Modified accrual |

SOURCE: Government Finance Officers Association, *Government Accounting, Auditing and Financial Reporting* (Chicago, IL: GFOA, 1988), p. 14.

current financial resources because the asset so acquired (e.g., equipment) is not "spendable" or "appropriable" while the asset surrendered (e.g., cash) was. Accordingly, capital outlays are reported as uses of current financial resources or "expenditures" in governmental fund operating statements. When a proprietary fund purchases a fixed asset, on the other hand, that transaction is considered to have no effect on the fund's *economic* resources because a fund is not *economically* better or worse off when one asset (e.g., cash) is exchanged for another asset (e.g., equipment). Therefore, capital outlays are *not* reflected in the operating statements of proprietary funds.

A second highly visible difference between the two measurement focuses involves the treatment accorded debt-service principal payments. As was the case for capital outlays, these payments represent a reduction in a fund's "spendable" or "appropriable" resources. Accordingly, governmental funds report the payment of debt-service principal as an expenditure in their operating statements. However, funds are not considered to be worse off *economically* when both debt and assets are reduced by the same amount. Therefore, proprietary funds do not report payments of debt-service principal in their operating statements.

A third difference between the two measurement focuses involves the use of depreciation accounting. Depreciation is an allocation methodology designed to assign the cost of fixed assets to the periods that benefit from the use of those assets. For example, if an asset is purchased for $10,000 and has a useful life of five years, depreciation accounting would result in recognizing $10,000 in "depreciation expense" during the five years of the asset's useful life (e.g., $2,000 per year if the "straight-line" method of depreciation is used). Proprietary funds, like commercial enterprises, use depreciation accounting and so report "depreciation expense" in their operating statements. This accounting reflects the fact that these funds are *economically* worse off as their assets are consumed. Governmental funds and similar trust funds, on the other hand, do *not* use depreciation accounting because the *financial* effect of the acquisition of a fixed asset occurs when it is purchased (i.e., capital outlay) rather than when it is consumed. In other words, the consumption of capital assets does not result in the reduction of "spendable" or "appropriable" resources and so is not reflected in the operating statements of governmental funds.

Finally, it should be noted that funds using the flow of current financial resources measurement focus do *not* report gains or losses, whereas both are reported in the operating statements of funds using the flow of economic resources measurement focus. For example, assume that both the general fund and an enterprise fund sell for $6,000 investments reported in those funds at $5,000. The enterprise fund would report the $1,000 difference as a "gain" in its operating statement, whereas the general fund would report the same $1,000 as revenue.

### *Basis of Accounting*

Accountants use the term *basis of accounting* to refer to the timing of transaction and event recognition. The concept of basis of accounting is closely linked to that of measurement focus. Funds using the flow of economic resources measurement focus (i.e., proprietary funds, nonexpendable trust funds, and pension trust funds), like commercial enterprises, use the accrual basis of accounting. Funds using the flow of current financial resources measurement focus (i.e., governmental funds and expendable trust funds) use the *modified* accrual basis of accounting.[17]

Funds using the accrual basis of accounting report revenues and *expenses* in their operating statements. Funds using the modified accrual basis of accounting, on the other hand, report revenues and *expenditures*. As might be expected from the use of different terms, the rules governing *expense* recognition differ from those governing *expenditure* recognition. Revenue-recognition criteria, however, also differ sharply between the two different bases of accounting.

Under accrual accounting, revenues are recognized when they are earned, regardless of when cash is received. Under the modified accrual basis of accounting, on the other hand, revenues can only be recognized when they are both *measurable* and *available* (i.e., collectible within the current period or soon enough thereafter to be used to pay liabilities of the current period).[18] Assume, for example, that a government plans to construct water mains on behalf of property owners in a new subdivision. Further assume that the government intends to recover the cost of this construction from the benefiting property owners by means of a special assessment, collectible from property owners during the next ten years. Under current standards, this activity could be reported in either a governmental fund or an enterprise fund, depending on the specific circumstances.[19] If an enterprise fund is used (and therefore the accrual basis of accounting), the entire amount of the special assessments receivable would be reported as revenue by the end of construction. On the other hand, if a governmental fund is used (and therefore the *modified* accrual basis of accounting), most of the special assessments receivable probably would *not* be recognized as revenue of the period because the assessments would not be collectible soon enough after the end of the current period to pay liabilities of the current period.

In most cases, the interpretation of what is "available" to pay liabilities of the current period is left to the discretion of individual governments using the modified accrual basis of accounting. For example, one government may consider revenue available if is collectible within 60 days of fiscal year end, whereas another government may consider the same revenue as available if it is collectible within 90 days of fiscal year end. Current authoritative standards, however, do set a specific limit in the case of property taxes: 60 days.[20]

The authoritative standards also appear to mandate a form of cash-basis accounting for income and sales taxes in funds using modified accrual accounting.[21] In practice, however, governments often have interpreted the authoritative standards broadly so as to allow the application of the same measurable and available criteria used for other revenue sources.

When accrual accounting is used, *expenses* are recognized when incurred, regardless of the timing of related cash flows. Most *expenditures*, however, are only recognized if they are expected to be "liquidated with expendable, available financial resources." Assume, for example, that it is probable that a fund will be required to pay a $300,000 claim at the end of a three-year period for an event that occurred in the first year. If the claim involved a fund using accrual accounting, the full $300,000 would be recognized as an expense of the first year. If the claim involved a fund using modified accrual accounting, however, none of the $300,000 would be recognized as an expenditure of the first year because none of the $300,000 is expected to be liquidated with expendable, available financial resources.

Modified accrual accounting has special expenditure recognition rules applicable to debt service principal and interest. Generally, both are reported as fund expenditures only when they are due. If, however, a government makes a transfer of resources to a debt service fund in anticipation of a debt service payment due early in the following year, the government has the *option* to recognize an expenditure in the debt service fund at the time of the transfer rather than when due.[22]

This treatment of expenditures related to debt service marks another important difference between accrual and modified accrual accounting. Assume, for example, that a government has a fiscal year end of June 30 and will be required to make a semiannual bond payment of $125,000 on July 15 ($100,000 principal, $25,000 interest). Under the modified accrual basis of accounting, a fund would not be required to report any expenditure in the current fiscal year because the principal and interest payments are not due. The fund would, however, be allowed to report the full $125,000 as an expenditure of the period if the early recognition option described above were selected. If, on the other hand, a fund using the accrual basis of accounting were reporting this same transaction, that fund would be required to report interest expense of $22,917 (i.e., 5½ months interest), while the principal portion of the debt service payment would have no effect on the operating statement of either the current period or future periods.

### *Account Groups*

Funds using the flow of economic resources measurement focus and the accrual basis of accounting report all assets and liabilities related to those funds within the funds themselves. This is not the case for governmental funds using the flow of current financial resources measurement focus and the modified accrual basis of accounting. As mentioned earlier in the discussion on measurement focus, capital outlays of governmental funds are reported as expenditures in the operating statement rather than as assets on the fund's balance sheet. Similarly, liabilities not expected to be liquidated with expendable, available financial resources are not reported immediately as expenditures and liabilities of governmental funds. Instead, such assets and liabilities are reported in two "account groups." These account groups report no operations and should not be confused with funds. Rather, the account groups serve simply as memorandum lists of assets and liabilities of the general government that would not otherwise be reported on the balance sheet because the flow of current financial resources measurement focus and the modified accrual basis of accounting are used.

*General Fixed Assets Account Group.* The general fixed assets account group (GFAAG) typically reports five categories of assets:

- Land
- Buildings
- Equipment
- Improvements other than buildings
- Construction in progress

Since double-entry bookkeeping requires that every debit be matched by a credit, fixed assets reported in the GFAAG (debit) are matched by a credit account entitled "investment in general fixed assets." In spite of its title, the "investment in general fixed assets" account should not be misunderstood to represent a government's equity in its general fixed assets.[23]

Under current standards, the reporting of infrastructure assets in the GFAAG is optional. For this purpose, infrastructure assets are defined as those that are "immovable and of value only to the governmental unit."[24] In practice, most governments elect not to report their infrastructure assets in the GFAAG. Governments similarly have an option to report "accumulated depreciation" in the GFAAG, even though depreciation expense may *never* be reported in a governmental fund. Once again, however, in practice, few governments elect to report accumulated depreciation in the GFAAG.

One reason governments decline to report infrastructure and accumulated depreciation is that they are sometimes not persuaded of the value of reporting such information on a historical cost basis, as required by GAAP. In other cases, governments may not report this information because they do not believe the benefits to be obtained would justify the additional record-keeping costs.

*General Long-Term Debt Account Group.* The general long-term debt account group (GLTDAG) typically reports the following categories of long-term liabilities:

- Long-term debt (e.g., bonds, notes, capital leases)
- Unfunded pension contributions (i.e., annual actuarial contributions not paid to the trust fund)
- Claims and judgments
- Compensated absences

Again, since double-entry bookkeeping requires that credits be matched by debits, these liabilities (credit) are offset by both an "amount available" account and an "amount to be provided" account. The former account represents resources set aside in the governmental funds themselves for debt service. The latter account is simply used to "balance" the remaining credits. It is important that neither of these two accounts be confused with assets, since they represent either the absence of resources (i.e., "amount to be provided") or resources already reported as assets somewhere else on the balance sheet (e.g., "amount available in debt service fund").

### *Other Financing Sources and Uses*

In addition to revenues and expenditures, the operating statements of governmental and similar trust funds also report "other financing sources and uses." This category is used to report sources and uses of current financial resources that could distort revenue and expenditure patterns if reported as revenues and expenditures in the operating statement.

The most common example of other financing sources/uses involves transfers between funds. For example, assume that the general fund transfers $500,000 to subsidize activities in a special revenue fund. In that case, the general fund would report the transfer to the special revenue fund as an "other financing use" and the special revenue fund would report the transfer from the general fund as an "other financing source."[25]

Debt proceeds are another common example of an "other financing source" found in governmental funds. In proprietary and similar trust funds, of course, debt proceeds (debit) are matched by the debt itself (credit) and there is no effect on the operating statement. Such a matching is not possible, however, in governmental funds since the debt (credit) is reported in the GLTDAG rather than in the fund. Therefore, the increase in *current* financial resources caused by issuing *long-term* debt is reported in governmental fund operating statements as an "other financing source" (credit).

Proceeds from the sale of general fixed assets reported in the GFAAG are a third example of an "other financing source." Because governmental and similar trust funds do *not* report gains and losses in their operating statements, as noted earlier, the entire amount of the proceeds would be classified as an "other financing source," regardless of the book value of the asset.

A second example of an "other financing use" (in addition to operating transfers to other funds) can be found in cases where governments issue new bonds to refund existing debt before the call date for that debt. In these situations, payments into an escrow account of amounts obtained through the issuance of new debt is reported as an "other financing use."

### *Residual Equity Transfers*

Another unique feature of governmental GAAP is the use of residual equity transfers. These transfers are reported separately from revenues, expenditures, and other financing sources and uses. Such transfers are defined as "nonrecurring or nonroutine transfers of equity between funds."[26] The most common examples of residual equity transfers involve

- Capital contributions to establish a new fund
- The return of capital upon the dissolution of a fund
- Contributions of capital assets

It is important to note that proprietary funds (i.e., enterprise and internal service funds) often report contributions from other funds as a direct increase in the balance sheet account "contributed capital" rather than as "residual equity transfers in." Accordingly, it is not uncommon for residual equity transfers in not to equal residual equity transfers out in governmental financial statements.

### *Reserves*

One of the goals of the flow of current financial resources measurement focus is to determine the balance of financial resources available for appropriation (i.e., spendable resources). "Fund balance" (i.e., the difference between fund assets and fund liabilities) is *not,* however, an adequate measure of this amount for two reasons. First, not all the assets reported in governmental funds are "spendable." For example, a long-term receivable, though a *financial* asset, is not a *current* financial asset because it will not be realized in cash soon enough after the end of the fiscal period to pay liabilities of the period. Second, sometimes current financial resources are not appropriable because there are legal restrictions on their use. Encumbrances are a good example of this latter situation. Therefore, if users of governmental and similar trust fund financial data are to determine the amount of fund resources available for appropriation, the types of items just described must somehow be separated out of "fund balance." GAAP achieve this goal by classifying "fund balance" into "reserved" and "unreserved" components. Fund balance reserves demonstrate the balance of a fund's net assets that may not be appropriated either because they are not appropriable or because there are legal restrictions on their appropriation. Unreserved fund balance, on the other hand, provides users of financial statements with a measure of the current financial resources that are available for appropriation.

Although the term *reserve* is also used in proprietary funds, its use there is different from its use for governmental funds. Proprietary funds have a different measurement focus than do governmental funds and it is not a goal of proprietary funds to provide users of financial statements with a measure of appropriable resources. Therefore, in practice, reserves are used in proprietary funds simply to inform financial statement users of legal restrictions on the use of net assets. For example, many enterprise funds report reserves of retained earnings related to assets whose use is restricted by the terms of bond indentures.

### *Designations*

Another categorization found in the equity section of governmental funds is that of "designations." Designations are designed to serve as indications of "tentative plans for financial resource utilization in a future period" and "reflect tentative managerial plans or intent."[27] To qualify, they must "be supported by definitive plans and approved by either the government's chief executive officer or legislature."[28] Unlike a reserve, a designation does *not* indicate that financial resources are unavailable for appropriation, only that they are being voluntarily set aside for some specific purpose (e.g., contingencies). Accordingly, "designated fund balance" is a subsection of "unreserved fund balance."

Traditionally, authoritative standards have been interpreted as not permitting the use of designations in proprietary funds.[29] The GASB has, however, recently mandated the use of designations in internal service funds in one particular instance.[30] Therefore, it is quite possible that designations may come to be used more frequently in proprietary funds in the future.

### *Basic Financial Statements*

Governments report a single balance sheet in their combined financial statements that contains a separate column for each fund type and account group used by the government. Because of differences in measurement focus and basis of accounting, however, governments normally report two different operating statements in their combined financial statements. Governmental and similar trust funds report their operations and changes in fund balance in one statement while proprietary and similar trust funds report their operations and changes in retained earnings/equity in a separate statement. Governments also are required to provide a combined statement of cash flows for their proprietary and similar trust funds. Account groups and agency funds are reported only on the balance sheet.

In addition to the financial statements just described, governments are also required by GAAP to provide a statement presenting budget-to-actual comparisons for all governmental funds that have annual appropriated budgets. Both the "budget" and "actual" columns on this statement must be presented on a budgetary basis and a reconciliation to GAAP must be provided either on the face of the statement or in the notes if the budgetary basis differs from GAAP. This required budgetary statement is presented in the combined financial statements, immediately following the operating statement for governmental and similar trust funds.

It should be noted that the Total columns often presented in combined financial statements are labeled "memorandum only." This language is used to notify readers of financial statements that the information contained in these columns is not presented in conformity with GAAP. Such a notice is also necessary because transactions between funds have not been "eliminated" as they would be in consolidated financial reports.

### *Note Disclosure*

Note disclosure, of course, is hardly a unique feature of governmental financial reporting. GAAP disclosure requirements in the public sector are, however, typically more extensive than similar requirements for private-sector entities. Traditionally, the more extensive note disclosure requirements found in the public sector have been justified by standard-setting bodies based on the need for a special, higher level of accountability for governmental entities.

One important difference between the notes presented in private-sector financial statements and those presented in the financial statements of local governments can be found in the summary of significant accounting policies (SSAP). While all GAAP financial statements contain an SSAP, those found in governmental financial reports are typically much more extensive because they are used to describe the many important differences between private-and public-sector accounting and financial reporting.

Two of the other more distinctive disclosures found in governmental financial reporting involve deposits and investments and participation in pension arrangements. GAAP require that deposits and investments of governmental entities be classified into one of three "risk categories" based on who is holding the collateral or investment (e.g., the government's agent) and how it is being held (e.g., "in the name of the government").[31] Required pension disclosures for governmental employers include information on the plan and its benefits, funding status and progress, contributions required and contributions made, and trend data.[32]

***Expanded Reporting***

Governments are required, at a minimum, to present a complete set of combined financial statements and notes in order to meet the requirements of GAAP. GAAP strongly encourage governments to go beyond this minimum requirement, however, and to prepare a CAFR or CUFR.[33]

A CAFR/CUFR is composed of at least three sections: introductory, financial, and statistical. The most important component of the introductory section is the letter of transmittal. This letter is used by management to provide users of the CAFR/CUFR with a general overview of the government's financial situation. Typically, the letter of transmittal should include information on the community's economic condition and outlook, a discussion of major government initiatives and summary financial data.

The financial section includes both the combined financial statements (including the notes) and combining and individual fund financial statements. Combining and individual fund financial statements are presented by fund type in separate "subsections" using the same order of presentation as on the combined balance sheet. These fund-type subsections also sometimes include schedules needed to demonstrate legal compliance (e.g., general fund disbursements).

The final basic section of a CAFR/CUFR is the statistical section. Information contained in this section typically is either nonfinancial in character (e.g., demographic data) or involves financial data for a ten-year period. GAAP recommend fifteen specific statistical tables.[34] In practice, however, not all fifteen tables may be applicable to a given government's circumstances. Moreover, governments are encouraged to provide additional statistical data that may be of special interest to users of their particular financial statements. For example, a school district or a state may wish to provide special information on enrollments or employment, respectively.

In addition to the three basic sections of a CAFR/CUFR just described, two other sections are sometimes found in CAFRs/CUFRs. Governments subject to the Single Audit Act of 1984 sometimes elect to present a fourth, "single audit" section in their report. This section would contain a schedule of federal financial assistance, findings and recommendations, and a number of required auditors' reports. Also, CAFRs/CUFRs for public employee retirement systems contain a separate fourth actuarial section.

### *Consolidated or "Popular" Reporting*

GAAP require that governmental financial data be presented by fund and account group. Many in the public sector believe, however, that such a detailed presentation of financial data may be difficult for nonspecialists to understand. Therefore, a number of governments choose to supplement their regular GAAP reporting by issuing non-GAAP "popular" reports. Often such reports are presented on a consolidated basis (i.e., information for the government as a whole rather than information by fund, with interfund transactions eliminated). Sometimes these reports are not only consolidated, but prepared in a manner similar to private-sector reports (e.g., depreciation is reported for general government fixed assets). Such reports may be useful tools for giving taxpayers and others a general overview of a government's financial position and results of operations, but they are not a substitute for GAAP financial reporting.

## *PENDING CHANGES*

The establishment of the GASB in 1984 marked a major turning point in governmental accounting and financial reporting. For the first time, state and local governments had a standard-setting body with the resources not only to provide timely guidance on emerging issues in governmental accounting and financial reporting, but to reexamine the governmental financial reporting model itself.

In May 1990, the GASB issued Statement No. 11, *Measurement Focus and Basis of Accounting—Governmental Fund Operating Statements.* This document is designed to serve as the keystone of the new financial reporting model for state and local governments. Perhaps the single most important change contained in this pronouncement is the move from the flow of *current financial* resources measurement focus to the flow of *financial* resources measurement focus. Because the emphasis in both cases remains on *financial* resources, governmental funds and similar trust funds will continue to report capital outlays and most debt service principal payments in their operating statements, unlike proprietary and similar trust funds. Because the emphasis has shifted, however, from *current financial* resources to just *financial* resources, the timing of cash flows will, for the most part, cease to be a consideration in the recognition of revenues and expenditures. In other words, the modified accrual basis of accounting will be replaced by the accrual basis of accounting. Accordingly, revenues will no longer have to be "available" to be recognized, nor will expenditures be reported only when liabilities are expected to be liquidated with "expendable available financial resources." Table 11-2 shows the changes that will occur to the measurement focus and basis of accounting of governmental funds in the wake of GASB Statement No. 11.

Another important result of the implementation of GASB Statement No. 11 will be a change in how long-term debt is treated in governmental fund

TABLE 11-2

*Comparison of Current and Future MFBA Governmental Funds*

| | Current MFBA | Future MFBA* |
|---|---|---|
| Measurement Focus | Flow of current financial resources | Flow of financial resources |
| Basis of Accounting | Modified accrual | Accrual |

* Per GASB Statement No. 11, *Measurement Focus and Basis of Accounting—Governmental Fund Operating Statements.*

operating statements. As mentioned earlier, under current standards essentially all long-term obligations of governmental funds to outside parties are reported in the GLTDAG. Therefore, when debt is issued, the proceeds received in a fund (debit) are balanced by an operating statement "other financing source" (credit). As a result, financing outlays with debt does not affect fund equity because the operating statement outflow (expenditure) is balanced by an operating statement inflow ("other financing source"). While GASB Statement No. 11 will retain this treatment for *capital-related* long-term debt, it will prohibit the reporting of an "other financing source" in connection with other types of long-term obligations. Therefore, under GASB Statement No. 11, debt issued for operating purposes (e.g., payroll), could not be used to avoid a reduction in fund equity.

The new measurement focus and basis of accounting, as mentioned earlier, is designed to serve as the keystone of a new governmental financial reporting model. Other aspects of this new model are the subject of several GASB projects that are scheduled for simultaneous implementation with GASB Statement No. 11 for fiscal years beginning after June 15, 1994. These other projects include financial reporting, capital reporting, pension accounting, and risk financing and insurance, as well as a project dealing with the possibility of broadening the definition of "capital debt" to encompass debt that is not directly related to the acquisition or construction of fixed assets but does provide long-term economic benefits to the government.

## CONCLUSION

Why should the nonaccountant take an interest in the accounting practices and conventions used to prepare local government financial reports? There are numerous possible responses to this fundamental question.

Perhaps the most important reason is that a basic knowledge of local government accounting and financial reporting is essential if users of local government financial reports are to obtain and interpret the data needed to make informed decisions. As noted throughout this chapter, local government accounting and financial reporting departs in many important respects from the accounting and financial reporting found in the private sector. An awareness of such key differences as the use of the modified accrual basis of accounting is vital to a proper understanding of local government financial reports.

Also, although accounting should not drive financial decision making, decision makers cannot afford to be unaware of the accounting and financial reporting implications of their actions. For example, changing the due date for property taxes could affect whether those taxes can still be recognized as revenue in the current year and thus whether they can be included in fund balance.

Accounting and financial reporting serve as the informational infrastructure of public finance. As such, a basic understanding of these disciplines should not be the domain of specialists, but the common knowledge of all involved in public finance. While accounting professionals play a vital role in establishing and maintaining this infrastructure, its usefulness must ultimately be judged in terms of how well it serves the wide array of nonaccounting professionals who must rely upon it.

## *NOTES*

1. For a more detailed discussion of these topics, readers are advised to consult *Governmental Accounting, Auditing and Financial Reporting* (*GAAFR*) (Chicago: Government Finance Officers Association, 1988).

2. See the American Institute of Certified Public Accountants' (AICPA) Statement of Auditing Standards (SAS) No. 55, *Consideration of the Internal Control Structure in a Financial Statement Audit* (New York: AICPA, April 1988).

3. These examples of transaction cycles and accounting applications are taken from *Government Auditing Standards* (Washington: General Accounting Office, 1988), pp. 5-8 and 5-9.

4. This article uses ALL CAPS to distinguish *budgetary* accounts from other accounts used in an accounting system.

5. Encumbrances are commitments of budgetary spending authority in unperformed (i.e., executory) contracts. For example, if a government has ordered $3,000 in supplies but has not yet received the supplies, it has committed $3,000 of its budgetary resources but has not yet incurred a liability or expenditure.

6. The net difference between debits and credits in budgetary accounts is recorded as BUDGETARY FUND BALANCE.

7. "Credits" are indicated by the use of parentheses.

8. See the *Codification of Governmental Accounting and Financial Reporting Standards* (Norwalk, CT: Governmental Accounting Standards Board, 1990), Section 1700.118–.119.

9. A recent Governmental Accounting Standards Board (GASB) research report by Professors Ingram and Robbins, *Financial Reporting Practices of Local Governments* (Stanford CT: GASB, 1987) indicates that "a majority of local governments are required to conform with GAAP by other levels of government" and that "a large majority are audited for GAAP compliance" (p. 79).

10. While the GASB has exercised complete jurisdiction over accounting and financial reporting by *all* governmental entities since its establishment in 1984, government

colleges and universities, hospitals, and gas and electric utilities have strongly urged that the accounting and financial reporting for these entities continue to resemble, as much as possible, the accounting and financial reporting used by their private-sector counterparts. To answer these concerns, the Financial Accounting Foundation, the GASB's oversight body, has requested that the GASB include in its mission statement a commitment to consider the special needs of these entities in setting accounting and financial reporting standards. At present, these "special entities" (i.e., government colleges and universities, hospitals, and gas and electric utilities) essentially use the same standards in preparing their financial statements as do similar private-sector entities. Nonetheless, they are still normally subject to the GASB's special disclosure requirements.

11. As of 1990, the precise authoritative status for governments of standards issued by the FASB is under review by the Financial Accounting Foundation.

12. GAAP allow the use of only a single general fund for financial reporting purposes (*Codification,* Section 1300.106).

13. See *Codification,* Section 1300.108.

14. Accounting systems can gather and maintain the data needed to demonstrate legal compliance by using detailed individual *accounts* rather than funds. These accounts can be aggregated for purposes of external financial reporting.

15. For example, if a government had a number of dissimilar enterprise funds, individual fund statements could be used to provide detailed information on the components of the "cost of goods sold" for each fund.

16. See *Codification,* Section 2200.101.

17. Agency funds cannot properly be said to have a "measurement focus" because they do not report operations. They do, however, use the modified accrual basis of accounting in calculating assets and related liabilities.

18. *Codification,* Section 1600.106.

19. *Codification,* Section S40.123.

20. *Codification,* Section P70.103. It should also be noted that property taxes must be due within the period to be recognized as revenue of the period.

21. *Codification,* Sections 1600.110 and S10.102.

22. *Codification,* Section 1600.121.

23. A true measure of a government's equity in its general fixed assets would require a reduction for outstanding related debt and capital consumption.

24. *Codification,* Section 1400.109.

25. Transfers are also reported in proprietary and similar trust funds, where they are presented in a separate transfers section of the operating statement, but are *not* classified as "other financing sources/uses." This latter term is only appropriate in funds using the flow of current financial resources measurement focus.

26. *Codification,* Section 1800.106a.

27. *Codification,* Section 1800.124.

28. *Audits of State and Local Governmental Units* (AICPA, NY 1986), Section 12.4.

29. 1988 *GAAFR,* p. 106.

30. GASB Statement No. 10, *Accounting and Financial Reporting for Risk Financing and Related Insurance Issues,* para. 67 (*Codification,* Section C50).

31. *Codification,* Section I50.

32. *Codification,* Section P20.

33. *Codification,* Section 2200.101. When governments that are themselves a part of another government issue separate reports, these are known as CUFRs rather than CAFRs.

34. *Codification,* Section 2800.

# 12
# *Auditing*

STEPHEN J. GAUTHIER

THE term *auditing* is a familiar one to all involved in public finance. Close examination, however, reveals that this term is commonly used in a variety of different ways. For example, the term *auditing* for many evokes images of the annual or biennial audit of a local government's financial statements. For others, auditing is primarily associated with a government's own internal audit function. Still others may see the term as applying to audits designed to evaluate the efficiency or effectiveness of one or more of a local government's activities or functions. This chapter will attempt to clarify the role of auditing at the local government level by providing an overview of the most common activities encompassed by that term.

## *OVERVIEW OF EXTERNAL FINANCIAL AUDITS*

Local governments normally prepare financial statements for the use of parties outside the government, such as taxpayers, oversight and legislative bodies, and investors and creditors.[1] Such financial reporting plays an important role in governments' meeting their obligation to be accountable. These financial statements contain management's assertions about a government's financial position, results of operations, and cash flows. Understandably, outside parties may not wish to rely upon the uncorroborated assertions of management, especially since these assertions could reflect favorably or unfavorably on management's own performance. Therefore, outside parties traditionally have turned to external or "independent" auditors for assurance that management's assertions in the financial statements can be relied upon.

A financial audit, therefore, requires the auditor to collect the sufficient, competent evidential matter needed to attest to the fairness of management's assertions in the financial statements. The auditor obtains this evidence by means of inspection, observation, inquiries, and confirmations from third parties.[2] The criteria used to judge fairness, in most cases, are generally accepted accounting principles (GAAP). The principal source of GAAP for local governments is the Governmental Accounting Standards Board (GASB), although other sources of GAAP (e.g., the American Institute of Certified Public Accountants) are also important.

### *Common Misconceptions*

Unfortunately, recent experience has shown that the public often misunderstands the role played by auditors of financial statements. Therefore, care must be taken to avoid some common misconceptions.

First, it is essential not to lose sight of the fact that the financial statements represent management's, not the auditor's, assertions about the government. Nor does management's ultimate responsibility for the financial statements change when the auditor is involved in their preparation. Rather, an auditor's role still remains the expression of an opinion on *management's* assertions.

Second, the auditor does *not* attempt to assure users of the financial statements that all the information contained in those statements is accurate. Rather, auditors do the work they consider necessary to provide *reasonable assurance* that the financial statements are not *materially* misstated. In other words, the auditor is not asserting that all of the data in financial statements are correct, but rather that the auditor is reasonably satisfied that the financial statements do not contain misstatements of such a nature as to seriously mislead readers.

Third, auditors do *not* examine all the transactions and events reflected in a government's financial statements. Except in extraordinary circumstances, such a detailed examination would not be cost-effective. Instead, auditors obtain the level of assurance they need by examining transactions and events on a test basis. For example, an auditor may select a small random sample of disbursements to obtain the evidence needed to reach a reasonable conclusion on all disbursements.

Finally, it is not the auditor's objective to detect all possible fraudulent activities that might have occurred during a fiscal period. Although the auditor should be alert to irregularities of all types that may come to light in the performance of the engagement, the audit itself is specifically designed only to detect those irregularities that could have a material effect on the fair presentation of the financial statements.

### *Independence*

Many local government audits are performed by firms of licensed certified public accountants (CPAs). Other local governments are audited by external government auditors (e.g., state auditor's office). In either case, it is essential that auditors of financial statements be independent if third-party users of financial statements are to rely upon their work.

Moreover, it is not enough for auditors to be independent *in fact,* they must also be so *in appearance.* Therefore, both CPAs and external government auditors must avoid any *personal* or *external* impairments that would reasonably lead others to question their objectivity or ability to perform the audit. For example, it would be inappropriate for an auditor to accept an engagement to audit a spouse or relative, regardless of the degree of objectivity that might be maintained. Similarly, unreasonable restrictions on the time allowed to complete an audit could impair independence. External government auditors must also be *organizationally* independent. To be so, external government auditors must meet at least one of the following criteria:

- They are auditing a different level of government (e.g., a state auditor audits a local government)
- They are auditing a different branch of the same level of government (e.g., a legislative auditor is auditing an executive branch agency)
- They are elected by the citizens
- They are elected by and report to the legislative body
- They are appointed by the chief executive, but are confirmed by and report to the legislative body

The question of independence is further complicated for local governments because the local government, as defined by GAAP, may comprise more than one legal entity. In such cases, the auditor of the "oversight entity" must not only be independent of the local government as legally defined, but must also be independent of all other "component units" included within the financial reporting entity as defined by GAAP.

### *Types of Audits*

Local governments typically receive one of three types of financial audits. These audits are categorized based on the standards used by the auditor to conduct and report upon the engagement.

*GAAS Audits.* At a minimum, an audit must be conducted in accordance with generally accepted auditing standards (GAAS). These standards are set by the Auditing Standards Board (ASB) of the American Institute of Certified Public Accountants (AICPA). There are ten fundamental GAAS, which are categorized into general standards, standards of field work, and standards of reporting. The ten basic GAAS have been the subject of a considerable authoritative commentary issued by the ASB in the form of Statements of Auditing Standards (SAS).

*GAGAS Audits.* In many cases, however, auditors of local governments are required to go beyond GAAS and follow generally accepted *government* auditing standards (GAGAS). These standards are established by the General Accounting Office (GAO) and are set forth in the publication *Government Auditing Standards* (1988), commonly referred to as the "yellow book." GAGAS do not replace the AICPA standards, but rather supplement GAAS to tailor them to the unique needs of the public sector. Accordingly, GAGAS incorporate by reference all the field work and reporting standards of GAAS. GAGAS do, however, establish separate general standards that replace those of GAAS. GAGAS are required for all federally mandated audits. In addition, a number of states and local governments have chosen to mandate the use of GAGAS even in the absence of a federal requirement for their use.

***Single Audits.*** A third type of audit encountered at the local level is the "single audit." Such audits were mandated for many local governments receiving federal financial assistance by the federal Single Audit Act of 1984 (Single Audit Act). Before the Single Audit Act, local governments receiving assistance from more than one federal grantor agency frequently were required to undergo multiple audits, often involving duplicative testing of the same internal control structure. The Single Audit Act eliminated such a duplication of effort by mandating one audit to meet the needs of all federal grantor agencies. As with all audits mandated by the federal government, single audits must be performed in accordance with GAGAS. Furthermore, these audits must meet additional requirements set forth in the Office of Management and Budget's (OMB) Circular A-128, *Audits of State and Local Governments.* Table 12-1 compares auditing standards under GAAS, GAGAS, and Single Audit requirements.

All GAGAS audits, including single audits, place a premium on a government's compliance with applicable laws and regulations. Accordingly, in the past such engagements were referred to as financial *and compliance* audits. Although this terminology has been modified in the most recent edition (1988) of *Government Auditing Standards,* the emphasis on compliance remains unchanged.

## *AUDIT PROCUREMENT*

### *Audit Quality*

Theoretically, licensure of auditors should assure recipients of audits that they will receive high-quality services. Unfortunately, experience has shown that licensure alone is not a guarantee that a government will receive a high-quality

TABLE 12-1
*Financial Auditing Standards*

| GAAS | GAGAS | SINGLE AUDIT |
|---|---|---|
| General Standards (AICPA) | General Standards (Yellow Book) | General Standards (Yellow Book) |
| Standards of Field Work (AICPA) | Standards of Field Work (AICPA + Yellow Book) | Standards of Field Work (AICPA + Yellow Book) |
| Standards of Reporting (AICPA) | Standards of Reporting (AICPA + Yellow Book) | Standards of Reporting (AICPA + Yellow Book) |
| | | OMB Circular A-128 |

audit.[3] The quality of audit services, like those of other professionals, depends on the skill and professionalism of the provider.

Of course, substandard audits are not a problem unique to the public sector. Nevertheless, several factors sometimes aggravate the problem for local governments.

One such factor is the specialized expertise that is needed to perform an audit of a local government. For instance, auditors need to be familiar with the specialized accounting and financial reporting practices and standards found in the public sector (e.g., GASB pronouncements). Likewise, as noted previously, auditors often are required to perform audits of local governments in accordance with standards that go beyond those used for audits of private-sector enterprises. As a result, expertise and experience in private-sector auditing does not ensure that a given audit firm will be able to perform a high-quality audit of a local government.

Another factor that may aggravate the problem of substandard auditing in the public sector is the misperception on the part of some audit firms that audits of local governments pose only a minimal risk of liability. Consequently, local governments sometimes find that audit firms assign less-seasoned staff to their engagements.

Also, auditors sometimes are unaware of all the interested parties who will rely upon the audit reports of local governments. Audits of public-sector entities not only must meet the needs of investors and creditors, as must audits of commercial enterprises, but they also must meet the needs of grantors and oversight bodies.

Finally, and perhaps most important, local governments often have placed too great an emphasis on price in the selection of an auditor. Such an approach can lead to the selection of less qualified or unqualified audit firms.

Given all the factors that sometimes lead to substandard audits of local governments, what steps can a government take to ensure that its audit meets high professional standards? A recent GAO study, *CPA Audit Quality: A Framework for Procuring Audit Services* (August 1987), established an important link between the quality of audits and the process used by a government to procure an audit. The GAO study established four critical attributes of a sound audit procurement process:

- *Competition.* Governments should consider no less than two audit firms in their selection process
- *Solicitation.* Governments should use comprehensive requests for proposals that contain all audit requirements
- *Technical evaluation.* Governments should consider the technical qualifications of proposers and not just price in making their selection of an auditor
- *Written agreement.* Governments should prepare audit contracts that delineate the respective responsibilities of both the auditor and the government

The GAO study found that of the audits reviewed, a full 46 percent were substandard when the government's audit procurement process lacked one or more of these critical attributes. Conversely, only 17 percent of audits were found to be substandard when all the critical attributes were present in the government's procurement process.

Accordingly, the GAO report included a recommendation that governments be provided with detailed guidance on how to obtain quality audit services. As a first step, the National Intergovernmental Audit Forum issued *How to Avoid a Substandard Audit: Suggestions for Procuring an Audit* (1988). This booklet provides an overview of each of the principal aspects of audit procurement and monitoring. Detailed guidance was then furnished in the 1989 *Audit Management Handbook*, issued by the Government Finance Officers Association (GFOA) in cooperation with the National Association of State Auditors, Comptrollers, and Treasurers.

### *Responsibility for Obtaining Audit Services*

In practice, governing bodies often delegate the responsibility of obtaining an external financial audit to an existing committee (e.g., the finance committee) or to an individual. Ideally, as discussed later in this chapter, this responsibility should be assigned to a special audit committee. Nonetheless, ultimate responsibility for engaging the services of an auditor rests with the governing body itself. Accordingly, when this responsibility is delegated to others those so delegated typically make a formal recommendation on auditor selection to the governing body, which then acts upon or rejects that recommendation.

Regardless of how a governing body chooses to delegate the responsibility for obtaining an external audit, it is vitally important that those selected corporately possess the expertise needed to make an informed recommendation to the governing body. In particular, the responsible individuals should collectively possess specific knowledge of governmental accounting, auditing, and financial reporting. Without such expertise, it is difficult, if not impossible, to design appropriate procurement procedures and to evaluate the relative merits of audit firms making proposals.

### *Planning for the Audit*

Once responsibility for obtaining the audit has been assigned, those responsible must identify the scope of the engagement. For example, what legal requirements are set in federal, state, or local law or regulation for the scope of the audit? Are there legal guidelines that must be followed by the government in its procurement of audit services? What auditing standards (i.e., GAAS, GAGAS, single audit) are to be used?

A decision must also be made concerning the level of assurance to be provided by the auditor. As noted in the chapter on accounting and financial reporting, local government financial reports take a "pyramid approach" to financial reporting, and may contain both individual, combining, and combined financial statements. At a minimum, auditors are required to provide an opinion on the fair presentation of financial data at the combined level. When this approach is taken, auditors judge the materiality of data in relation to each of the combined fund types and account groups.[4]

Governments may, however, wish to ask their auditors to provide a "full-scope" opinion on the fair presentation of the financial statements. Using this approach, auditors judge the materiality of data in relation to each of the individual funds and account groups. Accordingly, full-scope audits provide local governments with a greater degree of assurance than do opinions based on the combined financial statements.

Both the GASB and the GFOA are formally on record in favor of the use of full-scope auditing, and full-scope audits are required by law or regulation in a number of jurisdictions.[5] Nonetheless, governments often decide not to seek a full-scope audit to avoid increased audit fees. In making a decision, individuals responsible for obtaining the audit should consider the view expressed in a GFOA policy statement that the additional cost of a full-scope audit "should be more than offset by the benefit of providing full assurance to all users with regard to the financial statements of every government."[6] Individuals responsible for obtaining an audit should also use the planning stage to consider the types and amounts of assistance that the government is willing to provide to the external auditor and the procedures and schedule that will be followed in the auditor selection process.

### *Soliciting Audit Services*

At the heart of the audit procurement process lies the preparation of a request for proposals (RFP). The RFP is an important informational document that, to be effective, must serve the needs of both potential proposers and the government.

The RFP needs to provide potential proposers with a broad range of information. For example, proposers need to know how and when they will be required to submit proposals and how those proposals will be judged. They also need to know the scope of the engagement and the auditing standards to be followed. In addition, proposers need to be informed about the nature of the government, including its fund structure, budget, and accounting system. They also need to know about any existing weaknesses or anticipated problems. Furthermore, proposers will desire information on the type and amount of assistance to be provided by the government, as well as on timetables for audit performance and required reports.

The RFP must also provide officials responsible for selecting the auditor with the information they will need to evaluate proposers' technical expertise. Accordingly, the RFP should ask for specific information about proposers' technical qualifications, prior experience, and proposed audit approach. Information on the anticipated audit approach is particularly useful in evaluating whether proposers have a sound grasp of the scope of the engagement and the government's unique environment.

### *Evaluating Proposals*

If a government has prepared a sound RFP, the proposals received by the government should provide all of the information needed to select an auditor.

In practice, a variety of approaches may be taken to selecting an auditor. One common approach is to request proposers to submit information on their technical qualifications and audit approach separately, but simultaneously, with information on their price bid. Separate "scores" are then assigned to each of the two pieces of the proposal, and the proposer with the highest overall score is selected. Another approach is initially to ask proposers only for information on their technical qualifications and audit approach. The government then invites only the most qualified proposers to submit price bids. Still another approach is the negotiated bid process. Under this method, proposers are not asked to submit price bids. Instead, the most qualified firm is identified on the basis of technical qualifications and audit approach and a price is negotiated with that firm. If a satisfactory price cannot be negotiated, then the government attempts to negotiate a price with the firm determined to be the next best qualified.[7]

Although price is an important consideration, it is vital that any auditor selection process place a premium on expertise. To accomplish this goal, governments must establish a scoring system for proposals that is clearly weighted in favor of technical qualifications rather than price. Moreover, governments must take care that such a system is properly applied in practice. If only a superficial evaluation is made of technical qualifications, then most or all of the proposers may receive the same technical score, even though important differences exist between them. In that case, price, rather than qualifications, becomes in effect the main determining factor in selecting among proposers.

For example, assume that a government is evaluating proposers' ability to audit the government's electronic data processing (EDP) system. The government could decide to give a perfect score on this item to all proposers who have experience auditing EDP systems. Not all EDP experience, however, is likely to be of equal value to the government. Some firms, for instance, may have extensive experience with hardware systems and software applications similar to those used by the government, while others may lack such experience. A sound proposal evaluation process should take such important differences into account in assigning scores to serve as a basis for auditor selection.

Once an auditor is selected, a contract should be drafted that carefully delineates the respective responsibilities of both the auditor and the government. In many instances, such a contract will incorporate by reference the specific provisions of the RFP used to solicit proposals. Governments are *not* well advised to allow an auditor's engagement letter to substitute for a well-drafted audit contract.

## *CONDUCT OF THE AUDIT AND REPORTING RESULTS*

### *Internal Controls and Audit Testing*

As mentioned previously, a financial audit is the process of systematically collecting the sufficient, competent evidential matter needed to attest to the fairness of a government's financial statements. The first step taken by an auditor in collecting this evidence is to gain an understanding of a government's internal control structure.

The government's internal control structure comprises three elements. The first element is the control environment, which includes the various factors that enhance or impede the effeciveness of policies and procedures. For example, a well-managed internal audit function, as discussed later in this chapter, can greatly enhance the control environment. Conversely, a dismissive attitude toward internal controls on the part of management can hamper the effectiveness of even the best-designed controls.

The second element of the internal control structure of a government is its accounting system. A government's accounting system consists of the

> methods and records established to identify, assemble, analyze, classify, record and report an entity's transactions and to maintain accountability for the related assets and liabilities.[8]

The third element of the internal control structure comprises the various control procedures, such as the segregation of incompatible duties, used to ensure that certain objectives will be achieved. Although a theoretical distinction is made between the accounting system itself and control procedures, in practice they usually function as two aspects of a single, integrated system.

Once the auditor has gained an understanding of the government's internal control structure and has documented that understanding in a manner (e.g., flowcharts, questionnaires, narratives) appropriate to the size and complexity of the government, the auditor is prepared to assess control risk. To understand the importance of this assessment, it is essential to distinguish first between two different categories of tests that may be performed by auditors.

On the one hand, auditors will *directly* test assertions related to material components of the financial statements. These assertions include existence/occurrence, completeness, rights/obligations, valuation/allocation and presentation/disclosure. On the other hand, auditors will also *indirectly* test financial statement assertions by testing the accounting system and control procedures that produce them. Tests of the first type are known in the auditing literature as "substantive tests"; tests of the latter type are referred to as "tests of controls." An example of each of the two types of tests may help to clarify the difference.

Assume that auditors wish to determine if the amount reported as "equipment" on the balance sheet is materially misstated. Also assume that the government has established procedures designed to ensure that all new equipment is automatically tagged and recorded in the accounts as part of the process of preparing a voucher to authorize payment to the vendor. As part of their effort, the auditors may decide to test the voucher system to determine that vouchers for equipment do, in fact, include tag numbers, as required indicating that all new equipment has been added to the equipment account. Such a test would be a "test of controls." Auditors also may conduct an inventory of equipment and compare the amount of equipment on hand, as determined by the inventory, to the amount of equipment reported in the accounts. Such an equipment inventory would constitute a substantive test.[9]

Although tests of controls may allow an auditor to place a high degree of reliance upon a government's control system, such tests can never eliminate the need for substantive testing. Nevertheless, the results of tests of controls can have an important effect on the nature, timing, and extent of substantive testing. The assessment of control risk is undertaken to determine the extent to which tests of controls may be used efficiently to modify substantive testing. If, based on the auditor's understanding of the internal control structure, a given set of internal controls appears well designed, the most efficient way to conduct the audit may be to rely extensively on those controls. On the other hand, auditors may find that certain controls are poorly designed or otherwise likely to be ineffective (e.g., insufficient staff for a proper segregation of incompatible duties). In that case, the auditor may be forced to rely heavily upon substantive tests. The specific type of substantive testing used (i.e., tests of details or analytical review procedures) also depends upon the auditor's assessment of control risk.

If the auditor determines in the assessment of control risk that it may be efficient to rely to a greater or lesser extent on certain controls, the auditor must obtain the evidence needed to ensure that those controls are, in fact, functioning as designed. Sometimes, such evidence may have already been collected as part of the process of obtaining and documenting the government's internal control structure. More commonly, the auditor has to conduct additional tests of controls after the preliminary assessment of control risk to gain the evidence needed to support that assessment. If the evidence gained through tests of controls does not support as high a degree of reliance on internal controls as the auditor had anticipated during the assessment of controls, the nature, design, and extent of substantive testing must be changed accordingly.

Single audits form something of an exception to the relationship just described between tests of controls and substantive tests. In single audits, auditors are required to perform additional tests of controls for all major federal financial assistance programs, regardless of whether they plan to rely upon those controls to modify substantive testing. Furthermore, if a government's major federal financial assistance programs do not comprise at least 50 percent of total federal financial assistance received by the government, auditors are then required to perform additional tests of controls for nonmajor programs, in decreasing order of size, until the controls on at least 50 percent of federal financial assistance have been so tested.[10]

***Control Weaknesses.*** In the course of obtaining the evidence needed to express an opinion on the fair presentation of the financial statements, the auditor may discover weaknesses in a government's internal control structure. If these weaknesses are significant, they must be communicated to management and are known as "reportable conditions."[11] Moreover, some reportable conditions are of such significance that they could result in material misstatements of the financial statements. Weaknesses in this subcategory of reportable conditions are known as "material weaknesses."[12]

*Compliance Testing.* One significant environmental characteristic of the public sector is the importance placed upon governments' complying with applicable legal requirements. Indeed, lack of compliance with legal requirements can sometimes have a material effect on the fair presentation of financial statements. Accordingly, all types of audits of local governments involve some testing of transactions for compliance with applicable laws and regulations.

In the case of federal financial assistance, auditors normally test for compliance with both *general* and *specific* requirements. General compliance requirements are those applicable to all federal financial assistance programs (e.g., Davis-Bacon Act, civil rights, cash management). Specific requirements, on the other hand, are the detailed guidelines that apply to particular federal financial assistance programs (i.e., types of services, eligibility, matching/level of effort, reporting, cost allocation, special requirements, and monitoring subrecipients). Suggested audit tests for general compliance requirements, as well as for specific compliance requirements applicable to the largest federal financial assistance programs, can be found in the OMB's *Compliance Supplement for Single Audits of State and Local Governments* (*Compliance Supplement*). The use of the tests recommended by the *Compliance Supplement* is voluntary, but auditors normally perform these tests because the *Compliance Supplement* has the practical benefit of serving as a "safe harbor" in any federal review of the quality of the audit. To determine specific compliance requirements for federal assistance programs not contained in the *Compliance Supplement,* auditors often turn to the *Catalog of Federal Domestic Assistance* or to the grant contract itself.[13]

### Auditor's Reports

An auditor's reporting responsibilities depend upon the standards used to conduct the engagement. Nonetheless, at a minimum, all audits will result in a report on the fair presentation of the financial statements. If the auditor determines that the financial statements are not materially misstated, the auditor will issue an unqualified or "clean" opinion. Alternatively, some deficiency (e.g., a lack of adequate fixed asset records to support the amount of fixed assets reported on the balance sheet) may require an auditor to issue a "qualified" opinion; in other words, the auditor will attest that the financial statements are fairly presented *except for* certain specified items. In extreme cases, auditors may not be able to express an opinion at all ("disclaimer of opinion") or may be compelled to state that the financial statements are *not* fairly presented ("adverse opinion").

Auditors also have reporting responsibilities for weaknesses in internal controls discovered in the course of an audit. In a GAAS audit, reportable conditions, including material weaknesses, are typically reported in a separate letter to management. This letter ordinarily is not published and may or may not be available to the public. In a GAGAS engagement, on the other hand, reportable conditions are communicated in a published report on internal controls. In a single audit, the GAGAS report on internal controls is further supplemented by an additional report on internal controls that specifically addresses controls over federal financial assistance programs.

Single audits and other GAGAS engagements also result in published reports on a government's compliance with applicable legal requirements. For a simple GAGAS engagement, the auditor is required only to provide positive and negative assurance on tested transactions; in other words, the auditor states in the report that all transactions tested, unless otherwise noted, complied with applicable legal requirements, and that there was no evidence to suggest that transactions not so tested were not also in compliance with legal requirements. In single audits, the GAGAS report on compliance is supplemented by up to three additional reports that specifically address compliance with laws and regulations connected with federal financial assistance programs. In one of these reports, the auditor is required to express an opinion on whether major federal financial assistance programs have complied with specific program requirements. The auditor issues a second report to address compliance by major federal financial assistance programs with general compliance requirements. Finally, the auditor issues a report to address compliance by nonmajor federal financial assistance programs. It also should be noted that single audits require auditors to report *all* instances of noncompliance, regardless of materiality.

Auditors in single audit engagements are also required to present a report on the fair presentation of the government's schedule of federal financial assistance. The auditor does *not* assert in this report that the schedule of federal financial assistance taken alone is fairly presented, but only that that schedule is not materially misstated *in relation to* the government's financial statements. Table 12-2 shows the various reports required under GAAS, GAGAS, and Single Audit standards.

In addition, it should be noted that GAGAS standards allow auditors to issue separate reports on illegal acts or indications of illegal acts.

### *Findings and Questioned Costs*

The reports on internal controls and compliance required by GAGAS and the Single Audit Act do not typically include detailed descriptions of reportable conditions and instances of noncompliance. Instead, these reports normally reference separate "findings" that accompany the reports. Ideally, findings describe a "condition" (i.e., control weakness or instance of noncompliance), set forth the criteria used to identify the condition (e.g., applicable law), discuss the cause and potential effect of the condition, and offer a recommendation on how the condition may be eliminated.[14]

In addition, single audits and other GAGAS engagements often present schedules of "questioned costs." These are charges to federal financial assistance programs whose allowability has been questioned by the auditor. The most common types of questioned costs are

- Unallowable costs (i.e., charges specifically not permitted by the grantor)
- Undocumented costs
- Unapproved costs (i.e., charges not contained in the grant budget or

charges requiring prior grantor approval when such approval was not, in fact, obtained)

- Unreasonable costs

### *Report Formats*

GAGAS and the Single Audit Act require auditors to issue a variety of reports, as described above. Ideally, these reports would be issued in conjunction with the auditor's opinion on the fair presentation of the financial statements and would accompany those statements.[15] Many governments, however, have encountered practical difficulties in preparing such a single report in a timely manner, or have decided for some other reason that their needs would be better served in some other way. Therefore, many governments publish required GAGAS and Single Audit reports—together with related findings, recommendations, and schedules—separately.

TABLE 12-2

*Required Auditors' Reports for Financial Audits*

| | GAAS | GAGAS | SINGLE AUDIT |
|---|---|---|---|
| Report on the Fair Presentation of the Financial Statements | X | X | X |
| Report on the Fair Presentation of the Schedule of Federal Financial Assistance | | | X |
| Report on Internal Controls | | X | X |
| Report on Internal Controls Related to Federal Financial Assistance Programs | | | X |
| Report on Compliance | | X | X |
| Report on Compliance with Specific Program Requirements for Major Federal Financial Assistance Programs | | | X |
| Report on Compliance with General Requirements for Major Federal Financial Assistance Programs | | | X |
| Report on Compliance for Nonmajor Federal Financial Assistance Programs | | | X |

### *Audit Monitoring*

A government is well advised to monitor the audit process. One important goal of such monitoring is to determine that the auditor is performing the engagement on schedule. For example, a government should verify throughout the engagement that the auditor is meeting deadlines set in the RFP and audit contract. Examples of important milestones of the engagement that should be monitored include the entrance conference, the beginning and ending of interim field work, the beginning and ending of year-end field work, the exit conference, and the issuance of the auditor's final reports.

Governments also need to monitor the audit to ensure that timely action is taken to remedy control weaknesses, instances of noncompliance, and potential audit qualifications that have been tentatively identified by the auditor.

### *Audit Resolution*

The final stage of the financial audit is audit resolution. As noted above, auditors normally identify weaknesses in the course of the audit and make appropriate recommendations, either in a management letter (for GAAS engagements) or in "findings and recommendations" that accompany GAGAS reports on internal controls and compliance. The audit resolution process should ensure that appropriate corrective action is taken to correct the conditions that remain unresolved at the close of the audit. One means of accomplishing this goal is to require the establishment of a corrective action plan that sets out the specific actions that must be taken by management and the timetable for such actions. The government should then monitor compliance with the corrective action plan and hold management accountable for any failure to meet its commitments.

## *PERFORMANCE AUDITING*

Traditional audits of financial statements focus on whether management is providing users of the financial statements with reliable information. They do not address the more fundamental question of whether management is meeting its responsibilities efficiently and effectively. To gain such assurance, interested parties must turn to the performance auditor.

Performance audits may be conducted by independent third parties or by internal audit staff within the government. When performance audits are performed by independent third parties, the same independence standards described earlier for financial audits normally would apply. When performance audits are performed by internal audit staff, staff members ordinarily should meet the special standards for independence discussed later for the internal audit function.

Although performance auditors and financial auditors use many of the same techniques, there are important differences between the two types of engagements. For example, financial audits are designed to attest to the fairness of *explicit management assertions* (i.e., the financial statements). Accordingly, the financial auditor's report is quite limited, taking the form of a commentary on what remains a management document. Performance audits, on the other hand, rarely involve explicit management assertions. Instead, such audits examine the *implicit* assertion of management that it is meeting its responsibilities efficiently and effectively. As a result, performance audit reports are essentially auditor documents, with management's participation in the published report being limited to responses to findings and recommendations.

Another important difference involves the respective scope of financial and performance audits. The scope of a financial audit normally encompasses the entire entity being reported on in the financial statements. It is not normally practical, though, for the scope of a performance audit to encompass an entire entity. Instead, performance audits typically focus on individual departments, agencies, activities, or functions within a government.

Also, the nature of the criteria used by the auditor in a financial audit differs from the nature of the criteria used in a performance audit. In financial audits, auditors judge the "fair presentation" of financial statements in accordance with GAAP. GAAP, in turn, are defined by a comprehensive authoritative accounting literature that has received general acceptance. There are no such uniformly accepted standards for judging whether management has performed its duties "efficiently" and "effectively." Accordingly, the performance auditor faces the difficult task of defining persuasive criteria of efficiency and effectiveness for each engagement.

Standards for performance auditing in the public sector are contained in the GAO's *Government Auditing Standards,* along with the standards discussed earlier for financial audits. These GAGAS for performance audits encompass general standards, field work standards, and standards of reporting.

The general standards used for performance audits are identical to those used for GAGAS financial audits. The field work standards and reporting standards, however, are specifically tailored to the needs of performance audits. Specialized field work standards for performance audits address the issues of planning, supervision, compliance, internal controls, and evidence. Specialized reporting standards for performance audits address the issues of form, timeliness, contents, presentation, and distribution of reports.

Performance audits normally follow a pattern that is similar, in many respects, to that followed in financial audits. The audit typically begins with a preliminary survey to gain an understanding of the department, agency, activity, or function to be audited, including the relevant internal control structure. After conducting this survey, the auditor is prepared to plan and conduct the engagement. Upon completion of the audit, an appropriate report is prepared. Finally, steps are taken to ensure that issues identified in the audit are resolved satisfactorily.

## THE INTERNAL AUDIT FUNCTION

Many local governments have established an internal audit function. Ideally, this internal audit function should serve as an independent appraisal mechanism within a government's internal control structure. Although the internal audit function may indirectly benefit parties outside of government, its primary responsibility is to aid government's management in fulfilling its responsibilities.

Internal auditors, like external financial auditors, often devote considerable effort to the study and testing of a government's accounting system. Indeed, as will be discussed later, this common focus often allows external financial auditors to build upon the work of internal auditors. Nonetheless, the focus of the internal auditor's work is broader than that of the external financial auditor and may encompass the testing and evaluation of the efficiency and effectiveness of programs, activities, and functions (i.e., performance auditing).

In the public sector, internal auditors often use the standards set forth in the GAO's *Government Auditing Standards* to conduct their audits. In addition, internal auditors may use the specialized standards issued by the Institute of Internal Auditors, which are consistent with those set forth by the GAO.

Because the internal auditor functions within the government and works primarily for the benefit of government's management, the internal auditor cannot be expected to meet the same criteria for independence that must be met by external financial or performance auditors. Nevertheless, an appropriate degree of independence is still necessary if internal auditors are to be effective in meeting their responsibilities. *Government Auditing Standards* states that to be considered independent, internal auditors should

- Report the results of their audits to the head or deputy head of the government
- Be accountable to the head or deputy head of the government
- Be organizationally located outside the staff or line management function of the unit under audit
- Be free of personal or external impairments to their independence

In addition, the GAO standards recommend that internal auditors, when feasible, "be under a personnel system in which compensation, training, job tenure, and advancement are based on merit."[16]

In practice, internal auditors often play a variety of roles in their government. In addition to testing accounting systems and evaluating performance, internal auditors also often are asked to investigate possible irregularities, to report on complaints or to work on other specific projects assigned by management or the legislative body. Moreover, because of their specialized expertise, internal auditors are often asked to provide technical support and assistance to management or the legislative body. For example, internal auditors may be asked to help prepare the RFP for audit services and to help evaluate the respective qualifications of proposers. Similarly, internal auditors are often involved in the design and implementation of new electronic data-processing systems and control procedures. Likewise, management often turns to its internal auditors for technical support in conducting reviews of the internal control structure that may be required under financial integrity legislation.[17]

External financial auditors often make use of the work of internal auditors in performing the annual or biennial audit of the financial statements. On the one hand, external auditors can build upon the work already performed by internal auditors. In that case, the external auditors treat the internal audit function as a separate "control" in its own right and perform appropriate tests to justify reliance upon that control. On the other hand, external auditors sometimes make use of internal audit staff to perform portions of the external audit engagement itself, under the external auditor's supervision. Close coordination of efforts between internal and external auditors can help both to achieve their goals more efficiently with scarce audit resources.

## *AUDIT COMMITTEES*

Ideally, governments should establish audit committees to advise the governing body on all matters related to the external financial audit, as well as on matters related to the government's internal control structure, including the internal audit function. Audit committees have been a common feature in the private sector for a number of years, but have only recently become common in the public sector as well.

Audit committees are particularly useful for several reasons. First, audit committees can serve as an excellent channel of communication between the external auditors, management, and the governing body. Second, audit committees can serve as a valuable pool of technical expertise upon which the governing body can draw in making decisions related to the external financial audit and the government's internal control structure. Also, audit committees serve as an important safeguard for the independence of the external financial audit.

In selecting an audit committee, a governing body should place primary emphasis on two considerations. First, the membership of the audit committee should collectively possess the technical expertise in accounting, auditing, and financial reporting needed to fulfill its duties. Second, the membership of the committee should be structured so that it cannot be dominated by the government's management. To achieve this second goal, governments may decide to require that a majority of the members of the audit committee come from "outside" the government. In other cases, independence may be achieved by insisting that any members of the governing body serving on the audit committee not exercise direct financial management responsibility within the government.

In practice, the size of audit committees can vary. What is important is that the audit committee be large enough to provide needed expertise, but small enough to form a practical working group. Normally an audit committee of about five members is appropriate on both counts.

An audit committee typically performs a variety of specific duties. Examples of such duties include

- Planning for the annual financial audit
- Preparing an RFP for the annual financial audit

- Selecting an audit firm
- Monitoring auditor performance
- Monitoring audit resolution
- Reviewing financial statement presentations (e.g., reasonableness of estimates, appropriateness of accounting principles selected)
- Reviewing the annual internal audit plan

The importance of audit committees has recently been underscored in the authoritative auditing literature by a GAAS requirement that auditors assure themselves that the audit committee (or its equivalent) is informed of certain specific audit-related matters. Examples of such matters include a change in accounting policies, significant audit adjustments, difficulties encountered in performing the audit, and disagreements with management.[18]

## PROFESSIONAL DEVELOPMENTS

In recent years, the auditing profession has taken important steps to improve the quality of audits. Two of the most important steps taken include mandating continuing professional education and peer reviews.

The 1988 edition of *Government Auditing Standards* mandates that both external and internal auditors performing audits in accordance with GAGAS meet certain specified levels of continuing professional education (CPE). At a minimum, auditors are required to receive 80 hours of CPE for each two-year period, with no less than 20 hours of CPE in any given year. Also, GAGAS now require that, in most cases, at least 24 of the 80 hours of required CPE be directly related to the government environment and governmental auditing.[19] Audit organizations are further required to establish and maintain a system to ensure that their staff meet these requirements.

The 1988 edition of *Government Auditing Standards* also introduced a new general standard of "quality control." This standard requires that both external and internal audit organizations be subjected to an external quality control review or "peer review" every three years. This review is designed to ensure that organizations have adequate policies and procedures and that these policies and procedures are being followed.

The GAO standards just described apply, of course, only to auditors conducting audits in accordance with GAGAS. The AICPA has recently adopted a change in its bylaws that sets similar CPE and peer review requirements for all of its members in public practice. Such standards would apply to all AICPA members conducting audits of local governments in accordance with GAAS.

## CONCLUSION

Auditing, in all of its forms, plays a vital role in local government finance. Internal auditors help to ensure the integrity of the government's internal control structure and assist management in meeting its responsibilties. External financial auditors provide users of local government financial statements with the independent assurance they need that data in those statements can be relied upon. Performance auditors, both external and internal, help to ensure that programs, activities, and functions are managed efficiently and effectively.

Auditing allows local governments to draw the contrast between what is and what should be. By doing so, local governments should be better prepared to meet the needs of their citizens and others with a vital interest in the government's finances.

## *NOTES*

1. Concepts Statement No. 1, *Objectives of Financial Reporting,* (Stamford, CT: Governmental Accounting Standards Board, 1987) paragraph 30, identifies these three groups as being the primary users of external local government financial reports.

2. See *Governmental Accounting, Auditing and Financial Reporting* (Chicago: Government Finance Officers Association, 1988), p. 131.

3. See the following reports published by the GAO: *CPA Audit Quality: Inspectors General Find Significant Problems* (Washington, D.C.: General Accounting Office, December 1985) and *CPA Audit Quality: Many Governmental Audits Do Not Comply with Professional Standards* (Washington, D.C.: General Accounting Office March 1986).

4. Combined fund types and account groups are recognized as the appropriate level for judging materiality in the AICPA's industry audit and accounting guide, *Audits of State and Local Governmental Units* (New York: American Institute of Certified Public Accountants, 1986), section 5.5.

5. See the *Codification of Governmental Accounting and Financial Reporting Standards* (Norwalk, CT: GASB, 1990), Appendix B, and the GFOA's policy statement, "Audit Coverage of Individual Funds" (Chicago: Municipal Finance Officers Association, 1983).

6. "Audit Coverage of Individual Funds" (Chicago: MFOA, 1983).

7. While negotiated bids are required in certain jurisdictions, they are often prohibited in others by law or regulation.

8. SAS No. 55, *Consideration of the Internal Control Structure in a Financial Statement Audit* (New York: AICPA, April, 1988).

9. While tests of controls and substantive tests serve conceptually different purposes, they are *not* mutually exclusive. Therefore, it is common for auditors to design tests that contain elements of both.

10. See *Audits of State and Local Governmental Units* (New York: American Institute of Certified Public Accountants, 1986), sections 21.11–.12.

11. SAS No. 60, *Communication of Internal Control Structure Related Matters Noted in an Audit* (New York: AICPA, 1988), defines reportable conditions as "significant deficiencies in the design or operation of the internal control structure, which could adversely affect the organization's ability to record, process, summarize, and report financial data consistent with the assertions of management in the financial statements."

12. SAS No. 60, *Communication of Internal Control Structure Related Matters Noted in an Audit* (New York: AICPA, 1988), defines a material weakness as "a reportable condition in which the design or operation of the specific internal control structure elements do not

reduce to a relatively low level the risk that errors or irregularities in amounts that would be material in relation to the financial statements being audited may occur and not be detected within a timely period by employees in the normal course of performing their assigned functions."

13. See SAS No. 63, *Compliance Auditing Applicable to Governmental Entities and Other Recipients of Governmental Financial Assistance* (New York: AICPA, 1989).

14. See *Government Auditing Standards* (Washington, D.C.: General Accounting Office, 1988), pp. 7-4–7-6.

15. See *Government Auditing Standards* (Washington, D.C.: General Accounting Office, 1988), p. 5-12.

16. *Government Auditing Standards* (Washington, D.C.: General Accounting Office, 1988), pp. 3-8–3-9.

17. The federal government and several states have passed "financial integrity" legislation mandating that management itself conduct periodic reviews of a government's internal control structure and report on the results of those reviews. The theory behind such legislation is that a government's internal control structure can be effective only if it enjoys the active support of management.

18. SAS No. 61, *Communication with Audit Committees* (New York: AICPA, 1988).

19. *Government Auditing Standards* (Washington, D.C.: General Accounting Office, 1988), p. 3-2.

# 13
# *Cash Management*

Girard Miller

Cash management can be defined as all activities undertaken to ensure maximum cash availability and maximum investment yield on a government's idle cash. Cash management is concerned with the efficient management of cash from the time revenue is earned to the time an expenditure payment clears the bank. At the local government level, cash-management activities can be categorized as follows:

1. Receipt and deposit of cash and negotiable payments
2. Custody of monies and securities of the government
3. Disbursement of funds upon proper authorization
4. Dealing with financial institutions
5. Investment of cash in money-market securities and related instruments
6. Cash budgeting and forecasting
7. Short-term borrowing

Numerous other activities also are performed by most cash-management personnel. For example, in some local governments, the treasurer is the chief fiscal officer and performs many other administrative duties. Because of the great variety in organizational structures, and the lack of homogeneity in how these functions are assigned to treasury or other finance personnel, this chapter focuses primarily on the cash-management functions common to most local governments, regardless of the department or administrative structure to which they are assigned.

The cash-management function generally is concerned with short-term investments. Some governments invest pension funds, debt-service funds, and trust funds for multiyear periods that could be considered long-term investing; these lie beyond the realm of cash management.

## OBJECTIVES: EFFICIENCY, SPEED, AND CONTROL

For years, local governments were much less cash conscious than private companies. Since the 1970s, however, expanding operations, increasing liquidity, high interest rates, and growing professionalism have resulted in increased attention to the cash-management function. In its simplest form, the cash-management function has three elements:

1. *Cash mobilization: Get the cash in as fast as you can.* Cash mobilization is simply the process of actively transforming financial claims into cash. For example, invoicing procedures should be reviewed to ensure that billings are current and actively monitored. Tax payments and other revenues should be deposited swiftly so that collected funds are available for investment. *Collection procedures* should be established to control aging receivables and to accelerate cash availability. Failure to pursue prompt payment can be viewed as an interest-free loan to a third party. Generally, taxpayers are entitled to earn interest on the funds to which they have a claim. Funds should be deposited as quickly as feasible to reduce "collection float."
2. *Controlled disbursement: Release cash at the last possible moment.* Although prompt payment is a virtue, premature disbursements result in lost interest income. Many governments have implemented techniques that enable them to disburse "just in time." Computerized accounts-payable systems now permit the cash manager to enter deadlines for receiving discounts or for net payment. Special care should be taken when handling large disbursements, such as debt service payments, so that cash is not released prior to the due date. In some cases, extra charges for wire transfers are justifiable considering the additional interest earned during the extra time held.
3. *The investment program: Do something worthwhile with the cash in the meantime.* A prudent investment program can help government officials generate additional income from their cash resources. Precautions should be implemented, however, to ensure that undue risks are avoided. Safety and liquidity come before yield in the design of a public-sector investment program. The sophistication of local government investment officials has increased dramatically in the past decade, as new technologies and techniques have become readily available.

With this general perspective of the goals of public cash managers, let us now examine the seven functions in greater detail.

## *RECEIPT AND DEPOSIT*

As cash and negotiable items (checks, wire transfers, and other payments) are received, the cash manager faces two immediate responsibilities. First, accountability must be established, so that precise records of cash receipts are available and auditable. Second, an aggressive program should be implemented to accelerate the deposit of cash receipts, so that funds become available for investment as quickly as possible.

In many governments, the accounting function is separated from treasury operations. Also, cash collections (e.g., tax payments) may occur through another jurisdiction, such as a county government, which subsequently transfers cash to other jurisdictions. Nonetheless, most treasurers' offices include cash-receipting equipment and record-keeping systems. With the advent of microcomputer technology, it is possible now to integrate sophisticated cash-receipt systems with the central accounting operation, thereby establishing point-of-sale records that tie into the general ledger. In smaller jurisdictions, however, simpler cash-receipt systems may exist, and the cost of automation may be unwarranted. The guidance of external auditors might be necessary to assist in determining the adequacy of the record-keeping system. Otherwise, the decision to employ advanced technology should be made on the basis of labor savings and speed.

Many jurisdictions retain the lockbox services of commercial banks to assist in the cash-receipts function. This helps to assure timely deposit of funds by eliminating the float between the public treasurer's office and the depository. Banks typically have high-speed, high-volume equipment available for receipts processing, which may add efficiency. Original documents can be provided to the contracting governmental jurisdiction so that accountability is retained. Some public treasury employees complain, however, that outside agencies such as bank lockbox offices fail to provide adequate service whenever exceptions arise. Therefore, the benefits of lockbox services should be weighed against possible complications. In general, the larger the jurisdiction, the more likely that economies of scale will make such services attractive. Some larger local governments are attempting to duplicate lockbox services internally in order to reduce costs while maintaining quality control.

Now that checking accounts pay interest, many individuals and corporate officials have become efficient cash managers; they delay payment until the due date. Therefore, local governments are less likely to receive early payments. Nonetheless, efforts should be made to accelerate cash receipts whenever possible. In some cases, tax collection schedules must be revised, and this frequently requires legislative action at the local or the state level.

Special attention should be given to high-dollar-amount receipts. Even at 5 percent interest, a $1 million deposit is worth $200 per business day (after averaging in weekends and holidays). Depository transfer checks (DTCs), the local automated clearing house (ACH), and messengers can be used to expedite collection of investable funds.

Large jurisdictions frequently receive cash at many locations, sometimes through operating departments that are otherwise unfamiliar with sound financial practices. The cash manager and other financial management personnel should take special care to review these remote receipt stations and design an appropriate control and connection network. Departments that receive large payments (e.g., state or federal aid, developer fees) must be informed of their responsibility to transfer such receipts immediately in order to maximize accountability as well as interest income. In general, auditors find that lax receipt practices present an opportunity for embezzlement.

## CUSTODIAL FUNCTIONS

Cash managers have important custodial responsibilities relating to both cash and securities. Five kinds of cash must be controlled by the cash manager:

1. *On hand:* This includes currency, checks, and other forms of money in the hands of the treasurer or other receiving offices that are available immediately for deposit.
2. *Demand deposit accounts:* These are the checking accounts to which funds are deposited and from which withdrawals, wire transfers, and checks are paid.
3. *Imprest cash:* Cash and change funds for cashiers.
4. *Petty cash:* Money that has been segregated for disbursement by the treasurer or other designated officers of the government, which can be used in limited amounts for specified purposes.
5. *Temporary investment:* Some cash managers regard their short-term investments—including repurchase agreements, bank accounts, and money-market fund balances—as cash equivalents.

Although embezzlement of cash from the public sector has been relatively rare, this constitutes a major political risk for public officials because of the attention such incidents draw in the local press. Generally, the chief financial officer should carefully review cash-control procedures with the internal staff as well as the auditor. Appropriate fiduciary and performance bonds should be purchased to protect the jurisdiction from the losses that could occur in the cash accounts. Although some jurisdictions "self-insure" their cash risks, such decisions should be approved at a level higher than the finance office, so that responsibility is taken to the appropriate level.

### Custody of Securities

Local governments have become major investors in money-market instruments. The custody of the investment securities has therefore become a significant cash-management responsibility. Access to securities must be tightly controlled, with no single person (even the treasurer) allowed access without a cosigner or witness.

Many securities are fully negotiable and may be sold by the bearer. These instruments pose the greatest security risk. Fortunately, book-entry and registered securities have become more prevalant in the past decade, and most local governments have access to bank safekeeping departments to serve as custodians for negotiable securities. Some local governments have entered into written agreements with commercial banks (or their trust departments) to serve as custodians for all their investment securities. Because banks' trust departments are legally separated from their commercial banking operations, some cash-management professionals prefer to isolate their safekeeping in the trust department if this can be accomplished at a reasonable cost. Important fiduciary protections are offered by trust departments under the regulatory controls required by federal and state bank examiners. Under such arrangements, the cash manager never sees the securities themselves, but instead receives verifiable receipts of ownership. The bank also can arrange for collection and deposit of interest earned. In general, instruments that are held by the same financial institution that acted as counterparty (seller) in a transaction are categorized as riskier than those for which independent (third-party) delivery is arranged. This independence can be enhanced through book-entry computerized custody at a Federal Reserve bank, provided that a third-party institution is used as the intermediary custodian. Many governments have entered into contractual agreements for their custodial services.

### *Collateral for Public Deposits*

Presently, 43 states require that public entities obtain collateral securities to protect public deposits. Generally, the statutes require that to protect uninsured deposits, marketable securities such as Treasury, federal government agency, or municipal securities be segregated and held as collateral. In the event of a bank or thrift failure, the receiver is expected to transfer the collateral securities to the investing government.

Three methods of collateralization are common. In some states, uniform statewide collateralization systems are administered by the state treasurer or a similar central office. All depository institutions are required to operate under the same rules, and local officials do not become involved directly in the administration of the collateralization program. In others, the state law may establish standards, but local officials remain responsible for preparing custodial agreements and monitoring the collateral. In 4 states (Connecticut, Florida, Oregon, and Washington), a partial collateral program is administered by a central state official, allowing depositories to pledge only a fraction of the total deposits—which are pooled and held as "insurance" against a bank or thrift failure.

Although collateralization practices differ from one state to another, recommended professional practices do exist.[1] As with repurchase agreements,[2] an additional margin of collateral should be pledged to protect depositors from adverse market price changes that occur during periods of rising interest rates. These economic periods are likely to produce bank failures, thereby necessitating the requirement that collateral exceed the amount of deposit plus accrued interest. Some states now permit nonmarketable securities (such as residential mortgages) for deposit pledging, but require considerably higher collateralization ratios (e.g., 150 percent or 200 percent).

## *DISBURSEMENT OF FUNDS*

Most governmental disbursement systems have become highly automated and routinized. Typically, disbursement activities center on payroll, debt service, capital outlay, and accounts payable.

*Payroll operations* typically are accomplished through computerized check-processing systems that are owned by the jurisdiction or obtained contractually through service bureaus. Master files are created for accounting purposes and a single cash transfer is made to "cover" the payroll. For jurisdictions with Friday payrolls, the opportunity exists for "playing the float" over the weekend by investing some of the funds that will not be collected through the banking system until the following Monday. As automated direct deposit payroll systems through local automated clearing houses (ACHs) become increasingly popular, however, the opportunity to derive interest income from the payroll has diminished in many jurisdictions.

For *debt-service payments,* most local governments employ a paying agent, which may require deposits well in advance of the date of disbursement. To the extent possible, funds should be wired on the last possible day, so that interest income is maximized. Larger jurisdictions with numerous outstanding bond issues sometimes can successfully negotiate or renegotiate their paying agent arrangements, so that interest income is maximized. As with payroll, the unique advantage of debt-service disbursements is the certainty of the disbursement date, which makes planning relatively simple. Fixed-term investments, such as bank certificates of deposit, can be selected to mature on the date required for disbursement, and investment income thus can be augmented because the cash manager is able to forego liquidity.

*Capital outlay* presents a "wild card" in the cash management function, because capital disbursements are less readily controlled. Construction contractors are notorious for encountering work stoppages or other delays in their projects; these cannot be planned in advance. Similarly, early deliveries of large equipment, such as fire trucks, have been known to foil the best-laid plans of public cash managers who invest their funds for the longest possible time. Department heads and consulting engineers generally are reluctant to provide accurate projections of needed capital outlays; they generally tend to err on the side of safety, which from their perspective is the earliest possible disbursement schedule. Some cash managers seek to overcome this problem by purchasing marketable securities that could be liquidated a few weeks or months prior to maturity in the event payment schedules are accelerated. Sometimes control over construction payments can be achieved through negotiation of contracted payment dates; the project manager should be consulted. Another alternative is to place construction funds into investment agreements, such as flexible repurchase agreements or guaranteed investment contracts that permit cash withdrawals at any time on or after the original drawdown schedule.

Routine *accounts payable* constitute the final dimension of the disbursement program, and these generally take one of two forms. Many governments process their accounts payable on a "batch" basis—payable monthly or semimonthly, or biweekly (off cycle from payroll). These large accounts payable disbursements are not entirely predictable, although most cash managers quickly develop an intuitive sense for their size and the extent to which float can be anticipated. For example, a $250,000 semimonthly accounts payable run might be projected during the previous week, based upon input available through the accounting system. Although the actual disbursements might prove to be $10,000 more or less on the day of disbursement, investment planning generally need not be quite that precise. Further, the cash manager should be able to estimate that on the first day following the disbursement, a certain percentage of the checks will still be in the mail, thereby permitting the jurisdiction to continue to invest perhaps $200,000. On the second day, however, as checks are presented against the jurisdiction's depository, additional funds must be provided, and investments must be liquidated to cover the disbursement.

Some jurisdictions have eliminated the use of batch processing, and instead pay on the last possible date according to a payables aging subprogram built into their accounts payable system. Such "just-in-time" techniques maximize investment income and tend to produce a steady flow of disbursements. For large jurisdictions, the rule of large numbers tends to work in the cash manager's favor, as the fluctuations in disbursements tend to cancel each other out. The result is that a minor liquidity pool (an overnight investment account or money-market fund) can be used to cover daily fluctuations.

### *Toward a Floatless Society*

The Federal Reserve, operating under the mandate of the Monetary Control Act of 1980, has aggressively acted to minimize the "float" in the banking system. Whereas checks drawn on geographically distant banks once required as much as a week or two to clear the banking system, the new operating procedures now have reduced this clearance time to two days, and even less in many locations. Thus, the opportunities for public cash managers to aggressively "play the float" have diminished considerably. Although a day of interest can still be significant, the opportunities for such earnings diminish as we gradually improve the payments system. To the extent that automated clearing houses and other systems eliminate the check as an instrument of payment, the disbursement side of the cash-management function will probably receive less attention as an area for opportunity to generate income.

## *RELATIONSHIPS WITH FINANCIAL INSTITUTIONS*

State and local governments are not in the business of making money: Cash management is a by-product of governmental operations. Specialized financial institutions, such as banks and securities dealers, therefore must be engaged to serve as agents or counterparties for most cash-management activities. Stated another way, a government's cash-management program cannot be conducted in a vacuum. Virtually all significant transactions must be accomplished through an intermediary. Most funds transfers at the time of purchase and maturity of investments are accomplished through a commercial bank. To control risk, many public investment officials have formalized their relationships through contracts with the institutions that conduct their investment transactions.

Deregulation of the financial services industry has somewhat blurred the lines separating banks, savings institutions and government securities dealers. Nonetheless, certain traditional functions performed by these industries remain concentrated in their respective sectors, and most local governments tend to rely on certain institutions for specific services.

For instance, routine cash-management services continue to be provided mostly by commercial banks. Although other financial service organizations now offer many of the same services, there often are significant advantages to conducting specific cash-management functions through commercial banks. On the other hand, the competitive interest rates offered by some savings institutions sometimes have lured public-sector investment officers away from commercial bank CDs. Finally, a variety of investments that might not otherwise be readily available through depository institutions can be purchased through securities dealers and investment companies.

The public cash manager's challenge is to take advantage of the specialty services and expertise provided by firms that compete to conduct business with their jurisdiction. Different analysis and judgment tools are needed, depending on the nature of the services, the risks associated with each, and the nature of the account relationship.

### *Depository Relationships*

Before funds can be invested, a government must first have a depository. Thus, the most appropriate place to begin the process of evaluating financial institutions is in the area of depository services. These are discussed below.

*Account-Maintenance Services.* For years, most commercial banks have provided basic account-maintenance services. Monthly statements of account provide the information necessary for the accounting division to reconcile transactions against the organization's own ledgers. Many modern financial institutions provide additional account-maintenance services that further benefit their customers. For example, many financial institutions now offer reconciliation services that provide for sequential listings of checks paid regardless of date of processing. For the accounting staff, this feature simplifies the reconciliation process.

A second service of perhaps greater importance to the investment officer is the account analysis report, which should include average daily balances per ledger, collected or available funds, service volumes, and fees. When this data is available, the disbursement float (lag between disbursement and payment by the bank) can be analyzed. Another popular service is direct computer access to account balances through treasury workstations or other electronic media. By providing current information on funds availability, the financial institution helps the investment officer minimize idle assets.

*Wire Transfer Facilities.* One of the most important investment functions of a commercial bank is wire transfer. By wiring funds, immediate payment is made, eliminating delays in the mail or through the check-clearing system. Institutions with direct access to the Federal Reserve system are preferred, because wire transfers can be subject to errors or delays. Small governments in particular complain that wire transfers conducted through correspondent banks for small, local institutions often become delayed in the wire system. Wire failure frequency should be considered when comparing depositories. Because of the risks associated with wire transfers, some banks and governments have adopted written agreements and procedures to govern wire transfer activity. Recently, the Federal Reserve invoked "daylight overdraft" controls over certain outgoing wire transfers, which could impede the activities of governments whose business represents a major proportion of a given financial institution's capacity.

*Concentration Accounts.* These are used to pull all cash into a single bank account through which investment transactions are made. Receipts may be realized in various other accounts, but the cash flows through the concentration account for investment purposes. Zero-balance disbursement accounts are an important part of the overall concentration account. Those accounts are used to pay disbursements, and needed funds are "swept" into the account at the end of the day. Meanwhile, idle cash is swept from the concentration account into interest-earning vehicles. The number of these accounts depends on the financial reporting system used by the jurisdiction. Use of a concentration account helps facilitate a pooled investment program and helps minimize leaks in the cash management system.

*Sweep Facilities.* A sweep facility enables a government to provide for daily transfer of available cash balances automatically from a demand deposit account to an interest-earning vehicle such as an overnight repurchase agreement. This system eliminates the possibility of lost income as a result of inaction by the public investor. Vacations, unexpected absences, emergency meetings, and other typical causes of investor inaction can be overcome through such systems. Before instituting a sweep facility, however, the bank's timing schedule should be explored. Some institutions require lags of one or two days before sweeping the funds. This lag can prove costly in terms of lost earnings.

*Investment Services.* Bank investment departments provide a useful vehicle for purchasing U.S. Treasury and agency securities, which are commonly traded by the financial institution. For some investors, the costs of conducting business through a depository's investment department might be less than the cost of making telephone calls to securities dealers. The bank investment department sometimes also can provide useful information and investment opinions. Investment purchases can be accomplished simply through a debit against the entity's concentration account, thereby eliminating the need for wire transfers. Safekeeping services also can be provided as part of this function, particularly if handled through the trust department of a nationally regulated bank. Use of the same bank's facilities for safekeeping remains controversial, however.

*Lockbox Services.* Lockbox collection can reduce collection float, thereby increasing the volume of funds available for investment purposes. A lockbox can often reduce personnel costs within the finance department, provided reconciliation systems are efficient and the workload is not duplicative of the tasks ordinarily performed by the treasury operation. A cost-benefit analysis may be needed to determine whether economies of scale and float reduction warrant a change.

*Credit Facilities.* Another service offered to public organizations is a standby or open credit facility. The availability of overnight or short-term loan facilities can be helpful if investment officials mismatch investment maturities and cash-flow needs. For example, if an unexpected claim arrives while cash is tied up in nonnegotiable bank CDs, it would be helpful to have arranged in advance for a standby credit facility. Some governments transact these short-term loans in the form of reverse repurchase agreements, whereby their governments' Treasury securities are exchanged temporarily for cash to meet bills. Upon maturity of the outstanding investment instruments, the reverse repo is "unwound" and the financial institution returns the original collateral securities.

### *Depository Selection*

As the foregoing overview suggests, the cash-management function involves complex services that must be evaluated systematically for the public's benefit. This section offers a brief summary of key concepts.

Competitive selection is best accomplished through a written request for proposal (RFP) for banking services. The RFP format can be flexible, but it always includes requests for information to facilitate the evaluation of facilities such as those described above, as well as costs and the financial stability of the institutions under consideration. Most banking services RFPs therefore include a specification of banking and investment facilities that are desired or expected, and they employ a format that allows the responding institution to describe its services, costs, and creditworthiness.

In the cost segment of the RFP, pricing structures are examined using several formats. Most jurisdictions receive proposals on a per-item basis, using estimated quantities and volumes provided by the initiating government. Others prefer a float-fee basis, with adjustments to be made in the event of above-normal volume. Some governments allow the bidding institutions to offer prices on a compensating-balance basis, in addition to direct fees. (Compensating balances are idle funds in a nonearning account that are used to compensate the bank for services.) Generally, reserve requirements imposed by the Federal Reserve Board make the compensating-balance approach less desirable, so most cash management experts advocate the direct-fee-payment method. Political, budgetary, and management considerations, however, continue to dominate in many governments where the compensating-balance method remains popular. Some governments also report unexpected success in negotiating favorable terms for their compensating-account earnings credits.

In addition to cost and available services, a third and final dimension of the competitive RFP for banking services involves financial statistics needed for the investing government's officials to evaluate the creditworthiness of the institution. Nobody wants to select as a lead bank an institution that is doomed to fail. To avoid such embarrassing and potentially costly errors in judgment, public investors turn to formal credit analysis. Financial statements, financial statistics, ratios, and ratings are collected as part of the evaluative process.

Unfortunately, the various factors studied when evaluating a financial institution for purposes of depository selection may be contradictory. The lowest-cost institution might bid aggressively for business—but could represent significant credit risks, or it might have a poor track record for providing efficient, accurate services. On the other hand, the most businesslike, reliable, and creditworthy financial institution might include a premium in its pricing structure, making it unduly costly for a local government to conduct business with this depository.

As a result, there is no single best way to score and evaluate proposals for banking services. In fact, the subjectivity of the process is certain to challenge even the most disciplined, price-conscious, and technically oriented cash manager. In the end, tradeoffs become necessary, and judgments are required. Because of the inherent politicization of the process and the absence of industrywide standards or rules of thumb, some government investment officials prefer to retain the services of independent consultants to aid in the process. The expertise of such consultants at least adds credibility to the process and relieves investment officials of potential charges of favoritism or bias. An additional benefit is that experienced consultants in the field of banking relations have developed some general sense for industrywide trends and practices that can provide useful benchmarks for appointed and elected officials.

### *Securities Dealers*

Increasing activity in the government securities market has attracted public investors to the facilities available through government securities dealers and related money-market brokers. Generally, these dealer-client relationships are beneficial, offering needed competition to the depository sector and providing diversification of public portfolios, but this trend toward increasing use of securities dealers has not been without casualties. During the 1980s hundreds of millions of dollars of public funds were lost through unsecured and sometimes imprudent transactions with a handful of government securities dealers.

Government securities dealers generally conduct their business in one of two ways. The most prominent of the dealer firms are subsidiaries of diversified national financial service organizations that serve retail and institutional clients in various markets, including the stock market, the bond market, the money market, and the government securities market. Their government securities operations are supported by capital provided by a parent organization, and the firms typically operate a network of regional and local offices that share space with other brokerage concerns. Research capabilities typically are provided through a central office, and many securities dealers who make markets in money-market instruments are specialists within the firm.

In some cases, the dealers are licensed by other regulatory agencies because of the firm's involvement in other markets. Primary dealers are regulated by the Federal Reserve, where they must make markets daily. Major houses offer their clients a relatively full plate of available government and agency securities. Because the size of their central trading desk, they can provide access to many markets for their clients.

The other common form of organization for securities dealers is the specialized dealer who participates exclusively in government securities or other money market instruments. These dealers tend to carve out a market niche. Some analysts refer to them as secondary dealers, a term that also refers to any firm that is not a primary dealer. Their niche is based on the instruments they offer, their clientele, or some other factor that sets them apart from the multipurpose broker-dealers. Within this category, some of the firms operate as large national firms with a few branch offices, while others serve only local or regional markets.

### *Other Financial Institutions*

In addition to securities dealers and banks, other financial institutions also are competing for public funds. In the United States, savings and loan associations (sometimes called S&Ls or thrift institutions) offer competitive interest rates on term certificates of deposits. Although most S&Ls lack the facilities to offer full-service banking, some are competing successfully for public funds. In a growing number of states, mutual fund companies also offer numerous cash-management services, either directly or through state investment pools. As with depository selection, public finance officials must be careful to assure propriety in the selection of these institutions.

## *THE INVESTMENT PROGRAM*

In many jurisdictions, the central focus of the cash-management program is the investment function. After all, the purpose of maximizing cash position is to marshal as many cash resources as possible to earn investment income. This investment process has become increasingly complex and sophisticated.[3] In general, the investment literature has developed sufficiently to permit generalization of the investment process as follows:

- An investor's opportunity, constraints, preferences, and capabilities must be identified and specified explicitly in written investment policies.
- Investment opportunities are identified and strategies are implemented through the purchase of financial securities and related instruments in the marketplace.
- The investor's circumstances, market conditions, and relative values of securities are monitored; results are documented and reported.
- Portfolio adjustments are made in response to new objectives and changing circumstances and results.[4]

Thinking about investments this way emphasizes that the investment process involves considerably more than simply picking out attractive assets as if selecting jewelry. For governments, the process outlined above requires a specific methodology that governs the actions of responsible officials. Policies must be based on a government's intrinsic characteristics and the preferences of its leadership. Procedures must be implemented to provide timely, thorough assessment of market conditions and strategy development.

As helpful as this conceptual framework might be, however, public sector cash managers have experienced difficulty in implementing these general concepts. Accordingly, an eleven-step checklist has been developed for short-term investors:

1. Identify the entity's objectives, constraints, preferences, and capabilities.
2. Develop investment policies.
3. Develop administrative systems and internal controls.
4. Prepare a cash forecast.
5. Determine the investment horizon.
6. Establish an investment outlook and strategy.
7. Analyze the yield curve.
8. Select optimizing instruments.
9. Monitor the markets and investment results.
10. Report results.
11. Adjust and rebalance the portfolio accordingly.

Note that these steps parallel closely the four-part description of the investment process discussed earlier. The value of this step-by-step approach is that responsibilities can be assigned to participants along the way, and the chronology of the investment process becomes clearer. Procedures and examples can guide public officials through each step, so that the overall process can be understood through its parts rather than in terms of the abstract concepts. Although this approach could still fail to produce optimal results, disciplined use of these basic procedures provides the framework for prudent investment of public funds.

### *Investment Policies*

Investment policies provide the formal structure that governs the activities of investment officials. Even when statutes regulate the activities of cash managers, investment policies are needed to clarify the entity's investment objectives, preferences, constraints, and procedures. The following subjects frequently are included in investment policies:

- Scope
- Objectives

- Instruments
- Maturities
- Diversification
- Credit and market risk
- Delegation and authority
- Prudence
- Ethics
- Indemnification of investment officials
- Controls
- Relationships with banks and dealers
- Investment committee composition and responsibilities
- Safekeeping and custody
- Interim and annual reporting
- Performance evaluation and operations audit

Modern investment policies provide considerable guidance to the cash manager by defining acceptable investments and risk parameters. Many policies written in recent years include the prudent-person investment clause, which places a considerable responsibility on the investment official. Although each jurisdiction is somewhat unique and therefore must customize its investment policy, much can be learned from studying policy language used by other jurisdictions—particularly those with full-time staff personnel responsible for policy development.

### *Cash Budgeting and Forecasting*

The goal of cash forecasting is to provide a projection of funds available for investment purposes for a specific time horizon, such as three months, six months, or one year. The purpose of cash forecasting is to provide a "road map" for the investment officer, so that short-term investments can be made on the basis of reliable projections rather than guesswork. Frequently, interest rates paid on longer-term investments are higher than those on shorter maturities. In the long run, investors who forego the liquidity of shorter-term investments expect to be compensated through higher yields. Thus, in theory at least, a cash forecast should help to produce superior investment results. Figure 13-1 illustrates how a cash forecast can help an investment official plan the year's investments so that funds are invested for the longest maturity possible.

To prepare a cash forecast, most cash managers first develop a cash budget. This can be prepared monthly or weekly using projections of cash receipts from various sources (such as taxes, bond proceeds, permits, fees, and grants) and cash disbursements (usually payroll, accounts payable, debt service, and capital outlay). The net cash inflow/outflow is projected for each forthcoming time interval, and this becomes an adjustment to the prevailing cash and investment balance. Historical cash and investment levels can be plotted and analyzed to reinforce the

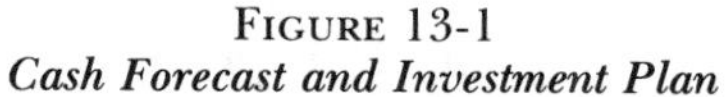

FIGURE 13-1
*Cash Forecast and Investment Plan*

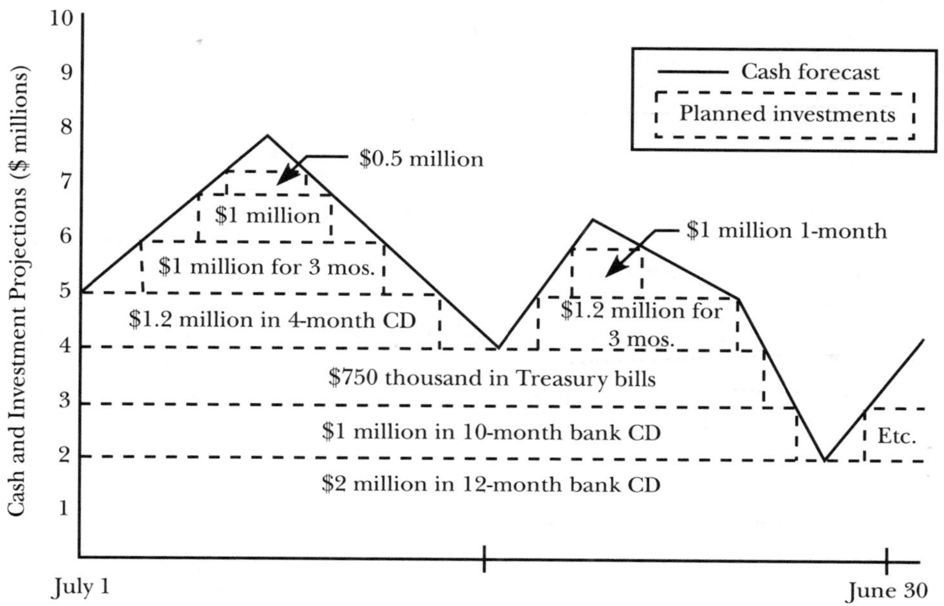


SOURCE: Girard Miller, ed., *Financial Management Handbook for Local Governments* (Chicago, IL: Government Finance Officers Association, 1986), p. 67.

reliability of the cash projections particularly when seasonal cash flows are important.

***Investment Instruments***

The selection of appropriate investment vehicles is an important stage of the overall cash-management process. State laws and investment policies generally establish the list of investment instruments from which the cash manager is permitted to choose. Among investment vehicles recommended for local governments are the following.

*U.S. Treasury Securities.* Short-term obligations of the U.S. government are permitted in all 50 states. Because the Treasury securities market is the world's largest and most liquid, these instruments offer a useful benchmark for all other money-market instruments. Typically, Treasury securities yield less than other instruments, because they are liquid and free of credit risk. Many public cash managers purchase Treasury bills, which are discount securities (priced at a discount from their face, or maturity, value). Also available are short-term notes and bonds that pay coupon interest every six months. Longer-term Treasury bonds also are available, although their use is discouraged for short-term cash managers, because the market prices of long-term fixed-income securities decline whenever interest rates increase. Price is inversely related to yield, and volatility increases as maturities are lengthened.

Also popular among some cash managers are so-called zero-coupon securities, which are created by separating the interest payment from the corpus of a Treasury bond. An investor, for example, might purchase a "bundle" of Treasury bond coupon interest payments due in 18 months, and pay for them at a discount from their maturity value. In some states, the legality of these instruments is still questionable unless they are purchased through the Federal Reserve's book-entry system. Most important, however, is the market price volatility of long-term zero-coupon securities. Because a change in interest rates must be reflected entirely in a price change, these securities lose 20 to 40 percent of their value whenever interest rates increase by 2 to 3 percentage points.

*Government Agencies and Instrumentalities.* Short-term discount securities are available from several federal agencies and instrumentalities (government-sponsored corporations). These instruments trade similarly to Treasury bills, although usually at higher yields that compensate investors for their reduced marketability and greater credit risk. Longer-term agency paper is also available, paying constant interest semiannually on coupon dates. Another type of agency security is the floating-rate note, issued by several government-sponsored corporations. Yields on "floaters" fluctuate with the market, protecting investors from future price risks. Other so-called agency securities include mortgage-backed instruments, which reflect partial ownership of a pool of mortgages. These longer-term securities generally are not appropriate in a cash-management context, but rather should be used by long-term investors such as pension funds.

*Bank Certificates of Deposit (CDs).* Commercial banks issue certificates of deposit. In many states, these instruments must be collateralized by marketable securities if they are purchased in amounts that exceed Federal Deposit Insurance Corporation limits. CDs are popular with public investment officials because the purchaser can select the maturity to match known disbursement requirements for payroll and debt-service payments. Yields typically exceed those of Treasury bills, although this is not always the case. Savings and loan associations also market their certificates of deposit to public cash managers. Some large banks also issue negotiable certificates of deposits, which typically are not collateralized, but can be sold to other investors in the open marketplace. These instruments trade much like other money-market securities, usually in $1 million blocks.

At the time of this writing, bank deposits typically are insured for $100,000 per bank per customer. Hence, a municipality investing in two $100,000 CDs at the same bank is federally insured only for $100,000. To protect the other deposits, most states require collateralization. The investment official should understand the collateralization mechanisms, if any, established under state law, and self-administer added protection if needed.[5]

*Bankers' Acceptances (BAs).* Some states now permit public entities to purchase bankers' acceptances. These trade instruments typically represent private financing in the form of a discount note. Often, the note is collateralized by goods in shipment, although receivables also may be used for security. A commercial bank then "accepts" the paper, adding its unconditional credit guarantee in the process. Instead of holding the note in its own portfolio, however, the bank often elects to sell it into the open market, which creates a "banker's acceptance" as a money-market instrument. Although public participation in the bankers' acceptance market began with domestic BAs, state and local governments in several western states also invest regularly in Japanese banks' acceptances. Because each transaction is typically independent, it is often difficult to detail ratings on individual BAs. Thus, some investors look to the credit rating of the bank's CDs or its long-term debt for hints about creditworthiness.

*Commercial Paper.* Instead of borrowing from commercial banks, major corporations frequently enter the money market in their own name. Their unsecured short-term borrowing is called commercial paper. Securities & Exchange Commission requirements for registration are waived for corporate debt maturing within 270 days, which is the practical limit for commercial paper. Much of the paper purchased by public entities is very short-term, with 5-, 15-, or 30-day maturities dominating the activity. Because there is no governmental credit guarantee (unless provided by a third-party bank), commercial paper is regarded as riskier than other money-market instruments. Accordingly, public investors typically purchase only top-rated (A-1, P-1) commercial paper. In large, well-diversified portfolios, however, the instrument can produce supplemental income without incurring undue risk. Smaller entities, however, must be careful to limit the size of their commercial paper investments because of the potential default risk.

*Money-Market Funds.* Investment companies offer money-market mutual funds whose portfolios consist entirely of short-term, high-quality investments. The funds offer the advantages of liquidity, safety, diversification, and professional management. In some market periods, the returns of money-market funds exceed those of other, competing instruments. For small jurisdictions lacking the resources needed to embark on active portfolio management, these funds offer a reasonable alternative to interest-earning bank accounts. In some states the authority for the mutual funds includes commercial paper, CDs, and BAs. This broader authority enhances their potential as a diversified source of higher returns. Investments that would be too risky in a small portfolio can be held prudently through a mutual fund.

*State Investment Pools.* Approximately 25 states have authorized state investment pools, which operate much like money-market funds under the supervision of the state treasurer or a governing board. The state pools combine assets of municipalities and special districts, purchase money-market securities, and distribute the income on a pro-rata basis. Some pools do not employ accrual accounting, however, so their cash-basis returns may be distorted. Some purchase long-term instruments whose yields differ from the current money market—making them attractive during declining-rate, or low-rate, market periods.

### Short-Term Investment Strategies

Cash managers can choose from several basic investment strategies, each of which may be appropriate under specific circumstances. The choice of a suitable investment strategy depends on such factors as the size of the portfolio, the sophistication of the investment staff, the availability of investment services through local financial institutions, and the support (or lack of support) from policy makers and chief administrative officials.

*Passive Management.* Although the term *passive* tends to connote inactivity and perhaps laziness, it should not be pejorative. A compelling argument can be made that many public cash managers lack the extensive investment training that professional portfolio traders draw on. Many small governments lack the financial and technological resources to support sophisticated money market trading. Most public cash managers carry other responsibilities that detract from the time they have to devote to the markets. Generally, one must ask whether a part-time official juggling three or four other tasks (such as budgeting, debt management, and tax collections) without access to on-line financial information can compete with professional traders in the nation's central financial exchanges. A considerable body of research has led numerous academic authors to the conclusion that the investment process is a "losers' game" in which amateurs generally can do no better than hope to obtain the market average rate of return less their transactions costs.[6] Accordingly, many public officials argue persuasively—and probably accurately—that there are only a few hundred public entities that should be attempting to "play the market." For the rest, a less exciting but equally deliberate and thoughtful investment strategy is appropriate. In general, this means that most investment officials and policy makers should seek to obtain market average rates of return through prudent strategies instead of seeking "maximization."

Passive investment management strategies usually begin with a liquidity pool. In the public cash-management sector, this ordinarily means use of repurchase agreements or short-term money-market instruments that can be liquidated readily. Alternatively, state investment pools and money-market funds offer competitive rates of return, safety of principal, and high liquidity. Many portfolio analysts and advisers would recommend that all passive investment-management programs should include a liquidity component. This function also could be fulfilled through the holding of marketable government securities, such as Treasury bills. The key ingredient here is for funds to remain invested systematically and earn interest without requiring local officials to analyze the markets.

Once the liquidity base has been established, passive portfolio strategies can then take one of several forms. A popular approach in many smaller jurisdictions is the purchase of certificates of deposit that mature on known disbursement dates, such as payroll and accounts payable dates. Using a first-in, first-out timing approach, the investment manager acts to ensure that funds are invested only as "far as the eye can see." Incoming funds are invested to the next "uncovered" disbursement date. By investing in specific maturities, incremental yield usually is obtained, and there is little risk that securities must be liquidated to meet disbursement requirements.

A variation on this approach is to use the cash forecast to invest for the longest maturity possible according to the cash budget. Thus, a cash manager might purchase a one-year money-market instrument, anticipating that future incoming cash receipts will provide the funding necessary for projected disbursements. This approach is suitable for entities whose cash flows are highly predictable, and works best when the term structure of interest rates (the yield curve) is positive. Under these circumstances, additional yield is obtained from the longer maturities that are purchased.

*Active Portfolio Strategies.* In addition to these passive strategies, some public cash managers also seek to maximize investment returns through active management. This can be accomplished in several ways, depending on the profile of the entity. Generally, active management can be classified as spread/swap oriented, yield-hunting, or market timing.

*Spread or "swap" strategies* focus on the relationship between different money-market instruments. Sometimes, because of various market factors, the yield differentials between various instruments widen or narrow. As these yield relationships reach historical extremes, opportunities sometime arise to adjust the portfolio by selling lower-yielding instruments and purchasing higher-yielding instruments. An example would be the purchase of Treasury bills whenever their yields near those of local bank CDs, and holding them until such time as their yields fall significantly below the CDs. This happens occasionally, providing cash managers an opportunity to augment their income by reinvesting through a "swap" at a later date.

Many securities dealers actively suggest swaps to their prospective clients, hoping to encourage sale of an existing portfolio holding and purchase of another. In some cases, such strategies can enhance returns; however, many swap suggestions offer little if any real value in the context of yield versus additional risk. Prudent cash managers should seek a second opinion if doubtful of the merits of a swap opportunity presented by a dealer representative whose primary motivation could be to earn supplemental commission income.

Another common strategy is to shop around for *yield.* Some public investors seek the highest yielding instrument, within the limits of the required maturities, and place their funds there. The risk of such strategies, of course, is that market conditions may change and they may find that a simpler buy-and-hold strategy based on the original cash forecast would have outperformed their yield-chasing approach. Nonetheless, in an environment in which insured or collateralized bank deposits may significantly outyield other money-market instruments, this approach sometimes has merit. Caution is necessary, however, when high yields reflect high risks. If instruments reflect yield well above the market, risk should be stringently analyzed.

*Market timing* is the most questionable of all public sector cash-management strategies. Advocates of efficient markets doubt that money managers consistently outperform the market through timing of purchases or sales. Despite the availability of numerous technical trading systems, very few traders seem able to consistently outtime the market in the management of their portfolios. Nonetheless, some public investors do seek to purchase longer maturities when yields decline (prices rise) and to shorten their maturities when yields are rising (prices declining). Although such trading strategies are possible, many observers note that the institutional environment in the public sector is not conducive to "taking losses," which is the required action when prices decline and yields rise in the open markets.

A popular strategy among a few cash managers, known as *riding the yield curve,* is the purchase of investments maturing on dates longer than the original cash budget would allow, with the intent to liquidate the position prior to the needed cash disbursement date. As long as the original investment yields a higher return, it is believed by some that they should be able to liquidate at a profitable level prior to maturity. Unfortunately, the academic research does not support this claim.[7] To the extent that the financial markets already anticipate rising interest rates through a positive term structure, the probability for success in riding the yield curve can be questioned.

Overall, considerable effort and expertise is required before public officials embark upon active portfolio management strategies. This need not, however, preclude the implementation of such approaches—provided that institutional capacity and support is available, and knowledgeable, competent officials manage the program.

### *A Note about Technology*

Rapid advances in microcomputer systems and distributed data processing now enable some public cash managers to exploit systems that previously were impractical. Spreadsheet software programs greatly enhance the process of storing, retrieving, and analyzing historical cash flow data. Treasury workstations are now available, often through banks, which enable cash managers to directly access their account information, place certain orders, and perform other administrative tasks. Electronic networks permit cash managers to obtain current market information via modem. Securities dealers and mutual fund companies offer order-placement linkages to simplify the investment process. Applications software has now been designed specifically for public cash managers to assist in their portfolio management function. Many governments also have learned to use facsimile machines to request and obtain quotations on their investments. The availability of relatively low cost office machines for performing financial functions makes the cash manager's job more interesting and challenging.

## *SHORT-TERM BORROWING*

Even the most well-managed finance operations may meet with temporary cash-flow shortfalls. Short-term borrowing is used to finance these shortfalls and enable governments to meet current obligations, such as payrolls, prior to the receipt of taxes and other revenues. Short-term borrowing is also conducted at times to provide temporary financing for capital projects.

Regardless of the specific cash need or reason for short-term borrowing, such borrowing is regulated at the state and local levels by laws and also by policies governing debt issuance. Local debt policies may stipulate how much money may be borrowed during a certain period of time, from whom money may be borrowed, and what types of debt may be issued. At the federal level, use of short-term borrowing is limited by arbitrage investment regulations.

Once the timing and level of cash shortfalls is ascertained, cash managers must decide on an appropriate source of funds for temporary financing. Generally, the sources available include local commercial banks, regional and national credit markets, and state liquidity pools.

Local banks are a common source of funds for short-term needs. Access to direct loans is facilitated by preestablished relationships between governmental entities and their local banks. Due to the tax-exempt status of most loans made to governments, the rate charged on these loans is usually lower than that charged even to the bank's most creditworthy corporate customers. Due to a frequent lack of competition in obtaining bank loans, however, the interest cost of bank loans is slightly higher than the rates on public short-term debt (i.e., tax-exempt notes) in the national and regional credit markets.

Tax-exempt debt financing is the second viable option for governments seeking short-term credit. Regional and national banks, investment banking firms, and other underwriters provide a competitive market for short-term municipal debt, typically offering lower rates of interest than those offered on direct bank loans. Short-term debt issuance can demonstrate to various constituents that the municipal entity is both creditworthy and capable of accessing national or regional credit sources. Options available to those considering short-term debt issuance include: tax anticipation notes (TANs), revenue anticipation notes (RANs), and grant anticipation notes (GANs).

Some states recently have developed and begun operation of "bond bank" liquidity pools, which are a third source of short-term funds. In these states (e.g., Michigan and Indiana), an agency of the state issues long-term debt and makes the funds available to local governments to assist them with their credit needs. Cost savings are attained through this method, first, since state governments may receive a higher rating and thus lower interest costs than the local entities. Second, costs are reduced when large blocks of long-term rather than smaller amounts of short-term debt are issued. Finally, costs are reduced since local entities need not pay to obtain debt ratings as they would on their own securities.

Strategies for borrowing depend on the direction of interest-rate movement at the time of a cash shortfall. For example, during periods of rising interest rates, the cash manager may wish to borrow the entire deficit amount in one lump sum. Conversely, during periods of declining interest rates, it may be more cost-effective to borrow incremental amounts as needed.

## *SUMMARY*

The public cash management sector has evolved considerably in the postwar era, and particularly in the past decade. Burgeoning levels of municipal cash have dramatically increased the importance of this professional discipline and the opportunities to earn substantial revenue to finance government operations. On the other hand, market risks have increased during the recent deregulation of financial institutions and the general liberalization of state investment laws. Sophistication among market participants in both the public and the private sectors now compels cash managers to familiarize themselves with modern techniques and pitfalls.

## *NOTES*

1. GFOA Committee on Cash Management, *Considerations for Governments in Collateralizing Public Deposits* (Chicago: Government Finance Officers Association, 1987), 35 pp.

2. GFOA Committee on Cash Management, *Considerations for Governments in Developing a Master Repurchase Agreement* (Chicago: Government Finance Officers Association, 1988), 31 pp.

3. Miller, Girard, *Investing Public Funds* (Chicago: Government Finance Officers Association 1986), 346 pp.

4. Maginn, John L., and Donald L. Tuttle, eds., *Managing Investment Portfolios: A Dynamic Process* (New York: Warren, Gorham & Lamont, 1983), 689 pp.

5. GFOA, *Considerations for Governments.*

6. Ellis, Charles, *Investment Policy: How to Win the Loser's Game* (Homewood, IL: Dow Jones-Irwin, 1985).

7. Cox, John C., and Stephen Ross, "A Re-examination of Traditional Hypotheses about the Term Structure of Interest Rates," *Journal of Finance* (September 1981): 769–99.

# 14
# Debt Policies and Procedures

JOHN E. PETERSEN AND THOMAS MCLOUGHLIN

THE ACT of borrowing, obtaining funds today in exchange for a promise to pay them back tomorrow, is one of the most potent and profound activities undertaken in government finance. Because it permits governments to break out of the constraints of their current resources, to raise large sums of money, and to obligate future legislatures and citizens to raise revenues, the power to borrow is one of the most tightly regulated and closely scrutinized activities of local governments. Governments may issue bonds for many purposes and on their own behalf or on behalf of others. The differences among borrowers, their uses of proceeds, and the technical attributes of each type of debt instrument used are important considerations in designing and marketing a particular issue. But, no matter how technical the specifics, the nature of the decisions to be made have many similarities.

This chapter focuses on the major characteristics, decision points, and players in the issuance of conventional long-term debt sold for the traditional purpose of financing capital facilities. It consists of five major sections. The first discusses debt financing in the larger context of the capital financing decision making process and recent major trends in the financing of capital expenditures. Next, there is an overview of the alternative methods of financing and the process of selecting one. This selection process occurs within a legal framework that governs and conditions the choice of financing techniques in general and that of debt obligations in particular. The next two sections review the various decisions about the structure and the type of instrument to be used, its design, its documentation, and the process of marketing it. The chapter ends with a discussion of hiring specialized services to assist in issuing the security.

## RECENT TRENDS IN CAPITAL FINANCING

Traditionally, capital financing in the public sector has meant the raising of funds for improvements to the physical structures upon which the daily operations of governments depend. Infrastructure, otherwise defined as the publicly owned facilities of a community, is composed of facilities that transmit goods and services (such as roads, water pipes, and stormwater and sanitary sewers) and facilities that function as origins and destinations (such as airports, schools, municipal buildings, and sanitary treatment plants). Expenditures on such long-lived assets are episodic and expensive. Once the funds are expended, new funds need not be spent again for that purpose until the asset has depreciated to the point where renovation or replacement is necessary.

An important distinction is drawn between capital expenditures and recurring, or operating, expenditures. Under the balanced-budget requirement that prevails for most local governments, operating expenditures normally are covered by current revenues. Both by law and custom, however, governments have been given latitude to incur debt to finance long-lived assets. As a result, the use of long-term debt in particular has added to the financing flexibility of governments. When viewed as a whole, state and local government capital spending can be financed from three major sources:

- Current revenues from a government's own sources
- Federal aid
- Borrowing in the credit markets

Figure 14-1 presents the average annual expenditures by state and local governments on fixed investment (structures and equipment) for five-year intervals 1955 through 1989. The composition of the major sources of funds used to pay for the spending is also shown. As may be seen, while spending levels systematically grew, the composition of the sources of funds changed over the years.[1]

In the 1950s, before the dramatic growth in state and local governments, their capital spending was largely financed by long-term bond sales. During the 1960s, federal aid for public construction grew, as did contributions from current revenues, and the importance of borrowed funds diminished. The 1970s saw a dramatic rise in the importance of federal aid as a source of capital funds and a continued decline in contributions from current revenues, as this source of funds came under the pressure of taxpayer revolts and recessionary conditions. In the 1980s the trend was one of diminished federal aid and a rapidly growing reliance on debt financing.

For reasons discussed below, it is evident that federal grants are unlikely to grow with any vigor. Financing from current revenues has been difficult to expand, although "non-debt" alternative means of financing have gained favor. The debt financing option once again has been increasing in importance.

### *Federal Aid for Capital Spending*

Federal assistance has been of major importance in financing state and local capital spending. The importance, of course, has varied by functional category. Federal assistance has been of greatest importance in the areas of highways, sewers, and transit.[2]

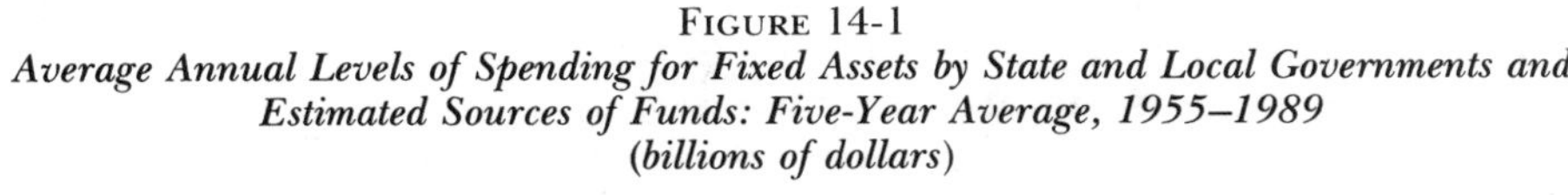

FIGURE 14-1
*Average Annual Levels of Spending for Fixed Assets by State and Local Governments and Estimated Sources of Funds: Five-Year Average, 1955–1989*
*(billions of dollars)*

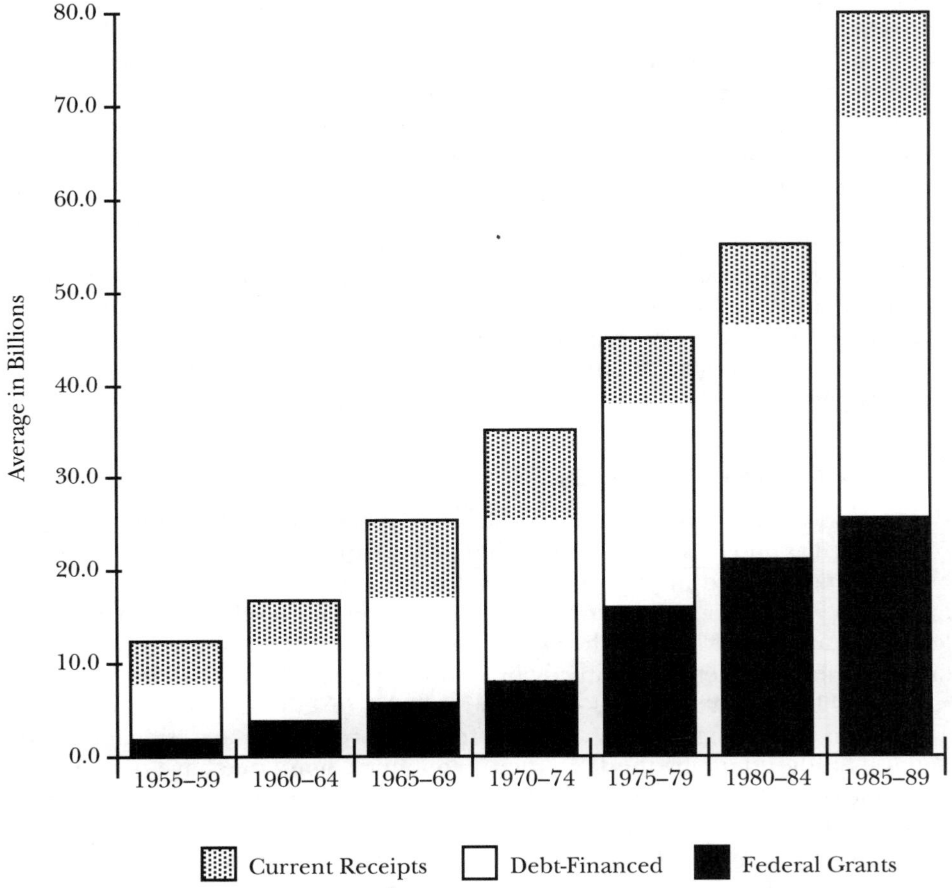

SOURCES: U.S. Bureau of the Census reports and GFOA Government Finance Research Center estimates.

There is little question that federal assistance has had a pervasive effect on both the types of capital spending state and local governments have undertaken and the way in which it has been financed. For the recipient governments, the often generous matching grants greatly lowered capital costs and tended to skew state and local budgets toward those project areas where federal assistance was available.[3] Also, the federal funds were substituted for funds that in many cases might have been raised by the states and localities themselves.[4]

Entering the decade of the 1990s, it is clear that federal aid in general, including that for capital assistance, has slowed down markedly. By all indications, federal aid will continue to decline in significance.[5]

Within the state and local government sector, intergovernmental assistance includes state payments to local governments. Such assistance may be in the form of grants, similar to the federal aid payments discussed above, or various forms of credit assistance (which, if they lead to debt on the part of localities, are treated as a form of borrowing). While state grants-in-aid are important to capital outlays in certain functional areas, such as local education, highways, and environmental projects, there is no nationally available information about the dollar value of these programs to capital spending, per se. Since states are themselves limited in current revenues, however, and often prefer that localities ultimately pay for improvements, there has been an expansion in various forms of credit assistance, such as state-sponsored loan and loan guarantee programs.[6]

Federal and state assistance may not always be a welcome windfall for local governments. Many times such programs are accompanied by a strong element of coercion if the local government is mandated to undertake an improvement it otherwise would not elect to have. In such cases, the assistance program may help lessen the local burden or remove the argument that the expenditure is not affordable.

### *Financing from Current Revenues*

Current revenues from state and local governments' own sources in the 1950s contributed as much as 50 percent of all funds to capital spending. But this source of funds has receded in importance steadily over the years, although it remains important in particular functional areas and at certain levels of government. A leading example has been in the area of highways, streets, and roads, where fuel tax revenues are often used directly by states or passed on to localities for capital spending. Local governments often use current revenues, some of which are earmarked for such purposes, to pay for their recurring and smaller capital outlays. Studies done by the U.S. Joint Economic Committee have documented that cities of all sizes on average financed about 40 percent of their general government capital spending from current revenue sources, either currently collected or accumulated in carryover balances from previous fiscal years.[7]

One problem in the use of current revenues for major expenditures is the relatively meager amount of revenue available to many local governments. Furthermore, attempts to accumulate funds in a "savings account" in the form of growing fund balances not only postpones the receipt of the benefits of the desired expenditure, but requires a political discipline that can seldom be sustained.

Historically, a major source of local revenues has been the property tax. The growth of this source has been legislatively constrained in recent years by the enactment of laws such as Proposition 13 in California and Proposition 2½ in Massachusetts. As a result of such legislation, governments frequently have had to reduce the level of long-term capital investment financed out of current revenues. A recent study that surveyed state and local government officials on the preferred ways of financing capital investment indicated that financing infrastructure through increases in local taxes is consistently the least attractive alternative available to public officials.[8]

A major change in public finance has been the shift to user fees to lessen the burden of general property taxation. Among the new "user-charge" forms of revenue is that of the impact fee, which has increased greatly in importance especially in areas where development precedes growth in the tax base. The linkage between impact fees and capital spending is particularly tight in view of the fact that necessary infrastructure improvements are usually the legal nexus for the imposition of such fees.[9]

A large, but unknown, amount of capital facilities are not purchased by governments but rather are "given" to them through dedications made by private developers. Such exactions are frequently required as a condition for many types of planned development. The character, location, and number of facilities to be dedicated for use by the general public are part of the negotiations surrounding rezonings and the approval of site plans. Projects of this nature may in fact be financed by special districts through the sale of tax-exempt bonds, but the security provided often is the credit of the developer, and payment of principal and interest is reflected in higher sales prices and rental rates, rather than through general tax receipts and user charges. Such techniques have been heavily employed in certain states and are best suited to rapidly growing areas.

In considering ways to obtain capital services by using current revenues, it should be noted that many financing techniques have been developed to obtain the use of capital goods and without purchasing the facilities outright or resorting to what is legally defined as borrowing. Lease-purchase financing, whereby the local government can finance the purchase of capital goods over time through periodic installment payments, has become increasingly popular. The use of service contracts, in which the unit of government purchases an entire service (as opposed to just the use of a facility), is another leading alternative. In this way, the government can enjoy capital services without assuming immediate ownership of the property or "borrowing" the funds as defined by state law.[10] Because of these devices, the underlying capital spending (and often the underlying borrowing) does not show up as governmental capital outlays but rather as a current operating expenditures. The extent of this behavior is unknown, but it probably amounts to the equivalent of several billion dollars in capital outlays each year.[11]

### *Debt Financing*

Borrowing traditionally has been of great importance to financing capital improvements. Developments of the late 1980s reinforced the significance of that source of funds. In examining the borrowing process, however, it is important to bear in mind that financing capital facilities, while the most important purpose of borrowing, is but one of the reasons governments go into debt. By the same token, not all debt nominally issued by state and governments should be viewed in the same light because of the different purposes for which it is undertaken and the different sources of its repayment.

The remainder of this chapter and all of the following chapters in this book discuss the borrowing process and the securities markets that deal in the obligations of state and local governments. Because the interest payments on these obligations in whole or in part are exempt from federal and most state and local government income taxes, the generic term "tax-exempt" is applied to this class of securities. There are, however, major distinctions that need to be made regarding the purposes for which borrowing is done and the types of security pledged to their repayment.

In recent years, the size and composition of the tax-exempt bond market have fluctuated greatly, under the influence of changing economic and financial conditions and changing federal government tax policies regarding various types of borrowing. After having peaked at over $200 billion in long-term bond sales in 1985, tax-exempt borrowing ebbed to slightly over $100 billion in sales in 1987 and grew at a more leisurely pace through the end of the decade. The principal factor in both the explosion in borrowing and its subsequent decline was the loosening and then tightening of the allowable uses of the tax-exempt security, most notably with the passage of the 1986 Tax Reform Act.[12]

The amount of debt outstanding and the future stream of payments of principal and interest that are needed to extinguish the obligation are of considerable long-term importance to the government issuer. Outstanding debt places a burden upon the local government obligated to repay the debt. Future revenue must be sufficient to provide services and repay previous capital obligations. The burden of debt only makes sense when its repayment is viewed in relationship to the government's underlying revenue bases available to support it. Among individual governments, the revenue base and the source of payment pledged to the payment of indebtedness will vary greatly, a subject discussed later.

While there are admittedly no perfect measures, municipal analysts rely on broad measures of economic activity or resources, such as gross national product (at the national level), personal income or gross state product (at the state level), and full market value of taxable property (at the local level) to come up with a denominator in calculating debt burdens. Examining the debt burdens of state and local governments requires care because not all debt sold in their name, in fact, constitutes their obligation. This has been especially so over the past decade because so much nominally "municipal" or tax-exempt debt in fact represents claims against underlying borrowers such as households, not-for-profit corporations, or for-profit companies, for which the government disclaims any liability for the obligation.[13]

Using the above distinctions in the nature of the revenues pledged and the underlying obligor, one can make meaningful statements about debt burdens. Taking total tax-exempt debt outstanding, including that of both governmental and private entities, one finds that as a percentage of GNP it has fluctuated over the past twenty years. First, the percentage fell from 14.2 percent in 1970 to 12.9 percent in 1980, and then grew rapidly in the early 1980s, when it peaked at

16.3 percent in 1985. It subsequently declined to approximately 15 percent by the end of 1989.[14]

These numbers mask what was happening to that borrowing in which a governmental unit is the ultimate debtor. During the above period, governmental purpose debt declined from more than 14 percent in 1970 to 11 percent of GNP in 1980; since then, it has fluctuated between 10 and 12 percent of GNP over the past decade. The more significant change, however, has been the shift from the tax-supported security to limited-obligation debt. The former has declined from nearly 8 percent of GNP in 1970 to 5.4 of GNP in 1980 to an estimated 4 percent of GNP in 1989.[15] In other words, governments have steadily decreased their reliance on tax-supported obligations. To a large degree the greatly diminished role of the tax-supported, tax-exempt security reflects the impact of the taxpayer revolt that dominated state and local finance during the decade of the 1980s. Reliance upon general government and tax revenues was reduced in favor of special districts and enterprises, and the corollary of greater reliance on user charges and fees.

## *CAPITAL FINANCING: EXAMINING THE ALTERNATIVES*

Ideally, a government contemplating capital financing needs to examine all the alternative sources of funds. The more common ones are current revenues or accumulated reserves, grants, contributions from private parties, funds from prior bond issues, or the receipts of new borrowings. By the same token, new borrowings may take a variety of forms or the government may elect to acquire capital services through various forms of leases or service contracts. As a practical matter, most governments usually can boil the options down to a few feasible alternatives once the nature and scale of the project and the government's current fiscal circumstances, legal powers, and the conditions of the market are considered.

The financing issue is usually couched in terms of own-source funds. Normally, when gifts or intergovernmental grants are available, such sources will be used unless there are overriding restrictions or delays. Of increasing importance recently has been the substitution of private financial sources such as impact fees for public resources. As noted, in states experiencing rapid growth, much public infrastructure is being provided for by private developers as a condition for development privileges through proffers and dedications.[16] In addition, governments may elect to take things a step further and "privatize" certain functions and facilities, either depending on their regulatory powers to protect the public interest or simply shedding the burdens of providing the service.

### *Guiding Principles*

In choosing a method by which to finance capital improvements, local government officials should be aware of three guiding principles: equity, effectiveness, and efficiency.[17] The equity, or fairness, of a proposed financing method is of considerable importance. The equity principle can be formulated to mean that those that benefit from an improvement should pay for it. Some improvements are in effect consumed in common, however, and one person's use does not deprive others of the benefits. In fact, some goods (such as education) are believed to benefit society as a whole, which is used as justification for general support. A contrasting view is that a user's ability to pay for the improvement should be considered. This view holds that income and wealth are themselves measures of benefit or, conversely, that certain goods and services are a right of citizenship and should not be allocated according to the means of citizens to pay for them.

An effective financing method is one that provides a sufficient sum of money when it is needed. Some methods of raising money are not effective because they may be less dependable than other methods or not productive enough in terms of revenues. For example, current revenue sources may be sufficient for meeting small-scale capital needs, but debt-financing may be needed to raise the large lump sums needed to make a major improvement. And, while a particular revenue source may be the most appropriate source of funds to pay debt service, an underpinning of general revenues may be needed to provide sufficient security to permit borrowing at reasonable rates.

Efficiency is the third guiding principle in choosing a financing method. The efficiency of the financing method refers to the relative costs of obtaining funds, whatever the financing method selected. For example, the overall cost of issuing bonds include fees for legal and financial advisory assistance, just as the total costs of collecting the property tax revenues include the costs of property assessment and the cost of collection.

Another aspect of efficiency is that of allocating limited resources. The ability of a financing method to price public goods and thereby convey information to consumers about the true cost of supplying government services can help allocate and conserve resources. For instance, water service charges can be determined by the amount of water consumed, a flat fee can be levied for the service, or the cost can be covered by general revenues. If the government charges a fee based upon the amount of water consumed, customers are more likely to consume their water more efficiently. Such a system, however, requires meters, an added capital cost, and people to read them, an added operating cost. Furthermore, allocation on the basis of price may conflict with notions of ability to pay, and it assumes that people are reasonably satisfied with the distribution of income or wealth.

### *Pay-as-you-go versus Borrowing*

For most jurisdictions, the key policy issue is that of paying out of current revenues (pay-as-you-go) versus borrowing.

There are advantages in using a pay-as-you-go option for a capital improvement program. For instance, interest savings realized from not going into debt can be used to expand future services or to reduce the tax rate. The use of current funding for capital improvements means that less of the budget is committed to fixed annual debt service payments, which permits greater flexibility in the future. Also, by restraining the level of borrowing, local governments can

conserve debt capacity and achieve a more favorable credit rating, thereby lessening interest costs when borrowing is necessary.

An argument for allocating at least a share of the capital improvement program to current financing is the desire to leave a legacy of paid-for infrastructure to the next generation of users. The concept of patrimony is implicit in the notion of paying for replacement and renewal out of current revenues and seems to make the most sense in established, stable communities.

Conversely, there are disadvantages to the pay-as-you-go option that argue for debt financing. First, facilities are frequently financed through the issuance of debt simply because it is impossible to raise enough money for them upfront. This is especially true when bond proceeds are used to build a new facility capable of generating revenue. Few users of a new water and sewer system are willing to pay charges prior to receiving the service in order to accumulate reserves for the improvement. More compelling is the argument that financing projects with debt over their useful life is equitable and efficient because those who will benefit from a facility should contribute to its costs as the services are consumed over time. The great mobility of individuals and families in American society makes this argument increasingly persuasive.

good point

In practice, pragmatic considerations typically will carry the day: if the capital requirements are recurring, of relative small scale, or are for short-lived improvements, the tendency is to build them into current spending levels (or to employ leases). On the other hand, major capital improvements that are not expected to recur and are long-lived are candidates for debt financing. In many cases, a combination of funds are used, with reserves or current revenues used to pay for a part of the project and debt proceeds paying the rest.

***Debt Policies***

Debt policies describe fiscal and management practices that seek to integrate a community's long-term physical needs with available financial resources. Most desirably, a debt policy is part of an overall capital financing policy that provides evidence of a commitment to meet infrastructure needs through a planned program of future financing.

!

Debt policies should be developed within the context of existing law and the present and prospective financial position of a local government. Debt policies should embody planned behavior that reflects both the capital needs of the jurisdiction and the parameters within which they will be met. Key factors typically found in policies have to do with acceptable levels of indebtedness, priorities among types of projects to be financed, policies regarding the use of tax-supported versus self-supporting debt, the mix between the use of current revenues and borrowing, and the appropriateness of and acceptable levels of short-term indebtedness.

Debt policies should be submitted to a jurisdiction's elected officials for consideration and approval. Through public adoption, the local government's appointed officials can implement programs and procedures in detail based upon general guidance and within accepted parameters. In order to remain effective, the policies should be reviewed at regular intervals.

In general, there are three reasons to establish a debt policy. First, the policies establish a criteria for the issuance of debt obligations so as not to exceed acceptable levels of indebtedness. Second, debt policies transmit a message to investors and rating agencies who value such evidence of a community's commitment to financial management. Third, debt policies can provide consistency and continuity to public policy development. Appointed officials are provided with a set of guidelines to govern their planning and execution of particular transactions and projects.

### *Legal Basis*

Borrowing, as is true with raising revenues and making expenditures, is an activity that must conform with state and local laws. For localities to issue debt of various types for specific purposes, the ability to do so must be expressly granted or implied by constitution or statutory authority. In some states, such authority is broadly conferred and may be embedded in the ability of cities to be chartered. But even in the case of the charter city, an ordinance or charter must directly authorize the incurring of debt.

Underlying the ability of governments to incur debt is the requirement that it meet a public purpose.[18] Generally, this requirement means that there must be a relationship between the improvement being financed and the public's benefit. While public-purpose requirements can be a barrier to certain types of projects, the vast majority of states (and courts) have greatly expanded the notion of what constitutes a public benefit, leaving it largely to the state legislature to make that determination.

State laws heavily regulate the types of debt that may be used and the process by which it may be issued. The nature of these restraints—which primarily are aimed at tax-supported debt—have had a major influence on the selection of the type of security to be used and the legal nature of the issuer. Not infrequently, tight restrictions have fomented conditions in which emphasis has shifted from the use of tax-supported obligations sold by general units of government to that of limited obligations sold either by general government (with requisite limitations on pledged revenues) or by special districts and authorities that do not possess general taxing powers.

The major limitations affecting indebtedness are debt limitations, referendum requirements, and various tax and expenditure limitations.

*Debt Limitations.* Municipalities in 44 states face direct constitutional or statutory limits on the amount of general obligation debt they are allowed to engender.[19]

These limits, usually related to some percentage of a municipality's real property levels, in practice have little impact, as municipalities generally maintain levels of indebtedness far below the cap.[20] The existence of debt limits is partly psychological. Credit analysts involved in municipal issues have demonstrated a desire to retain the limits even while acknowledging that the limits are seldom tested. The importance to creditors of the limitations' existence increases as the general credit rating of a municipality decreases, even though the troubled city is not near its legal debt margin. For cities with strong financial resources, market analysts often favor retention of the limits because removal would introduce a potential source of volatility into fluctuations in the rates of interest demanded by the market.[21]

Statutory interest-rate limits are also used to control municipal debt in 40 states.[22] The relevance of this limit is dubious due to states' willingness to adjust the limits as needed to respond to the credit market and the exemption of many types of debt.

***Referendum Requirements.*** Another major form of control of general obligation debt is the referendum requirement on local indebtedness. Voter approval of general-obligation bond issues is required in 42 states. The impact of this constraint is strongly felt by local officials who believe more capital expenditures are needed; more than one-third consider referendum requirements as the major restraint to indebtedness.[23] As a result of these requirements, municipalities have found several methods of issuing debt without voter approvals, including:

- Issuing general-obligation debt in amounts or maturities below the statutory minimum that would require a referendum
- Issuing less-regulated securities, such as revenue bonds, for activities previously financed by general obligation bonds
- Shifting the cost of capital construction forward to developers by rebating the cost through tax incentives or abatements

Although referendum requirements are commonly evaded, they do have their supporters. Analysts have shown in surveys that they consider the existence of the referendum requirements to be the most desired constraint on government debt, especially as the general financial health of a municipality declines.[24]

***Tax and Expenditure Limitations.*** Tax and expenditure limitations have had a detrimental effect on all forms of local government spending, including capital spending, especially when the latter is financed by current revenues. In the face of legislated revenue restrictions, governments have tended to postpone capital spending. Although borrowing may appear to constitute a method of avoiding certain revenue-related limitations, restrictions on future revenue-raising powers tend to reduce the reliability of prospective debt service. More directly, they have negated the ability of governments in many states to make the traditional "full faith and credit" pledge of property taxes, unlimited in rate or amount, in support of debt. Less directly, but of substantial importance, is the impression left by the adoption of limitations that retroactively affect the ability of governments to meet outstanding obligations. Major downgradings of existing credit ratings followed the adoption of such limitations in California and Massachusetts, and the cost of borrowing and market access were adversely affected.[25]

## *STRUCTURE OF INSTRUMENT*

Once having decided to borrow, an issuer faces numerous structural questions involving the type of security to be used, the maturity structure, issue size, call provisions, and, for limited-obligation securities, the design of the trust indenture. In addition to these questions on the design of the instrument, there are questions on the method of sale and the basis of award and the timing of sales—all considered in the section below. Typically, most issuers will require outside assistance in making these decisions, since they are affected by both legal and market considerations that need expert technical consideration.

The structure of the security must be devised in such a way as to permit prompt repayment of the obligation while abiding with legal requirements and adhering to the adopted debt policy. For instance, if the debt policy of the community requires rapid repayment, the final maturity of the obligation should not exceed a certain number of years. If the local government prefers a level annual debt-service requirement, then the obligation should be structured with increasing principal requirements.

In addition to conforming to the local government's own policies, the debt obligation may be structured so as to take advantage of the bond market's desire for a specific type of investment. In some markets, the obligation can be designed to attract long-term institutional investor interest. At other times, the design may make them attractive to individuals.

### *Forms of Security*

State and local government debt securities can be categorized into two major types, depending on the nature of funds pledged to their repayment:

*General Obligation Bonds.* These securities are commonly referred to as "full-faith-and-credit" bonds because they are based on the pledge of a governmental unit to levy the taxes necessary to pay the debt. An unconditional promise is made to pay the interest and retire the principal.

*Limited-Liability or "Revenue" Bonds.* Funds to pay interest and retire principal on these securities come only from restricted revenues or user fees. As a class, these bonds are classified by what they are not: they are not backed by the taxing power. As a result, they are not included in the usual debt limits, and often do not require voter approval.

There are four major classes of limited-liability bonds:

*Enterprise Revenue Bonds.* Bonds issued for governmental enterprise projects that generate revenues from user charges to pay the debt. This form is commonly used for public utilities such as water, sewer, gas, and electric facilities.

*Lease-Rental Bonds.* Bonds to finance facilities that are leased under contract to a local government, which pays rent sufficient to service the debt. They have been used to finance schools, public buildings, parks, transportation facilities, and hospitals. They frequently are used to circumvent borrowing restrictions on governmental powers that levy taxes to pay the debt.

*Conduit Revenue Bonds.* Bonds to finance private facilities such as homes, hospitals, and factories in order to increase employment opportunities, promote economic development, or achieve a socially useful goal. Facilities are leased or funds are lent to a private entity. Rental or loan payments cover the debt service on the bonds. The term conduit refers to the fact that the sponsoring government undertakes no commitment to pay or guarantee the debt service, but merely gives the underlying obligor access to the tax-exempt market.

***Special Tax Bonds.*** Bonds the principal and interest of which are paid from a specific tax such as a gasoline tax; a special-purpose tax such as that levied by a development district; or a special assessment. Depending on the extent of the tax, these securities can be close cousins to the general obligation security.

Table 14–1 provides a summary of the advantages and disadvantages of using general-obligation versus limited-obligation securities. The full-faith-and-credit pledge of a state or local government is viewed as the strongest type of security because it obligates the issuer to apply its unlimited taxing power to assure repayment. For a local government this typically has meant its ability to levy ad valorem property taxes that are unlimited in rate or amount. A limited tax pledge is often used when the local government's taxing authority is restricted

TABLE 14-1

*Advantages and Disadvantages of General-Obligation and Limited-Liability Bonds*

| GENERAL-OBLIGATION BONDS | |
|---|---|
| **Advantages** | **Disadvantages** |
| 1. Strongest pledge of local government usually produces lowest interest cost. | 1. Necessity for vote may delay capital financing. |
| 2. Administrative aspects of preparing to borrow are simpler and normally cost less. | 2. Is constrained by legal debt limit. Can be a problem if limit is less than state limit because of local legislation. |
| 3. Typically sold at competitive sale rather than negotiation, usually reducing the interest cost. | 3. If paid by taxes, may not align benefits to cost. |
| 4. A vote of the people confirms that the project or program is popularly supported. | 4. Project costs may not be aligned to useful life of improvement. |
| **LIMITED-LIABILITY BONDS** | |
| **Advantages** | **Disadvantages** |
| 1. Allow for quick action because voters' approval is not required. | 1. Usually require a higher interest rate. |
| 2. Do not contribute to the legal debt margin. | 2. No voter approval: elected officials less accountable. |
| 3. With revenue bonds, cost of debt is distributed to the benefiting users of the service. | 3. Greater preparation and administrative costs. |
| 4. Financing costs must be paid within the useful life of the project. | 4. Bonds are more apt to be sold through negotiations, thus increasing interest costs. |

Copy This

in rate or amount by state statutes. In these instances, the taxing authority, while broad, is considered to incur a limited obligation.

A local government may issue special tax bonds in cases where the capital improvement benefits a specific class of user. For instance, a highway bond issue may be secured by the imposition of a gasoline tax or an improvement district may issue by a bond secured by the levy of a special tax on benefiting property owners. Revenue bonds are traditionally issued when the local government expects a revenue-producing enterprise to be able to repay the debt. By securing repayment of a debt obligation in this way, users of the facilities pay for the improvements without reliance upon the general taxing authority of the jurisdiction.

### *Maturity Structure*

Municipal bonds have a face value (par value) that is repaid to investors at a specific date (maturity date). While the bond is outstanding, periodic payments of interest (usually every six months) are paid at some specified interest percentage of the face value. Alternatively, the bond may be sold at discount and all or part of the interest is accumulated until the bond is repaid at par at the final maturity date.

When bonds are issued, they typically consist of a bundle of maturities, bound up in a single bond issue. There are two basic approaches to designing the maturity structure of bonds. First is the serial bond issue, where there is a range of individual maturities, extending from the first to the final year of the issue. The second major type of maturity structure is the term bond, where there is a single final maturity for all the bonds in the issue. Municipal securities often are structured to include both types of securities in the same bond issue.

Annual debt-service requirements depend upon the pattern of principal and interest payments adopted by the issuer. Local governments can structure their debt service for a level, declining, or ascending repayment schedule. In a level-debt service pattern, the annual sum of interest and principal repayments is held constant over the life of the issue (much like the amortization schedule of a home mortgage). The level-principal repayment pattern, on the other hand, often is used by issuers interested in the rapid retirement of outstanding debt. The process of repaying equal installments of outstanding principal each year results in higher initial debt service payments. The use of these alternatives often is taken as evidence of the issuer's ability to repay its outstanding obligations without difficulty.

An ascending debt service schedule that grows over time, on the other hand, may result in greater scrutiny of the issuer's operating performance by independent credit analysts to ascertain if the delay in repayment is attributable to financial difficulties. There are, however, a limited number of instances when the use of an ascending debt service schedule is viewed as the most appropriate pattern of debt service. For instance, utility systems and other municipal enterprises often finance substantial capital improvements through the issuance of long-term debt obligations. The improvements expand the capacity of the enterprise system to provide public services and generate higher revenues. In these circumstances, an ascending debt-service schedule enables the issuer to capture more user charges over time and repay a greater amount of debt service without difficulty.

### *Trust Indenture for Revenue Bonds*

Revenue bonds require a specific contract between the borrower and the investor. This contract is embodied in the trust indenture, a document that sets forth in detail the pledge of revenues, how they will be obtained and disbursed, and various other covenants that control the construction and operation of the facility and the handling of funds. General-obligation bonds are secured by the full faith and credit of the issuer and therefore do not require such an agreement. In contrast, limited-liability bonds are secured by the more restrictive pledge of revenues or use fees derived from the facility.

The trust indenture usually covers the disbursement of bond proceeds, application of revenues, and the applied rate for services and other covenants.

*Disbursement of Bond Proceeds.* Because the revenues of the facility being financed are the source of debt service payments, it is important that use of bond proceeds be controlled. This is done by the trust indenture, which requires bond funds to be placed in a special construction account to make sure that capital project funds are not diverted to other uses, such as expenses. Payments from this account may be made only in the manner prescribed in the indenture. Upon completion of the project, any monies left in the construction account are typically used to meet the payment of the outstanding debt.

*Application of Revenues (Flow of Funds).* The trust indenture prescribes how the facility's revenues are applied to the cost of operation and maintenance, debt service, reserve maintenance, and contingencies. This sequence of deposits is called the "flow of funds." Typically, a revenue fund is established to receive all income from the facility's operations. Monies in the revenue fund are then distributed to other funds in the order described below.

1. *Operation and maintenance fund*—First, all operating expenses are met, under the theory that the facility must operate to generate revenues.
2. *Debt service fund*—Next, funds sufficient to pay principal and interest are set aside. With serial bonds, typically a monthly amount is deposited equal to one-sixth of the next maturing semiannual interest payment plus one-twelfth of the next annual principal payment.
3. *Reserve fund*—Next, funds sufficient to pay principal and interest, in case of a deficiency, are placed in the debt service reserve fund. It is usually accumulated in the first 60 months after the issuance of bonds. The amount accumulated may be expressed as the maximum annual debt-service requirement, the average annual debt service, or a specified sum.
4. *Contingencies fund*—Last, funds are deposited to meet emergency operating expenditures, usually during the months following issuance at a specified level.

*Rate and Other Covenants.* The establishment of a rate covenant, which pledges that rates will be maintained sufficient to meet the cost of operation and maintenance, pay debt service, create reserve, and meet contingencies, is very important. Specifically, a borrower will pledge to maintain a margin of safety referred to as "debt service coverage." The coverage, which is expressed as a ratio of net revenues to annual debt service, may range from 1.0 to 1.5 or higher. A coverage of 1.2 means that the local government covenants to maintain rates adequate to generate *net* revenues (operating revenues minus operating expenditures) sufficient to pay 1.2 times a specified amount of debt service. The debt service to be covered may be expressed as the maximum annual amount, the average amount, the amount due in the next year, or a specified sum.

Trust indentures, which may run to over a hundred pages, can contain a myriad of other covenants designed to assure the operation of the facility and to protect the interests of the investor. Among items commonly covered by covenants are the use of consulting engineers, the retention of a trustee, annual audits, insurance coverage, restrictions on offering additional bonds, acts of default and remedies, and prohibitions against free services and misappropriation of funds. Typically, a trustee is appointed to oversee the enforcement of the trust indenture.

### Sizing the Issue

Deciding how much needs to be borrowed can be a fairly complicated decision. In addition to the amount needed to pay for the improvement, various items may need to be capitalized and paid out of bond proceeds. Offsetting this is the ability of the issuer to earn interest income on bond proceeds before they are disbursed. To complicate the process, restrictions by the U.S. Treasury on the investment of bond proceeds must be considered when sizing a bond issue.

To size a new bond issue accurately, the issuer first must consider the estimated project cost. Bond proceeds must be sufficient to meet the expected cost of acquisition or construction. For construction projects, an accurate construction schedule must be obtained from the contractor. The schedule by which bond proceeds are to be drawn upon can be calculated accordingly. Interest earnings on invested funds held in the construction account can be used to reduce the initial size of the bond issue.

The bond issue's size also is affected by the extent to which other funds are available to pay for the improvements. If these can cover a portion of the capital improvement program, the principal size of the bond issue is reduced accordingly.

The size of the issue is also determined by whether the issuer chooses to capitalize certain issuance costs. For example, the issuer may elect to pay the costs of bond insurance and engineering, legal, financial advisory, and underwriting services from the bond proceeds. While these "soft costs" are candidates for capitalization for most bond issues, they are limited in the case of certain private-activity bonds by U.S. Treasury regulations to 2 percent or less of the total amount borrowed.[26]

The nature of the security plays an integral role in determining the size of the bond issue. Limited-obligation bonds, for instance, are often structured with reserve funds to provide additional security to the bondholder in case the pledged revenue stream is insufficient and the issuer defaults on its obligation. The size of the reserve fund is restricted by U.S. Treasury regulations; in general, they cannot exceed the lesser of maximum annual debt service, 10 percent of the par amount, or 125 percent of average annual debt service. Reserve funds will increase the size of the bond issue if funded from bond proceeds. Interest earnings on the reserve may be used to defray annual debt service, however, and may be used to pay all or part of the final year's debt-service payment.[27]

Capitalized interest is also an increasingly common component of the limited obligation bond. When funded from bond proceeds, the amount of the issue will be increased. Capitalized interest is deposited into a separate fund and used to pay semiannual interest on the bond issue until the improvements are completed. The inclusion of capitalized interest is a two-edged sword. On the one hand, it provides the investor with additional security in case of a delay in the construction schedule or damage to the property being improved by granting additional time before larger debt-service payments from the issuer's own resources must be made. On the other hand, it does result in a larger bond issue and heavier debt-service payments in the future.

### *Call Provisions*

Many issuers structure their bond issues with an optional redemption, or "call" feature. A callable bond is one that grants the issuer the privilege of paying the obligation prior to the stated maturity date. The issuer provides the bondholder with a notice of redemption in a manner specified in the bond indenture.[28] The ability to accelerate the redemption date of a bond is of particular value to the issuer in case interest rates decline. If the outstanding securities can be called early for redemption, an equivalent amount of new debt can be sold at the lower rates. Considerable savings can be realized as a result. Of course, the investor recognizes this risk and normally will demand a higher initial yield to offset the risk of reinvestment at lower yields.

The inclusion of an optional redemption feature provides the issuer with additional advantages besides the potential for future debt-service savings. The early call enables the issuer to alter the maturity schedule of outstanding debt obligations more easily. The payment schedule of outstanding debt may be lengthened to better match the stream of revenues pledged to repay the debt or revised to reduce debt service payments in those years when the pledged revenue stream is not expected to be sufficient.

A third reason for the inclusion of a call provision is the ability to relieve the issuer of onerous bond covenants. Limited-obligation bonds often curb the issuer's ability to sell additional debt unless certain debt-service coverage ratios are satisfied. For example, existing bond covenants may restrict the issuer from selling additional debt when that becomes necessary or may require the issuer to raise rates sufficient to generate a level of net revenues inconsistent with the issuer's financial policies. Once the bonds are redeemed or legally defeased through an advance refunding, the issuer can proceed under a new set of covenants.[29]

## *THE MARKETING PROCESS*

The marketing of even a small municipal bond issue entails the coordination of several players to take the required steps and to produce the documents needed for the sale. Since the method of sale will dictate the players in the process and their assignments, that subject will be taken up first, followed by a discussion of the basis of award and the timing of sales. Issuers will have assembled a team to assist in various phases of preparing for the sale and to help produce the key sales-related documents, and these activities are discussed next. The section that follows contains a discussion of obtaining specialized legal, financial, and other services to assist the issuer in the design and selling of securities.

### *Method of Sale*

The municipal bond issuer may sell securities in one of two ways. Unlike the market for corporate debt instruments, in which the sale of securities through negotiation is almost universal, municipal bonds are often sold through competitive bidding.[30] In a competitive sale, the bonds are awarded at an auction to the underwriting firm that provides the issuer with the best bid for its securities. The bidding parameters are established prior to the sale date and are used to determine which offer will result in the lowest effective interest cost.

In a negotiated sale, the issuer chooses the initial buyer of its securities (usually an underwriter that plans to reoffer them) in advance of the sale date. The terms of the sale are subject to negotiation between the issuer and the initial purchaser. State statutes often require certain types of municipal bonds, usually general obligations, to be sold through a competitive bidding process. The proliferation of limited obligation bonds has, however, contributed to a pronounced trend toward the negotiated sale.[31]

The inherent protections afforded by open competition are absent when negotiation is chosen as the method of sale. Although relieved of some duties, the issuer assumes many others in the negotiated sale. The finance official must monitor market conditions to assure the receipt of the lowest rates of interest and also must take an active role in determining the level of compensation for the underwriter in a negotiated sale.

Several factors should be considered in choosing between a competitive sale and negotiation. The first is the relative complexity of the issue. Municipal securities with complex security features require a greater sales effort on the part of the underwriter. In a competitive sale, the underwriter does not know whether it will have bonds to sell until after the bids are opened. As a result, its sales force may be unwilling to spend much time marketing a competitive issue in advance of the sale date. To offset weaker or more complex security features of limited-obligation bonds, the issuer may be best advised to identify potential purchasers early in the issuance process in order to convince them to make the investment.

As a consequence, the negotiated sale can be preferable if the issue requires a stronger marketing effort.

The volatility of the municipal market is the second important factor that must be considered in the choice of a sale method. When the municipal securities market is subjected to abrupt changes in the interest rates demanded by investors, state and local governments frequently use the negotiated sale. When markets are volatile, underwriters are reluctant to bid aggressively; as a consequence, competitive sales can result in the receipt of fewer and more conservative bids. When the market became more volatile during the decade of the 1980s, the proportion of bonds sold through negotiation increased.

Third, the familiarity of the underwriters with the credit of the issuer also has a direct impact on the willingness of the underwriters to bid aggressively. General obligation securities of infrequent issuers still can be sold on a competitive basis, but additional effort must be made to familiarize investors with the issuer's creditworthiness.

The fourth and final factor for consideration is the size of the issue. For example, the probability of attracting many bids for an issue in excess of $200 million is limited, especially in volatile markets. A large issue size can induce the formation of bidding syndicates that are so large as to reduce the number of potential bidders to one or two syndicates. For issues of great size, it is unlikely that the competitive process results in lower costs of capital.

### *Basis of Award*

In order to determine which one of the competing groups of underwriters is offering to purchase the issuer's securities for the lowest cost, the issuer must determine the effective interest cost of each bid. There are two methods for making this interest cost calculation.

The first method is a calculation of the bid's effect upon the net interest cost, or NIC, of the bond issue. The net interest cost is the average interest cost rate on a bond issue calculated on the basis of simple interest.[32] The aggregate amount of interest payable over the life of the bonds is simply divided by the aggregate amount of bonds sold multiplied by the average life of the issue. Although simple to calculate, the NIC has a major drawback in that it treats a dollar of interest paid today in the same way as a dollar paid twenty years from now (i.e., it does not discount future interest payments). The net interest cost method of calculating the effective interest cost of a bond issue originally was applied to term bond issues, each of which carried a single maturity date and interest rate.[33]

The preferred method of calculating the effective interest cost of a bid is the calculation of true interest cost (TIC). The TIC is the rate that will produce a present value precisely equal to the amount of money received by the issuers in exchange for the bonds when it is used to discount all the future debt-service payments.[34] The use of the true interest cost as a method of calculating the lowest effective interest cost in effect forces the bidder to eliminate high interest rates, or "penalty yields," on early maturities. The complexity of calculating TIC was once a discouragement to its use, but with the advent of the microcomputer, the complexity of the calculation is no longer an issue.

### *Scheduling Issuance*

There are numerous considerations to review before scheduling the sale of debt. In a negotiated sale, the timing becomes less critical because it is much easier to reschedule the sale of the bonds until market conditions are more favorable. When the bonds are to be sold competitively, however, the sale date should be chosen with great care.

Some general rules of thumb are helpful. The chosen date should not conflict with the scheduled sale by units of government that compete for investors. In addition, the sale date should not fall on a date when the U.S. Treasury is selling its obligations, because this may distract potential investors. Or worse, the outcome of the sale may adversely affect all fixed-income investments.

Generally, bond issues are sold in the beginning of the week to permit the market sufficient time to sell the obligations before the next spate of issues the following week. Tuesdays are the most popular days, although Monday and Wednesday also are chosen frequently. The distraction of a holiday is often cited as reason enough not to schedule a bond sale for the same week.

### *Issuance Team: Players and Roles*

The operational heart of a bond issuance is a team that consist of participants that help design the issue, make key marketing decisions and develop the documentation accompanying the offering. Depending on the markets, the size of the issue, the type of sale employed, the use of proceeds, and other variables, the players and procedures will differ in detail; but, as discussed below, the primary roles are clear.[35]

At a minimum, the team consists of the governmental issuer (usually represented by a chief financial officer), bond counsel (a specialist in municipal securities law), and a financial advisor (acting in the capacity of a financial specialist to assist in the transaction). If the sale will be negotiated, an underwriter is selected by the issuer prior to the sale and becomes a member of the issuance team. An underwriter will not join the team in a competitive offering until the sale is consummated, but will be present during the presale period in a negotiated transaction.

In larger issues, the team also may contain other specialists, such as an engineer or other project-related consultant (who opines on the feasibility of the project if the issuance is to be secured by project-generated revenues), an auditor (who opines on the financial reports of the issuer), and perhaps an attorney to represent the underwriter, if the transaction is a negotiated one. A credit enhancer, a legal counsel for a credit enhancer, or a specialist in tax law also will join the team on occasion. The function of these professionals acting together is to structure the instrument and transaction and to assist the issuer in the marketing of the offering, including the production and dissemination of the offering-related documents.

In terms of actual management of the issuance process and informing the market of a pending sale, the assignment of duties within the team can be distributed in a variety of ways. An early step in the process is an allocation of the responsibilities among team members and the establishment of a calendar of activities. This allocation and coordination of duties may be done by the issuer, but more likely will be handled by the financial advisor or, in the negotiated offering, by the bond underwriter.[36]

### *Disclosure Roles of Participants*

Although not subject to direct federal regulation, governments and government officials that issue bonds must be concerned about the securities laws and their liabilities under them. The official statements and other sales documents produced in conjunction with the sale of securities play a pivotal role in providing information about the issuer and issuances so that investors can make informed investment decisions. Accordingly, issuers must take care that they provide full and accurate disclosure of pertinent information in these documents. Failure to do so may mean running afoul of the federal securities laws, not to mention state statutes and common law.

The disclosure roles of the participants in the municipal bond market are flexible, a situation that arises from the unique regulatory framework of the municipal securities market. Issuers typically look to local and state laws, custom, and professional standards such as the GFOA's *Disclosure Guidelines for State and Local Government Securities* (Disclosure Guidelines) for guidance in the process.[37] Underwriters and financial advisors rely on the same sources, with formal requirements regarding their duties provided by the rules of the Securities and Exchange Commission (SEC) and the Municipal Securities Rulemaking Board (MSRB). Bond Counsel and other experts also rely on established custom as well as their professional standards. All participants must be attuned to their responsibilities as implicit in the antifraud provisions of the federal securities acts.[38]

### *Sales-Related Documents*

A number of important documents and other informational items are generated before and at the time of sale of a newly issued municipal security by the issuer, typically assisted by its specialized advisors.

The *notice of sale* is an essential document in the issuance of bonds by competitive means. It is an official publication by the issuer that describes the terms of sale of a planned new offering of securities. Custom, law, and individual circumstances can dictate documents of greatly varying lengths and detail. In most cases, however, the notice of sale contains the date, time, and place of the sale; the amount of the issue; the nature of the security; information concerning the official statement and delivery of bonds; and the method of delivery. The notice of sale also serves as the basis for an official advertisement for the offering, which typically is printed in the *Bond Buyer* and in local newspapers.

The *official statement* is a document (or series of documents) that is prepared in conjunction with sales of state and local government securities to provide information to prospective purchasers of the securities. The official statement thus functions as the principal disclosure document. Although other terms such as "prospectus" or "offering circular" are sometimes used in reference to the official statement, there are significant differences between these documents and the official statement. The offering circular often is not the "official" document of the issuer, but rather an informational piece that may be put out by the underwriter or advisor to generate interest in the proposed financing. The official statement, on the other hand, has the approval or authorization of the issuer, thereby making it the issuer's document; and it is a "statement," a direct exposition of information concerning the offering.

The official statement provides a complete and accurate written statement that presents information in such a manner as not to misrepresent or omit any material fact that the investor needs in making an investment decision. Guidance to those items to be considered for inclusion in the official statement is provided by GFOA's *Disclosure Guidelines.* The *Disclosure Guidelines,* since their introduction in 1976, have enjoyed wide acceptance in defining the content of official statements, a fact evidenced by the growing uniformity and completeness of official statements. In practice, an issuer will publish two versions of the official statement: The *preliminary official statement,* or "POS," is a presale document that is distributed by the issuer and its agents to elicit interest in and provide information about the forthcoming sale. The POS is a draft document and subject to amendment and completion prior to delivery of the final version. The document is made available upon request, although the issuer will send a copy to potential underwriters (in a competitive sale), the rating agencies, and major institutional investors before the scheduled sale. Dealers, in a negotiated sale, must provide the POS, if one is produced, to potential buyers.[39] In the case of the competitive sale, the POS will typically be distributed one to two weeks before the sale of the bonds.

Once the bonds are awarded, the underwriter supplies additional information, including the yields at which the securities are reoffered to the public. The issuer will incorporate the established interest rates into the draft debt service schedules. Once the official statement is modified in this manner, the document is referred to as the final official statement and is delivered to the underwriters for distribution to investors.[40]

In some cases, the issuer may take the lead in producing the official statement and other sales-related documents. Local governments, in particular, have become increasingly sophisticated users of microcomputers. Their familiarity with this technology will result in more official statements being published in-house. In other cases, the issuer's job is focused upon providing basic information to be incorporated into the disclosure document and reviewing that document and to attest to the veracity and comprehensiveness of the information contained therein.

### *Rating Agencies*

Most municipal bond issuers will request a rating on the creditworthiness of the securities to be issued. The rating agency provides an independent assessment of the relative creditworthiness of debt obligations for the municipal market. The rating system consists of letter grades that convey the agency's assessment of the issuer's ability and willingness to repay the debt. Ratings expedite the marketing process by providing the market with information that can be used to determine the level of risk contained in the repayment of the debt to investors. Because of their wide following, they influence the interest rates that issuers pay on their obligations.

Moody's Investors Service, Standard & Poor's Corporation, and Fitch Investors Service are the principal rating agencies for municipal debt. For a fee, each of the agencies provides ratings of the securities being offered for sale based on information supplied with the issue and supplemented by their own research. There are nuances regarding how ratings should be interpreted, but essentially they speak to the credit quality, that is, the relative likelihood that bonds will pay interest and principal in full and on time. In the process of creating categories of comparable credits, the agencies classify groups of bonds from prime quality down to those that are in default.

Applications for ratings are typically made by the issuer or its advisor prior to the sale of new issues. If an application is not made and ratings are in effect for outstanding parity issues, the ratings may be withdrawn or the new issues may be rated without a request. In the case of all the agencies, after analysis by assigned specialists, the rating is subject to review by a committee, communicated to the applicant or its advisor, and then released to the general public. The major agencies continue to review ratings throughout the life of an obligation as long as information is regularly supplied. If the required information (e.g., annual financial reports, budgets, capital plans) is not supplied, the rating is withdrawn and the withdrawal is noted in the agencies' publications.[41]

### *The Sale, Reporting Results, and Closing*

The mechanics of the sale will depend upon on the method of sale used and will be discussed in the next section under the subject of underwriters. In summary, however, once the terms have been settled and the transaction agreed to (the bonds awarded), a number of additional steps need to be undertaken. As noted, the final official statement needs to be prepared and, following the SEC rule, should be available to the underwriters within seven days of the sale.

Immediately after a sale, the results are published in the *Bond Buyer,* the trade journal of the municipal securities market. The results are typically reported by the issuer's financial advisor or the underwriter. The *Bond Buyer,* using its listing of sales, follows up on advertised sales to obtain the results. In addition, many sales results are collected by the Public Securities Association, the MSRB, and the U.S. Treasury for purpose of tax compliance. Traditionally, the results of major new-offering sales will be evidenced by "tombstone" advertisements frequently taken out by the winning underwriting firms in national circulation newspapers, typically *The New York Times* or the *Wall Street Journal,* and trade journals.

Also, immediately after sale, information about the bonds, if printed in a certificate form, needs to be submitted to the bond printer. In the case of bonds sold in book-entry form (without certificates), the repository must be notified of the results to set up its records. Approximately three weeks after the sale, the closing is held, at which time the bonds and other sales documents in final form are presented to the winning syndicate and a final check is presented (or funds wired) to the issuer. For certain transactions, such as the sale of short-term debt, the closing period can be as short as the day after the sale.

## *SECURING SPECIALIZED SERVICES*

Most issuers retain advisors to assist in the structuring of the transaction and the provision of documents. In some cases, the specialized services are limited to the employment of bond counsel. In others, an independent financial advisor, consulting engineer, and special legal counsel also are employed. These advisors may be selected in a variety of ways and may be engaged on an issuance-by-issuance basis or for an interval of time. Smaller and infrequent issuers are, as a practical matter, very reliant on the advisory team to assist them with the mechanics of issuing debt. The bond counsel, financial advisor, and, in the case of a negotiated transaction, the underwriter and its counsel are the most common outside advisors in the debt-issuance process. In the case of revenue bonds, the role of fiscal agent and trustee can also be an important one.

Many sales are more complicated. As a result, a bevy of other experts may be involved in the production of various aspects of the transaction that require special expertise. Auditors may be needed to provide audit reports, which may be required prior to the issuance of additional bonds. For example, this function is found for utility revenue bonds where the original indenture requires a minimum debt service coverage prior to additional bond issuance. Engineers and market analysts provide feasibility studies and engineering reports. These reports contain independent confirmation of the project's necessity and the likelihood that sufficient revenues will be generated to repay the bonds. Another important player in a transaction may be the provider of a credit enhancement, which may be represented by its own legal counsel. The underlying documents generated in conjunction with such studies, reports, or the provision of additional credit backing (the insurance policy, letter of credit, and the like) may be included in part or in whole in the official statement or incorporated by reference, with their availability noted.

### *Bond Counsel*

In both negotiated and competitive sales, bond counsel may perform numerous duties, but its traditional responsibilities revolve around providing an opinion on the validity of the issue and its tax status. Bond counsel also prepare and review sundry legal documents such as the form of the bond and the transcript of the bond sale. The additional roles of bond counsel in preparing transactions for market and their corresponding responsibilities concerning disclosure are extensive and flexible, and form the subjects of professional debate.

The key activities of bond counsel typically are as follows:

- Determining whether there is legal authority to issue the bonds
- Drafting a bond ordinance, resolution, or, in the case of revenue bonds, a trust indenture
- Examining transcripts of proceedings to determine that bonds were legally offered and sold
- Determining that bonds were properly executed
- Answering legal questions about bonds by prospective purchasers

Especially in negotiated transactions, the bond counsel's role may be supplemented by the underwriter's counsel, which historically has primary responsibility for the assembly of the disclosure documents in a negotiated sale and the provision of a disclosure letter that opines on the adequacy and accuracy of disclosures. As the term implies, the client of the underwriter counsel is the underwriter. Issuer's counsel may be involved in the preparation of disclosure information, but the role is usually limited to opinions regarding the organization and good standing of the issuer, various procedural matters, and the existence of pending litigation.

Other counsel may get involved in the transaction, such as that of a credit-enhancing entity, where bond insurance or a letter of credit is involved, or that of a private beneficiary, as in the case of a conduit borrowing where the ultimate security is based on a private party's credit.

### *Financial Advisor*

The principal role of a financial advisor to a state or local government is to provide assistance to issuers on matters relating to the issuance of municipal securities. Typically, the nature of that assistance depends upon the method of sale. For instance, in a competitive sale, the financial advisor assists the issuer in designing the debt structure, preparation of the official statement, and marketing the securities to potential investors.

The role of the financial advisor differs when the bonds are being sold through negotiation. More often than not, the advisor acts as an advocate for the client government to assure that the underwriter is treating the government fairly. An important duty may be to assist in the selection of the underwriter. In negotiated transactions, the bonds are structured by the underwriter, whose own marketing staff contacts institutional and retail investors directly. During the pricing of the bonds, however, the advisor may be used by the municipal officials to provide assurance that the interest-rate scale for the proposed issue is reasonable in light of existing market conditions.

The pressures of a pending bond sale do not create the best environment for developing a long-term financial strategy. The terms of the bond sale, however, including restrictions in the bond indenture and the maturity and interest-payment structures, have long-term implications for the issuer's financial operations.

As a result, the financial advisor's role can encompass a broader scope of activities. For instance, the establishment of a long-term capital improvement program and the investment of proceeds from the sale of securities are activities in which most financial advisors now participate. In some instances, the independent advisor assists in the development of a long-term capital financing plan, which integrates the capital improvement plan; examines alternative sources of revenue; explores alternative financing arrangements to replace or augment the issuance of bonds; oversees or conducts project-feasibility analyses; and recommends alternative debt-management practices.

The method by which the advisor is compensated also has evolved as financial advisors assume more varied duties on behalf of their clients. The financial advisor's fee can be based upon a flat annual retainer, hourly charges based upon services rendered, or a percentage of the total dollar amount of all financings in which the advisor participates. While all three methods are used, an increasing number of local governments have chosen to pay their advisors on the basis of an hourly fee for a comprehensive array of services. By separating the advisor's fee from the necessity to issue bonds, local governments are assured of impartiality of advice and relieve the pressure to issue debt as the most effective means of financing improvements. For example, it may not be in the issuer's best interest to finance a certain project through the sale of bonds, or to enter the market in a period of volatile interest rates. A financial advisor whose compensation depends on the successful completion of bond sales may be under pressure not to recommend alternative financing sources, such as the use of current revenues or a postponement of the sale.

***Underwriter***

The role of the underwriter (sometimes called banker) is to purchase the bonds from the issuer and to sell (reoffer) them to investors. As was discussed, the exact nature of the underwriter's role depends upon whether the issue is negotiated or sold competitively. If the issue is negotiated, the underwriter may perform many of the consultive and support roles performed by a financial advisor, such as structuring the issue, preparing the disclosure information, and obtaining ratings from the rating services. In those cases where the underwriter also serves as the financial advisor, it is subject to special MSRB rules to avoid or disclose potential conflicts of interest between the two roles.

On most large issues, the managing underwriter will form a syndicate that will offer the issuer a price at the sale date. Other members of the syndicate will be securities firms or banks that, depending on the nature of the underwriting agreement, will have the opportunity to reoffer the bonds, but also assume responsibility that the sale will raise the needed funds on a timely basis.

In a negotiated sale, the syndicate knows that it will get the bonds and therefore will be able to discuss the issue before their offering with potential investors, feeding back information and perhaps influencing the designing of the issue to meet market desires. The final purchase price is decided upon when a firm bond purchase agreement is submitted to the issuer. As has been noted, a major advantage is one of timing, since the sale date is flexible and can be decided very quickly.

In a competitive sale, the underwriters or syndicates bid against one another. Generally, the underwriters decide on bids by reviewing how comparable issues are doing, canvassing potential purchasers, noting the overall supply of bonds in the market, and making a judgment about the level of competition for the offering. Key to an underwriting by competition are the rules, established in the notice of sale and the bid form, that are to be used in comparing bids (basis of sale), various restrictions carried on the coupon rates, and whether the bonds can be sold at a discount. Underwriters are compensated for their efforts in different ways. In a negotiated sale, the underwriter receives a gross spread or discount that is a percentage of the face amount of the bonds and is often expressed in so many dollars per $1,000 on bonds (such as 1 percent or $10.00 per bond). In a competitive sale, the compensation may come either from buying the bonds at discount or from buying them at par and reoffering them at a premium. In either case, the lead underwriter will be paid more (a management fee) than other members of the syndicate to compensate for its management services and will also be reimbursed for issue-related expenses. Other members of the syndicate will receive sales commissions (takedowns), as will dealers that assist in the sales efforts (concessions). In addition, after the initial reoffering period, underwriters may experience either losses or gains on bonds held in inventory.

### *Fiscal Agents and Trustees*

The traditional role of the fiscal agent (often called the paying agent) is to maintain interest and redemption funds, paying out interest and principal as due. This function is frequently performed by financial institutions. Since bonds issued after July 1, 1983, have been required by federal law to be registered, an additional duty has been to maintain a list of registered owners and to perform duties of transferring the ownership of bonds when they are traded in the secondary market.

The fiscal agent task is frequently combined with that of trustee in the case of limited-obligation securities that have a trust indenture. The role of the trustee in public finance has assumed greater importance with the increased use of the revenue security and the often complicated relationships and responsibilities found in certain transactions. Although hired by the issuer, the trustee has the fiduciary responsibility to protect the interests of the investors and to oversee the execution of the trust indenture. The trustee's activities can cover an extensive range of responsibilities, including making sure covenants are observed, the disbursement of bond proceeds, managing the investment of unspent bond funds, processing call provisions, and making purchases of bonds in the open market with surplus funds.

### *Cost of Services*

The use of specialized services entails costs that, in conjunction with a bond sale, are termed the *costs of issuance*. In addition to the major advisors listed above, other activities (such as printing) and professional services (such as accounting) are carried out in support of a bond issuance and may be capitalized into the issue and paid from bond proceeds.

Comparisons among the costs of issuance are difficult, because of the range of activities that various participants may play, including the issuer, which may elect to carry on certain activities using its own resources.

A survey of issuance costs performed in 1988, provides general indications of the costs of external services. The most notable result was that all costs tended to decline on a per-dollar-borrowed basis as the size of issuance grew. For all issues of $5 million or less in size, the average total cost of issuance was 2.7 percent of issue size. For issues of $75 million or more, the total cost fell to 1.1 percent. Generally, revenue bond issues and those sold by negotiated bid sustained higher issuance costs per dollar borrowed than did general-obligation issues on those sold competitively.[42]

The largest component of costs is that paid to the underwriter, with average costs ranging from 1.3 percent for issues of $5 million or less to slightly below 1 percent for issues of $75 million or larger. The fees paid to financial advisors and bond counsel, using the above size measures, ranged from 0.6 and 0.5 percent, respectively, on small issues to approximately 0.05 percent on the largest issues.[43]

## *CONCLUSION*

Local government debt policies and procedures are primarily focused on the issuance of debt to help finance capital improvements. As such, they are part of the larger question of capital financing, in which numerous alternative sources of funds should be examined. Because the power to borrow means binding future taxpayers and ratepayers to raise revenues, it is subject to many constraints and procedural requirements.

When entering the capital markets, local governments need to attune their needs for funds to the desires of investors. Thus, they must make decisions regarding the structure of the instrument, such as funds pledged to repayment and maturity structure, with an eye to what the market is buying. Borrowers must also make decisions about the method of sale and assembling a team of advisors to assist them in the preparation and distribution of documents related to the sale. Such documents not only are needed to meet various state and local legal requirements, but have become increasingly important to informing investors and satisfying the requirements of disclosure under the federal securities laws. Thus, obtaining and managing expert professional services from lawyers, financial advisors, and others is a critical part of the issuance process.

## *NOTES*

1. For a discussion of defining government capital spending and estimating by what sources it is financed, see John E. Petersen, *The Future of Infrastructure Needs and*

*Financing,* a study commissioned by MBIA Corporation (Washington: Government Finance Officers Association, December 1988), chapter 2.

2. *Ibid.,* p. II–5.

3. U.S. Congressional Budget Office, *Federal Policies for Infrastructure Management,* Washington: U.S.G.P.O., June 1986, pp. 80–86.

4. John E. Petersen, *Financing Clean Water,* New York: First Boston Corporation, 1985.

5. The contraction of federal aid and its implications for state and local governments is documented in United States General Accounting Office, *Federal–State–Local Relations: Trends of the Past Decade and Emerging Issues* (Washington: GAO, March 1990).

6. See John Petersen, et al., *Credit Pooling to Finance Infrastructure* (Chicago: Government Finance Officers Association, September 1988).

7. John Petersen and Deborah Matz, *Trends in the Fiscal Condition of Cities: 1983–1985* (Washington: U.S. Joint Economic Committee, May 1985), pp. 12–13.

8. Touche Ross and Co., *Financing Infrastructure in America* (Chicago: Touche Ross and Co., 1985), p. 1.

9. Cynthia Angell and Charles A. Shorter, "Impact Fees: Private Sector Participation in Infrastructure Financing," *Government Finance Review,* October 1988, p. 20.

10. John Petersen, et al., *Non–Debt Financing of Public Works* (Washington: Government Finance Officers Association, July 1986).

11. *Ibid.,* p. I–12.

12. Petersen, *The Future of Infrastructure,* chapter 3.

13. Such obligations are often called "conduit securities" since the governmental issuer of the security merely acts as a conduit to the tax–exempt bond market. See Petersen, *The Future of Infrastructure,* pp. II–21–II–24.

14. *Ibid.,* pp. II–33–II–36. The estimates have been updated by the authors.

15. *Ibid.*

16. For a discussion of the various growth–related financing techniques and privatization arrangements that may be used, see Susan Robinson, ed., *Financing Growth: Who Benefits? Who Pays? And How Much?* (Chicago: Government Finance Officers Association, 1990).

17. For a discussion of the process of selecting among financing alternatives and the applications of the principles under constraint, see National Association of Counties, et al., *Building Together: Investing in Community Infrastructure,* (Washington: National Association of Home Builders, 1990), chapters 3 and 4.

18. David Gelfand, ed., *State and Local Government Debt Financing* (Deerfield, Ill.: Callaghan and Co.), volume 1, chapter 1.

19. John Petersen, et al., *Constitutional, Statutory and Other Impediments to Local Government Infrastructure Financing* (Washington: Government Finance Officers Association, 1987), p. 40.

20. *Ibid.,* p. 41.

21. New York State Legislative Commission on State–Local Relations, *New York's Limits on Local Taxing and Borrowing—Time for a Change?* (Albany, N.Y.: State Legislature, 1983), p. 119.

22. Petersen, et al., *Constitutional and Statutory Impediments,* p. 42.

23. Michael Pagano, *How the Public Works: Major Issues in Infrastructure Finance* (Washington: The National League of Cities, 1986), p. 16.

24. New York State Legislative Commission, *New York's Limits,* p. 151.

25. Petersen, et al., *Constitutional and Statutory Impediments,* pp. 15–24.

26. The various restrictions on tax–exempt borrowings are very complex. For a convenient summary, see Virginia Horler, *Guide to Public Debt Financing In California* (New York: Packard Press, 1987), pp. 20–39.

27. *Ibid.,* p. 222.

28. Lennox Moak, *Municipal Bonds: Planning, Sale, and Administration* (Chicago: Government Finance Officers Association, 1982), p. 348.

29. For a discussion of advanced refunding and other debt reorganization techniques, see Moak, *Municipal Bonds,* pp. 313–330.

30. As of the late 1980s, approximately 25 percent of the dollar volume of tax–exempt bonds were sold competitively, according to *The Bond Buyer Yearbook 1989* (New York: Thomson Publishing, 1989).

31. Thomas McLoughlin, "Choosing an Underwriter for a Negotiated Bond Sale," *Government Finance Review,* June 1990, p. 28.

32. Lennox Moak, *Municipal Bonds,* p. 356.

33. *Ibid.,* p. 182.

34. *Ibid.,* p. 361.

35. For a discussion of the team and their roles, see John Petersen, *Information Flows in the Municipal Bond Market* (Chicago: Government Finance Officers Association, February, 1989), pp. 3–11.

36. *Ibid.,* pp. 8–9.

37. Government Finance Officers Association, *Disclosure Guidelines for State and Local Government Securities* (Chicago: GFOA, 1988).

38. The area of regulation of municipal securities has been evolving rapidly with the adoption of the new SEC rule 15c2–12. See John Petersen, "The New SEC Rule on Municipal Disclosure: Implications for Issuers of Municipal Securities," *Government Finance Review,* October 1989, pp. 17–20.

39. *Ibid.,* p. 20.

40. Final official statements need to be supplied to underwriters within seven days of sale. See Petersen, "New SEC Rules," p. 18.

41. See Petersen, *Information Flows,* pp. 24–29.

42. Ronald Forbes, "Cost of Issuance on Tax–Exempt Debt, Results of a 1988 Survey," *Municipal Finance Journal,* Summer 1990, pp. 129–40.

43. *Ibid.,* p. 135.

# 15

# *Debt Markets and Instruments*

John E. Petersen

Local governments depend upon the securities markets to raise the majority of funds needed for large-scale capital projects and programs, as well as to meet their cash-flow needs.[1] Both the financial markets for these securities and the ways they are tapped by governmental borrowers are subject to changes (sometimes rapid and severe) in response to the changing economy, the purposes for which governments borrow, and the tax laws and other laws and regulations that influence the financial environment.

Although seeds were planted earlier in many cases, the rate and scope of changes during the 1980s proved to be unprecedented, for it was a period that saw much innovation in the design and marketing of the tax-exempt security.[2] Some of the innovations were fleeting and did not last long, but several have proved enduring and have transformed the classic fixed-income debt instrument and the way it is offered to investors. Underlying the innovations was the need to attract new investors during periods of market turmoil, and this meant the introduction of greater flexibility in how investors and governmental borrowers trade off risks and rewards.

This chapter provides an overview of how the tax-exempt market—the special (but by no means exclusive) domain of state and local borrowers—has been transformed by new techniques, why these new ways of doing things were developed, and how they operate. The subject is a broad one and, by its nature, dynamic; therefore, concentration will be on those new devices that appear to have had the greatest staying power. The chapter starts with brief descriptions of the municipal bond market, the demand for and supply of municipal securities, and how these intersecting forces interact to cause changes in the design of instruments and the nature of transactions. Next, there is a discussion of how tax-exempt rates are determined and the components of risk, followed by an analysis of how new risk and reward tradeoffs are accomplished in the creation of innovative techniques. Subsequent discussion covers several major categories of innovations in instrument and security design: tax-exempt commercial paper, variable-rates, putable securities, call options, refunding, zeros, direct issuance, hedges, forward delivery, swaps, and taxable municipals. The chapter ends with a review of the varieties of credit enhancements and credit assistance, both public and private. None of these topics is treated in depth: the array of options presented demonstrates the vitality and dynamism of a securities market where governments must configure their capital-raising activities to comport with the latest trends in investment demands arising from the private sector.

## *CONTOURS OF THE MARKET*

The tax-exempt securities market has changed dramatically over the years, and especially during the last decade. Figure 15-1 presents a summary of new issuances of long-term and short-term tax-exempt securities since 1966. In terms of overall volume, the tax-exempt market, after years of relatively steady growth, exploded in the mid-1980s, with long-term bond sales more than doubling from $48 billion in 1981 to over $220 billion in 1985. Subsequently, under the impact of the Tax Reform Act of 1986, the market retreated to annual long-term volumes of $120

FIGURE 15-1
*Volume of New Issues of Long- and Short-Term Municipal Securities 1966–1989*
*(in billions of dollars)*

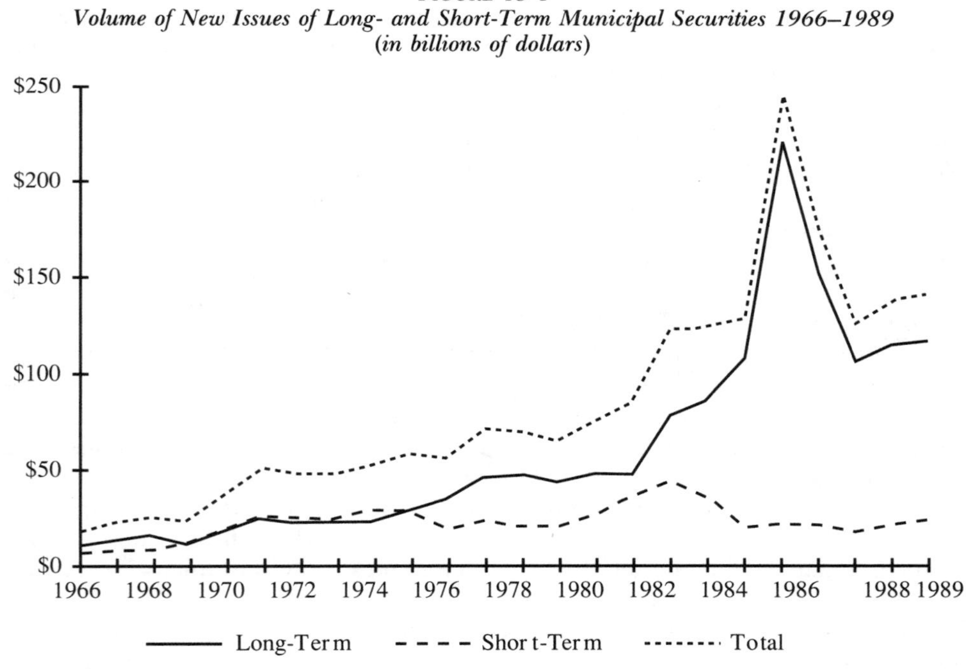


SOURCE: *The Bond Buyer.*

TABLE 15-1
*Long-Term, Tax-Exempt Bonds by Size of Issue and Number of Issues (1988 data)*

| Par Amount ($ Millions) | Volume ($ Billions) | Percentage of Total Dollar Volume | Number of Issues | Percentage of Total Number of Issues |
|---|---|---|---|---|
| 0.0– .9 | .67 | 0.6 | 1419 | 18.7 |
| 1.0– 4.9 | 7.78 | 6.8 | 3019 | 39.9 |
| 5.0– 9.9 | 8.32 | 7.3 | 1205 | 15.9 |
| 10.0–49.9 | 30.94 | 27.1 | 1402 | 18.5 |
| 50.0–99.9 | 18.82 | 16.5 | 279 | 3.9 |
| 100.0 and greater | 47.79 | 41.8 | 248 | 3.3 |

SOURCE: Investment Dealer Digest/Public Securities Association Municipal Database, New York.

billion. Short-term debt sales averaged about $20 billion over the period, having declined in the mid-1980s in contrast to the growth in long-term issues.

By convention, short-term debt is defined as debt with a stated final maturity at the time of sale of 13 months or less. One of the consequences of the innovative financing of the 1980s was that distinctions between long-term and short-term debt became blurred as securities have taken on characteristics of both. Thus, the decline in short-term debt throughout much of the decade was partly explained by the substitution of long-term debt with short-term features.

There are a large number of new issues sold each year in the tax-exempt market: approximately 7,000 new bond issues come to market annually. As may be seen in table 15-1, most new-issue tax-exempts are relatively small in size (the average issue size is about $15 million, but more than half of all issues are less than $5 million). For issuers, the small size of an issue can mean a limited geographic appeal in terms of potential investors, who often are concerned about the liquidity of a small investment and the difficulties of monitoring it. As discussed later, the information needs of investors and the desire to reach broader markets helped stimulate the credit-enhancement business. Among the major changes that occurred during the 1980s was in the uses of tax-exempt bond proceeds. Tax-exempt financing has traditionally been used for public facilities (like schools, roads, water supply) that are usually owned and operated by governments. The early 1980s, however, saw a rapid rise of nontraditional uses that involve the channeling of tax-exempt borrowing proceeds to nongovernmental projects or persons. By 1985, over 50 percent of new long-term issues were used for nontraditional purposes—including industrial pollution control, residential home mortgages, nonprofit hospitals, and industrial or commercial enterprises. (After the passage of the Tax Reform Act of 1986, this growth of the nontraditional debt was greatly curtailed.)[3]

Accompanying the changing purposes for tax-exempt borrowing have been changes in the types of security pledged to repay debt. Traditionally, most government projects were financed by government units that pledged their taxing power as security—the full faith and credit, unlimited-tax, general obligation (GO) bond. In the early 1970s, GO bonds represented about 60 percent of all tax-exempt bonds sold. By the 1980s, however, the GO bond's share of the market had been eclipsed by that of the limited-liability obligation, or "revenue bond," as it is popularly called. The latter bonds are generally repaid from user charges or from enterprise earnings and do not rely on taxing powers for their security. Securities sold for local utility operations—such as water, sewer, and electric power—are typically enterprise revenue bonds. The form proved to be very flexible and the scope of its usage expanded to cover a variety of uses where there was a need not to pledge taxes. The ascendancy of the revenue bond has several explanations. One is the need or the desire to finance traditional projects without pledging the power to tax, reserving this power for other services. In other cases, the choice of the revenue bond is based on the belief that those who benefit directly by an improvement or program should be responsible for the  repayment. In yet other cases, the limited-obligation revenue bond is a product of practical expediency, because these bonds typically do not require voter approval and usually are not restricted by various debt limitations.

During the 1980s, the nature of borrowers changed as well. The general government was supplanted by the statutory authority as the major category of borrower. A statutory authority is a special-purpose public corporation that usually does not have the power of taxation but does have the authority to float bonds. By the mid-eighties, statutory authorities, such as housing and educational loan authorities, accounted for over one-half of all long-term tax-exempt borrowing. Such entities often are established to accomplish purposes beyond the normal purview of general governmental activity: sometimes they are created solely to circumvent debt or expenditure limitations that restrict general units of government; in other instances, the statutory authority has served as a conduit for financing nongovernmental activities in the tax-exempt market (as in the case of housing bond authorities).[4]

The importation of several financing instruments—such as put options, lines of credit, and commercial paper—from the taxable to tax-exempt markets accompanied the shift of private-purpose borrowers to this market and the growing use of the statutory authority. The greater managerial and legal flexibility typically afforded to statutory authorities made it easier for them to accommodate the sometimes complicated arrangements of creative financing. Nonetheless, traditional governments have also been able to incorporate new borrowing techniques as they find them useful.

## THE CHANGING DEMAND FOR TAX EXEMPTS

The primary appeal of state and local tax-exempt securities is that investors don't have to pay (or pay as much) federal or (in some cases) state or local income taxes on the interest income.[5] This appeal has limited the market to those potential investors with higher marginal income-tax rates. Because of their tax status, three major investor groups traditionally supplied the buying power for the tax-exempt market: commercial banks, property and casualty insurance companies, and higher-income households.

In years gone by, the dynamics of the market have largely been explained by the changing fortunes (mainly, profitability) of the banks and insurance companies, alterations in their tax status, and the array of competing investment vehicles available to them. The story, a complex one, is treated at length elsewhere, and need not detain us here.[6] The high points of the ebb and flow of demand for tax-exempts are illustrated in figure 15-2, which presents the percentage composition of holdings of municipal securities for selected years 1960 through 1988. Throughout the 1960s, commercial banks were the bedrock of demand for tax-exempts, being briefly superseded by the insurance companies in the late 1970s as the latter enjoyed a cyclical run of profitability. Except for brief intervals of special circumstances, however, the financial institutions faded as major holders of tax-exempts during the 1980s, being supplanted by households and mutual funds.[7]

The household sector traditionally filled the gap between the supply of new tax-exempt securities and the demand by institutional investors. During the 1960s and 1970s, the individual investor was called on only infrequently to pick up the

FIGURE 15-2
*Trends in Holdings of Municipal Securities: National, State, and Local Issues 1960–1988*

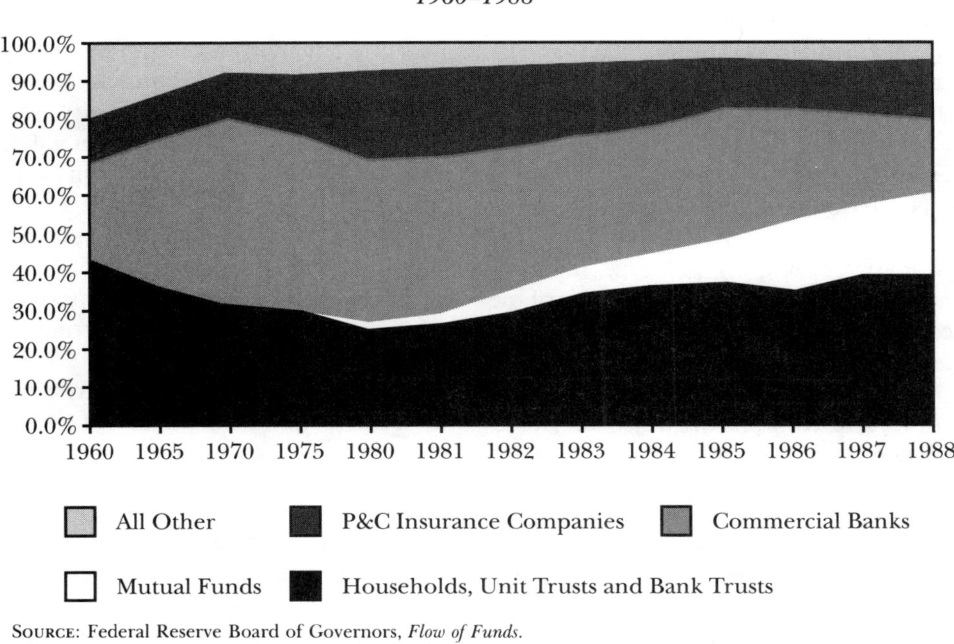


SOURCE: Federal Reserve Board of Governors, *Flow of Funds*.

slack. During the 1980s, however, individual investors and their institutional surrogates—managed bond funds and unit investment trusts—absorbed record volumes of new tax-exempts. The dominance of the household sector as the primary buyers of tax-exempts proved a major factor in the development of new financing techniques. Individual investors are far more heterogeneous in their investment objectives than institutions. Moreover, the small size of their transactions imposes higher distribution and processing costs. Individuals are also less likely to have the time or expertise to analyze the complex borrowing instruments that are now common. Recognizing the gaps and needs, professionally selected and managed funds stepped into the breech to mobilize individual investor funds.

By the end of the decade of the 1980s, the importance of tax-exempt funds had grown greatly. In the face of a relatively meager supply of new tax-exempt bonds, funds have greatly concentrated new purchasing by the household sector. Consequently, their buying power has placed a premium on tailoring new issuances to meet the needs of a relative few, highly sophisticated primary market buyers,[8] the mutual funds and unit trusts.

## *DETERMINING THE TAX-EXEMPT INTEREST RATE*

As noted, the primary appeal of the conventional tax-exempt bond has been that its interest income is exempted from federal and most state and local income taxes. Because of this, the tax-exempt borrower can offer a lower interest rate than it could if the interest were subject to taxes.[9] While tax exemption is the primary attraction, several other considerations influence the interest rate on a particular municipal security. But it is equally clear that, given the maturity of the debt (the period before the principal comes due) and the credit quality (which is largely determined by the ratings conferred by the major credit-rating agencies), the rate of return that the investor will require on a tax-exempt security is at least equal to that available after taxes on a comparable taxable investment. For example, investors in the 28 percent marginal tax bracket pay 28 cents in taxes on each dollar of added taxable income; for these investors, a tax-exempt security yielding a 7 percent return would be equal on an after-tax basis to a taxable security yielding 9.7 percent.

Historically, in those periods of high rate ratios, which coincided with periods of "tight money," the participation of the household sector was important as institutions retreated from the market.

By the 1980s, institutional interest waned and the need to market increasing volumes of new securities to the household sector required dramatic increases in tax-exempt interest rates. Early in the decade, the long-term tax-exempt interest rate reached the double-digit level and the ratio of tax-exempt rates to taxable rates climbed to 79 percent. The growing importance of the household sector coincided with the most significant reduction in individual tax rates in the past two decades and the creation of many other forms of tax shelters with passage of the 1981 Tax Act. Thus, the level of tax-exempt rates was driven higher to provide returns equivalent to those on competing tax shelters and on taxable investments with a higher after-tax value because of lowered tax brackets. Later, in 1985 and 1986, the ratio of rates was wildly tossed up and down by the pending Tax Reform Act and huge surges of new offerings as worried participants sought to market bonds before deadlines contemplated by the Tax Act. But the end of the decade saw the ratio stabilize at approximately 75 percent; as a result, investors in a 25 percent marginal bracket were on the borderline of tax-exempt buyers.

## THE COMPONENTS OF RISK

### The Yield Curve

The yield curve refers to the relationship between the maturity of debt and the interest rate it carries. Generally, the yield curve slopes upward: the longer that an obligation is outstanding, the higher the rate of interest that investors receive to compensate both for the use of their money and to reward them for a variety of risks that they face as time goes by.[10] These types of risk will be discussed in more detail shortly, but the major ones have to do with (1) possible fluctuations in interest rates (market risks) that may impair the expected rate of return and (2) the ability of the debtor to pay interest and principal on time and in full (credit risk). Thus, the farther into the future debt runs, the less certain investors can be about the probability of avoiding both these major risks, and the more they require additional interest above the "riskless" rate on capital.

The more favorable (for borrowers) ratio of tax-exempt to taxable interest rates is found in the short end of the yield curve. This may be attributable to several factors. First, investors are much more certain about their tax status in the near term than in the distant future. That is, when investors buy a 20-year bond, they are assuming not only their need for shelter for that interval of time (or that their fellow investors will need to shelter income) but also the future value of the shelter (the future tax laws). Second, the tax laws favor institutional investment in the short term securities market. In the short-term market, this opportunity involves little risk of capital in return for tax-exempt income. Last, very short term investments that mature quickly expose the investor to relatively little danger of illiquidity through price fluctuations (because the principal returns so quickly), and this is an important attribute for investors who wish to preserve capital value. In addition, certain institutional factors encourage buying by the tax-exempt mutual and money-market funds that need short-term investment outlets to "park" their assets while awaiting longer-term and higher-yield obligations in which to invest. In subsequent discussions of financing instruments, we will return to the yield curve, focusing on short-term borrowing; namely, securities that mature in as short a time as a day or a week and that allow the investor the option of specifying when the maturity will occur.

### Credit Quality and Credit Ratings

An important element in determining the interest rate that jurisdictions must pay on their borrowings is the perceived quality of their credit. Investors always

TABLE 15-2

*Moody's, Standard & Poor's, and Fitch's Bond Rating Classifications*

| | RATING SYMBOL | | |
|---|---|---|---|
| General Quality Characteristic | Moody's[1] | Standard & Poor's[2] | Fitch's[3] |
| Prime Quality | Aaa | AAA | AAA |
| Excellent Quality | Aa | AA | AA |
| Upper Medium Quality | A | A | A |
| Lower Medium Quality | Baa | BBB | BBB |
| Marginally Speculative Quality | Ba | BB | BB |
| Very Speculative Quality | B, Caa | B, CCC, CC | B, CCC, CC |
| Default Quality | Ca, C | C, D | C, DDD, DD, D |

[1] Bonds rated by Moody's with the suffix "-1" (e.g., A-1) indicate the stronger credits in that category.
[2] Standard & Poor's uses a suffix of "+" or "−" (e.g. A+) to indicate relative position in the rating category.
[3] Fitch uses a suffix of "+" or "−" (e.g. A+) to indicate relative position in the rating category. Fitch also assigns trend indicators (arrows) to indicate if fundamentals are improving (↑), stable (↔), declining (↓), or uncertain (↕).

SOURCE: John Petersen and Ronald Forbes, *Innovative Capital Financing* (Chicago: American Planning Association, 1985); and Fitch Investors Service, *Fitch Insights* (New York, 1989).

face the risk that borrowers will default; that is, not pay their obligations on time or in full. Because of the large number of tax-exempt issues and their greater diversity, certain quality assessments of credit are widely followed by market participants. Those most widely followed are Moody's Investors Service and Standard & Poor's Corporation but with those of Fitch Investors Service getting increased attention. The rating symbols used by the firms and brief characterizations of them are shown in table 15-2. The vast bulk of ratings conferred are in the top four major rating brackets (Aaa/AAA through Baa/BBB, using Moody's and Standard & Poor's symbols, respectively), which are considered to be "investment grade" ratings.

The significance of the ratings for the cost of borrowing can be seen in figure 15-3, which plots the differential in yields for 20-year general-obligation borrowings in the years 1980 through 1989. The differential in borrowing costs between the Moody's prime quality (Aaa) and the lower-medium quality (Baa) has fluctuated between less than half a percentage point to nearly two percentage points. The message is clear: borrowers that can improve their ratings can reduce interest cost, although the value of that savings will vary.

Two things about ratings should be noted. First, the rating agency is primarily interested in the strength of the security pledged to the repayment of the debt; the lighter the burden of the debt in relation to the resources pledged to repayment means a higher rating, everything else being equal. Second, although many of the factors that enter into the rating are beyond the immediate control of the borrower (health of the local economy, various constitutional and state

FIGURE 15-3
*Interest Rate Spread Between Aaa-Rated and Baa-Rated Municipal Debt Issuances*
*January 1983–August 1989*

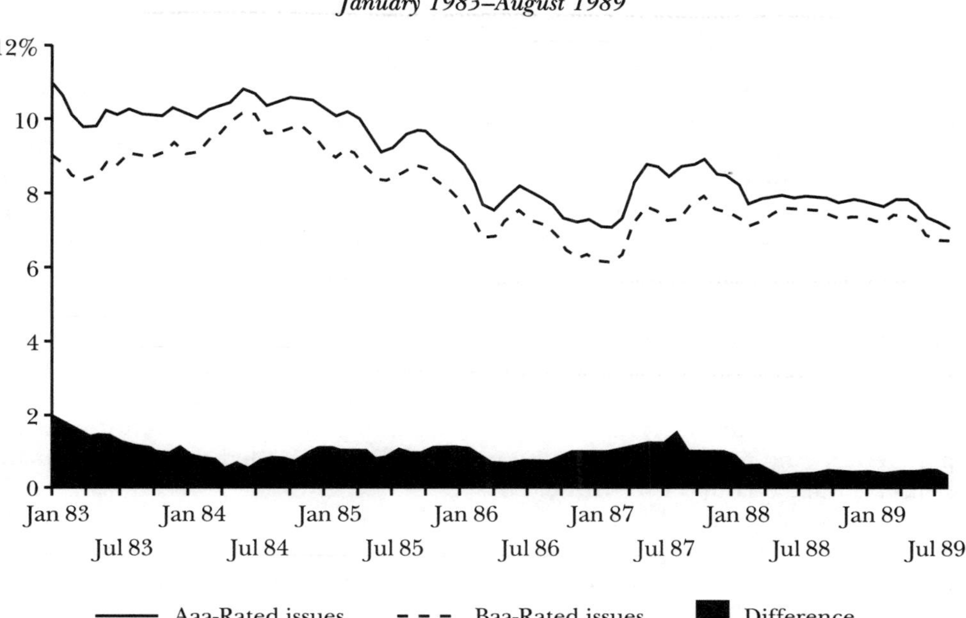


SOURCE: Moody's Bond Record.

statutory constraints, etc.), borrowers frequently can control or at least influence factors that can enhance or impair the quality of their credit. Designing transactions to strengthen the security pledged and to improve the ratings on them is a major theme of many of the newer financing techniques.

### *Repackaging Traditional Debt*

The earlier overview of the tax-exempt bond market established the foundation for examining recent trends in debt financing techniques. Understanding what is different about these new techniques first requires an examination of what is orthodox in the sale of tax-exempt debt and how the methods of borrowing have repackaged the basic instrument to accommodate changing market conditions and shifting investor preferences.

The traditional package in which tax-exempt bonds are sold is that of an annual cash flow of fixed interest payments (typically paid semiannually) for each maturity with the principal due at maturity. The investor in a 20-year bond with an 8 percent coupon thus receives 40 semiannual cash payments of $40 per $1,000 invested and the payment of the principal at the end of 20 years. Moreover, since most issues are made up of sets (or "strips") of serial bonds maturing each year and each having its own coupon, a 20-year bond issue is in reality a collection of 20 distinct securities, each with its unique price and maturity characteristics.

The above traditional package associated with long-term debt maturities fell from favor with many investors because of three pervasive uncertainties associated with it: the uncertainty of present values; the uncertainty over future accumulated wealth; and the uncertainty over future value.

The uncertainty over present values is a consequence of the greater volatility of interest rates in recent years. Yearly variations in interest rates of two to three percentage points between the highs and lows became common during the 1980s (as contrasted with variations of less than one percentage point during the 1970s). Greater volatility translates into more uncertainty over market values. With fixed coupon rates, the only way that an outstanding bond can be sold to a new investor to provide a current yield—when market rates of interest have risen—is through a discount in its price.

Regardless of the intended investment horizon at the time of purchase, most investors are concerned about the current market values of their investments. Because of the mathematics of bond pricing and discounting formulas, price changes are greater on long-term bonds for a given change in interest rates than on short-term securities. Thus, the upward-sloping schedule of interest rates in part reflects the need to compensate investors for the added risks they bear in long-term, fixed-coupon securities.

But investors have different investment objectives, and some are less sensitive to market fluctuations in prices. For example, some accumulate financial resources for use at a future date—for retirement or for children's education. For such investors, the traditional stream of semiannual coupon payments from a long-term bond is not particularly valuable. In that instance, semiannual coupon payments must be reinvested to accumulate, or compound, interest over the planned investment horizon—but the actual interest rate earned on reinvesting the interim coupons will be known only after the fact. Thus, the total realized return and future wealth cannot be known at the time the bonds are purchased.

Another element of future value is the ability of an issue to maintain its value relative to other borrowers, its relative credit quality. Investors are concerned about the credit quality of their investments. Deteriorating credit quality both diminishes the market value of investments and raises concerns over the safety of principal. On the other hand, as was illustrated in the foregoing discussion of ratings, higher bond ratings and enhanced credit quality can allay investor concerns, especially those of the individual investor.

The creativity of the 1980s in the municipal bond market amounted to repackaging the traditional fixed-income, long-term security sold on the basis of its own rating into new products designed to meet the evolving risk/reward demands of investors. Before turning to the specific varieties of instruments that emerged, it is useful to review the fundamentals of the new debt packaging techniques.

### *Canons of Creativity*

Financing techniques have been designed to alter the traditional risk/reward relationships between borrowers and lenders in a variety of ways. These can be conveniently summarized as follows:

- Shifting interest-rate risk from the lender to the borrower
- Enhancing the creditworthiness of borrowers by shifting credit-related risks to third parties
- Increasing the types of returns available to investors beyond those available from the regular receipt of interest-income payments

These general types of "creative financing" actions can be examined in the framework of the typical yield curve as shown in figure 15-4, which shows the cost of capital on the vertical axis and the maturity on the horizontal axis. Depicted are

FIGURE 15-4
*Creative Financing Techniques and Net Cost of Capital*

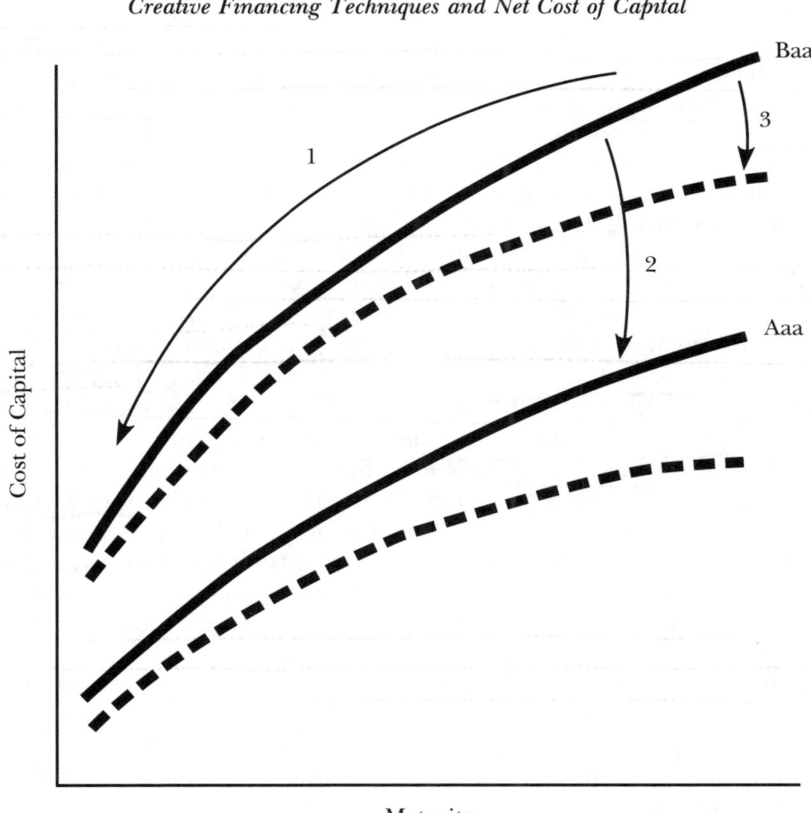


Explanation:
1. Move down yield curve (shorten maturity)
2. Enhance credit quality
3. Employ other economic returns and/or lessen net debt service

SOURCE: John Petersen and Ronald Forbes, *Innovative Capital Financing*, PAS Report #392 (Chicago: American Planning Association, 1985).

two yield curves, one for a lower-grade credit (shown as Baa) and one for a prime credit (Aaa). One method of reducing costs is to shorten the maturity, taking advantage of the traditionally lower rates of interest in the short-term markets, as is shown by the movement depicted by arrow 1. A subsequent discussion of short-term market instruments and the adaptation of long-term obligations to take on the characteristics of short-term instruments (variable rates and put options), will demonstrate how this shortening of obligations has been performed and its cost implications. But it is essential to note that a radical shortening of debt involves risks and costs to issuers that may offset much of the apparent savings suggested by simple comparisons of the interest costs.

Another move to lower borrowing costs is to improve the credit quality and rating of the obligation. This is illustrated by the shift from the lower-grade to the prime yield curve, labeled as movement 2. Credit improvement can be accomplished in two ways: either by the borrowing unit taking steps to strengthen the credit pledged from its own resources or, more commonly, using third-party credit enhancements such as insurance, guarantees, or various types of credit backstops. Again, the borrower engages in the process of shifting risk from the investor onto itself or onto a third party. And, again, this movement usually entails additional costs such as insurance premiums or increased uncertainties about future financing costs. The third major movement depicted in figure 15-4 involves either altering the nature of the economic returns to investors or lowering the net cost of capital to the borrower or both. This is illustrated as movement 3, where the yield curve seen in the conventional securities market is supplanted by one that reflects new, lower costs. Three major varieties of creative financing techniques can create these new, lower-yield curves. The first involves those actions through which the borrower changes the nature of the interest payments to protect the investor against reinvestment risk by, in effect, guaranteeing the reinvestment of interest earnings at a stated rate. A good example of its application is found in the original-issue discount, or zero-coupon bonds. Of course, the borrower assumes the burden of a much larger payment at the end of the investment period and the requisite problems of managing sinking funds or other resources that will be needed to meet the final payment.

The second technique that changes the nature of the economic returns to investors is to design transactions that take advantage of various tax preferences other than the tax exemption of interest income. A leading technique to accomplish this was the design of joint public/private financings in which private investors—by acquiring ownership interests—could enjoy the benefits of tax preferences such as accelerated depreciation and investment tax credits. The opportunities for this cost-saving maneuver were virtually eliminated by the Tax Reform Act of 1986. A third set of innovative financing techniques that can lower the net cost of capital to state and local governments involves the structuring of transactions to take advantage of the opportunity to earn interest through the investment of assets, including investment in bond proceeds and in taxable securities that yield more than the interest costs of tax-exempt borrowings (a practice called arbitrage). Arbitrage techniques for lowering the net cost of capital remain of interest in some transactions, but their availability and profitability were greatly curtailed by the Tax Reform Act of 1986.[11]

## *SEEDBED OF CHANGE: SHORT-TERM SECURITIES*

The steeply sloped yield curve of the early 1980s and the high level of rates focused attention early on the opportunities to tap the relatively low cost of capital available in the short-term tax-exempt market. At the outset, issuers reexamined their traditional methods of borrowing short-term and to think creatively about their use.

The traditional forms of short-term borrowing are tax or revenue anticipation notes (TANs, RANs) and bond anticipation notes (BANs). The equivalent of working capital loans, TANs and RANs provide temporary sources of funds to bridge cash-flow gaps between revenue collections and operating outlays. BANs are used to provide interim funds during construction progress; upon project completion, they are replaced with long-term bond financing.

These traditional forms of short-term borrowing share several features with long-term bond financing. Each note issue carries a fixed interest rate, and each note sale requires a separate borrowing resolution, accompanying sales documentation (such as a legal opinion and an official statement), and frequently a formal competitive bidding procedure. Not surprisingly, the effort necessary to issue traditional short-term notes discouraged repeated offerings with very short maturities—of, say, 90 days or less.

The positively sloped yield curve typically found in the tax-exempt market stimulated the development and growth of a variety of financing techniques designed to lower the cost of borrowing by sliding down the yield curve. During the 1980s, new varieties of short-term debt were designed to capture the vast pool of investor funds that wanted tax-free income without exposure to the interest-rate risks inherent in long-term bonds. In addition, before the tight restrictions were placed by the U.S. Congress on tax-exempt short-term financing for arbitrage purposes, the low yields on tax-exempts in relationship to taxable investments greatly favored the earning of arbitrage profits by tax-exempt issuers.

### *Tax-Exempt Commercial Paper*

Tax-exempt commercial paper proved an early and flexible solution to accessing the short-term market. It is a financing device that can be defined as short-term unsecured promissory notes, possessing the following characteristics.

It is of short-term maturity (usually 30 to 60 days) and may be as short as one day or as long as 365 days. Because of the short maturity, it has continuous offerings (the paper may be made available as frequently as on a daily basis). Commercial paper maturities are a matter of negotiation and set to coincide with issuer and investor preferences. Because of their flexibility, repayment of the paper is backed up by a credit facility (line or letter of credit) from a commercial bank. Last, there is same-day settlement; that is, purchases made in the morning by investors are settled with immediately available funds by the close of business the same day.

Commercial paper first entered the tax-exempt securities market in 1973 but did not rise to prominence until the early 1980s. The slow takeoff was caused by a combination of legal and procedural difficulties that needed to be worked out by governmental issuers in the early years. Exceptionally low rates of interest in the very short term prime-paper market, however, made commercial paper very attractive, and it grew rapidly until 1985. The advent of the tax reform proposals undercut its growth by presenting the problem of reissuance, which effectively blocked certain issuers from ongoing access to the market.[12]

### *Variable-Rate Securities*

Variable-rate securities were developed first in the short-term market but rapidly extended to long-term debt as well. Their chief characteristic is that, instead of a fixed interest rate throughout the life of the obligation, the rate is allowed to fluctuate in response to the changing market. In the case of tax-exempt commercial paper, the same effect is achieved by the short maturities that allow investors frequent options to continue lending at the new rate by "rolling over" their investment (replacing retiring paper with a new loan) or to cash in their loan. In the case of the variable-rate security, the new rate is assigned to the outstanding paper without maturing.

In the early 1980s, variable rates were incorporated into a new debt instrument that had its yield periodically changed or "reset." Initially, the rate was recalculated to reflect market rates using a fixed formula. These early efforts, called "flexible rates" or "low floaters" had fixed, albeit short, maturities and experienced difficulty sustaining par values as the rigid formulas lost touch with market conditions.

Later, such resets of rates were made more flexible and based on judgment, without recourse to a formula. This new instrument had attached the important added inducement of a demand feature that allowed investors at their election to cash in their investment by putting it back to the issuer for repayment. Such a "put option" feature, as it is called, greatly enhances the liquidity of the investor, who, upon short notice, can get back the principal amount of the investment and is not exposed to the risk of capital deterioration found in fixed-coupon obligations.

### *Putable Securities*

A put option allows bondholders the choice of holding or redeeming at par their investments at specified future intervals. Depending on the frequency of the put-option interval, otherwise long-term bonds may behave as short-term investments.

Variable-rate demand securities, discussed above, can have extremely short deferrals—as little as one day or one week—from the sale date before the put option can be exercised by the investor. Such instruments, where the put option can be exercised frequently between short intervals of time (30 days or less), are called continuing puts. Other instruments may carry less frequent put options, such as one year or at the end of five or ten years.

The put option effectively allows investors to convert long-term bonds into short-term securities. Thus, the interest rates on these bonds are generally established by the put interval; for example, weekly continuing-put bonds carry a rate approximately equal to the rate on seven-day investments. Alternatively, the coupon rates on put bonds can be fixed at the time of original sale, in which case the cost to the borrower is also fixed until bonds are redeemed.

While conceptually simple, a put option can require an elaborate supporting cast of players. In a typical variable security, when the interest rate is reset, the investor has the option of holding for the next period or putting ("tendering") its bonds back. To make sure funds are available to meet investor demands, three parties are needed: a tender agent, a remarketing agent, and a credit facility.

If investors choose to tender their bonds, a firm acting as tender agent exchanges bonds for cash. The tender agent next notifies the remarketing agent, who then attempts to resell tendered bonds at a new interest rate after reference to an interest index. Typically, the remarketing agent can reset the new rate within a range around an interest index in order to reoffer the bonds at par. As new sales occur, the cash is then delivered to the tender agent. If not all bonds are remarketed, the remaining cash needs of the tender agent are met by the standby credit agreement with a commercial bank, which serves as a backup credit facility to ensure sufficient funds will be on hand to pay off investors.

The cost of packaging such bonds with short-term rates is a factor to consider. Typically, the letter or line of credit that constitutes the credit facility will cost $\frac{3}{8}$ to 1 full percentage point on the dollar amount of the bonds covered, and the remarketing agent is paid an annual fee on the outstanding balance of $\frac{1}{8}$ to $\frac{1}{4}$ percentage point (12.5 to 25 basis points). Thus, the cost of accommodating the increased investor liquidity may be 50 to 100 or more basis points.[13] The interest cost savings that are possible, if there are wide differences in cost between very short term rates and rates on long-term bonds, must be weighed against these costs.

In addition to the interest cost savings, variable-rate issues have other attributes that make them attractive to issuers. First, they are typically convertible to long-term, fixed-rate issues at any interest reset date at the election of the issuer. Thus, when long-term rates drop to a desirable level, the issuer can opt to "fix out" the bonds, remarketing them in the form of long-term, fixed-interest obligations. By the same token, the obligations can be called at any interest-adjustment date at the election of the issuer with no call premium. Last, the underwriting charges on variable-rate demand notes and bonds tend to be lower ($5 to $7 a bond as opposed to $10 to $15), with a traditional fixed-rate long-term bond.[14]

The disadvantage of the put bond resides primarily in the interest-rate risk borne by the issuer. The issuer is unsure from one interest-rate adjustment to the next what its debt service will be. This uncertainty can be hedged by stating interest rate maximums or by building in an interest-rate reserve or "guard" fund that can be used to smooth out fluctuations in interest cost. Also, should there be a need to use the credit facility by the issuer, the cost of borrowing can escalate sharply because the lending rate is typically pegged to the bank prime rate or higher. There is also the risk that the credit rating of the credit facility provider may drop and force a substantial putting back of the issue to the remarketing agent, who then would have to increase interest rates sharply or make a new backstop arrangement, perhaps under unfavorable market conditions.

To help solve the above problems, remarketing agreements have been designed so that bonds put back for redemption may be redistributed in a variety of ways. The remarketing alternatives are refined to include conversion options that permit the issuer and the remarketing agent to change the interest payment structure (from fixed to variable or from variable to fixed). These conversion options may also be combined with options by the borrower to terminate the put with advance notice. The termination option, combined with a conversion option, permits issuers to sell fixed-rate, long-term debt at a future date when interest rates have fallen, without the necessity of first calling variable-rate bonds for redemption.

Perhaps the apogee of flexibility in tax-exempt debt structuring is reached with "multimodal" bonds. Multimodal bonds permit the underwriters to structure all or part of the issue in a unit-price mode (similar to commercial paper in that the remarketing agent has liberty to establish interest scales and investors select the maturity they want); a variable-rate mode; and a fixed-rate mode (the traditional structure that can range from one year to final maturity). The bonds, over their life, may be converted among the modes upon notice, thus establishing great flexibility on the part of the issuer.

### *Call Options*

Most government borrowers (even in the face of an upward-sloping yield curve) choose to issue long-term, fixed-coupon debt knowing that, while it is somewhat more expensive, a ceiling has been placed on future debt-service outlays. By the same token, they like a back door so they can refinance their debt if rates drop. A technique called refunding permits issuers the flexibility to reduce remaining debt-service costs at some future date. The key to refunding is the optional redemption provision, popularly known as the call option.

If future interest rates decline well below the coupon rates on outstanding bonds, borrowers with the call option can redeem outstanding high-coupon debt without unknown market risks and finance the redemption with new, lower-cost debt. Repurchase of noncallable bonds carry a price. As an example, a noncallable bond issued with a 9 percent coupon with 20 years to maturity would command a market price of $134.67 per $100 par value if market rates declined to 6 percent.

The cost to borrowers of incorporating the call option takes the form of a higher rate on redeemable bonds. Rates on callable bonds range from 10 to 50 basis points higher than rates on otherwise comparable bonds that are noncallable.[15] The market routinely places a higher value on the call option when interest rates are near cyclical peaks, anticipating that the high levels in rates during these periods cannot be sustained over the long term.

Most often, bond indentures carry "call protection," which prohibits the exercise of a call option for a period ranging from five to ten years after the sale date of the bond. Moreover, most call provisions require issuers to pay a call premium to investors if bonds are subsequently redeemed ("called"). These premiums generally range from 2 percent to 5 percent above par value (e.g., a redemption price of $102 or $105 per $100 par value) and are designed to compensate investors if there is an early retirement of the debt.

### *Refunding Strategies*

Issuers can follow two general strategies for exercising the call option when interest rates decline: refunding and advance refunding. At the end of the call deferment period, usually five to ten years from the sale date of the "old" bonds, issuers may elect to do a refunding. A refunding involves the sale of new bonds, the proceeds of which are used concurrently to redeem "old" bonds. Refundings are usually done to save on interest costs but may be undertaken to overcome restrictions in bond covenants.

An important alternative, however, is for issuers to do an advance refunding. Advance refunding requires the sale of new bonds, as in a refunding, but the proceeds are not used immediately to redeem outstanding bonds. Instead, proceeds are typically invested in U.S. government securities and placed in escrow. This escrow fund is used to meet debt-service payments on "old" bonds until the first call date, at which time the remainder of the escrow fund is used to redeem outstanding bonds. Under the traditional advance refunding technique, the "old" bondholders look to the escrow fund for their security (which has been funded by the proceeds from the refunding); whereas under "straight" refunding, bondholders look to the original pledged revenue source for their security. Consequently, the owners of the bonds that are refunded by the escrow enjoy an elevation of the credit quality of their holdings.

Advance refundings are complex financial transactions that are structured in a number of ways and they are subject to a variety of constraints imposed by federal tax laws and regulations and by bond indenture provisions.[16] Generally, however, once an issuer provides for the payment of an outstanding bond issue, that issue is considered "defeased," or no longer a liability of the issuer.

### *The Zero-Coupon Bond*

The zero-coupon bond (zero) is a security that does not pay interest coupons but, being originally sold at discount, over its life accumulates (or accretes) interest that is paid at the maturity of the obligation. Zeros may be especially attractive to investors who wish to accumulate future wealth or who anticipate that future reinvestment rates may be lower than present coupon rates. In short, for these investors, the zero can be viewed as a way of avoiding reinvestment risk. Table 14-3 provides examples of alternative reinvestment returns to demonstrate the concept.

Panel A of table 15-3 compares a zero that costs $1,000 today and has a final payment of $5,112 in 20 years with a coupon-bearing bond that also costs $1,000 today but pays coupon income of $85 each year until maturity. As noted,

TABLE 15-3

*Importance of Reinvestment Returns to Realized Yield: 8.50% Zero Coupon Compared to 8.50% Coupon Bond with Alternative Reinvestment Rates (20-Year Bonds with Initial Price of $1,000)*

| | Panel A | | Panel B | |
|---|---|---|---|---|
| | 8.50% Coupon Bond 8.50% Reinvestment Rate | Zero Coupon with 8.50% Yield | 8.50% Coupon Bond 7.00% Reinvestment Rate | 8.50% Coupon Bond 10% Reinvestment Rate |
| Coupon Income | $1,700 | 0 | $1,700 | $1,700 |
| Reinvestment Income | 2,412 | 0 | 1,785 | 3,168 |
| Return of Principal | 1,000 | 0 | 1,000 | 1,000 |
| Total Return (20 Years) | 5,112 | 5,112 | 4,485 | 6,868 |
| Realized Yield | 8.50% | 8.50% | 7.79% | 9.25% |

SOURCE: Based on John Petersen and Ronald Forbes, *Innovative Capital Financing* (Chicago: American Planning Association, 1985).

in order for the current coupon bond to produce the same total return at the end of 20 years, the interim coupon payments must be reinvested at 8.5 percent. Note that interest earned on interest, or reinvestment income, is the most significant portion of total return for long-term investors in coupon bonds.

Panel B points out that the final realized return on coupon bonds at the end of 20 years is very sensitive to the reinvestment rate. If the stream of coupon payments are reinvested at a rate of only 7.0 percent, the total return falls to $4,485; in contrast, when the reinvestment rate is 10 percent, the total return rises to $6,868. For the zero, the realized compound yield is 8.5 percent. For the 8.5 percent coupon bond, the realized compound yield with reinvestment at 7.4 percent is only 7.79 percent; at a reinvestment rate of 10 percent, the realized compound yield is 9.25 percent.

These examples illustrate that the zero can be an attractive investment alternative to coupon bonds for investors with an investment objective of assured asset accumulation. By guaranteeing reinvestment rates, zeros reduce the risk of uncertain future investment rates to investors.

A disadvantage to the issuer of zeros is that a much larger par value of bonds must initially be used in order to realize a given amount of net proceeds, which can cause legal problems in regard to the treatment of indebtedness. Deferral of interest payment until the bonds' maturity can also create uncertainties about the ability of issuers to meet the balloon payments.

An important variant of the zero is the capital-appreciation or accumulator bond. Like the zero, all debt service is postponed until maturity. Unlike the zero, however, the bonds are not sold at an original discount but are sold at par.

Meanwhile, the interest component is held by the issuer and compounded at the stated rate so that the investor receives a lump-sum multiple of the principal amount at the end of the holding period. Otherwise, the accumulator operates in much the same way as the zero.

The greatest advantage to the accumulator is a legal one: because most debt limitations (including caps on single-family housing and industrial development bonds) are expressed in terms of the par value of debt, accumulator bonds permit conventional sales that retain investor benefit of the locked-in reinvestment return.

### *Direct Issuance and Minibonds*

Most issuers elect to market their bonds through an underwriting syndicate whereby the securities are bought first by investment bankers who then redistribute the offering to the ultimate investors. In some cases, however, the issuer may choose to place its bonds directly with the investors. When this occurs, it typically has been restricted to short-term borrowings or specialized and small issuances.

One exception to the rule, however, has been the use of direct issuances where a government decides to offer from its own offices securities to its own citizen-investors. In order to appeal to small investors and encourage broad distribution, the bonds were usually offered in small denominations ($100 to $500 as opposed to the typical $5,000 of the conventional bond). Although such "minibond" offerings were fairly uncommon because of the relatively high administrative costs and uncertainty about raising the needed funds, innovations elsewhere in the market have put them in a much more favorable light during recent years. The growing use of the original issue discount bond, coupled with the registered form of security (which replaced the bearer form by federal law in the early 1980s) and the introduction of the put option, all combined to greatly lower the administrative costs involved in issuance of the minibond, making it much more cost effective.[17]

Recent offerings of minibonds have adopted the capital-accumulator instrument (eliminating the need for issuing semiannual interest checks) and the put option to provide investor liquidity (in exchange for making the instruments nontransferable, eliminating the need for transfer agents). Reducing the paperwork and the need for outside services makes the costs of raising capital competitive with those in the conventional market (especially if the issue is done in conjunction with a conventional offering). In addition, the minibond can have important public relations advantages in developing local support for and understanding of a jurisdiction's capital financing program.[18]

### *Hedges, Forward Delivery, and Swaps*

The Tax Reform Act of 1986 placed many new and exceedingly complicated restrictions on tax-exempt borrowing in the latter half of the 1980s. Meanwhile, the generally declining interest rate encouraged issuers to seek long-term financing, either to lock in the low rates currently available or to refinance outstanding debt that had been sold in a high-interest environment. Accomplishing either of these objectives under the new restrictions spawned an array of new techniques in the market at the end of the decade.

The 1986 Tax Act, by its restrictions on arbitrage, removed the advantages of delaying bond issuance and quickened the interest of issuers in issuing bonds as a hedge against future increases in the rates of interest. For example, the issuer might have a series of identified projects to be financed and would wish to lock in the low interest costs, or it might simply be speculating that somewhere in the future it might need money and, if so, would have raised low-cost capital. Such a borrowing, designed as a hedge against future increases in rates, would have its proceeds placed in escrow at a "restricted" yield so as not to violate the arbitrage restrictions, and the various legal and underwriting fees associated with the transaction would be on a contingent basis and paid only when the funds were actually expended as planned. In 1988 and 1989, Congress passed laws to restrict the practice of such transactions, effectively eliminating the ability of issuers to hedge against future rate increases unless they had projects firmly in mind and ready to go.[19]

The Tax Reform Act also left large volumes of tax-exempt bonds outstanding that were precluded from advance refunding. In addition, the Act placed constraints on the volume of tax-exempt borrowing that might be done for non-governmental purposes by the imposing of state volume caps, which created timing problems for issuances that would exceed annual limits. The challenge became one of locking in the low rates in the tax-exempt market without issuing tax-exempt bonds. One way this is accomplished is through a device called forward delivery or refunding escrow deposit securities ("REDs"), in which investors enter into forward purchase agreements to buy tax-exempt refunding issues when the old issues were eligible for call. The investor's money is placed in escrow invested in U.S. Treasuries that are designed to mature just before the maturity of the old bonds to be refunded. Investors are paid from the earnings on the escrowed notes (the interest is taxable) until they come due, at which time the principal is used to refund the old bonds. At that point, the investors become owners of tax-exempt securities.

There are, of course, bets being made in all of this. Investors are betting that rates will go down or maybe that tax rates will rise. On the other side, issuers risk that rates may go down further and that their savings might have been greater had they waited. But in any event, the issuer is locking in a savings in comparison to the coupon rate on the old high-coupon bond.[20]

Another technique used extensively in the international markets and gaining some acceptance in the tax-exempt market is the use of interest-rate swaps. As with escrow deposits, the major impetus for swaps appears to have evolved from the need to accomplish debt-management goals (such as changing the nature of the interest-rate-payment pattern) without resorting to a new issue (which, as in the case of advance refunding, might not be possible).

In the municipal swap, parties swap their interest payments, which usually involves an exchange of floating for fixed rates. Neither the original obligation nor the principal payments are affected by the switch. Payments are made on a net basis; whichever party owes more pays the other the difference. Opinion differs over whether the swap represents a speculation on interest rates or a way of obtaining more flexibility in debt management. But, speculation or not, it does offer the possibility to reorganize debt payments without a reissue.[21]

### *Taxable Municipals*

It once would have been thought to be an oxymoron to use the expression "taxable municipal," but that is no longer the case. Although there were a few early experiments, there emerged in earnest following the Tax Reform Act of 1986 a new class of state and local obligations on which the interest income was taxable under the federal income-tax laws. These are bonds sold for purposes that, because of the degree of nongovernmental involvement in the transaction, no longer were eligible for tax exemption or that exceeded the bounds of limitations placed by the federal tax code on bonds of that type (such as exceeding volume caps or total issuance costs).[22]

The leading example of taxable financing is the economic development bond, in which private firms are aided by state or local governments. Because it is subject to the federal income tax, the taxable security carries higher interest rates than the tax-exempt—it may nevertheless possess advantages. Advantages arise principally from the fact that interest income is exempt from state income taxes, the sponsoring governments may extend certain pledges that improve the creditworthiness of the issue, and the financed improvement may enjoy sales-tax and property-tax exemptions.[23]

The taxable municipal market, while growing, is small in comparison to the conventional tax-exempt market, representing only 2 to 3 percent of total state and local government borrowing.[24]

## *CREDIT ENHANCEMENTS*

Credit enhancements are contractual arrangements involving third parties that are designed to improve the creditworthiness—as represented by the credit rating—of transactions and issuers. The risk of default is of fundamental concern to the rating agencies and investors, and developments in the municipal bond market were often not reassuring on that score during the 1980s. Aside from the massive $2.25 billion default of the Washington Public Power Supply System (WPPSS) in 1983, the municipal market had to contend with a variety of lesser disruptions and disappointments. Although the payments record on the municipal security remained good throughout the decade, the opinions of the rating agencies were subject to numerous revisions; in the case of Moody's there were upwards of 500 to 600 credits having their ratings changed annually. Moreover, throughout much of the decade downgradings predominated over upgradings, a source of concern to investors and issuers alike.[25]

A contributing factor to the importance of enhancements has been the growth of the individual investor as the primary buyer in the market. As stated earlier, the municipal bond market is distinguished by the large number and heterogeneity of the securities offered. Individual investors generally do not have portfolios of sufficient size to allow for diversification and have limited skills and information to follow particular credits. Accordingly, bond underwriters and the bond funds have found it a useful marketing tool (and a protection against accusations of securities fraud) to reduce credit risk by acquiring obligations with credit enhancements.

Three types of credit enhancements will be examined below: bank credit supports (found predominantly, but not exclusively, in the short-term market); bond insurance as provided by private insurers; and state-sponsored credit assistance programs for local governments.

### *Bank Credit Enhancements*

Bank credit supports (or credit facilities, as they are called in the aggregate), may be grouped into two generic types: lines of credit and letters of credit. The weaker form of bank support is the line of credit. This type of agreement generally provides only temporary liquidity for the issuer's debt and can be subject to numerous provisions. For example, the line often cannot be used if the borrower is in default on its obligation.

Lines of credit are used primarily in the short-term market for governmental units of superior credit standing and where there is only a temporary need for financing. Banks generally impose two charges on lines of credit—a commitment fee and a draw-down rate. The commitment fee (usually from ⅛ to ¾ of 1 percent of the amount of debt) is like an insurance premium; it is the charge for ensuring access to cash at a future date. The draw-down fee is the loan rate charged by the bank if it actually makes a loan on the line. Loan fees can range from 60 percent of the U.S. Treasury bill rate to 100 percent or more of the bank's (taxable) prime rate, with the rates geared to the value of tax-exempt income to the bank.[26]

The more important form of credit enhancement is the letter of credit (LOC). LOCs are commitments between the bank and the investors (or trustees) in which they have direct claims against the bank for payment in the event that debt service is not paid in full and on time. Nearly all LOCs are irrevocable and, hence, constitute a direct guarantee of the borrower's obligation by the bank, regardless of subsequent actions by the issuer. LOC commitment fees are higher than fees for liquidity agreements, ranging from ⅛ of 1 percent to 1.5 percent of the amount of debt.[27]

Generally, the term of an LOC is shorter than the life of the bonds. Terms typically run from five to ten years, with future renewals at the bank's option. In the event a bank notifies an issuer that it chooses not to renew, the agreement with investors in the enhanced borrowing may stipulate that substitute supports (of equivalent rating) will be supplied or the bonds will be subject to mandatory redemption. Thus, while investors receive some additional assurances about the safety of their expected future income, the duration of this added safety is uncertain.[28] The experience of the last few years has shown that the providers of enhancements themselves are subject to downgrading, thus presenting an added dimension of risk.[29] In addition to credit facilities, financial institutions provide other devices designed to alleviate various risks that either investors or issuers may encounter. Banks, for a fee, can engineer interest-rate guards (which put maximums on interest rates paid in the case of variable-rate securities); investment agreements (which guarantee the spreads between the cost of borrowed and invested funds); and interest-rate swaps. These devices can neutralize or hedge against various risk, but at a cost.

### *Private Bond Insurance*

Following many of the same impulses of the market that have led to the development of the LOC, the demand for insured tax-exempt obligations has grown rapidly. New issues of insured bonds in 1989 amounted to $30 billion or about 25 percent of the total volume.[30] In contrast to LOCs, which may be ended short of bond maturity, bond insurance is an unconditional promise to pay over the life of the bond issue. The bond insurance companies are typically made up of major property and casualty insurance companies with assorted large financial institutions also appearing in consortiums. They are regulated by the state insurance commissions. To be accepted in the market, insurance companies typically must be of the highest rating category.

At present, there are three major private municipal bond insurance companies: Municipal Bond Investors Assurance Corporation (MBIA); American Municipal Bond Assurance Corporation (AMBAC); and Financial Guaranty Insurance Company (FGIC). The standard bond insurance provides that, in the case of an issuer who fails to make principal and interest payments in full and on time, the insurer will do so. The payments are made according to the original maturity schedule, and such payments continue to be tax-exempt.

Premiums are scaled to risk, and the insured borrower's underlying credit quality must meet certain standards to be eligible for insurance. In practice, the borrower must be rated equivalent to Baa or BBB or better by one of the rating agencies. Premiums range from 0.1 percent to 2 percent of the combined principal and interest due over the life of the issue and are typically payable at the beginning of the policy. The savings enjoyed by issuers that elect to buy insurance vary with the level of interest rates, the relative spreads on interest rates between the grades of bonds, and the insurer. Because the premium is usually paid up front, the interest cost savings (which occur over several years) need to be compared to the cost of the premium in present-value terms.[31]

There has been considerable innovation in the area of bond insurance. Bond insurance has been used to "front end" LOCs from low-rated or unrated banks, with the bank providing a liquidity agreement and the insurance company providing surety insurance to cover longer-term liquidity and credit risk. Another innovation is the insurance of debt-service reserves. Under this program, the insurer may insure a portion of interest and principal, allowing the issuer to dispense with a debt-service reserve.

A final development in the area of insurance has to do with increased competition among insurers. Issuers are well advised to ask for competitive bids on insurance, as well as having their bond offerings bid on an insured and uninsured basis, thereby letting the market determine the cheaper way to borrow.

### *State Credit Assistance*

Local governments often have the opportunity to improve the marketability of their debt by availing themselves of state credit assistance. States have a multitude of forms in helping local governments meet their capital financing needs. The major types of state assistance are guarantees, various forms of loan pools, banks, and other special-purpose lending authorities to assist in marketing bonds.[32]

The simplest and most straightforward form of credit assistance is a state guarantee of local government debt, pledging the state's full faith and credit in support of the local debt. If the state itself is highly rated, such a guarantee provides the greatest degree of credit support and the greatest savings in interest cost (aside from a state giving a direct interest subsidy). But direct guarantees are comparatively rare. Some states cannot extend credit supports to localities because of constitutional restraints. In other cases, the state does not wish to dilute its own creditworthiness and have its bond ratings threatened. This can happen because a state's direct guarantee counts against the state's debt limitations, and, even if the local debt is currently self-supporting, the guaranteed debt still will represent a contingent liability.

When assisting localities, states generally attempt to insulate their own credit quality by applying certain conditions on local governments whose debt is to carry a state guarantee. For example, a state backup may provide that there be prior recourse to the following sources of funds:

- A lien on revenues of a local project that is financed through the state-guaranteed bonds (The lien might entail state requirements on the levies that a locality must make to ensure debt-service coverage.)
- A lien on the general obligation (taxing power) of the local government unit to ensure that sufficient taxes will be raised to meet required debt service
- A lien on state assistance payments to the locality so that they are diverted to the repayment of debt if necessary
- A lien on a debt-service reserve that is equal to the maximum annual debt service

States have other ways of "softening" the degree of credit support they give to localities. A common technique is a "moral obligation" backing of a borrowing. Under this arrangement, the state is not legally bound to assume responsibility for repayment of loans. Should there develop a deficiency in the debt-service reserve fund, the legislature would have to appropriate funds to meet the deficiency. Moral obligations are a weaker form of obligation than a direct guarantee and of less value to local issuers in reducing their borrowing costs.

The most popular form of credit assistance involves the creation of state-sponsored borrowing entities, such as a special-purpose lending authority or a general-purpose bond bank, that finance local governments through the purchase of their obligations. The authority collects several local bond issues and consolidates them into a single bond issue that is sold in the national bond market. Typically, such entities have no taxing power and exist solely for the purpose of facilitating debt issuance by governmental units. Although the state may provide some direct subsidies to particular types of borrowers or for certain borrowing purposes, the interest rates paid by the lending authority generally form the basis for what the local borrowers must pay.

To enhance the marketability of the lending authority's obligations and lower the costs of borrowing, some form of state-sponsored credit support, such as those discussed above, is often provided so that the authority has a credit rating close to that of the state. In addition, the authority, by pooling smaller issues into a big one, is able to enjoy certain economies of scale, such as lower costs of issuance (printing, legal costs, and the like) per dollar of borrowing and typically lower rates of interest that larger issues are able to attract.

Most state authorities are geared to financing particular types of projects (such as housing, hospitals, school facilities, economic development, and water and sewer projects), but some are relatively open-ended in the types of projects they can assist. Municipal bond banks, which are designed to finance a broad range of local government functions, operate in a handful of states, including Arkansas, Alaska, Vermont, New Hampshire, and Maine, and a new one has just been formed in Indiana. Generally speaking, the bond banks are especially aimed at helping small governments; most large local government borrowers, if they have sufficient credit quality, find it more economical to borrow directly on their own.

## *SUMMARY*

No area of finance in recent history has been subject to greater change and tumult than the municipal securities markets. The high and volatile interest rates of the early 1980s, coupled with investor groups and mounting investor concerns over both interest-rate and credit risk, led to a repackaging of the traditional fixed-income, fixed-maturity debt instrument sold on the basis of its own, unenhanced credit quality. Also abetting the cause of innovation in the market was the rapid expansion in the uses of tax-exempt bond proceeds, the greater importance of the special-purpose authorities (as opposed to general units of government), and provisions in the federal tax code that either accommodated or stimulated the issuance of tax-exempt securities. In the flux of change, several innovative instruments emerged to better meet the needs of investors and to improve the market for borrowers. Tax-exempt commercial paper, variable rate securities, putable obligations, zero-coupon and capital-appreciation instruments blossomed into existence.

With the passage of the 1986 Tax Act, the municipal market in the last half of the decade found itself adjusting to another source of change as many of the earlier innovations found their attractiveness or availability greatly diminished. In an atmosphere of dramatically smaller volumes of borrowing and lower interest rates, the municipal market returned to focus on traditional borrowers and conventional instruments. The lessons of tailoring issues to meet shifting markets had, however, been learned and practitioners continued to develop new borrowing techniques to suit changing times, albeit at a reduced pace. Taxable municipals, pooled borrowings, swaps, forward delivery, and direct issuance by issuers reflected areas of continuing innovation.

## NOTES

1. By the late 1980s, it is estimated over half of all capital outlays of state and local governments were being debt financed and the trend was upward. See John E. Petersen, *The Future of Infrastructure* (Washington, DC: Government Finance Officers Association, Government Finance Research Center, 1989), Chapter II-2.

2. The terms "tax-exempt" and "municipal" are used interchangibly to refer to obligations of state and local governments and their agencies and certain other borrowers (namely, 501(c)3 not-for-profit entities) that receive preferential treatment on the interest income of their obligations under the federal tax code. Earlier, useful reviews of the changes in the tax-exempt bond market are found in John Petersen and Wesley Hough, *Creative Capital Financing for State and Local Governments* (Chicago: Municipal Finance Officers Association, 1983); John Petersen and Ronald Forbes, *Innovative Capital Financing* (Chicago: American Planning Association, 1985); Ronald Forbes, "Innovations in Tax-Exempt Finance" and John Petersen and Ronald Forbes, "The Impact of Tax Reform on the Tax Exempt Securities Market" in J. Peter Williamson, ed., *Investment Banking Handbook* (New York: John Wiley, 1988).

3. Nontraditional borrowing has been variously defined but for practical purposes constitutes those forms of private-activity debt that were either terminated or restricted by the Tax Reform Act of 1986. See John Petersen, *Tax Exempts and Tax Reform* (Chicago: Government Finance Officers Association, 1987), pp. 2-1-2-7. The Tax Reform Act of 1986 gutted much of the supply of private activity bonds, which sank to account for less than 20 percent of all bond sales by the end of the decade. However, sales of one nontraditional form (not-for-profit corporations) continue to be important to the tax-exempt market since they are not subject to state volume limits.

4. For a thorough discussion of the linkage between the rise of the revenue bond and the authority, see Ronald Forbes, Phillip Fisher, and John Petersen, "Recent Trends in Municipal Revenue Bond Financing, in George Kaufman, ed., *Efficiency in the Municipal Bond Market* (Greenwich, Conn.: JAI Press, 1981).

5. Because of changing tax laws, the statement is subject to numerous, complicated caveats. See Petersen, *Tax Exempts and Tax Reform,* pp. 3.1-3.12. Since the passage of the Tax Reform Act, state and local income tax treatments have become a more important factor in explaining tax-exempt bond yields. See Petersen, p. 3.10.

6. Petersen, chapter 1.

7. Commercial bank ownership of municipal bonds decreased by nearly $100 billion during the three years 1986 to 1988, an amount equal to 40 percent of their holdings at year end 1985. The Tax Reform Act of 1986 sapped an already depressed appetite for municipal bonds on the part of commercial banks.

8. By the end of 1988, $443 billion (58 percent) of all tax-exempts were held by the household sector ($299 billion) and mutual funds ($144 billion). Included in the household section's $289 billion are $105 billion of Unit Investment Trusts and $65 billion in bank administered trusts, leaving only $123 billion held directly by individuals. Author's estimates based on Flow of Funds data and other sources.

9. The standard analysis is that the tax-exempt yield, $I_e$, is equal to one minus the marginal tax rate, $T_m$, times the alternative taxable yield, $I_t$: i.e., $I_e = (1 - T_m) I_t$.

10. For a discussion of the yield curve and its meaning for investors, see Girard Miller, *Investing Public Funds* (Chicago: Government Finance Officers Association, 1986), pp. 183-206.

11. The favorable spread between tax-exempt and taxable securities provided powerful inducements for tax-exempt issues to borrow more and earlier than was needed to meet a particular project need. In effect, most issuers could enjoy unlimited arbitrage earnings for up to three years and, beyond that, could use earnings to cover underwriting and other costs of issuance. The 1986 Tax Act gutted most arbitrage opportunities by tightly restricting the period during which unlimited earnings could be enjoyed and by forcing jurisdictions to pay over any excess earnings in the form of rebates to the U.S. Treasury. Definitions were changed to further limit earnings opportunities (including the disallowance of issuance costs) and to create recordkeeping requirements. Although the 1986 Tax Act stifled most arbitrage opportunities, it did engender some innovative techniques. For example, the arbitrage restrictions did not apply to bond proceeds invested in tax-exempt securities. This allowed tax-exempt issuers to invest in partially taxable tax exempts (those subject to the Alternative Minimum Tax). In addition, governments issuing less than $10 million annually had their securities qualified for special tax treatment in bank portfolios (Bank Qualified Bonds).

12. Forbes, "Innovations in Tax-Exempt Finance," p. 357.

13. *Ibid.*, pp. 362-63.

14. *Ibid.*

15. *Ibid*,. p. 367. Investors demand a payment for providing borrowers with the call option because the exercise of the optional redemption will require them to reinvest at a lower interest rate.

16. See Lennox Moak, *Municipal Bonds: Planning, Sale and Administration* (Chicago: Municipal Finance Officers Association, 1982), pp. 321-25. Recent federal tax laws have significantly limited the ability to advance-refund. Certain types of tax-exempt bonds may not advance refunds at all while others may do so only once. See Petersen, pp. 2-9.

17. For an extensive treatment of the minibond's development and applications, see Lawrence Pierce, Percy Aguila, and John Petersen, with Catherine Holstein, *Municipal Minibonds: Small Denomination Direct Issuances by State and Local Governments* (Chicago: Government Finance Officers Association, February 1989).

18. Daniel Katzenberg, "Minibond Programs Pay Public Relations Dividends," *The Bond Buyer*, June 1989, p. 2.

19. See Perry Israel, "Arbitrage: General and Refunding," *National Association of Bond Lawyers Washington Conference Notebook*, January 12, 1990, Tab II.

20. For a fuller discussion, see *Financing with Forward Delivery* (New York: First Boston Corporation, 1989).

21. Steven Dickson, "Municipal Swaps: A Growing Market Could Challenge Merrill Lynch Stronghold," *The Bond Buyer*, December 11, 1989, p. 1. For a discussion of a municipal swap by a local government, see Harold Boldt, "Reducing Interest Costs with an Interest Rate Swap in Columbia, Missouri," *Government Finance Review*, June 1988, pp. 23-26.

22. John E. Petersen, "Taxable Bonds at Home and Abroad," *Government Finance Review,* February 1987, p. 12.

23. See *New York's Local Industrial Development Agencies* (Albany, N.Y.: New York State Legislative Commission on State and Local Relations, 1989), pp. 41-49.

24. Steven Dickson, "Taxable Municipal Volume Climbed 34% in 1989," *The Bond Buyer,* January 11, 1990, p. 1.

25. John Petersen, *Information Flows in the Municipal Securities Market* (Chicago: Government Finance Officers Association, 1989), p. 2.

26. Forbes, "Innovations in Tax-Exempt Financing," p. 378.

27. *Ibid.*

28. In the case of long-term obligations or where there might be a weaker form of support, the issue is rated by the rating agencies both on the basis of the bank's credit for the period covered by the irrevocable LOC and on the credit rating of the underlying issuer, since the assumption is made that the LOC may not always remain in effect.

29. Forbes, "Innovations in Tax-Exempt Financing," p. 378.

30. Matthew Kreps, "Muni Sales Rose 2% in 1989," *The Bond Buyer,* January 2, 1990, p. 1.

31. Thomas McLoughlin and Catherine Holstein, "Does Bond Insurance Make Sense?" *Government Finance Review,* December 1989, pp. 37-38.

32. For a recent comprehensive study of credit pooling, see John E. Petersen *et al., Credit Pooling to Finance Infrastructure* (Chicago: Government Finance Officers Association, 1988).

# 16
# *Leasing and Service Contracts*

PERCY R. AGUILA, JR. AND JOHN E. PETERSEN

A FEW years ago, the headline "Oakland Sells Its City Hall" appeared in a national publication. It did not spell the doom of San Francisco's sister city across the bay. Oakland was not going out of business; rather, the headline reported the city's creative use of a lease financing transaction to fund local government needs. Through a sale-and-leaseback of City Hall and twenty-three other municipally owned buildings, Oakland used the financing proceeds to fund police and fire pension-fund liabilities.

This transaction can be viewed in three distinct phases. First, an issuing entity acting on behalf of Oakland sold certificates of participation to investors to finance the purchase of the buildings from the City. The proceeds from the sale were used to purchase annuities for the fire and police pension fund. Second, Oakland entered into a lease agreement with the issuing entity that allowed the City use of the buildings. The lease payments by the City are construed as debt-service payments on the certificates of participation. Finally, when the amortization is complete at the end of thirty years, the City will regain ownership of the buildings.

Oakland used sale-and-leaseback financing in essence to take advantage of the equity it had in its municipal buildings. The financing allowed the City to borrow against the value of the buildings, which it sold to private investors who could use the tax preferences. The lease secured use of the structures by the City over the life of the transaction.

Oakland's innovative financing (which, due to changes in the federal tax code, is much less attractive than it used to be) provides an example of how lease financing has been used by state and local governments to raise funds or acquire capital assets. Above all, it illustrates the flexibility of the lease, historically a hallmark of its use. Indeed, over the past decade, municipal leasing has evolved from a seldom used means to acquire capital equipment and real property to an often considered financing mechanism that competes with traditional capital financing methods.

Accurate volume figures of the municipal leasing market are not possible because most of the "market" for leases is unorganized and the lease transaction comes in so many forms. At a minimum, it is possible to say that sales of debt backed by leases which are evidenced in certificates of participation or lease-rental bonds, have increased greatly in recent years. Less than a billion dollars in annual volume of new issuances in 1980, by the late 1980s there was an estimated $7 to $8 billion in lease-secured debt issuances a year. If one adds those leases that do not result in credit market obligations sold in the capital markets, the annual volume of new leases is clearly much higher. Moody's Investor Service rated $5.3 billion in lease-backed debt in 1988 and Standard & Poor's Corporation, about $3.6 billion. Since not all issues are rated by both agencies, and some issues are unrated, the total is probably around $7 to $8 billion. The volume of true leases for equipment and space by governments is not available, but undoubtedly runs to billions in leasehold value.

The growth in government leasing at the state and local level is the result of several economic and legal factors that reflect a blend of expediency and efficiency.[1]

- In most cases, a lease obligation is not included as long-term debt in calculating legal debt limitations, nor is it generally subject to voter approval. These characteristics may be attractive to communities that have federal or court-mandated capital investment requirements or where voters are reluctant to approve a new bond issue.
- Certain issuance costs of a bond sale—including legal fees, preparation of the official statement, and bond referendum—may be avoided through leasing, which may compensate for the higher interest rates typically built into lease payments.
- Leasing often is a suitable method for financing capital assets that are too expensive to fund for one period, but that have useful lives too short to justify their financing by the issuance of long-term bonds (fleets of automobiles and other equipment fit this description).
- Finally, certain types of equipment and facilities (such as computers and telecommunications equipment) lend themselves to leasing because rapid changes in technology make ownership impractical, or the equipment's maintenance and modernization require the expertise and service facilities of the vendor.

In the past, leases traditionally were used by government units to contract with a second party for the short-term and intermittent use of property (e.g., office space, voting machines, office equipment) in exchange for the payment of rent. Over the years, a rich variety of transactions under the general heading of leases has emerged in response to the changing needs of governments and the changing legal environment in which those needs are met.

In the remainder of this chapter, we will first look at the major varieties of leases and the structure of typical lease transactions. This is followed by a brief discussion of the service contract, the lease's first cousin. Next, there is a review of tax treatments. The chapter concludes with a discussion of the characteristics of tax-exempt leases, in particular a discussion of their use in financing capital projects.

## *MAJOR TYPES OF LEASES*

A lease is a contract or agreement that allows one party ("the lessee") the right to use and possess the equipment or property of another party ("the lessor") for a specified period of time. The lease agreement may evidence a single transaction involving a specific item or items of equipment or property; or, it may be a "master" lease governing a continuing arrangement, with the specific descriptions of equipment or real property evidenced by separate schedules that are updated from time to time. In either case, the agreement requires the lessee to make periodic payments to the lessor for the use of the leased asset.

Another closely related form of contract that will be discussed later in this chapter is the service contract. Unlike a lease, which serves the primary function of acting as a financing source for the use or acquisition of a capital good, the service contract accomplishes more for the government by acquiring services of which use of the capital good is only a part. A "full" service contract, for example, when involving capital facilities that require highly sophisticated and technologically competent management, allows the government to enter into an agreement with another entity (usually a private-sector firm) that designs, constructs, operates, and owns the capital facility. Examples of such service contracts range from those involving office machines, such as copiers, to waste-energy plants that represent massive, sophisticated investments.

### *True or Operating Leases*

The place to start the discussion of leases is with the concept of "true leases." A true lease is an arrangement in which the lessee acquires use, but not ownership, of leased property and the lease term is shorter than the asset's useful life. Thus, at the end of the lease, the property is returned to the lessor, although the lessee often has an option to purchase the property at fair market value. True leases are common between parties in the private sector, where lessors may claim the tax benefits of ownership—principally depreciation. In the public sector, the tax benefits of ownership that may be claimed by lessors that lease to governments may be somewhat reduced. True leases in the public sector are also characterized by the fact that payments under the lease are not treated as principal and interest payments (as they would be if the property were to be acquired) and therefore no exemption is permitted the lessor from federal or state income taxes for any part of the lease payments.

True leases are defined specifically as operating leases for accounting and financial reporting purposes by Financial Accounting Standards Board's (FASB) Statement 13. In general, an operating lease is classified as such when the term of the lease covers only a portion (usually much less than 75 percent) of the leased property's useful life. Another version of the true or operating lease is the service lease. In a service lease the same characteristics that define a true or operating lease hold true. Additionally, the service lease requires the owner or lessor to maintain the leased property and typically includes other executory obligations as well.[2]

True leases or operating leases, as their definitions suggest, are used for short-term and intermittent purposes, such as during an emergency or when a program is temporary and ownership is not desirable. In addition, lack of sufficient funds to acquire an asset because of budget constraints may prompt a government entity to use this type of lease. Frequently, true leases are considered appropriate when financial considerations are not as important as other factors. For instance, computers may be leased, rather than purchased, due to the high obsolescence factor, regardless of the availability of more favorable financial terms were they to be purchased.[3]

### *Tax-Exempt Leases*

Another, very different form of lease is the lease-purchase agreement. For reasons discussed below, these are called "tax-exempt leases" when employed by state and local governments and are used as a means of purchasing equipment and facilities over time as in an installment sale. This type of lease has become extremely popular and has financed the acquisition of equipment such as telephone systems, fire trucks, and water meters, as well as real property and major facilities such as jails, office buildings, and sewer plants.

Under a municipal lease-purchase agreement, financing may be provided by the manufacturer or vendor of the leased property or by third-party investors. The periodic lease payments of the municipality must be separable into principal and interest components, and the interest portion is considered tax-exempt income to the party providing the financing. But to generate tax-exempt interest, a lease-purchase contract (also referred to as condition-sales or installment purchases) must meet the requirements of a "government obligation" as defined by the Internal Revenue Code.

What is considered an obligation in the eyes of the federal tax laws, however, need not be viewed as such by state and local laws. Thus, the tax-exempt lease typically includes what is called a "nonappropriation" or "fiscal funding" clause to avoid having the agreement classified as long-term debt under most state and local laws. Such a clause allows a government lessee to terminate, without penalty except for the loss of the leased property, a lease for which funds are not appropriated beyond the current fiscal year. The security of the lease agreement may be strengthened by various means to be discussed later. Because it can be canceled at the option of the lessee, the lease is a weaker pledge than a bond. Ownership of the asset usually does not transfer to the government upon successful completion of the lease term, although for tax purposes it resides with the government during the lease-purchase period.[4]

Because of the federal tax exemption of the interest component of the lease payment, lessors are willing to charge lower interest rates on tax-exempt leases than on other, comparable conditional sales made to the private sector. The higher risk that investors face with the nonappropriation clause, however, usually means that the interest rates are higher on such leases than on traditional debt financing, although that need not always be the case.

The greatest dollar volume of leases in the state and local sector are structured as lease-purchase agreements and, thus, are tax-exempt leases. Such transactions are designed so that the lease payments are considered installments for the purchase of an asset. Typically, at the end of the lease and upon extinguishing its obligations to the lessor, the lessee acquires title to the asset. This is largely a formality, however, since in fact the lessee has possessed and used the leased asset from the inception of the lease term.

### *Master Leases*

One version of the lease-purchase agreement that is of special importance is the master lease. Under a master lease, a lessee can acquire several types of assets over a period of time that extend beyond the initial financing date of the transaction. The transaction is called a master lease because one set of documents, the "master," controls and sets forth the conditions under which the lessee can acquire the use of assets. The innovative feature of this type of transaction comes from the ability of the master lease to eliminate the creation of separate documentation and security for the different types of assets to be leased. Governments typically use master leases when they want to centralize the leasing of equipment under one department and in the context of larger financings. Since master leases contain "all or nothing" nonappropriation provisions, they also improve the security pledged behind any particular leased asset and thereby lower risk and reduce interest cost.[5]

Through the master-lease financing approach several benefits can accrue to the government entity, particularly if the jurisdiction wants to expand its use of this financing tool. With a master-lease financing, the government entity can

- Reduce overall financing costs (that is, receive better interest rates on large, more secure financings than are possible on individual and smaller transactions)
- Consolidate the financing of equipment needs of several departments into one transaction
- Centralize the financing procedure within one department
- Reduce market risk and exposure inherent in multiple financings
- Eliminate unnecessary expense and labor involved in repeated financial bids and analysis
- Utilize one standard documentation package for the entire financing

The master-lease financing approach can be used for real property acquisition as well as equipment—for which it is especially well suited.

In a typical master-lease transaction, the government entity or lessee first identifies equipment needs for a period of time that can be deemed essential for a necessary governmental function (e.g., school buses, data-processing equipment, road-maintenance equipment). The equipment being financed may also include equipment under existing lease agreements that include a buy-out option, or equipment purchased outright within the past year that the government entity would prefer to be reimbursed for and pay for over time.

The next step is to analyze the list of equipment to be financed and prepare a schedule of financing categories that segregates the equipment by approximate purchase date and the useful life of the equipment acquired. This step is taken to allow for the financing to be structured such that the obligation related to any piece of equipment will be retired before the end of the equipment's useful life. Once the above step is completed, and the structure and size of the master-lease financing is established, the government entity can proceed to take the steps that it would typically take when offering a debt security to investors in the capital markets.

### *Sale-Leasebacks and Asset Transfers*

As described in the City of Oakland example mentioned at the onset of this chapter, a sale-leaseback is a financing arrangement in which the owner of a capital asset sells the asset to another party and simultaneously executes an agreement to lease the asset back from the buyer. Sale-leasebacks and lease-leaseback, also known as asset transfers, have been undertaken for a variety of purposes over the years, such as raising funds by selling off an existing asset (at least for tax purposes) or for improving the security and pledging the cash flows of an already existing asset. In certain cases, the sale-leaseback can be used to eliminate the need to build up reserve funds or capitalize interest since already existing money flows exist.[6]

Sale-leasebacks and lease-leasebacks had a run of popularity for a period of time in the 1980s when federal tax laws favored their use by governments as financing vehicles. As will be discussed under "Tax Treatment" later in this chapter, changes in tax laws have lessened the attractiveness of such transactions for purposes other than enhancing creditworthiness.

## *LEASE FINANCING STRUCTURES*

Before examining the characteristics and documents of tax-exempt leases in greater detail, it is useful to illustrate a few of the basic financing structures used in leases. There are at least two parties to the municipal lease: the lessor and the local government lessee. The lessor may be an equipment vendor, a lease broker, or a financial institution. In the simplest case, the lessor would enter into the lease and receive rental payments from the lessee. The basic two-party lease, or "client form" as it is often called, is illustrated in panel A of figure 16-1.

Figure 16-1 Municipal Lease Structures

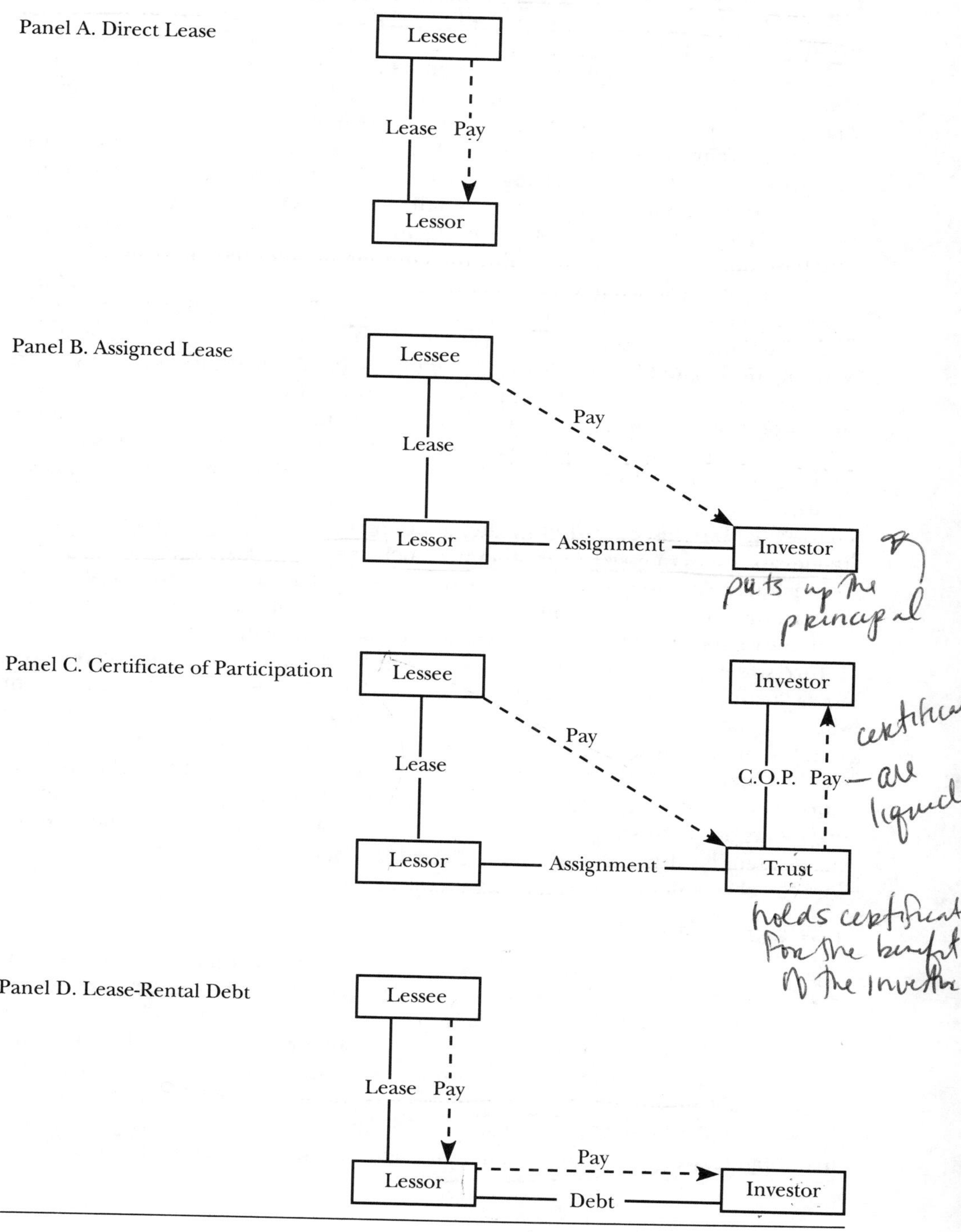

More likely, as illustrated in panel B of figure 16-1, the lease structure will have the lessor assign interest in the lease payments to one or more investors who put up the principal needed by the local government lessee in exchange for assignment of the right to receive the payments under the lease. In the case of the lease purchase, the interest component of these payments is tax-exempt. This characteristic makes ownership of the lease obligation most attractive to investors that benefit by tax-exemption, the same as is true with tax-exempt bonds.

The assignment of the lessor's rights, title, and interest in the lease to the investor may be direct or through a trust agreement. In the direct form, the investor receives payments directly from the government. This arrangement may be facilitated by employing a transfer agent who invoices the government, forwards payments to investors, and carries out other administrative tasks.

The trust agreement version, as is depicted in panel C of figure 16-1, involves the creation of a trust and the assignment of the lease payments to a trustee. In a trust arrangement, the lessor acts as trustor and enters into a trust agreement, with the designated lease or leases going to designated investors as beneficiaries. The trustee is usually a trust company, which oversees the operation of the lease and represents the interests of investors that hold certificates of participation. The certificate of participation has become a very important financing structure and we will return to how it has been used to broaden the market for leases shortly.

Panel D of figure 16-1 illustrates another version of lease structure, in which the lessor itself is a governmental entity, such as a school building authority. The government entity-lessor may do the financing and act as agent for construction and acquisition of the equipment or structure and lease it to the lessee government. The lessor sells to investors its own debt obligations, which are secured on the future stream of payments by the lessee. These obligations are typically referred to as "lease-revenue debt" since the debt is secured only on the revenues from the lease payments. These structures are frequently employed to assist governments that have insufficient borrowing powers; the lessor acts merely as a conduit to the financial markets for the lessee. Since the issuer of the debt and the underlying obligor and user of the facility are both governments, the interest payments are tax-exempt. The lease-rental obligation is a very common device at the state level in particular and is used to finance school construction at the local level in several states.

### *Certificates of Participation*

The participation of many investors in the lease transaction allows the transformation of what would otherwise be a straightforward financing instrument, executed between a lessee and a lessor, into a marketable security. This means that the lease enjoys much greater access to funds and greater liquidity for investors. In a certificate of participation (COP) financing, title to the leased asset is assigned by the lessor to a trustee that holds it for the benefit of the investors, the certificate holders.[7] The idea behind the COP-based borrowing is to make the certificates marketable and transferable, generally behaving like conventional debt instruments. Other parties participate in the COP lease, which makes it look similar to debt financing, including underwriters, underwriters' counsel, registrar, and bond counsel. These parties play essentially the same roles in accessing the tax-exempt capital markets as they would play in assisting a governmental entity to undertake a conventional debt financing.

Not surprisingly, when COP-backed debt is used (which typically occurs for capital needs of $5 million and above), the financing costs, while similar to those for conventional bond issues, usually are higher. Three major factors account for the higher costs associated with COP financings. The first is that the issuance costs (that is, the costs of preparing documents, designing the transaction and executing the sale) associated with a certificate of participation financing are similar to those of bond financing. Thus, the COP presents no economies here that may be available under other tax-exempt leases.

A second factor is the higher interest costs of the lease-purchase financing than, for example, those on bonds backed by a "full faith and credit" general-obligation pledge. This interest differential reflects the added risks of nonappropriation in a lease-purchase financing structure. The differential depends on the given credit ratings and market factors and has typically ranged from one-tenth of a percentage point to one full percentage point above the lessee's general obligation interest costs.[8]

A third factor is the requirement of debt-service reserve funds. Debt-service reserve funds, which typically equal 10 percent of the total principal borrowed, are not required for general-obligation borrowings; the risks present in COP financings, however, often do require debt-service reserve funds. As a result, issuers must borrow more funds than are needed for the capital acquisition—the additional amount being the required debt-service reserve fund. Thus, even if the interest rate charged on the COP financing compares favorably with the amount that would otherwise be charged on general-obligation debt, the state and local government borrower will be paying for financing on a larger principal because of the debt-service reserve fund.

## SERVICE CONTRACTS

Leasing arrangements may be used by governments simply to acquire use of a capital item for a limited period of time or as a method of purchasing such an item over a period of years. In cases where government entities wish to acquire services as opposed to just the item itself, another type of arrangement is a candidate for consideration—the service contract. A service contract may be defined as follows: A legal contract between a private company and a governmental entity that requires the private company, in return for a specified fee, to provide certain services that would otherwise be provided by the governmental entity.

Service contracts can cover the spectrum of facility development, ranging from short-term operation of a facility by a private firm to complete private design, construction, operation, ownership, and financing of a public works facility. Or a service contract may entail the establishment of long-term relationships between the government entity and the other party, the private entity or service provider. Service contracts used for the short-term (five years and less) operation of a facility are entered into by government entities for many of the same reasons that are considered when entering into true lease or operating lease arrangements. Economic considerations enter into the equation, but government entities primarily utilize short-term operating arrangements when "use" and "access" to the capital asset or facility is important for only a short period of time, when governmental control of the capital asset or facility is not relevant or is a secondary goal, and when ownership of the capital asset or facility is not highly valued by the governmental entity.[9]

Prior to passage of the 1984 Tax Act and the Tax Reform Act of 1986, the tax benefits available in a service contract arrangement included accelerated depreciation, the investment tax credit, and the use of tax-exempt (typically, industrial development bond) financing. Subsequent to the passage of the Tax Reform Act of 1986, only depreciation benefits are applicable to private owners of equipment and facilities. These may still play a role in determining the fees that are charged for service contracts entered into by government entities, but they are of much less importance than was formerly the case.[10]

With the curtailment of the tax benefits, tax-related cost savings no longer offer the primary reason for entering into service contract arrangements. Thus, continued use of service contracts for construction, acquisition, or operation of facilities is based on other factors. Among the factors that may lead a government entity to consider a service contract with a private entity or service provider are the following:

- Provision of a service that is not otherwise available under existing constraints
- Potential for high-quality service
- Sharing the risks of operation
- Ability to establish the service in a shorter time than were the government to develop the project itself

Against these benefits, the governmental entity must consider the disadvantages that can be present in the "full" service contract. These disadvantages can include[11]

- Loss of control of the facility
- Complicated legal proceedings to structure and finance the project
- Reduction in the municipal workforce
- Ongoing need for monitoring the quality of the service provided
- Difficulty in determining the net cost of the project on an equitable basis
- Requirement to buy the facility at the end of the term of the agreement

Solid-waste facilities or wastewater-treatment plants, for example, present types of facilities the financing of which can be structured under a service contract. In general, a government entity may opt for total private sector design, construction, operation, financing, and ownership responsibility, or it may rely on public ownership with private-sector design, construction, and operation. Under what has come to be called the "full" service contract approach, the private sector would have responsibility for design, construction, operation, financing, and ownership. This approach offers the government entity the potential of gaining the benefits mentioned above, and perhaps lower costs, since the service contract may allow for tax benefits claimed by the private-sector owner to be partially shared with the government entity.

## *TAX TREATMENT*

Tax considerations, primarily those in the federal income-tax code relating to the treatment of ownership and the recovery of capital costs and tax exemption of certain forms of interest income, have played a major role in the design and use of municipal leases. As has been indicated in the foregoing discussion, a series of federal tax changes have greatly altered the economics of governmental leases and service contracts, rendering certain transactions obsolete, especially when used in conjunction with the sale of tax-exempt bonds.

Figure 16-2 provides a summary of the use and ownership characteristics of leases and service contracts and the related federal tax treatments. The true lease, or operating lease, provides depreciation benefits for the private lessor/owner of the asset. If the lease involves a governmental lessor and exceeds a short-term arrangement, however, then the depreciation benefits may not be accelerated, but must be taken using a straight-line method over the midpoint life of the asset or 125 percent of the lease term of the lease, whichever is longer. The impact of this is to delay the recovery of capital for the private owner and to effectively reduce its rate of return on invested capital.

Under the tax-exempt lease, the interest component of lease payments is tax-exempt, but there are no capital recovery advantages to be enjoyed since the owner of the asset for federal tax purposes is not a taxable entity. In the case of the service contract, depreciation may be taken and, if the service contract qualifies, it may enjoy the benefit of shorter depreciable lives, unless there has been financing by use of a tax-exempt bond, in which case longer-lived depreciation schedules are required.

Determining whether the arrangement with the government entity is a lease or a service contract still remains important since those transactions qualifying under service contracts receive depreciation benefits that are superior to those available under leases. Under federal tax laws, service-contract status exists only when certain minimum conditions are met. These conditions are used to help distinguish a service contract from a lease, or as is sometimes mentioned, a "lease in disguise":

FIGURE 16-2

*Leases and Service Contracts: User and Owner of Asset and Related Tax Benefits*

| Type of Arrangement | User | Owner | Tax Benefits |
|---|---|---|---|
| "True" Lease | Public | Private | Depreciation† |
| Tax-Exempt Lease | Public | Public | Tax-exempt interest |
| Service Contract‡ | Private | Private | Accelerated depreciation† |

† Depreciation is generally less favorable on all leases in excess of three years for equipment and properties used by governments and other not-for-profit entities because of longer depreciation periods that must be used. Depreciation in the case of qualifying service contracts can be for the shorter periods (ACRS) allowed private owners. When equipment and properties are financed by use of a tax-exempt security, however, the depreciation must be taken on a straight-line basis.

‡ Certain service contracts, which have less restrictive guidelines to distinguish them from leases, are restricted to wastewater treatment, solid-waste, and energy facilities.

SOURCE: Based on John Petersen and Ronald Forbes, *Innovative Capital Financing* (Chicago: American Planning Association, 1985), p. 33.

- The government entity may not operate the facility
- The government entity may not bear significant financial burden for the facility
- The government entity may not receive significant financial benefit
- The government entity may exercise a purchase option only at a fair market price

Generally, when the above conditions are met, service contracts allow the passing along of tax benefits to the private contractor that would not be allowed under a lease with a government entity or in a project that involves tax-exempt financing.

## CHARACTERISTICS OF TAX-EXEMPT LEASES

Tax-exempt leasing, once thought of as an alternative to annual out-of-pocket purchases of capital assets, has become a full-fledged competitor of long-term debt financing. Accordingly, evaluations by state and local governments have moved away from contrasting the benefits and costs of a lease transaction with outright purchase. Instead, lease financings are being compared to debt financings for the acquisition of major, long-lived capital assets. It is important to understand, however, how leases are distinguished from bonded indebtedness. The key characteristics of the tax-exempt lease that distinguish it from bond indebtedness include the nonappropriation clause, nonsubstitution, essential purpose, security of interest, and insurance and reserve requirements.

### Nonappropriation Clause

The nonappropriation or fiscal funding clause means that payments of the lease are dependent upon an annual appropriation by the governing body. This is a key point in differentiating the lease from indebtedness because with the nonappropriation provision, the present-year government's action does not bind succeeding ones to pay the obligation.

The ability to enter into a contractual obligation that is not considered debt is the principal reason lease-purchase financing is used by governments for major capital projects. This occurs when governments are constrained by restrictive debt limitations or referendum requirements regarding the issuance of debt or when they do not themselves have the power to borrow. But there is no "free lunch" when using lease-purchase financing to avoid debt constraints. The nondebt classification of lease-purchase financing does not eliminate the need to fund lease payment expenditures nor does it eliminate the responsibility of the government to disclose the obligation in its financial statements.

A typical example of a nonappropriation clause, which would be found in the lease purchase agreement, is the following:

> Notwithstanding anything in this Agreement to the contrary, the City's obligations to pay the cost of performing its obligations under this Agreement and the Trust Agreement, including without limitation its obligations to pay all Base Payments, shall be subject to and dependent upon appropriations being made from time to time by the City Council for such purpose; provided, however, that the City Manager or other officer charged with the responsibility for preparing the City's annual budget shall include in the budget for each fiscal year the amount of the Base Payments and all other amounts required to be paid under this Agreement and the Trust Agreement during such fiscal year, and the City Manager or such other officer shall use his best efforts to obtain the annual appropriations of the Base Payments throughout the Lease Term. Throughout the Lease Term the City Manager shall deliver to the Trustee within ten days after the adoption of the budget for each fiscal year, but not later than June 15, a certificate stating whether an amount equal to the Base Payment which will be due during the next fiscal year has been appropriated by the City Council in such budget.[12]

The commitment to make lease payments is a far cry from the commitment that underlies the issuance of general-obligation debt. The absence of "full faith and credit" support for the lease-purchase financings, however, evidently has not resulted in a large number of default situations. In fact, the number of issuers that have "walked away" from their lease-purchase obligations have been few.[13]

### *Nonsubstitution*

The nonappropriation clause allows the lessee government to design a transaction that will not constitute debt, but it leaves the lessor in the unsecured situation of not having a long-term obligation. Hence, the lessors, to strengthen their security under a lease purchase, ask for a nonsubstitution provision. This amounts to a declaration by the government that it will not substitute a new facility or equipment for that which is leased.

A nonsubstitution clause often reads as follows:

> In the event the Lease-Purchase Agreement is terminated because of nonappropriation of funds, the State agrees not to purchase, lease, rent, or otherwise acquire equipment or contract for services to perform the same functions as, or functions taking the place of, those performed by the equipment for a period of 12 months, except as permitted by the Lease-Purchase Agreement.[14]

Providing a form of "comfort" for lessors and investors, the nonsubstitution clause found in lease-purchase agreements can vary from a term of 30 days to a term of up to 180 days and even up to a year. Despite its use, the role of the nonsubstitution clause as a reducer of risk of early termination of the lease is sometimes questioned. As discussed below, lease-purchase agreements are also characterized by a statement of essential purpose of the asset or facility being leased and some lawyers have argued that the nonsubstitution clause is not enforceable since enforcement of the governmental liability means that the government is stripped of its ability to perform an essential function (e.g., using school buses or police vehicles).[15]

### *Essential Purpose*

Another strengthening provision for the lessor is a statement by the government that the public facility or equipment is being acquired for an essential public purpose and that, by implication, the government will continue to make the appropriations needed to make the lease payments.

A typical essential-purpose letter is a one-page document that briefly describes the use to which the leased equipment or property will be put and an expression of the fact that the purpose is essential to the lessee's operation. Statements of essential purpose are not taken at face value and need to be substantively backed in fact. The way one determines which projects are necessary to a government's operation varies case by case. While there is no precise way to judge a facility's importance, potential investors ask the following questions when evaluating lease issues:

- Is the lease project vital to the community, without which the community could not function properly?
- How does the project tie into the governmental entity's total delivery system?
- What would be the impact of not providing the project or terminating the lease agreement before the end of the lease term?
- Would it be practical (in terms of time and dollars) for the issuer to replace the leased property or equipment?
- Has a needs assessment study or other feasibility study been completed by either the government lessee or an outside consultant?[16]

### *Security of Interest*

Security of interest is an important concept that functions as an assurance to the lessor that if the government lessee fails to make the required lease payments, then the lessor has the right to take possession of and operate or sell the property without a legal contest. Certain states, including Texas and Florida, constitutionally restrict municipalities from granting the lessor a security interest in lease-purchased municipal property. The issuer's inability to grant the lessor a security interest has credit implications for lease-secured obligations in these states. The lessee does not stand to lose use of, or title to, the leased property by failing to pay for its use. Under such circumstances, the project's essentiality is an even more crucial factor.[17]

Initially, in the development of the lease-purchase financings, the varieties of state and local laws caused problems in designing marketable and conventional transactions. Nonetheless, the above complexities in constructing the lease-purchase have been mastered in most jurisdictions. Still, state and local laws that govern leases and lease-purchases are complicated and diverse and lead to a heterogeneous family of obligations.[18]

### *Insurance Coverage and Reserve Funds*

Insurance during the construction and operation of lease-secured transactions is particularly important. Insurance proceeds can be used to repair or replace damaged or nonoperating facilities and to provide for rental payments during periods of downtime. This is particularly important in states where there may be abatements in rent if the facility is not operating. Insurance coverage may either be purchased or supplied by the lessee through self-insurance, if it has adequate reserves.[19] By the same token, reserves protect against construction delays, rent abatement risks, and delays in appropriations and insurance receipts. Funding reserves may, however, create problems. Because of limitations under the 1986 Tax Reform Act, funding of reserves from tax-exempt bond issues may not exceed 10 percent of the initial offering. Therefore, the reserve may not reach an amount equal to the maximum amount of annual debt service. Various forms of surety bonds or insurance may be used, however, to provide the required coverage.[20]

## *THE LEASE VERSUS BORROWING DECISION*

The avoidance of debt limitations or referendum constraints has been credited with fostering the use of lease-purchase financing. While this is largely true, these are not the only factors that enter into the decision to use lease-purchase financing. When properly structured and, especially, when applied to smaller transactions, a lease-purchase agreement may be more efficient and less expensive than the traditional bond issue.

The economics of the lease-purchase contract may be found in a number of areas, such as (1) the elimination of the expense and delay caused by a bond referendum; (2) its usefulness to small governments that have limited access to the capital markets; and (3) its ability to finance relatively small capital needs that are too large to be funded from current revenues, yet too small even to be considered for bond financing. However, a "present value cost analysis" should be done to determine if leasing is more economically feasible than borrowing for specific capital items. Even in cases when the interest rate embodied in a lease is higher than the projected rate of interest on a bond issue, leasing can be more economically feasible than bond issues. An evaluation of a "lease vs. borrow" decision for acquisition of capital items using a "total present-value cost analysis" should be undertaken to determine if that is the case. In such an analysis, it is necessary to add all the costs that occur over time under each alternative, to adjust them for the time-value of money through discounting to present values, and then to compare the net present-value costs to each other. A lease for a smaller project may have few, if any, costs other than those involved in making the lease payments. A straightforward, simple contract may be used and easily executed. However, a bond issue may have referendum costs, legal fees, printing costs, rating costs, fiscal advisory fees and accounting fees, all in addition to the debt service payments. The tradeoff, as noted, is that the lower transaction costs of the lease will be offset by a higher rate.

## *CONCLUSION*

The hallmark of the lease over the years has been its great flexibility. Originally, the lease was conceived of as a means of obtaining the services of capital or land on a temporary basis, and, accordingly, its use was restricted to the short-term hiring of space and equipment. More recently, lease purchase arrangements were developed for the acquisition of capital through installment payments. Otherwise called "tax-exempt" leases, an important attribute of these arrangements is that the interest component of lease payments is exempt from federal income taxes, the same as the treatment of conventional state and local government indebtedness. In their most advanced formulation, lease purchase transactions in many ways are tantamount to borrowing. The difference, however, is that the lease obligation does not represent bonded indebtedness because the lessee typically has the right to terminate the arrangement through a failure to appropriate funds.

The weaker security behind the lease purchase means that obligations secured on them usually carry higher rates of interest than tax-supported bonds. Nonetheless, because the lease obligation typically does not count against statutory debt limits and are not subject to voter approval, their popularity continues to grow as a means of financing large-scale capital projects. Much of the development of the mechanics of the lease arrangement has been directed to strengthening the lessee's pledge. Likewise, innovations have been in the direction of structuring transactions so as to enhance the marketability of the lease obligation. Among the financing tools available to governments, the lease-purchase has evolved into a somewhat more expensive but more flexible alternative to conventional debt financing.

## *NOTES*

1. Petersen, John, and Ronald Forbes, *Innovative Capital Financing* (Chicago: American Planning Association, 1985), p. 31.

2. Vogt, A. John, and Lisa A. Cole, *A Guide to Municipal Leasing,* (Chicago, IL: Municipal Finance Officers Association), 1985, p 5.

3. Harrell, Rhett D., Jr., "Governmental Leasing Techniques," *Government Finance,* March 1980, p. 16.

4. Technically, title to property in a lease-purchase may either stay with the lessor until all lease payments are completed or pass to the lessee at the lease's inception, with the lessor having a security of interest. In either event, the agreement can be structured as a tax-exempt obligation. While passage at the indebtedness for accounting purposes and under state laws. In some states (such as California) passage at the outset is effectively precluded because the lease would constitute indebtedness. Moreover, in other states, it is not possible to grant a security of interest in property owned by governments. A large transaction involving third-party investors (such as certificates of participation) typically finds the title held in trust for the benefit of the lessor or its assignees. See Virginia L. Horler, *Guide to Public Financing in California,* San Francisco: Packard Press (September 1987), pp. 134–141; and Vogt and Cole, *op. cit.* pp. 104–5.

5. A key characteristic of the master lease is that a government cannot selectively appropriate for some leased items and not for others. See Standard & Poor's Corporation, "Governments Embrace Lease Financings," *Credit Review,* March 13, 1989, p. 4.

6. *Ibid.,* p. 5.

7. Technically and legally, a COP is a financing instrument that represents "interests" or a participation in an underlying lessee contract. Thus, when COPs are used, two contracts actually are created. For ease of reference, the term certificate of participation leases refers to financing that utilizes the creation of certificates in conjunction with a lease-purchase agreement.

8. Smith, James, and Anilkamar J. Hoffberg, "Municipal Leasing," in Mid-Atlantic Municipal Advisory Committee, *Governmental Bonds after the Tax Reform Act of 1986 Conference,* July 22, 1987.

9. While true leases, operating leases, and service contracts are referred to as short-term arrangements, it is important to know that federal tax considerations make it a point to classify each of them differently. Accordingly, the tax treatment of each type of arrangement is different and, thus, is an important factor in determining the tax consequences for the owner of the capital asset or facility subject to the arrangement. In turn, the tax benefits play a role in determining the pricing that is established between the governmental entity and the private-sector owner.

10. Prior to the Tax Reform Act of 1986 the question of whether the private owner of a facility was performing services for a government entity, or rather was leasing the facility to it, was very important for two reasons. First, longer depreciation life applied to assets leased to governments than to those used in service contracts to governments. Second, the investment tax credit was not generally available if the facility was leased to a government entity.

11. Scully Capital Services, Inc., *Impact of the Tax Reform Act of 1986 On Privatization* (prepared for the National Council of Public Works Improvement, June 26, 1987), pages 5–6.

12. City of Virginia Beach, Virginia, $7,080,000 Certificates of Participation, Series of 1987, Real Property Lease Agreement dated: October 1, 1987.

13. According to Moody's Investors Service, the rate of nonappropriation or default on outstanding leases has been extremely low. "The Rating Process for Municipal Leases," *Moody's Municipal Issues* (March 1989), p. 4.

14. The State of West Virginia, Department of Finance and Administration,

$9,740,000 Certificates of Participation, Lease-Purchase Agreement, Dated: April 1, 1986.

15. "Evaluating the Lease Structure and Financing Plan," *Moody's Municipal Issues* (March 1989), p. 4.

16. Standard & Poor's Corporation, "Lease Financings," p. 4.

17. *Ibid.*, p. 10.

18. Cone, Pamela, and Julie Van Horn, "Governmental Leasing: A Fifty State Survey of Legislation and Case Law," *The Urban Lawyer* 18 (Winter 1986): pp. 1–187.

19. "Moody's Views on Lease Rental Debt," *Moody's Municipal Issues* (March 1989), pp. 3–5.

20. *Ibid.*, p. 3.

# 17
# Purchasing

STEPHEN B. GORDON

THERE are those who might argue that purchasing requires no definition—nor, for that matter, a separate chapter in this book. After all, purchasing is buying, and everybody knows what buying is. Yet a definition and a separate discussion *are* necessary because governmental purchasing—whether at the local, state, or federal level—is very different from and far more complex than the buying that occurs in supermarkets and stores. Unlike everyday consumer buying, governmental purchasing involves the expenditure of someone else's (i.e., the taxpayer's) money to obtain products and services that still other parties (i.e., the government managers and employees who deliver public services) request and use. The legal requirements, which cover everything from who is authorized to purchase a particular item to who can (and who cannot) supply the item, complicate the seemingly simple task of securing needed goods and services.

As a result, this outwardly low-profile but critical support function has evolved into a highly controlled and accountable process that is governed, even in the smallest local jurisdictions, by a myriad of laws and ordinances, rules and regulations, judicial and administrative decisions, and procedures and practices. To be able to supply what is needed, when it is needed, without wasting taxpayers' money (and indeed, if possible, while saving it), and to be able, while doing so, to demonstrate compliance with the law is the challenge that confronts the local government purchaser.

This chapter examines the role and organization of the purchasing function and reviews the three major phases of the purchasing cycle: (1) planning and scheduling, (2) vendor selection, and (3) contract administration. In addition, the chapter takes a look at several policy and management issues that have influenced local government purchasing, including ethical considerations, intergovernmental cooperation, and automation. Before we begin, however, it would be helpful to spell out more exactly what we mean by purchasing.

## *THE ROLE AND ORGANIZATION OF PURCHASING*

As used in this chapter, *purchasing* encompasses the total process of supplying goods and services to user agencies and disposing of surplus property. It includes the acquisition of services as well as the procurement of equipment and supplies. It involves outright purchasing, lease purchasing, and rentals. And it covers inventory management, term contracting, and other measures that are taken to ensure the continued availability of certain items to user departments and agencies.

Depending on the size of the local government, what and how much it purchases, and other considerations, one entity may choose to have a very centralized purchasing department with a staff of fifty; and another, a decentralized activity with a part-time staff of one. No matter who is authorized to make purchases, however, the ultimate authority and responsibility for ensuring that the function is administered competently and within legal requirements should be assigned by law to a single position. The individual who occupies this position must be able to hold accountable those to whom purchasing authority is delegated.

Whether purchasing is a centralized or decentralized function, if it is done well, it offers public managers an opportunity to "save money without cutting back or eliminating services, discharging employees, or otherwise disturbing the operations of the local government."[1] If it is properly organized and administered, the function can be a "sentry at the tax exit gate" because purchases represent up to 40 percent of the budgets of many jurisdictions.[2] Given this potential for savings, it is therefore not surprising that purchasing at the local government level is more often than not located under the umbrella of the finance department.[3]

Purchasing in local government has several responsibilities that are clearly supportive of its fundamental charge to achieve economy and value while maintaining openness and integrity. These responsibilities include

- Assisting user departments to select the most appropriate purchasing methods, and to develop and write purchase specifications, statements of work, bid evaluation formulas, and proposal evaluation methodologies
- Compiling and maintaining lists of potential suppliers
- Participating in decisions whether to make or buy services—that is, whether to provide a service in-house or contract it out
- Securing quotes, bids, and proposals and working with the user departments to evaluate the offers received
- Awarding contracts on behalf of the user departments
- Maintaining continuity of supply through coordinated planning and scheduling, term contracts, and inventory
- Seeking to assure the quality of needed goods and services through standardization, inspection, and contract administration
- Advising management and user departments on such matters as market conditions, product improvements and new products, and opportunities for building (proper) goodwill in the business community

FIGURE 17-1
*Local Purchasing Process*

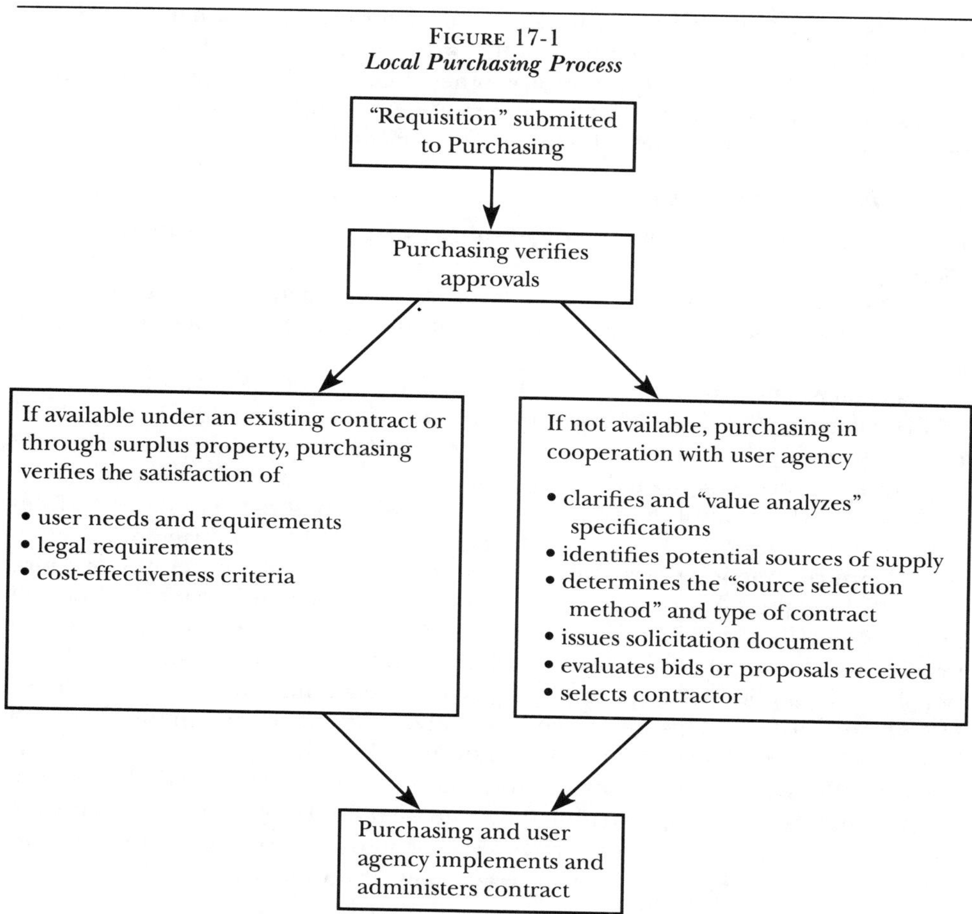


Through standardization and coordination, local governments can attain economies that otherwise might not be possible if the purchasing function was carried out entirely by user agencies.

The procurement cycle in a local government begins with the determination of need for a product or services and includes a variety of tasks, functions, and responsibilities (see figure 17-1). For products, the cycle generally concludes with the consumption or disposition of the item. For services, it generally ends with final payment for services rendered. The three key phases in the process are planning and scheduling, vendor selection, and contract administration.

## PLANNING AND SCHEDULING

Purchasing and the user agencies should work together to ensure that product/service needs are met at the lowest total cost. In today's complex and rapidly changing marketplace, this means such things as agreeing on acceptable quality levels, deciding how and when to purchase, determining whether to carry an item in inventory, and evaluating whether to provide a particular service in or out of house. Governments can improve their planning and scheduling of purchases through consolidation of requirements, inventory management, market research, value analysis, and scheduling of acquisitions.

### *Consolidation of Requirements*

In general, quantity purchases will result in better pricing and increased responsiveness by vendors. Even so, a user agency frequently does not consolidate its requirements for products that it, as an individual agency, uses repetitively. An even less frequent practice is joint purchasing by user agencies of similar or identical items used by each.

Purchasing, or in its absence a lead department, should collect, maintain, and regularly analyze such historical data as quantities purchased, frequency of purchases, unit prices per transaction, and vendor performance to determine the appropriate procurement methods and timing. As a result, purchasing may schedule one or more quantity purchases, with preestablished delivery dates and delivery points during the year; alternatively, it may establish a term contract.

Term contracting is a procurement technique that establishes one or more sources of supply for a repetitive-use product or service "for a specified period of time."[4] Term contracts come in a variety of arrangements, but typically they provide for the supply of an "estimated or definite minimum quantity, with the possibility of additional requirements beyond the minimum, all at a predetermined unit price."[5] This approach generally elicits better pricing and overall service as a result of the increased quantities and the higher stakes involved. It also eliminates the administrative effort and expense of "repeatedly preparing and issuing invitations for bids for the same item, and of receiving, processing, and evaluating the offers that are received."[6] Moreover, term contracting enables a few staff personnel to manage large volumes of purchases.

### *Inventory Management*

This subject is discussed here only briefly because inventory management is a functional responsibility in its own right. It is also not discussed in great depth because the trend now "is away from maintaining warehouses and stores toward relying on 'stockless' term contracts."[7] The goal of inventory management, if it is utilized in a local government, must be twofold:

1. To ensure that certain items (e.g., power transformers) are immediately available
2. To keep at a minimum both the local government's investment in the inventoried items and the overhead costs incurred as a result of purchasing, maintaining, and dispersing such products.[8]

### *Market Research*

No matter who it is, someone in the local government should be given the responsibility of keeping up with the market for the more critical products and services. This person should be called upon to, among other things, stay abreast of product improvements and new products. He or she also should be asked to track market conditions in order to be able to recommend whether sources for an item should be solicited for a term contract or a one-time purchase. This responsibility is generally shared by purchasing, user agencies, and economic analysts in the larger jurisdictions; it is generally handled by the finance department and the user agency in the smaller entities.

### *Value Analysis*

Value analysis (VA) is an analytical technique for studying given function(s) to determine the lowest total cost for performing those function(s) "at the lowest total cost . . . consistent with requirements for performance, reliability, quality, and maintainability."[9]

Much more than a cost reduction, or for that matter, a purchasing technique, VA is a means by which a local government can save money without sacrificing necessary performance or service levels. Value analysis, in essence, looks at a product, a service, or a function and asks four questions:

1. What is the function that must be performed?
2. How is it being performed right now, and at what cost?
3. What are the alternative means of accomplishing the required function, and how much would each of these cost?
4. Considering the cost of the current approach and the projected cost of each of the alternatives, which approach should be chosen in order to perform the required function at the lowest total cost?[10]

There are a number of areas in which VA can be used. Generally speaking, however, the technique is used to

- Exclude inferior-quality merchandise from even being considered for purchase by including performance standards as well as design requirements in bid specifications (requirements analysis)
- Facilitate the purchase of higher-quality, and sometimes higher-priced, goods and services by awarding contracts on the basis of lowest total cost *(as defined in the particular solicitation)* rather than lowest initial price (life-cycle cost bid evaluation)
- Reward vendors in bid evaluation for offering products or services that pollute less than competitive offerings (value purchasing bid evaluation)
- Determine whether a service should be provided in-house or by contract (make or buy service decisions)
- Decide whether a piece of equipment should be leased or purchased

The inclusion of performance requirements (e.g., 28 miles per gallon) in specifications and the award of contracts on the basis of more than just initial acquisition price (e.g., fuel costs over a projected life) have increased significantly within the past two decades. These changes have, however, been driven more by industry and user agency officials than by purchasing staff. Purchasing staff have tended more to react to user interest and to mimic their peers in other jurisdictions than to develop and utilize performance requirements and total-cost bid-evaluation formulas of their own.

Similarly, in the 1980s, many local governments gave increasing consideration to privatization of services. A principal outcome of such scrutiny was an overall improvement in the cost and quality of services, regardless of whether services were contracted out or performed in-house. The factor of added competition, it seems, provided incentive for increased productivity.[11]

### *Scheduling of Acquisitions*

Purchasing and user agencies should jointly develop and adhere to an "annual buy schedule" for needed products and services. In addition to item descriptions, this schedule generally includes a timetable with deadlines and dates for requisitioning services and products, letting and submitting bids or proposals, and awarding contracts.

## *VENDOR SELECTION*

The next phase in the procurement cycle encompasses those steps entailed in selecting vendors or suppliers, including identifying sources of supply, soliciting offers (i.e., bids or proposals), and evaluating offers and making awards.

### *Identifying Sources of Supply*

Most local governments are legally required to obtain at least some competition on all but the smallest of purchases. Many are, moreover, required to "formally advertise" in "newspapers of record." Because newspaper advertisements are an ineffective way of soliciting bids, local governments traditionally have relied upon the bidders (mailing) list to produce an adequate number of responses. In order to reasonably ensure that only "live" and interested vendors are solicited, and to keep the current bidders' pricing as competitive as possible, local governments should

1. Use a proven commodity-coding system to organize the bidders on their list according to the specific products and services they sell
2. Require or at least encourage bidders, when they submit an application for the bidders list, to sign up only for the specific items they wish to bid on
3. Establish and implement a procedure to purge those companies who do not respond to solicitations after a specified number on mailings
4. Seek out continuously, especially in the product and service categories where very few possible sources are known, additional firms and individuals who may have an interest in selling to the jurisdiction

The Texas commodity-coding system, which at the level of vendor classification utilizes a three-digit class and a two-digit item system, is probably the most popular in use at the local level. Many local governments have abandoned codes developed on their own or those based on the Standard Industrial Classification (SIC) or the Federal Supply Code (FSC) in favor of the Texas approach. The commodity code distributed by the National Institute of Governmental Purchasing (NIGP) is based on the Texas system, as is BidNet's Product/Service Code.

Because they have experienced a problem with companies who sign up for far more product and service categories than they could ever bid on, some local governments have instituted charges for being placed on their bidders lists.

Removing bidders from the bidders list for a specific product or service is generally carried out after the bidders' failure to respond to three successive solicitations.[12] Removal from a bidders list does not mean, however, that a vendor is ineligible to respond to a particular solicitation. Even the poorest performers on past contracts may *respond* to a solicitation; but, as shall be discussed later, there is no guarantee that its offer will even be considered by the jurisdiction. As automation of the purchasing function becomes more widespread, vendor performance increasingly will be scored quantitatively—which may be utilized to determine whether a particular bidder should remain on the bidders list.

There are several effective means for adding new potential sources of supply to the bidders list that may cost the jurisdiction little or nothing. The most cost-effective approaches include networking with nearby jurisdictions and local business-development organizations, such as chambers of commerce and federally funded Small Business Development Centers. Obviously, the Yellow Pages and any of a number of national directories of suppliers also are affordable options for increasing the competitive base. Moreover, bidding information services such as BidNet, which are free of charge to local governments, are very helpful in locating new sources.

### *Soliciting Offers*

As one leading authority has noted:

> The process of going into the market is a continuous one. Some purchasing offices issue 20 to 30 solicitations daily. This frequency requires that there be a structured method or system for carrying it out. Yet the process should not be seen as a perfunctory or simple one. It needs, instead to be considered in terms of the perceptions it creates and results it produces.[13]

An effective system for soliciting offers emphasizes and facilitates the use of the most appropriate source-selection method and the most appropriate type of contract. It also is concerned with making the solicitations inviting and productive. Purchasing's effectiveness will depend in large degree on the amount and quality of competition its solicitation documents can generate.[14]

***Source Selection Methods.*** The terminology varies from state to state. The fundamental methods utilized in the competitive purchasing of products and services includes, however, what the *Model Procurement Code for State and Local Governments* labels as competitive sealed bidding, multistep competitive sealed bidding, and competitive sealed proposals. Additional information regarding these methods and when each should or can be utilized is provided in table 17-1. Local governments also may choose from several types of contracts to procure supplies and services.

*Types of Contracts.* Contracts can be classified in a number of ways, including

- Whether they are of the fixed-price or the cost reimbursement type
- Whether they call for a definite or an indefinite quantity
- Whether they involve a performance incentive for the vendor
- Whether they are for a one-time requirement (a "spot" purchase) or span a period of time (a "term" contract—see previous discussion)
- Whether they are for a purchase, a lease-purchase, or a true lease

Almost all contracts established by local governments fall into the fixed-price category, because most products and services required by these entities are commercially available. As such, these items can be reasonably specified and their cost can be reasonably estimated. Forms of fixed-price contracts that are authorized for use in many states include firm fixed-price, fixed-price with readjustment, and fixed-price with a performance incentive.

As for classifying contracts based on the quantity to be purchased, recent data indicates that, at the state level at least, the use of definite quantity contracting is increasing.[15] This trend and a parallel trend toward term contracting most likely will increase as the automation of the procurement function enables local governments more easily to collect, manipulate, and analyze historical data.

*Quality and Effectiveness of Solicitation Documents.* Few local governments have adopted standards or control measures for assuring the quality, content, or effectiveness of their solicitation documents. Moreover, governments generally are known for documents that are verbose, difficult to understand, and often illegible. A poorly written purchasing document usually deters competition. A "well-designed solicitation document does more than merely ask for prices . . . it also stimulates the competitiveness of individual responses and the overall quality of competition."[16]

### *Evaluating Offers and Awarding Contracts*

The evaluation of bids and proposals brings together two of the most fundamental objectives of governmental purchasing: economy and fairness. The significance of the evaluation process and how it works must, therefore, be clearly understood by whoever does the purchasing, those for whom the purchasing is done, and the community of vendors. Otherwise, favoritism and waste could result, and the local government and its officials, managers, and employees could enjoy a less-than-favorable reputation.

A jurisdiction's criteria for awarding contracts will, of course, depend on

TABLE 17-1
*Obtaining Bids or Proposals*

| Competitive Sealed Bidding | Multistep Competitive Sealed Bidding | Competitive Sealed Proposals |
|---|---|---|
| Competitive sealed bidding is the method most often used by local governments for acquiring goods, services, and construction. It provides for award of the contract to the responsive and responsible bidder whose bid price is lowest, thereby making the bid evaluation process more objective than it is when competitive sealed proposals (see below) are evaluated.<br><br>Competitive sealed bidding, which *does not* include negotiations with bidders after bids are opened, is normally used when:<br><br>Clear and adequate specifications are available.<br><br>Two or more responsible bidders are willing to do business with the government in accordance with the government's requirements and criteria.<br><br>The dollar value of the purchase is large enough to justify to both buyer and seller the expense associated with competitive sealed bidding.<br><br>Sufficient time is available for the solicitation, preparation, and evaluation of sealed bids.<br><br>Even though competitive sealed bidding is the easiest method to audit, there are certain circumstances under which this method may not be practical. Provided that they have the legal authority to do so, jurisdictions may find that multistep competitive sealed bidding, or requesting competitive sealed proposals, is more appropriate. | Multistep (generally, two-step) sealed bidding is a variant of the competitive sealed bidding method. It may be used when a jurisdiction wishes to award a contract on the basis of price, but available specifications are inadequate or too general to permit full and free competition without technical evaluation and discussion. It is a multiphased process that combines elements of both the request for proposals method (in the first phases) and "regular" competitive sealed bidding (in the final phase).<br><br>The first phase consists of one or more requests for information, or unpriced technical offers. The second phase resembles competitive sealed bidding. Bidders who submitted technically acceptable offers in the first phase are invited to submit sealed bids based on their technical offers. The contract is awarded to the lowest responsive and responsible bidder. Multistep bidding, if used properly and within appropriate circumstances, can introduce price competition into purchases of complex items. | If a jurisdiction has to purchase relatively new technology or a nonstandard item, it may choose to request competitive sealed proposals *if* its laws permit it to do so. Some reasons for going this route are:<br><br>The contract needs to be other than a fixed-price type.<br><br>Oral or written discussions may need to be conducted with offerors concerning the technical aspects and price of their proposals.<br><br>Offerors may need the opportunity to revise their proposals, including price.<br><br>The award may need to be based on a "comparative evaluation" that takes differing price, quality, and contractual favors into account.<br><br>Jurisdictions should be sure that they have the ability to use this approach fairly and effectively before they actually request sealed proposals. This method provides more flexibility than competitive sealed bidding, but it also allows more room for error. |

SOURCE: Adapted from Stephen B. Gordon, "Purchasing," in *Management of Local Public Works*, edited by Sam M. Cristofano and William S. Foster (Washington, D.C.: International City Management Association, 1986). Originally published in National Institute of Governmental Purchasing, Inc., *Public Purchasing and Materials Management*.

the particular source-selection method that is utilized. On the one hand, a contract based on competitive sealed *bidding* should (and generally will) be awarded to the responsible bidder whose offer is responsive to the solicitation and lowest in price. On the other hand, a contract based on the competitive sealed *proposals* method (and perhaps, but not necessarily, involving negotiations), should be awarded to the offeror whose proposal is deemed to represent the best combination of offeror responsibility and responsiveness. A *responsive* offer is one that at a minimum "conforms in all material respects to the invitation for bids."[17] Factors that should be considered in determining whether the standard of responsibility has been met include whether a prospective contractor

1. Has available the appropriate financial, material, equipment, facility, and personnel resources and expertise, or the ability to obtain them, necessary to indicate its capability to meet all contractual requirements
2. Has a satisfactory record of performance
3. Has a satisfactory record of integrity
4. Has qualified legally to contract with the local government
5. Has supplied all necessary information in connection with the inquiry concerning responsibility

The responsiveness of an offer is determined at the time it is opened (i.e., removed from the sealed envelope). Only minor irregularities should be waived. The purchasing decision must be an objective one based on the evaluation criteria stated in the solicitation document.

According to the ABA's *Model Procurement Code* (MPC), the *responsibility* of a bidder can be determined anytime after opening and prior to award. Data needed to determine responsibility may (again, according to the MPC and most but not all local governments' legal requirements) be obtained after bid or proposal opening. Determination of responsibility should be an objective *and* subjective decision based on the judgment of the procurement officer.

Under no circumstances should an offeror or an offer ever be evaluated for any requirement or criterion that is not disclosed in the solicitation. The local government's objective in the solicitation must be to provide offerors with exacting guidelines on how pricing and other data is to be submitted and how it will be evaluated to determine the successful offeror.

Increasingly, decisions on more complex government procurements are based upon the recommendation of an evaluation committee rather than upon that of one or two individuals.

## *CONTRACT ADMINISTRATION*

Only within the past decade or so has contract administration consisted of much more than following up on orders and inspecting delivered merchandise. And, generally speaking, the merchandise has not been inspected as frequently or as well as it should have been.[18] Now that local governments are procuring expensive hi-tech systems, however, and relying on outside contractors to provide a range of functions, contract administration has assumed an especially important role. To protect their financial interests and to ensure the quality of government services (whether provided in-house or out-of-house), local officials should

- Ensure that *all necessary* contractual requirements (for the local government as well as the vendor) are spelled out clearly, correctly, and concisely in the purchase order or contract
- Ensure that both local government and vendor staff *understand* their responsibilities under the purchase order or contract
- Flush out and resolve as many potential problems as possible before the purchase order or contract takes effect
- Check to see if the vendor provides goods or services in accordance with the purchase order or contract
- Document problems and take the appropriate action to resolve them and/or minimize their impact
- Take the lessons that are learned and utilize them (to the extent possible) to improve future contracting arrangements

Local governments increasingly use "start-up" conferences to ensure that contractual requirements are understood and that as many potential problems as possible are identified and addressed up front.

## *ETHICAL CONSIDERATIONS*

Most local government managers subscribe to the premise that "purchasing is an operation of government that ought to be run in a businesslike way, ought to produce good results, and ought to serve the best interests of everyone concerned: the departments, the vendors, and the taxpaying public."[19]

Nevertheless, management must be continually on the alert in order to prevent corrupt practices from occurring and to identify and confront them when they do. Ethical violations not only result in indictments and embarrassment; they also do great damage to purchasing's ability to conserve public funds and inspire the confidence of the vendor community. Favoritism and decreased competition inflate prices, and could, in the worst of circumstances, make it difficult to obtain a needed product or service. The American Bar Association has identified several practices that *can be* (but are not necessarily) evidence of ethical violations. These practices, which frequently can be difficult to detect and equally difficult to distinguish from errors and other "honest" shortcomings, include

*Circumventing competitive bidding requirements by*

- "splitting" purchases so that they can be made through less competitive small purchase procedures

- requesting or making an "emergency" purchase when no true emergency exists
- requesting or making a "sole source" purchase when competition is available

*Denying one or more vendors the opportunity to bid or propose on a particular contract by*

- using unnecessarily restrictive specifications
- prequalifying the bidders on a discriminatory basis
- removing the companies from the bidders list without just cause
- requiring unnecessarily high bonding

*Giving favored vendors an unfair advantage by*

- providing them with information regarding their competitors' offers in advance of the bid opening
- making information available to the favored vendors but not to the others
- giving the "unfavored" vendors inaccurate and misleading information[20]

Management can never eliminate the possibility of ethical violations. It can, however, hold them to a minimum by setting forth standards of conduct in a written code of ethics and making it clear that the code has management's complete and unwavering support. Moreover, managers can promote adherence to these standards through employee training, code enforcement, and personal example.[21]

## *PURCHASING AS AN INSTRUMENT OF PUBLIC POLICY*

Local government purchasing dollars represent an enormous share of total spending in the United States (approximately $200 billion, or 6 percent of GNP, in 1988). For this reason, they long have been used to facilitate the attainment of political and socioeconomic goals. Policymakers have sought to increase the wealth of their local economies, or certain defined groups within those local economies, by enacting various forms of *preferences.*

Regardless of the specific form, a preference obviously has the effect of restraining free trade, and thereby can result in fewer bidders, rejection of low bids, and potentially higher prices. Perhaps of greatest concern, they also invite other local governments to retaliate on behalf of their "own" vendors.[22]

Even when their effects are viewed favorably, some preferences, specifically racial preferences, at least, may not, in the long run, be able to survive legal challenges. According to Michael Love, the U.S. Supreme Court in *J. A. Croson Co.* v. *City of Richmond,* 822 F.2d 1355 (4th Cir. 1987), while it did not "formally [eliminate] a racial preference to remedy past wrongs, . . . may have effectively done so."[23] The *Croson* decision, which dealt with the constitutionality of minority business set-asides, indicates that the Supreme Court is "unlikely to uphold any but the most carefully composed, extensively factually supported affirmative action plans by state or local governments," states Love.

Also because of its clout in the marketplace, local government purchasing power potentially could play an important role in bringing about product improvements and new products that consume less fuel and pollute less. The Buy Quiet Program, a joint effort of the U.S. Environmental Protection Agency, the National League of Cities, and the National Institute of Governmental Purchasing, was a short-lived effort directed at doing just that. The funding for the program was eliminated in 1982 by the Reagan administration when the program was only three years old. In that brief period, however, commitments to purchase on a more environmentally conscious basis were received from more than one hundred local governments. Entities as diverse as the State of California and Prince George's County, Maryland, continue to use purchasing specifications and bid-evaluation formulas developed nearly a decade ago in Buy Quiet.[24] The Buy Quiet specifications and a variety of other specifications that local governments can use to develop their own environmentally conscious solicitations are available through clearinghouses such as the National Institute of Governmental Purchasing.

## *INTERGOVERNMENTAL COOPERATION*

Since the early 1970s, local governments have been working together more closely in many areas, including purchasing. Governments enter into cooperative agreements to obtain lower prices on goods and services, reduce administrative costs, and stay abreast of improvements in products and services as well as purchasing techniques.

Four ways in which local governments commonly cooperate in the procurement area include

- Intergovernmental cooperative purchasing
- Joint administrative (consolidated) purchasing
- The joint use of facilities
- The interchange of personnel, information, and technical services with other local governments

Intergovernmental cooperative purchasing, as defined by NIGP,[25] refers to "a variety of arrangements under which two or more governmental entities purchase a good or service from the same supplier as a result of a single invitation for bids (or request for proposals)." There are, as NIGP notes, "several types of IGCP and several forms within each type"; however, the most common types are the *piggybacking* method and the *joint-bid* method. Under piggybacking, "a large purchaser of an item (or group of items) invites bids, enters into a contract, and arranges, as a part of the contract, for other governmental units to purchase the same item (or items) under basically the same terms and conditions." Under the joint-bid approach, "two or more governmental entities agree on specifications and contract terms and conditions for an item of common usage and combine their requirements for this item ['up front'] in a single invitation for bids." Some successful joint bid cooperatives, such as the one administered by the Purchasing Officers' Committee of the Metropolitan Washington, D.C., Council of Governments, are large and supported by professional staff. Others are small, volunteer-supported groups such as the Eastern Iowa Governmental Purchasing Association.

Joint administrative (consolidated) purchasing is a formal arrangement under which "part or all of the purchases of two or more governmental units are made by a shared administrative agency created for that purpose." Two examples of successful consolidated purchasing programs include those serving the City of St. Paul and Ramsey County, Minnesota, and the City of Louisville and Jefferson County, Kentucky.[26] Several school districts in the north central and northeastern United States have consolidated purchasing and other support functions.

Two examples of the joint use of facilities for purchasing operations involve the City of Greensboro and Guilford County, North Carolina, and the City of Minneapolis and Hennepin County, Minnesota. In both instances, the city and county purchasing agencies are separate but housed in the same building. The principal benefit in both cases is "the exchange of information on problems, solutions, and product/service innovations." In addition, local governments might save on costs by sharing a facility, such as a warehouse or testing laboratory, that they both need.

Finally, even if local governments (for whatever reasons) are unable to purchase cooperatively, consolidate their purchasing, or jointly use facilities, they at least can help one another by sharing information, loaning their staff, or letting others use their facilities. Such interaction can be as simple as one jurisdiction letting another jurisdiction use its specifications for a product as a starting point.[27]

## *THE AUTOMATION OF PURCHASING*

The automation of the purchasing function offers several potential benefits for local governments, including opportunities for price savings, cost savings, and increased responsiveness to user needs. Local governments can effect price and cost savings by utilizing historical data (made analyzable by automation) to aggregate requirements for one or more agencies and plan spot purchases and term contracting biddings, as appropriate. Automation also can assist local governments to keep track of vendor performance, eliminate paperwork, and spend more time, generally, on purchasing management. Despite the benefits, the progress of purchasing automation (beyond merely generating purchase orders on the computer) has been slow. And, for the larger local governments, it also has, in many instances, proved to be an expensive, labor-intensive, and not always successful process as entities have struggled to adapt mainframe packages developed for industry to a government environment. Automation is moving more smoothly for many of the smaller and mid-sized local governments, because they typically rely on proven microcomputer software.

## CONCLUSION

Government purchasing practices are shaped largely by laws that emphasize an open, competitive, and accountable process. Because of this emphasis, purchasing procedures are designed foremost to ensure compliance with applicable laws and regulations. As a consequence, government purchasing has often been plagued by red tape and inefficiency. There is a growing awareness, however, that important safeguards need not be jeopardized in a streamlined procurement process.

Local government purchasing has gained many efficiencies through the increasing use of cooperative arrangements and technology. Whether and how well they will use these same resources to pursue social goals through the procurement process—be it to purchase more energy-efficient products and services or to develop the capabilities of minority-owned businesses—is the fundamental question to be answered.

## NOTES

1. Stephen B. Gordon, "Purchasing," in Sam M. Cristofano and William S. Foster, eds., *Management of Local Public Works* (Washington: International City Management Association), p. 148.
2. Gordon, p. 148.
3. The Council of State Governments, *State and Local Government Purchasing,* 1st ed. (Lexington, Ky.: 1975), table B-17.
4. Gordon, p. 151.
5. *Ibid.*
6. *Ibid.*
7. *Ibid.,* p. 152.
8. *Ibid.*
9. National Institute of Governmental Purchasing, Inc., *Public Purchasing and Materials Management* (Falls Church, Va.: National Institute of Governmental Purchasing, 1973), pp. 106–7.
10. *Ibid.,* p. 107.
11. Stephen B. Gordon, *Contracting Out for "Support" Services by U.S. Counties and Municipalities: The Political Aspects,* Ph.D. dissertation, Department of Government and Politics, University of Maryland-College Park, May 1984.
12. "Vendor Contractor Rating Systems," Subject Matter Workshop at the 45th Annual Conference of the National Institute of Governmental Purchasing, Inc., Atlanta, Georgia, July 28–August 1, 1990.
13. Willis Holding, Jr., *Invitations for Bids; Requests for Proposals: Content and Composition* (Rockville, MD: BidNet, Inc., 1987), p. 1.
14. *Ibid.*
15. The Council of State Governments, *State and Local Government Purchasing,* 3rd ed. (Lexington, Ky.: 1988), 39.
16. Holding, p. 1.
17. American Bar Association, *The Model Procurement Code for State and Local Governments; Recommended Regulations* (Chicago: ABA, 1981), Regulation 3-401.

18. National Institute of Governmental Purchasing, *Intermediate Public Purchasing and Materials Management* (Falls Church, Va.: National Institute of Governmental Purchasing, 1983), pp. 195–96.

19. National Association of Counties, "The Case for Cooperative or Centralized Purchasing," *Information and Education Service Report,* 17 (1962): 1.

20. American Bar Association, *Identifying and Prosecuting Fraud, Waste, and Abuse in State and Local Contracting* (Chicago: American Bar Association, 1984).

21. Ethics Resource Center, "Management Ethics: A View from the Top" (Washington: Ethics Resource Center, 1984): videotape.

22. J. W. Stevenson, "In Opposition to Preferences in Purchasing," *The BidNet Link,* Vol. 1, No. 4 (May 1986), pp. 1–2.

23. Michael K. Love, "Legal Ease," *The BidNet Link,* vol. 4, no. 2 (May 1989), pp. 5–11.

24. National Institute of Governmental Purchasing, final report submitted to the U.S. Environmental Protection Agency, 1982.

25. National Institute of Governmental Purchasing, *Public Procurement Management,* Part 1 (Falls Church, Va.: National Institute of Governmental Purchasing, Inc.: 1985), pp. 6-1–6-6.

26. *Ibid.,* pp. 6-6–6-7.

27. *Ibid.,* pp. 6-7–6-9.

# 18
# *Risk Management*

R. Bradley Johnson and Bernard H. Ross

In the past decade, risk management has emerged as an important part of local government management with significant impact on public financial management. This emergence has been fostered by governments' need to provide services, guard against economic loss and ensure public safety during a time of uncertain legal liability and increasing litigation. The insurance crisis of the mid–1980s, which threatened government's ability to carry on basic operations, also encouraged the growth and visibility of public risk management. Local governments began to realize the need to reexamine operations and protect their increasingly limited resources. Public managers now recognize risk management as an ongoing management control tool applicable at all levels of operation.

## *BEYOND INSURANCE*

Mention risk management and most government officials think of insurance. This is not surprising, as insurance was—and continues to be—the traditional way by which governments protect their assets. Although insurance is important, it is only one way to deal with losses.

Because every government operation involves some level of risk, risk management is one of the broadest fields in local government administration. Its practice is interdisciplinary, involving finance, environmental management, public works, safety, transportation, parks, recreation, health, education, personnel, purchasing, and law. In all such areas, risk management is a tool for exercising better operational control.

When a government official examines the potential for loss and takes steps to protect organizational assets, he or she is, in effect, performing the duties of a risk manager. Most local governments practice risk management; their efforts, however, are often fragmented and uncoordinated. A formal system of policies and decision processes is critical to successful risk management. Risk management resembles a typical planning process. It provides a formal method to (1) identify risks, (2) evaluate their frequency and potential severity, (3) decide which method is best for dealing with them, and (4) implement the chosen method(s).

## *WHY MANAGE RISK?*

Why should governments look beyond insurance and develop full-fledged risk management programs? Here are some answers:

- Risk management results in more effective use of funds that might otherwise be diverted to purchasing unnecessary or expensive insurance, replacing damaged property, or paying liability or workers' compensation claims.
- Overall costs are decreased while productivity is increased. Risk management aids in preventing worksite accidents and injuries, reducing medical expenses and other costs related to lost workdays, replacement workers, etc.
- Risk management identifies exposures that can be covered by means other than insurance—or that can be avoided completely.
- Risk management also helps make communities more attractive to insurance companies, which can increase insurance availability.
- Risk management can lower expenditures by reducing the overall "costs of risk."
- Risk management reduces uncertainties associated with future projects—by highlighting better ways to prevent and pay for accidental losses.

Although risk management may not be the definitive answer to all liability and insurance problems, it does help make operations safer, less costly, and more efficient.

The risk management process answers the following questions: What are the loss exposures facing our organization? What is the potential for loss and probable effect? What is the best way to deal with these risks? To reiterate, the steps in this process are

1. Risk identification—outlining the potential exposure to loss
2. Risk evaluation—analyzing the potential for loss both on a historical basis and for future frequency and severity
3. Risk treatment—reviewing alternatives available to deal with risks (including control and financing)
4. Implementing the best alternative

Figure 18-1 illustrates the key steps in public risk management.

FIGURE 18-1
*Risk Management Process*

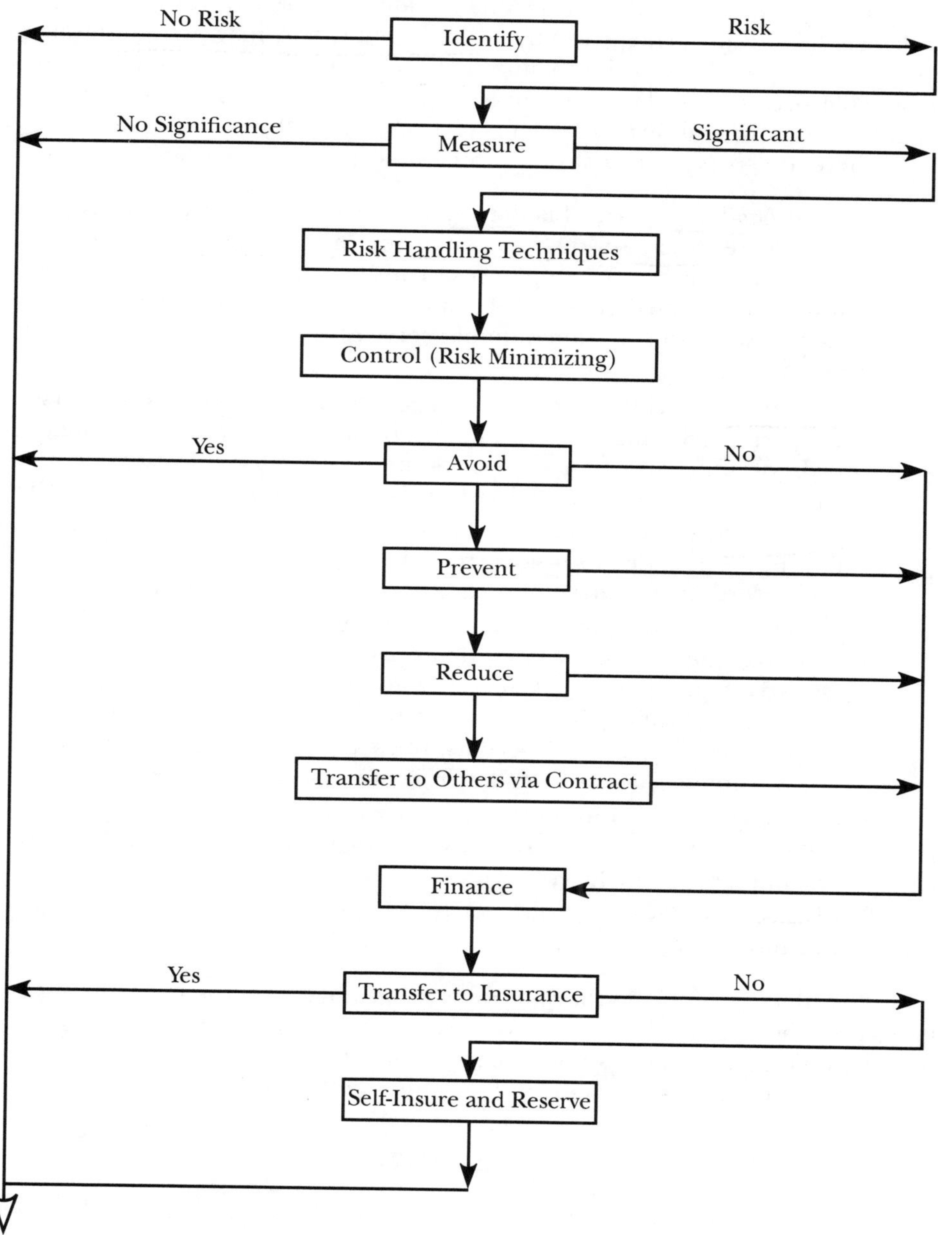


SOURCE: Reprinted with permission from *Risk Management and Insurance: A Handbook of Fundamentals*, copyright 1983, National Association of College and University Business Officers.

## *RISK IDENTIFICATION*

Many local governments do not adequately identify loss exposures, so risks go undetected until an incident occurs. Risk identification may not locate all exposures to potential losses, but it does help to spot trouble areas and to make reasonable predictions. This is a ongoing process, since exposures change—as do government operations and legal climates.

There are six types of risks that can result in economic loss:

1. *Legal liability to others:* Liability claims involving injuries and property damage represent serious loss exposures for public agencies. Claims may result from actions of employees or public officials (e.g., intentional or unintentional negligent acts). Claims involving contractual liabilities may surface with privatization of public services or intergovernmental service arrangements.
2. *Property loss:* Accidental loss or damage can occur to both real and personal property, including public buildings, parks, swimming pools, public records, desks, chairs, typewriters, computers, and tools. Losses may result from carelessness, natural disasters, faulty equipment, or fire and theft.
3. *Extra expense:* After some losses, governments incur additional expenses to renew or maintain services from cleanup or repair of damaged property, overtime, or hiring and training of replacement workers.
4. *Loss of income:* Unfortunately, loss-of-income exposure is often overlooked by governments. For localities that operate revenue-producing facilities (such as stadiums, gymnasiums, and fairgrounds) destruction of or damage to these facilities means a loss in income. In addition, taxes, charges for services, licenses and permits, fines and other sources could be lost if governments' ability to collect revenue is somehow disrupted.
5. *Human resources loss:* Job-related illnesses and injuries mean higher medical and hospital expenses plus costs associated with replacement of workers and lost productivity.
6. *Crime and fidelity loss:* Dishonest, fraudulent, or criminal acts committed by employees or others can also result in losses.

Risk identification asks the question: "What and where are the risk exposures in each of these areas?" Governments use any of several investigative tools for uncovering unique and not-so-unique risks, including field inspections, exposure checklists, and analyses of claims history and accident reports.

## *RISK EVALUATION*

Once risk exposures are identified, the financial risks of each need to be determined. Potential financial loss is measured by frequency and degree of loss. In other words, how often is a loss likely to occur, and how severe could it be? By evaluating loss exposures, decisions can be made on how best to handle them.

A review of prior loss expenses is the best predictor of future losses. This loss history data should go back at least five years and should show the number of losses and the dollar amounts involved (those paid by the government or another party).

Unfortunately, evaluating loss severity is speculative, especially for liability exposures, and is the most difficult part of risk management. This is why accurate records of claims, incidents and settlements are absolutely vital.

The following steps may be used to estimate the severity of liability exposures:

1. Assess the liability exposure by reviewing state laws on public liabilities and immunities, local claims history (three to five years), liability suits in nearby communities, recent court cases, jury award amounts, settlements, and common defense costs.
2. Identify liability exposures most likely to affect the organization. While it's difficult to accurately predict which lawsuits might befall a jurisdiction, records of recent cases within the area and state can help identify potential claims.
3. Estimate the potential losses from all events that might occur. Consider all costs, including defense costs, settlements, property and income losses, and costs related to personal and bodily injuries.

In estimating the severity of property loss exposures, values should be assigned to real and personal property. Property valuation should include two estimates of the potential total losses: maximum probable loss and maximum possible loss.

### *Maximum Probable Loss*

This projects the worst loss occurring under average conditions. For example, in estimating the severity of fire loss for a building, the type of structure, fire detection/prevention systems, and building contents must be considered. If a building has smoke detectors and sprinklers, a fire probably would not destroy it completely (assuming all safety devices work). A property valuation, then, would estimate what portion might be destroyed and what parts are most susceptible to fire.

### *Maximum Possible Loss*

This is a worst-case scenario predicting the greatest conceivable loss assuming all safety measures fail. It assumes the total destruction of a building and its contents, as well as damage to nearby structures. Estimates of maximum possible loss identify exposures not covered by property insurance policies, so they can be integrated into other coverages.

Estimates of loss severity should also project indirect costs stemming from disruption of daily operations, loss of income and other expenses (e.g., rental equipment, etc).

FIGURE 18-2
*Types of Risks and Their Treatment*

| | | Frequency: Low | Frequency: High |
|---|---|---|---|
| Severity | Low | A<br>Operating funds<br>Claims reserves | B<br>Operating funds<br>Claims reserves |
| | High | C<br>Insurance<br>Pooled risk | D<br>Insurance |

The matrix presented in figure 18-2 is used as a guideline to determine how to handle each exposure based on its frequency/severity analysis.

Low-frequency, low-severity losses in quadrant A do not occur often, and when they do, are not severe. Examples include petty theft, vandalism, and minor building damage. Governments usually pay for such losses with operating funds or claims reserves.

High-frequency, low-severity losses in quadrant B occur fairly often, but are not costly. They include minor vehicle accidents, small workers' compensation claims and general liability claims, such as slip-and-fall accidents. These losses are also paid from operating funds or claims reserves.

Low-frequency, high-severity losses in quadrant C are very serious but do not occur often. Examples include natural disasters, boiler and machinery accidents, major fires or theft, large liability suits, permanent disability injuries, and environmental claims. A single claim can have a devastating effect on a jurisdiction, so insurance or pool coverage is generally the best way to protect against these sizable claims.

High-frequency, high-severity losses in quadrant D are the most serious of all claims. They include major liability suits against law enforcement officials, serious accidents resulting from faulty road maintenance, and severe workplace injuries. Loss control is important in terms of these exposures and transfer of risk through insurance is often the best financing strategy.

## *RISK TREATMENT*

After identifying and evaluating exposures, the next task is to determine how to treat these exposures. Typically these exposures are handled either through control or finance measures. Risk-control techniques can be categorized as either risk avoidance or loss prevention and control.

### *Risk Avoidance*

Some governmental activities or services carry risks so great, it is best to avoid the activity altogether. In the strictest sense, avoidance is the most complete way to manage risks, because it eliminates any chance of a loss. Governments avoid risks by either avoiding or discontinuing the activities that create risk. For example, a town planning to build a skateboard park may determine that the liabilities and safety risks involved are too great, and therefore it avoids these risks by not building the park.

Often, however, avoiding one risk may create others. The town children, in the example here, may ride their skateboards on public streets instead of in a park, endangering themselves and others and exposing the town to other liability risks.

While risk avoidance is the most complete way to handle exposure, it is rarely used by governments because some loss exposures cannot be avoided. Some public services must be provided regardless of risk. In these instances, it is the risk manager's job to find safe ways in which government services can best be delivered.

### *Loss Prevention and Control*

Steps can be taken to reduce the likelihood that risks will occur and reduce the severity of losses when they do occur. Fire-safety training programs, rules for storage and handling of flammable materials and fire inspections of public buildings can help prevent fire loss. These are common *loss-prevention* measures.

Smoke detectors, fire extinguishers, fire alarms, and sprinkler systems cannot prevent fires, but they help minimize fire damage. These are *loss-control* measures.

Governments can benefit from the creation of safety and loss-control committees, although community size and accident and claim levels can affect the size of the benefit. Loss-control committees usually include key supervisors and staff from various agencies. Committee duties include creating safety policies and procedures; developing inspection programs; designing safety orientation programs for new employees; creating accident and claims investigation systems; identifying safety measures needing funding; developing disciplinary procedures; and establishing review boards to investigate fatalities, serious injuries, or major accidents.

A variety of other risk-control techniques, such as contingency planning and claims management, are also available to local governments.

Even if every effort is made to avoid or control risks, governments must still be protected financially in case accidents occur. Risk-financing techniques fall into either *transfer* or *retention* categories.

### *Risk Transfer*

The most common method of financing risks is transferring the financial burden of loss to another party. Transfer is usually more feasible than avoidance because it ensures continued service provision while protecting the jurisdiction. Insurance is the most popular form of financial risk transfer, but other methods may also be used successfully.

*Insurance.* Commercial insurance is the most common way to pay for losses, with most public agencies buying one form or another. Problems arise when governments buy insurance with little idea of their own loss exposures or how they can be controlled. As a result, they may not purchase enough insurance or, when premiums are low, they may buy more coverage than is needed. The decision to purchase coverage must be made in conjunction with other measures.

Insurance is designed in "layers" of coverage. Primary coverage is the first layer, covering the first dollar of losses (usually after a deductible) up to a specified limit. Excess insurance pays beyond the primary level, up to a specific amount. For example, a city may carry $1 million of primary coverage and $5 million in excess coverage. If the city has a $2 million claim, it probably would pay a deductible and the primary coverage would pay the first $1 million, with excess insurance paying the balance. Umbrella coverage is one type of excess insurance and, as its name implies, it covers all primary liability insurance as well as some self-funded retentions not covered by any insurance. Umbrella coverage does not provide complete coverage for all perils, types of losses, or amounts of losses. Because its coverage is so broad and limits are usually high, it is not always available.

Governments face losses associated with many types of exposures. As a result, they need different types of coverage:

- *Property insurance* protects against damage or loss of property or its ability to generate income.
- *Liability insurance* covers losses related to a government responsibility (legal or contractual) not being met.
- *Fidelity bonds* cover losses from embezzlement, fund misappropriation, and loss of money or property from dishonest acts committed by employees or volunteers. These bonds obligate insurance companies to reimburse governments for such losses.
- *Workers compensation* provides employees with coverage for all medical bills resulting from job-related injuries or disabilities.

Employers also must offer protection from loss of income and rehabilitation or other services, as specified by state law.

*Noninsurance Transfers.* Insurance is one method of risk transfer. Other methods can also be used to transfer risk but may, at the same time, shift the risks of other organizations to the government. "Hold-harmless agreements" are one form of noninsurance transfer. In these agreements, one party agrees to indemnify, or hold another party harmless, for all claims and legal expenses incurred in specified situations. For example, local governments can hold a contractor harmless or a contractor can indemnify and hold the government harmless according to some states' laws.

Hold-harmless agreements impose different levels of responsibility. For example, a contractor could hold a government harmless against

- Suits resulting solely from the contractor's negligence
- Claims arising from joint negligence
- all possible suits

### *Risk Retention*

Governments may also retain some risks; that is, assume financial responsibility for some losses. For example, paying for slip-and-fall claims from a general fund (rather than purchasing insurance coverage) or carrying deductibles on automobile insurance (paying for claims up to the point where insurance coverage begins). Unfortunately, many jurisdictions retain risks unknowingly because they are unaware of their exposures and have neither budgeted nor planned for payment of losses.

Various mechanisms allow governments to provide their own risk protection, outside of the commercial insurance marketplace. Two alternatives that can help protect against catastrophic loss, if properly used, are self-insurance and intergovernmental pools.

*Self-Insurance.* When a government self-funds or self-insures, it accepts all or part of its operational exposure by using (or combining) the following options to pay for losses:

- Using operating funds (treating losses as expenses)
- Establishing loss-reserve funds to cover estimated claims
- Establishing lines of credit at financial institutions for preapproved loans
- Purchasing "excess" insurance for catastrophic losses

Self-insurance is often advantageous for governments with large budgets, but it is generally not an option for smaller jurisdictions. The adept use of deductibles is, however, a feasible form of self-insurance for a government of any size.

Most organizations that self-insure pay for losses only up to a certain amount, with insurance coverage paying for losses over that amount. For example, a government may decide to budget funds to pay for the first $100,000 of claims and purchase insurance to cover any claims above that amount. Very few organizations can afford to be fully self-insured. Property exposures, in particular, do not lend themselves well to self-insurance. Replacement of a $10 million building would have to compete with new capital improvement projects for limited capital funds.

An important decision in self-funding is determining which exposures will be retained. The most common of these exposures are: low-frequency/low-severity losses (e.g., minor bodily injuries, fender-benders), and high-frequency/low-severity losses (e.g., broken windows or other minor property damage).

Self-insurance offers several advantages over commercial insurance:

- *Cost-avoidance*—insurance transactions entail certain additional costs (e.g., premium taxes, commissions)
- *Cashflow*—funds reserved for self-insurance are held until claims are paid, providing additional investment opportunities
- *Service control*—government decides with which claim adjusters and loss-control professionals to contract
- *Enhanced awareness*—public officials and managers become more aware of risk liabilities and consequently should manage risks better[1]

These advantages naturally must be weighed against the disadvantages of experiencing fluctuations in claims payments and incurring extra costs associated with administration and contracting with service providers.

Recent surveys indicate an increase in nontraditional risk financing in the public sector. In a PRIMA member survey,[2] 79.5 percent of the respondents reported some form of self-insurance in three liability areas (general, public-official, and police professional) as well as automobile, property, workers' compensation, and employee benefit coverage. Only 20.5 percent reported the use of commercial insurance for all these areas.

Roughly 60 percent of those surveyed were self-insured for workers' compensation; 55.4 percent for general liability; 53.7 percent for auto liability; and 47 percent for public-official liability.

In this survey, *self-insured* meant having no primary insurance coverage; it did not distinguish, however, between formal self-insurance and merely going without coverage. In either case, respondents did not have primary coverage through a traditional insurer and therefore would pay claims directly from public funds. As noted earlier, self-insurance is often a tool of larger governments whose fiscal capacity allows them to retain loss rather than transfer it. Of the 320 self-insured governments surveyed, the average operating budget was $195 million compared with $48 million budget for those who do not self-insure. More than one-third of the self-insured group had operating budgets in excess of $100 million, while two-thirds of the remainder had budgets of less than $25 million.[3]

***Intergovernmental Pools.*** One of the fastest-growing risk-financing alternatives, intergovernmental pools, enable governments to pool funds for loss payments among contributing members.

Group self-insurance pooling began in 1974 when the Texas Municipal League created the first risk-sharing pool in the United States. Today, 200 pools serve as a risk-financing alternative for over 25 percent of the estimated 80,000 general and special-purpose local governments in the United States.

Pools operate as cooperatives with members paying contributions, receiving coverage, and making claims. Many public agencies also rely on pools for assistance with risk-management operations. These groups normally operate within state boundaries, either on a regional or statewide basis, and function under statutory authorization. Generally, they use three levels of coverage:

1. Members pay for their own losses up to a specified amount, with an annual limit. For example, members cover their own losses up to $1,000, with an annual limit of $25,000. Thereafter, the pool pays for any additional losses.
2. The pool pays for losses over the individual limit, up to its own limit. For example, the pool pays for losses between $1,000 and $100,000.
3. Pools use membership funds to purchase insurance for losses exceeding the pool's own limits. For example, the pool purchases coverage for losses ranging between $100,000 and $5 million.

Forty percent of the PRIMA survey respondents indicated that they belonged to an intergovernmental risk pool. Market analysts expect up to 50 percent of the existing property/casualty market to shift from traditional insurance to other alternatives, such as pools, in the near future. They foresee pools expanding into new areas, such as pollution/environmental impairment liability and employee benefits and expect an increase in pool usage among regional and interstate special districts and other quasi-public bodies.[4]

***Implementation of Risk Management***

Selecting appropriate risk-treatment strategies is a significant part of managing risks. Unless risks can be avoided, governments should apply (at a minimum) one risk control and one risk-financing technique to each major loss exposure. While it is possible to substitute techniques of like kind, it is usually not wise to substitute risk financing for risk control or vice-versa. Any risk-control technique (except avoidance) can be used with any risk-financing option or with another control method. Similarly, any risk-financing technique can be used along with any risk-control method or other risk-financing option. In deciding which techniques to use, three criteria are recommended for risk analysis:

1. *Frequency and severity:* estimating how often losses occur and how much they may cost.
2. *Effectiveness:* analyzing how effective a technique will be in achieving the objective. For example, if workers experience back injuries, teaching proper lifting may not be the only answer. Analyzing the work procedures with an eye toward redesign could eliminate movements which cause injuries.
3. *Costs:* analyzing the costs (cash outlays and maintenance expenses) and benefits of each technique.

Governments should design and implement a risk-management plan to carry out these strategies. Risk management is a function that covers all operations and whose principles must be instilled in all employees.

The growth of risk management in the last ten years has developed with a variety of administrative structures and organizations used to operate public risk-management programs. About one-third of PRIMA's 1987–88 survey responses noted the existence of a separate risk–management department. This option gives the risk-management function more authority to work with other top-level administrators and report directly to top management.

When a separate risk-management department does not exist, the risk-management function typically is assigned to a finance, administrative, or personnel agency. PRIMA's survey found that most governments place risk management within finance departments (30.6%), administration departments (18.5%), or human resources/personnel offices (16.4%). In contradiction to one view of risk management, as a purchasing function, only 4.3 percent of respondents identified risk management as a function of purchasing departments.

Despite its recent growth, risk management is often handled by staff whose primary duties are not risk management. This is particularly true in smaller communities. It is interesting to note that finance directors make up the largest percentage (9%) of those handling these responsibilities. This is indicative of the strong financial element involved in managing risk.

Risk managers must open channels of communication with elected officials and department heads, agency supervisors, and the public. They must work closely with elected officials to develop and disseminate comprehensive policy statements regarding their risk and insurance management objectives. These policies should aim to eliminate fragmentation in managing risk across agencies.

Program objectives should identify the risk-management function as protecting the general public and public assets against accidental loss, so government can continue to provide services, even after a catastrophe.

## *CONCLUSION*

Risk management, like most government functions, provides officials with both problems and opportunities. Because its scope is broadly based, risk management has the potential to affect all departments and operations. How public officials organize and implement this function can have a profound effect on the organization's financial and administrative health.

Today government managers are aware of the many risks involved in urban crime, hospital emergencies, recreation areas, and fire fighting. Already on the horizon, however, are new and emerging risks associated with AIDS, drug testing, toxic emissions, and solid and hazardous waste disposal. Each of these potential risks poses a series of new managerial and financial challenges. Events during the 1980s indicate that public risk management will continue to grow in scope and importance. The need to focus new resources on public risk-management activities will continue to grow as jurisdictions move toward greater internal control of risk-management activities and funding.

## *NOTES*

1. Excerpted from "Self-insurance," a presentation by David M. Randall at the Public Risk Management Association at its 11th annual conference, June 10–13, 1990, in Reno, Nevada.

2. *Public Risk Management: State of the Profession, 1987–88,* (Washington: Public Risk Management Association, 1988). For further discussion of these survey results, see Bradley R. Johnson and Bernard H. Ross, "Risk Management in the Public Sector," *Municipal Yearbook* (Washington: International City Management Association, 1989).

3. For information on accounting and financial reporting issues of risk financing, see *Accounting and Financial Reporting for Risk Financing and Related Insurance Issues,* Statement 10 (Norwalk, Conn.: Governmental Accounting Standards Board, 1989).

4. For additional information on pooling, see *Pooling: An Introduction for Public Agencies* (Washington: Public Risk Management Association, 1987).

# 19

# *Public Employee Retirement Systems and Benefits*

WERNER PAUL ZORN

THERE are approximately 9,000 public employee retirement systems (PERS) in the United States today. These systems provide over $27 billion annually in benefits to 3.7 million retirees and their beneficiaries and cover 11.8 million state and local government employees. In order to meet the obligations of their promised benefits, state and local PERS have accumulated $650 billion in assets, an amount equal to approximately 25 percent of all public and private pension assets in the United States.

PERS are complex entities, requiring a wide range of legal, actuarial, accounting, and investment expertise. During the past two decades, PERS trustees and administrators have become more sophisticated in the performance of their duties; oversight officials have begun to recognize the power of pension assets; and standard-setting bodies have undertaken the herculean task of creating a set of unified and consistent standards. The purpose of this chapter is to discuss the administration, management, and financing of PERS. The chapter will provide an overview, discuss benefit design and administration, catalog obligations and contribution policies, describe management of system assets, and discuss accounting requirements. It will close with a discussion of current trends and the prospects for public retirement plans.

## *OVERVIEW OF PERS*

Of the nearly 9,000 PERS in the United States, over half are concentrated in five states: Pennsylvania, Minnesota, Florida, Illinois, and Michigan. Generally, PERS may be categorized by their administrating jurisdiction—that is, the state, city, county, special district, or other jurisdiction that is responsible for administering the plan. According to a recent survey, 71 percent of PERS are administered by cities, 12 percent by counties, 10 percent by special districts, 4 percent by states, and the remainder by school districts and other local jurisdictions.[1]

Many of these plans are very small, however, and cover only a few employees. In 1978, the Pension Task Force of the U.S. House of Representatives Committee on Education and Labor found that the vast majority (at least 60 percent and possibly as high as 80 percent) of state and local systems had fewer than 100 members. These small plans covered less than 5 percent of total membership among all plans. On the other hand, the 390 systems with more than 1,000 members covered more than 95 percent of total membership.[2]

Research done by the U.S. Bureau of the Census indicates that most of the very small systems pay premiums for the purchase of annuity policies from private insurance carriers to make retirement contributions.[3] Substantially more is known about the 2,500 to 3,000 plans that make up the sample contained in the U.S. Bureau of the Census periodic study *Employee-Retirement Systems of State and Local Governments*. Consequently, many of the statistics presented in this chapter are drawn from the Census studies.[4]

PERS can also be categorized by the type of employees covered by the plan, such as general employees, teachers, other school employees, police, fire fighters, etc. During the twenty-year period between 1962 and 1982, Census studies show that the number of and distribution of PERS among the different types of employees has remained relatively stable.[5] Systems covering general governmental employees grew slightly from 503 in 1962 to 553 in 1982, constituting approximately 21 percent of surveyed plans in both years. Systems with coverage limited to police or fire personnel have also grown slightly from 1,651 in 1962 to 1,685 in 1982, constituting approximately 70 percent of surveyed plans in 1962 and 66 percent in 1982. PERS with coverage limited to teachers and other school employees declined from 70 in 1962 to 57 in 1982, falling from 3 percent of surveyed plans in 1962 to 2 percent in 1982. Finally, plans with coverage limited to other personnel (i.e., special districts, etc.) grew sharply from 122 in 1962 to 264 in 1982, more than doubling during the period.[6]

Although the total number and distribution of PERS has remained relatively stable during the past quarter century, the number of plan members has increased dramatically from 5.3 million in 1962 to 11.8 million in 1987. Much of this growth resulted from increases in the number of covered general employees (which grew from 3.0 million in 1962 to 7.4 million in 1982), and the number of covered teachers and other school employees (which grew from 2.0 million in 1962 to 3.5 million in 1982).[7] It is interesting to note that while police and fire plans constitute about two-thirds of the total number of PERS, police and fire membership made up less than 3 percent of all covered employees in 1982. On the other hand, the school employees and teachers category made up over 30 percent of covered employees.[8]

PERS may also be classified by their scope of operations. Some plans are statewide and cover many governmental units, while others are single-employer plans that cover only specific classes of employees. As one might expect, almost all the smaller state and local plans are maintained by a single employing unit of government. A substantial percentage of the large state and local plans, however, are "multiple-employer" plans covering the members of a number of jurisdictions. A survey conducted by the Government Finance Officers Association (GFOA) in 1987 found that 65 out of 183 sampled plans (36 percent) identified themselves as multiple-employer PERS, acting on behalf of a number of employers. Most of the multiple-employer plans were administered at the state level.[9]

## *PERS BENEFITS*

The purpose of PERS is to provide plan members and their beneficiaries with retirement income. The 2,580 public retirement plans sampled by the Bureau of the Census in 1987 had 11.8 million members, of whom 10.7 million were "active" (that is, covered persons currently employed by state and local governments).[10] In general, PERS's provide coverage for most state and local employees. The ratio of active system members to full-time equivalent (FTE) employees grew from 84 percent in 1962 to 93 percent in 1982. This ratio slipped between 1982 and 1986, however, falling to 91 percent. Part of this decrease may be due to an aging public-sector work force. As older workers retire, they are replaced by younger workers who are new to the system and may take several years to become covered by the plan. This could lead to a temporary reduction in the ratio of active members to FTE employees.

While the number of active members has grown over the past twenty years, so too has the number of plan beneficiaries. Figure 19-1 shows that the total number of plan beneficiaries grew from 739,000 in 1962 to 3.7 million in 1987 (note that the scale for the number of beneficiaries is presented on the right axis). In current dollars, the average annual payments per beneficiary grew from $1,704

FIGURE 19-1
*Number of PERS Beneficiaries and Average Annual Payments (current and inflation-adjusted dollars)*

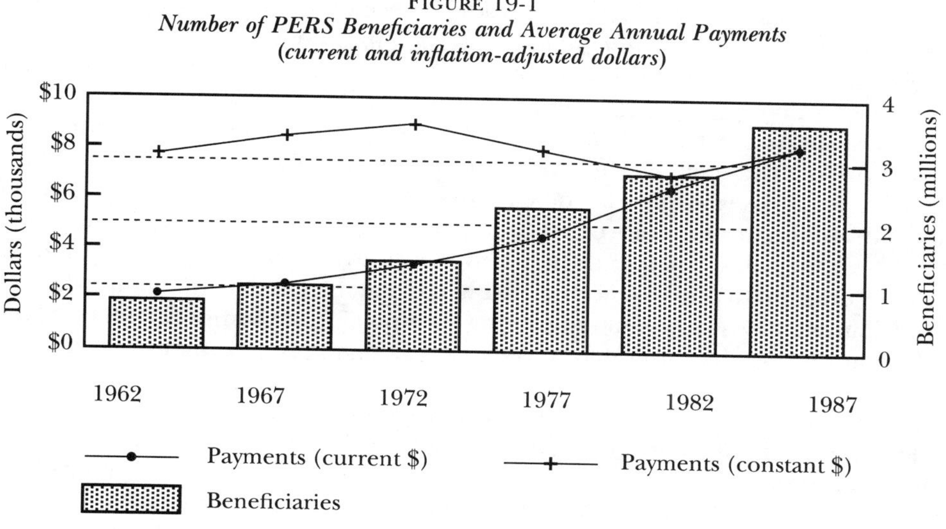


SOURCE: U.S. Bureau of the Census, *Employee-Retirement Systems of State and Local Governments*, various years.

to $8,249 during the same period. When viewed in constant dollars, however (i.e., adjusted to reflect the impact of inflation on spending power), the average annual payments per beneficiary actually fell during the later 1970s and early 1980s, and ended up in 1987 at about the same level as in 1962. Although benefit payments have recovered from the buffeting that they took from the high inflation in the 1970s, figure 19-1 illustrates the sensitivity of retirement income to inflation.

### *The Nature of Retirement Benefits*

The history of retirement plans illustrates the evolution of the retirement benefit promise. Pensions originated as gifts provided by sovereigns as acts of grace to faithful servants. Although efforts were underway in the early nineteenth century to redefine pensions as deferred pay, these were generally defeated. Around the turn of the twentieth century, however, several national reform movements, including the National Civil Reform League and the National Assembly of Civil Service Commissioners, called on each U.S. state, city, and county to establish and maintain a system of deferred annuities for all employees entering civil service. Soon after, in the years immediately before and after World War I, the number of public employee retirement systems in the United States grew rapidly.[11] Today, the interpretation that pensions represent a deferred compensation has been largely accepted, and is reflected in the two general types of retirement benefit plans: defined benefit plans and defined contribution plans.

Defined benefit plans are the best-known and most frequently used form of retirement plan offered by public employers. Defined benefit plans offer employees a specific ("defined") benefit when they retire, usually based on the length of the employee's service and final average salary. Defined contribution plans are more recent creations, but have been growing in acceptance. Under a defined contribution plan, the employer sets aside a specific ("defined") contribution into the employee's account on a periodic basis. This amount (plus any of the employee's contributions and the interest accrued on the account) is given to the employee when he or she retires.

Defined contribution plans shift the risk of financing future retirement benefits from the employer to the employee, since the employer's obligation to provide retirement income to the employee ends when the employer has made its contribution to the employee's retirement account. Consequently, the employee must bear the risk of whether the total amount contributed (plus or minus interest) will be sufficient to provide income during retirement. On the other hand, defined contribution plans are generally more "portable" than defined benefit plans, allowing the employee to retain possession of the account even after leaving the employer.

In addition, it should be noted that the benefit definition is still evolving and some benefit plans are being augmented by "cafeteria" plans that allow greater choice on the part of the employees and that reduce risks to the employer. In the private sector, these cafeteria plans allow employees to "mix and match" a selection of benefits, ranging from retirement income to health benefits, vacation time, and even legal advice. Although the greater choice provided by such a selection has been showcased as a means of providing greater employee satisfaction, the adoption of cafeteria plans in the public sector has been limited, and the results inconclusive.

### *Types of Benefit Formulas*

The benefit formula for defined contribution plans is conceptually simple. The employer's annual contribution is the product of the employee's salary times the employer's contribution rate. Defined benefit arrangements, however, are much more complex and warrant a discussion of the basic formulas used to establish the defined benefit payments.

In general, there are two types of defined benefit formulas: flat-benefit formulas and unit-benefit formulas. Flat-benefit formulas provide a retirement benefit based on some flat percentage of compensation. Such a formula might promise to pay members 50 percent of their salaries upon retirement after 20 years of service. Flat-benefit formulas were used by only 8 percent of the systems in the 1987 GFOA survey and were used more frequently by the smaller systems.[12]

The majority of public pension funds use unit-benefit formulas. Unit-benefit formulas have two basic variations: "single-rate" formulas and "step-rate" formulas. Generally, unit-benefit formulas promise to pay retirement benefits equal to the "unit benefits" that have accumulated over the employee's years of service times the employee's final average salary. Unit benefits are usually computed as a percentage (e.g., 1.5 percent) times the number of years of the employee's service. For example, an employee who works for 30 years at a unit-benefit rate of 1.5 percent per year would earn benefits equal to 45 percent of final average salary upon retirement. The specifics of determining "final average salary" are discussed below.

Under a "single-rate" unit-benefit formula, the benefit rate is fixed over the service life of the employee. Under a "step-rate" unit-benefit formula the benefit rate applicable to the first years of an employee's service is different from the rate applicable during the remaining years. For example, during the first ten years of service an employee may accumulate benefits at a rate of 1.5 percent per year and during the remaining years of service the rate may rise to 2.0 percent per year. In some plans, the initial rate is higher than the rate that applies in future years, i.e., 1.5 percent during the first twenty years and 1.0 percent for the remaining years of service. Single-rate formulas are conceptually easier to communicate to employees and to administer. This may be the reason that over half of the PERS offering defined benefit formulas use the single-rate formula.[13] On the other hand, a step-rate formula offers more flexibility to the employer and can be tailored either to attract new workers (i.e., by applying a higher rate to the first years of service), or to retain workers (by applying a higher rate to the later years of service).

### *Final Average Salary*

Most PERS calculate benefits as a percentage of final average salary multiplied by the single-rate or step-rate formulas discussed above. Consequently the method for determining the final average salary will have an important effect on the calculated benefit. In most plans, final average salary is defined as the employee's average salary during his or her last three or five years' of service, or during the three or five years when the employee received his or her highest level of pay. As many as 14 percent of the GFOA's survey respondents, however, based benefits on the last year's salary alone, and one plan based benefits on the last month's salary.[14] Since salary is likely to increase through the service life of the employee, retirement benefits will generally be higher when final average salary is defined as being closest to the last years of employment.

### *Integration with Social Security*

Before 1951, state and local government employees were not eligible for coverage under the federal Old Age Survivors Disability Income (OASDI) program, commonly referred to as Social Security. At the time of the program's enactment in 1935, it was considered unconstitutional for the federal government to tax state governments. Since Social Security is financed from taxes paid by employers and employees, state and local government employees were not included in the program. In keeping with the movement to extend Social Security coverage, however, legislation was enacted in 1950 to allow voluntary coverage of state and local government employees at the employer's option. Under this legislation, state and local governments could elect Social Security coverage in addition to the coverage provided by their retirement plans. At that time, Social Security coverage for the group could also be terminated by giving two years' notice, but, more recent legislation (i.e., the Social Security amendments of 1983) ended the option for state and local governments to withdraw from Social Security.

Approximately 75 percent of state and local government employees are now covered by Social Security under voluntary participation arrangements.[15] Upon retiring, these members receive Social Security benefits in addition to the benefits provided by the PERS. Although some plans have benefit formulas that explicitly take into account the benefits provided through federal programs, public systems have shown a reluctance to explicitly coordinate their plans with Social Security.[16] According to the House's *Pension Task Force Report,* only about 15 percent of state and local plans utilize a benefit formula that explicitly takes into account the benefits provided through the OASDI program.[17]

Two basic approaches to Social Security integration are found among PERS. Approximately half the integrated plans use an "offset" approach, with the other half using a "step-rate" approach. Under the offset approach, a recipient's pension benefits from the plan are reduced by a set percentage (e.g., 50 percent) of the recipient's Social Security benefit. Under the step-rate approach, a higher "benefit accrual rate" is applied to compensation above the "integration level" and a lower rate is applied to compensation below that level. The integration level used in this instance is usually the maximum taxable wage base for Social Security. The benefit accrual rates applied to compensation above the integration level range from 1.5 to 2.5 percent for each year of service, while rates below the integration level range from .75 to 2.0 percent for each year of service.[18]

While there has been no conclusive study of why state and local plans are reluctant to explicitly coordinate their plans with Social Security benefits, there may be several explanations. The first is that a single-rate unit-benefit formula without integration is easier to understand and communicate than an integrated formula. The second is that the changing nature of Social Security might result in frequent changes to the benefit formulas, making the integrated plan more difficult to administer.

### *Cost-of-Living Adjustments*

In order to mitigate the effect that inflation has on retirement income, many PERS provide members with cost-of-living adjustments (COLAs). Many of the systems that provide these adjustments do so on an *ad hoc* basis, after special consideration by the retirement board, legislature, or other official body. Some systems, however, provide automatic cost-of-living adjustments, using either a fixed percentage (e.g., 3 percent per year) or a percentage indexed to a measure of inflation (e.g., 60 percent of the Consumer Price Index).[19]

## *PLAN ADMINISTRATION*

PERS generally come into being through legislative enactment. State statutes provide the legal basis for retirement benefits among the majority of plans (63 percent of the GFOA survey's respondents). In addition, the governing bodies of home-rule cities, counties, special districts, and other political subdivisions may be able to establish retirement plans with the approval of their electorates.

Procedural guidelines for the operation of the system are usually set forth in the enabling legislation and bylaws that are prepared and adopted by the system's board of trustees to provide administrative direction. These bylaws usually define the authority granted the system in meeting the benefit promise, the composition and election of trustees, the procedures for holding board meetings, the officers of the system, and the role and authority of the board's subcommittees.[20]

### *The Board of Trustees*

The overall management of the retirement system is the responsibility of the system's board of trustees. They fulfill this responsibility by making policy decisions within the framework of the system's enabling statutes, and by employing an administrator to carry out the day-to-day operation of the system. The board may also employ consultants who provide advice on the technical aspects of system operations.

The board approves procedures and policies that ensure the proper performance of system operations, such as

- adopting interest-rate and mortality tables for use in actuarial calculations
- approving methods for system control and reporting
- setting investment policy

It is important to note that, in setting investment policy, the trustees are acting as fiduciaries and are entrusted to invest the funds in a way that ensures the safety of the assets and a sound return on the investments. More will be said about the role of fiduciaries later in this chapter.

### *The System Administrator*

The system administrator (often called the director, executive director, or executive secretary) is responsible for the day-to-day operation of the system. In this capacity, the administrator acts as coordinator for the board, directs the system staff, and deals with membership and other constituencies such as taxpayer organizations, the legislature, and the community.

The administrator's key tasks include overseeing the receipt of payments made to the retirement system and ensuring that they are properly deposited or invested; authorizing payments for benefits or services rendered; informing the board regarding the payment of benefits and expenses as well as the purchase and disposition of investments; maintaining all records, files, and accounts; maintaining proper communications with all interested parties; and representing the board during legislative sessions and hearings. In addition, the administrator is usually given responsibility for hiring administrative staff and advising the board on selection of technical consultants and other outside help.

### *Technical Consultants*

The management of PERS is complex and requires a broad range of expertise. As a result, retirement systems often enlist the services of a number of assisting professionals, including legal counsel, actuaries, investment advisers, auditors, and fund custodians.

Legal counsel must be consulted on questions arising in the areas not covered by the enabling statue or bylaws and on problem cases that must be settled in court. Legal counsel can also be helpful in areas such as interpreting changes in federal tax laws and arbitrating disputes arising from overpayment of claims. Most retirement systems authorize the appointment of legal counsel. In some instances, the state's attorney general may serve in that capacity.

The actuary is a technical adviser who analyzes the demographic and economic characteristics of the retirement system and recommends the assumptions used by the system to determine the cost of the benefits promised. The actuary also prepares the actuarial portion of the annual report to the board, submits valuations of liabilities and reserves, and makes periodic studies of the operating experience of the system. Actuaries also evaluate proposed benefit amendments in order to estimate the cost of a change in benefits before the change is adopted.

The investment adviser makes recommendations to the board regarding the appropriate allocation of assets among the different investment options. Many systems also hire investment managers, who are given discretion to make investments on behalf of the system and who must present information to the board periodically on the performance of the investments.

The auditor examines the financial statements prepared from the system's accounts and supporting records in order to verify that the statements are presented in accordance with generally accepted accounting principals and that they comply with pertinent statutes. System audits are usually made at the close of each fiscal year by an independent certified public accountant or by an auditor employed by the state.

Fund custodians keep the cash and securities of the retirement system in safekeeping, subject to the direction of the board. The custodian must maintain proper records of transactions and is generally bonded for proper performance of its duties with respect to the conservation of monies and securities under its control and supervision.

## *BENEFIT OBLIGATIONS/ACTUARIAL VALUATION*

In establishing the retirement plan, a public employer is promising to pay benefits that will come due in the future. Generally these benefits can be paid in one of two ways: either through a "pay-as-you-go" approach or through a "reserve funding" approach.

Under a "pay-as-you-go" approach, the monies required to pay retirement benefits are appropriated by the employer when the benefits come due, and no attempt is made to accumulate monies or to make long-term investments. Under the "reserve funding" approach, periodic contributions are made in excess of the amounts necessary to pay benefits to current retirees.

Reserve funding offers a number of advantages. As assets accumulate, they can be invested and income from the investments can be used to defray a portion of the required contributions. These investment earnings can be substantial and may, over time, meet 25 to 50 percent of total pension costs.[21] It follows that, over time, the reserve funding approach will result in lower contributions than the pay-as-you-go approach, since investment income can be substituted for contributions. Reserve funding also increases the security of pension benefits by accumulating assets in a systematic manner and provides equitable treatment of different generations of employees and taxpayers by assigning plan costs more closely to the years in which the benefits were earned.

### *Reserve Funding Methods*

Most public plans use the reserve funding method and rely on an actuarial analysis to determine the amount of assets that must be accumulated in order to pay plan benefits. The GFOA's 1987 survey found that approximately 80 percent of the respondents providing defined benefit plans used some form of reserve funding method and conducted actuarial valuations on an annual basis.[22]

An actuarial valuation is a procedure for measuring the expected value of a plan's future benefit payments and assigning portions of this value to past years, the current year, and future years. The main purpose of this analysis is to determine the contributions necessary to adequately fund the retirement plan over a period of time. In conducting an actuarial valuation, the actuary uses information about the demographic characteristics of the covered employees and assumptions about rates of investment return, pay increases, withdrawal from employment, and mortality to estimate the contributions necessary for the orderly accumulation of plan assets necessary to pay plan benefits.

Technically, the expected value of a plan's future benefit payments is referred to as the *actuarial present value of total projected benefits.* This term can best be understood if thought of in two parts: *actuarial present value* and *total projected benefits. Total projected benefits* is the sum (as of the actuarial valuation date) of all benefits payable to

- retirees, beneficiaries, and terminated employees who are entitled to benefits
- current covered employees who are entitled to benefits as a result of their past service
- current covered employees who are entitled to benefits as a result of their expected future service[23]

The *actuarial present value* (APV) is the value (on the actuarial valuation date) of the total projected benefits, discounted to reflect the time value of money and the probability of payment. Thus, the actuarial present value of total projected benefits is the amount that would have to be invested (as of the actuarial valuation date) so that the amount invested, plus investment earnings, would provide the money necessary to pay the total projected benefits.

Generally speaking, the portion of the APV of total projected benefits attributable to a given year is commonly called the *normal cost* for that year. The sum of the costs assigned to years before the valuation date (plus the interest accrued on those costs) is called the *actuarial accrued liability*. The difference between the actuarial accrued liability and the total assets that have accumulated in the plan is called the *unfunded actuarial accrued liability.*[24] This amount must be funded by future contributions, and is usually amortized over a period of 30 to 40 years.[25]

After calculating these values, the actuary determines the contribution that provides for current funding of the normal cost and amortization of the unfunded actuarial accrued liability, if any. This contribution may be expressed as a dollar amount or as a percentage of covered payroll. The method used to determine this contribution amount (or rate) is referred to as the actuarial funding method.

### *Actuarial Funding Methods*

Although a large number of actuarial methods exist, only a few are used frequently by PERS. These include

- unit credit actuarial methods
- the entry-age-normal actuarial method
- the aggregate actuarial cost method[26]

It is important to note that all the above methods will, when applied consistently, result in sufficient assets being available to meet benefit payments over the long run.[27] Different actuarial methods will, however, result in different patterns of contributions over time. These patterns may be important to an employer, since some patterns offer greater consistency in the level of benefit contributions from year to year. This consistency may be useful in the budget process, since it allows for a more predictable series of payments.

*Unit Credit Actuarial Methods.* There are basically two forms of unit credit (or unit benefit) actuarial methods: the accumulated benefit method and the credited projected benefit method. These unit credit approaches differ in their treatment of the effects of (a) projected salary increases and (b) step-rate benefits and benefit enhancements.

The accumulated benefit approach credits benefits using the employee's service and salary history *as of the valuation date.* Under this approach, the actuarial accrued liability at a given time is a function of current salary and the number of years of the employees' credited past service up to that point in time. This liability is referred to as the accumulated benefit obligation. If salaries increase in the next year, then the accumulated benefit obligation increases by a factor that not only includes the additional year's service, but also applies the new salary to all previous years' service. Thus, under the accumulated benefits approach, costs can increase sharply as employees approach retirement.[28]

The credited projected benefit approach is similar to the accumulated benefits approach but is modified to take into account the effect of projected salary increases. This approach credits benefits using the employee's service history as of the valuation date and *the projected salary on which the benefits will be based.* The actuarial accrued liability measure produced by this approach is called the pension benefit obligation. Under this measure the actuarial accrued liability for each employee may increase more gradually than under the accumulated benefits approach.[29]

*The Entry-Age-Normal Actuarial Method.* The entry-age-normal actuarial method does not focus on the benefits earned by employees as a result of service through the valuation date. Instead, it computes the total cost of funding projected benefits *(including benefits arising from expected future service)* and then allocates the total cost to the years of past credited service and expected future service. This approach is designed to allocate the total cost on a level basis to all years of service, (i.e., in equal amounts or percentages of payroll).[30]

*The Aggregate Actuarial Cost Method.* Under the aggregate actuarial cost method, the difference between the APV of projected benefits for the group (rather than each individual) and the actuarial value of assets is allocated on a level basis over the period between the valuation date and the projected exit date. The benefits not covered by current assets are amortized over the remaining working career of the covered group, and the actuarial accrued liability is set equal to the actuarial value of the assets. Consequently, by definition, there is no unfunded actuarial liability under the aggregate actuarial cost method.

### *Actuarial Assumptions*

The assumptions used by actuaries to calculate the funding requirements of PERS play an important role in determining the amount of the employer's contributions. By controlling the actuarial assumptions, one can influence the level and timing of employer contributions. For some plans, the actuarial assumptions are legislated by state statute. For other plans, the retirement board must accept or reject the assumptions made by the actuary. This gives the retirement board greater control over the assumptions that drive plan costs.

Because it is impossible to know the future, a variety of assumptions must be made concerning rates of investment return, pay increases, withdrawal from employment, and mortality. Of these, the assumptions regarding investment return and salary increase are especially critical, since even small changes in these assumptions can result in large changes to computed contributions. For example, a relatively small increase in the discount rate used to compute contributions from 5.0 to 5.5 percent can have a large effect on a plan's normal costs, reducing them by 12 to 14 percent.[31]

A fundamental tenet of the actuarial profession is that all assumptions should be conservative in nature. This is done so that the employer's contributions will be large enough to cover the actual costs of future benefits. If the actuary assumes a rate of investment return that is too high, or a rate of salary increase that is too low, then future contributions must be higher to make up the difference.

The GFOA survey found that, for fiscal year 1986, the assumed rates of investment return used by two-thirds of the responding PERS fell between 6.75 and 8.25 percent, with a mean of 7.44 percent, slightly lower than the 7.68 percent rate of return earned that year on ten-year U.S. Treasury bonds.[32] Assumed average salary increases for fiscal year 1986 ranged over a wider scale, with two-thirds of the respondents reporting assumed increases between 4.75 and 7.25 percent. The mean actuarial assumption regarding salary increase was 5.92 percent, somewhat higher than the 5.2 percent increase in the U.S. Bureau of Labor Statistic's Employment Cost Index for state and local government workers in 1986.[33]

Although each of the assumptions is important in its own right, the difference between the assumptions is important as well. Just as the difference between rate of return on investments and the rate of increase in prices is used to calculate a real rate of return on investments, so the difference between the assumed rate of return on investments and the assumed average salary increase might be used to calculate an assumed real rate of return for a pension fund. For the respondents of the GFOA survey, the assumed real rate of return was 1.52 percent for fiscal year 1986.

### *Actuarial Valuation of Assets*

If the plan is funded on an actuarial basis, substantial assets will accumulate. Establishing the value of the assets is important, since they will ultimately be used to finance the benefits promised to the employees and thus play a substantial role in the calculation of the required contribution.

There are three methods that can be used to determine the actuarial value of plan assets: the cost method, market method, and moving average method.

Under the cost method, investment return is the sum of ordinary income plus the capital gains and losses that result from the sales of investments during the period. A variant of the cost method, referred to as the amortized cost method, allows the original premium or discount on fixed-income securities to be amortized over the investment period.

Under the market method, the value of an investment is its market price on the date of the actuarial valuation.

Under the moving average method, the value of an investment is calculated by a formula that smoothes short-term market fluctuations in a manner that better reflects the long-term values of the investment.[34]

Public plans generally use the cost method somewhat more frequently than the market or moving average methods. Thirty-four percent of the GFOA survey respondents indicated that they use the cost method to value their securities for actuarial purposes; 28 percent use the market method; and 24 percent use some variant of the moving average method.[35]

## EMPLOYER AND EMPLOYEE CONTRIBUTIONS

The monies used by PERS to pay benefits (and accumulate assets) are received from employer and employee contributions as well as from the income earned on PERS investments. Combined, these receipts amounted to $99.4 billion in 1987. Total employer and employee contributions amounted to $41.6 billion, or 41 percent of total receipts in 1987. The remainder, 59 percent of annual receipts, was obtained from investment income.[36]

### Employer Contributions

State and local employers contributed $30.4 billion to retirement systems in 1987. In most cases, public employer contributions to the retirement plans are subject to the appropriation process within the employing government. Consequently, the plans compete with other governmental programs for funds. In many cases, statutory funding requirements would appear to give the state plans a prior claim on state revenues. In some cases, however, the laws may have less substance than they appear to provide. For example, in the early 1970s, the Illinois Supreme Court upheld the right of the Governor of Illinois to reduce state pension fund appropriations below statutorily mandated levels.[37] In addition, maximum tax rates set by state laws have hampered some local plans from achieving adequate funding.[38]

### Employee Contributions

Approximately three-fourths of PERS are contributory systems, requiring plan members to contribute to the plan.[39] According to the 1987 Census of Governments, public employees contributed $11.2 billion to state and local retirement systems in 1987.[40] When members contribute to the plan, they usually do so through a fixed contribution rate that ranges between 4 and 10 percent of pay.[41] Contribution rates for employees not covered by Social Security tend to be larger than for employees covered by Social Security.[42]

Employee contributions generally play a more important role in PERS than in private systems. Yet, although the total amount of employee contributions has risen over the past 20 years, it makes up a declining percentage of annual plan receipts. This may be due, in part, to the fact that some employers "pick up" their employees' contributions in a manner specified under Section 414 (h) of the Internal Revenue Code. Under this provision, employee contributions that are designated as having been made by the employer are given favorable tax status under the Code.[43] It is also likely that the substantial rise in investment income that has occurred over the past two decades has reduced the need for contributions.

## ASSETS

The investment of plan assets is an issue of immense consequence to plan participants and their beneficiaries, to taxpayers, and to the economy as a whole. If the assets invested by the retirement system earn low yields, then the sponsoring government must contribute additional funds to pay retirement benefits that have been promised to plan members. This places an additional strain on the sponsoring government and may require tax increases. Proper investment requires careful thought about the plan's funding structure, the potential risks and rewards inherent in different investment policies, the legal constraints governing the investment of assets, and proper monitoring and control of currently invested assets. As was noted at the beginning of this chapter, PERS assets now total approximately $650 billion and represent a major source of investment capital in the United States.

### *Asset Growth and Distribution*

Over the past twenty years PERS assets have grown rapidly. Between 1962 and 1989, the assets of state and local retirement systems increased from $24.5 billion to $647.1 billion, with annual compounded rates of growth ranging as high as 14.6 percent.[44] If PERS assets continue to grow at this rate, they will climb to over a trillion dollars by the end of the century.

In addition to the growth in the amount of assets, there has been a substantial shift in the distribution of investments. In 1962, 44 percent of state retirement system assets were invested in corporate bonds; 26 percent in U.S. government securities; 4 percent in corporate equities; 9 percent in mortgages; and the remainder in short-term and miscellaneous securities. By 1989, the percent of assets in corporate bonds had fallen dramatically to 27 percent, while investments in corporate equities and U.S. government securities had grown to 36 and 31 percent, respectively.

Much of this shift is probably due to a growing sophistication on the part of PERS administrators regarding investment selection and the importance of asset allocation. This growing sophistication has clearly been beneficial to state and local governments. PERS assets earned $58 billion in 1987, amounting to 59 percent of total plan receipts for that year. Historically, earnings on investments have grown rapidly as a percentage of receipts and make up a larger and larger share of the monies available to pay benefits.

### *Investment Policies, Asset Allocation, and Investment Risk and Return*

The long-run investment objective of a pension fund should be to obtain a good return on investment consistent with the risk tolerances of the plan sponsors, the trustees, and the fund itself. In order to specify the fund's investment policy properly, administrators and trustees should be knowledgeable about the effects of asset allocation, the tradeoffs between risk and return, and the legal and fiduciary constraints that pertain to PERS investments.

*Asset Allocation.* Empirical research suggests that the biggest portion of investment return over time is attributable to the basic *asset allocation* of the portfolio. Asset allocation refers to the distribution of assets among the traditional asset classes (e.g., stocks, bonds, real estate, cash, etc.). In GFOA's publication *Pension Fund Investing,* Girard Miller reports on a study by Jeffrey Diermeier, which found a close correlation between the basic allocation of assets and investment return.[45] Diermeier reported that the basic allocation of assets among traditional asset classes was correlated with 86 percent of total variation in investment returns. Girard Miller interprets the results as follows:

> if the entire universe of pension portfolio's long-term returns averaged 10 percent over a decade, it is likely that an unmanaged portfolio would have obtained an annual return of 8.6% by simply investing in the same asset classes as everybody else and ignoring market timing and securities selection.[46]

This result is significant, since it argues that public investors will obtain most of their returns as a result of the percentage of assets that they invest in the major types of securities, rather than as a result of the individual securities selected or the time that they are purchased.

*Investment Risk and Return.* Over the past sixty years, investors have received positive returns on their investments, even after inflation and major economic shocks are taken into account. Generally, the rate of return has been related to the riskiness of the investment class. When examined over the period between 1926 and 1986, common stocks (one of the riskiest investments) earned an average annual return of 10 percent, despite the stock market crash of 1929-32. Over the same period, long-term bonds (a moderately risky investment) earned an average annual return of 5.1 percent, and U.S. Treasury bills (the least risky investment) earned 3.5 percent. By comparison, the Consumer Price Index grew at an average annual rate of 3.0 percent during the period.[47]

It should be noted, however, that the long-term trend of an investment class does not guarantee that the trend will continue, or that any individual investment within the class will earn the same rate of return as the class as a whole. All investments are subject to risk.

Investment risk is measured by the volatility of investment returns for the different classes of investments. Volatility is a statistical measure of the size and frequency of deviations from the average return. An investment that fluctuates widely around its long-term average rate of return is statistically more volatile (i.e., more risky) than an investment that deviates very little from its average return. Historically, the annual returns on stocks have been much more volatile than the return on bonds.[48]

Investment risk is managed through a technique called "diversification," which involves reducing the portfolio's overall volatility by managing the number and types of investments. Basically, there are two forms of risk: "systematic" risk and "unsystematic" risk. Unsystematic risk is the potential for loss associated with an individual security (i.e., the potential that a specific stock's price will fall or that a specific bond will default). Unsystematic risk is reduced by holding a large number of different securities so that if one investment loses value, the others combined may still produce an adequate return.

Systematic risk is the risk associated with owning an entire class of securities (e.g., stocks, bonds, real estate). This risk is not reduced by increasing the number of individual securities held. For example, if the stock market crashes, the pension plan is not protected by owning 2,000 stocks instead of only 50. Rather, systematic risk is reduced by allocating assets among different, unrelated classes of securities. Ideally, the investor should find classes of investments that have good long-run potential for returns but move opposite each other in the short term, thereby cancelling each other's short-term volatility.

In order to fully utilize the benefits of asset allocation and diversification, the fund must decide in advance what kinds of risks it can afford to take. Younger, growing plans may be able to invest more of their assets in the stock market, since they have very small cash payments and a longer time to absorb the risk. Older plans with a growing number of retirees may decide to place more of their assets in fixed-income securities or cash equivalents, given their need for stable income and liquidity. In making these decisions, however, the fund will be constrained by a variety of legal statutes and fiduciary requirements.

### *Investment Constraints and Fiduciary Requirements*

Pension fund administrators and board members are *fiduciaries,* that is, they are entrusted to invest the funds in a way that ensures the safety of the assets and a sound return on the investments. The two basic fiduciary responsibilities are loyalty and reasonable care. Both principles have long histories and are established by common law, state statutes, and federal regulations.

Loyalty requires that fiduciaries do not place their own interests above the interests of plan members. Reasonable care requires that investments be made by informed individuals, acting prudently, to meet the retirement needs of their members. The principle of prudent investment dates back to 1830 and the decision of *Harvard* v. *Amory,* in which the court decided that the soundness of an investment was a function of the investor's "prudence, discretion, and intelligence." This phrasing is echoed in the statutory fiduciary requirements of states and localities.

***Federal Fiduciary Requirements.*** Federal fiduciary requirements leave much of the direct control of PERS investments to the states. Indirectly, the federal government regulates most PERS through two mechanisms: the Internal Revenue Code (IRC) and the Employee Retirement Income Security Act (ERISA).

The Internal Revenue Code sets forth provisions that pension funds and institutional investors must meet in order to qualify for tax-exempt status. A key provision of the IRC is that investments must be made for the "exclusive benefit" of system members. If this provision were strictly interpreted, it might well prevent pension plans from making investments targeted to promote economic development—whether or not the investments were prudent. In Revenue Ruling 69-495, 1969-2 CB, however, the IRS has chosen to interpret "exclusive" to mean "primary" and, as a result, retirement systems may retain their tax-exempt status while making investments that benefit members and other parties, provided:

- the cost of the investments does not exceed their fair market value
- the investments offer a rate commensurate with that offered in the market
- prudent investor and diversification requirements are met

Prudent investor and diversification requirements are explicitly set forth in the Employee Retirement Income Security Act of 1974 (ERISA). Although PERS are exempt from many of ERISA's requirements, the Act provides an authoritative definition of the prudent investor principle, which is echoed in many state and local statutes. To comply with the standard of prudence, fiduciaries must

- exercise the care, skill, and diligence of a prudent individual
- select investments solely in the interests of plan participants
- diversify investments, unless it would be imprudent to do so

*State Statutes and Policies.* While the IRC and ERISA indirectly regulate the investments of PERS, state statutes directly control many of the investments made by them. The variety of state legal provisions relating to public employee retirement investments is extensive. Most of the states rely on some form of the prudent investor standard, while other states specify the nature of investments that can or cannot be made.

Usually, state laws control investments by specifying the maximum percentage of system assets that can be placed in a particular type of security. For example, many states limit the percentage of assets that can be placed in equities to 50 percent or less. Other common state investment restrictions include limiting the maximum percentage of assets that can be placed in one company, in foreign stocks or bonds, or in real estate mortgages.

Many PERS themselves adopt investment policies that limit the types of investments they can make. Often these policies take the form of investment options approved by the system's board of trustees and restrict the maximum percentage of assets that can be held in one or another kind of securities.

Frequently, a system will be governed by both a prudent investor standard and authorized investment options. While this may be considered redundant, it can also be viewed as a means of providing some security for the system's fiduciaries. Prudence is a vague concept. Fiduciaries may find it reassuring to have specific guidelines to follow when deciding how to place investments.

*Changes in Investment Restrictions.* Between 1978 and 1988, 25 states changed their investment restrictions. In almost all cases, these changes have permitted greater discretion on the part of investment managers:

- 10 states have added the prudent investor standard
- 8 states have increased the maximum percentage of assets that can be held in equities
- 3 states have added a "basket clause" allowing a certain percentage of assets to be placed in investments that are not otherwise permitted
- 5 states have specifically authorized investments in venture capital[49]

## *ACCOUNTING AND FINANCIAL REPORTING*

Public employee retirement systems (PERS) often issue separate "stand-alone" financial reports. In other cases, the financial statements of a PERS are combined with those of one or more other entities as part of a single report for a larger financial reporting entity (e.g., a city or state). In either case, PERS are classified as "pension trust funds" in governmental fund accounting and are reported using the accrual basis of accounting.

In current practice, generally accepted accounting principles (GAAP) permit PERS to select one of three different methods for purposes of financial statement display:

- National Council on Governmental Accounting (NCGA)[50] Statement No. 1, *Governmental Accounting and Financial Reporting Principles*
- Financial Accounting Standards Board (FASB)[51] Statement No. 35, *Accounting and Reporting by Defined Benefit Pension Plans*
- NCGA Statement No. 6, *Pension Accounting and Financial Reporting: Public Employee Retirement Systems and State and Local Government Employers*

In practice, NCGA Statement No. 1 and FASB Statement No. 35 are the methods most commonly selected by PERS.

Both NCGA methods provide for two basic financial statements: the balance sheet and the statement of revenues, expenses and changes in fund balances.[52] The FASB option, on the other hand, provides for four basic PERS financial statements:

- statement of net assets available for benefits
- statement of changes in net assets available for benefits

- statement of accumulated plan benefits
- statement of changes in accumulated plan benefits

NCGA Statement No. 6 also provides that assets should be valued at cost or amortized cost. In practice, this same valuation methodology is also followed by PERS using NCGA Statement No. 1, although that statement does not specifically address asset valuation. FASB Statement No. 35, on the other hand, calls for PERS to value their assets in the financial statements at market value.

It also should be noted that FASB Statement No. 35 does not allow future salary to be considered in determining the benefit obligation. NCGA Statement No. 6, on the other hand, *requires* the inclusion of future salary in the calculation of the benefit obligation. NCGA Statement No. 1 allows the pension obligation to be calculated using any one of several acceptable actuarial cost methods.

It can be seen from the foregoing discussion that current GAAP allow for considerable diversity in financial statement display among PERS. The Governmental Accounting Standards Board (GASB) hopes in the near future to eliminate much of this diversity by setting a single set of standards for PERS display that will be applicable to all public-sector pension plans. Regardless of the option selected for financial statement display, all PERS are required to provide a common set of disclosures prescribed by GASB Statement No. 5, *Disclosure of Pension Information by Public Employee Retirement Systems and State and Local Governmental Employers*. Required disclosures include a description of the plan, a summary of significant accounting policies, information on funding status and progress and information on contributions required and contributions made. In addition, GASB Statement No. 5 requires PERS to present certain 10-year trend data as "required supplementary information" (RSI). RSI is different from other required disclosures in that it is not subject to audit, although the auditor is required to make certain basic inquiries regarding the presentation of the data, and the absence of the data or any known deficiencies in the data must be disclosed in the auditor's report on the PERS' financial statements.

Like other government entities, PERS commonly issue a comprehensive annual financial report (CAFR)/component unit financial report (CUFR). Like other CAFRs/CUFRs, PERS reports contain an introductory section, a financial section and a statistical section. However, unlike other CAFRs/CUFRs, PERS reports also contain a separate actuarial section that normally includes the following information:

- actuarial certification letter
- schedule of active member valuation data
- schedule of retirants and beneficiaries added to and removed from rolls
- summary of accrued and unfunded accrued liabilities
- solvency test
- schedule of recommended versus actual contributions
- analysis of financial experience (when applicable)

Moreover, the financial section of a PERS CAFR/CUFR normally contains the following specialized schedules:

- schedule of administrative expenses
- investment summary
- summary schedule of cash receipts and disbursements
- summary schedules of compensation of administrative officials and commissions and payments to brokers and consultants

Finally, it should be noted that GASB Statement No. 5's provision requiring the presentation of RSI has lowered the number of tables normally presented in the statistical table for a PERS CAFR/CUFR to four schedules: retired members by type of benefit; investment results; average benefit payment amounts; and participating employers (if applicable).

## *LOOKING TO THE FUTURE*

If current trends are borne out, it is likely that public employee retirement systems will face substantial challenges in the future.[53] This conclusion is suggested by the following demographic and economic trends:

- The large increase in the number of births after World War II (the baby boomers) will result in a sharp increase in the number of persons retiring after the first decade of the twenty-first century.
- The decrease in mortality rates that occurred in recent years has increased life expectancy. When the baby boomers reach 65, their remaining life expectancies will range from 13 to 18 years, almost 5 years longer than is currently the case.
- The large decrease in the number of births during the 1960s and 1970s will reduce the number of people who will be working during the first and second decades of the twenty-first century and reduce the ratio of workers to retirees from about 3:1 at present to 2:1 early in the next century. Although this change would not affect the funding of retirement plans that use reserve funding methods, it could substantially strain plans that use a "pay-as-you-go" approach to funding.

It is likely that, 25 to 30 years from now, employees will be working longer and retiring at later ages. As health and life expectancy improve, and as growth in the workforce subsides, aging employees will probably remain in the workforce past the age of 65, perhaps taking part-time or less strenuous jobs toward the ends of their careers.

It is also likely that employers will reevaluate the benefits that they promise their workers upon retirement. Longer life expectancies will mean higher costs for defined benefit plans and increased risks on the part of the employer.

It is possible that public entities, particularly those that do not have a sound tax base, will develop two-or three-tiered retirement programs, providing different sets of benefits to different groups of employees. It is also possible that employees will be expected to play a greater role in financing their retirement. While employers will still provide substantial retirement benefits, employees will be expected to bear more of the future risk through the partial restructuring of benefit arrangements. For example, more public employers may provide defined contribution plans (in addition to defined benefit plans) in order to encourage employees to set aside some of their own funds for retirement.

In addition, other issues such as post-retirement medical care and the solvency of Social Security will play important roles in determining the future amount and types of benefits that public employers promise their employees. In order to accommodate this future, public plans would be well advised to review their benefit packages to determine whether the benefits that they promise will satisfy their employees' needs and can be realistically provided.

## NOTES

1. Corporate Profiles, *The Directory of Public Employee Retirement Funds* (Woodbridge, NJ: Corporate Profiles, Inc. 1988), p. v.

2. U.S. Congress, House, Committee on Education and Labor, *Pension Task Force Report on Public Employee Retirement Systems,* 1978, p. 53.

3. U.S. Bureau of the Census, *Finances of Employee-Retirement Systems of State and Local Governments in 1985-1986* (Washington, DC: Government Printing Office, 1987), p. x.

4. U.S. Bureau of the Census, Census of Governments, *Employee-Retirement Systems of State and Local Governments* (Washington, DC: Government Printing Office, various years). Although the Census sample represents a subset of all the public retirement systems in the United States, it contains most of the largest state and local systems. It also offers consistent time-series data, allowing the examination of trends over time.

5. The following statistics are taken from, Census of Governments, *Employee-Retirement Systems,* Vol. 4, No. 6, for the years 1962 and 1982. At the time of this writing, the 1987 statistics were not available for coverage classes.

6. *Ibid.*

7. *Ibid.*

8. *Ibid.*

9. Paul Zorn and Michael Hanus, *Public Pension Accounting and Reporting: A Survey of Current Practices* (Chicago: Government Finance Research Center of the Government Finance Officers Association, December 1987), p. 12.

10. Census of Governments, *Employee-Retirement Systems,* p. 24.

11. Archibald L. Patterson, *Public Pension Administration* (Athens, GA: Univ. of Georgia, 1982), pp. 5-7. Readers interested in a concise, readable history of public pensions and the benefit promise should turn to this book.

12. Zorn and Hanus, p. 26.

13. *Ibid.*

14. *Ibid.,* p. 27.

15. A. Haeworth Robertson, *The Coming Revolution in Social Security* (Reston, VA: Reston Publishing Company, 1981), pp. 17-18.

16. Zorn and Hanus, p. 32.

17. U. S. House, *Pension Task Force Report,* p. 111.

18. *Ibid.*

19. Zorn and Hanus, p. 27.

20. A detailed description of public employee retirement administration may be found in the Municipal Finance Officers Association Committee on Public Employee Retirement Administration, *Public Employee Retirement Administration* (Chicago: Municipal Finance Officers Association, 1977).

21. William F. Marples, *Actuarial Aspects of Pension Security* (Homewood, IL: Richard D. Irwin, 1965).

22. Zorn and Hanus, p. 40. Defined contribution plans can be considered fully funded at all times, since the benefits promised to plan members are based solely on the contributions placed in the members' accounts, plus accumulated interest.

23. Governmental Accounting Standards Board, *Disclosure of Pension Information by Public Employee Retirement Systems and State and Local Governmental Employers* (Stamford, CT: Governmental Accounting Standards Board, 1986), p. 54.

24. The reader should note that pension terminology is not uniform and that actuarial terms vary. The definitions given above are general but will not apply to every actuarial method. For example, under the "aggregate cost" method, the unfunded actuarial accrued liability is not separately identified.

25. Zorn and Hanus, p. 87.

26. This list does not include all the actuarial methods used by PERS; it does list the methods used by the majority of systems.

27. Barnet N. Berin, *Pensions: A Guide to the Technical Side* (Chicago: Charles D. Spenser, 1981), p. 1.

28. Governmental Accounting Standards Board, *Disclosure of Pension Information,* pp. 58-59.

29. *Ibid.,* p. 59.

30. *Ibid.*

31. U.S. House, *Pension Task Force Report,* p. 161.

32. Actuarial assumption statistics regarding the rates of investment return were obtained from Zorn and Hanus, p. 44; the rates of return for ten-year U.S. Treasury bonds in 1986 was obtained from the U.S. Department of Commerce, *Statistical Abstract of the United States* (Washington, DC: U.S. Government Printing Office, 1989), p. 503.

33. Actuarial assumption statistics regarding salary increases were obtained from Zorn and Hanus, pp. 44-46; U.S. Bureau of Labor Statistics Employment Cost Index was obtained from the U.S. Department of Commerce, *Statistical Abstract of the United States* (Washington, DC: U.S. Government Printing Office, 1989), p. 408.

34. Richard G. Roeder, *Financing Retirement System Benefits* (Chicago: Government Finance Officers Association, 1987), p. 4.

35. Zorn and Hanus, pp. 67-68.

36. Census of Governments, *Employee-Retirement Systems,* p. 1.

37. U.S. House, *Pension Task Force Report,* p. 140.

38. *Ibid.,* p. 141.

39. *Ibid.,* p. 54.

40. Census of Governments, *Employee-Retirement Systems,* p. 1.

41. Zorn and Hanus, p. 95.

42. U.S. House, *Pension Task Force Report,* p. 138.

43. Municipal Finance Officers Association, *Public Employee Retirement Administration,* p. 108.

44. Board of Governors of the Federal Reserve System, *Flow of Funds Accounts 1964-1987;* and *Flow of Funds Accounts 2nd Quarter, 1989,* (Washington, D.C. Board of Governors, 1988 and 1989).

45. Girard Miller, *Pension Fund Investing* (Chicago: Government Finance Officers Association, 1987) p. 9. Diermeier's article, "Economic Inputs and Their Effect on Asset Allocation Decisions," appears in the booklet *Applying Economic Analysis to Portfolio Management* (Homewood, IL: Dow-Jones Irwin and the Institute of Chartered Financial Analysts, 1985).

46. Miller, p. 9.

47. *Ibid.,* p. 11.

48. *Ibid.,* p. 13.

49. Economic Development Administration, *Capital Financing and Development: An Inquiry Into Credit Pooling, Bank Community Development Corporations, and Public Employee Pension Funds* (Washington, DC: U.S. Department of Commerce, 1988), p. IV-21.

50. The NCGA was the Governmental Accounting Standards Board's predecessor as the authoritative accounting standard-setting body for state and local governments.

51. The FASB is the authoritative accounting standard-setting body for all non-governmental entities.

52. The NCGA had also established a third basic financial statement for PERS, the statement of changes in financial position, but this statement was eliminated for PERS by the Governmental Accounting Standards Board (GASB) Statement No. 9, *Reporting Cash Flows in Proprietary and Nonexpendable Trust Funds and Governmental Entities That Use Proprietary Fund Accounting.*

53. For a sobering look at the future of public plans, see Haeworth A. Robertson and Robert Kalman, "What Is In the Future for Public Retirement Systems?" *Government Finance Review,* October 1986, p. 23.

# 20

# *Government Enterprises*

Lawrence W. "Chip" Pierce and Kenneth L. Rust

"Government enterprise" may appear, at first glance, to be a contradiction in terms. The word *enterprise* generally connotes economic activity directed both toward the generation of revenues and toward economic efficiency that results in capital formation. Thus, placing the word *government* in front of *enterprises* may seem like attaching a Winnebago to a Ferrari. In fact, government enterprises have existed in some form as long as there have been governments. For example, the Roman aqueducts that provided water to Roman citizens over two thousand years ago were constructed through the collection of a crude form of benefit-based taxation.

In modern times, governmental provision of revenue-generating services is commonplace. A partial list of such services includes

- Water supply
- Wastewater treatment
- Electric utilities
- Solid waste collection
- Stormwater management
- Road maintenance
- Toll facilities
- Public parking
- Public mass transportation
- Port facilities
- Airports

Some services listed above can successfully be provided by the private sector, but this chapter will emphasize the financial and administrative requirements of providing revenue-generating enterprises by the public sector.

## *THE ESSENCE OF THE ENTERPRISE*

In order for a service to generate revenue, the service provider must be able to identify two factors: the users of the service and their level of consumption of the service. In certain cases, for example with police services, identifying these factors may be difficult.

An important feature of public enterprises is their dependence on service fees and charges to support operations. This assumes that the product being offered by the enterprise activity is demanded by the general public, and that the general public will pay to consume or enjoy the product being offered. Demand and willingness to pay for such services is simplified if the public enterprise is the sole service provider. Where the public enterprise acts as a monopoly (e.g., water, sewer, electricity), user charges are cost-driven and are the result of a detailed cost-allocation process. For enterprise activities where the public entity does not enjoy a monopoly, the development of user charges may also need to reflect what the market will bear and the charges levied by competing activities.

Regardless of the type of competitive environment within which a public enterprise operates, the development of user charges should consider the following criteria:

1. *Equity.* To what extent does the user-charge system recognize differences in service demand by individual customers?
2. *Revenue stability.* Does the user-charge schedule produce stable and predictable revenues over time?
3. *Flexibility.* Does the user-charge system have the flexibility to accommodate customers with widely varying demand and usage characteristics?
4. *Ease of administration.* How difficult is it for administrative staff to prepare, levy, and collect bills, and can charges be updated easily?
5. *Public acceptance.* Does the design of the user-charge schedule encourage public acceptance?

No one user-charge system is perfect. User-charge systems that are very simple may be inequitable and result in poor public acceptance. To treat all customers fairly may require an extremely complicated rate structure that would be extremely cumbersome to administer and to explain to system customers. The user-charge system that best meets the above-stated criteria is likely to fall between the two extremes of simplest and fairest.

It is clear that user charges have increased significantly in their importance to local governmental entities. User-charge revenue as a fraction of total current revenues increased dramatically between 1977 and 1987.[1] This trend is likely to continue as other sources of funding dry up or are constrained by state-imposed or voter-imposed restrictions.

The increases in user-fee generation is at least partly a result of governments becoming more "enterprising" in charging fees for services that have traditionally been supported through general governmental funds. For example, user fees are now commonly charged for a wide variety of recreational activities and services, as well as for specialized public-safety services.

The two principal attractions in such fees stem from the fiscal and regulatory role that user fees play. That is, user charges (1) generate revenue and (2) regulate service demand by curbing the abuse that is sometimes associated with free public services. The combination of diminishing intergovernmental and local tax revenue sources and the attributes of benefit-based charges portends further growth of this area of public finance in years to come.

## *LOCAL GOVERNMENT ENTERPRISES*

Governmental units provide a variety of revenue-generating services. The extent to which fees are charged to defray the costs of providing service depends on the nature of the service, the size and characteristics of the customer base, and the public policy objectives of the jurisdiction. The following eleven public enterprises are the most common to local government. The sections below discuss the unique characteristics of each service and how these characteristics affect financial management of the enterprise.

### *Water Supply*

The federal government has been less active in the realm of water supply than in many other areas of infrastructure in terms of regulation, operation, and provision of financial assistance. The Safe Drinking Water Act establishes upper limits for concentration of certain harmful substances such as lead and organic compounds. The 1986 amendments to the Act greatly increased the federal government's role in water-supply regulation by increasing dramatically the number of compounds that must be limited and by mandating treatment of surface water sources for many communities. The amendments may have a significant impact on capital and operating costs for many systems.[2] Many communities will see user charges, which have been fairly low, increase greatly in the next few years.

Large water utilities have generally established declining-block rate structures. They set two or three "blocks" of water use. The first block covers all water typically used by residential customers and carries the highest rate per gallon (or per cubic foot). The second block usually includes water-consumption levels typical of commercial customers and has a somewhat lower unit cost. The third block, if used, covers industrial, wholesale, and irrigation use and has the lowest rates. Many utilities add a service charge component that covers fixed costs of reading meters, billing, and customer service.

The rationale for the declining-block rate structure is that water utility costs have two primary causes. The first is overall demand for water, which determines the size of the supply, filtration systems, and storage. The second is peak demand, which determines the size of the distribution system. Because commercial and industrial water use is fairly even throughout the day and the year, while residential use is characterized by peaks and valleys, residential users are charged a higher share of the costs related to peak demand and thus pay higher rates for each gallon used.

There are a number of alternatives to the declining-block structure. Communities without significant nonresidential use often eliminate the rate blocks, opting instead for a uniform charge for each gallon used. Communities without water meters have to have some other way of estimating water use. Some charge a flat-rate for households and charge commercial users based on an estimate of their water use in "household equivalents." Some small water systems charge all users the same monthly or quarterly charge. Many water enterprises establish a charge against the community's general fund to recover the costs of supplying fire hydrants. The charge is usually based on an estimate of water used in fire fighting and of the peak demand generated by a large fire. A general rule in setting water rates, or charges for any enterprise, is to use the simplest rate structure that still provides customer equity. A system with only residential users does not need a complex set of rate blocks, while a community with a number of different industries probably does.

A recent trend in water enterprise charges has been toward the use of increasing-block rates. The rate structure is the reverse of the traditional declining-block structure, with users paying a higher per-gallon rate as their use increases. This type of rate structure provides a powerful incentive to conserve water and it also minimizes the cost of water for residential users. It can create heavy burdens on large industrial users, who may be tempted to seek other sources for their water or to relocate their operations. A simple alternative that reduces water costs for lower-income residents is to modify the increasing-block (or flat-rate) structure so that the first few thousand gallons are offered at the lowest rate.

### *Wastewater Treatment*

Unlike water supply, wastewater treatment has been a public service since its inception. Until the past few decades, however, treatment standards were minimal and costs low. As a result, many communities did not establish their wastewater systems as enterprises; they simply paid the costs from general revenues. Adoption of the Federal Water Pollution Control Act in 1972 and the Clean Water Act in 1977 raised the standard, cost, and visibility of wastewater treatment. Local governments across the nation are still adjusting to this new environment.

While the Environmental Protection Agency (EPA) offered billions of dollars in grants for treatment facility construction, many local governments delayed making necessary capital improvements, since EPA was slow in enforcing requirements to improve treatment. Beginning in the mid-1980s, however, EPA stepped up enforcement efforts and began reducing the amounts available for grants. As a result, many communities faced the need for major capital investments in their wastewater collection and treatment systems. The need to borrow large sums for capital needs and to operate the expensive new facilities placed new emphasis on the need for fully self-supporting wastewater enterprises.

Like water supply, charging for wastewater treatment services is now standard among local governments. Also like water supply, the objective of most wastewater treatment utilities is the recovery of revenues from operations sufficient to pay for both the utility's capital costs and operation and maintenance costs. The EPA requires that communities that have received federal grant funds recover operating and maintenance costs through user fees. The mechanisms used to recover costs should ensure that utility customers are treated equitably and that the system is efficient and, to the extent possible, simple.

There are some special characteristics of wastewater service that must be kept in mind when setting rates. Cost recovery depends on cost identification. It is essential that the wastewater utility identify all costs that are to be recovered from rates and realistically estimate how those costs will increase during the life of a given rate structure. Labor costs are probably the single most important cost factor in operating a wastewater utility. Materials and supplies include chemicals (generally around 10 to 15 percent of the operating budget), spare parts for mechanical equipment, supplies for testing, and office equipment. Utility costs include costs for electricity (which can be second only to salaries as an operating cost), fuel oil, water, gas, and telephone service. Equipment replacement is a cost category generally included in the capital budget for replacing items such as pumps, motors, and vehicles. Funds for equipment replacement may be collected in an equipment-replacement reserve. Capital costs are often financed through the issuance of bonds. In that case, debt-service costs (principal and interest) must be considered in establishing user fees.

To develop equitable rates, the utility must determine the relationship between the characteristics of the waste it treats and the cost to treat it. Wastewater differs from one community to the next and from one user to the next in its (1) flow, (2) biochemical oxygen demand (BOD), (3) suspended solids, and (4) heavy metals contents. If a utility serves only residential customers, flow may be the only operating data necessary. When there are industrial and commercial customers as well, more extensive data on the strength (concentration) of the flow will be necessary.

Once total flow and the content of the waste are known, the utility must determine how each waste characteristic contributes to its cost. Collection costs, for example, result from the flow and the number of customers. Sludge disposal costs vary with solids content, while treatment costs depend on both the flow and the strength of the waste. Other costs, such as administration and customer service, depend only on the number of customers and not on the characteristics of their waste. Once costs of each component of the system and characteristics of all waste treated are known, the utility can calculate the unit cost of serving each customer, treating each gallon of waste, and removing each pound of solids, BOD, or metal.

To determine the rate structure, the utility staff should estimate the content of waste from the typical residential customer and thus the cost to serve that customer. Rates can then be established to recover that cost of service from every residential customer. The same can be done for commercial and industrial customers, though it may be necessary to look at differences between industries or businesses more carefully. The rate structure will depend on the mix of customers and the ability to measure the wastewater characteristics and water consumption of the utility's customers. The most common rate structures include

- *Flat rates (e.g., $7.00 per month:* the simplest rate structure, used when there are no water meters and all users are residential
- *Volume rates (e.g., $2.50 per thousand gallons):* used when there are flow records but no ability to differentiate the strength of flow among users
- *Volume rates plus surcharge (e.g., $2.50 per thousand gallons for all customers plus $1.00 per thousand pounds of BOD for customers with high BOD levels):* used when the volume and strength of sewage can be identified
- *Ad valorem taxes:* can be used if there is a close relationship between ad valorem taxation and the level of use of the wastewater utility

A monthly service charge is often used in conjunction with volume and surcharge rates.

### *Electric Utilities*

In 1986 operating revenues for electric utilities in the United States amounted to $184.6 billion. Of this total, $21.7 billion (11.7 percent) flowed to public electric systems. Investor-owned utilities accounted for $135.8 billion (73.6 percent). The balance of revenues were accounted for by Rural Electrification Administration borrowers and federal systems. Public systems served 14 million customers, compared to 77.7 million for investor-owned utilities.[3] With the exception of the profit motive found in private utilities, the pricing decisions for electric utilities are based on similar criteria.

Residential rates are made up of three components. *Customer costs* are established per customer and are essentially unaffected by the size and pattern of individual customer use. These costs include meter reading, billing, bill collecting, and consumer records. *Demand costs* relate to the size of the electrical capacity of the system and are often expressed as so much per kilowatt of demand. Demand costs include the costs of investment in production facilities and demand charges in wholesale power bills. Demand costs change as production or consumption varies and are expressed as so much per kilowatt of demand. They include the costs of investment in production facilities and demand charges in wholesale power bills. *Energy costs* change as production or consumption varies and are expressed as so much per kilowatt of energy used. Energy costs include those associated with fuel usage expenses for generating plants and the energy charge in wholesale power bills.

There are a number of different rate-setting techniques for residential customers. Without going into great detail on the calculations under the alternatives, it is fair to say that residential customers usually pay a rate with a specified customer charge plus a charge per kilowatt-hour of energy used. The demand cost is generally recovered through an added charge per kilowatt-hour.

The prices that electric utilities charge for service to industrial customers are generally made up of four components. Two, energy and demand costs, are identical to those found in establishing residential rates. *Fuel adjustment cost* reflects increases in the electric utility's fuel costs, expressed in dollars per kilowatt-hour, and the *power factor* measures the ratio of the apparent power available to the customer (after accounting for resistance) to the true power provided by the utility. Electric utilities generally charge a penalty to customers with a low power factor as a result of the additional generating capacity needed to make up for power resistance.[4]

The typical industrial electric bill may be determined through a formula that combines the four factors in a way that covers costs in an equitable fashion. Prices must be responsive to the sometimes competing goals of sound financial management and sound public policy.

### *Solid Waste Collection*

One of the most immediate and widespread problems facing metropolitan areas is disposing of the massive volume of debris that cities produce. The National Council on Public Works estimates that this country annually produces between 130 and 165 million tons of solid waste.[5] The vast majority of this waste finds its way into one of the thousands of landfills operating around the United States.

Clearly, municipal solid waste poses a threat to the environment. It is also a threat to the fiscal health of many municipalities. Not only are the tip fees (the charge per ton for disposing of waste in a municipal landfill) that cities pay growing, but transportation costs for solid waste are climbing as urban areas expand and nearby landfills close. Suburban communities in the New York City metropolitan area have begun to ship waste to landfills in Pennsylvania and upstate New York. Philadelphia has been forced to transport waste to landfills as distant as Maryland and Virginia. Once the waste arrives at the landfill, jurisdictions are facing ever-increasing costs for disposing of that waste. Tipping fees, which were commonly in the $10 range as recently as ten years ago, have risen to over $100 in some areas as landfills become more scarce and environmental regulations more costly to abide by.[6]

Municipal landfills operated by governmental entities should collect revenues sufficient to pay for the following:

- The cost of acquiring the land for the landfill
- Development costs, including geotechnical, environmental, siting, permits, civil engineering, legal, and financial services
- Capital equipment
- Operating and maintenance expenses
- Debt service on bonds issued for site construction
- Final closure costs
- Post-closure maintenance and monitoring

Revenues may be obtained from three principal sources: tipping fees may be charged for each ton of waste delivered; a periodic utility charge may be applied to customers of the service; and the jurisdiction may support solid-waste disposal through general revenue sources. Tipping fees are generally not charged to municipal waste collectors, private haulers under contract with the municipality, or private citizens living within the jurisdiction of the entity. Tipping fees are, however, generally charged to municipal haulers from other jurisdictions, private haulers not under contract with the municipality, and individuals not within the jurisdiction.

An increasing number of communities that collect garbage at curbside are establishing enterprise mechanisms for the collection process. This trend can be expected to continue as landfill costs rise and as public officials develop recycling programs and seek ways to discourage unnecessary solid-waste production. Collection fees can cover both the cost of picking up the solid waste and the cost of landfilling it. As with most utility charges, this is usually done by estimating the annual solid waste collected from the average customer and setting charges so that all users pay that average amount. "Metered garbage charges," in which users pay on a per-container basis (often requiring the use of community-provided containers), are also gaining in popularity due to their role in encouraging conservation.

### *Stormwater Management*

Although often treated as the poor cousin of sewerage treatment and disposal, there is growing recognition of the importance of managing stormwater runoff and urban drainage in a municipality's overall public utilities system. This recognition will likely increase in the future as current and proposed EPA water-quality standards for the nonpoint discharge of urban runoff are adopted and enforced.

The problem of urban runoff and stormwater management affects both older urban communities and developing suburban areas. Older urban cities with combined sanitary and stormwater collection and disposal systems often suffer from combined sewer overflows during peak storm events. Regulatory action by the EPA to limit these overflows, either through separating the two systems or through building on-line storage, would impose significant cost burdens on these cities.

Urbanizing areas are faced with a different problem. While the sanitary and storm sewer systems may have been constructed as separate systems, existing drainage culverts and channels are often incapable of meeting the runoff associated with new development. As development occurs and the percentage of impervious land area increases, the volume of stormwater runoff and its intensity increases. This development pattern burdens existing downstream drainageways and retention facilities, often resulting in increased incidents of flooding. If federal water-quality standards are imposed by the EPA on point stormwater discharges, retrofitting these facilities to provide needed treatment will add yet further costs to these systems.

Recognition of drainage and urban runoff as a separate public utility service has not won universal acceptance within the public works profession. Historically, drainage facilities have been planned in conjunction with the construction of streets and roadways and therefore are felt to be in the domain of the transportation or street maintenance department. In communities with a combined sanitary/storm sewer system, stormwater collection and treatment is often the responsibility of the sewer utility. Urban runoff and drainage is, however, increasingly becoming an issue of water-quality management, and for this reason more logically belongs within the purview of the sewer utility.

To fund stormwater capital and ongoing maintenance needs, municipalities have begun establishing drainage utilities, either as part of an existing sewer utility or as a separate enterprise activity. These drainage utilities are typically patterned after sewer utilities and in most cases utilize a cost-of-service-based user-charge system to recover their annual revenue requirements from properties within their service area. In some communities, regional drainage utilities have been created in order to provide a consistent level of drainage services to all properties within a single drainage basin or within overlapping basins.

Annual revenue requirements for stormwater utilities can be divided into capital costs and operating costs, and then further allocated to parameters of the rate model according to the services provided by the utility. Property characteristics are used to allocate costs to customer classes and develop rates and charges. Factors such as property front footage, property square footage, and ratio of impervious area to total area can all be used to allocate costs and establish fees. Bills can either be incorporated in the regular sewer bill or—in the case of a separate drainage utility—be sent out separately on a periodic basis. In some instances user fees are billed on the property-tax statement.

### *Road Maintenance*

Another example of financial innovations for funding infrastructure improvements is the creation of road-maintenance districts or utilities. The purpose of these entities is to provide road-maintenance services (e.g., street cleaning, pavement maintenance, signing) to property owners within a defined service area. Instead of relying on general government revenues or dedicated funds such as gas taxes to pay for these services, road-service districts are funded by fees and charges that reflect the cost of providing service to individual properties.

Funding for a road-maintenance district typically comes through fees and charges collected from property owners within the district. Fees and charges, as opposed to a general tax, are used as the cost-recovery scheme for two important reasons: (1) Unlike taxes, which must be apportioned uniformly, fees and charges can be linked to particular cost-causative factors. This enables some degree of price discrimination between different types of properties. (2) Fees and charges, because they are not taxes, apply to all properties within the road-service district, including public nonprofit activities.

Road-maintenance fees can be based on a cost-of-service framework that is utilized by other utilities. Revenue requirements can include both operating and capital costs. Operating costs would include items such as personal services or materials and services required to perform various road-maintenance activities.

Also included as operating costs are administrative expenses associated with preparing bills and collecting charges from properties. A road-service district may also incur capital costs. These capital costs might include expenditures for major equipment or for building or rebuilding roadways. Capital costs could also include debt service on bonds sold to finance capital expenditures.

Like other types of utilities, developing cost-of-service rates and charges requires establishing customer classes based on homogeneous usage characteristics. For a road-service district, demand and usage factors will often be linked to the number of trips that a particular type of property generates. Trip-generation factors can be obtained either through actual measurement using counters placed at driveways leading to/from a particular property or through estimation using trip-factor data published by the Institute of Traffic Engineers. Trip factors can be further refined to reflect average trip length, vacancy rates, etc. Property size or property front footage can also be used to estimate a property's demand for service, particularly for those cost items that vary with the length of roadway.

Operating and capital costs can be allocated to customer classes based on unit costs of service (e.g., cost per vehicle-mile traveled, per front-foot) and customer-class demand. Fees and charges for road-maintenance services can be designed on either a flat or variable rate basis. Homogeneous customer classes lend themselves to flat charges, calculated either monthly or annually. Customer classes with wide variation in size or usage can be based more equitably based on their property and trip-making characteristics.

### *Toll Facilities*

As of 1985 there were a total of 240 toll facilities (including bridges, tunnels, and roads) in operation as part of the nation's highway system. Of this total, 210 were publicly owned and operated, including 65 of the 72 toll roads.[7] Toll roads are primarily an East Coast and Midwest phenomenon. No publicly owned toll roads are currently in operation on the West Coast, although some are under consideration. Of the 5,176 miles of toll highways in operation across the country, the majority of this mileage is part of the Interstate highway system.

Most publicly owned toll facilities are operated by either special-purpose public corporations or by state highway departments or transportation agencies. For the most part, these facilities are constructed and operated solely from toll revenues, or revenues collected in conjunction with toll operations (e.g., concession revenues).

Federal law prohibits toll collection on any portion of the federal highway system that has received federal funding. There have, however, been some exceptions to federal law, although these exceptions generally apply only to toll bridges and tunnels or toll road approaches that are incorporated into the Interstate highway system. These "Section 129 Agreements" (named after Section 129 of Title 23 of the U.S. Code, which deals with federal prohibitions against toll collections on federally supported highways) restrict the use of tolls to the costs of building, operating, and maintaining the toll facility, with the further requirement that tolls be discontinued after all construction costs have been paid for.

Toll facilities are operated using either closed or open toll-collection facilities. Closed collection systems utilize barriers at facility access points to collect tolls from all users. This type of collection system works particularly well for bridges and tunnels where access is relatively easy to restrict. Toll roads using a closed toll-collection system tend to limit access along the toll route and rely on toll plazas at each end and toll booths at exit/entrance ramps to collect tolls from vehicles. Open systems, on the other hand, are not designed to collect tolls from all users, but instead enable certain local trips to be made toll free. Open systems rely on toll barriers placed at selected intervals to collect tolls from vehicles.[8]

There is a wide disparity in the per-mile charges for toll facilities. On average, interurban toll roads are less expensive to travel than their urban expressway counterparts. Passenger car tolls for interurban roads vary from 1.8 to 9.1 cents per mile, as opposed to a range of 5 to 7 cents per mile on urban toll roads.[9] The wide range in per-mile fees can be explained by differences in construction costs, interest rates on bonds sold to finance construction, right-of-way acquisition costs, etc. Toll fees typically vary by type of vehicle (passenger car, multiaxle truck, etc.). For toll roads, trip length is also used to determine the toll amount.

Like many other public infrastructure improvements, toll facilities require enormous initial capital expenditures to build or extend facilities. To finance these capital expenditures and smooth out cash-flow requirements over time, debt financing is heavily relied on. Most of the bonds sold to finance toll facilities have been issued as revenue bonds, with principal and interest on the bonds paid from toll revenues.

Toll facilities are highly leveraged systems that are subject to competition and are susceptible to external economic events. Given this operating environment, revenue bonds payable solely from toll revenues, assuming no credit enhancement, are not likely to receive upper investment ratings. For example, of the 46 toll-backed revenue bond issues rated by Standard & Poor's Corporation, only one issue is rated higher than A+. Issuers could choose to place more stringent requirements on their financial operations (e.g., higher debt-coverage ratios, larger maintenance reserve funds); these requirements, however, would put additional pressure on toll rates and might end up being counterproductive. Significant improvements in the credit ratings assigned to toll-backed revenue bonds will likely come only through credit enhancement (bond insurance, letter-of-credit liquidity support) or through an additional revenue pledge such as state motor vehicle revenues.

### *Public Parking*

To enhance the viability of a central business district for both commercial and retail activities, many municipalities have established enterprise funds as a means to operate off-street parking facilities. These enterprise funds are designed to be self-supporting through the collection of parking fees and charges. In some instances, separate public authorities are created for the purposes of financing and operating the parking structures.

Parking enterprise funds depend primarily on revenues collected at parking structures to pay operating and capital costs. Parking fees and charges vary widely from city to city and are heavily influenced by overall parking demand and the cost of parking and transportation options. Parking rates can also reflect public policy decisions. For example, some cities structure their parking rates to encourage short-term, shopper-oriented parkers to bolster downtown retail activities. Multistory parking facilities in downtown core areas often devote the ground floor level to retail activities, with the resulting lease revenues helping to support garage operations. Some parking systems also include on-street parking revenues in their revenue base, further enhancing the system's financial stability and ability to manage public parking within a defined service area. Some parking enterprises assess a fee against benefitting property owners (e.g., retail stores, office buildings) to pay some or all of the costs of operating facilities.

Unlike public enterprises such as water and sewer utilities, which act as monopolies in the delivery of services, parking enterprises often compete with privately owned facilities for market share. If ownership of parking facilities is widely dispersed, the ability to raise rates in a timely manner may be affected. While other utilities develop a schedule of rates and charges based on the cost of providing service, parking enterprises, because they often do not control the supply of parking available to consumers, are more likely to be forced to charge rates that are based on what the market will bear. This pricing practice may or may not result in a rate structure that produces sufficient revenues to maintain strong financial operations. Parking enterprises are also subject to competition from other modes of transportation. As parking rates are increased, users may switch to mass transit or car pooling, thus reducing parking system revenues.

### *Public Mass Transportation*

Public mass transportation enterprises operate a variety of transportation modes including motor buses, light and heavy rail vehicles, street trolleys, van pools, ferryboats, and cable cars. Although all mass transit systems were initially privately owned and operated, almost all major mass transit systems within the United States are now operated by public agencies. The mass transit industry was characterized in its early years of operation as largely self-supporting, with farebox collections providing sufficient revenues to meet operating expenses. This industry trend continued until the early 1960s, when rising operating costs and declining ridership combined to force many transit systems into the red.

Passage of the Urban Mass Transportation Act of 1964 served to breathe new life into the ailing transit industry by providing substantial federal assistance to help fund capital outlays. Transit systems expanded throughout the country with the federal government financing two-thirds of the capital cost. Even with system expansion, ridership during the last two decades has continued to decline. To support ongoing transit operations, state and local governments have had to take a much larger role in financing transit operations, usually through a dedicated tax (e.g., sales, payroll) or through direct appropriations.

Few transit systems now recover all operating costs from fares, much less the costs of capital and debt service. Fares are not set on a full-cost-recovery method, as they are for most utility operations. Instead, the fare is set at a level that attempts to maximize the contribution from fare revenue, considering such factors as the cost of making the same trip by automobile, the cost of transit trips in similar communities, and the expected ridership loss due to fare increases. Most transit systems have a flat fare for all trips, with senior citizens, the handicapped, and children receiving discounts. There is a trend to charge higher rates for premium services such as express buses. Many transit systems have surcharges for rush-hour service or for very long trips.

### *Port Facilities*

The nation's port facilities consist of 188 major deepwater ports (ports with a minimum depth of 25 feet adjacent landside dock and cargo-handling facilities) located along the Atlantic, Pacific, Gulf, and Great Lakes coasts, and 175 inland waterway ports served by 21,100 miles of shallow-draft (less than 14 feet deep) waterways. The bulk of the inland waterway ports and terminals are located along the Mississippi River.

While the federal government has assumed responsibility for developing and maintaining harbors and inland waterways, state and local governments and the private sector have largely been responsible for the development and operation of landside facilities, including construction of wharves and piers, docking and terminal facilities, cargo loading/unloading equipment, and dockside rail and truck transport improvements.

The organization of public port enterprises varies widely and can include independent authorities governed by an independent board, agencies of the state government, or city departments. Port enterprises are designed to be self-supporting from revenues collected through port operations, including fees charged for shipping services (dockage, wharfage, storage, etc.), facility rentals, and other fees and charges collected in conjunction with port operations. Some ports have diversified their revenue base by leasing unused waterfront property for commercial/retail developments.

To help support the investment in new facilities, some ports have received voter approval to collect property taxes either to support ongoing operations or to pay debt service on bonds sold to finance port improvements. These additional sources of revenue provide port enterprises with more operating flexibility while helping to provide access to capital at a reasonable cost. Public willingness to support port operations with taxes is indicative of the role these facilities play in a community. Ports are an important part of a local economy and can play a crucial role in economic development.

Successful, self-supporting port systems generally share the following characteristics:

1. Proximity to major sources of export products
2. Diversity in export/import product mix and a balance between imports and exports
3. Proximity to a growing population or distribution center
4. Access to inland transportation modes
5. Modern and efficient terminal facilities and equipment

While port operators and managers will always be affected by external economic and political factors that are beyond their control, the overall management plan should focus on developing as many of the preceding attributes as possible. Effective management and a diverse revenue base will enable port operations to adapt to changes in the national and global economy.

### *Airports*

Like the development of port systems, airports represent joint undertakings of the public and private sector. Initially, the federal government played a major role in the development of airport facilities through contracts awarded to private carriers to haul postal freight and through grants awarded to municipal airports for the construction of airfield and terminal improvements. Federal construction grants were funded by a tax on airline tickets, with the tax revenue paid into a trust fund dedicated to funding airport improvements.

Up until 1975 the airline industry operated under a system of regulation established by the Civil Aeronautics Act of 1938. Under this act, routes and fares were subject to federal review and approval, and competition between airlines was limited. A feature of this regulatory framework was airline route systems that followed a linear pattern, with passengers moving between airlines in route to their final destination. The deregulation of the airline industry that began in 1975 transformed the manner in which airlines competed for customers. As low cost carriers entered the marketplace, existing airlines cut back service to small communities and improved their service between major markets. To handle increased passenger volumes, hub-and-spoke route systems were developed to provide more efficient service throughout a carrier's route system.

Most airports with commercial service are origin and destination (OD) airports, whose sole purposes is to move people to and from one urban area. While the airline industry itself has experienced substantial changes over the past decade, the success of OD airport operations as a public enterprise is still heavily influenced by one major factor that is key to their overall success: strength of the local economy and the demand for air travel. If the local market area served by an airport enterprise is strong and vibrant, this will create demand for air travel. The competitiveness of the airline industry will respond to this demand in the form of improved levels of service, which in itself further increases the demand for air travel by making travel more convenient.

Airport operations are typically financed from four major revenue sources:

- Rental income from airlines
- Revenue from fixed-base operators and concessionaires
- Landing fees from airlines
- Revenues from parking operations

Rental income usually represents the largest portion of airport revenues. To help provide revenue stability and to assist in administering the collection of revenues, airline-use agreements are negotiated between the airport and its carriers. Airline-use agreements set forth the manner in which landing fees, terminal rents, and other charges will be calculated and assessed to the carrier airlines. Because landing fees are charged on the basis of aircraft landing weights, landing-fee revenues will vary with airline activity. Terminal rentals, on the other hand, are based on the amount of terminal area occupied by each airline and tend to be fixed.

Although airline-use agreements add to revenue stability, the financial success of an airport is ultimately linked to underlying passenger demand.

If financially weak airlines discontinue service, the air traffic demand will be met by other carriers. While this fact insulates O&D airports from the financial problems of individual airlines, it does leave them vulnerable to downturns in the local economy, which affect passenger demand.

While the trend in the airline industry has been toward the development of hub airports (thirty-five are now in operation or under construction), hub airports may not necessarily enhance airport financial operations. Airports that issue additional debt to fund facilities that serve the needs of a weak carrier assume substantial risk if the hub carrier's traffic projections fail to materialize, or if the hub carrier ceases operations. An airport, however, with strong OD passenger demand, a growing local and regional economy, and strong hub carriers could improve overall financial performance through hub development.

## *ORGANIZING THE ENTERPRISE*

Governmental enterprises are organized in a variety of ways that reflect the type of service, the regulatory environment, and the breadth and scope of the market. Under any form, the effective management of a governmental enterprise depends on direction and control of operations under a single administrator who performs management functions within the guidelines established by the enterprise's governing authorities. The following is a brief review of the most common organization forms of enterprise management.

### *Single Community*

The most common administrative pattern for governmental enterprises involves service provision by one community that owns and operates the facility. In this case, the administration of the enterprise may be directed through the public works department of the local government or a separate department devoted to the specific enterprise (i.e., the water works department).

Day-to-day operation of the enterprise is generally the task of administrative staff and managers. The broader policy decisions, such as pricing and capital-investment decisions, are usually made by the community's elected officials or by a board appointed by elected leaders. Under this form, the finances of the enterprise are accounted for in the community's financial statements and generally reported within its enterprise funds.

### *Joint Ownership*

There are occasions when two or more communities may opt to jointly operate an enterprise. This may be advantageous when it is economically infeasible for one jurisdiction to offer the service because of a limited market, limited expertise, or other limiting factors.

The ownership of the facilities is generally proportional to the capital investment by the participants. In the case of debt financing, debt is issued by, and remains an obligation of, each of the participating jurisdictions rather than the facility under joint ownership. This is true even though the primary revenues pledged to repay the debt are those received from each jurisdiction's interest in the facility.

Clearly defining the administration and responsibilities of the participating jurisdictions at the inception of a jointly owned enterprise is critical. The procedures for administering and financing the needs of the facility need to be ironed out, as well as the methods for billing and collections. It is common for the participating jurisdictions to form a joint body composed of elected or appointed officials from each.[10]

### *Special or Multipurpose District*

The difference between the joint ownership arrangement described above and a special district approach lies in the degree of financial and administrative autonomy practiced by the enterprise. While formation of special districts is usually closely defined in state law and can vary considerably from one state to another, a special or multipurpose district generally possesses more authority to combine the resources of member communities and plan the operations of the facility.

Contrary to the joint ownership case, where financing and fee collection are initiated and conducted by the jurisdictions themselves, the district approach establishes an authority empowered to collect user charges and may issue debt in the district's name, even though the debt may carry the full faith and credit of each of the member jurisdictions. Sometimes the member jurisdictions will individually issue debt for capital investment in the district facilities, as in the case of joint ownership.

The district is generally administered and managed by an elected or appointed board that represents the participating jurisdictions. This board will manage the planning, construction, and operation of district facilities, will develop the collection and distribution techniques, and may have powers extending to the definition of district boundaries and service area.

### *Independent Authority*

Although an independent authority may be characterized by a multijurisdictional scope, its administration and operations are conducted with a greater degree of independence from communities within its service area than in the cases of joint ownership and the service district. Typically, an authority is established to provide some revenue-generating service and is empowered to issue revenue bonds in the authority's name backed solely by the stream of user charges. The authority usually lacks the ability to levy taxes against property within its service area, although there are examples to the contrary.

The lack of taxing power is a double-edged sword. On one hand, the authority does not face debt limitations that may apply to the communities within the authority service area. On the other hand, because of the greater risk involved, debt backed solely by revenues requires a higher interest cost than debt supported by a full faith and credit (general-obligation) pledge.

The management and administration of an authority is conducted by a body that resembles the board that oversees the operations of a service district. The nature of representation of the communities within the service area is often a matter of state statutes.

## *EVALUATING FINANCIAL PERFORMANCE*

Enterprise activities must use effective financial planning in order to minimize long-run costs. Sound financial performance, both historical and projected, is essential to demonstrate the ability to meet long-term financial obligations and in obtaining capital at the lowest possible cost. Financial planning must also consider the effects that changes in demand impose on system unit costs and financial performance. Enterprise activities must be able to anticipate what impact changes in demand will have on financial performance to ensure that long-term financial health will be maintained.

For many enterprise activities and other governmental services, the measurement of financial performance is limited to determining whether enough funds are on hand to pay bills when they become due. For enterprises with outstanding debt, performance standards may have to be extended to include the calculation of debt-service coverage to determine compliance with outstanding bond ordinances. Given the complex environment in which municipal enterprises operate, these limited measures of financial performance cannot provide managers with sufficient information to ensure long-term financial health. A more comprehensive set of performance indicators derived from several sources—including enterprise fund financial statements, system operations, service area demographics, and comparable activities—will provide a much clearer picture of current financial status.

The measurement of financial performance is accomplished through the calculation of financial ratios, with the financial statements (operating statement and balance sheet) serving as the starting point for their calculation. Each ratio can help to provide insight about the ability of an enterprise to meet certain aspects of its overall financial operating requirements. These measurements of financial performance can be designed to evaluate both the short-term and long-term financial health of the enterprise. Table 20-1 shows four ratios that can be used to evaluate short-term financial performance. The first three ratios use balance-sheet information to determine the ability of an enterprise activity to generate cash flow sufficient to meet current liabilities. The fourth ratio utilizes budgetary information to calculate the amount of unappropriated funds that are available to meet unforeseen operating expenditures.

Although financial ratios provide a very important picture of a system's historical and current financial performance, in addition to providing useful guidelines for developing financial plans and forecasts, other ratios and indicators can also be useful in developing a comprehensive picture of financial health.

TABLE 20-1
*Financial Performance Ratios*

| Ratio | Formula for Computation | Significance | Recommended Level |
|---|---|---|---|
| Current or working capital ratio | current assets ÷ liabilities | Primary test of short-term liquidity. Indicates ability to meet current obligations from current assets as a going concern. Measure of adequacy of working capital. | At least 2.0 |
| Acid-test or quick ratio | quick assets ÷ current liabilities | A more severe test of immediate liquidity than the current ratio. Tests ability to meet sudden demands upon current assets. | At least 1.0 |
| Working capital to total assets | working capital ÷ total assets | Indicates relative liquidity of total assets distribution of resources employed | Sufficient to provide at least the minimum levels |
| Fund balance ratio | unappropriated ending fund balance (operating fund) ÷ operating expenses | Indicates ability to meet unforeseen operating expenditures | 10% |

SOURCE: Adapted from Glenn A. Welsch and Charles T. Zlatkovich, *Intermediate Accounting*, (Homewood, IL: Richard Irwin, Inc., 1976), Exhibit 24-7, p. 1026.

These other performance ratios and standards are somewhat more subjective and should be tailored to meet the particular needs of each enterprise activity.

Table 20-2 provides additional performance indicators that can be used to assess the overall health of an enterprise activity. Although the performance ratios shown in this table are designed for use by a water or sewer utility, they could be adapted for use by other utility operations. While some of the ratios shown in the table are based on financial information, broader service area and demographic information are also utilized to assess issues such as service affordability and market penetration. Another important performance standard is a cost comparison with adjacent communities or with communities of a similar size. This cost-comparison information enables an enterprise's competitiveness to be assessed and is often used as a partial justification for additional rate increases (assuming that the rates to be increased are lower than those charged by surrounding jurisdictions).

Financial and performance ratios are an effective means of evaluating historic and current financial performance. Inclusion of these financial ratios in a comprehensive financial model provides enterprise managers with the means to

TABLE 20-2

*Other Performance Ratios*

| Item | Formula for Computation | Significance | Recommended Level |
|---|---|---|---|
| Delinquency ratio | delinquent bills ÷ total billings | Measures effect of utility cost and/or local economic performance on timely payment. | 2% or lower |
| Revenue growth ratio | % increase in operating revenues ÷ % increase in operating expenditures | Measures ability to maintain revenue growth in excess of inflation and real cost increases. | Greater than 1.0 |
| Affordability | annual single family bill ÷ median service area household income | Measures overall affordability and ability to pass on higher rate increases. | 1.5% or less for water or sewer |
| Customer growth ratio | % increases in new connections ÷ % increase in service area population | Measures market penetration with respect to increased service area growth. | Greater than 1.0 |
| Comparable rates* | NA | Measures relative rates by comparing with other local and regional utilities. | NA |

* Requires compiling rate information from neighboring cities or from cities of comparable size to compare relative costs.

evaluate quickly the strengths and weaknesses of their financial plans and to make incremental refinements as needed. The use of ratios in the financial planning process should not serve as a substitute for management input and decision making, but rather should be used as a means to better understand how alternative plans and strategies affect long-term financial performance.

## *CAPITAL AND RELATED FEES*

Rapid growth in many areas of the country has put intense pressure on many communities' infrastructure systems. They must grow in order to serve new residents and businesses, but the costs of growth can be staggering. One method of reducing the burden on existing customers is the user of capital-related fees, often known as impact fees or system development charges. A related technique is to guarantee that capital costs will be recovered regardless of future demographic changes through the use of availability or dedicated capacity charges. Many enterprises use some or all of these fees to assign the cost of new development to the new residents or businesses. Often, they recover not only the direct costs of extending water, sewer, or electric lines, but also recover a contribution for prior investments in capacity of the existing system.

### *Availability and Dedicated Capacity Charges*

A developing trend within enterprise finance is to establish dedicated-capacity charges for larger commercial and industrial customers. These are charges designed to recover the ongoing costs of plant capacity required to serve customers with a significant portion of demand. Dedicated capacity charges serve to protect the utility from investing in greater plant capacity for a limited number of large customers, only to find that those customers demand less than anticipated. Some communities structure their charges to protect against business closures as well. Two types of dedicated-capacity charges are the availability charge and the demand contract charge.

The availability charge is designed to recover a utility's capital and operating costs related to the construction of facilities that benefit identifiable future customers and require increased plant capacity. The charge is generally made between the time when the service is available to potential customers and the time when the service actually goes into effect. The availability charge does not defray the costs of services rendered, but pays the costs of increasing the plant's capacity whether that capacity is utilized or not.

An availability charge may be appropriate for a new water system in which the existing connected-customer base is small, but where a minimum level of revenue is necessary to make installation of an extension to an existing water system financially feasible.

The demand contract charge protects an enterprise when a small number of large customers make up a significant proportion of the utility's revenue stream, and loss of the business of any one of these customers would adversely affect the utility's ability to continue operations. In such a circumstance it is to the benefit of the utility and the customer to establish a service contract that sets forth the terms between the two parties related to the conditions under which service will be provided. Generally, a demand contract involves an agreement by the major customer to pay the fixed costs related to additional capacity for a stated period of time, whether the usage implied by that contract is taken by the customer or not.

### *System Development Charges*

As the service area for a utility expands or the demand for service shifts, a utility's capital plant must evolve to meet those changes. The costs to expand capital facilities can be extensive. Essentially, the system development charge (SDC) is a technique in which new customers become equity contributors to the costs of system expansion, including adding capacity to the existing plant and extending the system to newly developed property. As a consequence, existing customers of the utility are not forced to bear an inequitable portion of the costs for capacity unrelated to existing demand.

System development charges come in a variety of forms and are appropriate when capital improvements to a system have no direct or indirect benefit on the existing customer base, but are performed solely as a result of expanded demand by new development and customers. The system development charge is an effective means to finance the capital needs generated from the growth in demand from an expanding customer base, as well as obtaining a fair contribution from new customers for a utility's existing facilities. SDC's can go by a variety of names, including facility charges, plant investment fees, developer fees, and impact fees. Their use is not limited to enterprises, either. A growing number of communities levy system development charges for schools, roads, and other more general purposes.

There are as many ways to calculate SDCs as there are governmental enterprises. Some enterprises base SDCs on a retrospective look at historical financing costs. Others look prospectively at projected future spending. SDCs are now being developed to account for inflation and the time value of money over the period that the SDC is in place. Four of the more common methods used to determine SDCs are discussed in the following paragraphs.

*System Buy-in Charges.* The objective of the system buy-in is to force new customers to pay an "entry fee" that places them on the same financial basis as the existing customer base. In other words, after the system buy-in fee is paid, all customers will have made the same capital contribution and then will be billed at the same rate. This assumes that the new customers are using the utility's existing facilities. If the system needs to be expanded to meet additional demand, charges to pay for that expansion may be levied in addition to the system buy-in charge.

The system buy-in charge is usually determined by calculating the depreciated cost of the capital system. From that total net cost, the net cost of the facilities that serve existing customers but not new ones is deducted, leaving only the costs that will be shared by both new and existing customers. In a water-supply system, for instance, these costs would include source-of-supply costs, treatment, and storage costs. The amount of outstanding bonds is deducted from the net shared costs, since new customers will be contributing to the retirement of outstanding bonds through their user charge payments. The balance is the net investment by the existing customers into the facilities that benefit all customers, both existing and future. The system buy-in charge in this example is calculated by dividing the number of existing customers into the total net investment. Each new customer pays this amount on joining the system to bring up their investment to equal that of each existing customer. New customers will usually be required to pay separately for expanding and extending the distribution system and the accompanying services, meters, and hydrants.

*Incremental-Cost System Development Charge.* An incremental-cost system development charge is designed to control or eliminate future rate increases that might result from new development. This objective is realized by setting system development charges at a level that supports the actual new investment required by the utility as a result of the growth of new customers. Consequently, this type of system development charge should be designed to derive the cost of the system expansion, as determined by recent construction cost experience or the estimated cost of planned future improvements.

*Growth-Related Cost Allocation.* System-development charges can be structured to pay for a system's capital expansion that may not actually be constructed for several years to come. A derivative of the incremental-cost pricing method, known as the growth-related cost allocation method, allows a utility to accumulate the resources necessary for financing proposed capital investment. This technique, like the incremental-cost pricing method, requires an estimation of the future number of individuals that will move into the growth area. The utility must first determine the charge that would reflect the cost per customer if the necessary investments were made immediately (using the incremental-cost pricing basis). For construction that will be delayed, the charge should reflect the adjustment to the ultimate construction cost as the date for construction is moved forward. If the utility can expect that the cost of construction will increase annually at a rate of 10 percent, system development charges can be adjusted to reflect the change in cost. Therefore, new customers who hook up to the system a year hence will pay a system-development charge that is discounted by 10 percent for each year until construction. The SDCs for the customers as they come on line will be 10 percent higher each year, reflecting the increased construction cost.

*Value-of-Service Method.* The value-of-service method, as the name implies, is a technique in which utilities establish a system development charge based on a survey of the fees that other jurisdictions charge for similar services to new customers. This relieves the utility of some of the technical estimating and projecting necessary in other methods. Of course, the value-of-service method does require that the utility have some sense of the capital demands that growth will have on the system, as well as the ability of new users to finance that growth. Using the value-of-service approach is most effective where there is ample comparable information available. It is of limited use when comparison information is limited. The following questions can be used to determine if the fee structure from other utilities is relevant to that of a utility attempting to establish SDCs:

- Is the size of the utility, both from a service area and financial perspective, comparable?
- Is the growth that necessitated the rate structure in the comparison case similar to what can be expected?
- How do the population demographics compare?
- Would the utility characterize its use of SDCs as successful, or are there aspects of the fee structure that have changed or are expected to change?

Successful utilities depend on a variety of benefit-based fees to generate the revenues necessary for operation and capital investment. Availability and dedicated-capacity charges have a proven track record with public enterprises. They allow a system to develop according to the existing customer base.

System development charges, on the other hand, are a proven viable and effective method of cost recovery for utilities that are experiencing pressure for expansion. SDCs allow a jurisdiction to accumulate sufficient revenue to finance existing or future expansions to the system in a fair and equitable manner. The use of all benefit-based fees is increasing among enterprises and is likely to continue as intergovernmental sources of revenue become more uncertain. In order to maintain a high level of service, it is incumbent on utilities to develop user fee structures that allocate costs equitably and provide a dependable source of revenue.

## *CONCLUSION*

Governmental enterprises are going to play an increasingly important role in providing public services in years to come. Data confirm that this trend is already well established. The days when local governments could expect, and received, extensive federal assistance for local public services are over. This reality will require that local governments distribute their limited resources in the most efficient manner. It also will require that beneficiaries of those services bear a larger share of the cost of service delivery than in the past.

Governmental enterprises is one area of local finance that is responding to these emerging realities. Local government are marshaling an ever-expanding array of financing mechanisms to pay for public services. The continued trend toward sophisticated benefit-based financing portends increasingly equitable and efficient public service provision.

## *NOTES*

1. Advisory Commission on Intergovernmental Relations, *Local Revenue Diversification: User Charges*, SR-6, (Washington: ACIR, October 1987), p. 10.

2. Safe Drinking Water Act, 42, U.S.C. 300 et seq. For the 1986 amendments, see PL 99-339.

3. 1988 Public Power Directory, American Public Power Association, page D-1.

4. Brown, Robert J., and Yanuck, Rudolph R., *Life Cycle Costing: A Practical Guide for Energy Managers* (Atlanta, GA: The Fairmont Press, Inc., 1980), pp. 84–85.

5. Clunie, Jeffrey F., et al., "Report on Solid Waste" (Washington: National Council on Public Works, 1987), p. 19.

6. *Ibid.*, p. 20.

7. *Ibid.*, p. 74.

8. Federal Highway Administration, *Toll Facilities in the United States* (Washington: Government Printing Office, April 1985), p. 6.

9. Schneider, Suzanne B., *Toll Financing of U.S. Highways* (Washington: Congressional Budget Office, December 1985), pp. 44–45.

10. U.S. Army Corps of Engineers, *Waterborne Commerce of the United States.* Part 5: National Summaries.

# 21
# *Computers in Local Finance*

Jerry Mechling

THE FIRST computers were for calculations involved with military code-breaking and ballistics, for the census, and for payroll recordkeeping in very large organizations, often government organizations. Throughout the fifties, sixties, seventies, and eighties—and now the nineties—computers have been applied heavily to financial recordkeeping and reporting. The management of computing has been the province, by and large, of technical and financial specialists.

No more. The costs of technology have decreased radically relative to manual methods. As a result, computing has moved out of its isolation in the "back office" and into pervasive use from the desks, cars, and even the briefcases of government organizations everywhere. These trends raise new problems as well as new opportunities for financial managers. This chapter will focus first on the evolution of computing in government, next on major applications, and finally on management issues and the future.

Our broad theme is that the essential nature of the "computing problem" has changed. We used to worry about the automation of preexisting, high-volume, routinized work; now, in addition, we need to think about using computers for entirely new ways of organizing and delivering government services. Success now and in the future will require political vision and skill even more than technical and financial expertise.

## *THE EVOLUTION OF COMPUTING IN GOVERNMENT*

Why are we more interested in computing than we used to be? A major reason is cost. The price of computing has fallen over the past thirty years by the almost unimaginable factor of 5,000 to 1! The unit costs of processing continue to fall about 25 percent per year, every year.[1] If you haven't looked at the cost effectiveness of an application within the last three years, it's probably time to look again.

Large changes in price lead to changes in usage. Relative to manual methods, computing has a high setup cost for systems acquisition and programming, then a low operating cost to return the investment over time. Early applications were affordable only for highly routine tasks such as payroll and accounting. These were well-structured and therefore relatively inexpensive to program; once programmed, the applications returned the investment quickly because they were stable and were run so often.

As technology has advanced, however, it has become cost-effective to computerize even less routine and more complex tasks; computing has become useful throughout the organization, among managers as well as clerks. We see widespread use of complex financial models, electronic mail, and external databases.

We can understand important managerial elements of the history of computing by dividing applications into several categories. Specifically, we can divide by the degree of change sought (efficiency, effectiveness, or transformation) and by the target group (individual worker, functional unit, or the entire organization and its relationships with external groups). Figure 21-1 presents these categories along with descriptive names for typical applications in each.[2]

### *Era I: Transaction Processing*

The first era of computing focused on financial transactions and "traditional" applications such as payroll. The typical goal was efficiency through reduction or avoidance of clerical costs. Since the routines to computerize were readily observable, programming costs were low. The back-office nature of applications permitted them to be run inexpensively in batch mode (i.e., data in on Friday, reports out by the following Wednesday). Success could be judged by measurable economic return.

A variant emerged when on-line systems made it possible to share resources

FIGURE 21-1
*Three Eras of Computer Applications*

| | Individual | Functional Unit | Client/ Organization |
|---|---|---|---|
| Efficiency | Task mechanization | Process automation | Boundary extension |
| Effectiveness | Work improvement | Functional enhancement | Service enhancement |
| Transformation | Role expansion | Functional redefinition | Service innovation |

*MANAGEMENT*
Innovation/change → Prototyping, senior management, leadership

and offer computing with a nearly immediate response for all users. Organizations could use computing for front-office as well as back-office operations (e.g., for order entry over the telephone, as with centralized dispatching of emergency vehicles). Projects then expanded beyond cost reduction to include new and more effective modes of operation. As with batch applications, however, the early on-line work was justifiable only if done in a high-volume or "production" mode.

Over the years, the greatest portion of computing resources have been invested in financial transaction processing. As a result, computing in government often reports to the head of administrative services or finance. Over the years, much has been learned about transaction-processing projects, especially about the value of good project management, participation by end users, and the use of purchased software packages rather than in-house programming for the traditional applications.

### *Era II: End-User Computing*

The second era of computing dominated the 1980s and was built around the personal computer. PCs, along with freer access to "user-friendly" software on minicomputers and mainframes, allowed end users to decide on their own what and when and how to computerize. As a result, managers and professionals began to use computers (almost always PCs rather than shared systems) to promote personal efficiency (faster word processing) and personal effectiveness (analysis of alternatives through spreadsheet models).

The growth of end-user computing has been phenomenal. From 1982 to 1986 the percentage of local governments using microcomputers rose from only 13 percent to 88 percent.[3] Governments now have more computing power in PCs than in mainframes, and applications that existed only in large jurisdictions are working their way down to jurisdictions of all sizes.[4]

Perhaps the major impacts of PCs, however, have been sociological and educational. No one could have successfully ordered government managers to spend nearly the time and energy learning about mainframe computing that they have willingly spent in learning about their own PCs. PCs have created a new cadre who speak the language of computing; the PC movement has fostered a "revolt of the masses" against central data processing.

For management, the end-user era has necessitated a rebalancing of power between user departments and central data processing (now usually called MIS, IRM, or IT).[5] In some governments, data processing has moved outside of administration or finance and reports instead to a steering committee representing a broader range of users. In general, the central data-processing staff is losing its monopoly powers. Its focus is being shifted to defining standards and providing for mission-critical and enterprisewide services; end users now are left to make their own computing decisions within an environment that operates much like a regulated market economy.

### *Era III: Strategic Applications*

Recent applications suggest we are entering yet another computing era, one whose projects may result in transformational changes internally (in the way people do their jobs) and externally (in government services and the way these reach their clients). In the private sector, such changes have already happened with airline reservations systems and hospital supply systems; in these and many other examples, market share has shifted dramatically to firms with better computer systems.[6]

In government, computerization can likewise support transformational change. At the federal, state, and local level, we see an increasing number of computer projects in which the target is not automating what already exists, but rather creating new services and new production and delivery mechanisms.

As an example, look at recent computerization in the Kings County district attorney's office (the DA's office of Brooklyn, New York). The business problem was reaching the victims and witnesses of crimes before having to decide on the charges to file in felony cases. Under the old system, victims and witnesses were asked to come to a boroughwide office for a hurried interview with an assistant DA; unfortunately, fewer than 5 percent actually did so (as it was extremely inconvenient and time-consuming). A further problem was a rapidly growing caseload, primarily because of narcotics cases.

Brooklyn has addressed this situation with new systems based on two-way video communications and an expert system. The victims and witnesses of narcotics cases can now stay at their local police precincts (or at any location where the video equipment may be installed) and talk via monitor with paralegal staff of the DA's office. The paralegals are supported by an expert system with readily accessible knowledge about the criminal code and about the DA's narcotics policies. The project shifts the boundary of the DA's office in much the way that automated teller machines shifted the boundaries of banks; the project also seeks to enhance the role of paralegals by empowering them to handle interviews that previously were handled by lawyers.

The Brooklyn project has been successful as an R&D project and has recently been expanded to full-scale field operations. Victims and witnesses are now telling their stories remotely and are enthusiastic about the system, as are senior managers of the DA's office and the outgoing DA, Elizabeth Holzman. What is important, however, is not the success or failure of a project in Brooklyn, but the fact that Brooklyn, like many others, is attempting to use computers to change how services reach the public and how government jobs are organized.[7]

Strategic applications require far more aggressive management involvement than earlier computing because the organizational changes are greater. In fact, without significant organizational change—in jobs, reporting relationships, reward systems, and culture—it is impossible to gain the benefits of strategic applications. The problem for Era III is primarily one of managing organizational change and only secondarily a problem of managing technology.

## *COMPUTING APPLICATIONS*

Finance managers, not surprisingly, have always been interested in computing for accounting and finance. The applications focused initially on transaction processing, then on decision support, and now increasingly on office automation. Let's look at each from a managerial perspective.

### *Transaction Processing*

Governments that computerize almost invariably include the "big four" financial applications: (1) payroll, (2) accounts receivable, (3) accounts payable, and (4) general ledger. For example, in cities over 100,000, over 90 percent have computerized these functions; smaller jurisdictions are also computerizing their accounting, especially as microcomputers get more and more powerful.[8]

The reasons are straightforward. Computerized financials are faster and more accurate since the data, once entered, can be updated and manipulated without error. Computerization saves clerical costs. It leads to better financial reporting, which in turn improves cash management and relations with oversight and funding agencies.

In general, computerization requires that financial data be explicit and consistent across the organization. This increases central control over departmental operations and the power of central officials such the budget director, treasurer, auditor, and mayor—precisely the officials responsible for initiating and funding most computerization. Over the past half-century, one of the major changes in local government has been the increasing power of financial oversight agencies (executive primarily, but also legislative), aided substantially by growing standardization and computerization.

Much of government's experience with computing comes from financial transaction processing. This does not mean that such applications are easy. In fact, trends and lessons from painful experience are important today and will remain so. Financial managers should be aware that:

1. Vendor-produced software "packages" are more cost- effective and often better than software programmed in-house. It is much rarer today for government to program its own financial applications; instead, it purchases software from a rich selection of market alternatives.[9] These are usually cheaper, better documented and programmed, more frequently updated, and more functional than applications programmed in-house. Modern financial packages make a wide variety of modules and functionality accessible to even the smallest government units.
2. Individual applications, while often available as stand-alone modules, are increasingly being designed and made more valuable as "integrated" packages. In an integrated design, transactions entered originally into the payroll module need not be reentered to be posted to the general ledger; data is captured once in the database and subsequently made available to all modules that require it.[10] The concept is simple but, in practice, the implementation can be complex because of the large number of government agencies, programs, funds, and funding sources involved and, sometimes, by conflicting accounting and reporting requirements.

Despite these problems, the trend today is clearly toward integrated packages.

3. Financial packages are being extended to include cost accounting and program performance data. Integration today is extending beyond the general ledger and other accounting modules to include advanced functionality such as: (a) grant reporting (for Medicaid, other specialized funding sources, affirmative action); (b) cost accounting (to handle the fixed versus variable cost analyses required for service cost and pricing decisions); and (c) performance and responsibility center reporting.

Over the next decade, due to aging systems and changes in reporting requirements, many jurisdictions will update their financial systems. An important decision will be how far to go to include cost accounting and performance reporting. In general, expanded integration is complicated technically and risky organizationally (departments may be sensitive about giving outside analysts easy access to detailed performance data); at the same time, integrating financial with program data promises far better analysis and control. Moves to expand the scope of integrated financial applications can be expected to provide high returns for relatively high risks; financial managers should be aware of both sides and strike a successful balance on a case-by-case basis.

***Decision Support***

Decision support emphasizes data analysis rather than data capture. Analysis helps managers avoid overload by having the computer rather than the manager search for critical data (those personnel with greatly higher-than-normal overtime) or summaries (e.g., changes in the volume of contracts with minority firms). Graphics can improve the communication of analytic results, as when maps are colored to show sites unsuited for sanitary landfills due to proximity to water supplies, the nature of underlying rock formations. Decision support makes it easier for end users to analyze the data to identify relationships, patterns, and implications.

The benefits of computer-based analysis are rarely a savings of analysis time (when answers get faster, more questions get asked), but rather an improvement in understanding. The costs for decision support are often low, because software is available on micros and because implementation, unlike the case with transaction processing, involves a few analysts and managers rather than the entire clerical workforce.[11]

A typical decision support application is revenue forecasting. Even for small jurisdictions, spreadsheet models have made revenue and cash-management projections easier to make and revise. And for some jurisdictions, sophistication is now available that was prohibitively expensive even a decade ago. In California, for example, the legislative analyst's office has built models to estimate more than $35 billion in revenues from more than fifty individual sources including taxes, fees, rents, royalties, and investments.[12] The system includes

- The use of Wharton Econometric's 400-plus equation national macroeconometric model to forecast nationwide economic variables (This model permits California to use its own policy-related assumptions when these differ from the Wharton assumptions.)
- A series of California-built submodels to forecast California economic variables, predict components of the state's revenue base, and translate these into expected revenues
- PC hardware with 640K memory and a 20-megabyte hard disk supported by software to download data from the Wharton service and to produce the unique analyses needed by California

The result, according to California, is a flexible and comprehensive revenue-estimating system without high costs for either personnel or on-line computer use.

The basic managerial guideline for decision support: Do it, try it, fix it—and don't plan it to death. Unlike the case with transaction processing, automating decision support is not automating something that was previously manual, but exploring the value of something that was previously unavailable. The best approach for such systems seems to be rapid construction of a prototype followed by iterative use and revision.

There are dangers, of course, in relying upon computer-based decision support. It is easy, even seductive, to play with impressive models whose assumptions are poorly documented (and possibly unrealistic). Managers must be appropriately cautious. Still, despite the problems of misuse, the low costs and high leverage of computer-based decision support make it an attractive target for financial and other managers. (If we lowered the qualifying age for the elderly shuttle bus service to 60, how many would then qualify in precinct 10 and what would we need for a budget?) Further, as externally collected data becomes available electronically, computer-based decision support will become even more important.

### *Office Automation*

Capturing and analyzing data—the target of transaction processing and decision support—is important for most managers and professionals, yet remains a very limited element of their work. Office automation seeks to go beyond traditional applications to computerize nearly all types of communication—not only the exchange and analysis of data, but also the exchange and analysis of text, graphics, and even full-motion video and sound. Office automation typically starts with word processing, but extends to electronic mail, voice mail, and ultimately to the creation of a world where electronics rather than paper becomes the dominant means of communication.

In such a world, computers reduce time and space as barriers to coordinated activity. Eventually, this will make possible a radical restructuring of what we mean by the word *office*. Office automation is thus something of a misnomer:

ultimately, we do not want merely to automate what we already do and the way we do it. For example, it will soon be possible to globalize office work much as we have globalized manufacturing. But will we want to do this? Should the major inner-city offices of the IRS or state revenue departments, for example, be dispersed to smaller regional and suburban offices? Should privatization of military health-insurance benefits be encouraged if the results include a shift of data-entry jobs to Bermuda or Ireland? Should specialized elderly care and penal institutions be replaced (at the margin) by in-house care supported by computerized communications much like the French Minitel?[13]

The managerial and political issues to be raised by such shifts will be enormous over the next decades. There is already a need to plan strategically in creating the networks and databases to serve as the computer and office-automation infrastructure of the future.[14]

Some jurisdictions are now moving to create integrated systems for data, voice, text, and video. Salem, Oregon, for example, has initiated a task force whose charter is not only to improve city services, but to address the communications infrastructure of the entire community.[15] As part of their effort, the task force is preparing an inventory of existing communications channels including telephone trunk lines, cable television facilities, government-owned transmission facilities, and microwave channels in the metropolitan area. Their goals:

- To establish a unified database management system for all city services
- To establish a single network to carry data, text, voice, and video transmissions
- To distribute the data-processing function
- To establish a management function to plan, coordinate, and monitor the work needed to bring the integrated infrastructure into being

The most useful managerial guidance for office automation is perhaps a warning: Beware of automating the past! It is of course possible to automate jobs in ways that capture detailed data for external control—the number of data entry errors per hour, time away from the workstation, etc. It is also relatively easy to justify incremental automation rather than the uncertainties of basic restructuring. But an overemphasis on incremental control-oriented automation may make it harder rather than easier to be successful in the future. So while government agencies are talking about creating the office of the future—with flatter hierarchies, broader jobs, improved responsiveness and innovation, etc.—many of our actual investments are aimed at something that looks instead like a paper-based version of factories of the past. There is danger as well as opportunity in office automation.[16]

## *MANAGEMENT ISSUES*

As computing becomes pervasive, what should be the primary concerns of managers, especially government financial managers? Here we will focus on classic issues related to planning, organizing, acquiring, implementing, and learning.

### *Planning*

Planning involves making commitments to improve the future. Thus arranging to meet someone for lunch is planning. So is deciding how to spend the next $10 million on information technology. With too little planning, the danger is in ending up with pieces that don't fit together; this is a serious danger with computer systems, as anyone who has spent an afternoon trying to translate and edit a file produced with an incompatible word processor can attest. On the other hand, with too much (or ineffectual) planning, the danger is that planning will substitute for action. We have all heard of (and likely participated in) planning whose only real output was delay and dust.

It is important for managers to shape an appropriate planning process. Planning should involve roughly the right people in roughly the right ways on roughly the right issues. Elements include plans for projects, for portfolios, and for strategic linkage.

*Projects.* The real danger for most computer projects is not in missing the targets for time or money (many systems considered successful today were originally late and over budget), but in missing essential user requirements. Planning for user requirements is thus extremely important (and, surprisingly, often overlooked). User requirements are often uncovered better by prototypes than by formal plans. Rapidly constructed and revised prototypes (built with fourth-generation languages or CASE tools), encourage early participation and feedback and are a preferred methodology that combines project planning with end-user involvement.[17]

*Portfolios.* It is not enough for individual projects to work, since computer investments must work and fit together. But as projects move outside the finance functions, it becomes impossible for the MIS director or finance director alone to make the substantive (and politically effective) tradeoffs required among contending proposals. Portfolio planning requires cross-departmental input, usually through some form of a steering committee. In settings where the technology is in flux, controversial, or perceived to be strategic, it is important that the steering committee secure deep involvement by senior managers (say department heads in quarterly half-day meetings); in more tranquil settings, a lesser and lower level of involvement may be adequate (perhaps an annual IT planning retreat among selected deputies).[18]

*Strategic Linkage.* Portfolios that fit together may nevertheless fall short of their true potential unless they are aligned with the strategic direction of the organization. Unfortunately, even in settings where technology is potentially strategic, there is often a gap between IT managers and senior general managers. Technology plans are too often developed without a full understanding of policy—and new policies are developed without knowing what technology might constrain or enable.

Forging a link between strategy and technology is widely considered to be the key problem in designing an effective planning process.[19] Solutions depend largely on

- Organizational design—on where the data-processing function(s) report and how technology issues are addressed in the organization's program-planning and career-planning systems
- Training—on giving technologists a firm grounding in the program and policy environment, giving managers an understanding of the process and potential impacts of computerization, and giving both the skills needed for collaborative work and conflict resolution
- Timing—on recognizing that major shifts in strategy, including important introductions of technology, depend on sensing when conditions are ripe and seizing the opportunity at the appropriate moment

If senior management does not believe in the value of technology or planning, little can be done. And in many cases it may take a crisis or specific application—say the need for an integrated financial system to recover payments from third-party health insurers—to make it credible to invest heavily in strategic IT planning.

### *Organizing*

In organizing for computer use, the major issues are acquiring and retaining competent technical staff and striking the balance between centralization and decentralization. Government pay scales do not compete well in the market for technical experts. As a result, systems work is increasingly handled by contractors. But where can government find the staff to monitor contractors? Some governments are turning to contractors to monitor other contractors.[20] While there seems to be no "silver bullet" for dealing with the staffing problem, some governments are concerned enough to be launching new initiatives to attract the skills and resources needed for serious IT work.

On the centralization issue, computers used to be centralized because big computers were more efficient than small ones. Recently, however, the tables have turned; now small computers are more efficient because small systems are the first to reach the market with new processors and other new and inherently more powerful technologies. Even so, centralization retains certain efficiencies, mostly in attracting technical staff and setting standards. What decentralization offers, in addition to cost-effective technology, is the ability to involve people who are close to the operational problems of service delivery. In general, the degree of computer centralization offered today can readily be tailored to fit the organizational culture—a centralized structure for paramilitary units, for example, with a dispersed structure for the R&D labs.[21]

### *Acquiring*

How should government acquire goods and services from markets that supply hardware, software, and data? While the markets themselves have been changing—with radically new suppliers, buyers, and ever-changing products and services—the acquisition practices of most governments have stayed constant. These practices assume, in general, that the central problem is controlling favoritism and abuse: as a result, policies generally require that requests be based upon a prior definition of (supposedly objective) needs, and that selections then be justified in terms of those (and only those) needs. While such a process enforces good discipline, elaborations of the process often require paperwork that is overly rigid and time-consuming. Little room is left for subjective judgment or for the learning that occurs (especially in the private sector) as organizations develop long-term relationships with vendors. Unfortunately, the systems that are acquired under today's procurement procedures are often costly, out of date, and not well supported by the vendors that supply them.

The goal for computer acquisition should be to encourage sensible decisions about when to buy (versus build) and how to gain good value for a fair price. Given the acknowledged problems with present practice, finance managers should analyze and update their procedures. Local governments could often improve their computer acquisitions by

- Getting advice and support from national associations such as the International City Management Association and the Government Finance Officers Association
- Leveraging the de facto standardization of state and federal procurements by allowing the prices and terms of those agreements to be accepted for local purchases
- Making it clear that vendor performance on present and past contracts will be a major factor in evaluating future proposals

In general, the thrust of acquisition should be to determine how the government can arrive at the best value rather than merely the least cost.[22]

### *Implementing*

How can computer projects be successfully implemented? The essence is managing the associated organizational change. When computer-based changes fail, it is usually because people are confused about what, exactly, is expected of them or, in those cases where the plan is precise and there is no confusion, because of conflicts over the promised results.

To resolve confusion—for example, to computerize successfully when there is uncertainty in figuring out how to proceed but the workers and management are clearly in support of automation—MIS directors (and consultants) have gotten much better over the years at systems analysis and project management. Experience helps.

To resolve conflicts, however, MIS directors and consultants often have little leverage. In high-conflict situations, there are two basic approaches to successful implementation:

***Participation and Negotiation.*** Giving participants adequate time and a serious role in systems design and implementation can result in overcoming many obstacles, especially when participants agree that some sort of change is called for.

FIGURE 21-2
*The Learning Curve*

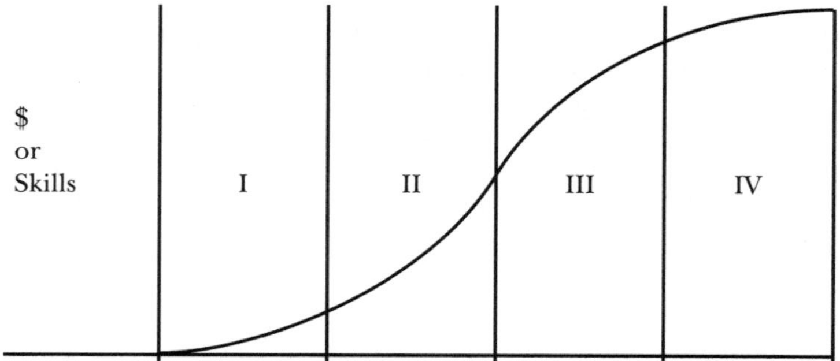

$ or Skills

I II III IV

| Stage | Initial | Growth | Control | Mature |
|---|---|---|---|---|
| Key Element | Tools | Users | Plans | Marketing |
| | Learn from mistakes | | Avoid mistakes | |

***Power and Top-Down Leadership.*** Moving forcefully can also be effective, using every power available to the leadership to remove obstacles and communicate that the proposed changes are, in fact, the new order of the day. This approach requires tougher political work than many managers are willing to handle unless the investment is seen as very necessary. While both participative and authoritative approaches can be successful, fast and forceful top-down implementation may be the only feasible approach with changes that threaten significant elements of the status quo.[23]

### *Learning*

Effectiveness with computers, as with anything new, requires learning. The most difficult learning with computers is not individual learning, but organizational learning. Over time, organizational performance tends to rise on the "S" curve of learning—slowly at first, then faster, then tailing off. (See figure 21-2.)

Senior managers need to understand that efficient performance with a given technology (e.g., with batch-transaction processing, personal computers, database systems) is not achievable without rising through the uncertain and rocky terrain of earlier learning. The goal of early projects should therefore not be to avoid mistakes so much as to learn from them. Management controls (plans, budgets, staffing) should be loose and supportive at first (as when educating children). Later, after the organization has learned to use a particular technology, stronger controls are appropriate (as when disciplining teenagers).[24]

For effective use of computers in the public sector, perhaps the biggest problem is getting the resources required for serious "learning." For managers in the glare of public scrutiny, pressures to avoid "mistakes" make it hard to experiment. Budget and finance directors bear a special responsibility here, since inflexible reliance on finance-oriented return on investment (ROI) criteria tends to screen out important opportunities for experimentation. With a more enlightened and longer-term view of the impacts of technology, however, public finance managers may also become key advocates for ensuring that resources are available for learning about potentially strategic technologies.

## *THE FUTURE*

For the future, expect rapid technological change to continue unabated. In addition, expect that the personal, organizational, and social impacts of this change will feel quite different to workers and management as the focus moves from individuals back to groups and organizations. While specifics are unpredictable, we foresee three major trends: growth in PC power, an increased use of networks, and further organizational changes prompted by computers.

### *PC Power*

New interfaces will (finally) introduce computers to "all of us." The personal computer of the mid-1990s will have the power of large mainframes of the 1980s. Much of this power will be directed at making the computer far easier to use.

It is clear that standardized graphics interfaces, such as the one made popular by the Apple MacIntosh, make it easier to learn software; Mac users typically use more software packages than IBM users. In the near future, as advances create a wider availability of software with a standardized graphics interface, the use of software will expand markedly. In addition, cost effective voice recognition will reduce the need for keyboard skills and initiate yet another huge wave of expanded use.

In general, computer use today involves a sizable minority of the workforce for a small part of the working day; soon it will involve nearly all of us for a large part of our working (and other) days. For finance managers there will be expanded ability to capture data on-line and accurately at the point of origin; there will be enormously increased importance in training and education; and there will also be a significant democratization of access to financial data. (This will make life messier for financial managers—as the opposition gains access to good numbers—but will also make financial data and analysis more important.)

### *Networks*

The basic unit of management concern will shift from the individual computer to the network and its associated distributed databases. In some ways this will make things harder, since individual freedom will be constrained by needs for standards and collective action. Still, the trends seem inevitable and powerful.

For what this shift may mean, financial managers can look at what has recently happened to the world's financial markets: currency trading and other services have now become electronic games played around the clock and around the world by a workforce tied to electronic workstations. Similar change should be expected in professions where access to detailed and timely information is key: in financial management, to be sure, and also in medical diagnosis, legal analysis, and a wide range of governmental services. With the assembly of large national databases, expect that budget reviews, even in small jurisdictions, will routinely include comparisons of per-capita costs and service measures against similar data from comparable jurisdictions.

### *Organizational Changes*

While applications will continue to lag what is technologically possible, there will be a shift toward newly designed electronic hierarchies and electronic markets. With the computerization we now see emerging, it will soon be possible to build organizations that are

- Simultaneously big and small (networked, and with access to significant capital, yet with operating units of 25 or so workers rather than thousands of workers)
- Coordinated via processes that are horizontal (cross-functional) and parallel (fast) rather than vertical (hierarchical) and sequential (slow)
- Dispersed to operate largely independently of geography and time

As organizations change, markets will also change. In general, much of the world's work will shift to coordination via markets rather than via the command and control decision-making of internal hierarchies. Thus we expect a continued privatization of government services, with production handled by contractors, much as has recently happened with human services and software development. The reason for shifting to market-coordinated activity will be the fact that electronic communications reduce the costs of shopping the market (since comparisons can be readily made on the screen). When travel agents became computerized, more airline tickets were purchased from agents (where market comparisons were easily made) than direct from the airlines; when government purchasing becomes computerized—for example with reliable on-line links to local vendors of vehicle maintenance services—government will shift even more of its maintenance work to outside suppliers. Government may of course be slower than private organizations to respond to the pressures and opportunities of electronic markets, but we expect that financial and other pressures will lead to significant restructuring over the next 10 to 15 years.

## *CONCLUSION*

Over the past thirty years, a 5,000 to 1 improvement in cost effectiveness has allowed computers to become a central tool for local government financial management. Computers are now in the front office as well as the back office, in services as well as administration.

The future promises continued exponential improvement on the technical front. As a result, interconnectivity will become practical across vendors and departments. Over time, government services will become highly individualized, comprehensive, and available wherever there is a connection to the network—that is, from home, from the office, from the automobile, from anywhere and at any time.

The management of computing has already changed irrevocably. The problem used to be getting difficult-to-use computers to fit into easy (routine) jobs. The problem now, however, is getting powerful and easy-to-use computers to transform difficult and nonroutine jobs. The earlier problem was appropriately delegated to technical specialists. The problem for now and the future cannot be appropriately delegated. In managing computers, the central problem has become the management of organizational change. Local government finance managers should understand these trends and provide much of the leadership needed to manage them effectively.

## *NOTES*

1. Processing costs per instruction executed have fallen about 25 percent per year and should continue to do so for another decade at least. Costs for storage have been falling closer to 40 percent per year, while costs for communications have fallen at about 13 percent per year. In general, hardware costs fall rapidly; total costs for computing are dominated by the costs of software and staff. Over a thirty-year period, relative costs of processing thus fall by a factor of $1/(.75)^{30}$ = 5600 to 1.

2. For a more complete treatment of this framework, see Gibson and Jackson, *The Information Imperative* (Homewood, IL: Richard D. Irwin, 1988).

3. John W. Ostrowski, Ella P. Gardner, and Magda H. Motawi, "Microcomputers in Public Finance Organizations: A Survey of Uses and Trends," *Government Finance Review*, February 1986, pp. 13–29.

4. For an extensive series of reports on the evolving uses of computing in local governments, see the publications of the Public Policy Research Organization, University of California–Irvine.

5. Data Processing (DP) is often ADP (automated data processing), EDP (electronic data processing), MIS (management information systems), IRM (information resources management), or most recently, IT (information technology).

6. Strategic computing in the private sector has been the subject of a growing literature in both specialized and general periodicals: see the *Harvard Business Review, Sloan Management Review,* and *MIS Quarterly*. For a textbook treatment see James I. Cash, F. Warren McFarlan, and James L. McKenney, *Corporate Information Systems Management: The Issues Facing Senior Executives*, 2nd ed. (Homewood, IL: Richard D. Irwin, 1988).

7. See "The Brooklyn DA's Office: A Client Contact System" (Cambridge, MA: Harvard Business School Case Distribution Office, 1988).

8. Kenneth L. Kraemer, John Wesley King, Deborah Dunkle, Joseph P. Layne, and Joey George, "Trends in Municipal Information Systems: 1975–1985," pp. 333–50 in P. Kovacks and E. Straub, ed., *Municipal Information Systems* (New York: North-Holland, 1988).

9. *Ibid.*

10. Database software or database management systems (DBMS) are specialized

programs that keep track of how data is defined and where it is stored on storage devices. Without database software, individual applications must maintain this information and must be individually updated when data such as names and ZIP codes are changed. Organizations may have hundreds or even thousands of applications to manipulate the same data, so the problem of updating and keeping data consistent can be extremely difficult without database software. With database software, a single change in the database (or a few changes) will suffice for all applications, since the applications do not maintain their own data but request it from the database program. Database software usually includes a "query and report writing" language that is easy for end users to learn (i.e., it takes less than two days to learn the basics) and that allows many reports to be generated on demand by end users rather than through a laborious programming project by the data-processing staff.

11. Over the past ten years, the growth of decision-support tools and techniques has spawned a substantial literature. The seminal work, and still one of the best, is Peter F. Keen and Michael S. Scott-Morton, *Decision Support Systems: An Organizational Perspective* (Reading, MA: Addison-Wesley, 1979).

12. Jon David Vasche, "The California Legislative Analyst's PC-Based Revenue Estimating Approach," *Government Finance Review,* June 1987, pp. 30–31.

13. The French have subsidized the placement of terminals into many households as part of basic telephone service, believing that these will help form the "critical mass" of a communications infrastructure that will support innovative new services of benefit to all society. In Sweden, it is common for elderly and penal services to be provided in private households through augmented communications, which have evolved over time from emergency dispatching services much like our own 911 services.

14. A number of proposals have been introduced to define the government role in building such infrastructures. For example, Senator Albert Gore of Tennessee has proposed, with others, that the federal government invest several billions to build a high speed computer communications network to connect the nation's research and educational institutions. Such proposals raise a variety of important public policy issues related to the funding, operation, and control of such investments. See U.S. Congress, Senate, 101st Congressional Session, *National High Performance Computer Technology Act of 1989,* Senate 1067, 1989.

15. Larry McCord, "Integrated Information Systems for Local Government: Developments in Salem, Oregon," *Government Finance Review,* April 1986.

16. This observation was a major conclusion to emerge from the workshop of senior government officials, "Technology and Organization in the Public Sector," held at Harvard in June 1989.

17. Fourth-generation languages (4GLs) are programming languages that typically include database commands within the language, thus substantially reducing the number of commands that need to be written (and the time required) for many recordkeeping and reporting applications. CASE tools (for Computer-Assisted Software Engineering) provide software support for an even broader array of software development tasks (typically including screen generation, database design, and requirements planning) and are also meant to speed up and improve the applications development process.

18. See James L. McKenney and F. Warren McFarlan, "The Information Archipelago-Maps and Bridges," *Harvard Business Review,* Sept.–Oct. 1982, pp. 109–119.

19. James I. Cash, F. Warren McFarlan, and James L. McKenney, *Corporate Information Systems Management: The Issues Facing Senior Executives,* Second Edition, 1988, pp. 231–254; much of the theory behind the integration of planning into organizational activity

was developed by Laurence and Lorsch in their seminal work: *Organization and Environment* (Boston: Division of Research, Harvard Business School, 1967).

20. With technical specialists tending to work for software firms rather than large general-purpose agencies and companies, the problems of attracting technical staff are severe in both the public and private sectors. General-purpose organizations are seeking to acquire technical skills through better pay, better training, and better ways to manage the work of outside consultants.

21. See Frederic Withington, "Coping with Computer Proliferation" *Harvard Business Review,* May–June 1980, pp. 152–164.

22. For perspective on state and local procurements of technology, see Donald A. Marchand, Sharon L. Caudle, Stuart I. Bretschneider, Patricia T. Fletcher, and Kurt M. Thurmaier, *Managing Information Resources: New Directions in State Government* (Syracuse, N.Y.: National Association of State Information Systems, 1989).

23. Cyrus F. Gibson, Charles J. Singer, Ava A. Schnidman, and Thomas H. Davenport, "Strategies for Making an Information System Fit Your Organization," *Management Review,* published by American Management Association, January 1984, pp. 8–14.

24. Cash, et al., *Corporate Information Systems Management,* pp. 91–96.

# 22
# *State Involvement in Local Finance*

Dennis Strachota

In the U.S. federal system, responsibilities for public services and goods are shared and divided among different levels of government. Providing for dual sovereignty, the U.S. Constitution authorizes both the federal and the state governments to raise taxes. It does not, however, specify the division of responsibility between the two levels of government. Moreover, the Constitution makes no mention of local government responsibilities leaving those to the states to define.

Local governments owe their existence, legal structure, and fiscal authority to their state. State constitution and law define many local government powers and responsibilities. Unless they operate under a grant of "home rule" authority, many of the functions performed by local jurisdictions will be delineated for them.

A discussion of state involvement in local finance would be incomplete without a closer look at the U.S. federal system. After delineating federal, state and local responsibilities, this chapter examines the states' roles as provider, preemptor and prescriber and how they are manifested in state regulation and assistance. Lastly, this chapter reviews five factors which seem to stand out as major influences on the type and extent of state involvement in local finance.

## *GOVERNMENT ROLES AT THE FEDERAL, STATE, AND LOCAL LEVELS*

The system of financing and delivering public services is one that has seen marked changes over time. John Shannon and James Edwin Kee identify three periods through which our federal system has evolved.[1] In the period from 1789 to 1929, the federal government's role was largely confined to those enumerated in the Constitution—national defense, postal services, customs, and foreign affairs. The states by themselves and through their local governments supplied most of the domestic needs of the nation.

A series of national crises between 1929 and 1954, beginning with the stock market crash, centralized power at the federal level, leading to federal involvement in areas previously reserved for the states. Bolstered by a lucrative income-tax system, the federal government increased its domestic commitments during this period—with the greatest spurt occurring in the creation of "Great Society" programs. Shannon and Kee conclude that this period of centralization ended in the late 1970s with the onset of tighter federal budgets and increased federal commitments to defense and transfer payments to individuals. Fiscal federalism is marked today by competition among the federal, state, and local levels for taxpayer support.

### *The Federal Role*

Although the federal role in financing state and local services has declined, federal influence in the state and local sectors has remained strong.

Both direct and indirect federal assistance has dropped since the dawning of "competitive federalism." Between 1978 and 1988, direct federal assistance to state and local governments fell by $17.2 billion in constant dollars. As a percent of state–local expenditures, this assistance dropped by one-third, from 27 to 18 percent.[2] Local governments have borne a larger share of these cutbacks because of the elimination of several federal–local programs, notably federal revenue sharing. Indirect federal aid to states and localities, in the form of tax subsidies, also took a downturn during this period. Elimination of deductions for state and local sales taxes and restrictions on tax-exempt bonds, enacted as part of the Tax Reform Act of 1986, represent a major portion of scaled-back federal tax subsidies.

Although federal aid fell off in the late '70s, federal regulatory requirements did not drop commensurately. Federal aid still has conditions attached. Those that go beyond the program requirements specific to the grant-in-aid are "crosscutting requirements" and "crossover sanctions." Crosscutting requirements—such as the Davis-Bacon Act provisions, which require the payment of prevailing wages to construction work financed with federal monies—apply to all federal aid programs. Crossover sanctions threaten the loss or reduction of aid provided under one aid program if the requirements of another program are not met (e.g., threatened loss of federal highway funds if states did not pass a minimum drinking age law). In addition to these grant requirements, a GAO study found federal regulations affecting state and local governments had increased between 1981 and 1986 in most of eighteen program areas examined (e.g., clean water, education, occupational health and safety).[3] Contributing to this heightened federal regulation have been several key U.S. Supreme Court decisions, in particular *Garcia* v. *San Antonio Metropolitan Transit Authority* (1986) and *South Carolina* v. *Baker* (1988), which have affirmed greater federal intrusion into state and local affairs.

### *The State Role in Federal System*

States have increased their prominence in domestic affairs during this period. In part, this greater role is the result of federal retrenchment manifested in the form of budget cuts, tax cuts, and the consolidation of categorical aid programs.

States have expanded their agendas, broadening their involvement in areas such as international trade, housing, health care, and the environment—areas previously dominated by the federal government. This venture into new areas was made possible in large part due to the modernization of state government and the strengthening of state revenue systems. Since World War II, states have made significant strides in increasing their capacity to govern through the emergence of cabinet government, full-time legislatures, and a professional workforce. At the same time, states have improved their revenue systems through revenue diversification and tax reforms. This increased role in domestic affairs was also reflected in increased state aid to localities during the period when direct federal assistance to localities declined.

Even more evident are costs that have been assumed by states. Most states have assumed the full costs of Aid to Families with Dependent Children and the entire nonfederal share of Medicaid costs. In addition, more states are assuming costs for the criminal justice system previously borne by localities (i.e., courts and prosecutors).[4]

### *Local Governments' Part*

Local governments have not remained idle as changes occurred at the federal and state levels. Local governments have shouldered an increasing portion of the raising of revenues for public services. Between 1977 and 1987, the local share of local general revenues increased 16 percent, from 60 to 69 percent.[5] Although the property tax remains the dominant source of local revenue, user charges and fees and sales taxes constitute a greater portion of the local revenue base.

Some of the major federal mandates imposed on the states are carried out at the local level. For example, many of the clean-water requirements fall to local general-purpose or special districts to satisfy. The states may set the standards, but the locals assume the responsibility for constructing and operating wastewater-treatment facilities. Local governments are the bulwarks of public-service providers and producers. In 1985, local general-purpose governments alone delivered 46 percent of all public services to state residents.[6]

## *LOCAL FINANCE SYSTEMS*

Despite the significant share of local service costs financed by federal and state governments, local governments are the major providers of public goods and services. A major component of service "provision" involves financial decisions. These decisions center on how to raise revenue and what to spend it on. Answers to these questions are the chief output of the local financial system.

The parameters for these financial decisions are established through financial policies. Financial policies, such as ones limiting the amount of debt issued by a locality, shape the final outcome. In the case of borrowing limits, should a local government reach its debt limit, its policymakers may have to either forego the desired outlay, choose another financing mechanism, or change its debt policy.

Financial policies are carried out through financial practices. Financial practices are those procedures used to plan, manage, and control the decision making process. They include, among others, accounting, auditing, financial reporting, budgeting, cash management, and debt administration.

### *Objectives of Local Finance*

Financial systems support the operations of organizations, making it possible for them to carry out their responsibilities and functions. Local government functions involve either the regulation of private activities or the production and provision of goods and services. Financial systems are designed to ensure and promote accountability, effectiveness, efficiency, and equity in the fulfillment of local regulatory and service responsibilities.

*Accountability and Control.* Governments must deal with legal constraints in carrying out their functions; they may do only what they are legally authorized to do. As we have already discussed, these limitations and restrictions are commonplace. Financial systems establish controls to ensure that public resources are spent for authorized purposes. Public managers are held accountable to legislative bodies, creditors, taxpayers, and grantors for financial decisions sanctioned in budgets, bond covenants, grants, contracts, lease agreements, intergovernmental agreements, and other legal documents.

*Effectiveness.* Financial systems should promote the effective use of public resources. Effectiveness is a matter of how well government programs and services meet their objectives. Effectiveness can be measured by whether a service or program is commensurate with user needs, desires, and willingness to pay. Budgeting allocates resources among government services and programs by sorting through competing objectives and service levels. Once resource decisions have been made, financial systems should assess the effectiveness of authorized programs and services to monitor performance and assist with future resource allocations.

*Efficiency and Equity.* Efficiency has several meanings. Economic efficiency is attained if citizens receive the services that they want and are willing to pay for. Inefficiency results if a government produces too little or too much service. Technical efficiency is attained if economies of scale (i.e., a decrease in the average unit cost of production as the scale of production increases) or cost effectiveness are achieved. Equity is achieved if fiscal disparities among local goverments are minimized. These disparities exist if taxpayers with similar incomes living in different jurisdictions pay different amounts for similar services. Financial systems should promote technical and economic efficiency and help ensure equity in the provision of public services. At its best, state involvement can help advance these financial objectives.

### *The State As Preemptor, Provider, and Prescriber*

States can take on three different roles in local finance: preemptor, provider, and prescriber. A state does not perform one role to the exclusion of the others. In fact, a state frequently serves in multiple roles at the same time.

As a *preemptor,* a state precludes certain local government finance decisions and practices. In their role as preemptor, states use their superior legal powers to usurp local discretion.

When a state serves as *provider,* it provides assistance to local governments. State financial assistance or assumption of local functions reduces local reliance on own-source revenues and mitigates fiscal disparities. States can also assist local units to improve their management of finances through technical assistance programs and state-run financial services.

Lastly, as a *prescriber,* a state dictates the manner in which local governments carry out finance functions. States regulate both local financial policies and procedures.[7] Enforcement of these regulations will vary with their degree of importance to the state.

## *STATE REGULATION OF LOCAL FINANCE*

States regulate local financial systems through a complex set of laws and regulations. State requirements frequently are created piecemeal over time without regard to their collective impact on local operations. They are rooted in constitutional and statutory law as well as in administrative regulation. Because it is rare to find one state agency with oversight responsibilities, fragmentation and duplication of state finance requirements can be pervasive. The degree to which state requirements are enforced will depend on their origin, purpose, and relative importance.

### *Financial Practice Regulation*

Local financial practices often are regulated to establish some "minimum standards." States are concerned that proper financial procedures are performed to ensure fiscal control and accountability. The interests of the state and the general public at large are served if some basic, uniform requirements are met by local governments.

***Accounting, Auditing, and Financial Reporting.*** State laws may set forth some basic internal control requirements, such as the separation of finance duties, to ensure proper fiscal control and accountability. When these requirements are so specific that they detail what, how, or when certain financial procedures are performed, however, they can result in conflicting or inefficient practices. For example, laws affixing responsibility for carrying out a certain finance duty to a particular local official may run counter to a more efficient division of responsibilities. In such instances, a local government may compromise its organizational effectiveness if it complies with the state's dictum.

States usually require local governments to prepare annual or more frequent financial reports. These reports may be the same as or different from the reports prepared by the jurisdiction for other purposes. If their primary purpose is financial disclosure, these reports should be prepared in accordance with generally accepted accounting principles (GAAP) for governments. Some states, however, do not adhere to these nationally recognized standards in their reporting requirements. As a result, local governments may face two different sets of reporting requirements intended to serve the same purpose. Many states also require localities to submit special financial reports. These reports may be used to monitor local government finances, estimate the fiscal impact of state legislation on local operations, enforce state levy limits and cost controls, calculate the distribution of certain kinds of state aid and serve a variety of other purposes.

Most states require annual audits of local governments. These audits may be performed by a state audit agency or a public accounting firm hired by the local jurisdiction. Typically these audits are financial audits performed in accordance with generally accepted auditing standards (GAAS) to attest to the fairness of the jurisdiction's financial statements. If a locality receives federal financial assistance passed through the state, the state may require a financial and compliance audit to determine the locality's compliance with grant conditions.

*Budgeting.* Because of its importance in allocating public resources, the local budgetary process may be prescribed by state law. Most states limit involvement in this process to requirements for annual budgets, public hearings on proposed budgets, and procedures for budget adoption and amendments. Some states may dictate specific budgetary procedures, including the type of budgeting (e.g., line-item, program), what information is included in the budget document, and the review process to be followed by the governing body.

A few states involve themselves directly in the local process. For example, New Jersey must review and approve local budgets before they can go into effect. In this instance, the state intervenes in the local decision-making process itself. State concerns over the financial solvency and stability of localities during the Depression led to the creation of this particular requirement. The state reviews local budgets to determine local compliance with other state requirements, notably revenue and spending caps imposed on counties and municipalities.

*Debt Management.* Another traditional area of state regulation is local borrowing. Because borrowing represents long-term commitments of future revenues, there is particular concern with these decisions. Additional concern is warranted because the failure to meet debt obligations by a single jurisdiction can jeopardize the debt ratings of other localities and the state itself. Aside from restrictions on the amount of local borrowing (discussed later), restrictions commonly apply to bond referenda, maximum maturities, and the method of bond sales.[8]

Depending upon the type and amount of borrowing, state law may require local governments to hold voter referenda to authorize debt issuance. Requirements for voter approval represent the ultimate exercise in accountability. Instead of delegating responsibility for borrowing decisions to elected officials, these requirements place decision-making authority in the hands of citizen–taxpayers themselves.

States may also establish maturity dates for various forms of debt, delineating the time period within which the principal and interest must be repaid by the local government borrower. These maturity dates ensure, in part, that the repayment period does not exceed the useful life of the capital asset financed with the borrowed funds. Much like requirements for competitive bids for the purchase of services and goods, state requirements for competitive sale of bonds are intended to lower borrowing costs.

Enforcement of these requirements is often actively pursued. Although some states require state approval of local bonds issues, most states rely on bond counsel who review bond covenants to attest to the legality of the transaction, including compliance with state laws. State debt laws can pose problems for local governments if favorable interest rates are foregone due to delays caused by state-prescribed borrowing procedures. State statutes may also limit local borrowing options if they are interpreted so narrowly that they do not accommodate new debt instruments. Again, localities may incur additional borrowing costs if state laws are not able to keep pace with advances in the marketplace.

*Purchasing.* Local purchasing practices are frequently subject to state regulation. States generally set some minimum standards for the local purchase of goods and services. Typical requirements may cover methods of purchasing, competitive bidding procedures, and conflict-of-interest provisions. State law may define which types of purchases are subject to competitive sealed bid versus competitive negotiation. Purchase of materials and supplies as well as construction contracts are frequently subject to competitive sealed bid, which awards the contract to the lowest responsible bidder. The statutes usually will specify the minimum purchase price subject to competitive bidding; these minimum prices can range from a few hundred dollars to several thousands of dollars. Competitive negotiation, which considers additional factors such as vendor experience and scope of services, is usually allowed for professional services. State law may set forth specific procedures governing the bidding process, including advertising requirements, inspection of bids, and recordkeeping requirements.

Enforcement of these statutory provisions is uneven, because usually no single state agency is involved in monitoring local purchasing practices. Enforcement is usually tighter if purchasing procedures are established for specific services or projects financed with state assistance. In these instances, the state grantor agencies promulgate rules on procurements made with grant funds. For example, state transportation agencies usually set specifications, let bids, and award contracts for local highway projects that are financed largely with federal and state funds.

*Grants Management.* Local governments, like other grant recipients, must comply with a variety of requirements as a condition of receiving intergovernmental assistance designated for specific purposes. State agencies responsible for managing federal pass-through aid and state categorical aid impose special financial management requirements on local grant recipients. These requirements usually cover grant accounting, cash management, reporting, purchasing, auditing, and other financial procedures. For example, a state grantor agency may require grantees to maintain separate financial records or prescribe minimum requirements for the grantee's accounting system. Where federal pass-through assistance is provided, a state grantor agency may add onto the federal requirements, which pass through with the federal dollars. In either case, these requirements may require the local government recipient to establish separate accounting records and procedures. This duplication of effort may not only increase administrative costs but also jeopardize the reliability and accuracy of financial information. This burden is greatly magnified if a local government receives financial assistance from more than one state agency, because each agency may establish its own requirements.

### *Financial Policy Regulation*

Financial policies set the parameters for a local government's revenue raising, spending, and borrowing decisions. A state may restrict or preempt these local policies to ensure financial solvency, reduce spillover effects, or protect state interests. Policy areas typically affected by state regulation are revenue diversification, debt limits, and spending policies.

*Revenue Diversification.* Many local governments establish policies to diversify their revenue base. For example, a locality may set a goal to rely more on user fees or charges to finance certain services or programs.

State law usually affects this policy in two ways. First, state statutes may prohibit local charges for particular services, such as immunization against childhood diseases, to remove any financial disincentives to use the service. Second, the state may limit the amount of the fee or charge to what is needed to cover the cost of the service or regulation. The fee or charge is subject to tests of reasonableness and equality. For example, parking meter fees may not be set so high that they generate "excess" revenue to support other programs and services.[9]

States can inhibit or promote local use of other revenue sources, notably income and sales taxes. States regulate local revenue use to reduce tax burdens, ensure uniform administration and lessen interjurisdictional tax competition, among others.

*Debt Limits.* Localities typically set policies on the amount of debt that they will incur as well as the purposes for which it will be incurred. For example, a government may limit general-obligation debt to a fixed percentage of general fund revenues so that it does not overcommit resources to debt purposes. State law may do the same. Frequently, state statutes will limit general-obligation debt to a fixed percentage (e.g., 5 percent) of the assessed valuation of taxable property within the jurisdiction.

Whether these borrowing limits constitute sound business practices or arbitrary requirements is a key question. If there is no strong correlation between the limitation and the debt capacity of a government, these restrictions may pose an unnecessary financial burden. A government with inadequate debt capacity may be forced to rely on lease-purchase or "pay-as-you-go financing" if it reaches its borrowing limit too quickly.

*Spending Policies.* As part of the budgetary process, local governments craft guidelines that limit the amount that agencies and departments may request or spend in their operating budgets. Some budget guidelines, such as salary ranges, cross departmental lines and may carry over from one budget year to the next.

Other guidelines, such as across-the-board cuts, are instituted only when financial conditions warrant substantial spending restraint. State requirements can supplant these spending policies by preempting local financial decisions.

Placing limits on taxes or spending is one preemption method available to state governments. Whether these restrictions are placed on local revenues or on expenditures, the goal is the same—to cap or reduce local spending. The two most widely used forms of limitation are property-tax-rate limits and caps on property-tax revenues. The tax-rate limit restricts the nominal tax rate; hence, it restricts the amount of tax that can be imposed on each dollar of assessed valuation. Limits on property-tax revenues restrict the percentage increase of that revenue from one year to the next. The annual permissible increase can be tied to a specific number (e.g., 5 percent per year) or to an economic indicator (e.g., the rate of inflation). Whether these limitations are effective will depend upon such factors as the percentage of increase allowed, exemptions to the limitations, and override provisions.[10]

Another means that states can use to preempt local finance decisions are mandates. Although any requirement that states impose on local governments can be labeled a "mandate," mandate here refers to a service or function local governments are required to perform. Because the legal basis for local government authority originates in state constitutional or statutory law, states have much greater latitude than the federal government to affect local programs and services. In many cases, states mandate programs or functions on equity and efficiency grounds. For example, state law may require cities to provide certain health services (e.g., home health care) to eligible individuals who might otherwise might be denied access to essential services because they are nonresidents. In other cases, states may require counties to perform some functions (e.g., criminal court systems) on behalf of the state because of the diseconomies of scale. Counties can provide such services at a lower cost per unit than the state could if it performed the function on its own. If the service or function is one that a locality has not previously performed, the cost to carry out the mandate can be high. On the other hand, a community that already provides the mandated services may experience no cost increases or only incremental ones as a result of the state action. In addition to the amount of prior activity, local demographic characteristics and local fiscal conditions are the most significant determinants of mandate-associated cost increases.[11]

## *STATE ASSISTANCE IN LOCAL FINANCE*

State assistance to local financial systems takes three principal forms—financial assistance, technical assistance, and financial services. Because it does not attempt to coerce local governments, assistance usually does not meet the local resistance that frequently confronts state regulatory action. States can employ a combination of assistance types as well as a combination of regulation and assistance to achieve their objectives.

### State Financial Assistance

Financial assistance affects revenue raising as well as spending decisions made by local governments. Although no monetary value has been placed on technical assistance and financial services, it is safe to say that financial assistance constitutes the most expensive form of assistance provided by state governments. Financial assistance involves both the direct payment of aid dollars to local jurisdictions as well as indirect assistance in the form of payments to individuals and state assumption of local services and functions.

*Direct Assistance.* Direct assistance is provided to local governments in the form of "categorical" and "unrestricted" aid. *Categorical aid* provides financial support for specific purposes; aid dollars must be spent only on designated programs and services. The single largest share of state categorical aid funds elementary and secondary education at the local level.[12] The primary purpose of categorical aid is to increase local spending on particular functions and programs in an effort to increase their effectiveness. Because certain programs, such as elementary and secondary education, have spillover benefits, the state has a socioeconomic interest in supporting educational programs. If categorical-aid dollars are distributed on the basis of program needs (e.g., number of students) or local revenue capacity (i.e., ability of locality to raise revenue to finance a given service level), then the financial assistance program also serves some efficiency and equity purposes.

*Unrestricted aid* takes the form of general assistance, shared taxes, and payments in lieu of taxes. Aid programs are considered "unrestricted" when states attach no strings; local governments are allowed to spend aid dollars for whatever purposes they deem appropriate.

*General assistance* usually is distributed to localities on the basis of origin, need and tax–base targeting, or a combination thereof. If distribution is based on origin, which is common for *shared taxes,* the state collects the revenues and returns all or a portion of them to localities "according to share of the tax base lying within its borders."[13] For example, a portion of income taxes collected by a state might be distributed to communities based on the amount of taxes generated in those communities. Distribution by this means does very little to address equity concerns. The opposite is true for financial assistance distributed on the basis of need or tax-base targeting, with the latter doing the best job of addressing equity concerns. Distribution on the basis of tax-base targeting, measured by tax capacity, tax effort, or another factor, reduces disparities between better-off and worse-off localities more efficiently.[14]

*Indirect Assistance.* Financial assistance is indirect if a state expends monies that benefit local governments but does not provide direct financial support to those local governments. Indirect assistance comes in all shapes and sizes: no systematic effort has been made, however, to catalog state efforts in this area. Two methods of indirect assistance that have been widely documented are circuit-breaker programs and state assumption of local costs.

The most common type of circuit-breaker program reduces the local property tax burden for low-and moderate-income taxpayers through the state income-tax system. Typically, an applicant files a supplemental form with the state income-tax return. An "excess burden" for the local property tax is calculated and the amount of the relief is deducted from the applicant's income-tax liability. If the applicant has no income-tax liability, the state will issue a refund. In many cases, these programs are taxpayer equity initiatives, reducing the disproportionate burden that local property taxes generally impose on lower-income taxpayers.[15] Although these programs do not provide additional revenue to local governments, they do reduce tax burden created by local government spending, which may in turn reduce taxpayer resistance to local property-tax increases.

State assumption of local programs and services has a more dramatic effect on the local financial system. When a state assumes the partial or entire cost of a local program or implements a program that competes with or supplants a local function, it offers localities the equivalent of financial assistance. In the 1970s and 1980s, states assumed a greater portion of health and welfare costs of programs administered at the local level. For example, most states have assumed the state-local share of the costs for the federal poverty programs—Aid to Families with Dependent Children (AFDC) and Medicaid. Most states also pick up the cost of general-assistance programs, the income-maintenance programs that provide coverage for indigents who do not qualify for the federal programs. A state might assume the cost of a local service or function because of spillover benefits, economies of scale, reassignment of responsibilities, or a variety of other reasons.

### *State Technical Assistance*

State technical assistance draws on state resources to improve financial policies and practices at the local level. In some cases, this assistance is designed to complement and reinforce state regulations; in other cases, it is specifically designed to meet local needs and problems.

When states reinforce regulation through technical assistance, they aid localities in changing or adapting their local financial practices and policies to meet state objectives. For example, states may train local finance staff to adapt state-prescribed charts of accounts to local accounting systems. These charts are used to classify and record financial information in a way that eases financial reporting to the state. Training is made more effective if state personnel are familiar with local systems and practices and can relate state requirements to local procedures. As a result, state assistance efforts can gain credibility and potentially greater acceptance among local officials.

Such efforts are more credible if they are not tied to, nor serve as a forerunner to, state regulatory action. In these instances, the state seeks to improve local practices and policies as ways to assist localities to manage more effectively their own programs and services. For example, state personnel may train local administrators in budgeting techniques so that they might make better resource allocation decisions. Whether state technical assistance reinforces regulation or helps local governments to help themselves, it usually takes the form of advice and consultation or training and publications.

*Advice and Consultation.* State officials with knowledge and expertise in finance can aid local officials to implement new and improved financial practices. This assistance usually takes the form of technical inquiry services offered by state finance or revenue agencies, state departments of community affairs, or state program agencies that work closely with their counterpart agencies at the local level. In its simplest and least expensive form, state personnel respond to written or telephone inquiries. This method can be fairly effective in responding to very specific inquiries, such as questions about the meaning of various state laws and regulations. Inquiry services also can be helpful if the inquirer is seeking general information or sources of information. In these latter cases, state personnel may be able to identify publications or individuals who can provide additional information.

On-site consultation may be the most effective method of technical assistance. State staff can observe first hand local problems and conditions and recommend improvements tailored to individual circumstances. For example, state audit staff might assist local finance staff with automating their accounting systems. Because this assistance is time-intensive and results in travel and other out-of-pocket costs, it is the most expensive form of technical assistance. Unless the state has a large staff and adequate budget to provide on-site help, however, it probably will be unable to reach a large number of local governments.

*Training and Publications.* Two ways to reach a larger audience at a lower cost are through training programs and technical publications.

Because travel and training budgets typically are very limited for local governments, efforts to offer training programs in different regions of a state or in conjunction with other meetings can have a positive affect on levels of participation. In the finance area, training generally serves two purposes: (1) to increase knowledge or awareness and (2) to build skills and technical competence. State officials are interested in enhancing local awareness of finance issues, laws, and techniques so that local officials might adapt them for their own governments. In more intensive training, state staff can train local staff in the use of specific financial practices and techniques. The skills-based training is more likely to effect change; it is also more time-consuming and expensive.

The state can also build awareness and technical capabilities through technical newsletters, guidebooks, and manuals. If they provide step-by-step guidance, these publications can be as effective as training. If combined with training, technical publications can have an even greater impact on local practices. It is important, however, for technical publications to offer detailed instruction that is tailored to local needs and problems. Otherwise, state technical assistance efforts will lose credibility. Newsletters can quickly disseminate information on innovative practices as well as on new laws and regulations that may be of interest to local officials.

Training and publications are provided by some of the same agencies that offer advisory and consultative services. They are not mutually exclusive forms of assistance. State agencies may also contract with private firms or universities to deliver this service. In some states, like Tennessee, the state offers training programs through its colleges and universities. Through economies of scale, the state is able to offer assistance that otherwise might be unavailable or too costly for individual governments.

### *Financial Services*

Economies of scale are the driving force behind another form of state assistance to local governments—financial services. Financial services are defined here as those financial management functions that the state performs on behalf of local jurisdictions. These services may or may not entirely supplant a local finance function; in most cases they provide another option for local decision makers. For example, state-run investment pools do not replace local investment activities but rather represent another investment vehicle in which local cash managers can invest their government's portfolio. On other hand, state retirement systems typically substitute for pension plans administered by localities.

Four of the most common financial services offered by states are investment pools, credit pools or enhancements, retirement systems, and cooperative purchasing.

*Investment Pools.* About half of the states offer local governments an opportunity to participate in investment pools. These pools combine the cash of local governments to invest in a diversified portfolio with earnings paid to government participants in proportion to their total investment. Typically, the pools are operated by state treasurers or state investment boards. In some cases, local funds are commingled with state funds. In other cases, a separate fund is established for local governments.

In either case, pools offer localities several advantages. Local jurisdictions, particularly small ones, may not possess or be able to afford the investment expertise needed to invest in higher-yielding securities. State pools are able to employ technical staff or contract with professional money managers to invest in more complex investments because they can distribute administrative costs among a large number of participants. State pools also offer the advantage of a more diversified portfolio. Because of state restrictions on local investment options, many localities are not able to purchase some of the higher-yielding securities (e.g., commercial paper) that are available to state pools.

The single greatest advantage afforded through state pools is liquidity. Because localities usually can withdraw their funds from the pool on short notice, they improve their cashflow picture without resorting to lower-yielding investments with short maturities.

*Credit Assistance.* States can help local governments lower their borrowing costs through a variety of credit-assistance programs.[16]

Through state guarantees, the state assumes an obligation to pay debt costs if a locality fails to meet its debt obligations. One popular program uses state aid entitlements as a form of guarantee—if a local jurisdiction cannot meet its repayment obligation, the state withholds sufficient state aid to meet the locality's debt payments.[17] Through these guarantees, localities are able to obtain higher credit ratings, which, in turn, lower borrowing costs. States provide debt financial services when they act as intermediaries, issuing debt then loaning the proceeds to local governments. Two credit pooling programs in use are bond banks and revolving loan funds. Through bond banks, states either sell bonds and use the proceeds to purchase bonds from local governments or pool several small local debt issues into one large issue that is sold in the bond market. Revolving funds differ from bond banks in the initial capitalization of the bonds. In addition, funds in the revolving funds are recycled to make additional loans. Because the federal government has provided seed money for state revolving funds to finance local wastewater-treatment facilities, revolving funds are likely to become the prevalent form of state credit assistance.

Like investment pools, credit pooling offers advantages of size. Because local governments share issuance costs through credit pools, they can proportionately reduce issuance costs such as rating agency fees and underwriting fees. Through credit enhancements, state credit pools can potentially reduce interest costs for local governments. In addition, these pools also afford small jurisdictions access to national markets which has the potential of lowering interest costs.

*Cooperative Purchasing.* Because they purchase goods and products in large quantities, states can often obtain more favorable terms and prices than smaller units of government. Except for very large localities, states generally possess the technical expertise to assess product quality and reliability. States can offer these advantages to local governments at little or no cost to themselves. Generally, states will permit localities to purchase from state contracts. Accordingly, localities can obtain volume discounts acquired by the state. The extent to which local governments can piggyback on state contracts will depend largely on the types of items purchased. If a jurisdiction has a need for a specific item or brand, for example, state contracts may not satisfy those requirements.

Even if state contracts do not offer price advantages, they may accelerate the purchasing process. Local purchasing staff can speed purchases if they do not need to develop product and bid specifications, solicit and evaluate bids, and award contracts. Frequently, state cooperative purchasing programs are exempt from purchasing requirements imposed by the states on local units of government. Hence, local governments can avoid some time-consuming and restrictive purchasing procedures. Among the other widely available state financial services, not discussed here, that offer economies of scale are state pension plans and state insurance pools.

## *FACTORS AFFECTING STATE INVOLVEMENT*

Many factors can affect the type and extent of state involvement in local finance. Five factors, however, seem to stand out as major influences on state involvement: tradition and law, the type of local government, centralization of service delivery, extent of federal involvement, and local revenue and technical capacity. States may choose to employ or emphasize one form of involvement over another as a result of one or more of these factors. Moreover, some of these factors may be so influential as to entirely preclude state activity in a given area of local finance.

### *Tradition and Law*

Local governments depend on state law for their very existence. In most states, states delegate to general-purpose local units of government all powers capable of delegation subject to preemption by general law.[18] Given the inferior legal status of local governments, states have virtually unlimited authority to define powers and functions. As a consequence, states generally have a strong legal footing to regulate any local financial activity. States do not always exercise that authority, however, for a variety of reasons.

First, states recognize that localities are best suited to deliver certain services and programs to their residents. For example, police patrol services, which have very low economies of scale and require quick response time to be effective, are better delivered at a community or neighborhood level.

Second, differences in local needs and problems will often dictate differences in the scope and level of local services. States are more likely to establish minimum standards for the local activities with interjurisdictional consequences than for those activities that affect only one jurisdiction. For example, states regulate local debt limits out of concern that the failure of one locality to meet its debt obligations will adversely affect all governments within the state.

Third, legal and political tradition can be an overriding factor in the type and extent of state involvement in local affairs. In states where there is a strong tradition of local self-government, resistance to state regulation will also be strong. In those instances, states may choose to use assistance as an alternative to regulatory action to achieve the desired results voluntarily. In other states where extensive regulatory involvement has been the tradition, local governments may not resist additional regulation if local officials consider it reasonable and appropriate.

### *Type of Jurisdiction*

Similar to tradition and law in its effect on state involvement is the number and type of local governments within a state. Local jurisdictions vary from state to state in their size and in their operations as well as in their numbers. Of the 83,186 local units, 38,933 are general-purpose jurisdictions—3,042 counties, 19,200 municipalities, and 16,691 township governments. The remainder are limited-purpose governments—14,721 school districts and 29,532 special districts. The average number of local units per state is 1,663; but Illinois has 6,627 while Hawaii has only 18.[19]

Jurisdiction type can be a major influence on the relationship between a state and a local unit of government. Municipalities (cities, towns, and villages) generally have more discretionary authority than do other types of local jurisdictions. As a consequence, they are better able to determine their own organization and functions than counties and limited-purpose districts. Although states may limit municipal discretion, they are less likely to intervene in the financial affairs of municipalities than in those of counties and school districts. On the other hand, states generally have stronger programmatic ties with counties and school districts than they do with municipalities.

Nationwide, on average, school districts received 52 percent of state intergovernmental payments in 1988 compared with 41 percent for counties and municipalities and less than 1 percent for special districts.[20] School districts receive a major portion of state aid because a major portion of state assistance is directed at elementary and secondary education. Although counties do not receive anywhere near as much state financial aid as school districts, they are a major partner with states in the administration of public-welfare and criminal-justice programs. Because counties act as agents of the states with respect to these programs, they are frequently subject to state fiscal rules and guidance.

Despite their numbers, special districts are less likely to bear the influence of state government than other local jurisdictions. As noted above, they receive virtually no state financial assistance. Moreover, they often rely on a single sources of revenue (primarily user charges and fees), for which they do not have to compete with the states or other local jurisdictions. Because they generally have a very narrow focus (e.g., fire protection, water supply) in program areas of little interest to state government, they typically escape state oversight.

### *Centralization of Services*

A widely accepted measure of a government's service responsibility is the amount of that government's direct expenditures for the service. That is, if a government assumes the cost of providing a service, it will make decisions about the level and composition of that service. In this line of reasoning, centralization of service responsibility or the extent to which the state provides services occurs in proportion to the state share of total state-local direct expenditures.

In states with greater centralization of service responsibility, at the same time, state involvement in local finance likely will be low. Because the state assumes the cost of the service, there is no need to provide financial assistance to local units for that service—nonetheless, state dollars may still flow to local governments if those units are involved in the production or delivery of state services. As in grants-in-aid, the state may set certain conditions in contracts with localities for service delivery that will affect local financial practices.

In states with decentralized service responsibility (i.e., localities provide majority of services), state involvement in local finance may be high if the state provides financial assistance to support the provision of those services. State financial assistance also may be extensive in states with centralized responsibility if that assistance is targeted to reduce fiscal disparities among local governments or reduce the local taxpayer burden.

### *Extent of Federal Involvement*

As discussed at the beginning of this chapter, the federal government also can have a major influence on local finance. Federal regulation and intervention in areas generally reserved for state and local governments in particular affect local spending decisions. This federal preemption heightens state involvement when the federal government directs the states to administer or enforce federal requirements. For example, states administer the federal limitations on the yearly volume of private-activity bonds issued by state and local governments. Through this federal requirement, states directly influence and even control certain local borrowing decisions.

The federal government relies on the states to pass through financial assistance to local governments. Because federal pass-through aid is not distinguished from state assistance in U.S. Census Bureau reports, it is difficult to estimate the amount that passes through. The most recent estimates put federal pass through assistance at 20 percent of total federal aid to state and local governments.[21]

Federal aid affects state involvement in two key ways. First, as federal assistance to localities has declined, states have moved to pick up the slack. State aid increases will depend largely, however, on a state's own financial situation. Those states facing economic downturns and subsequent budget deficits are unlikely to make up for lost federal funds.[22] Although the effects will vary with the type of federal grant (e.g., matching), there is evidence that funds spent at the state-local levels will increase significantly in proportion with the federal assistance received.[23] Second, states extend their involvement in local finance in their management of federal assistance programs. States assume oversight and administrative responsibilities for federal pass-through programs. Accordingly, they enforce local compliance with program and administrative requirements (including financial procedures) set forth in federal law and regulations. Frequently, states add on their own requirements to satisfy their own needs as well as to ensure state compliance with federal requirements. The Omnibus Budget Reconciliation Act of 1981 gave states greater responsibility over federal assistance programs by consolidating nearly 80 categorical grant programs into 9 state-administered block grant programs. With passage of this legislation and elimination of federal revenue sharing, focus of federal assistance clearly shifted from localities to state governments.

### *Revenue and Technical Capacity*

A local government's revenue or technical capacity can be a major determinant of state involvement in its financial affairs. Revenue capacity is defined as a local government's ability to raise revenues relative to the cost of its service responsibilities. Revenue capacity typically is measured to identify fiscal disparities among communities. Fiscal disparities exist when residents of one community must incur higher taxes to obtain levels of services comparable to those in another community.

These disparities create both efficiency and equity problems. Taxpayers in poorer communities face higher tax burdens to deliver reasonable levels of public services and may relocate to avoid higher taxes, making matters worse for those who remain.

State involvement can provide relief to fiscally disadvantaged communities. Disparities can be reduced if state categorical aid is distributed on the basis of program needs, not the ability of local taxpayers to finance programs with local revenues.[24] Centralizing service delivery at the state level and relaxing state restrictions on local revenue-raising authority can also reduce the size of these fiscal disparities.

Technical capacity is defined here as a local government's ability to manage its finance relative to its size and needs. Specialization of tasks generally occurs in proportion to the size of an organization. Large governments usually are better equipped to handle technical functions such as financial management, because they can hire professional staff who possess specialized knowledge and skills. Smaller local governments either cannot compete in the labor market for highly skilled professionals or rely on fewer staff to perform multidisciplinary tasks (e.g., budgeting and treasury management).

States with a large number of small local jurisdictions may be compelled to offer assistance. They can help bridge the gap in the technical capacity of small governments through financial services and technical assistance efforts. These state programs allow local units to acquire at little or no cost the technical capacity to manage better their financial affairs.

## *CONCLUSION*

A discussion of state involvement in local finance usually focuses on state mandates and state aid. Although they provoke the most debate in state legislatures and city halls, there are other forms of involvement that may well have a more lasting impact on local budgets.

State mandates and aid affect both sides of the local finance equation. State aid constitutes a sizeable portion of local revenue, and mandates comprise a significant share of local spending. State assumption of local functions and prohibitions against the use of certain revenue sources, however, may have greater implications because they preempt local finance decisions. Whatever form it takes, state involvement is usually influenced by a number of factors. Some factors, such as federal involvement and centralization of services, make dramatic shifts. Others, such as tradition and the makeup of local governments, change gradually. In turn, a state's response to these changes will be shaped largely by its own history as preemptor, provider, and prescriber.

## *NOTES*

1. John Shannon and James Edwin Kee, "The Rise of Competitive Federalism," *Public Budgeting Finance,* Winter 1989, Vol. 9, No. 4 (New Brunswick, N.J.: Transaction Periodicals Consortium): 5-20.
2. U.S. General Accounting Office, "Federal-State-Local Relations, Trends of the Past Decade and Emerging Issues," GAO/HRD-90-34 (Washington: GAO, March 1990), p. 15.
3. *Ibid.,* p. 28.
4. Gold, Steven D., *Reforming State-Local Relations: A Practical Guide* (Denver, Colo.: National Conference of State Legislatures, December 1989), p. 98.

5. U.S. General Accounting Office, "Communities in Fiscal Distress, State Grant Targeting Provides Limited Help," GAO/HRD-90-69 (Washington: GAO, April 1990), p. 10.

6. *Ibid.*

7. For a comprehensive study of state regulation of local financial management, see John E. Petersen, C. Wayne Stallings, and Catherine Lavigne Spain, *State Roles in Local Government Financial Management: A Comparative Analysis* (Washington: Government Finance Officers Association, June 1979).

8. Petersen, John E., Lisa A. Cole, and Maria A. Petrillo, *Watching and Counting: A Survey of State Assistance to and Supervision of Local Debt and Financial Administration* (Washington: National Conference of State Legislatures and Municipal Finance Officers Association, October 1977), p. 3.

9. Advisory Commission on Intergovernmental Relations, *Local Revenue Diversification: User Charges* SR-6 (Washington: ACIR, October 1987), p. 41.

10. For a survey of revenue and spending limits, see Steven D. Gold and Martha A. Fabricius, "How States Limit City and County Property Taxes and Spending" (Denver, Colo.: National Conference of State Legislatures, March 1989) (35 pp.).

11. Fix, Michael, and Daphne A. Kenyon, eds., *Coping with Mandates: What Are the Alternatives?* (Washington: The Urban Institute Press, 1990), p. 34.

12. Advisory Commission on Intergovernmental Relations, *Significant Features of Fiscal Federalism,* Vol. 2: Revenues and Expenditures, M-169-II (Washington: ACIR, August 1990), table 25, p. 29.

13. U.S. GAO, "Communities in Fiscal Distress," p. 26.

14. *Ibid.*

15. Advisory Commission on Intergovernmental Relations, *Property Tax Circuit-Breakers: Current Status and Policy Issues,* M-87 (Washington: ACIR, February 1975), pp. 1-17.

16. For a review of the major state credit assistance programs, see John E. Petersen, Susan Robinson, Percy Aquila, Joni L. Leithe, and William Graham, "Credit Pooling to Finance Infrastructure: An Examination of State Bond Banks, State Revolving Funds and Substate Credit Pools" (research report) (Washington: Government Finance Officers Association, September 1988).

17. Standard & Poor's, "State Provide Powerful Credit Enhancements," *Credit Review,* April 10, 1989, p. 1.

18. Advisory Commission on Intergovernmental Relations, *Measuring Local Discretionary Authority,* M-131 (Washington: ACIR, November 1981), p. 20.

19. U.S. Bureau of the Census, "Government Organization," Volume 1, No. 1, *1987 Census of Governments,* GC87(1)-1 (Washington: U.S. Government Printing Office, September 1988), p. *v.* 20. ACIR, *Significant Features of Fiscal Federalism,* table 27, p. 51.

21. Steven D. Gold and Brenda M. Erickson, "State Aid to Local Governments in the 1980s," Legislative Finance Paper 63 (Denver, Colo.: National Conference of State Legislatures, January 1988), p. 3.

22. U.S. GAO, "Federal-State-Local Relations," p. 24.

23. Advisory Commission on Intergovernmental Relations, *State and Local Roles in the Federal System,* A-88 (Washington: ACIR, April 1982), p. 55.

24. U.S. GAO, "Communities in Fiscal Distress," p. 24.

# *About the Editors*

JOHN E. PETERSEN is senior director of the Government Finance Research Center of the Government Finance Officers Association of the United States and Canada (GFOA), responsible for the association's municipal finance and management research programs. Petersen also served as director of the Center for Policy Research of the National Governors' Conference, director of public finance for the Securities Industry Association, and economist for The Urban Institute and the Board of Governors of the Federal Reserve System. In addition, he has been a consultant to many nonprofit and private organizations including the Twentieth Century Fund, National Science Foundation, Time-Life Corporation and federal agencies.

Petersen has authored books on public finance, including *Creative Capital Financing for State and Local Governments, A Guide to Registered Municipal Securities,* and *Disclosure Guidelines for State and Local Governments.* His articles have been published in the *Nation's Cities, Investment Dealer's Digest, Federal Reserve Bulletin, The Daily Bond Buyer, National Tax Journal,* and *Government Finance Review.* Mr. Petersen received a bachelor's degree from Northwestern University, a master's degree in business administration from the Wharton School, and a doctorate from the University of Pennsylvania.

DENNIS R. STRACHOTA is director of the Educational Services Center of the Government Finance Officers Association of the United States and Canada (GFOA), responsible for the association's conference and training programs. Strachota also directs GFOA's technical assistance programs in budgeting and cash management, including the Distinguished Budget Presentation Awards Program. Prior to joining GFOA, he served as director of Local Government Services and a budget and tax policy analyst for the State of Wisconsin.

Strachota is the author of several studies on state–local fiscal relations and co-author of GFOA's forthcoming *Best of Budgeting,* a guidebook on the preparation of local budget documents. He received a bachelor's degree in political science from the University of Wisconsin–Madison and a master's degree in public administration from Harvard's Kennedy School of Government.

# *About the Contributors*

Percy R. Aguila, Jr. is a senior vice president and manager of the Public Finance Group of Guzman Company. Since joining Guzman Company in 1990, Aguila has managed the firm's investment banking and financial advisory activities. Aguila's public finance background includes serving as financial advisor on over $300 million general obligation, revenue-backed and lease-secured financings. He is a former assistant director, Government Finance Research Center of the Government Finance Officers Association of the United States and Canada (GFOA) and vice president of Municipal Lease Insurance Managers, Inc., where he was responsible for the underwriting of municipal lease transactions. Aguila has also worked for state government, having served in an analytic capacity for four years with the New York State Financial Control Board.

Aguila received a bachelor's degree in urban affairs from George Washington University and a master's degree in public administration from New York University's Graduate School of Public Administration. He co-authored the GFOA publication *Municipal Minibonds—Small Denomination Direct Issuance by State and Local Governments.*

Michael E. Bell is a principal research scientist at the Institute for Policy Studies, John Hopkins University. Bell's previous positions include senior research associate at The Urban Institute, deputy executive director of the National Council on Public Works Improvement, and senior economist at the U.S. Department of Commerce. He has also served on staff at the Office of State and Local Finance, U.S. Department of Treasury.

Bell has authored, co-authored and served as editor on numerous books, monographs and articles in professional journals. In addition, he has written several book chapters and has conducted a number of presentations on various issues in public finance.

He received a master's degree in economics from Simon Fraser University at Burnaby, British Columbia, Canada in 1972 and a doctoral degree in economics from the Graduate School of Public Affairs, State University of New York at Albany in 1975.

JOHN H. BOWMAN is professor of economics at Virginia Commonwealth University. Prior positions include associate professor of public and environmental affairs at Indiana University, senior resident in public finance at the U.S. Advisory Commission on Intergovernmental Relations, and chief of tax planning in the Ohio Department of Taxation. He received his doctoral degree in economics at Ohio State University.

Bowman specializes in state and local government finance and intergovernmental fiscal relations. His research has appeared in several academic journals, including the *National Tax Journal, Public Finance Quarterly, Land Economics, Public Administration Review,* and the *American Journal of Economics and Sociology,* among others. In addition, he has contributed chapters to various books and presented papers at a number of professional conferences. In addition, he has served as a consultant in the area of property taxation to a number of governmental bodies, including state tax study commissions in Arizona, Maryland, Minnesota, Nevada, New Jersey, and West Virginia.

JOHN J. FORRER is a doctoral candidate in public administration at George Washington University. He has extensive research and management experience in public finance, economic development, and technology transfer. Recent research activities include an analysis of the tax capacity of counties in the greater Washington, D.C. area, a survey of software used by local governments to conduct financial analysis of economic development issues, and a comparative assessment of state manufacturing technology extension programs. Forrer is currently a senior associate with Technology and Management Services in Germantown, Maryland.

Forrer received his master's in public administration degree in 1980 from the Maxwell School of Government, Syracuse University and his bachelor's degree in 1978 from Miami University.

STEPHEN J. GAUTHIER is director of the Technical Services Center of the Government Finance Officers Association of the United States and Canada (GFOA). Before joining the association's staff in 1987, Gauthier served as the research and technical review manager for the Tennessee Division of State Audit in Nashville.

Gauthier is co-author of GFOA's 1988 *Governmental Accounting, Auditing and Financial Reporting* and the editor of the association's monthly accounting and auditing publication *GAAFR Review*. He is also the author of the *Audit Management Handbook* and the co-author of the *GAAFR Study Guide*. He is a licensed certified public accountant in both Tennessee and Illinois and a member of the American Institute of Certified Public Accountants (AICPA) and the Illinois Society of Certified Public Accountants.

Gauthier received his bachelor's degree from the University of Wisconsin–Milwaukee. He holds advanced degrees from both the University of Wisconsin–Milwaukee and Vanderbilt University.

STEPHEN B. GORDON is the associate administrator for professional services at the University of Maryland's University College, Graduate School of Management and Technology. He previously served as director of corporate products and services for BidNet, Inc., an information services firm serving purchasers and vendors in the public sector. He also served on the staff of the National Institute of Governmental Purchasing (NIGP) where he developed and managed NIGP's professional development and research programs. Gordon is the author of several publications relating to governmental contracting and service delivery.

He received a doctoral degree in government and politics from the University of Maryland and a master's degree and a bachelor's degree in political science from Mississippi State University.

FREDA S. JOHNSON is a consultant with Government Finance Associates, specializing in advisory work with both domestic and international governments. Formerly, she served for ten years as executive vice president and director of the Public Finance Department of Moody's Investors Service, Inc. Prior to 1990, she spent her entire career as a municipal analyst at both Moody's and Moody's parent corporation, Dun and Bradstreet, Inc.

Johnson is currently a member of the Anthony Commission on Public Finance, the Citizens Budget Commission, the Government Accounting Standards Advisory Council, the Society of Municipal Analysts, the Municipal Analysts Group of New York, the Women's Economic Roundtable, the Financial Women's Association, and the Women's Bond Club. Formerly, she served as president of the Board of Governors of the Municipal Forum of New York.

Johnson received her bachelor's degree from Queens College and attended the Advanced Management Program at the Harvard University Graduate School of Business Administration.

R. BRADLEY JOHNSON is executive director of Public Risk Management Association in Washington, D.C. where he has served in several positions since 1986. His publications include *Employee Assistance Programs: Strategies for Local Government Workplaces, Public Risk Management: State of the Profession, 1987–1988,* and *Risk Management: A Guide for Nonprofits*. He has also contributed an article to the International City Management Association's *Municipal Yearbook, 1989* titled "Risk Management in the Public Sector."

Johnson holds a master's degree in public administration from The American University in Washington, D.C. and a bachelor's degree in political science from Vanderbilt University in Nashville, TN.

JAMES EDWIN KEE is an associate professor of public administration for the School of Business and Public Management at George Washington University, Washington, D.C. Previously, he was the first executive director of the Utah Department of Administrative Services, responsible for the financial management and administration of the state. He has also been Utah's State Budget Director and Utah's State Planning Coordinator, before which he was a legislative assistant and counsel to the New York State Assembly. Kee has also served as Governor Scott M. Matheson's liaison to the National Governors' Association and president of the National Association of State Budget Officers.

Professor Kee has served as managing editor of *Public Budgeting Finance* for four years and has published articles on federal and state budget and fiscal policy, intergovernmental relations, and managing for excellence. He co-authored *Out of Balance* (1986, Peregrine Smith Books) with former Governor Matheson. Professor Kee received his bachelor's degree from the University of Notre Dame and his master's degree in public administration and a doctorate of law from New York University where he was a Root-Tilden Scholar.

EDWARD ANTHONY LEHAN is president and principal consultant concentrating on finance and budgeting at Cantabrigia, a New England–based consulting, training and publishing firm. His experience includes assignments as chief administrative officer, New Haven, Connecticut; finance director, Rochester, New York, West Hartford, Connecticut, and Cambridge, Massachusetts; town manager, North Kingstown, Rhode Island; local government program manager, National Science Foundation; and executive secretary to the city manager, Hartford, Connecticut.

Recently, Lehan completed a four-year engagement as an advisor to the Government of Jamaica on finance organization and budgetary procedures, including the introduction of performance budgeting. He has written extensively on finance procedures, including budgeting, cash management, risk management, and the application of technology to finance work. His writings include *Simplified Governmental Budgeting* and *Budgetmaking–A Workbook of Theory and Practice.* Lehan has also authored specialized workbooks on police and education budgeting.

THOMAS MCLOUGHLIN is manager in the Government Finance Research Center of the Government Finance Officers Association of the United States and Canada (GFOA). McLoughlin is responsible for financial advisory services and research related to issues in municipal finance and capital investment, including debt issuance methods and costs and capital financing alternatives. Prior to joining GFOA, McLoughlin was a municipal securities analyst for Moody's Investors Service, Inc.

McLoughlin authored revisions to GFOA's publication *Disclosure Guidelines for State and Local Government Securities.* He has published a number of articles, including "Choosing an Underwriter for a Negotiated Bond Sale" and "Does Municipal Bond Insurance Make Sense?" in GFOA's *Government Finance Review.*

He received a master's degree in urban and regional planning from George Washington University and a bachelor's degree in political science from the State University of New York at Albany.

JERRY E. MECHLING is director of the Strategic Computing and Telecommunications Program as well as an adjunct lecturer in public policy of the John F. Kennedy School of Government at Harvard University. He teaches management information systems in graduate and executive programs, and his research and consulting focus on the impacts of computer-based technologies on organizational behavior and strategy. In addition, Mechling is a principal in Hayes-Mechling-Kleiman, Inc., a management and systems consulting company.

Formerly, Mechling served as an aide to the mayor and assistant administrator of the Environmental Protection Administration for Mayor John V. Lindsay of New York City and as Director of the Office of Management and Budget for Mayor Kevin H. White of Boston. He has consulted to numerous public and private organizations including federal, state, local and international agencies and corporations such as AT&T, CBS, Cadbury-Schweppes and IBM.

He was a fellow of the Kennedy Institute of Politics at Harvard. He is co-author of *Linkages: Integrated Systems for Financial Management* (The Urban Institute, 1982). He holds a bachelor's degree in physical sciences (mathematics and physics) from Harvard College, a master's degree in public administration and a doctoral degree in economics and public affairs from the Woodrow Wilson School at Princeton.

GIRARD MILLER is vice president of government markets at Fidelity Investments Institutional Services Company in Boston, Massachusetts. His responsibilities include working with Fidelity's clients in the design of prudent portfolios, as well as new product design, legislative and technical support for the public sector, and research assistance to finance officer organizations. Previously, Miller was director of the Technical Services Center of the Government Finance Officers Association of the United States and Canada (GFOA). He also served as director of fiscal services for the City of Southfield, Michigan, and as president of the Michigan MFOA. His government career includes employment by the cities of Farmington Hills, Michigan, and West Windsor and Princeton, New Jersey.

Miller founded GFOA's investment newsletter, *Public Investor,* and is the author of numerous GFOA publications, including *Investing Public Funds,* and *Pension Fund Investing.* He contributes a monthly investment analysis article in Fidelity's public–sector newsletter, *Investment Exchange.* He is a Chartered Financial Analyst (CFA).

Miller holds a master's degree in public administration from the Maxwell School of Public Affairs, Syracuse University, and a master's degree in economics from Wayne State University in Detroit, Michigan.

Lawrence W. "Chip" Pierce is a Consultant at Public Financial Management, Inc. His experience with debt issuance includes refundings, general obligation bonds, revenue bonds and direct-sale minibonds. Pierce has focused on feasibility studies, financial forecasting, and the structuring and execution of bond sales. He has worked with governmental enterprises throughout the northwest, including Portland, Oregon and the Washington Public Power Supply System.

Prior to joining PFM, Pierce served as a project manager with the Government Finance Research Center of the Government Finance Officers Association of the United States and Canada (GFOA), where he managed the first direct sale of small denomination bonds from the issuer to the marketplace in Virginia.

Pierce has published several articles on public finance topics. Most recently, he wrote an article for GFOA's *Government Finance Review* that examines financing techniques for convention centers in the post-tax reform world.

Pierce graduated Phi Beta Kappa with a bachelor's degree in American political history from the Colorado College and holds a master's degree in public policy and management from the Wharton School at the University of Pennsylvania.

Robert W. Rafuse, Jr. is a visiting senior fellow at the U.S. Advisory Commission on Intergovernmental Relations (ACIR), on leave from his position as director of the Office of Regional Economics at the U.S. Department of the Treasury. Previous positions include deputy assistant secretary of the Treasury for State and Local Finance, president of Phoenix Associates, a consulting firm in Washington specializing in state–local public finance and intergovernmental fiscal relations, regional economics, and project evaluation in developing countries, and deputy chief economist and director of the Research Center of the National Planning Association. In 1969–1971, he was Assistant Director of the Economic Research Division of Mathematica, Inc.

Rafuse has taught public finance at Princeton University, the University of Illinois at Urbana–Champaign, and George Washington University. His experience with the federal government includes service with the Bureau of the Budget (now OMB), the Council of Economic Advisers, and the ACIR.

Rafuse received a bachelor's degree from Harpur College (State University of New York at Binghamton) and a doctoral degree in economics from Princeton University. He was a Fulbright Scholar at the Institute d'Etudes Politiques, University of Bordeaux, France.

Susan G. Robinson, as manager with the Government Finance Research Center of the Government Finance Officers Association of the United States and Canada (GFOA), is responsible for a variety of research, training and advisory projects in the areas of financial management and planning. Prior to joining GFOA, Robinson analyzed and wrote extensively on economic development issues and public/private partnerships for Partners for Livable Places. She also held management positions with local governments in Utah and California.

Robinson was principal author of *Building Together: Investing in Community Infrastructure*, co-published by GFOA. She also was editor of the 1990 GFOA publication *Financing Growth: Who Benefits? Who Pays? and How Much?*.

Robinson received a bachelor's degree in political science from the University of Utah and a master's degree in public administration from George Washington University.

BERNARD H. ROSS is professor of government and public administration at the School of Public Affairs at the American University where he is chair of the Department of Public Administration. Ross has served as a consultant to numerous local governments and corporations. He has also served as director of urban affairs and public administration programs at the American University.

Ross has published *Urban Management, How Washington Works,* and *Business Regulation and Government Decision Making*. His textbook, *Urban Politics,* will have a fourth edition published next year. Ross has also published numerous articles and monographs on urban politics and management.

DIANA L. ROSWICK is a vice president and assistant director in the Public Finance Department of Moody's Investors Service, Inc. She has been with Moody's since 1983. Currently she is manager of the Product Planning and Design group and Managing Editor of Public Finance publications. Formerly, Roswick managed the Great Lakes Regional Ratings group. Prior to joining Moody's, she held various analytic positions at the New York State Financial Control Board and at Corporate Contributions, Inc. She has also worked for the New York City Board of Education.

Among her published works are "The City's Role in Health" in *Setting Municipal Priorities,* and *Alternatives to the Medicaid Formula—Issues of Equity and Fiscal Relief.*

Roswick received a master's degree in management and urban professions from the New School for Social Research, a master's degree from the Bank Street College of Education, and her bachelor's degree from Cornell University.

KENNETH L. RUST joined Public Financial Management, Inc. in May 1989 as a managing consultant. He specializes in economic and financial analysis and has provided financial planning and advisory services to a wide range of municipal clients. His financial planning work centers around enterprise fund activities, particularly water and sewer.

Rust has served as guest lecturer in municipal finance for graduate programs in public administration. Rust began his public finance career as a project manager and economist with CH2M Hill, a national engineering consulting firm, where he specialized in utility rate-making, financial planning, economic feasibility analysis and microcomputer modeling.

Rust received his bachelor's degree in economics and business administration with honors from Portland State University.

LON SPRECHER is president of EPIC Insurance Corporation. Previously, he was senior vice-president for finance and information systems with Central Life Assurance Company of Des Moines, Iowa, where he was responsible for corporate strategic planning, resource allocation and management information systems. Before that, he served as state budget director for the State of Wisconsin from 1982–1987. Sprecher also served as city budget director and executive assistant to the mayor of the City of Madison, Wisconsin, and director of program management, Wisconsin Department of Administration.

Sprecher received a degree in economics and a master's degree in public administration from the University of Wisconsin–Madison. He is currently an adjunct professor at the LaFollette Institute of Public Affairs, University of Wisconsin–Madison.

HOLLEY H. ULBRICH is alumni professor of economics at Clemson University and a senior fellow at the University's Strom Thurmond Institute for Excellence in Government and Public Affairs. Professor Ulbrich received her doctoral degree in economics from the University of Connecticut in 1968. She has been on the faculty at Clemson since 1967. Her particular areas of research and teaching interest are state and local public finance and international trade. She has served as a policy analyst for the U.S. Advisory Commission on Intergovernmental Relations (ACIR) and has consulted with various public agencies at the national, state, and local level on tax policy issues.

Ulbrich is the author of five textbooks as well as numerous journal articles and other publications. In the area of state and local public finance, her recent publications include two monographs for the ACIR on *Local Income Taxes* (1988) and *Local Sales Taxes* (1989).

C. KURT ZORN is currently director of state relations for Indiana University. In 1989, he was appointed commissioner of Indiana State Board of Tax Commissioners and was associate director of the Regional Economic Development Institute in 1988. He joined the faculty of the School of Public and Environmental Affairs at Indiana University–Bloomington as a lecturer in 1980. He was promoted to assistant professor in 1981 and to associate professor in 1987.

Professor Zorn is the author of numerous articles, monographs, and book chapters in the areas of state and local public finance, economic development, and transportation. He has served as consultant to numerous state agencies, the U. S. Transportation Department and the President's Commission on Aviation Safety.

He received a bachelor's degree in economics in 1976 from the State University of New York at Albany. He did his graduate work at Syracuse University and received his doctoral degree in economics in 1981.

WERNER PAUL ZORN is a consultant with the Government Finance Research Center of the Government Finance Officers Association of the United States and Canada (GFOA). He has conducted numerous studies of public pension plans, including examinations of their accounting, reporting, benefit, actuarial, and investment practices. His recent report on these topics, *A Survey of State Retirement Systems Covering General Employees and Teachers,* was written for the GFOA in conjunction with the National Association of State Retirement Administrators. Prior to his current position, Zorn served as an assistant director at the GFOA research center. Zorn obtained his bachelor's degree from the University of Michigan and master's degree in public policy from the University of Chicago.